Psychology

PSYCHOLOGY
THE ESSENCE OF A SCIENCE

BRUCE H. HINRICHS
CENTURY COLLEGE

PEARSON

Boston   New York   San Francisco
Mexico City   Montreal   Toronto   London   Madrid   Munich   Paris
Hong Kong   Singapore   Tokyo   Cape Town   Sydney

Executive Editor: Karon Bowers
Editorial Assistant: Lara Torsky
Senior Marketing Manager: Wendy Gordon
Editorial-Production Administrator: Anna Socrates
Manufacturing Buyer: JoAnne Sweeney
Cover Administrator: Linda Knowles
Compositions and Prepress Buyer: Linda Cox
Editorial-Production Service: Susan McNally
Text Design: Suzanne Montazer, Monotype
Electronic Composition: Monotype

Library of Congress Cataloging-in-Publication Data

Hinrichs, Bruce H.
    Psychology : the essence of a science / Bruce H. Hinrichs
        p. cm.
    Includes bibliographical references (p.) and index.
    ISBN 0-205-36095-5
    1. Psychology–Textbooks. I. Title

BF121.H584 2004
150–dc22   2004051964

Printed in the United States of America

10 9 8 7 6 5 4 3 2   10 09 08 07 06 05

Contents

TO THE STUDENT

This textbook was written with you in mind. How do I know you, you wonder? Well, I've taught psychology for many years, and although I don't know you personally, I believe that I know what most psychology students need in a textbook. This book was carefully written and organized to present the fundamental facts of psychology in an interesting way and in a way that makes them easy to learn. Here are some tips to help:

1. Important terms are in **bold type.** These terms will likely show up on tests! Make flashcards, or use some other study technique to learn those terms.

2. A glossary in the back of the book defines the most important terms, but don't depend on it too much. Try to understand the terms in their contexts. You should be able to understand the meanings of those terms by reading the text, and you should use the glossary only as a backup.

3. Read the text slowly. Don't try to read a whole chapter, or even a large section of a chapter, all at once. Read a bit, paying careful attention, and when you feel overloaded or "full," then stop reading. Come back later and review what you read before. Then read a little more. If you do it this way, you will retain information much better and will not need to cram before a test. Tons of research has found that spaced practice is much more efficient than massed practice (Willingman, 2002).

4. Read actively, not passively. Many students who do poorly on tests complain that they can't understand why they don't do well even after they read the chapters many times. But that's not reading; it's turning pages in front of your eyes. You must read *actively.* Underline, highlight, circle words, number things, write in the margins, make flashcards, make an outline, take notes. Do anything to be actively involved in your reading.

5. Use the study guides. Each chapter has study items with answers. When you complete the fill-in-the-blank items, you will have a complete summary of the chapter. Also, in the text you will find critical thinking questions in boxes labeled "Think Tank." These questions require deeper thought and will engage you in active thinking. Research shows that people remember what they think about. (Isn't that obvious?) So if you want to recall, be sure to think! What you think about during learning is what you will later remember, so be sure to organize your thinking to give you cues to later trigger your memory. Critical thinking questions also appear in the study guides. These will also help you to remember and understand. Boxes labeled "Connecting Concepts" connect material in one chapter to ideas from another chapter. These will help you make associations; they are also helpful for learning and recall.

6. "I Link, Therefore I Am" boxes suggest Web sites that will be useful for studying or getting more information. This resource is organized by chapter and located at the end of each chapter.

7. Ask questions. Approach your professor, and ask for examples or explanations of things that are unclear. Professors love that! Don't be shy. Whatever you have a question about, you can bet that other students do too.

8. Form study groups. Interact with other students. Discuss the material. Whether you like psychology or not, pretend that you like it. It's easier to learn about something you like. Talk about what you've learned. Tell someone about it. All of these things will help you remember the material you are learning.

Good luck, I wish you well. I hope you learn a great deal and find psychology fascinating.

Bruce H. Hinrichs

I Link, Therefore I Am

General information about psychology and
   psychologists:

http://stange.simplenet.com/psycsite/

http://www.psy.pdx.edu/PsiCafe/

http://www.psychlinks.cjb.net/

http://www.alleydog.com/

http://www.personalityresearch.org/

http://psychclassics.yorku.ca/

Study skills:

http://www.mtsu.edu/~studskl/

http://gwis2.circ.gwu.edu/~gwvcusas/

http://wsrv.clas.virginia.edu/~rjh9u/howstudy.html

http://www.psy.pdx.edu/PsyTutor/

Time Management tips:

http://www.csuchico.edu/cdoe/timemanag.html

TO THE PROFESSOR

Psychology textbooks are in a rut. They have become encyclopedias of every topic in psychology. They blend fundamental principles with innumerable specialized facts. By covering everything, they are sure to include what each professor wants. But what about the students? It is not possible for them to absorb everything, differentiate basic information from details, and form a unified concept of psychology. Introductory textbooks have too many chapters, segregating topics into seemingly unrelated, disjointed disciplines. Professors skip around in their text and omit many chapters entirely. How can students put it all together into a coherent picture? How can students go beyond shallow understanding to deep processing?

It's time for something different. You will find that this text includes essential foundations without loads of secondary information or excessive details that overload and confuse students and distract them from focusing on basic principles. This text is designed to enhance recall, deep processing, and critical thinking. An attempt has been made here to (a) compress the number of chapters into a more manageable package that makes it easier for students to grasp psychology as a whole and to form a more unified schema; (b) organize material logically and coherently; (c) integrate effective pedagogical tools into the text, including a study guide for each chapter; and (d) keep the text short enough that you can add information and supplement the reading to individualize your course.

Here are the main features of this textbook:

1. The focus is on essentials—the foundations of scientific psychology. Basic principles, theories, and people are included, as well as classic and the latest citations. A rigorous scientific approach is taken, but with a casual, conversational, and often humorous tone. Students will find this book very easy to read, fun to read, and easy to learn from.

2. Numerous pedagogical aids are integrated into each chapter to encourage deep processing of

information. This book is designed, in the writing style, the organization, and the pedagogy, to encourage students to think, because we want more than rote memory from students. The emphasis here is to encourage deeper understanding. "Think tanks" contain provocative critical thinking questions that not only stimulate student thinking but also can be used in lecture, discussion, or small groups or as assignments. "Connecting Concepts" help students refresh their learning and bridge material throughout the course. Each chapter concludes with a study guide containing different types of questions. The fill-in-the-blank items, when completed, make a good chapter summary. The "I Link, Therefore I Am" list of relevant Web sites is organized by chapter and located at the end of each chapter. Finally, the text itself uses a number of tools to help learning and memory. Difficult vocabulary is eased by using context and subsequent sentences that reword hard terms. Pronunciation guides, mnemonic devices, FYIs, applications, frequent recaps, stimulating quotations, metaphors, examples, and analogies are prominent features that are intended to motivate students and enhance their memory of the material.

3. The number of chapters has been compressed to ten, divided into five units of two chapters each. Topics such as emotion, motivation, social psychology, stress, states of consciousness, and development do not have their own chapters but are blended into the five basic units. This structure is easy to learn from and to teach from. It organizes easily into a semester or quarter system; helps your students to form a whole concept of psychology; and allows you to customize your course to fit your particular students or your special knowledge, background, or interests. You can easily add supplemental reading, for example.

4. The first unit, **Introduction,** gives an overview of what psychology is, where it came from, and how it uses scientific methods. The focus is on ideas, such as dualism versus monism and conscious versus unconscious mind. The most current ideas are included, such as evolutionary psychology, research on automaticity, and cognitive neuroscience. The second unit is **Biology,** helpful for later topics. But the brain chapter does not begin with neurons, as occurs in traditional textbooks; a top-down approach is more accessible, so brain anatomy and function are covered before axonal and synaptic transmissions. The third unit is **Cognition,** a well-organized and current discussion of learning and memory, including lots of examples that students find so helpful. The fourth unit is **Personality,** which incorporates intelligence, personality testing, social psychology, theories, emotions, and motivation. Personality approaches are contrasted with social psychology in a unique organization that gives students an easy schema for these two areas of psychology. The last unit, **Disorders,** includes chapters on psychopathology and therapies. These topics come last because they rely and build on knowledge of biology, cognition, and personality.

5. The content is contemporary with many recent references and includes important information that is not found in other general psychology textbooks, such as (a) the latest on taste receptors (umami) and their locations; (b) multicultural views of the Big Five personality traits, eating disorders, attribution theory, and psychological disorders; (c) meta-analysis; (d) the most contemporary thinking about the nature-nurture question and evolutionary psychology (including instincts and adaptations); (e) the fusiform face area; (f) asymmetry of hemispheres; (g) EEG used to identify what words and sentences are being read; (h) current atypical neuroleptics and their side effects; (i) the latest on the influence of infections on disorders such as schizophrenia and OCD; and (j) hippocampal neurogenesis and its relationship to depression.

Though more concise, this textbook is similar to traditional books in presenting fundamental information in a science-based, clear, readable format. So far, students and professors have loved this book's style and organization. Please feel free to contact me with your opinions, criticisms, and suggestions.

Best regards,
Bruce H. Hinrichs
b.hinrichs@century.mnscu.edu

ACKNOWLEDGMENTS

I will begin by giving thanks to the people at Pearson Educational who published this textbook in a custom version and to the pioneering psychology professors who used that prototype book: Doug Pearson, Beth Lanning, Debra Matchinsky, and Megan Rogers. They provided me with great encouragement and feedback, and I am very grateful for their efforts; this book is much better because of them. Next I wish to thank the people at Allyn & Bacon, particularly Sales Representative Leslie Ortiz, my editor, Karon Bowers, her assistant, Lara Torsky, and the production team, especially Susan McNally and Anna Socrates. An author also needs emotional support, so I send my thanks and deepest appreciation to my family, Danielle and Chris, Nicole and Franck, and little Solenne, who carries our hopes

for the future. Finally, my sincere thanks to the reviewers of this textbook, who gave me wonderful, thoughtful suggestions that helped enormously. The many voices of wisdom include: Mary A. Waterstreet, St. Ambrose University; Karsten Look, Columbus State Community College; Michael J. Zickar, Bowling Green State University; Martin F. Marino, Atlantic Cape Community College; Jay Alperson, Palomar College; Charles Blose, MacMurray College; Debbie Podwika, Kankaka Community College; Marisa McLeod, Santa Fe Community College; Michael Berkowitz, SUNY Westchester Community College; Douglas Pearson, Normandale Community College; Lindette Lent, Arizona Western College; Nancy Digdon, Grand MacEwan College; and Pam MacDonald, Washburn University.

ABOUT THE AUTHOR

Bruce H. Hinrichs is a professor of psychology at Century College in White Bear Lake, Minnesota, and previously taught at Anoka-Ramsey Community College, in the Compleat Scholar program at the University of Minnesota, as an Honorary Fellow at the University of Wisconsin–Madison, and as an artist/teacher-in-residence at the University of Illinois. Mr. Hinrichs is also a professor of film studies and an

artist whose works have appeared in galleries across the country. Mr. Hinrichs has published numerous articles on psychology, art, and film, and two other books: *Film & Art* (1999), an analysis of the film medium as an art form, and *Mind as Mosaic: The Robot in the Machine* (2000), an introduction to cognitive neuroscience.

INTRODUCTION

"The true science and study of man is man."
—PIERRE CHARRON

We begin our journey of the discipline of psychology with an overview of the many vast dimensions of this fascinating field and a look at the experimental methods that psychologists use. Here you will find a description of the many diverse subfields of psychology and of the scientific methods that provide the discipline of psychology with the tools for meeting its goals: to describe, explain, predict, and control the behavior and mental processes of animals, including, of course, humans.

The first unit includes these two chapters:

Chapter 1 The World of Psychology—a description of the many areas that constitute modern psychology; a brief history of the development of the discipline; an introduction to the latest trends, including cognitive psychology, cognitive neuroscience, and evolutionary psychology; and an illustration that ties together a wide range of research findings and ideas in psychological science, demonstrating the breadth as well as the interconnectedness of psychological topics. This chapter provides a complete and thorough look at where psychology came from, what topics it tackles, its diverse subfields, and how they connect into a unified, cohesive science.

Chapter 2 Methods of Scientific Research—a description, with examples, of the many research methods that are part of the scientific process of finding facts. This chapter includes a detailed discussion of correlational studies and controlled experiments. Also included here are important ideas about how to avoid myths and misconceptions about psychological ideas and how to interpret the results of scientific studies.

The World of Psychology

PLAN AHEAD...

- What is psychology? What are its subfields? What do psychologists study?
- How does psychology compare to other fields of study?
- How does one become a psychologist or a psychiatrist?
- Where did psychology come from—how did it begin?
- What are the different theories within psychology?
- What is the unconscious mind, and what are some examples of it?
- How do psychologists study dreams?
- Who were Freud, Skinner, and some other influential psychologists? What were their main ideas?
- What are some of the newest ideas or trends in psychology?

WELCOME TO THE WONDERFUL WORLD OF PSYCHOLOGY!
Right now students all around the earth are studying the very same fascinating sub-
jects that you will be in this course. In Norway, Brazil, China, Portugal, Kenya, Australia,
Iceland, and everywhere else in the world, college students are learning about Freud,
Skinner, Piaget, how the brain works, perception, mental illnesses, heredity, conditioning, memory, and all the other exciting topics that are covered in a general psychology
course. In fact, of all the courses offered in colleges around the world, Introduction to
Psychology is the course most frequently taken. You are beginning a marvelous journey
of amazing ideas, facts, theories, and principles.

Because this is such a common, fundamental, and popular course (and has been for
many years), millions of people around the world are aware of the concepts of psychology. Now you will be one of them. Having this knowledge and this experience will not
only be fun, it will be valuable to you in many ways.

But don't make the mistake of thinking that learning is valuable only as a means to
an end. It is far too common today to think of college and learning as things we must
endure to get a good job. Learning is valuable and desirable in its own right, regardless of
what ends it might serve. The pursuit of truth and knowledge has always been a human
drive, an intellectual need, and an expression of human curiosity. We study and learn not
only to attain certain selfish ends, but also because we want to live a good life, a moral
life, and a fulfilling life. We want to do the right thing, and that requires knowledge. Psychology will be an important part of living a good life and being a good person. As
Socrates said, "The unexamined life is not worth living." This course could be the impetus,
or perhaps a major ingredient, in your journey to understand yourself and others.

So welcome to psychology. Many students find this course to be the most fascinating course in their college careers. I hope you do too. It is full of mind-boggling ideas,
concepts, research findings, principles, and examples from life. If you don't find something in this course to interest you, then you must be made of wood!

DEFINITIONS

"Art is myself, science is ourselves."
—CLAUDE BERNARD

One should begin a college course with definitions, so we shall. The problem is
that it is very difficult to give a definition of psychology. The subject is so broad, it covers so much ground, and its terms are so ambiguous, so open to different interpretations, that it is quite hard to get students off on the right track. One really needs to study
psychology to get a good feeling for what it is! At the end of this course, you will know
what psychology is much better than can be explained to you now.

Pop Culture

In addition, popular culture and the media have, to some extent, already taught you what psychology is—and guess what? They have sent you down the wrong path! The concept of psychology that is portrayed on TV, in movies, newspapers, and magazines, and even in many high school psychology courses not only is skewed, it is often quite wrong! Psychology is not what you probably think it is.

Popular culture teaches us that psychologists are either mind readers or therapists. But this view is both misleading and wrong. Psychology is a tremendously broad field that includes everything from therapists to researchers who put electrodes into the backs of frogs' eyes. Psychology is a wide-ranging discipline and definitely is not limited to people who listen to others talk about their emotions or their dreams. Well, what is psychology then?

What's Official

The official definition of psychology is a good place to begin: **Psychology** is the science of behavior and mental processes.

This definition needs a good deal of elaboration. First notice that this definition describes the science of psychology, not the practice of psychology. There are two quite different categories of psychology. One is a purely scientific approach that tries to identify laws and principles, just as in biology, physics, or chemistry. The other is the application of those laws in business, schools, industry, personal relationships, or therapy. We have two different enterprises, both called psychology. One is the process of finding scientific laws; the other is the practical application of scientific principles. The single term *psychology* refers to two very different things.

In this class, as always in general psychology, we study the scientific side of psychology, not the practical application or therapy side. There are college courses that focus primarily on therapy and helping people with psychological problems—classes in human services, counseling, chemical dependency, and so on—and they also include some study of psychological principles. But therapy and application are not the main emphasis in this course.

General psychology is more like a course in physics, chemistry, or biology. In this course you will learn about basic concepts, principles, theories, people, events, and research findings in the scientific study of behavior and mental processes. We do not learn how to be therapists or how to read minds, and we do not talk about what feelings or dreams we have had. In this course, we study the results of scientific research, theories, and ideas about behavior and the mind.

The good news is that the breadth of psychology makes it very likely that you will find something that you like and something that you are good at within psychology.

THINK TANK

What are some ideas that you have about psychology?

What does a psychologist do?

Where do you think people get their ideas about psychology and other disciplines?

How accurate do you think these ideas are?

Why did you decide to take this course?

What do you hope to get out of it? How could you or your professor make this course a good one?

Divisions of Psychology

As I hope you are starting to realize, psychology is not one unified discipline, but rather a broad field that includes many diverse topics of study and various applications of its findings and theories. There is no one kind of psychology; there are many disparate subfields. The most common subtype is **clinical psychology**, in which psychologists provide therapy and counseling to people with behavioral or emotional concerns. However, most psychologists are not clinical psychologists. Some psychologists work in schools, institutions, or agencies. Many psychologists work in colleges or universities as researchers or teachers who study a wide variety of issues and problems. Some common fields of study by psychological researchers include human development, animal behavior (**comparative psychology**), learning and memory, personality, intelligence, emotion, physiology, sports, health, business, school, **human factors** (designing equipment for efficient use by people), social issues, and mental illness (**abnormal psychology** or **psychopathology**). As you can see, there is a wide range of topics in psychology.

TABLE 1.1 Some Subtypes of Psychology

Subtype	Focus
1. Clinical	Therapy for people with emotional problems
2. Social	Study of how people are influenced by other people or by groups
3. Comparative	Animal behavior
4. Industrial/organizational (I/O)	Improving worker efficiency and satisfaction
5. Developmental	Study the principles of maturation and development
6. Experimental	Laboratory research of psychological principles

There are two large organizations of psychologists. The oldest is the **American Psychological Association (APA)**. It has many thousands of members around the world and is divided into dozens of divisions including Teaching, Counseling, Personality and Social, Experimental, Industrial and Organizational (popularly known as I/O), Developmental, School, Statistics, Sport, Humanistic, Consumer, Aesthetics, Substance Abuse, Women, Family, Gay Issues, Health, Population, and even Peace Psychology. If you meet a psychologist, be sure to ask what kind she or he is.

The **American Psychological Society (APS)** was formed to meet the needs of scientific psychologists. This group publishes information and hosts meetings aimed at the scientific exploration of behavior and the mind rather than focusing on psychological applications, such as issues of therapy. The APS is more

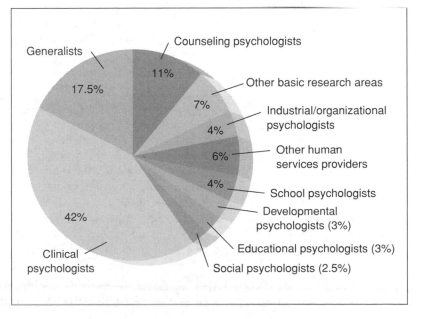

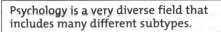

Psychology is a very diverse field that includes many different subtypes.

a scientific group, while the larger APA leans more toward the concerns of counselors and therapists.

THINK TANK

Name some different topics that you think psychologists might be interested in studying.

Match those topics with the different subfields of psychology.

Connecting Concepts

In Chapter 8, you will learn about the most common theories of personality; in Chapter 9, you will learn about mental illnesses; and in Chapter 10, you will learn about the various treatments that clinical psychologists and psychiatrists use to help people with psychological disorders.

Psychiatry

Psychology is not the same as psychiatry. A **psychiatrist** is a medical doctor who specializes in helping people with emotional and behavioral problems. To become a psychiatrist, you must go to medical school and earn an M.D. degree. **Psychiatry** is a branch of medical practice. Some psychiatrists, maybe 5%, receive additional training in the theory and methods that were developed by Sigmund Freud about 100 years ago. Psychiatrists who conduct Freudian therapy are called **psychoanalysts,** a term that is often abbreviated as *analysts.*

Psychologists earn degrees in one or more of the many subfields of psychology. A psychologist might study learning, behavior, human development, motivation, and many other topics. Psychologists who study emotional and behavioral problems can set up a practice to help people. They are called **clinical psychologists.** A clinical psychologist is similar to a psychiatrist but does not have a degree in medicine. Medical doctors are licensed by the federal government and can legally prescribe drugs, give electroshock treatment, set a broken arm, and perform other medical procedures. A practicing psychologist, by contrast, is licensed by the state government, and licensing rules vary somewhat from state to state and are administered by a board of psychology.

Psychologists in any of the various subtypes, such as school psychology or applied psychology, must be licensed in their state if they are providing consumer services. In most states, to be granted a license to practice psychology, one must earn at least a master's degree in some branch of psychology, pass a test administered by the board, and pay a fee. However, licensing laws do vary, and some psychology practitioners are not licensed, so potential clients should be knowledgeable and careful consumers of psychological services. Of course, most psychologists who do research, teach, or work for an institution (but do not charge a fee to clients) do not need to be licensed.

Return of the Definition!

Look again at the definition of psychology: The science of behavior and mental processes. There are three important terms here. First, psychology is a science. Psychologists use scientific methods and reasoning. Chapter 2 outlines the common scientific methods used in psychology. Second, psychologists try to understand behavior. Behavior means anything that an animal does. It is not what happens to an animal, but the actions of the animal. Some behavior is directly observable, such as walking, talking, or moving about. Some behavior, such as heartbeat, is not directly observable but can be detected with fairly simple procedures. Some behavior, such as brain activity, requires sophisticated equipment to observe and measure. Psychology tries to scientifically study behavior and find the laws that explain it.

Third, psychology is interested in mental processes. This means the mind. Psychologists want to know everything about mental states, consciousness, awareness, perception, memory, thinking, dreaming, and so on. Unfortunately, mental processes are not observable in any direct way, so the workings of the mind must be inferred by studying something else that is observable, such as brain waves, eye movements, body language, or what a person says or does. The mind is not open to direct scientific observation. This is a problem that will be discussed later.

So even scientific psychology (what we cover in this course) really has two fields of interest: observable behaviors and mental experiences.

Psychology Alphabet

A good way to define scientific psychology is to focus on its domain, its topics of interest. A nice way to describe the domain of psychology is to divide it into three categories that can be represented with the letters A, B, and C. Psychology includes the study of the following:

- **Affect,** which refers to the emotions, moods, or temperaments that we experience. Fear, love, depression, nervousness, anger, and happiness—these are states of affect.
- **Behavior,** which refers to actions, to what an animal does. Psychology is not limited to the study of humans; lower animals are also studied. Psychologists try to uncover the laws of animal (the broad definition, including humans) behavior.
- **Cognition,** which refers to mental acts, whether conscious or unconscious. Memory, learning, perception, thinking, reasoning, intelligence, problem solving, and similar processes performed by our brains are all included in the concept of cognition.

So psychology is the study of the ABCs! The goals of psychology are to describe, explain, predict, and control emotions, actions, and cognitions.

Pyramid of Sciences

As you know, there are many different sciences, and each one attempts to understand a certain portion of the world around us. Psychology is one of these sciences, and it has its own domain, its own topics of study. However, it is often useful to think about how psychology fits into the whole scheme of the sciences. One interesting way to do this is to consider the **pyramid of sciences,** an organization of scientific disciplines that is based on their domains.

At the bottom of the pyramid is physics, the scientific study of the laws of the physical universe. In a sense, physics studies the smallest particles in the natural world—atoms, subatomic particles, and so on. Above physics on the pyramid is chemistry, the study of how those atoms and molecules come together, form bonds, and eventually create elements, the fundamental chemical units of our natural world. The domain of chemistry is just a bit larger than that of physics. Above chemistry is biology, the scientific study of living things. Biologists need to know about chemistry, and even about physics, to accurately describe the complicated functions that define biological life.

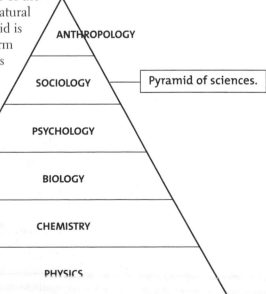

Pyramid of sciences.

Above biology on the pyramid of sciences is psychology. Psychology focuses on the individual—the personality, memory, learning, development, and other characteristics of an individual organism. Unlike biology, psychology does not center its attention on the parts or the processes of biological life but instead directs its main scientific gaze at the whole living organism. Psychology is interested in the actions, emotions, and cognitions of all animals, not just humans. The focus is on the individual, however, rather than on the organism's parts or on groups of individuals.

Above psychology is sociology. This is the science of groups of individuals. Sociologists study societies and attempt to uncover laws and principles that describe and explain the actions of the group. Naturally, sociology sometimes overlaps with psychology. For example, there is a branch of psychology called social psychology that studies how an individual is influenced by other individuals. Its topics include conformity, aggression, prejudice, obedience, and attraction.

At the top of the pyramid of sciences, above sociology, we find anthropology, the scientific study of the origin of humans and the study of the physical, social, and cultural development of humans over long periods of time.

Recap

— Psychology is difficult to define because it has so many different divisions and because there are many misconceptions about it.

— Popular culture gives the idea that psychology is only about therapy; the scientific side of psychology is often ignored.

— The official definition of psychology is: The science of behavior and mental processes.

— Psychology studies the ABCs: affect (emotional feelings), behavior (actions), and cognition (thinking, perceiving, memory, and reasoning).

— Psychology has many subfields that are often quite different from one another. The most common is clinical psychology; others include developmental, social, dustrial/organizational, and experimental.

— Psychologists are different from psychiatrists, who are medical doctors.

— Psychology is a science that falls between biology and sociology on the pyramid of sciences (physics on the bottom, anthropology on the top).

A BRIEF HISTORY OF PSYCHOLOGY

"Human history in essence is the history of ideas."
— H. G. WELLS

Next we tackle the issue of where psychology came from: How did it get to be what it is today? People have been interested in the issues of psychology for eons, but as a scientific discipline, psychology is very young. That is why in 1908 pioneer researcher Hermann Ebbinghaus said of psychology: "It has a long past, but only a short history."

Earliest Beginnings

All sciences in Western civilization had their origins in ancient Greece about 2,500 years ago. Some ancient Greeks were curious about the world and began to reason logically and carefully about things, trying to determine facts and truths about the universe. These early thinkers were called philosophers. The term *philosophy* comes from the Greek language and is a combination of *phil*, meaning "love," and *sophia*, which means "wisdom." (The term *sophomore*, by the way, is a combination of *sophia* for wisdom and *moros* for foolish, meaning that sophomores are people who have just enough knowledge to foolishly think they know everything!) So a philosopher is a lover of wisdom. Are you a philosopher?

The best-known ancient Greek philosophers were Socrates, Plato, and Aristotle. I'm sure you've heard of them. ("SPA" will help you recall their names; just picture them sitting in a hot tub!) These were truly philosophers; they were obsessed with the love of wisdom. For instance, Socrates said, "There is only one good, knowledge, and only one evil, ignorance," and Aristotle wrote, "Plato is dear to me, but dearer still is truth."

The ancient Greek philosophers believed that the mind and the soul were essentially the same thing. Their word for the mind/soul was *psyche*. Therefore one might say that one subdivision of their study of philosophy was psychology, literally *the logical study of the mind* (*logos* means "logical study"), even though the word psychology was not invented until many centuries later.

Socrates was accused of "denying the gods recognized by the state, and corrupting the young." He was found guilty and forced to die by drinking poison.

So in a sense, psychology began thousands of years ago as a subset of the thoughts of ancient Greek philosophers, and the word itself reflects these origins. Today we use the Greek letter psi (ψ) to stand for psychology because it is the first letter in the Greek word psyche (ψυχη). This will be a handy shortcut when writing notes.

Ψ = the Greek letter psi, used as an abbreviation for psychology.

One of the early Greek philosophers was a man named **Hippocrates** who is today credited as being the first medical doctor in Western civilization. Physicians today take the **Hippocratic oath** (named for Hippocrates), promising to always try to help and never harm people. This oath is based on Hippocrates' advice: "As to diseases make a habit of two things—to help, or at least, to do no harm."

Hippocrates was far ahead of his time in thinking about medical problems. Thousands of years ago (just as today, I'm sorry to say!) many people believed that physical disorders were caused by supernatural forces. A person who had a seizure, for example, was thought to be possessed by divine spirits. Yes, epilepsy (abnormal electrical functioning of brain cells) was known as a divine illness. Hippocrates, however, did not believe this. He attributed disorders to problems in the body. He believed in **somatogenic** (caused by the physical body; *soma* means "body," and *genic* means "causes") medicine. Epilepsy, he believed, originated in the brain. Hippocrates wrote, "There are two things, science and opinion; the former begets knowledge, the latter, ignorance."

Mental Tricks

One of the disorders that was common in ancient Greece and has continued to be a problem over the years was known as **hysteria.** In these cases, people would experience physical impairments (blindness, deafness, paralysis, numbness, pain, etc.) without any apparent organic illness or trauma. A woman might claim to have a paralyzed arm, for instance, yet a medical examination will find nothing wrong with her arm, and in fact she often moves it when she is distracted.

People with hysteria believe that they really do have something wrong with their body, but doctors can't find anything physically or organically dysfunctional that could cause their complaints. It's not that these patients are pretending. It's rather that they actually seem to be experiencing some body impairment in their mind but not in their body.

For example, a man went to a doctor and said that he was completely blind. The doctor asked whether he had experienced a bump on the head or something. No, the

Connecting Concepts

In Chapter 3, you will learn a great deal about how brains work, including some ideas about how a brain may "see" something that the mind does not. Hysteria is now called conversion disorder and is discussed in the chapter on psychological disorders (Chapter 9).

man said that nothing like that had happened to him. The doctor asked how it came about then that he suddenly went blind. The man said that he was on his way to his wedding when it occurred. The doctor then asked the question we always ask when we suspect hysteria: "What does it mean to you to have this problem?" The man answered, "I really want to get married, but I guess I can't now."

Although he claims that he wants to, we suspect that the man might not want to get married. When asked, he insists that he does. Apparently, the blindness is some sort of defense against getting married that the man is unaware of. Apparently, he really thinks that he is blind. However, if we walk him down the hall toward a pillar, he goes around it. He doesn't bump into things. If we ask him why this is so, he claims to be psychic or lucky or something. He persists in feeling that he is blind, although he is not. His brain is able to "see," and so he does not bump into things. But his brain is preventing his conscious mind from "seeing." His brain sees, but his mind doesn't. Do you see?

Wandering Wombs

What could cause hysteria? What could cause people to believe that they have some physical impairment that in fact they do not have? For thousands of years, the majority of people believed that such an odd thing was caused by evil forces or supernatural possession. But Hippocrates and other philosophers did not agree. They thought that hysteria must have a physical cause. Now here's an amazing thing: They believed that hysteria was produced by a woman's uterus, her womb, moving around inside of her body, perhaps yearning to become pregnant. Yes, that's right. Hippocrates and others were far ahead of their time in eschewing supernatural causes, but they were not well informed about the fact that our internal organs do not roam around inside of us!

In fact, the word *hysteria* comes from the Greek word for "uterus" (as in the word *hysterectomy*). For years, psychiatrists believed that hysteria was a problem only women could have. Men were not diagnosed with hysteria. And what was the treatment for hysteria? If a woman had such a problem—suppose, for example, that she complained of a numb arm—the ancient Greek doctors would rub foul-smelling manure on her arm to entice the womb to leave that area, and they would place a bouquet of nice-smelling flowers in her crotch to lure the womb back where it belonged! I guess they thought wombs had a sense of smell.

The Unconscious

We no longer use the term *hysteria*, since it is both anatomically incorrect and sexist. This fascinating condition is now known as a **conversion disorder.** Many people still experience this problem; for example, recently, in Europe, many people thought they were sick from Coca-Cola because they had heard that it contained a harmful substance. They experienced many vague body symptoms. In fact, the Coke was perfectly normal.

Sigmund Freud (1856–1939), who was trained as a neurologist and practiced psychiatry, was one of the first to say that hysteria could occur in men. He was jeered at and derided for what was then considered an outrageous idea. It turns out, of course, that Freud was right. Freud was the first to give us a good understanding of hysteria. His first book, written in 1896 with his colleague Dr. Joseph Breuer, was titled *Studies in Hysteria*; in the book, he described this condition in a number of people and outlined his ideas about its cause and a possible therapy. Freud believed that the problem was in his patients' minds—not in the conscious part, but in an **unconscious.** Hence, Freud made an important distinction: The mind can be divided into two components: things we are aware of (conscious) and things we are unaware of (unconscious). Our brain knows some things that it doesn't tell our aware consciousness. Our aware mind doesn't know everything!

So according to Freud's **psychoanalytic theory,** the man who thought he was blind thought so only in the conscious part of his mind. His unconscious (his brain activities that he didn't know about) knew that he didn't want to get married, but it kept this information from his awareness (by a technique that Freud called **repression**). Freud taught that the cure for hysteria was to help patients become aware of their unconscious. In most cases of conversion disorder, Freud's approach continues to be the most successful treatment.

Today when we say that psychology studies the mind, we are using the term "mind" in a broad way, broad enough to include both conscious and unconscious brain activity. But it wasn't always like that. Most early scientific psychologists focused only on the conscious mind—things that we are aware of, such as perceptions, memories, dreams, and sensations. However, it was the ancient Greek philosophers who started the whole enterprise with their logical, reasoned approach to the mind. Next let's continue this story by turning to modern philosophy.

Focus on Mind

The first modern philosopher is usually considered to be a Frenchman named **René Descartes** who lived from 1596 to 1650. Descartes was a genius in mathematics; in fact, he invented analytical geometry (the graphs that we make are named after him—they are known as Cartesian planes). Descartes is known for his rational approach to philosophy. That is, he wanted to discover the truths about the world through logical reasoning.

Perhaps you have wondered the same thing that Descartes wondered. As a young man (23 years old) he began to doubt the things he had been taught. He began to wonder just what things he should believe—what was true in this world and what was not. Should we believe something just because someone said that it is so? What is the best way to decide what to believe and what not to believe? Can we trust our own senses? What if we are hallucinating or dreaming and we don't know it? What if our senses are not accurate windows of the real world?

René Descartes decided to reject everything he had been taught and to construct his ideas of truth through careful, logical reasoning. He began with a simple idea that has become very well known and important. The first, most basic truth that Descartes recognized as undeniably true was the now well-known maxim "I think, therefore I am" (in Latin: "*Cogito, ergo sum*"). Descartes believed that because he was able to experience his own thoughts, memories, and awareness of the world, he must therefore exist. This idea became the basis for his other conclusions about the truths of the universe around us. Notice that Descartes's reasoning was centered on his mental experiences—the fact that he was aware of his own mind. This is one of the reasons that Descartes is called the first modern philosopher. He put the focus on the mind. We are defined not by our bodies, but by our minds.

Descartes's idea can be extended. If my mental awareness proves my reality, then I must not be a dream. Someone who is dreamed is not real and therefore cannot have a mind. Only things that are real can have a mind, since mental activity proves existence. If something has a mind, it is real. If it is not real, it must not have a mind. Does this sound reasonable to you?

Many psychologists believe that using only logical reasoning to reach accurate conclusions will not be enough. They argue that sometimes we must observe and measure things to find out what's true. For example, we cannot use reasoning to determine how many students at a college wear glasses. That is something that we can, however, determine by observation and measurement. This idea is known as **empiricism,** compared

Sigmund Freud, founder of psychoanalytic psychology.

René Descartes, leading proponent of dualism.

to Descartes's method of **rationalism**. An **empirical question** is one that can be answered through observation and measurement. In science today, empiricism is the most important foundation.

The Inaccessible Mind

But perhaps you have noticed one of the major problems that we have in the scientific study of psychology. Because scientific progress and accuracy depend on empiricism, we must observe and measure things to find out what is true (what is empirically true). Remember that psychology is the science of two things: behavior (what animals do) and mental processes (memory, thoughts, dreams, and so on—in other words, the mind). On the one hand, behavior is observable and measurable. So a scientific study of behavior is possible.

Mental processes, on the other hand, are private, subjective, personal experiences that we can know only in ourselves; we cannot measure or observe them in others. So psychology cannot be a science of the mind, at least not directly. Psychologists must infer things about the mind by observing behavior. With most humans we can ask them what is in their minds. Of course, we can know only what people tell us or demonstrate; we cannot observe their minds directly. In those who can't talk, such as babies and animals, we must infer mental states on the basis of what they do.

For example, in a recent study (Terrace & Brannon, 1998), a computer screen was divided into four quadrants. In each quadrant was a picture of a number of objects—either one, two, three, or four. A chimpanzee who touched the quadrants in the correct order—one object, two, three, then four—would receive a nice piece of food. Soon the chimps learned to touch the screen in the proper order. Next comes

THINK TANK

How should we define the "mind"?

What do we mean by *mental*?

Is the mind the same thing as the brain?

Does the mind include emotions?

Does the mind include everything that the brain does, even biological housekeeping functions such as metabolism?

Do animals have minds?

What about insects?

What about bacteria?

Is mind the same thing as conscious awareness?

If so, isn't the mind private and subjective?

If so, how can we have a science of the mind?

How would we know if a robot or a machine had a mind?

What would it have to do?

the interesting part. The researchers placed larger quantities of objects in the screen's quadrants: five, six, seven, and eight objects. The chimps had never seen this before. What would they do? You guessed it—they touched the screen in the proper order. Chimpanzees can count!

We do not know what was going on in the minds of the chimpanzees. We can conclude only that their brains apparently have the ability to compare different quantities of objects and to arrange them sequentially by amount. Are they consciously thinking? If so, what are they thinking? We do not know. Minds are private and personal. Science cannot get at them directly. Psychologists who want to scientifically study mental things—the mind—must be satisfied with assumptions and indirect measures. The mind cannot be observed directly.

Sleep and Dreaming

Another good example of the unobservable nature of mental events is dreaming. I assume that you dream, but I do not know it empirically. It is often said that psychologists study dreaming. But this is not true. At least, it is not true that scientists *empirically* study dreaming; that is impossible. Dreams must be studied indirectly. Dreams are mental states and therefore are not accessible to direct experimentation.

How do we know when someone is dreaming? Look at their brain waves, you say? Well, how do we know that certain brain waves occur during dreaming? How do we know that people are dreaming when they have those certain brain waves? Look at their eye movements, you say? Well, how do we know that certain eye movements occur during dreaming? How do we know that people are dreaming when their eyes are moving rapidly?

It's strange, I suppose, but the answer is that we *cannot* know empirically when someone is dreaming. What researchers do, of course, is wake people up and ask them. That is the only way we have to try to determine whether someone is dreaming. We cannot know by any physical measurement. Do dogs dream? There is no way to know empirically. Do babies dream? I do not know, and neither does anyone else—except the babies. Do college students dream? They say they do, but I do not empirically know. I have no way of measuring dreams. I must wake people up and ask them. Mental states, awareness and consciousness, memory and thinking, dreaming, and all other conditions of the mind cannot be known empirically. Psychologists who say they study dreaming are actually studying what people *say* about dreaming. A dream and what a person reports about it are two entirely different things.

People have always been interested in sleep and dreaming, I suppose, but the scientific study of these enigmatic processes benefited immensely from the invention of the **electroencephalograph** (EEG). This technique uses sensitive electrodes placed on a person's head that can detect the electrical firings of groups of brain cells. The patterns detected are called **brain waves.** When people are asleep, their brain waves go through a number of changes and are categorized by their physical characteristics.

Sometimes when people are asleep, their brain waves are active, as if they were awake. At the same time, the sleeping person's eyes are darting around rapidly. This stage of sleep is therefore called **REM sleep** (pronounced "rem"), which stands for *rapid eye movement.* The other stages of sleep grouped together are simply called **NREM** (pronounced "non-rem") and are numbered 1 through 4, stage 4 being the deepest sleep.

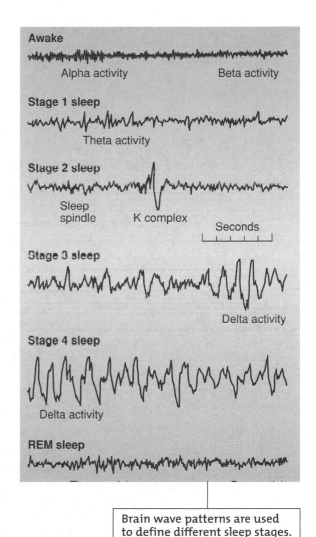

Brain wave patterns are used to define different sleep stages.

When people are awakened during REM sleep, they report dreaming about 85% of the time; people report dreaming only about 15% of the time when they are awakened from NREM sleep. For this reason, REM sleep is often known as *dreaming sleep*. All other mammals and most birds also have REM sleep, as indicated by their brain waves and eye movements. Do they dream? We don't know. With electrodes we can measure only brain waves and eye movements. We cannot measure mental activities. That is the problem. If psychology wants to be a science of mental activity, it is going to be difficult because mental activity cannot be measured directly. Psychologists must ask people what's going on in their minds or use some other indirect means of getting information about mental states. (You can learn more about sleep in Chapter 4.)

Dualism

René Descartes contributed to psychology by making an interesting claim about the mind. Descartes was a religious person, and the Church authorities had ruled that people should not study certain things. Galileo and other scientists had been put into prison for making scientific statements that went against the Church's teachings—for example, that the earth revolves around the sun. To avoid problems with the Church, Descartes separated the mind from the body and declared that they were two different kinds of things. Descartes argued that our bodies are made of physical substances—molecules, atoms, and so on—and as such were subject to the physical laws of the universe and could legitimately be studied. On the other hand, the mind, he argued, was not a physical thing; it was like a ghost or a spirit, and therefore was not subject to physical laws. The mind was free, Descartes said, completely separate from the physical world.

Descartes's view, dividing the universe into two categories (physical and nonphysical), became known as **dualism.** As you are probably well aware, this is a very popular view among the general public even today. Most scientists and philosophers, however, do not believe that this is a well-reasoned idea. A modern neuroscientist would argue that mental phenomena emanate from the physical brain and are therefore physical products that do follow physical laws. This view is known as **monism** (one kind of thing—the physical).

Descartes had reasoned that our brains control the movements of our bodies but that our brains receive their instructions from our minds. Other thinkers disagreed, arguing that there is no way that a nonphysical thing could make a physical thing move. Descartes believed that our minds interact with our brains via a small gland, known as the **pineal gland,** located about in the middle of the brain. For Descartes, the pineal gland was where the mind and soul connected with the brain. How a nonphysical thing can interact with a physical thing is one of the challenges to dualism that has been posed.

Dualists believe that the mind is a nonphysical thing, a ghost or spirit, that is free and not subject to laws or predictability and that it can somehow influence the brain to send signals to the muscles of the body and thereby direct behavior. Monists, on the contrary, believe that the mind is a subjective experience produced by physical, biological activity in the brain and that therefore the mind is predictable and subject to laws.

Here is another way to look at it: Dualists say that the mind controls the brain; monists claim that the brain controls the mind. Descartes said that if you want to move your arm, first you must freely think this idea in your nonphysical mind/soul. The mind/soul then tells your brain to send a signal to your arm muscles. By contrast, monists say that a nonphysical thing cannot think things and cannot send signals to a physical brain. They argue that the brain, not the mind, is where thoughts and signals originate. Whereas dualists say that the mind controls the

FYI

Dualism is the philosophy that behavior is controlled by a nonphysical mind, while monism says that the mind is a phyical creation of the brain (awareness results when brain cell networks are in a certain state).

brain and body, monists say that the brain controls the mind and the body. Philosophers still argue about this issue, although scientists are firmly in the monist camp.

Philosophy has always been, and continues to be, an important ingredient of psychology. In a manner philosophy was the "mother" of psychology. However, modern scientific psychologists also rely heavily on empirical research. Philosophy is not enough. In fact, philosophical ideas and reasoning are less common in psychology today than are mathematical and experimental procedures. Knowing that, let's turn next to the story of how the empirical, experimental science of psychology got its start.

FYI

Descartes was hired to tutor Queen Christina of Sweden but became ill in the cold climate and died of pneumonia. To fit his corpse into a box, his head was cut off. What an ironic thing to happen to a dualist—to have his head separated from his body! Descartes' decapitated head was stolen and not found for nearly 100 years. He is now buried in Paris but is missing a finger that was also stolen.

Recap

— Psychology began as a branch of philosophy in ancient Greece.

— The unconscious part of the mind is at work in hysteria—a condition in which people have physical symptoms without organic causes.

— Ancient Greek philosophers, such as Hippocrates, believed that hysteria was caused by a woman's uterus moving in her body.

— Sigmund Freud was a psychiatrist (trained as a neurologist) who put great importance on unconscious mental processes. Freud's psychoanalytic theory taught that hysteria resulted from repression.

— Minds are not objectively measurable. Dreams and other mental experiences must be studied in indirect ways.

— The EEG measures brain waves and is used to define stages of sleep and alertness.

— REM sleep is associated with rapid movement of the eyes, active brain waves, and dreaming.

— René Descartes promoted the philosophy of dualism, which says that the mind is a nonphysical thing. Monists, by contrast, say that the mind is a physical brain state.

EARLY SCIENTIFIC PSYCHOLOGY

"People are trapped in history and history is trapped in them."
—JAMES BALDWIN

The person who is most often regarded as the first experimental psychologist was a German professor of physiology named **Wilhelm Wundt** (1832–1920). In 1879 Wundt established a laboratory at the University in Leipzig, Germany, for the scientific study

Wilhelm Wundt, the first experimental psychologist in 1879, shown with the clock he used in his attempt to time thinking.

FYI Wundt was a teacher to nearly every famous psychologist of his time. He was an avid experimentalist and published 53,735 pages in his lifetime.

of the conscious mind. In 1979, one hundred years later, Wundt was recognized by the American Psychological Association as the initiator of the empirical approach to psychology. If philosophy is the "mother" of psychology, then physiology is psychology's "father."

Wundt was not a psychologist by education; there was no such thing yet, because psychology as a separate discipline was just being formed. Wundt brought scientific thinking and methodology from his study of physiology to his attempts to measure the conscious mind. He wanted to move psychology out of the subjective field of philosophy and into the objectivity of science. He said, "We take issue with every treatment of psychology that is based on simple self-observation or on philosophical presuppositions." Wundt wanted psychology to be a science, like physiology. But psychology, of course, would be the science of the conscious mind. That was his goal.

In his laboratory, Wundt attempted to measure such things as the speed of thinking, using a clock with a pendulum that he had fashioned for just that purpose. He was measuring people's mental ideas about stimuli they experienced; today this branch of psychology is called psychophysics, and it is discussed in Chapter 4. Wundt's emphasis was on conscious awareness, and he found that to measure the mind, it was necessary to ask people questions about what they were thinking, feeling, sensing, or remembering. Recall what was said above, that the mind is not subject to direct experimental investigation. An empirical science of the mind is a bit of a paradox.

What Is Mind?

Wundt had a student named **Edward B. Titchener** (1867–1927), who came to Cornell University in New York and set up a laboratory to study the conscious mind. Titchener believed that psychology should be like chemistry and should try to find out what things are made of. For example, the periodic table shows the elements that everything physical is made of. Titchener thought that there might be something like that for the conscious mind. He wanted to find the structures of the mind; therefore, his approach is known as **structuralism.**

Titchener asked people to tell him what they experienced in their minds when they engaged in certain activities, such as eating an apple, or when they thought of certain concepts. This technique is called **introspection** because it asks people to look inside themselves and report on their mental experiences. Introspection is self-report. Because the mind is not directly observable, introspection is a common means of trying to discover what is in it. Psychologists today often rely on introspection. For example, as was mentioned above, researchers who want to study dreaming or other mental states must ask people to look inside their minds and report their experiences. (In fact, introspection is a very poor scientific method. Can you imagine if other sciences used such a subjective technique? What if your chemistry professor said that today you would imagine what happens when chlorine is mixed with hydrogen?)

Titchener drew conclusions about what the mind is made of that today sound quite strange. For example, he concluded that a certain concept in the mind consisted of a small yellow triangle partially stuck inside a blue rubbery substance. I suppose early chemists found that it sounded strange to people when they were told that water was made of hydrogen and oxygen, too. The idea that the mind is made of something as abstract as yellow triangles is a weird idea by today's standards. In fact, the whole idea of finding out what the mind is made of is a bit odd—well, other than the idea of studying the brain and its functioning. Today's modern psychologists no longer attempt to find out what the mind is made of in the manner of Titchener. Instead, scientists study the biological events that go on in the brain that correspond to mental phenomena.

Whole Patterns

In Germany, about one hundred years ago, a group of budding psychologists argued that structuralism was a meaningless approach, a dead-end, because the mind could not be meaningfully divided up into its parts. These thinkers argued that the mind must be understood as a whole, with attention to the relationships between its parts. Their approach became known as **Gestalt psychology.**

The German word *Gestalt* has no exact equivalent in English. Its meaning is easier to understand if you know the Gestalt psychology motto: "The whole is greater than the sum of the parts." The Gestalt psychology movement was led by Max Wertheimer (1880–1943), Wolfgang Köhler (1887–1967), Kurt Koffka (1886–1941), and Kurt Lewin (1890–1947).

The word *Gestalt* literally means "form," or something like it. But in psychology, the term *Gestalt* is used to mean something like the relationships between parts that make a whole pattern emerge. Think of the tiles in a mosaic and how they form an image by the way they are positioned. You can also think of the term *Gestalt* as roughly equivalent to the idea of "whole."

Gestalt psychologists studied human perception and identified many important principles that describe how we perceive the world. For example, they studied optical illusions and discovered rules regarding depth perception and other mental processes, rules that describe how our brain and mind create perceptions. A good example is the **phi phenomenon.** If similar images appear within a split second of each other (such as the frames in a film or pictures on cards fanned quickly in front of your eyes), a brain does not perceive separate images; it perceives one image that is in motion. In this instance, the perception of motion is created by the brain. This is an example of Gestalt. Gestalt psychologists also studied insight learning—suddenly grasping an idea or solution. The leaders of Gestalt psychology were nearly all Jewish, and they all fled Nazi-controlled Germany and came to the United States, where they continued their work; hence, many Gestalt ideas originated in the United States.

How Does the Mind Work?

While Wundt, Titchener, and the Gestalt psychologists were developing their ideas of what the new discipline of psychology should be, a professor at Harvard, **William James** (1842–1910), was giving the first lectures on scientific psychology and published an acclaimed textbook in the field, *Principles of Psychology* (1890). James was a professor in two fields, philosophy and physiology (the field of Wundt). Even today a fairly good definition of psychology is that it is a blend of those two areas of study.

William James did not agree with structuralism. He did not believe that this new discipline of psychology should be like chemistry and try to find the structure of the conscious mind. James reasoned that if you sent someone to study the Mississippi River and they returned to tell you that it is made of hydrogen and oxygen, something would be wrong. Psychology's goal, James argued, should not be to find the elements or structures of the mind; rather, psychology's goal should be to find the functions of the mind. What is the mind for, and how does it work? How do we remember, think, learn, and reason? Because James's focus was on how the mind functions, this approach to psychology became known as **functionalism.** James wrote, "I wished by treating psychology like a natural science, to help her to become one."

Edward Titchener, proponent of structuralism.

Connecting Concepts

The principles of perception that were studied by Gestalt psychologists are discussed in Chapter 4 along with other interesting facts about how our brains sense and perceive the world around us.

William James, the first American psychologist, proponent of functionalism.

William James was an influential, charismatic, and caring professor and a gifted writer. Many of his students went on to become famous psychologists themselves. His brother was Henry James, the great American novelist. The famed author Gertrude Stein was one of many influential and gifted people who studied with William James. On her philosophy final exam, Ms. Stein wrote only that she did not feel like doing philosophy that day. Professor James gave her an "A+" and wrote that sometimes he didn't feel like it either. (Why don't you try that with your professor?) In the development of scientific psychology in the United States, no one was more important or influential than William James; hence, he is known as the father of American psychology.

William James is well known for his view that the conscious mind is like a stream that flows from one thing to another. Perhaps you have heard or read his term *stream of consciousness.* For James the conscious mind was a flowing awareness that should be studied to find out how it works, and that knowledge should be then used to help people learn, remember, and function. The functionalist psychologists were interested in practical matters of psychology. How do people think? Structuralists, by contrast, were interested in finding out what the mind is made of.

The functionalists, like James, were influenced by **Charles Darwin**'s (1809–1882) theory of evolution: **natural selection.** James and his followers attempted to apply Darwin's ideas to the conscious mind. Perhaps mental functions exist, they reasoned, because they have been selected for their usefulness, just as physical features are selected via genetics for their survival value.

Functionalism is no longer an approach used in psychology, but it was a major contributor to the practical, applied side of psychology. Much of **educational psychology today**—the study of how people learn and remember and how we can help students in practical ways to do better in school—was influenced by the contributions and ideas of William James. We might say that the laboratory, scientific side of psychology—the pure research—was initiated by Wundt, and the applications, the practical side of psychology—applied psychology—began with James.

TABLE 1.2 Early Approaches to Psychology

Approach	Leaders	Basic Idea
Structuralism	Edward Titchener	Find the structures of the conscious mind using introspection.
Functionalism	William James	Find out how the conscious mind functions; how it works.
Gestalt	Max Wertheimer Wolfgang Köhler Kurt Koffka Kurt Lewin	The whole is more than the sum of the parts—find the basic principles of perception.

Recap

— Scientific psychology began in 1879 when Wilhelm Wundt established a laboratory in Leipzig, Germany.

— Wundt's student, Edward Titchener, used introspection to try to find the structures of the conscious mind. This early approach to psychology is known as structuralism.

— Gestalt psychologists believed that the mind should not be broken down into its parts but should be studied as a whole. They studied principles of perception, including optical illusions.

— William James was the father of American psychology. He also rejected structuralism and promoted functionalism, the early school of psychology that attempted to discover the functions of the conscious mind.

MODERN SCHOOLS OF PSYCHOLOGY

"The history of the world is but the biography of great men."
—THOMAS CARLYLE

Into the Depths

Modern psychology began with the ideas of Sigmund Freud (1856–1939). Freud was born in a place in Europe called Moravia, which is now part of the Czech Republic. When Sigmund was only four years old, his family moved to Vienna, Austria, where he lived nearly his whole life. Freud studied to be a physician, was trained in neurology, went to Paris to learn psychiatric techniques such as hypnosis, and returned to practice psychiatry in Vienna.

Freud began developing his ideas about the unconscious because of the things that his patients said. He began to believe that behavior was often caused by things a person doesn't know about, perhaps traumatic events that had been somehow pushed out of awareness. Freud's patients talked about sexual experiences with their parents, and Freud came to believe that sexuality and childhood were important components of personality development. His approach is called psychoanalytic theory. Freud also developed a number of therapeutic techniques aimed at revealing the contents of a patient's unconscious. This therapeutic method is known as **psychoanalysis.**

Freud's psychoanalytic theory says that most human behavior is caused by ideas in the unconscious part of the mind. That is, your behavior is typically the result of something you don't know about. Freud believed that the mind is capable of protecting itself from horrible or traumatic thoughts and events. This process, in which the mind pushes threatening things out of awareness, is called repression. However, Freud proposed that things repressed into the unconscious could still exert their influence over personality and behavior. Most repressed things, he said, came from childhood experiences when the mind was immature and irrational. Freud believed that by revealing the contents of the unconscious, a person could learn to deal with them more rationally and would become psychologically healthier.

Sigmund Freud's ideas about the unconscious became very popular among other psychiatrists and even spread to other thinkers, such as artists, philosophers, and literati. For instance, **surrealist** artists and writers attempted to reveal the contents of their unconscious minds in their art and literature. Freud's ideas were cemented in his landmark book *The Interpretation of Dreams* (1900), in which he argued that the best way to find out what is in the unconscious is to decode a person's dreams. Freud said that dreams were "the royal road to the unconscious." Freud's psychoanalytic theory (and corresponding techniques of psychoanalysis) was the most influential intellectual idea of the early twentieth century.

Freud's Life

Sigmund Freud regularly smoked cigars, which led people to wonder if this was a reflection of what was in his unconscious—perhaps a need for power or authority. It is said that Freud replied to such queries, "Sometimes a cigar is just a cigar." Freud's remark meant that he didn't believe that *all* behaviors emanated from the unconscious. A cigar might or might not be a symbol of an unconscious desire for power, but it certainly is a carcinogen. Unfortunately, because of his smoking, Freud developed cancer of the jaw and had thirty-one surgical operations on his face. They were ultimately unsuccessful.

In 1938, Freud left Vienna and traveled to London with his wife and his daughter Anna (who later also became a famous analyst, having been taught by her father). Freud was Jewish and therefore was hated by the Nazis. Freud and Albert Einstein (who left Germany for Princeton University) were favorite targets of the Nazis, who often burned their books and threatened their lives. Today you can go to Vienna and see Freud's apartment and some of his belongings; you can also visit a Freud museum in London, which houses his famous couch. Freud told his doctor that if he ever became too ill to function properly, he wanted an overdose of morphine. That day came in 1939. Some books say that Freud died of cancer; others say he died of suicide. To be precise, Freud died of assisted suicide because of his cancer.

Focus on Behavior

In the early twentieth century, while Freud's psychoanalytic theory was enjoying its greatest glory, a young man named **John B. Watson** (1878–1958) was finishing a Ph.D. in psychology at the University of Chicago. Watson did research on the behavior of rats, and he was asked by his professors to speculate on what was going on in the minds of his animals. Watson believed not only that was this scientifically impossible (because minds cannot be directly observed), but also that it was irrelevant information. He argued that looking to the mind for the causes of behavior was equivalent to past thinkers' looking for a life force to explain the movement of animals. Watson was convinced that psychology should give up its aspirations of being a science of the mind and should focus instead on being a science of behavior. This approach is called **behaviorism.**

John B. Watson, the founder of behaviorism, the approach to psychology that emphasizes the scientific study of observable behavior.

Watson argued that knowing what is in someone's mind would not help us to explain behavior. Watson was not a dualist—he did not believe that the mind controls behavior. Watson speculated that the causes of behavior could be found in environmental circumstances. He was like a physicist trying to discover fundamental laws that explain why animals acted the way they do. He wanted to control variables within the environment and see what effect that had on behavior. For example, he taught a two-year-old child (Little Albert) to be afraid of a furry rat by making a loud, frightening noise whenever Albert touched the rat. Watson thus showed that an emotional reaction (fear, in this instance) could be learned through a predictable set of circumstances (here, association with a loud noise). Watson believed that all human behaviors were shaped by experiences within the environment.

Watson rejected the notion that human behavior was influenced by unconscious processes or that behavior was guided by inherited factors. His idea of behaviorism argued that behavior was shaped mostly by experiences in the world. One of his most famous quotes indicates his confidence in the effects of experience:

> Give me a dozen healthy infants, well-formed, and my own specified world to bring them up in and I'll guarantee to take any one at random and train him to become any type of specialist I might select—doctor, lawyer, merchant-chief, and yes, even beggar-man and thief, regardless of his talents, penchants, tendencies, abilities, vocations, and race of his ancestors. (Watson, 1924 p. 94)

Psychologists today would agree that Watson's statement is extreme, but they would also agree that his basic contention is sound; it is undeniable that experience plays a profound role in making us what we are.

It is sometimes said that Watson believed that a newborn was like a **tabula rasa** (a "blank slate"), with no inherited tendencies, capable of being shaped in any direction by experiences. Although Watson did put great emphasis on experience, this is not an entirely accurate statement of his beliefs. Notice in the quote above that he refers to "healthy, well-formed infants." Watson undoubtedly did not give enough weight to inherited factors, but neither did he completely ignore them.

Watson was not able to complete his research into the laws of behavior because he was forced to resign from Johns Hopkins University. Why? Because he had an affair with his graduate assistant (Rosalie Rayner, who helped with the study of Little Albert) and was divorced by his wife. Watson went on to a successful career in advertising, and the study of the laws of behavior was left to others.

If you have been wondering why all the important people in the development of scientific psychology were men, it was because women were not allowed to receive Ph.D. degrees in early America. Why? Because they were women! What do you think of that reasoning? (Today, we have nearly the opposite problem: Many fewer men than women study psychology.) In a most flagrantly unfair act, **Mary Whiton Calkins** (1863–1930) was denied a Ph.D. from Harvard in 1895, though she had completed all the requirements and was recommended by the psychology professors at Harvard, including William James. She went on to become the first woman president of the American Psychological Association in 1905.

Margaret Floy Washburn (1871–1939) was the first woman to receive a Ph.D. in psychology. She was awarded the degree from Cornell University in 1894 for the work she did under Titchener. She became president of the APA in 1921.

Anyway, back to our story about behaviorism—John B. Watson's search to discover the laws of behavior fell to another important thinker. **B. F. Skinner** (1904–1990) had studied English at Hamilton College in New York, and he wanted to be a writer. Skinner published his first literary work when he was only ten years old. After graduation from college, he discovered that as a young, inexperienced man, he had nothing to write about. He read a book by John B. Watson detailing the ideas of behaviorism. Skinner then went to Harvard University to study psychology, telling people that he was a behaviorist. No one seemed to know what that was, but it was the beginning of the biggest revolution in modern psychology.

B. F. Skinner, the foremost behaviorist.

Connecting Concepts

The laws of behavior that were uncovered by Watson, Skinner, and other experimental psychologists are presented in Chapter 5. These laws have very practical value; they are often used by psychologists for research purposes, and they are commonly used in the treatment of behavioral problems.

In 1931, Skinner received his Ph.D. from Harvard and secured a job at the University of Minnesota, where he began his research on behavior. He initially used pigeons in his studies because they were plentiful, cheap, and easy to keep. Skinner placed the pigeons in cages (what we now call **Skinner boxes**) in which he could carefully measure changes in their behavior (pecking a disk on the wall, for example) while he manipulated variables, such as giving them food when they pecked. Skinner wrote a number of books detailing his results and the laws of behavior that he discovered. Over the years, Skinner's fame and influence grew, surpassing even that of Freud. In 1947, Skinner returned to teach at Harvard. He continued to argue against the study of the subjective mind and urged psychologists to stick to the scientific study of how experiences influence actions. Skinner believed that cognitive topics, such as language and thinking, should be studied by defining them in behavioral terms. His book *Verbal Behavior* (1957), for example, analyzed language as a type of observable behavior. Because his views were so persistent and extreme, his point of view became known as **radical behaviorism.**

Skinner's support of radical behaviorism continued up to his death from leukemia in 1990. Eight days before he died, Skinner addressed the American Psychological Association and repeated his belief that psychologists should stick to the scientific study of observable, measurable behavior. Many psychologists, however, had become fascinated with cognition and were seeking indirect ways of measuring mental processes. Today, behaviorism remains an important and influential part of psychology, though its influence is somewhat weaker than it was during Skinner's career.

Becoming a Person

We consider psychoanalytic theory (Freud) to be the first modern approach to psychology and behaviorism (Watson and Skinner) to be the second. There is a third school of psychology that emerged, a point of view that is sometimes simply called the third approach. This new way of approaching psychology was initiated by **Abraham Maslow** (1908–1970), who as a young man from Brooklyn told friends that he was going out West to become a famous psychologist. He went to the University of Wisconsin–Madison, which is way out West if you're from New York.

Maslow was disenchanted with Freud's psychoanalytic theory because it focused on abnormality and ignored the conscious mind. He was unhappy with behaviorism because it didn't focus on the mind at all and dealt with behaviors that were common in lower animals, giving little or no attention to characteristics that were uniquely human. Maslow believed that psychology should include an approach that centered on the normal conscious minds of humans, an approach that came to be called **humanistic psychology** or **humanism.** Maslow created humanism as an approach to

THINK TANK

If psychologists decide to study only objective, observable behavior, does this mean that they cannot study the mind?

Is the mind behavior?

It is not directly observable, is it?

What if we find indirect ways of studying the mind, such as brain scans?

Would that provide acceptable data on which to draw conclusions about the mind?

Or would it be too subjective?

psychology that would (1) focus on humans, not lower animals; (2) be concerned with good, normal human traits, not abnormality; and (3) study conscious awareness and feelings, not behavior or the unconscious.

Humanism is not a scientific approach like behaviorism, nor does it use case studies of people with psychological disorders, as does psychoanalytic theory (although Maslow was interested in case studies of gifted and successful people). Rather, Maslow's technique was to focus on the subjective feelings of people about such normal, good human concerns as love, creativity, self-esteem, integrity, fulfillment, and life satisfaction. The cornerstone of humanistic psychology is the idea of **self-actualization.** To Maslow, self-actualization is not an end result, but a process—the process of becoming true to our inner selves. He reasoned that all people have a drive to be honest, whole, genuine, and complete, a drive to actualize the inner self. Interestingly, a very new subfield of psychology called **positive psychology** is a *scientific* approach that is interested in many of the same good human qualities that humanism stresses. For example, positive psychology studies happiness, how optimism can affect health, and how to create a better sense of well-being and success.

These three approaches—psychoanalytic theory, behaviorism, and humanism—define the basis of modern psychology. But psychology has grown and today is a wide-ranging discipline with dozens of approaches, many that had their roots in these three fundamental views. However, psychology is still a young field and therefore is changing rapidly; there are many new trends and avenues of interest in contemporary psychology that veer from the three fundamental approaches. Next we will explore some of the most important of these new areas of interest within psychology.

Abraham Maslow, founder of the third force in psychology: humanism.

TABLE 1.3 Modern Schools of Psychology

School	Leader	Main Idea
Psychoanalytic	Sigmund Freud	The unconscious
Behaviorism	John B. Watson B. F. Skinner	Behaviors are learned
Humanism	Abraham Maslow	Self-actualization

Recap

— Sigmund Freud proposed that the unconscious part of the mind was more important than the conscious and developed an influential modern theory known as psychoanalysis.

— Behavioral psychologists John B. Watson and B. F. Skinner believed that psychology should experimentally study the laws of objective behavior.

— Behaviorism became an influential school of psychology that stressed the importance of scientifically studying observable behavior and ignoring the mind.

— Humanistic psychologists, led by Abraham Maslow, argued that psychology should focus on normal, good, human characteristics, such as self-actualization. Positive psychology is a new subfield that scientifically studies similar topics.

LATEST TRENDS

"All experience is an arch to build upon."
—HENRY BROOKS ADAMS

Minds from Brains

Perhaps the hottest trend in psychology today is the interest in the physiological bases of behavior and the mind. **Neuropsychology** is the branch of psychology that studies the biology of actions, emotions, and mental experiences. What is going on in the brain and in the body that produces a certain emotion, thought, dream, memory, or behavior? What is the biology of vision? What physiological changes in the brain represent learning and memory? What is the chemistry of perception, attention, and consciousness? How do our hormones influence our emotions? These are examples of the many exciting questions that many researchers in contemporary psychology have begun to examine, often using sophisticated new technology.

The answers that are being discovered not only are fascinating bits of scientific knowledge, but also have enormous potential for use in treating mental illnesses and helping people improve their lives. For instance, three researchers in this field were awarded the Nobel Prize in Medicine in 2000 for their progress in elucidating the details of the brain chemistry involved in Parkinson's disease and the formation and storage of memories in the brain. A number of drug treatments have been developed because of these findings. We can expect a good deal more progress in areas of research involving stem cells (basic cells that can develop into brain cells), brain implants, and memory enhancement and a deeper understanding of the precise physiological events that are involved in mental disorders and psychological experiences, even consciousness and identity.

Thinking about Thinking

Another very popular interest of psychologists today is cognition. **Cognitive psychology** is perhaps the fastest-growing branch of psychology. In 1985, Harvard psychologist **Howard Gardner** wrote a popular introduction to this young field titled *The Mind's New Science*, in which he refers to a **cognitive revolution** in psychology. Cognition is today one of the most studied topics by psychological researchers.

The term *cognition* includes the concepts of perception, learning, memory, problem solving, and all other mental acts by which people understand their world and themselves. Interest in cognition, of course, goes back to the earliest scientific psychologists, Wundt, Titchener, James, and the Gestalt psychologists, approximately one hundred years ago. It is ironic that contemporary psychologists are returning to the study of the conscious mind, something that went out of fashion when psychology became more scientific (because of the difficulty of empirically measuring mental states). However, with modern technology, psychologists are finding creative and interesting ways of measuring cognition indirectly, often by means of brain images.

A Biologist from Switzerland

One of the first catalysts for the current trend in cognitive psychology came in the 1960s when psychologists became aware of the groundbreaking studies of a Swiss biologist named **Jean Piaget** (1896–1980) who was trying to determine how cognition develops in childhood. Piaget wrote, "If only we could know what was going on in a baby's mind while observing him in action we could certainly understand everything there is to psychology" (Evans, 1973).

Piaget (pronounced "Pee-ah-ZHAY") was interested in how children thought and reasoned—how they used logic and problem-solving abilities. But more than that, Piaget wanted to find a pattern in the way these cognitive abilities emerged. Today we say that Piaget was studying cognitive development, and the ideas that he devised are known as a theory of cognitive development.

Piaget performed experiments on children in which he asked them to reason about events. For example, which of these glasses contains more water: a fat, wide glass that is filled halfway or a skinny, narrow glass that is filled to the top? When Piaget analyzed the answers that children gave to many such problems, he concluded that children's ability to reason develops in a regular pattern. The theory that Piaget proposed to describe and explain the results that he found included four stages of cognitive development.

Piaget said that cognition begins with an infant's simple sensory-motor awareness of the physical world. A baby has not yet developed the ability to hold things in imagination, according to Piaget. A young infant, for example, will not seek a toy that is out of sight. In a sense the infant's mind lives only in the arena of what can be sensed. For young babies the world is "out of sight, out of mind." But infants begin to develop mental ideas of things, **schemas,** through their reflexes, sensory experiences, and movements in the world. Hence this stage is known as the **sensory-motor period.**

At the beginning of this stage, the infant is unable to differentiate between his or her own sensations of things and the things themselves. The infant does not have a mental representation of objects. The infant does not understand, for example, that objects are permanently in the environment, that they exist outside of our sensory experiences of them. The infant does not understand **object permanence.** This cognitive ability will emerge gradually during the first two years of life.

In the second of Piaget's stages, preschoolers begin to imagine; that is, they begin to hold representations of objects in their minds. As was noted, these mental representations are called schemas. They are the mental ideas that people have about objects. A preschool child has a schema of her teddy bear, and if the bear is not where she last left it, the child will look for it elsewhere. She understands object permanence.

But preschoolers are **egocentric.** They see the world only from their own perspective or point of view and cannot reason logically, cannot hold multiple things in mind at the same time. For instance, a preschool child will say that a flat, pancake-shaped piece of clay is not the same amount as a piece of clay rolled into a ball. A tall, thin glass full of water when poured into a short, wide glass results in less liquid, according to the average preschooler, because the level of the water is lower. Preschoolers do not reason logically; instead, they rely on what things look like or seem like. They are unable to juggle more than one dimension in mind at a time, such as height and width. Because preschoolers are not capable of doing these kinds of mental operations, this stage is known as the **preoperational period.**

In the third of Piaget's stages, school-aged children begin to understand basic physical concepts, such as **conservation,** the notion that the amount of liquid or substance does not change if you change only its appearance. However, this stage is known as the **concrete operational period** because the school-aged child can perform mental operations only when the contents of such mental figuring are concrete or easily imagined. This child has difficulty in abstract reasoning—doing mental operations

Jean Piaget, pioneer of cognitive developmental psychology.

FYI

Piaget published his first essay at the age of 10. He published 21 articles and was offered a curator's job before finishing high school. He became interested in cognition because of his uncle, who was a philosopher of epistemology, the study of the nature and origin of knowledge. Piaget applied the scientific methods of biology to the philosophy of epistemology. In fact, Piaget called himself a genetic epistemologist.

about things that are not real. In early childhood, children can solve logical problems about concrete things. If we show school-aged children a red square that is larger than a blue square and then show them that the blue square is larger than a green square, the children will be able to mentally deduce that the red square is larger than the green square without actually seeing the two squares together at the same time. However, suppose we pose the following problem: Mary is taller than Jane, and Jane is taller than Betty. Who is taller, Mary or Betty? The children will not be able to solve this problem because the girls are fictional, not concrete; they are abstract. A child might even ask us which Mary we are talking about because he knows two of them! Children in the concrete operational stage (ages about six to twelve) are good at solving mental problems only about concrete things. Subjects such as algebra are difficult for these children because such subjects require abstract thinking.

TABLE 1.4 Developmental Periods and Piaget's Stages

Developmental Period	Piaget's Stage	Key characteristics
Infancy	Sensory-motor	Absence of object permanence; focus on sensing and moving
Preschool	Preoperational	Egocentric, illogical, absence of operational thinking
Early childhood	Concrete operational	Capable of mental operations such as conservation, focus on one thing at a time, absence of abstract thinking
Adolescence	Formal operational	Abstract thinking

Piaget's fourth and final stage is called the **formal operational period** and is defined by the person's ability to think in the abstract. Beginning in adolescence, children begin to reason outside the concrete world and can reach logical conclusions about abstract concepts (values, philosophy, religion, and theoretical concepts, for example). Adolescents enter a new mental world because they are able to apply the rules of reasoning and logic to a whole set of new and interesting ideas—abstract ideas. Hence adolescents often come to question their own lives and values. Abstract thinking means being able to think logically about things that are not concrete—topics that are outside the physical, that are theoretical, and abstruse. Research shows that many adults in the United States do not reach this final stage.

Piaget's research was so unusual and so fascinating that many psychologists began to build on his work. In the 1960s more than half of the research in **developmental psychology** (the scientific study of how people develop and mature) was based on Piaget's theory. As is usually the case, however, many competing theories have emerged since Piaget's initial work, and most psychologists today recognize that Piaget's concepts were not correct in every detail.

A preschool child (in Piaget's preoperational stage) thinks there is more liquid in a tall, thin glass than in a short, wide one. This lack of conservation occurs because the child has difficulty keeping two things in mind at the same time.

In addition, there has been some criticism of contemporary research on Piagetian concepts because it has become too concerned with *quantity* and not enough with the *quality* of thinking. Piaget himself was firmly committed to finding general principles and not measuring differences between children, an approach that is today very common. In fact, the focus on individual differences and the question of how to push children through the four stages as fast as possible is known as the **American question** because it is the most common approach in the United States. Piaget said that he did not care about individuals; he was seeking the *universal* principles of development. Current research is full of references to Piaget's ideas and methods. It is clear that Jean Piaget introduced to psychology an amazing way of thinking and an approach to doing research that continues to be extremely influential.

Moral Development

One of the major offshoots of Piaget's theory came from an American psychologist named **Lawrence Kohlberg** (1927–1987), who was interested in how people reason about right and wrong. Kohlberg used Piaget's methods of investigating people's thinking about moral situations. For example, he presented the following dilemma to children, adolescents, and adults: A man's wife is dying, and she needs a certain medicine that is far too expensive for them. The man begs for the medicine but is told that developing this medicine required a lot of money and the medicine cannot be given away. So the man steals the medicine for his wife. After presenting this dilemma, Kohlberg asked people why they thought the man's theft was right or wrong. Kohlberg's interest was not in what people concluded, but in what their reasoning was. That is, how do people reason about morality?

 FYI Lawrence Kohlberg was born into wealth but chose to become a sailor in the U.S. Navy during World War II. After the war, he helped to smuggle Jews through the British blockade of Palestine and was caught and put into prison. While in prison, Kohlberg began thinking about morality—why it was right to do certain things.

TABLE 1.5 Kohlberg's Stages of Moral Thinking

Stage	Key Characteristics
1. Obedience and punishment	What is right is to obey and to avoid punishment
2. Instrumental purpose	What is right is what gets you what you want, though you might have to give someone else what they want (the man shouldn't steal the drug if he doesn't love his wife)
3. Conformity	One should be nice and please others
4. Law and order	It's wrong to break the law; the law is the highest moral authority (this is the most common stage for adults)
5. Social contract/individual rights	We should uphold the rights of individuals within the society; laws are created as a kind of contract that we all agree to
6. Universal ethical principles	One's morality should follow inner principles of conscience based on careful reasoning and ethics

THINK TANK   If Piaget is correct that children's cognitive abilities develop in steps or stages, each one qualitatively different from the other, then what should we recommend to elementary schools regarding the education of children?

Are there certain educational approaches that will take advantage of Piaget's findings?

Kohlberg used many such dilemmas in his research. He then classified people's answers according to certain criteria and discovered a pattern. Kohlberg developed a **theory of moral development** that included six stages.

The main points of Piaget's and Kohlberg's theories are as follows:

- Focus on cognition (thinking)
- Focus on development (maturation)
- Focus on stages (development by steps rather than continuously)
- Stages differ from each other in quality of thinking
- Higher stages represent more complex thinking

Another important impetus for the cognitive revolution was an idea called **information processing.** Some years ago, psychologists and other thinkers from many different disciplines began to view the brain as an organ that analyzes or processes information, much as a computer does. Naturally, the emergence of interest in computer science and artificial intelligence helped to propel this line of thinking. Psychologists began to think of memory, for example, as a *process* rather than a thing in the brain or mind—the focus was on *how* one remembers rather than on what a memory is.

Unraveling Consciousness

The combination of neuropsychology and cognitive psychology has today led to a remarkably active study called **cognitive neuroscience,** a multidisciplinary field that includes philosophy, psychology, neuroscience, and computer science. Researchers in this field of study are attempting to uncover the exact details of the brain events that produce various cognitions, behaviors, and emotions.

Some researchers are even daring to investigate the biggest mystery today: consciousness. **Francis Crick,** who, with James Watson, won the Nobel Prize in Medicine, for determining the shape of the DNA molecule, has used the term *The Astonishing Hypothesis* (1994) for the idea that the biochemical activities in our brains produce our minds, consciousness, and mental identities. So far, great strides have been made in mapping the functions of the brain and identifying regions associated with many cognitive processes. Using brain-imaging devices and recording electrodes placed into brains, scientists have been able to see memories being formed, locate the brain areas involved in hundreds of cognitive acts, and help manufacturers to develop drugs and brain implants that are helping to relieve the symptoms of Parkinson's disease, depression, schizophrenia, and other mental problems.

The brain performs a great number of cognitive operations without a person's conscious awareness. In fact, most cognition (perception, memory, and thinking) that a brain does is kept separate from consciousness. Apparently, the conscious mind is needed only for certain cognitive tasks. Most of the time brains simply do their cognitive business—making sense of the world, making decisions about how and when to act, what to perceive and to remember, when to be afraid, when to be happy, and so on—without conscious awareness. Many of these functions must be done quickly, and the consciousness system is too slow. Other times, consciousness is required. Then brains create a certain biological state that produces the mind—the conscious, aware mind.

A new subject in psychology called **automaticity** studies behaviors that occur without conscious control. Researchers in this area believe that the vast majority of our behaviors are controlled nonconsciously. Daniel Wegner (2002 pp. 96–98; Wegner & Wheatley, 1999) has conducted numerous automaticity experiments and concluded, "The experience of will is the way our minds portray their operations to us, not their actual operation . . . the real causes of human action are unconscious . . . unconscious and inscrutable mechanisms create both conscious thought about action and create the action as well, and also produce the sense of will."

Cognitive neuroscience is becoming an even broader discipline. An emerging area of study is social cognitive neuroscience, which attempts to link social behavior (interactions between individuals) to cognition and to physiology, particularly brain functioning and evolution (Ochsner & Lieberman, 2001). This very new area of study helps to connect psychology and biology with sociology.

People working in the field of artificial intelligence have also contributed to the field of cognitive neuroscience. They have been able to develop computer systems that replicate many brain cognitive functions, including vision, dyslexia, playing chess, and moving around in the environment. Perhaps in the not-too-distant future, we will be able to record the network activity of our brains and upload that information into a computer. We might eventually be able to store our consciousness on a silicon chip. Computer expert Raymond Kurzweil calls this "reinstantiation" and predicts that it will be possible in 30 years. Would you like to be reinstantiated?

The Seeds of Our Past

One more area of intense interest today is the field of **evolutionary psychology.** This subdivision is almost a blend of psychology and anthropology; researchers want to learn how evolution and heredity have influenced our behaviors, our minds, and our emotions. Humans are viewed as biological beings that have inherited tendencies (so-called **instincts**) that are attributable to the survival and reproduction advantages of our predecessors.

Two of the leaders in the field of evolutionary psychology are **Leda Cosmides** and **John Tooby.** They argue that this field is not simply a branch of psychology, but rather a way of thinking about psychology that can be applied in all of psychology's diverse branches. Their fundamental goal is to understand human behavior; therefore, they turn to the biological roots of behavior, through the work of Charles Darwin (1809–1882) and other biologists who have described the process of evolution. In *The Origin of Species* (1859), Darwin proposed that evolution occurs through a process of natural selection. That is, characteristics that led to survival would be passed from one generation to the next, while characteristics that were a disadvantage for survival would necessarily drop out. This weeding-out process not only allowed for a species to develop physical attributes, such as an opposable thumb, but also contributed to the emergence of certain behaviors, such as walking upright, and instincts, built-in tendencies to act a certain way (the ability to learn language, for example).

 FYI

One of the latest specialized fields merges the study of genetics, evolution, and development. This interdisciplinary field is called *evo-devo.* Tell your guidance counselor you want to be an evo-devoer or evo-devoist.

Connecting Concepts

The nature-nurture question unfairly divides things into two interacting, overlapping categories. It is misleading. This issue is discussed in more detail in Chapters 3 and 8.

Cosmides and Tooby have proposed a number of principles for psychologists who want to follow the approach of evolutionary psychology. These principles include the idea that the brain is a physical system, that brains were designed by natural selection, that most brain processing is not conscious, that different parts of the brain are specialized for solving different problems, and that our brains are essentially designed for the tasks of the Stone Age.

Cosmides and Tooby also have provided some very useful reasoning about the **nature-nurture question,** the question that asks what things about us are inherited and what things are learned. They rightly point out that this question is bogus—evolutionary psychology rejects the idea that nature and nurture are ends of a dichotomy. Instead, evolutionary psychology argues that nature and nurture are simply two ways of looking at the same thing: human development. For example, what is meant when someone asks whether a particular trait or human characteristic is "inborn"? Such questions confuse the "initial state" of a person (look at a baby—that's what's inborn!) with the "evolved state," the end result of any given moment of the combined effect of developmental forces. For example, a newborn baby does not yet have teeth. Teeth are not "inborn." We should not conclude that they therefore are learned!

TABLE 1.6 Latest Trends in Psychology

Trend	Focus
Neuropsychology	The biology of behavior and mental states; how the brain and body work.
Cognitive psychology	Thinking and other mental processes; information processing model.
Cognitive neuroscience	Multidisciplinary study of how the brain produces cognitive processes such as attention.
Evolutionary psychology	How heredity and evolution influence behavior and mental states.

Recap

— The latest trends in psychology include neuropsychology, which studies how the mind and behavior are influenced by the physiology of the body.

— Perhaps the hottest trend is cognitive psychology, which has been influenced by the theory that the brain is an information-processing organ.

— Jean Piaget studied children's cognitive development and proposed an influential theory of four stages, each differing in quality of thinking involved.

— Piaget's four stages are: (1) sensory-motor (unable to understand object permanence);

(2) preoperational (egocentric, illogical, unable to solve conservation problems); (3) concrete operational (unable to think abstractly); and (4) formal operational (beginning of abstract thinking).

— Lawrence Kohlberg developed a theory of moral thinking with six stages.

— Cognitive neuroscience is a multidisciplinary field that attempts to discover the biological details of mental states.

— Evolutionary psychology applies principles of evolution and heredity to the interpretation of human behavior and mind.

AN ILLUSTRATION

"If you look closely enough at anything, you will see that there is nothing more exciting than the truth, the pay dirt of the scientist, discovered by his painstaking efforts . . . observation is the ultimate and final judge of the truth of an idea."
—RICHARD FEYNMAN

Here is an extended illustration intended to give you an understanding of the complexity of the discipline of psychlogy, how broad is its reach, how diverse are its interests, yet how interconnected and symbiotic (mutually dependent) are its theories and research findings.

Deprivation

In the 1930s, several psychologists around the world reported their observations of children raised in deprived environments, such as orphanages, in which the infants did not receive proper social attention. These psychologists suggested that babies have more than just physical needs—that babies also have psychological needs that are important for healthy development. Researchers reported observing many children who did not thrive or develop normally because of the deprivation they had suffered. Some even died. **René Spitz** reported what he called **marasmus** among children, a sense of despair and hopelessness when the children did not receive physical touching, hugging, and movement.

British psychologist **John Bowlby** recalled the ideas of Sigmund Freud regarding early infant needs. Freud had argued that babies have a biological drive for love and affection. Bowlby noticed that infants who were deprived of normal mothering were impaired in many ways. Bowlby rejected the details of Freud's psychoanalytic theory but recognized that for normal human development it is important for babies to develop a close relationship with their mother or with other significant adults. Bowlby coined the term *attachment* to refer to this relationship.

Meanwhile, an **ethologist** (a scientist who studies animal behavior) named **Konrad Lorenz** was studying ducklings and discovered what he called **imprinting**. Lorenz noticed that baby ducklings would begin to follow their mother (learning to swim, find food, and hide from predators) at a specific age. Perhaps you have seen a line of ducklings or goslings waddling behind their mother. Lorenz found that the peak time for this imprinting to occur was about 16 hours after hatching. Newly hatched ducklings are not yet ready to follow. On the other hand, if you wait too long to present the ducklings to their mother, they will show a fear response and will not imprint. Lorenz called

Ducklings imprinted on Konrad Lorenz.

the peak time for the expression of imprinting the **critical period**. Then Lorenz discovered that if he removed the mother duck, and instead he himself walked around in front of 16-hour-old ducklings, they would follow him. A long line of ducklings followed him wherever he went. The key variable appeared to be the presence of a large animal moving around the ducklings shortly after they hatched. Lorenz argued that this imprinting behavior was inborn in ducks and geese.

Lorenz and other scientists suggested that all animals, including humans, have such inborn predispositions, which are expressed at certain times during development. Because humans are the most flexible of all animal species, the time of expression of these inborn behaviors was sometimes called a **sensitive period** rather than a critical period. Developmental psychologists proposed that normal development in human babies required certain environmental events to stimulate the expression of imprinting-like behaviors during these sensitive periods. It was argued that development might be retarded if a person was deprived of certain experiences or conditions at crucial times during his or her **maturation** (natural and normal development of the individuals within a species, such as growth, that occurs regularly and orderly as a result of heredity).

Early Experience

Though Konrad Lorenz had assumed that imprinting in ducklings was an inborn characteristic, the leading behaviorist, B. F. Skinner, had his doubts. Skinner believed that behaviors are learned and couldn't see any reason why the ducklings' following behavior would be any different. He set up a study to test his idea. Skinner reasoned that the ducklings were following their mothers to get closer to them (for food and other **reinforcers**). If following did not lead to getting closer to the mother, Skinner proposed, the ducklings would not learn that behavior. Skinner built a wooden mother duck that he could move by remote control. As the ducklings moved toward the decoy, Skinner quickly moved it away from them. When the ducklings turned away from the decoy, Skinner moved it quickly to their side. As he had predicted, the ducklings began to move *away* from the substitute mother duck, rather than toward it. Skinner showed that behavior is learned; what is inborn is the desire for reinforcements, not any specific behavior.

Meanwhile, **Harry Harlow,** a psychologist at the University of Wisconsin, was planning a study on infant monkeys. He was rearing the monkeys in cages in his laboratory. Harlow met developmental psychologist John Bowlby, who predicted that Harlow's laboratory-reared monkeys would be developmentally abnormal because they were being deprived of mothering (attachment) during their early critical periods. On the basis of this prediction, Harlow abandoned his original experimental plan and decided instead to test the hypothesis that Bowlby had suggested—that the development of the infant monkeys would be harmed if they did not form proper attachments with mothers.

FYI Harlow had poor relationships with his own children; one of them said, "We never were father and son." Harlow's real last name was Israel, but he was told that a university would not hire him because the name sounded Jewish (anti-Semitism was common in the 1930s). He said, "I am the only scientist who has ever been named by his major professor."

Harry Harlow discovered that infant monkeys became emotionally attached to the surrogate mother that provided contact comfort.

Harlow built two surrogate (substitute) monkey mothers made of wire—one that held a bottle of milk and one that was covered with terrycloth, thereby providing a huggable surface, a condition that Harlow called **contact comfort.** Harlow found that the infant monkeys became emotionally attached to the terrycloth surrogate but not to the surrogate from which they received food. In addition, just as Bowlby had predicted, the infant monkeys that developed an emotional bond, an attachment, showed many fewer developmental problems than did the infant monkeys that did not form an attachment. These unattached monkeys demonstrated a large number of abnormalities. In addition, Harlow discovered that emotional attachment occurred only within a critical period of about three to four months. He concluded that contact comfort was an important experience for the normal development of monkeys and that it had to be present early in life. Harlow even suggested that his experiments showed that to be able to love later in life, one must first be loved as a baby.

Strange Situations

Harlow's findings led researchers to begin observing human infants in search of similar attachment needs. Psychologist **Mary Ainsworth** invented an experimental condition called the **strange situation** in which babies and children could be tested for the extent of their emotional attachment to their mothers. A child and mother are in a room, a stranger enters the room and approaches the child, the mother leaves the room, the stranger leaves the room, and then finally the mother reenters the room. Researchers observe the child's reactions and look for **separation anxiety** and **stranger anxiety,** two normal developments in children who have successfully formed emotional attachments to their mothers. Ainsworth argued that children who do not form a successful attachment are more likely to have problems later in life. This general notion and its theoretical offspring are known as **attachment theory.**

Researchers at the University of Minnesota tested Ainsworth's hypothesis. They observed babies and young children in the strange situation to determine whether they were **securely attached** or not. They then did follow-up evaluations of those same children over many years to find out how they turned out. They found that the **non-securely attached** children, on the average, had significantly more problems both in school and in their social relationships than did the children who had formed a secure attachment to their mothers. The researchers concluded that a secure attachment is an important event for very young children. It has even been suggested that insecure attachments might cause permanent changes in brain neurochemistry that result in problems in adulthood (van der Kolk, 1987).

A 6-month-old baby is *cognitively* beginning to understand object permanence and *emotionally* developing attachments to caregivers.

Recently, many psychologists and researchers have stressed the importance of the early years of life (up to about age four) for healthy, normal development. This point of view sees infancy and early childhood as a kind of critical period for maximizing successful development in all areas—cognitive, social, and personality. Some scientists who hold this view have even argued that employers should be required to give parents time off to be with their young children.

Some theorists, however, have argued that this view is too extreme. These scientists believe that infancy and early childhood are not as critical as attachment theory suggests. They argue that humans are more malleable than these studies suggest and that children who are brought to daycare or who stay with relatives while their parents work will still develop normal emotional attachments and their development will not be adversely affected. Obviously, this issue is still being debated.

Recap

— Ethologists, such as Konrad Lorenz, believed that animal behavior is highly programmed by genes—such as imprinting behavior in ducks and geese.

— Behavioral psychologists argued that specific behaviors are learned.

— Developmental psychologists discovered that newborns have psychological needs (such as attachment) that must be met for normal development to take place.

— Harry Harlow discovered the importance of contact comfort in the early development of monkeys.

— Mary Ainsworth invented the strange situation to experimentally measure babies' emotional attachment.

— It was found that securely attached children later did better in school and in social situations than did non-securely attached children.

— Bonding, the formation of emotional attachment right after birth, was found to be an important factor in babies' development.

— Today scientists and policymakers debate the extent to which the first few years of life are important, or even critical, for healthy human development.

I Link, Therefore I Am

Learn more about ancient Greek philosophers at the Greek philosophy archive:
http://graduate.gradsch.uga.edu/archive/Greek.html

Find more details about famous psychologists from history at these Web sites:
http://www.oklahoma.net/~jnichols/famous.html
http://inst.santafe.cc.fl.us/~mwehr/X1-6PsyFa.htm
http://www.800therapist.com/history/

Read more about women who have contributed to psychology at
http://teach.psy.uga.edu/dept/student/parker/PsychWomen/wopsy.htm

A list of resources related to neuropsychology can be found at
http://www.neuropsychologycentral.com/index.html

The Jean Piaget Society is as http://www.piaget.org/

Read more about Kohlberg and his theory at
http://gsep.pepperdine.edu/gsep/class/ethics/kohlberg/

The research lab in cognitive neuroscience at the National Institute of Mental Health can be explored at http://lbc.nimh.nih.gov/

Some Web sites for evolutionary psychology are http://www.psych.ucsb.edu/research/cep/
http://www.evoyage.com/ and http://www.hbes.com

Take a virtual tour of Freud's London home at http://www.freud.org.uk

STUDY GUIDE FOR CHAPTER 1:
THE WORLD OF PSYCHOLOGY

Key terms and names (Make flash cards.)

psychology
clinical psychology
comparative psychology
human factors
abnormal psychology
psychopathology
American Psychological Association
 (APA)
American Psychological Society (APS)
psychiatrist
psychiatry
psychoanalyst
psychologist
clinical psychologist
affect
behavior
cognition
pyramid of sciences
philosophy
Hippocrates
Hippocratic oath
somatogenic
hysteria
conversion disorder
Sigmund Freud
unconscious
psychoanalytic theory
repression
René Descartes
empiricism
rationalism
empirical question
electroencephalogram
brain waves
REM sleep
NREM sleep
dualism

monism
pineal gland
Wilhelm Wundt
Edward B. Titchener
structuralism
introspection
Gestalt psychology
phi phenomenon
William James
functionalism
stream of consciousness
Charles Darwin
natural selection
educational psychology
psychoanalysis
surrealism
John B. Watson
behaviorism
tabula rasa
Mary Whiton Calkins
Margaret Floy Washburn
B. F. Skinner
Skinner box
radical behaviorism
Abraham Maslow
humanistic psychology (humanism)
self-actualization
positive psychology
neuropsychology
cognitive psychology
Howard Gardner
cognitive revolution
Jean Piaget
schema
sensory-motor period
object permanence
egocentric

preoperational period
conservation
concrete operational period
formal operational period
developmental psychology
American question
Lawrence Kohlberg
theory of moral development
information processing
cognitive neuroscience
Francis Crick
automaticity
evolutionary psychology
instincts
Leda Cosmides
John Tooby
nature-nurture question
René Spitz
marasmus
John Bowlby
attachment
ethologist
Konrad Lorenz
imprinting
critical period
sensitive period
maturation
reinforcers
Harry Harlow
contact comfort
Mary Ainsworth
strange situation
separation anxiety
stranger anxiety
attachment theory
securely attached
non-securely attached

Fill in the blank

1. Of all the courses offered in colleges around the world, _____ is the most common one taken.
2. Psychology is the science of _____ and _____.
3. In this course, as in every course in general psychology, we study the _____ side of psychology.

4. The most common subtype of psychology is _____.
5. A subfield of psychology in which researchers study animal behavior is called _____.
6. The subfield of psychology known as I/O stands for _____.
7. A _____ is a medical doctor.

8. Psychiatrists who conduct Freudian therapy are called _____.

9. _____ refers to emotions, moods, or temperaments.

10. On the pyramid of sciences, psychology lies just above _____.

11. All sciences in Western civilization had their origins in the field of _____.

12. The best-known ancient Greek philosophers were _____, _____, and _____.

13. The ancient Greek word for the mind/soul was _____.

14. The word *psychology* literally means the _____ of the _____.

15. The first medical doctor in Western civilization was _____.

16. When people experienced physical impairments without any apparent organic illness or trauma, this was called _____.

17. Hippocrates and other philosophers thought that hysteria was caused by a _____.

18. Sigmund Freud believed that the cause of hysteria was in the _____ mind.

19. A mental technique of keeping information out of awareness is called a _____.

20. The first modern philosopher was a Frenchman named _____.

21. The first, most basic truth that Descartes recognized as undeniably true was the now well-known maxim: _____.

22. Descartes's view, dividing the universe into two categories (physical and nonphysical), is known as _____.

23. An _____ question is one that can be answered through observation and measurement.

24. The _____ measures _____ _____.

25. Active brain waves sometimes occur during sleep. This stage of sleep is called _____.

26. When people are awakened during _____ sleep, they report dreaming about _____% of the time. When awakened during _____ sleep, dreaming is reported about _____ % of the time.

27. _____ sleep is often known as dreaming sleep.

28. A modern neuroscientist would argue that mental phenomena emanate from the _____. This view is known as _____ (one kind of thing—the physical).

29. The person most often regarded as the first experimental psychologist was a German professor of _____ named _____ _____.

30. The first laboratory for the experimental study of psychology was established at the university in _____, _____ in the year _____.

31. If _____ is the "mother" of psychology, then _____ is psychology's "father."

32. Titchener wanted to find the basic elements of the mind; therefore, his approach is known as _____.

33. The technique called _____ asks people to look inside themselves and report on their mental experiences.

34. The Gestalt psychology motto is that the whole is _____ than the sum of the parts.

35. The approach to psychology associated with William James is known as _____.

36. William James said the conscious mind is like a _____ of consciousness.

37. Sigmund Freud's theory is called _____, and the therapeutic methods based on his theory are known as _____.

38. _____ artists and writers attempted to reveal the contents of their unconscious minds in their art and literature.

39. Freud said that _____ were "the royal road to the unconscious."

40. John B. _____ was convinced that psychology should give up its aspirations of being a science of the mind, and should focus instead on being a science of behavior.

41. The psychological approach that focuses on observable behavior is called _____.

42. B. F. _____ placed pigeons in experimental cages that we now call _____.

43. There is a third school of psychology that emerged called _____ psychology. A new subfield based on the same ideas is called _____ psychology.

44. Abraham _____ believed that psychology should include an approach that centered on the normal conscious minds of humans.

45. The cornerstone of the humanistic approach is the idea of _____.

46. Neuropsychology concentrates on finding _____ causes of behavior.

47. _____ includes perception, learning, memory, problem solving, and all other mental acts by which people understand their world and themselves.

48. Cognitive development was studied by the Swiss biologist Jean _____.

49. The infant does not understand _____ permanence.

50. Piaget called mental representations _____.

51. Since preschoolers are not capable of doing mental _____, their stage is known as _____.
52. _____ is the notion that the amount of liquid or substance does not change if you only change its appearance.
53. Children in the third of Piaget's stages are not capable of doing _____ thinking.
54. Piaget's fourth and final stage is called _____ _____.
55. Lawrence_____ used Piaget's methods to investigate people's thinking about _____ situations.
56. An influential idea that contributed to the _____ revolution in psychology was the idea of comparing a brain to a computer by the approach known as _____ processing.
57. The subdivision of psychology that is almost a blend with anthropology is _____ psychology.

58. Inherited tendencies are called _____.
59. The biologist Charles _____ is known for describing the process of evolution.
60. Evolution occurs through a process of _____ selection.
61. John Bowlby coined the term _____ to refer to the emotional relationship between infant and mother.
62. Konrad Lorenz studied ducklings and discovered what he called _____.
63. The peak time for the expression of developmental characteristics is called a _____ period.
64. Harry Harlow showed that _____ was important for normal development of infant monkeys.
65. Mary Ainsworth invented an experimental condition called the _____ situation, in which babies and children could be tested for the extent of their emotional attachment to their mothers.

Matching

1. Jean Piaget _____
2. Abraham Maslow _____
3. comparative psychology _____
4. clinical psychology _____
5. attachment theory _____
6. Konrad Lorenz _____
7. Sigmund Freud _____
8. Titchener _____
9. Wilhelm Wundt _____
10. Hippocrates _____
11. John B. Watson _____
12. William James _____
13. dualism _____
14. evolution _____
15. Gestalt psychology _____
16. psychiatrists _____
17. wandering womb _____
18. Lawrence Kohlberg _____

a. first experimental psychologist
b. structuralism
c. behaviorism
d. John Bowlby
e. psychoanalysis
f. medical doctors
g. study of animals
h. cognitive development
i. moral development
j. ethology/imprinting
k. humanism
l. first medical doctor
m. hysteria
n. the whole
o. René Descartes
p. natural selection
q. functionalism
r. provides therapy

Multiple choice

1. You meet a psychologist who says she works for a company that is designing equipment that will be safe and efficient for the workers. What type of psychologist is she?
   a. social
   b. developmental
   c. comparative
   d. I/O

2. Your friend went to a therapist who used Freudian techniques to help him with his problems. The therapist is a
   a. psychoanalyst
   b. personality psychologist
   c. social psychologist
   d. structuralist

3. Which of these would a comparative psychologist be interested in?
   a. how to help people with anxiety disorders
   b. how children's maturation can be affected by food
   c. the mating behavior of chimpanzees
   d. why people conform to others' behaviors

4. A computer expert is trying to figure out how different software systems work. This is most similar to what type of early psychology?
   a. Gestalt
   b. I/O
   c. functionalism
   d. structuralism

5. If you want to scientifically study memory, you will have to do it
   a. using social psychological principles
   b. indirectly by measuring behavior
   c. with children
   d. using structuralism

6. What was B. F. Skinner's interpretation of imprinting?
   a. It must be inherited.
   b. It cannot be possible.
   c. Like any other behavior, it is controlled by reinforcers.
   d. It is the result of mothering instincts.

7. The school of psychology that tried to determine what the conscious mind was made of was called
   a. functionalism
   b. Gestalt
   c. structuralism
   d. behaviorism

8. The idea that the conscious mind is a nonphysical thing is known as
   a. empiricism
   b. introspection
   c. dualism
   d. psychoanalytic theory

9. The idea that the conscious mind should not be studied is a part of
   a. behaviorism
   b. humanism
   c. structuralism
   d. functionalism

10. "The whole is greater than the sum of the parts" is the motto of _____ psychology.
    a. psychoanalytic
    b. behavioral
    c. humanistic
    d. Gestalt

11. When newly hatched ducklings follow their mother, this behavior is called
    a. attachment
    b. bonding
    c. behavioral contagion
    d. imprinting

12. The strange situation is used to study
    a. psychological needs
    b. attachment
    c. cognitive development
    d. instincts

13. Which science is at the base, the bottom, of the pyramid of sciences?
    a. chemistry
    b. psychology
    c. physics
    d. biology

14. The first of Piaget's stages involves
    a. sensory-motor learning
    b. operational thinking
    c. egocentrism
    d. conservation

15. Piaget's stage of formal operations involves
    a. emotional intelligence
    b. abstract thinking
    c. obedience and punishment
    d. unconscious mental processes

16. Psychoanalytic psychology focuses on
    a. observable behavior
    b. the conscious part of the mind
    c. the unconscious
    d. empiricism

17. The idea of monism says that the mind is
    a. created by the physical brain
    b. separate from the brain
    c. identical to the brain
    d. a nonphysical entity

18. Who developed a theory of moral development?
    a. Lawrence Kohlberg
    b. Jean Piaget
    c. B. F. Skinner
    d. Wilhelm Wundt

19. The idea that the mind is a stream of consciousness was suggested by
    a. Sigmund Freud
    b. B. F. Skinner
    c. William James
    d. Jean Piaget

20. Psychology was originated by the
    a. ancient Greeks
    b. Romans
    c. Egyptians
    d. Chinese

21. If a man believes that he is blind, but he is not, he is suffering from what was once called
    a. neurosis
    b. psychosis
    c. object permanence
    d. hysteria
22. Self-actualization is a key idea in the school of psychology known as
    a. functionalism
    b. humanism
    c. behaviorism
    d. psychoanalytic theory
23. A child who believes that a tall, thin glass contains more water than a short, wide glass does not yet understand the concept of
    a. conservation
    b. egocentrism
    c. abstract thinking
    d. universal principles
24. You ask your friend to tell you all of his thoughts and feelings about a certain experience he had. This is similar to the technique used by early psychologists called
    a. unconscious repression
    b. introspection
    c. dream interpretation
    d. functionalism
25. Which of these questions would be most interesting to a behaviorist?
    a. How do people remember details?
    b. What do dreams mean?
    c. In what situations do people talk faster?
    d. What are the thinking processes common to preschool children?

26. A friend of yours is very interested in how ballet dancers move around the stage to interact with each other and with the space they are in. Which type of psychology would your friend most probably enjoy?
    a. Gestalt
    b. behaviorism
    c. functionalism
    d. psychoanalytic theory
27. Your four-year-old daughter sees an elephant at the zoo, but she is with her aunt while you are going to get snacks for everyone. Later, your daughter asks you a question about the elephant as if you have seen it. Piaget would say that she is
    a. using abstract reasoning
    b. beyond formal operational thinking
    c. unable to grasp object permanence
    d. egocentric
28. The first experimental psychologist was
    a. William James
    b. B. F. Skinner
    c. John B. Watson
    d. Wilhelm Wundt
29. The most multidisciplinary of the many subfields of psychology is
    a. cognitive neuroscience
    b. comparative psychology
    c. clinical psychology
    d. ethology
30. Which stage of sleep is associated with dreaming?
    a. stage 2
    b. REM
    c. NREM
    d. deep sleep

Short answer and critical thinking

1. What did Ebbinghaus mean by "Psychology has a long past but a short history"?
2. What is hysteria? How did early Greek philosophers explain it? How did Freud explain it?
3. Define and contrast dualism and monism.
4. Compare and contrast structuralism, Gestalt psychology, and functionalism.
5. What does it mean to say that one can't scientifically study dreams?
6. What things does evolutionary psychology focus on?
7. How is psychology portrayed by popular culture? Give examples. How is this view different from the actual scientific discipline of psychology?
8. Why is psychology said to be a very broad science?
9. What is meant by *the ABCs of psychology*? Give an example of each.
10. What is the difference between rationalism and empiricism?
11. Which of the latest trends in psychology seems most interesting to you? Why? Which seems most valuable to society? Which seems most valuable for discovering the laws of behavior and the mind?
12. What does the term *attachment* mean to developmental psychologists? Cite some research on this topic.
13. What things that you learned about psychology in this chapter surprised you?

Chapter
2

Methods of Scientific Research

"Science is the search for truth."
—LINUS PAULING

PLAN AHEAD...

- Why is scientific research necessary? Can't we just use common sense?
- What are some different types of research methods that scientists use?
- What is a correlation? What is a negative correlation?
- How do scientists do controlled experiments?
- What is a placebo? What does *double-blind* mean?
- What ethical guidelines do scientists use when doing research?

WHEN PEOPLE FIND OUT THAT I ONCE TAUGHT MATH, they often remark that psychology and math are an odd combination. You know this is wrong. You know that psychology is a science. But what does that mean? What is a science? I am also an artist, which is very different from a scientist. What differentiates science from art? You might say that the answer is the topics studied. But that is only partially correct. Yes, science can study only empirical subjects, topics that are measurable. But that is because of the kinds of *methods* that are used in scientific pursuits. Science is limited to certain methodology. In fact, science is best defined not by what it studies, but by *how* it studies—not by its topics, but by its methods. In this chapter, we discuss the methods that psychologists use to do scientific research.

THE MEASURE OF MEASUREMENT

"In the fields of observation, chance favors only the prepared mind."
—LOUIS PASTEUR

Because science is empirical, the analysis of scientific research depends strongly on mathematics, particularly on statistics. Statistical analysis gives us a tool for deciding whether our results are accurate and believable. Mathematics provides not only a technique of gathering data, but also a method of determining the probability that the results could have happened by chance. Statistical analysis is always a component of the scientific method.

Scientists are free to use any of numerous methods of research, as long as they are empirical. Many possible methods are available to scientists. Each, however, is based on the principle of public verification. Each study must be replicable (repeatable) and capable of being disproved.

Good, Not Common, Sense

Science cannot be based on common sense. Far too often in the past, the ideas of the majority (the *common* sense) were in fact wrong. Albert Einstein defined common sense as "the collection of prejudices acquired by age eighteen." Science is designed to help us discover whether empirical statements are true or not. Science cannot take beliefs for granted. It is necessary to verify even common beliefs that everyone assumes. Sometimes science discovers that what we all "knew" was true in fact is false. For example, all of the following statements are false:

- People who wear eyeglasses have higher IQs than those who do not. (There is no relationship between eyesight and intelligence.)

"Truth does not change because it is, or is not, believed by a majority of the people."
—GIORDANO BRUNO (WHO WAS BURNED AT THE STAKE FOR HIS VIEWS)

- Eye color is inherited. (We do not inherit any traits; we inherit the DNA sequences or recipes for the development of traits. For example, a person could have two eyes of different colors.)

- Alcohol is a stimulant. (Alcohol slows down—depresses—the nervous system. For example, reflexes are slowed by alcohol.)

- Suicide is most common among teens and young adults. (Suicide rates tend generally to increase with age. Older adults have the highest suicide rate.)

- Mentally ill people tend to be dangerous. (People who are diagnosed as mentally ill have a lower rate of dangerous behavior than do the non-mentally ill.)

- There is a place in the brain where memories are stored. (Memories are scattered throughout the brain in networks that extend to various brain regions.)

- Schizophrenia is the same as multiple personality. (No, these are two separate disorders.)

- People can change only if they want to. (Change occurs because of many different variables. Having motivation is not necessary in most cases.)

- Most mental illnesses are incurable. (The overall rate of success in treating mental illnesses is as high as 80%. Naturally, some mental illnesses have higher cure rates than others.)

- Human behavior is influenced by the full moon. (The phases of the moon have no effect on human behavior.)

The last myth is a good example of how easily people accept ideas that are false. Hundreds of scientific studies have attempted to find an association between the full moon and many different human behaviors, and the results consistently show no relationship (Kelly et al., 1996). These results should not surprise us because the gravitational effect of the moon on a person is extremely small; it is about equal to that of a nearby mosquito! In fact, a person standing next to you has about 10 million times more force on you than the moon does. Still, surveys show that many people believe this myth.

Why do people believe things that are demonstrably wrong? There are many reasons. First, brains are not perfect logic machines; they are quick to draw conclusions on the basis of coincidental occurrences. Second, people have selective perception. They remember the occurrences that supported their ideas and forget the times when their belief is not supported by observation.

For instance, a vast number of people believe in ESP and other psychic powers, yet one hundred years of research has found no evidence whatsoever of such forces. Of course, this makes sense. How could such a thing exist? The magician James Randi has a bank account containing one million dollars that he will give to anyone who can demonstrate psychic power. Although this offer has been available for decades, no one has claimed the prize. Randi (1982) also has demonstrated how easily people can be fooled. He trained students to fake psychic ability, and they fooled psychologists and scientists as well as the general public. It would be a very different world if people really had psychic powers. We could use psychics to diagnose and treat illnesses; work in schools, industry, and the government; and help people in many ways. It is not a coincidence that psychics are found in only one profession: entertainment. There are a multitude of similar myths that are common among the public. Science historian Michael Shermer's book *Why People Believe Weird Things* (1997) lists many of them and his ideas about why people persist in these beliefs.

Obviously, we cannot trust that something is true on the basis of how many people believe it or how reasonable it seems. We need to turn to appropriate scientific investigation to help us decide what is true about our empirical world. But be cautious. Brains were not designed to reason perfectly, so they make many errors. In fact, one study found that the number of myths that students believed *increased* after they took a course in general psychology! I hope that doesn't happen to you. Be careful out there.

A Sample of Scientific Methods

Many different methods are legitimate for scientific research, each with its own advantages and disadvantages. Here we provide short descriptions of three commonly used methods for scientific research.

Case Study

A **case study** is just what it says: the study of a case. Here we do not mean a controlled experiment, only an observation. In a case study, one or a few individuals are described, sometimes in great detail. Case studies are fascinating to read and highly engrossing, but they do not give us the big picture, since they concentrate on describing only one or a few people. Case studies can often be found in journals that deal with psychiatric disorders or psychological counseling, although the *American Psychiatric Journal* now tends to focus more on controlled experiments of large groups of individuals. Case studies are often the main type of information provided in medical journals, such as the *Journal of the American Medical Association* (JAMA); they are more rare in psychological journals such as the *American Psychologist*.

The main fault of case studies is that we cannot trust generalizations made from them. Because one person acts, thinks, or feels a certain way does not mean that others do. In fact, case studies are often of most interest when they describe a condition that is rare. In this sense, they are useful not for building a science that is universal, but rather for providing exceptional instances. Their strength is in providing the details of one person's situation.

Sigmund Freud developed an entire complicated theory of personality and mental illness known as psychoanalytic theory not by doing experiments, but by listening to and observing individuals—by collecting case studies. Quite amazingly, Freud got the idea for the **Oedipus complex** (what he called his most important idea: the notion that children are unconsciously attracted to their opposite-sexed parent and feel fear and resentment toward their same-sexed parent) from the case study of one little boy whom Freud met only once. Freud received letters from the boy's father telling of the boy's strange fear of being bitten by horses and of the boy's comment that his father, while shaving, resembled a horse.

Case studies have been a common part of medical science and in the past were an important part of early psychology. In contemporary psychology, however, they have been pushed somewhat to the side by the overwhelming interest in more scientifically accurate, large-scale experimental studies. Case studies continue to be an interesting and well-received component of psychology, however, as evidenced by the many popular books that become best sellers each year by incorporating this methodology. Perhaps the most successful are those by **Oliver Sacks** (who is a neurologist, not a psychologist), who has published *The Man Who Mistook His Wife for a Hat* (1987), a series of case studies about people with brain disorders that produce odd behaviors, and *An Anthropologist on Mars* (1995), a description of people who have an inherited form of color blindness. Although not as common today, the case study continues to be a fascinating form of research about the most extreme and unusual psychological conditions.

Naturalistic Observation

Sometimes scientists gather information by observing people or animals in their natural setting, a technique known as **naturalistic observation.** We can go to a playground and observe the children there. We can carefully and objectively count the number of times they do something, such as interact with each other, act aggressively or cooperatively, communicate, or remain isolated. By careful observation, we can collect data about behavior in its natural conditions. Of course, we want to be unobtrusive and not cause a distraction because that would interfere with attaining objective results (since people behave differently when they know they are being watched). Careful observation can provide us with statistical data about the behavior of individuals or groups.

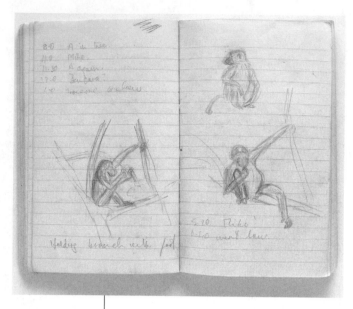

Jane Goodall uses the method of naturalistic observation as shown in her notebook.

Naturalistic observation is used more often in the study of lower animals than in studying humans. The famous humanistic psychologist Abraham Maslow began his career at the University of Wisconsin by observing and recording the sex lives of monkeys. **Jane Goodall** has spent a career meticulously noting the detailed behavior of chimpanzees in their natural habitat. Psychologists who study animal behavior are called **comparative psychologists.** Their observations not only provide us with information about lower animals in their natural habitats, but also provide a basis with which to make comparisons with human behavior.

Survey

Quite unlike the case study, which focuses on an individual, **surveys** attempt to gather data about large numbers of people. With a survey, we do not objectively observe the behavior of animals or people in their natural surroundings; rather, we ask people to give us answers verbally. A survey asks a large group of people about their various behaviors, emotions, thoughts, or problems by means of either a questionnaire or an interview. The data can then be statistically analyzed and used to draw conclusions, make decisions, or develop hypotheses and theories.

Perhaps the most famous survey in history was that undertaken by **Alfred Kinsey** (1894–1956) in the 1940s and 1950s. Kinsey was a biologist at Indiana University. He was a world-renowned expert on bees. One day, after he gave a lecture on the sexual behavior of bees, it struck him as outrageous that more was known in science about the sexual behavior of bees than about the sexual behavior of humans. He set out to correct that.

Kinsey and his team surveyed many thousands of American men and women about their sexual behaviors. The books describing his results were extremely popular. Today there is still a Kinsey Institute for research on the sexual behavior of humans. Interestingly, Kinsey discovered that people reported engaging in a number of sexual activities that were frowned on and even against the law in many states. Kinsey found that a number of sexual behaviors that people thought were rare were reported as quite common. Once again, scientific research sometimes proves popular knowledge to be wrong.

However, we must remember that surveys (interviews and questionnaires) are self-reporting methods. Therefore, surveys are notoriously unreliable and must be accepted cautiously. People do not always report accurately about themselves. Sometimes they do not know the answer, sometimes they have forgotten, sometimes they inadvertently fudge, and sometimes they fib. Precisely when these inaccuracies will occur depends on many variables. For example, how risky is the situation? Using self-report to determine how many people cheat on their spouses, how many people are gay, how many people steal things from work will probably not be very successful because these are risky behaviors to report.

Another phenomenon that helps to illuminate the fact that self-reports are sometimes not accurate is that a person will often give different answers to the same question if asked by two different interviewers. For example, the answer given might depend on whether one is asked by a man or by a woman. A related complication is the fact that most people believe self-reports to be more reliable than they are; that is, most people overestimate the truthfulness or reliability of self-reported information. The vast majority of people put their faith in what others say or report. This is a big mistake. We need to be cautious in drawing conclusions from research based only on the results of surveys.

The three methods mentioned above—case study, naturalistic observation, and survey—are still common in modern scientific study. However, there are two other

THINK TANK

Give some examples of things that would be best studied by case study, by naturalistic observation, or by the survey method.

What are the advantages and disadvantages of each?

Name some fields of study or disciplines, such as medicine or sociology, that rely on each method.

methods that are far more common and far more important, that often provide more useful information, and that are more difficult to explain. Because of the importance and the difficulty of these two methods, we will take a good deal of time here to describe them. They are correlation and the controlled experiment.

Variables

The characteristics that are studied in science are called **variables.** Variables are characteristics that can vary, that is, that can have varying values. The length of an object, the frequency of a behavior, how long a phenomenon lasts, scores on a test, height, weight, and eye color are all variables—all characteristics that can vary. In psychology we are interested in variables relating to the ABCs: affect (emotion and mood), behavior (actions), and cognition (perceptions, thoughts, and memories). We want to know everything about those variables. We want to describe them, explain them, predict them, and control them. Those are the goals of psychology.

To gather information about variables, we use the three methods that are mentioned above and many others. However, the two most common and important research methods are the correlational study, which attempts to discover to what extent variables are related to each other, and the controlled experiment, which is a carefully designed attempt to find out which variables have an influence on a specific variable.

Recap

— Sciences are empirical; they cannot be based on common sense but must use objective observation and measurement.

— A case study focuses on one individual. This method was used by Freud and is often used to study unusual cases or medical problems. Oliver Sacks is well known for his case studies of people with odd brain disorders.

— Naturalistic observation measures people or animals in their natural setting, such as Jane Goodall's study of chimpanzees.

— A survey gathers information about large numbers of participants. Kinsey's survey of human sexual behavior is a good example.

— Variables are the characteristics that science studies; they can have varying values.

— The goals of psychology are to describe, explain, predict, and control the ABCs: affect, behavior, and cognition (behavior and mental processes).

CORRELATIONAL STUDY

"Marriage is one of the chief causes of divorce."
—ANONYMOUS

Look at the word *correlation*. It is essentially a co-relation, meaning a relationship between two things. With this method of research, we attempt to discover whether two variables are related to each other (do they co-vary) and, if so, by how much. For variables to be correlated, it means that if we know someone's score on one variable, then we will be able to predict his or her score on the other variable. If two variables are not related, then knowing a score on one does not help at all in predicting a score on the other variable.

The Concept of Correlation

Suppose it was true that students who get high grades tend more often to sit in one area of the classroom, maybe the front row or the back row. Regardless of *why* this were so, if it were true, then we would say that there is a correlation between grades and where students sit. Suppose that highly creative people are more likely to be vegetarians. Regardless of why, we would say that there is a correlation between creativity (a variable) and food choice (another variable). Suppose there is absolutely no correlation between one's height and the number of dates one has. That is, suppose that tall, short, or medium people on average have the same number of dates. If there were no correlation, then we would have no advantage in guessing how tall someone is even if we knew how many dates that person had. Likewise, we would not be able to predict any better than chance how many dates a person had if we knew his or her height. There would be no correlation between the two variables. Suppose that all of the football teams in a certain division finished in nearly the same order this year as they did last year. We would say that there was a correlation between the standings. If the teams finished in exactly the same order from one year to the next, we would then say that there was a **perfect correlation.**

These examples show what correlation means. Correlation does not tell us why something is true, nor does it necessarily provide for perfect prediction. It tells us that variables are related to each other by a certain amount—it shows us that knowing one score will help to predict the other. If we know all the variables that are correlated with a particular mental illness, for example, we can then predict with a higher probability than chance who will develop that mental illness. But remember: Correlation does not tell us *why* variables are related, it tells us only that they *are* related.

In a correlational study, two variables are measured. For example, we might want to know whether intelligence is in any way related to socioeconomic status (SES). That is, do people who are in different social classes have different intelligence test scores? Is there any pattern between these two variables? We want to find out whether there is a relationship between these two things. The procedure is the same no matter what variables are chosen. We need to measure the variables for a select group of people (or animals), and then we need to analyze the data that we collect to see whether there is a correlation of any amount. Finally, we need to use statistical mathematics to determine whether our data are fair, that is, to determine whether we can trust that the results we obtained are accurate for the whole group in which we are interested.

Conducting a Correlational Study

We begin by selecting a **sample**. The group that we are interested in drawing conclusions about is called the **population**. We might be interested in finding out something about college students, for example, or about people who work in manufacturing, about children between the ages of five and ten, and so on. The population is the group of people or animals about which we want to reach a conclusion. Because this group is invariably too large (typically we cannot measure every individual in the population), we must select some members of that group to represent the whole population. The group that we select is called the sample. The conclusions that we draw about the **participants** (previously called subjects) in the sample will be extrapolated to the population.

Samples should be large enough to draw accurate conclusions (this is a matter of mathematical probability statistics) and should be selected at **random** from the population. If we do not have a random sample, the people we measure might not accurately reflect the population as a whole. For example, a telephone poll of voters in 1948 predicted that Thomas Dewey would win the presidential election. The poll, in fact, was accurate as far as it went—more people who owned telephones did vote for Dewey. But more people who did not own telephones voted for Harry Truman, who was elected. The poll was wrong because it did not include a random sample of the correct group—people who will vote. Samples must be large and should be randomly selected from the appropriate population.

Stop and think about the idea of a random sample. Random means that every member of the population has an equal chance of being selected into the sample. It is common for people to draw conclusions about a large group based on a nonrandom section of that group. For example, one of my colleagues once concluded that Americans don't like modern art because none of his friends liked modern art. Need we be reminded that our friends do not constitute a random sample? I informed my colleague that all of my friends liked modern art. He missed my point and concluded that my friends must be very strange. We cannot make an informed judgment about a large group based only on our friends.

In science we need to be careful not to draw conclusions based on a sample that does not fairly represent the population we are interested in. Most scientific studies in psychology, for example, include participants selected from college students. As you can imagine, it is difficult to have a completely random sample. Therefore, if you ever disagree with the results of a research study, you can complain that the sample was not randomly selected, and you will likely be right. It is rare for a study to have random selection of participants. Therefore, we should be aware of the limitations created by the particular participants included in a study.

Into the Abstract

A scientific study must have a **hypothesis**. The most common definition of a hypothesis is that it is an "educated guess." This is entirely wrong. You do not have to be educated to have a hypothesis; that has nothing to do with it. Also, a hypothesis does not involve guessing. Rather, a hypothesis is a statement (or a prediction) about some variables that we intend to measure to find out whether the statement is true. A hypothesis is a statement or prediction that a scientist wants to test. In a correlational study, the hypothesis will always be of the form "X is related to Y" (X and Y are variables). We want to know whether this is true and, if so, what is the extent of the correlation. As an illustration, let's take the hypothesis that intelligence is related to SES.

In psychology, the variables that we are interested in often, maybe usually, are not physical things (as in physics, chemistry, and biology), but abstract concepts. We are interested in studying variables such as intelligence. You cannot get a jar of intelligence and study it directly. Love, creativity, conformity, shyness, and happiness are similar abstract variables. These are technically called **hypothetical constructs.** Our problem is that in science, we need to measure variables, and hypothetical constructs are not directly measurable. Therefore, we need to think of a practical way to define these variables so that we can operate with them scientifically—so that we can measure them. We need a definition that makes them measurable. Such a definition is called an **operational definition,** and scientists say that they need to "operationalize a construct."

For example, if we want to study intelligence, we need to define it in a way that makes it measurable, or operational. We might say that intelligence is the length of your nose. That would be an operational definition, but obviously, it is far from what most people mean by intelligence. No one will take your research seriously if you use such a silly operational definition. The point is that scientists can use any operational definitions they want; but we need to know what those definitions are to understand their research findings. A better operational definition of intelligence might be a person's score on a test that measures abilities such as vocabulary, verbal ability, numerical ability, problem solving, memory, and so on. In our example, let's use IQ score as our operational definition of intelligence.

If our hypothesis is that intelligence is related to SES, we will also need an operational definition of SES. We can measure that with a questionnaire that asks people about their income level, type of job or career, amount of education, and so on. We can then give a score that will indicate what social class a person is in; for example, the highest class (upper-upper) will be given a score of 9, middle-upper class will be given an 8, lower-upper class a 7, upper-middle class a 6, middle-middle class a 5, and so on, to lower-lower class a score of 1.

Harvesting Numbers

The next step is to collect the data. We now need to measure the participants on the two variables. We will give each person an IQ test and an SES questionnaire, and we will then tabulate the scores. This sounds easy, but it is normally the most time-consuming part of the experiment. The data that we collect can easily be listed in two columns:

Participant	IQ Score	SES Score
1	98	5
2	135	9
3	75	2
4	120	6
5	88	4
6	149	8
7	100	5
8	79	1
9	96	3
10	133	7

Although ten participants is a very small sample size, let's stop there because we are merely giving an illustration of how a correlational study is done. Notice that each person has two scores—in this case, intelligence and SES. We want to determine whether there is a pattern, a correlation between these two sets of scores that we got by measuring these ten people. I purposely made up these scores so that it would be easy to see a pattern (notice that high scores on IQ go with high scores on SES and low scores go with low scores), although in a true correlational study, we do not simply look at the data, we must analyze the scores mathematically. A scientist must use mathematics to determine whether there is a relationship and how strong it is.

Connecting Concepts

The concept of intelligence is discussed in Chapter 7. There you will learn about IQ tests—what they are, what they measure, and how they are scored—as well as various definitions of intelligence.

Making Sense of the Data

The next step is to analyze the data. We take the scores that we got from our participants, and we put the numbers into a special formula. (It is not necessary in this course for you to know that formula or to do the calculations. But if you want to, you can easily learn how to do this in a statistics course—a plug for the math department!) The formula we use will give an answer between 0 and 1. This number is called a **correlation coefficient** and is represented by the letter r. The mathematical formula for calculating correlation is adjusted so that the answer, the r, cannot be greater than 1. If you get a correlation of 3.65, then something is terribly wrong!

If $r = 0$, then there is no relationship, no pattern between the two sets of numbers that were obtained. The closer the coefficient is to 0, the smaller is the degree of correlation between the two variables. A correlation of 0.08, for example, would indicate a very small relationship, a meager pattern, with a great many exceptions. On the other hand, if $r = 1$, then there is a perfect relationship between the sets of numbers (there are no exceptions to the pattern). Perfect correlation never happens. However, the closer the coefficient is to 1, the higher is the degree of correlation between the two sets of scores. For example, $r = 0.95$ represents a very high correlation.

In summary, a correlational study results in a number, a correlation coefficient, that tells us the degree of relationship between the two variables that we measured; the higher the number, the stronger is the relationship. The correlation coefficient might be a number such as 0.63, meaning a moderately strong relationship between variables but far from perfect. It is tempting to think of 0.63 as a normal decimal number that can be converted to 63%. But this is *not* correct with correlation coefficients. Do not convert them to percentages. If it helps to think of a percentage, then square the coefficient. For example, $0.63 \times 0.63 = 39.69\%$. In other words, if $r = 0.63$, there is about 40% overlap between the two variables. What this means is that if we hold one variable constant, the other variable will be about 40% reduced in its range of scores. If we attempt to predict one variable from the other variable, we will do about 40% better than if we predict by chance. An r of 0.63 means that we improve our prediction by about 40%.

Correlation Examples

Colleges use correlations to help in making admissions decisions. The relationship between college grades and scores on an aptitude test (such as the ACT or SAT) is about 0.45. If we add high school rank to test scores, the correlation increases to about 0.60. By using scores on those two variables, colleges can reduce their admissions errors (choosing the wrong students) by about 36%.

Here is another example: We can measure IQ scores of various people and then compute correlation coefficients. Identical twins (they have the same inherited DNA patterns) who are raised together in the same home have IQ scores with a correlation of about 0.90. (They are very similar in IQ.) If one twin has a certain IQ score, the other twin usually has a similar score. However, identical twins who are raised apart, in different homes, have IQs with a correlation of about 0.75. This means that they are not as similar in IQ—environmental experiences matter. However, the correlations are high enough that it is apparent that heredity is an important contributor to IQ score. If you want a high IQ, the first step is to choose your parents carefully! Incidentally, the IQ scores of mothers and their children have a correlation of about 0.50, and those of cousins have a correlation of about 0.20.

Positive and Negative

The formula that we use will give us a correlation coefficient that is either positive (+) or negative (−). This does *not* tell us the amount or degree of relationship; it tells us the *direction* of correlation. A positive *r* means that the relationship is direct, as in the examples above. A **positive correlation** is one in which scores that are high on one variable tend to go with high scores on the other variable, and low scores on one variable tend to go with low scores on the other variable. This is sometimes described as a direct correlation. A **negative correlation** (or indirect, or backward, or inverse) is one in which people who have high scores on one variable tend to have low scores on the other variable and vice versa. For example, rates of schizophrenia are negatively correlated with social class (higher rates of schizophrenia occur in lower-income groups). Also, school grades are negatively correlated with absences (higher grades go with smaller numbers of absences). Here is an example from psychology: There is a negative correlation between depression and REM latency.

Depression refers to the mental and emotional suffering that some people experience when they have a very low mood, problems sleeping and eating, feelings of hopelessness, and other disturbances. REM (pronounced "rem") stands for "rapid eye movement," is a stage of sleep during which people's eyes move around rapidly, and is associated with dreaming. **REM latency** is the amount of time after falling asleep before a person enters REM sleep. We measure how long it takes after people fall asleep before their eyes start darting around. This amount of time is called REM latency. It varies from person to person and, it turns out, is negatively correlated with the amount of depression people are experiencing.

What does this mean? A negative relationship between these two variables means that people with more depression on the average have shorter REM latencies (remember, a negative *r* means high scores on one variable go with low scores on the other variable). This means that on the average, depressed people move into dream sleep faster than do nondepressed people. Similarly, this negative correlation means that, on the average, people with less depression will have longer REM latencies; that is, they will sleep longer before beginning dreaming. Please note that we do not know why this relationship exists. We know only that there is a negative correlation between these two variables. Knowing someone's REM latency, we can predict his or her level of depression more accurately than by chance, and knowing a person's level of depression will allow us to predict that person's REM latency better than by chance. This is what a correlation means.

THINK TANK

Name some variables that are most likely positively correlated, such as height and shoe size.

Name some variables that are likely negatively correlated, such as creativity and conformity.

Getting Graphic

Not only can we calculate a number (the correlation coefficient, *r*) from the data we collect in a correlational study, we also can make a graph. On a standard Cartesian plane with two axes we label and number the axes from the bottom up and from left to right for our two variables. Then we simply place a dot on the graph for each participant. If we had 50 participants in our sample, we will have 50 dots on our graph. Each dot will represent one person, but it will indicate two things about that person. Each dot will be placed directly above and directly across from the scores of one person.

The pattern of dots on the graph will indicate the relationship between the two sets of scores. If the dots are randomly scattered all over the Cartesian plane, then the two variables were unrelated to each other, and their correlation coefficient will be 0. If the

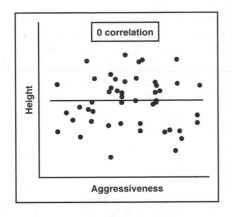

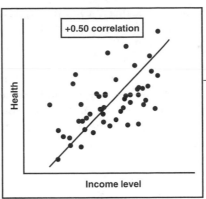

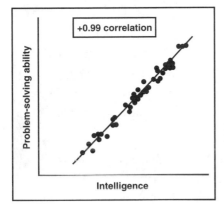

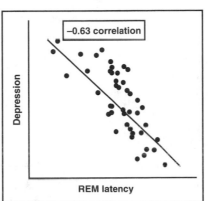

Each dot on a scatter plot shows two scores for one participant. The pattern of the dots indicates the degree of correlation between the two variables. The more the dots form a straight line, the higher is the correlation. When there is no correlation between the two variables, the dots will be randomly spread out.

dots line up in a perfect straight line, then the variables are perfectly related, and $r = 1.00$. If the pattern of dots moves up from left to right, then the correlation is positive (direct). If the pattern moves down from left to right, then the relationship is negative (indirect or backward). The closer the dots are to forming a straight line, the higher is the correlation. The more spread out the dots (the looser their arrangement), the lower the correlation.

Being Probable

Finally, there is one more important bit of analysis to do. Because we did not measure the whole population (we measured only a sample of people), we do not know whether our data accurately reflect the entire group. It is possible that our data are skewed in some way. There might be a relationship in the population that we did not find, or there might be no relationship but we were unlucky in selecting a sample that did have a relationship. We need to determine mathematically how likely it is that our results could have happened if in fact there is no relationship in the population from which we randomly selected our sample.

To do this, we use mathematical probability statistics. The data are placed into a special formula, and a probability is calculated. The result is called a **p value.** This number tells us the probability that the results we found could have been produced if there were no relationship between those variables within the population. The number is expressed as a decimal, for example, 0.05 or 0.12 or 0.001 or 0.03 or 0.24. For instance, if the *p* value is 0.05, it means there is a 5% chance (5 times out of 100) that the results could have happened even if there is no correlation in the population.

Now here's what is important: A large *p* value means that our results could have occurred by chance, and so we do not trust that there is a real correlation between the variables within the population. However, if we get a small p value, it means that there is a small probability that our results could have happened by chance. A small p value means that our hypothesis is more likely correct, that it represents a real correlation in the population. But how small is small? To consider their results reliable, most scientists require a p value of 0.05 or smaller (less than a 5% chance that these results could happen if there is no correlation). In that case, the results are called **statistically significant.** This means that we can be quite sure that our results did not happen by chance, that in fact there really is a relationship between those variables within the population. The smaller the p value, the more certain we can be. But we are never totally certain because it is possible for a sample to indicate a relationship that does not exist in the population.

Recap

— A correlational study attempts to find the degree of relationship between two or more variables. Correlation means a relationship.

— Experiments begin with a hypothesis, a statement about variables. Any hypothetical constructs (abstract ideas) must be operationally defined (defined in a way to make them measurable).

— In a simple correlational study, two variables are measured, and then a coefficient, known as r, is calculated. The closer r is to 0, the smaller the relationship, the closer to 1.00, the higher the relationship.

— A positive correlation means that high scores on one variable tend to go with high scores on the other variable. A negative correlation means high scores on one tend to go with low scores on the other. For example, IQ is positively correlated with SES, and depression is negatively correlated with REM latency.

— A scatter plot graph can be made of the data. If the dots move upward from left to right, there is a positive correlation; if the dots move downward, the correlation is negative. The closer the dots fall into a linear pattern, the stronger is the relationship.

— A p value is calculated to give the probability that the correlation occurred by chance. A small p value (usually less than 0.05) is called statistically significant.

CAUSE AND EFFECT

"Lucky is he who has been able to understand the causes of things."
—VIRGIL

When we find a correlation between two variables, it is important to remember that we do not know why there is a relationship. In a correlational study, we do not control any variables; we merely measure them. Using a correlational study, we can discover the extent of relationship between variables but not why it is there. If there is a relationship between X and Y, there are three possible reasons for it:

1. X causes or influences Y.
2. Y causes or influences X.
3. There is some other variable (that we did not measure) that is influencing both X and Y.

For example, if we went to cities in the United States and measured the number of churches and the number of bars we found there, we would find a high positive correlation. For instance, New York City would have a high number of both, and Podunk, North Dakota, would have a small number of both. We could then conclude that religion drives people to drink or that drinking makes people more religious. This silly example was chosen to help you see that sometimes there is an unmeasured variable that influences the relationship between the two measured variables. In this case it is the population of the cities.

Here's another example: Researchers have found a negative (inverse) relationship between Parkinson's disease (PD) and coffee consumption. People with PD on the average drink less coffee than do people without PD. Why might this be so? There are three possible reasons. First, perhaps having PD causes people to drink less coffee. Second, perhaps drinking coffee reduces the risk of PD. Third, maybe there is a third unmeasured factor, such as occupation (farmers have a higher rate of PD because they are exposed to more chemicals), that gives people an increased risk of PD but also is associated with less coffee consumption. Well, which one is it? Do you have a guess? Researchers think it's the first explanation. PD decreases the brain chemical dopamine, which is what gives caffeine its kick. It's likely that people with PD do not get much satisfaction from coffee.

As was noted above, there is a negative correlation between depression and REM latency. We do not know why this relationship exists; we know only that it does. It might be that depression causes REM latency to be shorter. It also might be that short REM latency causes people to be depressed. Finally, there might be a third variable (maybe brain chemistry?) that is influencing both depression and REM latency.

For each correlational study, we do not definitively know which of the three possibilities is correct. We say that *correlation does not prove causation.* We can theorize about which is true, but we cannot prove any of them from the correlational results. To prove cause and effect, we need to do a **controlled experiment.** Before we describe the procedures of a controlled experiment, it is wise to think about the concept of cause and effect.

THINK TANK

Suppose a positive correlation was found between the wearing of watches and students' grades. That is, suppose that students who wore watches got higher grades on the average than those who did not.

Give three explanations using the model X causes Y, Y causes X, or Z causes both X and Y.

Now try this one: Cigarette smoking is positively correlated with depression and suicide, and smoking is negatively correlated with serotonin activity in the brain (Malone et al., 2003).

What are the three possible explanations for this?

The Meaning of Cause

The terms *cause* and *effect* are commonly used in science. These terms are also used among the general public. I'm sure you can see it coming: Scientists are not using these terms in exactly the same way that the general public does. It is normal for nonscientists to think of cause and effect as a single notion; that is, if we say that A causes B, many people take this to mean that every time A is present, B will result. It is also believed that if B is present, there must have been an A before it. This is not correct.

For example, if we say that smoking causes lung cancer, people regularly say that they know someone who smoked for many years and did not get lung cancer. Or they say that they know someone who has lung cancer who did not smoke. They believe that "A causes B" means that every A results in B and that every B is always preceded by A. But consider this analogy: If we say that war is dangerous, would it be correct to reject that idea because we know someone who went to war and came back unharmed or because we know someone who was harmed who had not been in a war?

Multiple Influences

The common notion of cause and effect is wrong. When scientists say that X causes Y, they do not mean that every instance of X results in Y. The variable Y may also result from things other than X. When scientists say that one variable *causes* another variable, they mean the same thing as *influences*. "X causes Y" means that the variable X has an influence on the variable Y. It means that the presence of X influences the presence of Y.

But most variables are caused (influenced) by multiple factors. What causes psychological depression? There are many paths that lead to depression. A particular behavior, mental illness, emotion, or cognition can have many different causes or influences. That is, it might be true that X causes (influences) Y, but it is more likely that to get Y, you need a combination of X with A, C, D, and E. Or you can get Y from A, F, G, and H. Human emotions, behaviors, and cognitions nearly always have multiple, interacting causes from culture, society, social situations, mental factors, and biology. Psychologists commonly use a *biopsychosocial* model. Psychological variables have multiple influences.

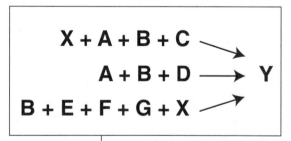

Variables nearly always have many causes, and the causes usually combine together like a recipe to influence the effect.

For example, many studies have shown that watching violent TV programs, movies, or video games causes aggression. On hearing this, most people say, "That's not true. I've watched violent movies all my life and I'm not violent." First, it is possible that you *are* more violent than other people who did not watch such movies (you might be more likely to fight, scream at people, hit your children or spouse, favor capital punishment, and so on). Even if you are not, it does not negate the fact that watching violent media influences aggression. The statement does not claim that *everyone* who watches violent media is aggressive. Some people who watch violent media are more aggressive, and some are not. Who is influenced depends on other variables. For example, we know that if parents talk to their children about the violent media that they watch, this does somewhat reduce the amount of aggression the children show. Some years ago, there was a movie on TV in which some teenagers set a homeless person on fire. The next day, in various places all over the United States, teenagers were setting homeless people on fire. I did not set anyone on fire. Most people did not set anyone on fire. However, scientifically, we would say that watching that movie *caused* (influenced) aggression. What we mean is that there was an increase in the average rate of aggressive behavior among people who watched the movie.

What correlations can you think of that do not prove causation?

Give examples of things (such as depression) that have multiple causes.

Give some examples (such as smoking causing cancer) of misconceptions about the idea of cause and effect.

CONTROLLED EXPERIMENT

"The scientist is a lover of truth for the very love of truth itself,

wherever it may lead."
—LUTHER BURBANK

Because a correlational study will not tell us convincingly whether one variable causes (influences) another variable, to determine causation, we need to do an experiment in which we control one variable to determine its influence on the other. This type of scientific study is exceedingly common, undoubtedly the most common in scientific research, and is simply called a controlled experiment.

Beginning a Controlled Experiment

The procedures for conducting a controlled experiment begin exactly the same as for a correlational study as discussed above. First you need participants (previously called subjects). The number of participants selected in the sample is represented by N. For example we might say that $N = 200$, meaning that 200 participants were selected for the study. This number needs to be sufficiently large to be mathematically representative of the population (the group of interest; for example, teenagers, college students, or adult males). Also, as was mentioned above, the participants should be randomly selected from the population. The participants who are selected in the sample will be studied, and the results will be generalized to the entire population from which the participants were drawn. That is why the selection of participants is so critical in reaching correct conclusions.

Next we need a hypothesis. In the case of a controlled experiment, the hypothesis will be in the form "A causes (influences) B." Naturally, A and B represent the psychological variables we are studying. In a controlled experiment, we are trying to determine whether one variable has any influence on another variable. Hence our hypothesis can always be stated in the form "A causes B."

In and Out

In a controlled experiment, we are attempting to determine whether one variable (in this example, A) is a cause or influence of something else (in this example, B). We call the causative (influencing) variable (in this case, A) the **independent variable.** This is the variable that will be controlled by the experimenter (it does not depend on the other variable—in that sense, it is independent). We are attempting to determine whether the other variable (B) is being influenced, that is, whether it is an effect. This variable (B) is known as the **dependent variable** because it will depend on the first variable. In every controlled experiment in which the hypothesis is of the form "A causes B," the first variable, the cause (A), is called the independent variable, and the second (B), the effect, is called the dependent variable. I need to warn you that for some weird reason, students tend to get these reversed. Therefore, you can either study this concept more than you think you need to or mark the opposite answer on your test! If you don't study enough, you will likely get them backward.

Here are some helpful ways to remember: The independent variable is the cause; it is the variable that the experimenter controls; it is what the participants are given by the experimenter; the independent variable goes "in" to the experiment; it does not depend on the other variable; it is independent. On the other hand, the dependent variable is the effect; it is not controlled; it is merely measured at the end of the experiment; it is what the participants are measured on; it is the outcome (what comes "out" of the experiment). The dependent variable depends on the independent variable.

Here are some examples:

1. Will rats run mazes faster if they are hungry? In the form "A causes B": Hunger causes faster running of mazes. Independent variable = hunger. Dependent variable = speed of running a maze.
2. Students who receive counseling will attend class more often than those who don't. In the form "A causes B": Counseling causes increased class attendance. Independent variable = receive counseling. Dependent variable = frequency of class attendance.
3. People will have fewer colds if they take vitamin C. In the form "A causes B": Vitamin C causes a reduction in the number of colds. Independent variable = vitamin C. Dependent variable = number of colds.
4. People who are afraid will want to talk with other people more than people who are not afraid. In the form "A causes B": Fear causes increased talking with others. Independent variable = fear. Dependent variable = amount of talking with others.
5. People will be more aggressive if they are in a frustrating situation. In the form "A causes B": Frustration causes aggression. Independent variable = frustration. Dependent variable = aggression.

Groups

Now we have participants and a hypothesis. If we were conducting a correlational study, we would proceed with measuring our variables. But in a controlled experiment, we want to determine cause and effect; therefore, we need to control our independent variable. To do that, we need to divide our participants into at least two groups. This should be done randomly; that is, the participants we have randomly selected from our population should next be randomly divided into two groups. We should not use any criterion whatsoever to divide them into groups because it could adversely affect the outcome of the experiment. The division into groups must be done randomly, meaning that each participant has an equal chance of being selected into either group.

One group is called the **experimental group,** and they will experience the independent variable. For example, if we are attempting to discover whether frustration has any influence on aggression, the members of the experimental group will be put into a frustrating situation. Because we normally are interested in variables that are hypothetical constructs (abstract, not concrete), as was mentioned above, we must operationally define those variables. In this case, we might have people put together jigsaw puzzles in which the pieces do not fit properly. That will be our operational definition of frustration.

The other group is called the **control group.** These participants will *not* be given the independent variable (frustration, in this example) but instead will be given what is called a **placebo,** a fake treatment. The members of the control group must be treated exactly the same as those in the experimental group in every way except one: the independent variable. Whatever we say to the members of one group, we must say exactly the same thing in exactly the same way at the same time of day to those in the other group. We need to make everything the same as much as possible because we do not know what might affect the dependent variable and therefore complicate the outcome of the experiment. The idea is that the participants are randomly divided into two groups, they are treated exactly the same in every way but one, they are then measured on something (the dependent variable), and if they are different on that, we can assume that the difference is due to the different treatment they got (the independent variable).

Recap

— Scientists attempt to find the causes of variables. *Cause* means the same as *influence*.

— Almost all variables have multiple causes, often in various combinations or interactions. There are many ways to develop depression, for example.

— Correlation does not prove causation. A correlational study shows only whether there is a relationship, not why there is.

— A controlled experiment can help to determine whether a variable is caused (influenced) by another variable.

— In a controlled experiment, participants are randomly assigned to one of two groups. The experimental group gets a treatment, while the control group gets a placebo (this defines the independent variable, which is controlled by the researcher). The independent variable is the hypothesized cause. The dependent variable is the effect, measured at the end of the experiment.

Please, Please Me

The control group must receive a placebo, a fake treatment. The word *placebo* comes from Latin and literally means, "I will please." Although the word was once used to refer to a fake pill, we now also use it more generally to refer to the fake situation that is given to the members of the control group to simulate the situation of the participants in the experimental group. The purpose of the placebo is to keep everything the same between the two groups except for the independent variable. If the experimental group is putting together jigsaw puzzles, as in the previously described example, then the control group must also put together jigsaw puzzles—except that their puzzle pieces will fit together easily and nicely. Everything must be the same for the two groups except the condition of the independent variable.

As you are likely aware, the participants in a controlled experiment must not know which group they are in; they must not know whether they are receiving the independent variable or a placebo. This is because of what is called the **placebo effect.** Sometimes knowledge can affect certain psychological variables. If people believe that taking vitamin C will reduce their number of colds and they believe that they are taking vitamin C, these beliefs might relax them, thereby improving the activity of their immune systems, and they might in fact have fewer colds—not from the vitamin C, but from the change in their body or their habits resulting from their belief. Similarly, they might be more cautious, eat better, or do other things that will reduce their number of colds if they believe that they are taking vitamin C.

If 100 people have headaches and are given a pain pill, about 80% will report that the headache is gone. If 100 people have headaches and are given a sugar pill that they believe is a powerful pain reliever, about 30% will report that the headache is gone. Their headaches really will be gone. That is the placebo effect. Of course, much of the change that occurs in psychological variables is due simply to time passing. If you have a cold and wait awhile, it will go away. People often conclude that something they did while they had a cold caused the cold to go away. But scientists need better proof— they need a control group to compare with.

The fact is, some things in our bodies are influenced by our actions and by our beliefs. Think about stress. If you are worried, certain biological events change in your body (hormones and digestion of food, for example). The placebo effect is a real effect; it is not fake. However, the placebo effect cannot influence everything. This point was emphasized by a recent study that criticized the use of placebos (Hróbjartsson & Gotzsche, 2001). The authors found that the placebo effect occurs only in some situations, most notably in reducing pain.

If you have a broken leg and I give you a sugar pill that you believe will straighten your leg, this belief will have no effect on your broken leg. Some things in your body (heartbeat, blood pressure, immune system, etc.) *can* be influenced by what you are thinking and by your degree of relaxation; other things cannot. Also, most things change with time, so we need to consider scientifically whether a change in a psychological variable was due to the independent variable, to the placebo effect, or to time passing. Because we do not know the full range of the placebo effect, every controlled experiment must protect against it so that we can determine whether the dependent variable was influenced by the independent variable.

One more important thing about the placebo effect: People often say that it doesn't matter as long as it works. This is wrong. It does matter. The goal of science is not to cure 30% of people. The goal is to determine which variables are influences and which are not. If your headache goes away because you believe you took a pain pill, even though you did not, we are happy for you; but science is not better off. In science we want to know which things actually reduce pain—in everyone, not just in you. No offense!

Help, I'm Blind!

It is not only the participants in a controlled experiment who must not know whether they are receiving a placebo or not; the experimenters who work with or have contact with the participants also must not know. This is because of what is called the **experimenter effect.** Any person who knows what group the participants are in might inadvertently treat them differently, and that different treatment might affect the outcome of the experiment. If I hand you a pill that I know is real, I might unconsciously smile, and if I hand you a placebo, I might frown. If I am scoring tests that I know came from the control group, I might unconsciously give them lower scores because I want my hypothesis to be found to be true, and so on.

An amusing example of the experimenter effect occurred in Germany some years ago. **Clever Hans** was a horse that could solve arithmetic problems. Hans's trainer, Herr von Osten, would pose an arithmetic problem, such as 3 times 2, and Hans would tap one forefoot the correct number of times—in this case, 6. But a curious young psychologist discovered that the horse could not solve arithmetic problems if the answers were not known by the questioner or anyone present. Hans, it turned out, was solving the problems using nonverbal cues (body language) given by the questioners. A problem was posed, then the questioner looked down at Hans's forefoot. This was Hans's signal to begin tapping. When the horse reached the correct number of taps, the questioner looked up at Hans's face to see whether he would stop tapping. This was the cue that Hans used to stop. Hans was not clever at arithmetic; he was clever at reading body language. Researchers who teach chimpanzees to use sign language or to use other methods of communication must control for the Clever Hans problem—the experimenter effect.

In fact, in any controlled experiment, anyone who deals with the participants in any way must not know which group they are in. This controls for the experimenter effect. And, of course, the participants must not know which group they are in. This controls for the placebo effect. When both these conditions are met, the experiment is called **double blind**—both the participants and those in contact with them are blind to which group they are in. If the experimenters who are in contact with the participants know which group they are in but the participants do not, then the experiment is called **single blind.** We want experiments to be double blind, but unfortunately, this is not always possible. We cannot give our complete trust to single-blind experiments. For example, if we want to know whether a new treatment works on schizophrenia, the psychologists who evaluate the patients should not know whether those patients received the treatment because that belief might distort the psychologists' clinical judgments of the patients' conditions. Experiments should be double blind for the results to be trustworthy.

THINK TANK

Can you think of some examples that are similar to the experimenter effect?

Give examples of things that people believe because of bias.

Can you think of examples of people using selective perception to draw conclusions? What about horoscopes or psychic powers?

Analyzing the Results

At the end of a controlled experiment, we must measure the dependent variable. For example, suppose we are attempting to determine whether frustration has an influence on aggression. Of course, we must operationally define those terms. Suppose that we define frustration as the experience of attempting to put jigsaw puzzles together that don't fit, and suppose that aggression is measured by how many times people will push a button that they believe gives an electric shock to a stranger in another room (no one gets a shock, but the participants are told that someone does). Both groups put puzzles together, but the experimental group has pieces that will not fit. Later, both groups of participants are tested on aggression (how many times they push the button), and the results of the two groups are compared. If, on the average, the people who were frustrated pushed the button more often than those who were not frustrated, we are tempted to conclude that frustration does have an influence on aggression—but not so fast.

It is possible that a larger number of aggressive people were accidentally selected into the experimental group than into the control group, even though we used random assignment. It might be that frustration has nothing to do with aggression, but that people in the experimental group pushed the button more often than people in the control group because of the luck of the draw. On the other hand, it might be that the results of the experiment are correct, that the dependent variable (aggression) was influenced by the independent variable (frustration). However, the results might have been the result of luck. Perhaps just by chance more aggressive people ended up in the experimental group. Which one is true? To decide which of these to believe, we need the help of mathematics.

Return to P

Just as with a correlational study, as described above, we need to calculate a p value for a controlled experiment. This number will tell us the probability that our results occurred by chance. In other words, if our dependent variable (aggression) really is not at all influenced by our independent variable (frustration), then what are the odds that our results would turn out the way they did just by chance? This can be determined by using probability statistics.

We put our data into a formula, and the answer we get (the p value) tells us this probability. If the p value is small (say, 0.01), it means that there is only a small chance (in this case, 1%) that these results could have occurred by chance. Therefore we trust that our hypothesis is correct. We are 99% sure. On the other hand, if the p value is large, then we do not put our faith in our hypothesis. We require more proof. How small is small? Again, most researchers require 0.05 (5%) or smaller. Scientists would rather *not* believe something that is true than believe something that is false. We can always do more research to determine what is true. We do not want to make the mistake of going forward believing that something is correct (and perhaps squelching further research on it) unless we are very certain, at least 95%.

When the p value is 0.05 or smaller, we say that our results are statistically significant. This does not mean that the results are important (they might or might not be); it simply means that we feel very certain (95% or better) that the independent variable had an influence on the dependent variable. It does not mean that it is true for everyone. Experiments are performed by using large groups of participants, and the scores are averaged. A controlled experiment is not a case study. The results refer to the group, not to individuals. If we find that frustration influences aggression (which, in fact, has been found in many experiments similar to the one described here), it means that this happens *on the average*, not in every person. Also, in some experiments (up to 5%), we get results that we accept as correct (affirming our hypothesis) but that occurred because of luck or chance.

Good Interpretations

Many modern scientists are beginning to question the logic of hypothesis testing as described here. New research methods and more complex statistical procedures now

THINK TANK   How can we reconcile the fact that psychology is interested in the behavior and mental processes of an individual, yet scientific research (except for the case study) provides information about a group?

If we know that people generally do something, how does this help us to understand a particular person?

allow for more complicated and meaningful analyses of data, and the trend is moving in that direction. One of the most common and valuable approaches emerging today is called **meta-analysis.** This is a statistical way of combining data from many studies to determine whether the hypothesis is true, how powerful the effect of the independent variable is, and why different studies found different results. In other words, meta-analysis is a mathematical way of examining the results of many different studies on the same topic.

"Not everything that can be counted counts, and not everything that counts can be counted."
—ALBERT EINSTEIN

Here are some examples:

1. Research on birth order and personality has shown inconsistent results. Are there certain personality traits that are associated with first-born, middle-born, and latter-born children in families? Some studies have found an association, and some have not. So a meta-analysis was done. The results of many different studies were analyzed together. The meta-analysis found that the differences between studies were due primarily to different operational definitions of personality traits and that there is, in fact, a small, but statistically significant, relationship between these variables (Sulloway, 1996).

2. Another tough research topic is schizophrenia, a brain disorder that causes a person to hear voices, think odd thoughts, and become socially and emotionally isolated. In recent years, about 2,000 studies have been published each year on this puzzling disorder—unfortunately often with inconsistent results about the biology and symptoms of schizophrenia. But meta-analysis can help to sort out the conflicting data. For example, Heinrichs (2001) looked at 54 studies and found that there was no one factor that marked schizophrenia but that cognitive problems were more associated with the disorder than were biological abnormalities.

Although meta-analysis and other techniques are becoming more common, most psychological research today is still founded on the principles of hypothesis testing that are described above. You still need to understand the logic of control groups, placebos, double blind, and p values. However, there are three things that are important beyond the p value in determining whether to believe a hypothesis.

First is **replication.** This means that experiments need to be done over and over again with different participants in different places. The more a hypothesis is replicated and found to be statistically significant, the more we tend to believe it. As the poet Tennyson wrote, "Science moves, but slowly, slowly, creeping on from point to point." Scientists have often noted how their work has built on the work of others. The first experimental psychologist, Wilhelm Wundt, said, "We are all epigones [successors]," and the great physicist Sir Isaac Newton (who was not known for his humility) said, "If I have seen further, it is by standing upon the shoulders of giants."

The second issue is to consider how well our results fit in with what we already know to be true. If the hypothesis is outlandish or is contrary to what we already are certain of or if our results do not coincide with a logical or rational analysis, then we have good reason to doubt the hypothesis, no matter how small the p value. The problem with using probability to determine truth is that if you measure something often enough, eventually just by chance it will come out to be true! Therefore we need to consider research results in light of what is rational and what we already know to be true. Results that contradict long-held scientific beliefs need careful attention and serious replication before being accepted.

The third issue might be the most important. When we say that a research finding is statistically significant, we do not mean that it is significant in its meaning and its application to people and society. We mean only that it meets the statistical criterion to be trusted and believed. Some results might be true but not important, useful, or interesting. As Einstein said, some things count. Science is one very valuable way of finding out what is true about nature. But, of course, there are many silly, insignificant findings in science; similarly, there are other ways than science of finding meaningful "truths" in our lives—the arts, literature, music, dance, love, friendship, and many more. Science is one very useful way of finding answers. But those answers are not everything.

THE VALUE OF SCIENCE

"Irrationally held truths may be more harmful than reasoned errors."
—THOMAS HENRY HUXLEY

For some terribly odd reason, far too many people today have a bias against science. Many people hate science, or fear it, or believe that it cannot help us in any way; in fact, many people think that science will harm us. This antiscience attitude is very common and, I believe, mostly wrong-headed. It is not science that harms us, since science is neutral. It is the way in which people use science that may be either helpful or harmful.

It is ironic that people who speak harshly against science happily use computers, cars, TVs, cameras, bridges, elevators, airplanes, DVD players, cell phones, and microwave ovens; run to the doctor for a flu shot or antibiotics; take their ailing cars to mechanics; consult engineers; and so on. Everyone seems to recognize that science has given us some remarkable things. Suspicion and caution about science are sometimes justified; however, suspicion should be aimed not at science in the abstract, but at the ways in which scientific knowledge is applied. Discovering the secrets of the atom will inevitably lead some people to want to build a bomb and some others to use that bomb. Knowing this, we might argue that people cannot be trusted with scientific findings. However, as is obvious, science can be used for progress if people apply its findings properly. For example, radiation therapy has extended the lives of countless cancer patients. But can we trust people to use science for good purposes? I leave the answer to you!

As you are undoubtedly aware, many people act unethically at times. Even many scientists act unethically at times because they too (surprise!) are people. To safeguard against some of the ethical lapses that can occur, scientists have instituted ethical guidelines and rules that apply to scientific research. Scientists now make their proposals for experiments to institutional review boards, and researchers are obligated to get informed consent from their participants, to not use deception, to debrief the participants, and in general to recognize the welfare of the participants as the primary concern. That was not always the case; there are many examples of past scientific studies that put people at risk of emotional, or even physical, harm. In medical research, there is the classic example of black men with syphilis who were purposely not given proper medication so that researchers could discover the long-term consequences of the illness (Jones, 1993). Yes, that happened in the United States, from 1932 to 1972. The President issued an apology in 1997.

Fortunately, current psychological research does not have extreme examples of unethical behavior. However, many years ago psychological researchers conducted a horrifyingly large number of experiments that harmed people. Early brain researchers, for example, applied intense electric shocks to people's brains, often resulting in permanent damage and even death (Fancher, 1990). Psychologists have also regularly used deception, lying to participants in experiments. Need we point out that it is wrong to lie? Most of these moral problems are addressed by today's ethical codes. But the most controversial ethical issue remaining in contemporary psychology regards animal research.

What rights should lower animals have? Does it depend on the species of animal? Should chimpanzees have more rights than worms? To what extent should animals be used in research? Is it legitimate if the animals are well treated and cared for, or is that wrong because it infringes on their right to live in their natural habitats? Is it reasonable to harm animals in research if the results might save human lives? Should monkeys be sacrificed if the research might lead to a cure for Parkinson's or Alzheimer's disease? These are some of the many thorny issues that today are being discussed and are, in fact, inciting protests and even riots at some universities and research centers.

I cannot tell you the correct answers to such questions. These, for the most part, are not empirical questions that can be answered by measuring something. These are questions whose answers must be discovered in the context of our social and cultural systems. The best answers will require philosophical and logical reasoning and understandings at a depth of analysis that is beyond most of us.

The emerging discipline of **bioethics** is a field of study that contemplates such issues and attempts to reach fair, correct conclusions. The latest branch of bioethics is **neuroethics,** a specialized study that had its first conference in May 2002. Experts met to discuss moral issues regarding brain-related scientific findings. Now that science has tools that can look at people's brains, could that information be used in unethical or disturbing ways (Hinrichs, 2001, 2002)?

As you probably already know, bioethicists often disagree on the answers to the profound questions that surround psychology and brain science. That can be disheartening. But be careful. Although even the experts cannot agree, and although at times it seems that there are no good answers to these deep ethical problems, that the answers are purely subjective, or that one answer is as good as the next, still we must not be deterred from asking these questions and considering these issues. We must try to do the right thing.

THINK TANK

What do you think should be the most important considerations for psychologists doing research?

Are there ever times when it would be okay to deceive participants?

Would it ever be okay to harm them, either physically or emotionally?

What about animals? The first genetically altered monkey was created in January 2001. His name is ANDi ("inserted DNA" backward). The idea is to create diseases in such animals that will be more similar to human diseases than those in transgenic mice. Is this ethical?

Recap

— The participants in the control group are given a placebo to control for the placebo effect, a possible influence on the dependent variable because the participants believe they are receiving a treatment.

— Similarly, the experimenters working with the participants must not know which are in the control group. This helps to control for the experimenter effect, the possible effect on the dependent variable by the experimenters. The case of Clever Hans, the horse that could supposedly count, is an example of the experimenter effect.

— A controlled experiment must be double blind; the participants, as well as those experimenters who come in contact with the participants, must not know which group the individuals are in.

— A p value is calculated to determine the probability that the results occurred because of luck or chance. A low p value (usually 0.05) means that the results are statistically significant.

— Meta-analysis is a statistical tool for examining many different studies to see whether a real effect is present. Replication and proper interpretation are important for all scientific research.

— Many people have an antiscience attitude. But science can provide very useful information if it is used properly.

— Scientific experiments are guided by rules of ethics, which have changed over the years and likely will continue to change. The field of bioethics deals with these issues.

I Link, Therefore I Am

The official Web site of Dr. Oliver Sacks is at http://www.oliversacks.com/

The Jane Goodall Institute has its Web site at http://www.janegoodall.org/

The Kinsey Institute is at http://www.indiana.edu/~kinsey/

There are many Web sites that discuss Clever Hans. For example, the Young Skeptics at http://www.csicop.org/youngskeptics/library/topics/cleverhans.html

If you enjoy using the Internet, you can find a good explanation of research methodology at http://www.georgetown.edu/grad/CCT/courses/method.html

Learn more about bioethics at the American Journal of Bioethics Web site at http://www.ajobonline.com/beginners.php or at the National Reference Center of Bioethics Literature at http://www.georgetown.edu/research/nrcbl

STUDY GUIDE FOR CHAPTER 2:

METHODS OF SCIENTIFIC RESEARCH

Key terms and names (Make flash cards.)

empirical	correlational study	positive correlation	placebo
case study	perfect correlation	negative correlation	placebo effect
Oedipus complex	sample	REM latency	experimenter effect
Oliver Sacks	population	p value	Clever Hans
naturalistic observation	participant	statistically significant	double blind
Jane Goodall	random	controlled experiment	single blind
comparative psychology	hypothesis	independent variable	meta-analysis
survey	hypothetical construct	dependent variable	replication
Alfred Kinsey	operational definition	experimental group	bioethics
variables	correlation coefficient	control group	neuroethics

Fill in the blank

1. Science can study only _____ subjects.
2. Journals that deal with psychiatric disorders often include _____ _____.
3. The books of Oliver _____, such as *The Man Who Mistook His Wife for a Hat*, are very popular accounts of case studies.
4. Jane _____ has spent a career meticulously noting the detailed behavior of chimpanzees in their natural habitat.
5. Psychologists who study animal behavior are called _____ _____.
6. Perhaps the most famous survey in history was that undertaken by Alfred _____.
7. Kinsey and his team surveyed many thousands of adult men and women about their _____ behavior.
8. The things that are studied in science are called _____.
9. The goals of psychology are to _____, _____, and _____ behavior.
10. If a set of teams finished in exactly the same order from one year to the next, we would then say that there is a _____.
11. The group about which we are interested in drawing conclusions in a scientific study is called the _____.
12. Samples should be large and _____ selected.
13. A _____ is a statement about variables that a scientist intends to measure.

14. Abstract variables that are not directly measurable are called _____.
15. A definition that makes abstract variables measurable is called an _____ definition.
16. A correlation coefficient is represented by the letter _____.
17. If there is no relationship between two variables then the correlation coefficient is _____.
18. A _____ correlation is one in which scores that are high on one variable tend to go with high scores on the other variable, and low scores on one variable tend to go with _____ scores on the other variable.
19. There is a _____ correlation between depression and REM latency.
20. If variables are perfectly related, then on a graph the dots will be in a _____.
21. A number that tells the probability that certain results could have occurred by chance is called a _____.
22. To consider their results reliable, most scientists require a p value of _____ or smaller.
23. When the p value is small, the results are called _____ _____.
24. Correlation does not prove _____.
25. In a controlled experiment, the hypothesis will be in the form _____.
26. We call the causative (influencing) variable the _____ variable.
27. The _____ variable is measured at the end of the experiment.

28. The participants in the _____ group are given the independent variable.
29. A fake treatment is called a _____ .
30. The Clever Hans problem is known as the _____ effect.
31. When both the participants and those in contact with the participants are unaware of which group the participants are in, the experiment is called _____ _____ .
32. A statistical technique of combining a number of different studies is called _____ .
33. _____ is the process of performing experiments over and over again with different participants in different places.

34. Many people have an _____ attitude.
35. Black men with syphilis were purposely _____ so that researchers could discover the long-term consequences of the illness.
36. The most controversial ethical issue remaining in contemporary psychology regards _____ _____ .
37. The emerging discipline of _____ is a field of study that contemplates moral issues in biological and psychological research.

Matching

1. uses case studies _____
2. Jane Goodall _____
3. Alfred Kinsey _____
4. empirical _____
5. Sigmund Freud _____
6. REM latency _____
7. correlational study _____
8. comparative psychology _____
9. dependent variable _____
10. hypothesis _____
11. moral issues _____
12. hypothetical construct _____
13. p value _____
14. control group _____
15. Clever Hans _____
16. independent variable _____

a. bioethics
b. measurable
c. the effect
d. survey method
e. relationship between variables
f. abstract variable
g. the cause
h. naturalistic observation
i. statistical significance
j. gets placebo
k. sleep
l. experimenter effect
m. study of animals
n. statement about variables
o. use of case study
p. Oliver Sacks

Multiple choice

1. If a psychologist found a statistically significant positive correlation between love and intelligence, which of these would be true?
   a. People in love are not very smart.
   b. The correlation was very high.
   c. The finding was very important to science.
   d. Highly intelligent people were more likely to have more love.
2. If I randomly divide students into two groups and I give one group a fair test and the other a trick test, and I then find that the students who took the trick test become more agitated than the others, what have I done wrong?
   a. did not determine a significant correlation
   b. used hypothetical constructs
   c. should not have divided them randomly
   d. did not make the experiment double blind

3. Only one or a few people are studied in a
   a. longitudinal study
   b. case study
   c. survey
   d. naturalistic observation
4. Jane Goodall is known for her research using
   a. survey
   b. correlational study
   c. case study
   d. naturalistic observation
5. How low must a p value be to be called statistically significant?
   a. 0.01
   b. 0.02
   c. 0.05
   d. 0.10

6. If neither the participants nor the experimenters who deal with them know which group each participant is in, the experiment is called
   a. single blind
   b. double blind
   c. statistically significant
   d. random

7. A negative correlation between variable X and variable Y means that a high score on X tends to be associated with a _____ score on Y.
   a. high
   b. low
   c. medium
   d. random

8. Which of these correlation coefficients represents the greatest degree of relationship between two variables?
   a. + 0.87
   b. + 0.56
   c. − 0.39
   d. − 0.94

9. In a controlled experiment, the participants in the control group must be treated exactly the same as the members of the experimental group in every way except for the
   a. independent variable
   b. dependent variable
   c. double blind
   d. correlation coefficient

10. Who is known for his classic survey of human sexual behavior?
    a. Arnold Schopenhauer
    b. Norbert Farraday
    c. Alfred Kinsey
    d. James MacKensey

11. A high negative correlation between anxiety and intelligence means that anxious people usually have
    a. lower intelligence
    b. higher intelligence
    c. medium intelligence
    d. It is impossible to say from this information.

12. If an experimenter finds that being in love causes people to have shorter attention spans, the dependent variable is
    a. length of attention span
    b. degree of being in love
    c. whether or not people are in love
    d. amount of attention the person gives to their partner

13. If it is found that where a student sits in the classroom has an effect on the student's grade, then the independent variable is
    a. where the students sit
    b. the grades
    c. the correlation
    d. how the students get good grades

14. In a controlled experiment, if the participants don't know which group they are in but the experimenters who work with them do know which group they are in, it is called
    a. replicated
    b. unethical
    c. statistically insignificant
    d. single blind

15. If we plot the scores of a correlational study on a graph and the dots are all over the place, this means that the two variables are
    a. negatively correlated
    b. positively correlated
    c. not correlated
    d. only weakly correlated

16. We should be careful about drawing generalizations from studies that are based only on one or a few individuals such as
    a. surveys
    b. naturalistic observations
    c. case studies
    d. correlations

17. The things that are measured and studied in science are called
    a. factors
    b. controlled factors
    c. empirical constructs
    d. variables

18. If every member of a population has an equal chance of being selected into a sample, it is called
    a. random
    b. independent
    c. dependent
    d. double blind

19. A hypothesis in the form "X causes Y" is appropriate for a
    a. correlational study
    b. survey
    c. controlled experiment
    d. independent variable

20. A student says that he thinks when his professor talks fast, the material is less likely to be on the next test. This statement is an example of
    a. the placebo effect
    b. a case study
    c. a hypothesis
    d. statistical significance

21. An anthropologist is interested in finding out whether people's personality traits are related to their birth orders. What sort of research method will she use?
    a. naturalistic observation
    b. correlation
    c. controlled experiment
    d. case study

22. A psychologist comes to your house to observe your children, but they act very different when the psychologist is there. This is a problem with the _____ method.
    a. correlational
    b. survey
    c. naturalistic observation
    d. controlled experiment
23. Suppose there is a negative correlation between drinking soda and college grades. This would mean that
    a. drinking soda causes students to get low grades
    b. drinking soda causes students to get high grades
    c. students who get low grades drink more soda
    d. students who get high grades drink more soda
24. If a study finds that people will eat more food if the food is presented in smaller pieces, then the dependent variable is
    a. the size of the pieces
    b. the amount of food eaten
    c. the correlation between the amounts of pieces
    d. the number of people who eat the small pieces
25. What is it that needs to be "operationalized"?
    a. dependent variable
    b. correlation coefficient
    c. hypothetical construct
    d. p value
26. If a variable is defined in such a way that makes it measurable, the definition is called
    a. operational
    b. significant
    c. a construct
    d. statistically valid
27. Scientists have found a _____ correlation between depression and REM latency.
    a. negative
    b. positive
    c. double blind
    d. variable
28. Scientists have found that people who watch violent media are
    a. less aggressive
    b. more aggressive
    c. less passive
    d. No relationship has been found.
29. If we want to know whether one variable influences another variable we must perform a
    a. controlled experiment
    b. correlational study
    c. naturalistic observation
    d. case study
30. If a scientist finds a correlation of -0.75 between creativity and intelligence, it means that
    a. high creativity causes people to be less intelligent
    b. high intelligence causes people to be less creative
    c. people who are high in intelligence are usually not very creative
    d. people who are high in creativity tend to be intelligent

Short answer and critical thinking

1. Give examples of appropriate topics for the case study method, survey, and naturalistic observation.
2. Explain what is meant by a perfect correlation. Give examples of positive and negative correlations.
3. What is meant by "Correlation does not prove causation"? Why doesn't it?
4. What is a p value? What does it tell us? What level is considered to be statistically significant? What does that mean?
5. What is the purpose of a placebo? What is the experimenter effect?
6. What is bioethics all about? Give examples of issues in its domain.
7. What do scientists mean by *cause*? Explain the concept of multiple causes.
8. What is double blind? Why is it important?

UNIT
2
BIOLOGY

"We are an intelligent species and the use of our intelligence quite properly gives us pleasure. In this respect the brain is like a muscle. When it is in use we feel very good. Understanding is joyous."

—CARL SAGAN

In this unit, you will learn about the brain, heredity, the senses, and perception. As you know, psychology is the study of the ABCs— affect (emotions and moods), behaviors (actions), and cognitions (perception, memory, and thinking). All of these are produced by the brain. Therefore knowing about the anatomy and physiology of the brain is an important step in understanding psychological processes. This unit presents fundamental information and explanations regarding how our brains function, how we sense and perceive things, and how heredity works. These topics represent the biological bases of the ABCs.

The two chapters included here are as follows:

Chapter 3 Brain and Heredity—includes a detailed discussion of brain anatomy and physiology, a clear explanation of axonal and synaptic transmission, split-brain surgery and localization of function, and, at the end of the chapter, an introduction to how heredity contributes to psychological phenomena.

Chapter 4 Sensation, Perception, and Consciousness—a description of the human senses (with special attention to vision), how they work, and how the brain interprets and gives meaning to sensory information. This chapter includes an introduction to the field of psychophysics, psychophysical laws, and the fundamental Gestalt principles of perception. The chapter concludes with a discussion of consciousness and altered states of consciousness, including sleep, dreaming, hypnosis, and psychoactive drugs.

Chapter

3

Brain and Heredity

"From the brain and the brain alone arise our pleasures, joys, laughter and jests, as well as our sorrows, pains and griefs."
—HIPPOCRATES

PLAN AHEAD...

- What does the brain have to do with psychology?
- What are the parts of the brain? Do different brain areas have different jobs or functions? Will damage in a certain brain region result in a certain kind of disability?
- How is the brain connected to the body? What are the parts of the nervous system?
- How do brain cells work?
- How does heredity work? What psychological characteristics do we inherit?

THE BRAIN OF A LAMPREY EEL IS SITTING IN A JAR AT Northwestern University in Chicago. Remarkably, that eel brain is controlling the movements of a small robot on wheels (Mussa-Ivaldi, 2000). The eel's brain sits in a cold, oxygen-rich saline solution and has two sets of wires connected to it; one set coming in and one going out. The brain receives electrical signals from light sensors on the robot and, in turn, sends electrical signals to the wheels of the robot. The eel brain moves the robot toward the light if the wires are placed in a certain part of the brain, away from the light if the wires are placed in a different part of the brain, and moves the robot in circles if the wires are placed in yet another part of the eel brain. This is the first time that two-way communication has been successful between a brain and a machine. Scientists hope that this research will lead to the development of brain-controlled prosthetic devices for humans.

A brain in a jar with wires leading to and from a robot—wow! Just as amazing, scientists at Duke University Medical Center recently were able to move a robot's arm via a signal sent from a computer 600 miles away at the Massachusetts Institute of Technology. But get this: The computer was programmed by using the signals from a monkey's brain to its arm. Electrodes recorded the impulses from the monkey's brain to its arm, and the signal was fed into a computer and then sent to Duke University, where the electrical signal was sent to a robot. The robot's arm moved just as the monkey's arm had (Nicolelis, 2001).

In a similar experiment in Philadelphia, electrodes were placed into a rat's brain and connected by wires to a robot arm. When the rat is thirsty, it can move the robot arm via electrical signals sent from its brain, and the robot brings water to the rat. The rat's brain is controlling the movements of the robot (Nicolelis & Chapin, 2002). Other researchers have fitted a monkey with a brain-machine interface that allows him to control a robot with his thoughts (Carmena, 2003). A rat with electrodes in brain areas that control its behavior allowed researchers to remotely control the movement of the rat (Talwar et al., 2002). Such research could lead to remote-controlled rats that could be guided to enter buildings or defuse bombs. Could humans be fitted with such electrodes? Naturally, experts in the new field of neuroethics are concerned with such issues.

In addition, two people who are paralyzed are able to move a computer cursor just by thinking. These two people have wires implanted in the parts of their brains that control body movement. The wires are connected to computers. When the people think about moving, the computer cursor moves on the screen. Obviously, such advances could help many paralyzed people.

How long will it be before brains in jars are controlling robots by remote control? What will the robots be able to do? What kinds of brains, other than an eel's, can be kept alive in a jar? I'll bet you can think of lots of wild possibilities for such scenarios, from science fiction to practical applications. It sounds like something out of *Star Trek*, but it is happening right now in neurobiology research.

Inside your head is a three-pound computer, one of the most powerful computers in the world. The three pounds are mostly water; in fact, less than one pound consists of living cells. These brain cells use electrical and chemical activity to compute your emotions, thoughts, memories, and behaviors. Oh, and tonight when you go to sleep, your three-pound computer will create your dreams.

The discipline of psychology is concerned with studying the ABCs: affect (emotions, moods, and temperaments), behavior (actions inside the body, as well as in the environment), and cognition (perception, memory, thinking, and reasoning). The amazing thing is that all of these—all of the ABCs—are produced by the brain, the computer in your head. That is why we will now give a great deal of attention to the brain. After all, it is the locus of the mind and the controller of behavior. It is where psychological experiences are created. It is where "it" is at.

BRAINY QUESTIONS

"Brain: An apparatus with which we think that we think. Mind: A mysterious form of matter secreted by the brain. Its chief activity consists in the endeavor to ascertain its own nature, the futility of the attempt being due to the fact that it has nothing but itself to know itself with."
—AMBROSE BIERCE

Let's begin with some fun. Here are some of the most frequently asked questions about the brain together with some facetious answers. These questions and silly answers are intended not only for your amusement, but also for the purpose of stimulating your interest and provoking your contemplation and understanding of these issues. Following the silly answers, the true answers are provided in an abbreviated form. You will learn a great deal more about these issues in this chapter. Then, equipped with this knowledge, you too will be an expert on brains and will be able to give your own answers, facetious and true, to the many questions that people ask about the computers in our heads.

1. Is it true that people only use 10% of their brains?

Yes, but only during election years.

True answer: This is an odd question because it implies that there is a person, a "you," that uses brain cells. What is the "you" that's using the brain cells? Where is the "you"? Isn't the "you" created by the actions of brain cells? Wouldn't it be more correct to say that brain cells are using you, rather than that you are using them?

Anyway, back to the question: No one seems to know where this fallacy originated, although there are many brain facts that could have inspired this myth. For example, brains consist of billions of cells, so a huge number of networks are possible, and you're certainly not using all of the potential connections between cells. Also, we can always store more information into our memories; no one is ever full. In that sense, too, there is always more potential than we are currently using. And brain cells are either alive or dead, so you are always using the cells that are living. Perhaps what is meant by this myth is that the brain has lots of potential for learning, thinking, and memory storage. That is true.

2. Can dead brain cells regenerate?

Yes, but then they become "zombie" cells that stalk the other cells at night! That's what causes bad dreams. The only way to deal with them is to eat lots of garlic.

True answer: Dead cells do not come back to life. Once they are dead, they are gone. However, new brain cells (**neurons**) are produced in a region of the brain called the **hippocampus.** This new growth is called **neurogenesis**. The newly created cells migrate out to other brain regions, such as the frontal lobe, where they apparently are used for learning and memory (Shors, 2001). However, some research shows that new cells actually eliminate old memories (Feng & Tsien, 2001). Also, neurogenesis apparently is related to anxiety and depression, is reduced by stress, and is required for antidepressant medicines to be effective (Santarelli et al., 2003).

Until very recently, scientists thought that brain cells stopped growing in adulthood and suffered a steady decline after childhood. In the past, it was assumed that an adult brain could not replace dead neurons. But it was recently discovered that adult human brains grow new brain cells in at least the hippocampus and the olfactory bulb (Gage & Kempermann, 1999). In addition, brain cell growth was discovered in the brains of adult macaque monkeys (Gould et al., 1999) and even in birds' brains (Scharff, 2000). It is estimated that you grow about 5,000 new brain cells per day; but they will normally die unless you use them for learning. (So keep studying!) However, current research shows that only certain regions of the brain can grow new neurons, and only one type of neuron is generated; for example, brains do not grow new sensory cells. These findings are giving some hope to researchers who are searching for treatments or cures for brain injuries and brain diseases, such as Alzheimer's and Parkinson's.

3. Because brain cells send electrical signals, do we therefore think at the speed of light?

No, we think at the speed of dark. In fact, some people's brains are black holes from which no thoughts can escape.

True answer: The electrical signals that travel through brain cells are not caused by the movement of electrons, but are created by chemical molecules moving into and out of brain cells. In addition, the communication from one brain cell to another is accomplished by the sending and receiving of chemicals. Therefore, the transmission of signals in a brain occurs much more slowly than the speed of light or electrons, more like 200 miles per hour. An example of this is reaction time. It takes quite a while to put your foot on the brake when you see a child run out in front of your car.

A German scientist named **Hermann Helmholtz** was the first to measure the speed of nervous system signals. He did this in a very simple way. Helmholtz touched a person on the toe and asked him to respond. Then he touched the person on the knee and asked him to respond. The difference between the two times was how long it took the signal to travel from the toe to the knee: about 200 miles per hour.

4. Do some people have psychic powers, such as mind reading ability or foreseeing the future?

I had this weird feeling you were going to ask that. Why don't you use your mind-reading ability to find out the answer? Yes, we all have psychic powers, so don't read this book. I'll send you the information telepathically!

True answer: No, of course not. Don't waste your time or money on such things. All human brains are the same in their essential anatomy and physiology. No one has a special or different brain that allows for such things. If people had psychic powers, they would be able to find many useful and profitable ways to use such abilities other than trying to dupe you out of your money by doing magic tricks. Of course, people do have intuition and unusual feelings that they cannot explain. And people experience coincidences, false memories, and knowledge that they do not know the source of. So it is easy for people to think that they are getting information through psychic powers. But ESP has been scientifically studied for nearly one hundred years, and no convincing evidence has been found for its existence. In fact, quite a bit of trickery and evidence to the contrary has been found.

5. How is Einstein's brain different from mine?

First, Einstein's brain was inside Einstein's head, and your brain is inside your head. Second, Einstein's brain is no longer inside his head, while I assume your brain is still in your head. Third, Einstein's brain could understand German, and I don't know about yours. Fourth, Einstein's brain was especially good at thinking, particularly thinking about complex issues of theoretical physics.

True answer: When Einstein died in 1955, his brain was removed (at his request) and saved by Dr. Thomas Harvey, a pathologist at Princeton Hospital, who now has Einstein's brain in two Mason jars at his house in Wichita, Kansas. Sections of Einstein's brain have been studied by scientists, who have discovered some differences from comparison brains. Einstein's brain was smaller than average, had a higher proportion of glial cells (nourishing cells), was thinner but denser than normal, and had an unusual pattern of wrinkles in the area associated with mathematics and spatial reasoning. Whether these differences are significant and how they came about are unknown. They might have resulted from hereditary factors, biological events, learning experiences, or some combination of those things.

6. Is brain size related to intelligence?

Yes, but don't tell that to a flea!

True answer: If we look at different species, we find that brain size probably is related to intelligence. For instance, a dog has a larger brain than an ant and probably would be judged to be more intelligent. However, we should consider body size. An elephant has a very large brain but also has a very large body. Perhaps the ratio between brain size and body size would be a more accurate indicator of intelligence. But there would still be many exceptions since it is not so much the size of the brain that matters (regarding intelligence) as what the brain does—how well it works.

Within a species (say, humans) it is much more difficult to find a relationship between brain size and intelligence. Some studies have found no correlation, and some have found a very small relationship. Some scientists have found that people with larger brains are less likely to develop Alzheimer's disease (Graves et al., 2001), and some research also has shown that certain areas of the brain, such as the frontal lobe, are larger in more intelligent people and that the size of these areas is greatly influenced by heredity (Thompson et al., 2001). However, these correlational findings have many exceptions. So the best answer is that brain size is somewhat related to intelligence across all species of animals but that within any one species, any relationship is small. The bad news is that we cannot increase the size of our brains. However, we can increase the number and quality of interactions between brain cells. There is considerable evidence that people who use their brains more will be better at putting off Alzheimer's. In this case there is some wisdom to the saying "Use it or lose it."

7. Do smart people use more brain cells than less intelligent people?

Don't bother me now, I'm busy using my many brain cells.

True answer: In fact, some research shows just the opposite. Newborns start out with a huge number of cells, a number that gets pared down early in life. Brain-imaging studies show that when adults solve a problem, people who know the problem well and can solve it easily use many fewer brain cells than do people who struggle with it. Perhaps learning results in using fewer brain cells to solve a problem. This is known as

efficiency theory, the idea that intelligent brains work more efficiently. If you have to use a lot of brain cells to solve problems, perhaps you are not as smart.

8. *Do different parts of the brain correspond to different activities?*

Yes, baseball is in the front of the brain, football is in the lower regions, marriage is in the brainstem, honesty is at the very top, meanness is at the very bottom, love of Jujubes is in the left parietal lobe, the ability to stick French fries up your nose is in the seventh wrinkle, and indecisiveness is smack dab in the middle.

True answer: To some extent, the brain works in modules. Some brain regions are much better at certain tasks (for example, language) than are other regions. However, these modules are limited to certain functions, and the idea of localized functions can be (and often is) taken too far. Most psychological functions involve the interactions between many brain regions. Brains are biological organs that act like modular computers. Some of the specialized regions involve vision, hearing, and the other senses; understanding and using language; emotional expression; and coordination of body movements. But the brain does not work according to simple words in English or in correspondence to the various activities of daily life that are a part of our culture.

9. *Is it true that if you dream that you are falling and you don't wake up before you hit the ground, you will die?*

Yes. Researchers at Columbia University interviewed 425 people who died in their sleep, and 81% of them said that they had that dream just before they died.

True answer: We do not know what people were dreaming who died in their sleep or whether they were dreaming. However, many people have said that they dreamed that they fell and hit the ground and did not die—in fact, did not even wake up. So apparently it is possible to dream that you fall and hit the ground and live to tell the tale.

10. *Is a brain like a computer?*

Yes, haven't you ever heard of having a chip on your shoulder?

True answer: A brain is not *like* a computer, it *is* a computer! There are many types of devices that do computations. The PC or Mac that you use is but one type of computer. A brain is also a computer—a computational machine. Brains use networks of cells to compute electrical and chemical data that are brought in through the senses. In this way a brain is a computer. But brains are very different from PCs or Macs. A brain is alive, for one thing. Unlike silicon chips, brains engage in biological processes that are important for their functioning. Also, a brain does not distinguish between hardware and software. Memories, for example, are stored in the brain in the same networks that process sensory information. There is no central processing area or memory storage area in a brain. A brain is a computer but of a very different sort than the one on your desk.

Connecting Concepts

Neurogenesis seems to be slowed when people suffer from depression, a disorder discussed in Chapter 9. Evidence in animals shows that antidepressant medicines, discussed in Chapter 10, stimulate neurogenesis and thereby help relieve symptoms (Santarelli et al., 2003).

THINK TANK

What are the most common statements or questions about the brain that you have heard?

What are the most common myths that people believe about the brain?

What do you hope to learn by studying the brain? How will this information be valuable?

THE WRINKLED TOP

"All beauty comes from beautiful blood and a beautiful brain."
—WALT WHITMAN

When one looks at a brain, probably the first thing that is noticed is the wrinkly part on the top. This is called the **cerebrum.** The cerebrum is responsible for higher mental functions such as sensations (vision, hearing, etc.), perception, language, mathematics, logic, music, purposeful body movement, memory, and thinking. The cerebrum is very large in humans, making up nearly 90% of the total brain. The cerebrum is a much smaller percentage of lower animals' brains, although the chimpanzee cerebrum is very similar to that of a human.

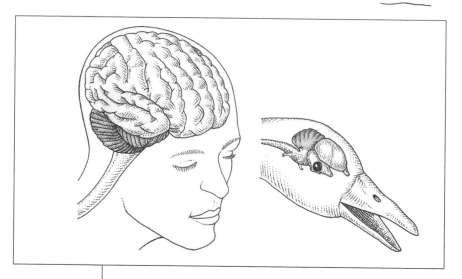

The human cerebrum is wrinkled which allows it to fit inside a head. The cerebrum is quite large, and if it were removed from your head and ironed, it would be about as large as a tabletop and very thin. Imagine a large piece of paper that must be crumpled to fit inside a smaller sphere. That is why the cerebrum is wrinkled. One can get an estimate of the size of an animal's cerebrum by looking at how many wrinkles it has.

The cerebrums of human and bird. The more wrinkles, the larger the area.

The wrinkles on the cerebrum are called **fissures** or **sulci** (singular = sulcus). The bumps that are formed by the wrinkling of the cerebrum are called **gyri** (singular = gyrus). These anatomical features are used as geographic boundaries for labeling and referring to parts of the brain. More about that in just a bit.

The cerebrum is divided from front to back by what is called the **longitudinal fissure**. This groove divides the cerebrum into left and right sides known as **hemispheres.** Don't take the term literally ("half-spheres"); the cerebrum is not shaped like a sphere—it is more ovoid. Differences between the left and right hemispheres have been studied extensively. In fact, researcher Roger Sperry won the Nobel Prize in Medicine for his studies of the left and right sides of the cerebrum. Let's look at some of what is known about the hemispheres.

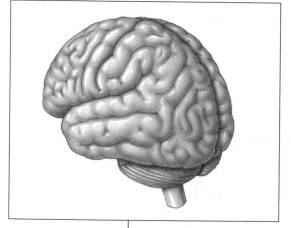

The left and right hemispheres are separated by the longitudinal fissure.

Two Highways

With only a few exceptions, the brain's left hemisphere is connected to the right side of the body and the right hemisphere is connected to the left side of the body. This connection is called **contralateral**, meaning "opposite sides." If a person has a stroke or other damage in the left hemisphere, the disability will be on the right side of his or her body, and damage in the right hemisphere will result in problems on the left side of the body. Also, if you touch something with your left hand, the signal is sent to the right hemisphere of your brain. Similarly, if you want to move your right hand, the signal must originate in the left hemisphere of your cerebrum. The brain is wired in reverse: The left side of the brain is wired to the right side of the body and vice versa.

The **spinal cord** is a series of cables (**nerves**) traveling up and down the back that carry signals to and from the brain and the body. These nerves carry signals only in one direction; they are not two-way highways. Some of the spinal cord nerves carry signals from the body to the brain—for example, when you touch something with your hand. If these signals are damaged or if the part of the brain that processes these signals is damaged, you will experience numbness, a lack of feeling in your body.

Other nerves in the spinal cord carry signals away from your brain to the muscles of your skeleton (so you can move). These signals travel from the brain

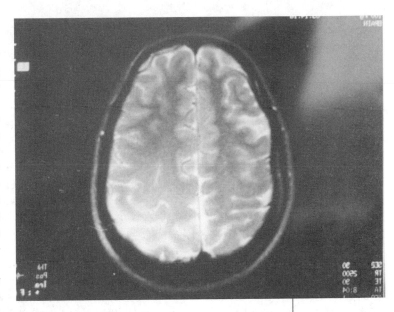

This MRI shows a woman's right hemisphere that is significantly smaller than her left, a condition that was probably caused by fetal alcohol syndrome. The woman complained of numbness and weakness on the left side of her body.

down the spinal cord. If they are damaged or if the part of the brain that originates these signals is damaged, then a person will experience paralysis. Please note that numbness and paralysis are *not* at all the same thing. They are different conditions that are caused by damage to different systems of brain and nerves.

The crossover points for the contralateral wiring of the nervous system are in the spinal cord and brainstem, depending on which nerves are involved. For example, if you touch something with your *right* hand, an electrical signal travels along your right arm to your spinal cord then crosses over to the *left* side of the spinal cord and travels up to the *left hemisphere*. Therefore, your left hemisphere feels something touching your right hand. Similarly, signals coming from the left hemisphere cross over and go to the right side of the body. To accomplish this, naturally, there are nerves that extend out of the spinal cord and carry signals to and from the body. These nerves carry signals only in one direction. So in effect, we have two highway systems of nerves. One set of nerves (known as the **afferent** or **sensory nerves**) carries signals from the body's parts to the spinal cord and brain, giving us the sense of touch and feeling in our body. Another set of nerves (known as the **efferent** or **motor nerves**) carries signals away from the brain and spinal cord to our body's parts, giving us movement of our skeletal muscles.

The above discussion refers to the nerves that extend up and down the spinal cord. There also are **cranial nerves,** 12 pairs of nerves that serve sensation and movement in the head (*cranium* means the skull). These nerves are not contralateral and sometimes have fibers that carry signals in two directions, thus conveying both skin sensations and muscle movement. As information travels through the brain, the pathways are known as **tracts**. For example, one would speak of the optic tract that carries signals from the optic nerves to various parts of the brain.

The Hard Body

If you think about the connections and highways of nerves described above, you will realize that there must be some way for the left and right hemispheres to communicate with each other. We do not have two hemispheres that act independently of one another—we have a system of coordination. This is accomplished by a bundle of fibers that carries information from the left hemisphere to the right and from the right to the left.

If we look down at the top of a cerebrum, it appears to be completely divided into left and right hemispheres. However, though the two hemispheres are divided at the top, deep down inside the cerebrum there is an area of connection called the **corpus callosum.** This term literally means a "hard body." If you had a brain in your hand and

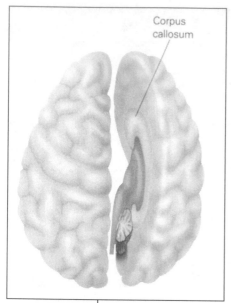
Corpus callosum

The left and right hemispheres communicate via the corpus callosum.

you pushed your fingers down between the two hemispheres, you would eventually (after an inch or two) feel the corpus callosum. This is the brain part (the tract) that sends signals back and forth between the two hemispheres so that one hemisphere can "know" what the other "knows." The corpus callosum is the communication tract between the left and right hemispheres.

Amazingly, some people have had their corpus callosum cut. This is done in rare cases of severe epilepsy to save a person's life. **Epilepsy** is a condition in which a person has repetitive **seizures**, or abnormal electrical firings of brain cells. It is as if there are short circuits occurring within the brain.

Epilepsy is fairly common and could affect anyone, although it is more common among children. Epilepsy has many causes, including genetic factors, birth problems, diseases and infections, and brain trauma. Sometimes epilepsy is mild, and there are few discernible problems associated with the seizures. Sometimes the seizures are more severe and more difficult to control. Many people with epilepsy take medication to control their seizures. In the most severe cases, the abnormal electrical activity can cross over the corpus callosum from one hemisphere to the other, and the person could die. In these rare cases, a surgical operation is performed to cut the corpus callosum.

The operation that is done could be called a corpus callosotomy, but it is more commonly called **split-brain surgery**. Don't be confused by the terminology; this has nothing to do with split personality, a psychological disorder that will be discussed in a later chapter. In split-brain surgery, surgeons sever the fibers that carry signals between the left and right hemispheres in the corpus callosum. The result is that the two hemispheres of the cerebrum are separated and act independently of one another; they are unable to receive signals from each other. The person who has had split-brain surgery, in effect, has two half brains that cannot talk to each other. Nothing whatsoever is done to the patients' abilities, such as their knowledge, their memories, their senses, or their intelligence. They are the same people as they were before the operation, except that their left and right hemispheres cannot send signals to one another.

FYI

Brains are electrical machines. A seizure results when there is an abnormality in the electrical firing of brain cells. Many things can cause a seizure; often they occur spontaneously because of internal biological functioning. However, seizures can be caused by a flickering light. Flash-induced seizures are most often caused by light flickering at a rate of 15 to 20 times per second. In 1997, hundreds of children in Japan suffered seizures while watching a Pokémon cartoon on TV. Seizures also have been caused by video games. Dramas and performances that use strobe lights often warn audience members in advance.

To the Side

A great deal of research has been done with split-brain patients, and from the findings, psychologists have learned a great deal about the differences between the left and right hemispheres. Sometimes, for example, a particular ability or psychological function is processed more in one hemisphere than in the other. This ability or function is then called **lateralized** (meaning "to the side"). For example, though a small percentage of people process language in their right hemispheres and an even smaller percentage use both hemispheres for language, in the vast majority of us, language is lateralized to the left. (This is easy to remember: *Language* is in the *Left* hemisphere.) The cerebrum's right hemisphere (in almost everyone) does not understand or create language. For most of us, to use grammar, syntax, semantics, sentence structure, and proper pronunciation, it is necessary to have a normally functioning left hemisphere.

On the other hand, the right hemisphere in most people is good at certain things that the left hemisphere is not. Most notably, the right hemisphere specializes in spatial perception, or visuospatial operations (being able to mentally picture things in space, such as a map of your surroundings, orienting in your space, or locating objects in the environment). The differences between the hemispheres are based not on the nature of the stimuli we sense, but on the type of cognitive operation the brain must perform to interpret our world (Stephan et al., 2003). Understanding what a word means is more a left hemisphere task; understanding where that word is on a page is more a right hemisphere task.

The differences between the hemispheres have led many people to devise wild ideas about left- and right-brained people. This is not a good idea. We have a corpus callosum that shares information between the hemispheres. Our right and left hemispheres communicate with each other. Yes, it's true that some people are better at some skills and psychological functions than are other people, but for the vast majority of mental functions, we are all two-hemisphere people! We do not have half a brain or even two brains. We have two halves that work together. The differences between the two hemispheres are mostly a matter of degree—one hemisphere does something a little better than the other. A good example is the brain's processing of music. Textbooks for years have stated that this is a right hemisphere function. But a recent study (Maess et al., 2001) used brain imaging to show that some music interpretation is computed in the area of the left hemisphere that processes grammar. It is better to think of the brain as a tightly organized bundle of interacting modules than to divide it into distinct regions with completely separate functions. After all, a brain is a communicating machine and is highly interconnected.

Recap

— Emotions, behavior, and cognitions are controlled by the brain, which uses cells to convey and process information. These cells use chemicals to create electrical and chemical signals.

— New brain cells are created even in adults. All living brain cells are functioning.

— Brains work in modules that have certain specific jobs. Those modules coordinate with each other to create psychological functions.

— The wrinkled top of the brain is the cerebrum, which is divided into two hemispheres, left and right, which are connected by the corpus callosum.

— The left hemisphere controls the right side of the body, and the right hemisphere controls the left side of the body.

— When a certain function is controlled more by one side of the brain than the other, it is said to be lateralized. In most people, language is lateralized to the left, and spatial perception (understanding maps) is processed in the right hemisphere.

Split-Brain Findings

If a person's corpus callosum has been cut, signals cannot be sent from one cerebral hemisphere to the other. The hemispheres are isolated from one another. For example, suppose we blindfold a split-brain patient and then place an object—say, a pencil—in her left hand. Her left hand feels the pencil and sends an electrical signal to her spinal cord. The signal crosses over to the right side of her spinal cord and ascends upward to the right cerebral hemisphere, which processes the feeling of the pencil. We might say that her right hemisphere "knows" about the pencil. The right hemisphere, however, cannot send a message over to the left hemisphere because the corpus callosum has been severed. So the left hemisphere "knows" nothing about the pencil. If we then take the pencil from her hand and place it on a table with a number of other objects and ask her to find it with her right hand (which is guided by the left hemisphere, which did not feel the pencil), she cannot identify the pencil as the object she was holding. However, if she uses her left hand (controlled by the right hemisphere that felt the pencil), then she identifies the pencil immediately. Students often ask whether this person knows about the pencil or whether she can feel the pencil. The answer is an astounding one: Her right hemisphere can feel the pencil and so knows about the pencil, but her left hemisphere does not.

Next, we ask the split-brain patient to *tell* us what she is holding in her left hand. Remember, the signal from the left hand travels to the right hemisphere, which does not control language. The left hemisphere controls language, so it will do the speaking. However, the left hemisphere does not know about the pencil. Therefore the left hemisphere will honestly say, "I do not know." She says that she does not know what she is holding in her left hand. Does she know? Well, again, although her left hemisphere does not know about the pencil, her right hemisphere does. How can we be sure? We can ask her to find it among a group of objects using her left hand, or we could ask her to draw a picture of the object using her left hand. Any task that asks the question of the right hemisphere will give us the answer. Her right hemisphere knows, but her left does not. Are you starting to see that you have two minds that communicate with each other?

But what about vision? What if she looks at an object? Eyes have cells in the very back that are sensitive to light. These cells send signals to the occipital lobe in the very back of the cerebrum. The way the eyes are wired to the brain is very interesting. The cells on the left side *of each eye* are wired to the *left* hemisphere, while the cells on the right side *of each eye* are connected to the *right* hemisphere. Now think about this: Cells on the left side of either eye are wired to the left hemisphere, while cells on the right side of either eye are wired to the right hemisphere. Cells on the left go to the left. Cells on the right go to the right.

But to accomplish this, because we have two eyes, some of the signals from the eyes must cross over from left to right, and some must cross from right to left. The cells that are on the outside of the eye (right side of the right eye and left side of the left eye) send signals to the hemispheres on the same side that they are on. That is, cells on the right side of the right eye are connected to the right hemisphere, and cells on the left side of the left eye are connected to the left hemisphere. That part is easy.

But the cells on the inside, toward the nose (right side of the left eye and left side of the right eye), send their signals to the brain hemispheres on the opposite side. That is, cells on the left side of the right eye are connected to the left hemisphere, and cells on the right side of the left eye are connected to the right hemisphere. The point where these cells must cross over is called the **optic chiasm**.

Each eye sends signals to both the left and right hemispheres. The cells on the left side of the eye send their signals to the left hemisphere, and the cells on the right side of the eye send their signals to the right hemisphere. However, those cells are

After the corpus callosum has been cut in split-brain surgery, the brain cannot communicate between left and right hemispheres. Typically, the left hemisphere controls language and sees things on the right. The right hemisphere does not use grammar but is good at maps and puzzles and sees things on the left.

responding to light that is coming from our environment, from things on our left and our right. The cells on the right side of the eye receive light from things on the left, and the cells on the left of the eye receive light coming from the right.

Because of the way the eyes are wired to the hemispheres of the brain, the result is that we see things that are on the *left* in our *right* hemisphere and we see things that are on our *right* in our *left* hemisphere. Think about this: If an object is in your *left* **field of vision**, then the light coming from it will strike the cells on the *right* side of the back of each eye. Thus an object in your left visual field stimulates cells on the right side of the back of each eye, and those cells on the right side of each eye are connected to the right hemisphere. Therefore an object on the left will be seen in the right hemisphere. Likewise, an object in the *right* visual field will stimulate cells on the *left* side of each eye, cells that are wired to the left hemisphere. So the left hemisphere sees things on the right. It's backward: Things on the left are seen in the right hemisphere, and things on the right are seen in the left hemisphere.

Suppose our split-brain patient sits in front of a screen and is shown pictures projected on the left and on the right sides of the screen. Pictures on the right will be

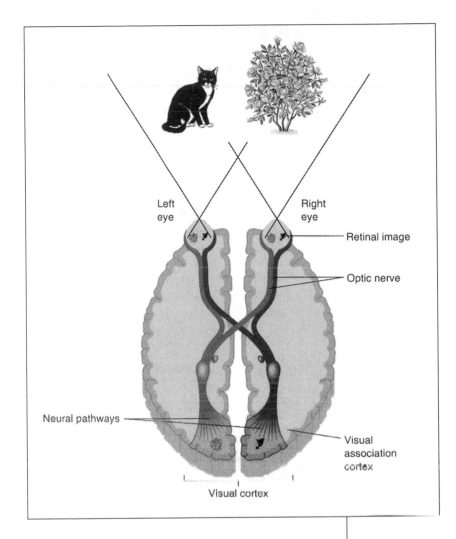

Left eye

Right eye

Retinal image

Optic nerve

Neural pathways

Visual association cortex

Visual cortex

The right sides of each eye are connected to the brain's right hemisphere. But the right sides of each eye receive light information from the left. Therefore, the right hemisphere sees things that are in the left field of vision. Similarly, the left hemisphere sees things on the right.

processed by her left hemisphere, and pictures on the left will be processed by her right hemisphere. Her corpus callosum has been cut, so the hemispheres cannot share information. If we flash a picture of a ball on the left side of the screen and a picture of a dog on the right side of the screen, her brain will see the ball in the right hemisphere and the dog in the left hemisphere. If we then give her a group of pictures and ask her to point to the object she saw using her left hand, she will point to a picture of a ball (the left hand is controlled by right hemisphere, which sees things on the left). However, if we ask her to tell us what she saw, she will say "a dog" because the left hemisphere controls speaking and it sees things on the right. Her left hand points at a ball, but she says, "dog."

The Interpreting Brain

A very interesting thing occurs if we ask our split-brain patient to explain her contradictory responses. For instance, if she points to a picture of a ball with her left hand (controlled by right hemisphere, which sees things on the left) but says that she saw a dog (left hemisphere speaking, sees things on the right), how will she explain this contradiction? Because she is not a brain scientist, she is not aware of the lack of communication between hemispheres in her head and the way that the eyes send signals to the brain. However, she knows what is in her mind. If we ask her to explain the contradiction with language, which brain hemisphere will take charge? Yes, the left. What

FYI

A certain woman who had split-brain surgery was found to have *spoken* language controlled by her left hemisphere, but *written* language was controlled in her right hemisphere. Words that were flashed to her left hemisphere could be spoken but not written, and words that were flashed to her right hemisphere could be written but not spoken. So at least in some people, these two functions of language are found in different hemispheres (Baynes et al., 1998).

does the left know? The left hemisphere saw a picture of a dog and then saw her left hand point to a picture of a ball and then heard her say, "dog." The vision and the speaking match, but pointing to a ball must be explained. She could simply say that she does not know why she is pointing to a ball. But she does not say that. The split-brain patient makes up a plausible-sounding reason for why she is pointing to the ball. She might say, "I saw a dog, and that made me think about playing fetch with a dog, and that's why I pointed at the ball." Humans give explanations. The process is called <u>confabulation</u>. Perhaps it is learned, or perhaps it is a part of our evolutionary development—this tendency, this disposition to explain our behavior, to confabulate. Whatever the cause, we do it automatically, without being aware of it.

Confabulation has been studied extensively by Michael Gazzaniga, who has written a number of books and articles about the differences between the right and left hemispheres. Working with a split-brain patient, Gazzaniga showed the right hemisphere the word *laugh*, and the patient began to laugh. When asked why he was laughing, he said, "You guys come up and test us every month. What a way to make a living!" When the word *walk* was shown to the split-brain patient's right hemisphere, he got up to leave. When he was asked where he was going, he confabulated, "I'm going to get a Coke." That's the patient's left hemisphere talking; it confabulates a reason to explain his behavior. We know that the reason for the behavior is the word shown to the right hemisphere. But because the corpus callosum has been cut, the left hemisphere does not know this, and it simply confabulates a reason for the observed behavior (Gazzaniga, 1992).

In another case, a split-brain patient was shown a snowy scene on the left (seen by her right hemisphere) and a chicken claw on the right (seen by her left hemisphere). Then the patient was asked to point to pictures that corresponded with what she saw. Her left hand (controlled by the right hemisphere) pointed to a shovel, and her right hand (controlled by the left hemisphere) pointed to a chicken. When asked why she was pointing to these things (remember, the left hemisphere does the speaking), she said she was pointing to the chicken because she saw a chicken claw, and she was pointing to the shovel because you use a shovel to clean out a chicken

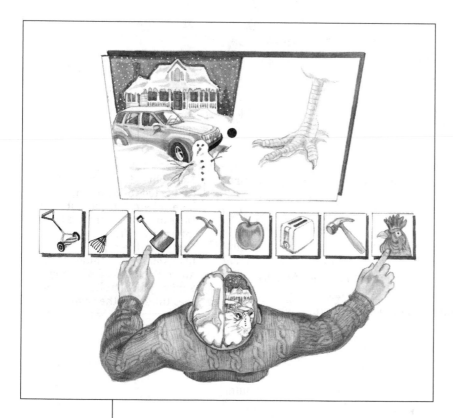

The left hemisphere confabulates a reason for why the left hand (controlled by the right hemisphere) is pointing at a shovel.

shed. That is confabulating (Gazzaniga & LeDoux, 1978).

This is fascinating! In each case, the patient's left hemisphere shows all indications that it believes the explanations it has made up. Our left hemispheres seem to have a tendency to interpret or explain behaviors. Apparently, we all do it. That is, the left hemisphere, the language hemisphere, does it. We make up plausible-sounding reasons for why we do things. Apparently, we really believe these reasons. However, they likely are not the true causes of our behaviors. It is good to differentiate between *reasons* (the explanations that people make up) and *causes* (the physical, biological things that actually lead to certain behaviors). Our left hemisphere seeks reasons, but scientists seek causes. The left hemisphere is especially designed to be in charge of interpreting behavior—of confabulating reasons to explain our behaviors.

BRAIN GEOGRAPHY

"If the brain were so simple we could understand it,

we would be so simple we couldn't."
—LYALL WATSON

The brain's cerebrum (the wrinkled part on the top) consists of layers of cells that are organized in columns. The outer, surface layer of the cerebrum is called the **cortex** (from the Latin for "bark," "rind," "shell," or "hull") or, more properly, the **cerebral cortex**. Think of it as the skin of the cerebrum. The cerebrum has many wrinkles, which are located roughly in the same places in each of us, though there are differences from individual to individual (as with fingerprints).

Scientists divide the cerebral cortex into various geographical areas. Remember, the cerebrum has both left and right hemispheres. There are two major fissures on each hemisphere. One fissure extends down from the top center almost vertically. It is called the **central fissure** or the **fissure of Rolando**. Another large fissure extends horizontally from the middle front of the cerebral cortex toward the back. It is called the **lateral fissure** or the **fissure of Sylvius**. These fissures are used as landmarks or boundaries in dividing each hemispheric cortex into four regions called **lobes**.

Frontal Lobe

The **frontal lobe** is the lobe that distinguishes humans from other animals. In humans, it is very large, bulging out in front, and extends from the very front of the head back to the central fissure. The frontal lobe is responsible for purposeful body movements, language and grammar (left side only), and the highest mental functions, including planning, holding things in mind, foreseeing future events, restraining us from carrying out our impulses, and other executive functions. It is like the leader or the overseer of the brain. Our working memory (when we hold thoughts in awareness) is generated here. Emotions are also a part of the frontal lobe's functions. The frontal lobe, more than any other brain region, is responsible for our most human characteristics.

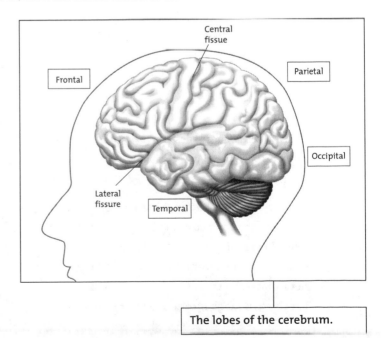

The lobes of the cerebrum.

Parietal Lobe

The **parietal lobe** is at the top back of the cerebral cortex. It is a very large lobe that has many functions, including body and skin sensations (more about this to come), pain perception, spatial perception, processing of music, and memories of various kinds. The parietal lobe stores information about where we saw things and helps us to navigate through the environment, acting as a computer for mapping our world. For example, damage to the parietal lobe can interfere with orientation in the environment. Our conscious maps of the world and our ability to move around directionally are created and processed by the networks of cells in the parietal lobe. Mathematics and imagery are also among the many functions of this brain region.

Occipital Lobe

The **occipital lobe** is in the back bottom of the cerebral cortex and is involved with processing and interpreting visual information. The cells in this lobe are organized into networks that process visual information not as a whole, but in parts. Visual processing is accomplished in parts, or modules. Damage to a specific region of this area will disturb only a particular characteristic of vision, such as movement, color, shapes, perceiving diagonal lines, or perceiving faces. More brain area is involved in the processing of visual information than in processing any other single function. Damage to the left occipital lobe will disturb vision in the right field of vision, and vice versa.

Temporal Lobe

The **temporal lobe** is the smallest lobe, located below the lateral fissure. One of its main functions is perceiving sounds. Areas of the temporal lobe, when electrically stimulated, cause a person to hear certain sounds. The ears are like the eyes in that the left and right ears each send some information to the left and right hemispheres. That is, the temporal lobe in the left hemisphere receives auditory information from both the left ear and the right ear. Similarly, the right temporal lobe receives information from both ears. Therefore, damage to only one temporal lobe will interfere with hearing in both ears. The temporal lobe also identifies objects. For example, a

Recap

— The left hemisphere sees things in the right field of vision, and the right hemisphere sees things on the left.

— A person who has had split-brain surgery cannot pass information between the right and left hemispheres. If the person's left hand touches something, the information goes to the right hemisphere. The person cannot say what it is, because language is controlled by the left hemisphere, but can point to it with his or her left hand.

— Split-brain research shows that the left hemisphere confabulates, or creates reasons for behaviors. Brains apparently have a tendency to interpret behavior.

— The cerebrum is divided into four regions called lobes: frontal (highest mental functions, language), parietal (skin sensations, where things are), occipital (vision), and temporal (hearing, identifying objects).

laboratory animal with damage to the temporal lobe will be able to see and move around in the environment but will not recognize objects that the animal saw before. The visual processing area of the occipital lobe sends signals to the temporal lobe regarding the identity of objects. While the parietal lobe processes *where* an object was seen, the temporal lobe processes *what* was seen. Another function of the temporal lobe is to understand the meanings of words. Damage in this brain area will not interfere with grammar or the pronunciation of words (those are frontal lobe functions) but will cause a person to have difficulty comprehending the *meaning* of words.

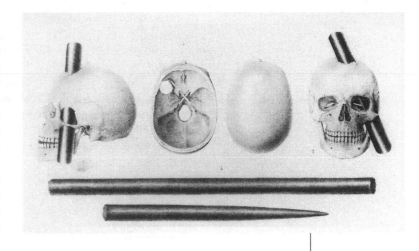

Amazingly, Phineas Gage lived through the experience of having a metal rod pass through his head.

A Metal Rod through the Head

In 1848, a railroad foreman in Vermont named **Phineas Gage** had an accident. Gage was tamping down a stick of dynamite with a long metal rod. His rod struck a rock, a spark ignited the dynamite, and the metal rod was propelled like a rocket through his head. The rod passed under Gage's cheek and through his frontal lobe and exited the top of his head (along with blood and bits of bone and brain). Amazingly, Gage did not die. He was taken to a doctor, who not only patched him up, but also wrote the first detailed case study of a person who had brain damage in a very specific area that was known to scientists. Today Gage's case is considered a landmark in neurobiology, and his skull and the rod that passed through it are kept at Harvard Medical School.

After his accident, Gage was a changed man. His friends said that he just wasn't the same Phineas anymore. He became compulsive in his behavior, carrying the metal rod around with him everywhere he went. He began to swear (which he had not done before), and he became anxious, neurotic, absentminded, and disorderly (though before his accident he had led a very orderly life). He showed poor self-control and was indecisive. Scientists today recognize these symptoms as common in people who experience brain damage to the frontal lobe similar to that suffered by Phineas Gage. But in 1848, most people, even doctors, did not recognize that personality and emotions were created in the brain. The case of Gage opened the door to a much better understanding of the functions of the brain and the idea that specific areas of the brain control specific mental and behavioral functions.

FYI Famous brain researcher Fred Gage, who discovered that age and exercise affect the number of neurons and recently showed that new neurons grow each day in the adult brain (neurogenesis), is a descendant of Phineas Gage.

FYI Many ancient thinkers, including Aristotle, believed that the mind was located in the heart. Today we have phrases such as "know it by heart" that derived from this idea. On Valentine's Day, instead of sending your loved one a heart, perhaps you should send a brain, the actual locus of emotions such as love.

Localization of Function

A hundred or so years ago, brain scientists argued over whether a brain worked as a whole, unified organ or was divided into separate areas, each with its own special functions or tasks. Some people believed that the brain was divided into hundreds of specialized areas and that the size of each area determined how well it worked. Further, some believed that the large brain areas, the areas that were especially good at whatever their function was, caused a bulging out of the skull. Consequently, a pseudoscience (fake science) called **phrenology** emerged. Belief in phrenology was remarkably widespread. The idea was that by feeling the bumps on a person's head, one could determine what the person excelled at. Many doctors had phrenology charts and busts to use as guides as they felt their patients' skulls. Phrenology, of course, turned out to be wrong. Larger areas of the brain are not necessarily better at their tasks than smaller areas, and the brain does not cause the skull to bulge out.

Although phrenology was wrong, its basic assumption had some truth in it. The brain *is* divided into modules that perform specific functions for some tasks. This is not the case for all psychological functions, nor does the brain divide its tasks according to simple English language concepts, and sometimes it's difficult to say exactly what a certain brain region specializes in. But in some cases, for some psychological functions, the brain does have separate (though interacting) modules. The idea that certain mental states and behaviors are controlled by a specific location in the brain is called **localization of function**. Here are some examples:

1. *Vision* is perceived by cells in the occipital lobe. These cells are organized in layers that are labeled V1, V2, V3, and so on. The pathway of visual processing begins with the V1 cells on the surface of the cortex in the back of the brain. The information flows forward in the brain and eventually divides into two pathways. One pathway processes and remembers visual information about what was seen. This pathway flows into the temporal lobe and is simply called the **what pathway**. The other system of cells carries neural information forward into the parietal lobe and processes and remembers where something was seen. This is called, as you might guess, the **where pathway**. Damage in the occipital lobe will adversely affect the processing of vision. The symptoms that occur depend on where the damage occurs. The cells are that specific in their jobs. For example, damage to one area disturbs a person's recognition of faces, a condition called **prosopagnosia.** In this case, a person does not recognize even very familiar people by sight; they need other stimuli, such as hearing the person's voice. Damage to a particular region of the brain (on the side just behind the ear) known as the **fusiform face area** (FFA) produces this problem. The FFA is a specialized area that allows quick recognition and memory of faces and also becomes involved when a person is an expert at identifying something visually. For instance, experienced bird watchers use their FFAs to quickly identify birds.

2. *Hearing* is perceived in areas located in the temporal lobes of each hemisphere. Each of these areas is an **auditory cortex**. Damage to one of these brain areas would cause a loss of some hearing in both ears because each ear sends some signals to the left and right hemispheres. The cells in the auditory cortex are arranged in layers that interpret the frequencies (pitch) of sound; interestingly, the layers are arranged very much like the keys on a piano. Wilder Penfield was a Canadian brain surgeon who, beginning in the 1930s, gently stimulated patients' brains with an electrode to locate the source of their epilepsy. Penfield discovered that the brain is highly localized. When he stimulated one area, for instance, the patient would hear a violin playing. When the electrical pulse was stopped, the sound ended. Stimulation of another area would result in the memory of a specific event. When stimulated in the visual area, one patient said, "Robbers are coming at me with guns."

3. *Body movement* is controlled by a gyrus, or bump, at the top of the cortex, at the very back of the frontal lobe just in front of the central fissure, extending from the top down vertically. This area is known as the **motor cortex**, the *motor strip*, or simply the *motor area*. (The term *motor* comes from the Latin and means "movement" or "motion.") The cells in this part of the brain send electrical signals to the skeletal muscles, initiating movement of the body. If you want to move your arm, your leg, or any part of your body, the cells in this region must be activated. The motor area is arranged upside down. That is, the cells at the top of the motor gyrus send signals to the feet, and the cells at the bottom of the motor strip control movements of the mouth and tongue. Damage to any section of the motor strip will cause difficulties in movement

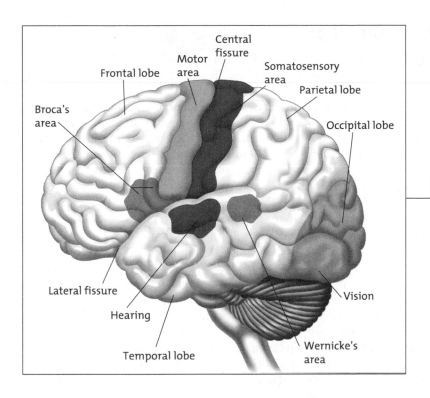

The primary localized areas of the cerebral cortex.

(*paralysis*) in the corresponding part of the body. For instance, a person damaged at the top of the motor cortex in the left hemisphere will have paralysis of the right foot.

4. *Body sensation* is processed by the cells in a brain gyrus just behind the central fissure in the parietal lobe. This brain bump is called the somatosensory cortex, *strip*, or *area*. It is located just behind the motor area. This place in the brain receives incoming signals from the body via the spinal cord. It might be thought of as the "touch" area of the brain. Like the motor cortex, the somatosensory cortex is organized upside down. A person who is injured at the top of this strip in the right hemisphere would have numbness, a lack of feeling, in the left toes.

In the past, psychology textbooks always included a drawing of a homunculus (small person) that illustrated the relative sizes of the subregions of the motor and somatosensory strips associated with different parts of the body (for example, a very big brain region feels the fingertips). It was believed that these subregions of the brain were precisely connected to movements and sensations in specific body parts. But recent research has shown that the motor and somatosensory strips are much more complicated (Helmuth, 2002). For example, a steady stimulation of a region of the motor strip causes a monkey's arm to move to its mouth no matter where the arm was originally positioned. We need to use caution in not oversimplifying the brain's organization, plasiticity, and complexity of function.

THINK TANK   "What" and "where" are processed in different areas of the brain.

Have you ever remembered something but not where you saw or heard it?

Have you ever recalled where you saw or heard something but not what it was?

Sensory Coordination

Although the brain regions mentioned above are specialized for certain functions, it is important to remember that brains are dynamic, living organs that are complex, interconnected, and changeable. The sensory systems are in communication with each other and act like instruments in an orchestra—they react to each other and create a symphony through teamwork. Each instrument (brain region) is modulated by other regions. In fact, scientists have found brain cells that receive signals from more than one sense, so-called **multisensory** (or **multimodal**) **neurons** (Driver & Spence, 1998). For instance, when people feel ridges on a pad that they cannot see, parts of their brains' visual areas become activated. In fact, disruption of the visual area interferes with feeling the ridges! Similarly, when blind people have activity in their visual areas disrupted, it causes them difficulty in reading Braille by touch.

There are many other examples of how the brain coordinates sensory systems. Some researchers now believe that all perception is multisensory (Stoffregen & Bardy, 2001). When adults had air blown into their faces, watched moving dots on a screen, or listened to sounds on headphones, not only did their touch, vision, and hearing brain areas become more active, but in each case, brain activity in three other areas increased (Bremmer et al., 2001). These brain regions presumably are cross-sensory. The **McGurk effect** is especially weird. When subjects watch a video of a person speaking a syllable but they hear a different syllable on the sound track, the subjects report hearing a sound that is some odd combination of the two. If they see lips say "ga," but hear "ba," the subjects report hearing "da." Could this be the result of a unification of sight and sound by the brain's multisensory neurons?

5. *Language*, as was mentioned above, is typically processed in several areas of the left hemisphere. Most right-handed people have a slightly larger left hemisphere, where language abilities are concentrated. Left-handers sometimes process language in the right hemisphere or on both sides of the brain but often also have their language areas in the left hemisphere. The result is that most people process language in the left hemisphere. (A gene contributes to being right-handed. When missing that gene, a person may become either a rightie or a leftie.)

By language, we do not mean just speech. A parrot that imitates sounds is not using language. Human languages have a structure, a grammar. For example, **syntax** refers to the proper order of words in a sentence. Using a grammatical language is a complicated computational problem that requires a large number of brain networks. Amazingly, children around the world learn language very easily and rapidly. This is because human brains are anatomically evolved to accomplish this wonderful feat.

Two brain regions are critically involved with language. French doctor **Paul Broca** (1824–1880) discovered that an area in the left frontal lobe is important for pronunciation and grammar. This brain area is now called **Broca's area** in his honor. One of Broca's patients was called "Tan" because that was the only word he could say. Tan's brain was somehow damaged in the left frontal lobe, the region now called Broca's area. If a person has damage in this region, say from a **stroke** (an accident in the blood vessels that deprives brain cells of oxygen, typically caused by a blood clot), the person is said to have **Broca's aphasia** or **expressive aphasia**. The term "aphasia" is used to designate any problem in the use or understanding of language. In Broca's aphasia a person will have difficulty pronouncing words and producing correct grammar. Such people might sound intellectually impaired because of their slurred speech or improper grammar, but it is important to note that Broca's aphasia does not interfere with intelligence or the understanding of language.

A German doctor, **Carl Wernicke** (pronounced "VER-nih-kee") (1848–1904), discovered another region of the brain involved in language. This area is located farther back from Broca's area, in the back of the temporal lobe. This brain region is involved in processing the meaning of words and sentences. The brain region discovered by Wernicke is now called **Wernicke's area** in his honor, and people with damage in this area have **Wernicke's aphasia** or **receptive aphasia.** Such patients have difficulty understanding language; that is, they have trouble comprehending the meanings of words. They may speak in ways that do not make sense, or they may create sentences that are very empty, using "like," "you know," and "whatever." Their sentences are often difficult to make sense of.

When a person wants to say something, Wernicke's area first creates the meaning of the words. Then Broca's area adds the grammar and pronunciation. Then the motor areas that control the mouth, tongue, and speech apparatus will express the language. The anatomy and physiology of these regions are primarily a matter of heredity, and a healthy human brain will learn language very easily and quickly when exposed to it at the right age. People who learn a second language early in life will use the brain cells in Broca's area for both of their languages. On the other hand, because Broca's area has a critical period, people who learn a second language later in life will have to rely on brain cell networks in regions other than Broca's area. This is why it is so much more difficult to learn another language as an adult.

Language

Language is one of the most studied of human behaviors. By language, scientists do not mean merely the sounds that many different kinds of animals use to communicate. Languages have **grammar.** This means that a language has a structure with specific rules for creating sentences that have meaning (**semantics**). The speech of young children shows that they are not simply mimicking words, but are applying the rules of grammar and syntax to their speech. For example, a preschool child might make an **overgeneralization**, such as saying, "I goed to the store" or "I saw a picture of two mouses." Although the past tense ("goed") and plural ("mouses") the child used are technically wrong, these statements show that the child understands the general rules for creating these parts of speech: Add an "ed" to indicate the past tense, add an "s" to make a noun plural. **Psycholinguistics** is a subfield of psychology that studies language development and the principles and behaviors that go with it. Naturally, this means an interest in the brain and how it is programmed to use language so skillfully and so early in life.

Contemporary ideas about language were influenced greatly by the linguistic theory of **Noam Chomsky.** Chomsky hypothesized a **language acquisition device,** a biological mechanism that is inborn in all humans and that provides a universal grammar. Chomsky's idea is that we all have a neurological system built into our brains that gives us tools for transforming meaning into sentences. Of course, children around the world learn different languages. But the fundamental rules of grammar are common to all languages, and Chomsky argues that they are not learned, but are part of the biological programming of our brains. Chomsky's theory says that every language has these fundamental ingredients and that the human brain is capable of understanding them (in the abstract form) without any learning.

Some behavioral psychologists have argued that Chomsky has gone too far, that he has not given enough importance to learning. Chimpanzees, for example, are capable of learning language at a rudimentary level and even appear to create words and use grammatical rules. Chimpanzees, however, do not have a speech apparatus that allows them to make

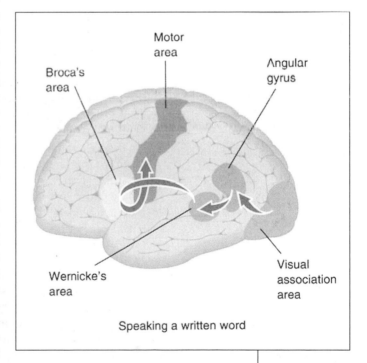

Motor area

Broca's area

Angular gyrus

Wernicke's area

Visual association area

Speaking a written word

Two language areas are typically in the left hemisphere: Broca's area, which controls grammar and pronunciation, and Wernicke's area, which controls the meaning of language.

FYI

In most people, the left hemisphere is best at processing and expressing language, and the right hemisphere leans toward music, rhythm, and melody. Interestingly, the Chinese language Mandarin uses lots of intonation (for example, a word can have different meanings depending on how it is pronounced). Brain images show that Mandarin speakers use both hemispheres for language, compared to English speakers, who use predominantly the left (Scott, 2003).

the sounds of language, so psycholinguists such as Gardner and Gardner (1969), Terrace and colleagues (1976, 1979), and Greenfield and Savage-Rumbaugh (1990) teach the chimps to use plastic symbols or computer icons in their language. Although some linguists believe that the chimps are not using complete grammar, that they are merely using a sophisticated kind of imitation, it appears that some chimps do create new sentences. In fact, Fouts (1997) has argued that such animals are capable of using language.

On the other hand, Chomsky's supporters argue, even deaf children learning sign language go through the same stages of language development and make overgeneralizations and other linguistic behaviors that hearing children make. Chomsky's view that people are born with language-specific skills is often called **nativism.** Other psychologists, such as Kyra Karmiloff and Annette Karmiloff-Smith (2001), lean toward a **cognitivist** view that humans are endowed with a wide variety of learning mechanisms that allow for language acquisition. It is true that children's ability to tell the difference between sounds improves for native speech and decreases for foreign speech. That is, by one year of age, children can distinguish between sounds in the language they are familiar with much better than they could previously but have lost their ability to differentiate sounds in unfamiliar languages. Does this mean that language is a unique brain system? Probably not, since it has been found that the same thing happens with vision: One-year-olds lose their ability to notice differences between faces they are not familiar with but improve in noticing differences in faces they know (Pascalis et al., 2002).

Interestingly, a human gene has been discovered called FOXP2 that is linked to language by guiding the development of the jaw. Apes do not have this exact gene. A British family in which about half the members suffer from language and speech difficulties has been studied since the early 1990s, and those members with aphasia were recently found to be missing two normal copies of FOXP2. It does seem that humans have a built-in advantage and predisposition for learning language, whether the rules of grammar are programmed into the brain in advance of learning or not. Preschool children all around the world, in every language community, very easily pick up the language that they hear and go through the same stages in their language development. However, learning is also part of the formula for developing language skills.

Evolutionary psychologists say that language is a good example of an **instinct**—an inherited tendency. That is, humans are not born with the ability to speak a language, but we are born with a predisposition to learn language very quickly. In *The Language Instinct* (1994), Steven Pinker writes about language:

> it is a distinct piece of the biological makeup of our brains . . . it is a complex, specialized skill, which develops in the child spontaneously, without conscious effort or formal instruction, is deployed without awareness of its underlying logic, is qualitatively the same in every individual, and is distinct from more general abilities to process information or behave intelligently. For these reasons some cognitive scientists have described language as a psychological faculty, a mental organ, a neural system, and a computational module. But I prefer the admittedly quaint term "instinct." It conveys the idea that people know how to talk in more or less the sense that spiders know how to spin webs. (p. 5)

Our brains are built for learning language. Perhaps this is part of a brain's propensity to find patterns—grammar, after all, is a type of pattern. Brains are pattern-seeking organs. And, of course, language had great survival value for our prehistoric ancestors. A genetic basis for language and speech has consistently been found in studies of families and twins, and now, for the first time, a gene has been located that is mutated in people with a language disorder (Lai et al., 2001). As with all human characteristics, this gene and others express themselves at certain times and interact with experience and other environmental factors. Any child, even one with perfectly normal genes, who is deprived of hearing language will not develop normal language ability. All psychological features, including language, are developed. Nothing is strictly inborn or strictly learned—everything about us develops.

The Body's Clock

Many aspects of physiology and behavior follow a cycle around day and night—sleep is an obvious example. These are called **circadian rhythms** (circles around the day). That is, many of our physiological processes (such as blood pressure), moods, and behavior patterns rise and fall at regular intervals during the day. This body clock is not automatically set at 24 hours. Travelers visiting another time zone often experience jet lag until their body clocks adjust to the new time.

The biological clock is set by incoming light. Certain cells in the eye (a subset of ganglion cells; see Chapter 4) contain a chemical (melanopsin) that is sensitive to the amount of light illumination (Berson et al., 2002; Roberts, 2004). These cells then send signals to a place in the brain known as the **superchiasmatic nucleus** (center above the optic chiasm). This area is the main brain region for regulating and setting the daily clock. That is, each day, the biological clock is reset by incoming light falling on cells in the back of the eye that connect to the brain. The brain then adjusts body physiology through mechanisms such as the hormone melatonin that is released by the pineal gland in the brain. The result of these physiological events is the circadian rhythms of the body.

THINK TANK

Language can be considered an "instinct" in humans, an inherited tendency or predisposition.

Are there any other human characteristics that could be considered instincts, using this notion? That is, what things about us make up "human nature"?

Plasticity

One of the most common myths about brains is that they are static and unchanging. People are always asking whether some psychological condition is inborn, as if we are stuck with whatever we have at birth. What is inborn is what a baby has at birth. Isn't it obvious that we change? Not only do psychological qualities change over time, but, of course, the source of those traits, the brain, also changes with experience. The brain's ability to change is called **plasticity.** Brains are not static; they are dynamic— they change with experience. For example, when people practiced five-finger piano exercises for only five days, researchers found that the area of the brain controlling the fingers was enhanced (Greenfield, 2001).

Research by Michael Merzenich (1998) is among the most commonly cited regarding brain plasticity. Merzenich showed that areas of the brain will increase in size with experience. For example, if a monkey is trained to touch something repeatedly with an index finger, the area of the monkey's brain that feels touch in that finger will increase in anatomical size. The number of brain cells used for feeling the index finger will increase. Brains are plastic.

FYI

Williams syndrome is a rare genetic disorder that causes a number of problems, including cognitive difficulties. Its sufferers resemble one another, have heart problems, age prematurely, have severe difficulty with spatial perception, and are mentally retarded. Despite their problems, children with Williams syndrome excel at language and social skills. Their language ability is extraordinarily good—precisely the opposite of autistic children. This finding indicates that language and cognitive skills are at least somewhat separate in the brain. Williams syndrome is caused when a group of genes on chromosome 7 is deleted during embryonic development. Interestingly, a gene on chromosome 7 has recently been discovered that apparently influences language ability (Lai et al., 2001). A mutation in this gene causes problems in grammar and pronunciation.

Similarly, when blind people listen to sounds, the cells in their *visual* cortex become active. Also, deaf people show activity in the *auditory* (hearing) area of the brain when they look at moving dots on a computer screen (Finney et al., 2001). Apparently, the brain recruits cells from other areas to help organize incoming information. Brains are flexible, dynamic organs. To determine just how flexible brain cells are, scientists rewired the brain of a ferret so that signals from the eyes were diverted to the auditory areas of the brain. Remarkably, the cells of the auditory cortex realigned themselves in a pattern similar to that of normal visual cells. However, the flexibility was not 100%, since the auditory cells did not completely copy the visual cortex.

If a young kitten has one eye blocked for only 24 hours, the number of cells in the brain that normally receive information from that eye will decrease, and the number of cells that receive information from the other eye will increase (Trachtenberg et al., 2000). Brain cells change; they are remodeled by experience. These findings remind us that the nature-nurture argument is a bit unreasonable. Nature and nurture work together—they are inseparable. Brains and experience are partners. Also, studies of brain plasticity remind us of **critical periods,** times when biological processes are more responsive to the environment. For example, a baby's brain will respond more to experience than will an adult's brain.

Another fascinating example comes from people who have lost a limb. A person whose arm has been amputated, for example, will still feel touch and pain in his or her arm. This experience is called **phantom limb.** The feeling persists even though the limb is not there. A missing arm will itch and hurt. Phantom limb demonstrates that the sense of feeling is not in our limbs, but in our brains. We feel with our brains.

In addition, brain cells that are not stimulated will begin to make connections with other cells. So if a person's arm is missing, the brain cells that were receiving signals from that arm will reach out to other cells. The brain cells will reorganize and form connections with nearby cells. The result is that the patient will eventually feel his arm when you touch his cheek! This is because the area of the brain that feels the arm is near the area that feels the face. Touch the patient's cheek, and he feels a sensation in his arm! The brain cells have organized themselves into a new pattern. Also interesting is that this apparently can be reversed: A man who received a transplanted hand had experienced a reorganization of his hand's cortical map after four months (Senior, 2001). Brains are plastic.

Of course, brains develop over time; the brain of a fetus is different from the brain of an adult. Brain development depends on experience: Cells in the eye and in the visual pathway depend on seeing (a newborn blocked from light will not develop normal vision), auditory cells depend on hearing (interestingly, noise can interfere with normal auditory cell development; see Chang & Merzenich, 2003), learning a language depends on hearing it spoken; and so on. Elderly brain cells also undergo changes. For instance, brain cells get thinner with age, slowing down reaction time and cognition. Also, elderly brain cells produce less of the transmitter GABA. Can anything be done to stop or reverse the effects of aging on brain cells? A recent study found that the visual cells of monkeys regained their youthful activity after being exposed to GABA (Leventhal et al., 2003). Perhaps this will lead to development of a drug that will help elderly people see and hear better.

Recap

— Brains have some localization of function, as has been demonstrated by cases of brain damage such as that of Phineas Gage. Unusual disorders such as prosopagnosia (inability to recognize faces) can result from damage to specialized brain areas.

— Vision is processed in the occipital lobe and divides into two pathways: the what and where pathways.

— Hearing, body movement, and body sensation all have specialized areas in the brain.

— Language is processed in at least two areas: Broca's area for grammar and pronunciation and Wernicke's area for the meaning of language. Damage to these areas results in aphasia.

— Some linguists, such as Noam Chomsky, believe that the human brain has a special ability to process language—a language acquisition device. This is an example of an instinct (an inherited tendency).

— A brain is plastic. It is capable of changing with experience.

BRAIN IMAGING

"The brain is a world consisting of a number of unexplored continents and great stretches of unknown territory. As long as the brain is a mystery, the universe, the reflection of the brain, will also be a mystery."
—SANTIAGO RAMÓN Y CAJAL

Today, there are a number of sophisticated technologies for recording and picturing a living brain. In the past, researchers had to rely on autopsy to look at a brain. In the past 50 years or so, scientists have invented several machines that can safely take images of the brain of a living person. These technologies not only are useful in diagnosing brain problems, but also are used extensively for research. Here are the most common brain-imaging techniques in use today:

1. The **Electroencephalogram (EEG)** has been around the longest. Prototypes of the EEG were used in the 1920s. In this procedure, very sensitive electrodes are placed on a person's scalp. It doesn't hurt. Each electrode records the electrical firing of cells in a certain region of the cerebral cortex. A number of pens record the electrical activity onto a long strip of paper. The EEG, of course, can detect abnormal electrical firing, as in epilepsy. Also, various patterns of cellular activity, called **brain waves,** can be measured and classified. For example, during REM sleep (when people are typically dreaming), brain waves are very active, rapid, and irregular (**beta waves**), and during deep sleep, brain waves are slow and rhythmic (**delta waves**). During relaxation, brain waves are low-intensity but regular (**alpha waves**). Recent research has shown that

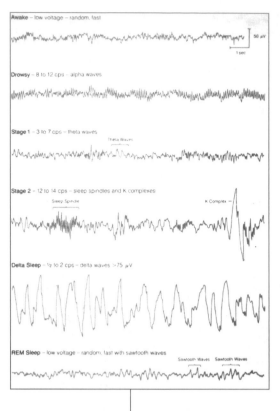

The EEG shows the intensity and frequency of electrical firings in the brain, known as brain waves.

EEG patterns are remarkably similar from person to person during the act of reading. Researchers have found that they could predict with 90% accuracy what sentence or word a person was reading by looking at his or her brain waves (Suppes & Han, 2000). Will this have practical applications in the future—uses in courtrooms, schools, counseling sessions, or corporations? What uses can you imagine for this technology?

2. Computerized axial tomography, or the **(CAT scan),** was first used in 1971. This technique is essentially a very sophisticated X-ray device. The CAT scan takes a series of X-rays that are put together by a computer. The result is a nice picture of anatomical structures. A CAT scan of a brain shows the major structural features, so it can be used to detect brain tumors and other structural problems. However, the CAT scan does not show functioning—only anatomical structure. Recently, the CAT scan has been used to take images of the inner ear, which it then sends to a computer that processes and analyzes them. The result is a digital video that provides a three-dimensional look at the structures inside the ear.

3. Positron emission tomography, or the **(PET scan),** allows researchers to make an image of a living brain in action. PET scans record brain activity—functioning—not structures. The PET scan does not give a picture of the parts of a brain; it gives a picture of which brain areas are most active. In this procedure, a person is first injected with a radioactive form of sugar. The most active cells of the brain use the most sugar. The radioactive trace particle decays rapidly and emits positrons, which are recorded by a large screen around the person's head. This way, we can detect which brain areas are active while a person is engaged in some task. That is, we can determine **localization of function.** The PET scan has been frequently used in this manner, and scientists have accumulated a long list of brain areas that are involved in different psychological functions. In this manner, scientists are creating a map of the brain, adding to the localized functions listed above.

4. Magnetic resonance imaging (MRI) was invented in 1952 and provides a more precise, higher-resolution image than does the CAT scan. MRI is more expensive, however. In this technique, electromagnets are used to align atoms in the brain, then

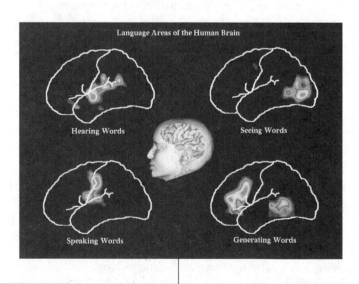

These PET scan images show where the brain is active during tasks involving words. When hearing a word, the temporal lobe and Wernicke's area are active; when seeing a word, it's the occipital lobe; when speaking a word, it's Broca's area and the motor strip; and when thinking up a word, the frontal lobe is most active.

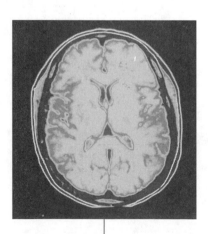

A CAT scan image of the brain shows brain structures.

radiowave pulses disturb the atoms, and finally, emitted radio signals are recorded. A clear picture of brain structures is the result. MRI, like CAT scan, provides an image of structure. However, a variation of MRI known as **functional magnetic resonance imaging (fMRI)** provides an image of brain functioning, similar to the PET scan but with better resolution. So fMRI, like PET, can be used to determine localization of function. Such research is common today in helping to map the functions of the brain.

5. Transcranial magnetic stimulation (TMS) is a safe, noninvasive procedure that uses powerful magnetic fields to determine the functions of brain areas. TMS can measure and modify the activity of brain cells and therefore can also be used for various therapies (see Chapter 10).

Brain Cross Section

Hidden deep inside the brain are a number of interesting areas that together are called **subcortical** because they lie below the cerebral cortex. These brain areas evolved earlier than the cerebral cortex and therefore are more intimately involved with the activities necessary for day-to-day survival, such as basic emotions, motivations, hunger, sensing the environment, the formation of memories, shifting attention to important stimuli, and maintaining body functions. Here is an illustration of some of the most important of these subcortical areas, as illustrated in a cross-sectional picture of a human brain, followed by descriptions of these brain regions.

1. At the top of the brain is the cerebrum, with its outer layer, the cortex, the center for higher thinking that was described just above in this chapter.

2. Deep down inside the cerebrum is the corpus callosum, the bundle of cells that connects the left and right hemispheres. Information to and from the left and right passes via these fibers. This is the brain area that is cut in split-brain surgery, as described above.

3. About in the center of the brain is the **thalamus**, a relay center for the senses. Sensory information consists of signals coming into the brain. These signals come from the eyes, the ears, the tongue, the skin, and different parts of the body. Before these signals are processed by the cerebral cortex, they first pass through the thalamus, where they are sorted and distributed to other areas of the brain. There is one exception: The only sensory signal that is received by the cortex first is smell. All other senses go to the thalamus first. The smell receptors in the nose send electrical signals to a brain area just at the bottom of the frontal lobe known as the **olfactory bulb**. This area represents a large proportion of the brain in some animals but is a relatively small part of a human brain. The thalamus, then, is a relay center for the senses. However, it not only sends signals to various cortical areas for processing, but also receives signals back from the cortex. Experts believe that this two-way communication is essential for creating consciousness.

4. An important brain area located just below the thalamus is the "below the thalamus," or the **hypothalamus**. This area acts as a regulator or control center for a number of motivations, such as hunger and thirst. Sometimes the hypothalamus is compared to a thermostat in that it measures bodily functions and then sends signals

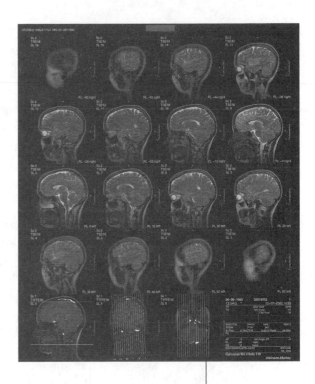

The MRI image also shows brain structures.

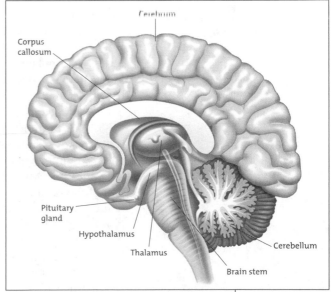

A cross section of the cerebrum showing major brain structures.

THINK TANK

If brain scans can indicate moods or certain broad characteristics of a person, when would such uses be appropriate?

Researchers Wagner (1998) and Brewer (1998) found that they could predict how well material would later be remembered by looking at brain activity during learning.

Some researchers can assess memories on the basis of brain activity. For example, a person who robbed a bank would have a visual memory of the bank teller.

Should schools use brain scans to identify which students have learned their lessons? How about employers, courtrooms, the government, or corporations that want to sell you something—should they be allowed to use brain scans? For what? How about dating services? Could a brain scan tell you whom you should marry? Would you want to know?

to the brain in response to those functions. The hypothalamus, for example, measures the amount of sugar in the blood (glucose) and, when it is low, sends out the signals that we interpret as hunger. Another part of the hypothalamus tells us when to stop eating. Thirst works the same way: A section of the hypothalamus measures things like water volume and cellular osmosis (sucking in water) in the body, and when the body cells are dry, the hypothalamus signals the brain. The result is that we feel thirsty. Damage to the hypothalamus therefore results in problems in motivations such as hunger and thirst. For example, damage to a certain region of a rat's hypothalamus causes a rat to overeat to the point of obesity. In humans, a rare genetic disorder called **Prader-Willi syndrome** causes the hypothalamus to malfunction; sufferers have an unending appetite and can even eat themselves to death. Another region of the hypothalamus has been dubbed the **pleasure center**. When electrically stimulated in this area, people say they feel pleasure. Rats with electrodes in this area will push a bar all day long to stimulate these cells. The pleasure center is surrounded by a **pain center**. With electrodes inserted into this brain region, rats will push a bar all day long to avoid receiving stimulation. The hypothalamus has been shown to be involved in many other motivations, such as anger, fear, and sex. An old joke says that the hypothalamus controls the four Fs: fighting, feeding, fleeing, and reproduction. (One of my students once reminded me that "reproduction" does not begin with the letter F.)

5. The **pituitary gland** is part of the **endocrine system**. The endocrine system consists of many glands located throughout the body. Glands are body organs that secrete chemicals into the bloodstream. These chemicals are called **hormones**, and they influence the functioning of various body parts and organs. The endocrine system is not part of the nervous system, but the two systems do work together cooperatively. Many of the glands throughout the body are stimulated by hormones that are released by the pituitary gland in the brain. Therefore, the pituitary has been called the **master gland**. The pituitary receives its signals from the brain, principally from the hypothalamus. Notice that the pituitary is located just below the hypothalamus, a prime location for the neural connections necessary for signaling the pituitary gland to release hormones. For instance, if a person is frightened, his or her brain signals the hypothalamus, which signals the pituitary, which releases hormones that travel through the bloodstream and influence other glands, such as the adrenal glands, which release adrenalin and other hormones that prepare the body to deal with a dangerous situation. Therefore, the endocrine system is important as a contributor to behavior.

6. The **hippocampus** (Greek for "seahorse") bends around in the inside of the temporal lobe and is critically involved in learning and memory, and according to new research, even emotions (Vogel, 2003). People with damage to the hippocampal area, as happens in Alzheimer's disease, lose the ability to form new memories. Later, in Chapter 6, we will give a much more detailed description of memory formation and storage, and the role of the hippocampus.

7. Near the end of the hippocampus is the **amygdala** (Greek for "almond"), which has an oval shape. There is one in each hemisphere. The amygdala is a center for emotions such as fear and anger and even for pleasant emotions. For example, a woman whose amygdalae were both destroyed lost her ability to recognize what emotion was being expressed in people's faces as well as her own ability to express emotions (Damasio, 1994). Researcher Joseph LeDoux (1996) has traced the formation of an emotional memory in the brains of rats and found that the network of cells involved is in the amygdala. The amygdala is part of the **limbic system**, a series of interconnected structures that lie between the brainstem and the cortex. The limbic system processes emotional feelings and reactions. Signals coming into the brain either go directly to the limbic system via the thalamus (for a quick reaction without thinking) or are processed by the cerebral cortex (for a slower, thoughtful response). If you see a snake in the grass in front of you, the visual information goes to the thalamus and then quickly to the amygdala and surrounding areas of the limbic system, which then alert the body: Your heart beats faster, adrenaline flows, blood pressure goes up, and so on. But information about the snake also takes another pathway to the cerebral cortex, where it is processed with thinking, memory, and judgment. This second avenue (via the cortex) involves awareness and takes longer than the limbic system route because it is more detailed and complex. So we have two brain pathways for responding to emotionally charged situations: one quick, for immediate body response, and one slower with more cognitive interpretation (Helmuth, 2003).

8. The **brainstem** is at the top of the spinal cord. It is the place where the brain and the spinal cord meet. The brainstem includes a number of **nuclei** (clusters of brain cells), each responsible for vital body functions necessary for survival and moment-to-moment functioning. For example, the **medulla** (full name: medulla oblongata) controls breathing, heartbeat, blood circulation, and muscle tone. The **pons** is a large bulging section of the brainstem that influences sleep, wakefulness, attention, and arousal. The **reticular formation** is an area that keeps one awake and attentive to things in the environment. Because of its role in "activating" us, the system of nerves that extends up from the brainstem into other brain areas is often called the **reticular activating system (RAS)**. It can be compared to the channel selector and volume control on a TV set. The RAS determines what we pay attention to and how intense our attention is. There are two general rules for the RAS: First, pay attention to things that are new or different. For example, if something changes in the environment (someone walks into the classroom during a lecture), the RAS in your brain directs your attention to that new, different stimulus. Often when teachers want to get your attention, they talk louder. This change in loudness will be noticed by your RAS. However, tell your teachers that talking softer will have the same, or even better, results. The RAS responds to *change*, not to loudness. When a stimulus occurs repeatedly, the RAS begins to tune it out. When your brain gets used to the sound of your alarm clock, for example, you need a new alarm clock with a different sound! Second, things that are meaningful get the attention of the RAS. If you are at a loud party and are concentrating on someone's conversation and suddenly somewhere else your name is spoken, you will shift your attention to the source of your name. Your RAS responds to things that are meaningful to you. Perhaps you should get an alarm clock that says your name instead of buzzing.

9. Attached to the back of the brainstem is the **cerebellum** (literally, "the little brain"). Don't confuse this word with the similar term *cerebrum*; notice the word *bell* in

Connecting Concepts

Psychology is like a brain. Psychology has many subfields that specialize in the study of certain topics (as described in Chapter 1), but these separate areas of psychology often interconnect in the common goal of understanding the mind and behavior. Similarly, a brain has many modules that do their own things, yet they often interact in the common goal of directing and controlling the mind and behavior. So psychology is like a brain!

cerebellum. (It is like a little bell hanging in the back of your head!) The cerebellum has a number of jobs as its cells process and store information and communicate with other parts of the brain. One of the cerebellum's most significant jobs is to store the programs for coordinated body movements. When we practice a movement—playing guitar, golfing, typing, playing piano, gymnastics, and so on—the cells of the cerebellum gradually get fused into a network that will automatically produce the coordinated movement. These coordinated movements do not require thinking; they are performed automatically. Practice might not make perfect, but it does make for cerebellar networks. Damage to these cells of the cerebellum means that a person would need to think carefully about every body movement, as if doing it for the first time, every time.

Recap

— Brain images can be made using a number of modern technologies such as EEG, CAT scan, PET scan, MRI, and fMRI. These are often used to map areas of the brain to determine their functions and to show brain structures.

— Beneath the cerebrum are the thalamus (a relay center for the senses), the hypothalamus (a regulatory center for motivations), the pituitary gland (which releases hormones), the hippocampus (which helps to form memories), the amygdala (emotional center), the reticular system (an arousal center in the brainstem), and the cerebellum (which coordinates body movements).

NERVOUS SYSTEM ORGANIZATION

The nervous system is a communication system. Its job is to communicate messages throughout the body. The cells of the nervous system receive and send messages. These messages are received from things outside of the body (in the environment) and from within the body. The signals that are sent are directed toward the brain (where they are processed or computed) or to various parts of the body, such as the endocrine system, the muscles, or the body organs. The nervous system communicates by receiving and sending signals. This communication system is divided into various components.

Nervous System Divisions

The brain and the spinal cord together are known as the **central nervous system (CNS)** because that is where all signals either go to or come from. The brain and spinal cord are at the center of the communications.

The nerves that bring messages from the body to the spinal cord, together with the nerves that send messages out from the spinal cord to the body, make up the **peripheral nervous system (PNS)**. These nerves are further divided into two categories:

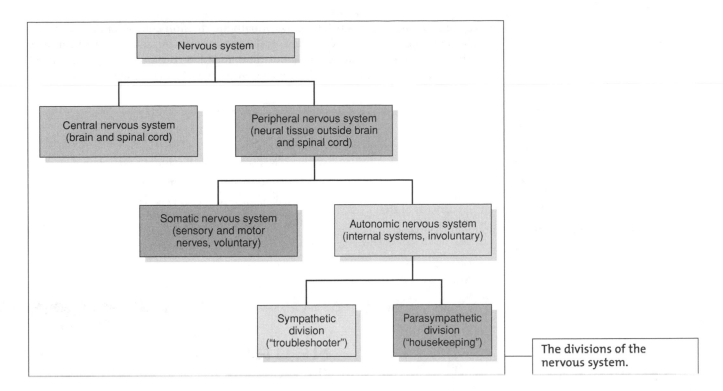

The divisions of the nervous system.

1. The **somatic nervous system (SNS)** consists of nerves that bring in messages about sensations (the senses) and the nerves that go to the skeletal muscles that move us around (the motor nerves). The SNS often operates under our conscious control. We are able to see, hear, and move about in our environment because of this system of nerves.

2. The **autonomic nervous system (ANS)** works mostly automatically in the control of body organs and basic life functions. When you go jogging, you don't need to remember to beat your heart faster; your ANS will take care of that. When you hear a sudden, very loud noise, you don't need to remember to jump; your ANS will do it automatically. When you are nervous, the nerves of your ANS will make you breathe harder to get more oxygen into your lungs. After you have eaten a big meal, you don't concern yourself with remembering to digest the food, because your ANS is on the job. The ANS works automatically but does intersect with the SNS; therefore, it can be affected somewhat by conscious thought. Most people have about 10% control over the ANS functions of their bodies. For example, you can change your heartbeat, your blood pressure, and other autonomic functions by about 10% by using conscious control, by thinking about it. Some people are much better at this than others, of course, and this control can be developed to some extent through practice. Still, the ANS mostly functions automatically.

The ANS is further divided into two divisions: The **sympathetic division** is made up of the nerves that use energy in situations of activation, such as danger. These nerves speed up your heart, increase your blood pressure,

FYI

A polygraph, commonly known as a lie detector, is a machine that measures a number of physiological responses, such as breathing, heart rate, blood pressure, and sweating (galvanic skin response). Supposedly, people who are lying will feel guilty and will be unable to control their autonomic nervous systems, which will become aroused and be detected by the polygraph. But sometimes people who lie do not get physiologically aroused, and some people telling the truth do! Because lie detectors are unreliable, they are not allowed as evidence in legal trials. In fact, polygraphs are often used to get people to confess; all suspects are told that the machine has caught them and they will get off easier if they confess. A brain scan would be a more reliable way of detecting lying. In fact, neuropsychologists found that fMRI showed activity in various brain regions (particularly the anterior cingulate cortex) when subjects were lying (Langleben, 2001).

release adrenaline, and so on. The **parasympathetic division** consists of nerves that do just the opposite. This set of nerves slows you down, relaxes you, and helps you conserve energy by digesting food and reducing heartbeat and blood pressure. These two systems work together (automatically, without conscious thought) in keeping your body working smoothly.

Recap

— The central nervous system (CNS) consists of the brain and spinal cord. The peripheral nervous system (PNS) consists of the somatic (senses and movement) and autonomic (reflexive reactions and automatic body housekeeping functions) nervous systems.

NEURONS

"I like nonsense; it wakes up the brain cells."
—DR. SEUSS

The fundamental unit of communication in the nervous system is the **neuron.** There are billions of neurons in the human brain. They are surrounded and nourished by another type of cell called a **glial cell** (Greek for "glue" and pronounced "GLEE-ul"). The neurons receive and send signals by both electrical and chemical processes. The glial cells help the neurons with communicating and do the housework and cleanup necessary to keep the nervous system functioning.

Beautiful Butterflies

Neurons were first described by Spanish doctor **Santiago Ramón y Cajal** (pronounced "eee-KA-HALL"), who made exquisite drawings of them and called neurons "butterflies of the soul." Neurons are organized into networks through which electrical and chemical signals pass. Sometimes signals are sent only very short distances, as from one brain center to another nearby; other times a signal might travel all the way from the toe to the brain. It is in these networks of neurons that our minds and behaviors are created and controlled.

Neurons come in different shapes and sizes, but they have certain similarities. The basic components of a neuron are (1) the cell body or **soma,** which includes (2) the **nucleus** (Latin for "kernel"), which houses the **chromosomes** (units of inheritance received from biological mother and father); (3) the **dendrites,** branches that extend out of the soma in order to receive signals; (4) the **axon,** the relatively long branch that extends out of the soma and carries a message to another location; and (5) the **terminals,** the branches at the end of the axon that send the signal to a muscle, an organ, or to another neuron. The dendrites receive a message, the axon carries it to another location, then the terminals send a message to a muscle or another neuron.

dendrites = receive   axons = carry   terminals = send

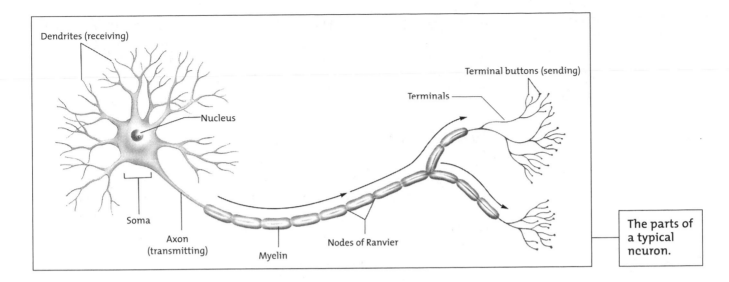

The parts of a typical neuron.

A Briefing on Neural Communication

Here is a brief explanation of how neurons accomplish the process of communication. This is the short version; the long version will come next!

A neuron has two methods of communication: One is electrical and the other is chemical. The electrical signal is created by the movement of electrically charged particles (**ions**) in and out of the neuron. The electrical process is responsible for moving the message from one end of the neuron (the soma) to the other (the terminals). To summarize: An electrical signal is created by the movement of ions into and out of the cell. This electrical signal travels from one end of a neuron to the other.

The chemical process occurs when a neuron sends or receives a signal. The dendrites have chemicals on their surface that are responsive to other chemicals. The dendrites receive a message via a chemical reaction. That chemical reaction starts the electrical process (ions moving into the cell). When the electrical signal reaches the end of the neuron (the terminals), chemicals are squirted out. A chemical reaction takes place at the receiving cell or muscle.

So an electrical process is responsible for signals traveling within a neuron, and chemical reactions are responsible for signals traveling between neurons. The transmission within a neuron is called **axonal transmission** and is an electrical process. The transmission between neurons is called a **synapse**. This is a chemical process. Got it? Now, the details!

AXONAL TRANSMISSION

"The body is an instrument, the mind its function."
—George Santayana

Neurons exist in a medium of water. The water in our bodies is not like tap water or Perrier. In our bodies we have salt water, like the ocean. Suspended in the water are particles—dissolved salts, for example. Particles such as chloride (Cl^-) that have more electrons than protons are said to have a negative charge. Sodium (Na$^+$), on the other hand, has a positive charge, because it has more protons than electrons. Both of these are greatly involved in the transmission of signals within neurons. Potassium (K$^+$), calcium (Ca$^+$), and other molecules are also involved. As was mentioned above, these electrically charged particles are called ions.

Open the Gates

When a neuron is at rest, not being stimulated, it has a certain arrangement of ions within and around it. A neuron has a surface, a **membrane,** which can be penetrated by certain small particles, but not by large particles. There are **gates** or **channels** on the surface of the neuron that can open to allow particles to enter. The surface membrane of a neuron is called **semipermeable,** because some things can enter and some cannot.

Large negative ions are trapped inside the neuron, unable to get out. Sodium and potassium ions, on the other hand, can move through the ion channels. However, the neuron has a sodium pump that regularly moves the positively charged sodium ions out of the cell. The result is that a neuron at rest has a negative charge on the inside. This is called the **resting potential** of the neuron. It measures precisely −70 millivolts (a millivolt is a thousandth of a volt; abbreviated mv).

Because there is an electrical difference between the outside of the neuron (more positively charged) and the inside of the neuron (more negatively charged) while the cell is at rest, the neuron is called **polarized** (meaning that there are two poles or extremes). Positive on the outside, negative on the inside = polarized!

The dendrites of a neuron have chemicals on their surface that respond to other chemicals, such as those released by another neuron, or those that come from outside our body and contact the cells in our eyes, ears, nose, skin, etc. When a dendrite has a chemical reaction, it causes the channels of the neuron membrane to open. Since the inside of the neuron is negatively charged, sodium ions will then enter the cell.

When the ion channels open up, the sodium ions want to join the party inside the cell because of the more negative charge inside. As positively charged sodium ions enter the cell, naturally the inside of the cell gradually becomes more positively charged. We say that the cell is experiencing **depolarization,** meaning it is becoming less polarized. The electrical potential inside the neuron goes up to −69 mv, then to −68 mv, then −67 mv, and so on. When the electric charge inside the soma reaches a certain point, called the threshold, then the channels on the axon open up. For a particular cell the threshold might be −60 mv, for example. When that level is reached inside the soma, then the channels of the axon open.

When the channels on the axon open, sodium ions enter the axon. This causes the channels next door to open. Sodium ions enter there. Then the next channels open. Sodium enters. And so on. All the way from the soma to the terminals, the inside of the neuron is becoming more positively charged, one section at a time. The whole process takes only a split second. This is called an **action potential**.

When an action potential occurs, the inside of the neuron becomes positively charged. We then say that the neuron has fired. The electrical charge inside the neuron goes up to +30 mv because the sodium ions are entering so furiously. The cell becomes completely depolarized. After firing, the cell returns to its negative resting potential because positively charged potassium ions flow out of the channels.

By the way, Novocain (used by dentists) and similar drugs work by blocking the sodium channels so that ions cannot enter the cell and therefore cannot send the pain signal to the brain. Therefore your mouth feels numb. Later, the Novocain wears off, and the sodium channels are free to admit sodium ions into the cell. Then you *do* feel the pain!

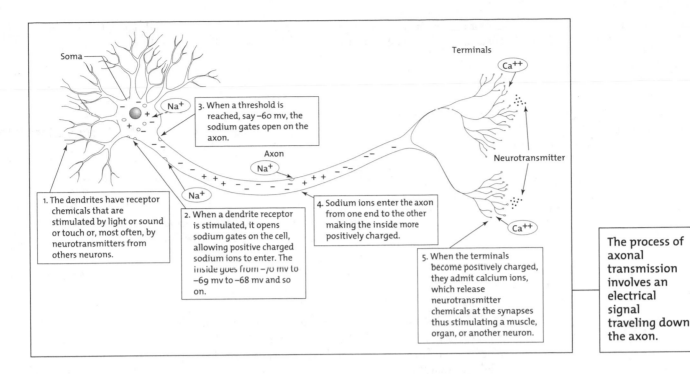

1. The dendrites have receptor chemicals that are stimulated by light or sound or touch or, most often, by neurotransmitters from others neurons.

2. When a dendrite receptor is stimulated, it opens sodium gates on the cell, allowing positive charged sodium ions to enter. The inside goes from −70 mv to −69 mv to −68 mv and so on.

3. When a threshold is reached, say −60 mv, the sodium gates open on the axon.

4. Sodium ions enter the axon from one end to the other making the inside more positively charged.

5. When the terminals become positively charged, they admit calcium ions, which release neurotransmitter chemicals at the synapses thus stimulating a muscle, organ, or another neuron.

The process of axonal transmission involves an electrical signal traveling down the axon.

The Going Rate

So are you getting this? It's complicated, but stick with it. Here is how neurons work: An action potential occurs when the inside of a neuron becomes positively charged owing to the invasion of sodium ions. That process is initiated by a chemical reaction at the dendrites. A positive charge then travels from one end of the neuron (the dendrites and the soma) to the other end (the terminals), and the inside of the cell increases in electrical potential from −70 mv to +30 mv. After firing, the cell returns to its resting potential, ready for another action potential.

Neurons are constantly firing: Negative, positive, negative, positive, negative, positive . . . that is the life of a neuron. Once an action potential begins, the signal travels all the way down to the end of the axon and to the terminals. The signal cannot go partway or be only partial in strength. The signal goes all the way and at full strength. This is called the **all-or-none law.** Every action potential, every firing of a particular neuron, is the same. What differs is the *rate* of firing; the rate at which the cell fires is what's important. The rate is different for different intensities of stimuli. Let's say a bee stings your toe. Neural signals are sent to your brain, to the pain center in your hypothalamus. How much pain do you feel? That depends on a number of things, but one of the most important is the rate at which those neurons from the toe are firing. A slow rate of firing means a weak stimulus and therefore not much pain. A strong stimulus will fire the neurons at a faster rate, resulting in a more intense feeling of pain. How bright is a light? A bright light will fire the neurons in your eye at a faster rate than will a dim light. So your brain perceives the brightness of light based on how fast the neurons are firing.

Mature neurons are covered with an insulating, fatty substance called **myelin.** This myelin surrounds portions of the axon. At one time, scientists thought that the complete axon was coated with myelin; hence, the covering was called a myelin sheath (a sheath is a coating, such as a case for a sword). But we now know that there are openings in the myelin covering. They are called **nodes of Ranvier** and are the places where sodium ions can enter the cell. With a myelinated neuron a signal can travel faster because it can skip from node to node. Sodium ions do not need to enter at every channel. Also, myelinated neurons are less likely to be accidentally fired by the firing of a nearby neuron—they are more efficient. So myelin is good. Unfortunately, there are a number of serious diseases that destroy myelin. **Multiple sclerosis** is the most common and best known of these.

SYNAPTIC TRANSMISSION

"I tend to think of human beings as huge, rubbery test tubes."
—KURT VONNEGUT, JR.

Messages also travel between cells, from one neuron to another. In this case, the message is passed by a chemical process. The place where this chemical transfer occurs is called a synapse, and the process is called **synaptic transmission.** Scientists believe that the synapse is the key to the physiological processes of learning, memory, and other cognitive functions.

Squirting

At the end of a neuron's axon are many branches called **terminals.** At the end of the terminals are enlarged regions called **buttons.** Inside the buttons are bags called **vesicles.** Inside the vesicles are chemical molecules known as **neurotransmitters** or just *transmitters.* Did you get all that? Again: Inside the terminals are chemicals (neurotransmitters) in bags (vesicles). Those chemicals will be released and will transmit messages to other cells; therefore, they are called transmitters.

When the inside of a terminal button becomes positively charged (when an action potential has reached the end of a neuron; when the neuron is depolarized), calcium ions enter the terminal button and cause some of the vesicles to open and to release their neurotransmitter chemicals. In other words, an action potential causes a neuron to squirt out a chemical. The transmitter chemical is squirted into the space between two neurons (the sender and the receiver cells), called the synaptic gap or **synaptic cleft.** The neurons do not touch each other; a chemical is released from the sending cell into the gap, where it can bond with other, complementary chemicals on the receiving cell.

The sending cell is called **presynaptic,** while the receiving cell is called **postsynaptic** (*pre* means "before," and *post* means "after"). The transmitter chemical passes from one neuron to the other. It is received by chemicals on the dendrites of the postsynaptic cell. The neurotransmitter chemical fits together with the chemicals on the receiving dendrite, chemicals that are called simply **receptors.** The process is usually likened to a key fitting into a lock: Each neurotransmitter fits into certain receptors.

When a neurotransmitter chemical binds with a receptor chemical on a receiving dendrite (when the key fits into the lock), a chemical reaction takes place. This causes the ion channels of the receiving cell either to open or to close. There are many different neurotransmitters; at least 50 have been identified. The transmitter chemicals that cause sodium ion channels to open are called **excitatory,** because they allow positively charged sodium ions to enter the neuron, causing depolarization and (maybe, if the threshold is reached!) an action potential. Some other transmitters are called

inhibitory. They cause the cell to become less positively charged, thus making it more difficult to fire the neuron (they inhibit firing). It is necessary to have both types of neurotransmitters (excitatory and inhibitory) and to have them working in a proper balance. When we move an arm, for instance, we want some of our muscles to expand and some to contract. If all transmitters caused excitation, you would have an epileptic seizure every time you opened your eyes! We need both excitation and inhibition in proper balance.

Whether or not a postsynaptic (receiving) cell will fire depends on the extent to which it receives excitatory and inhibitory neurotransmitter chemicals. This is a **more-or-less process.** Each neuron receives chemicals from many other cells. On the average, a cell receives signals from 1,000 other cells. It is the summation of these chemical messages that determines whether the cell will depolarize enough to fire. Imagine: A neuron decides whether to fire on the basis of the relative inputs of hundreds or thousands of terminals squirting chemicals onto its dendrites. If the receiving cell becomes positively charged enough to reach its threshold, then the cell will fire. In Chapters 5 and 6, we will learn that synapses are changed by experience. That is, synapses can become easier to fire because of chemical and anatomical changes that occur. Brains are dynamic. They can change. You can learn!

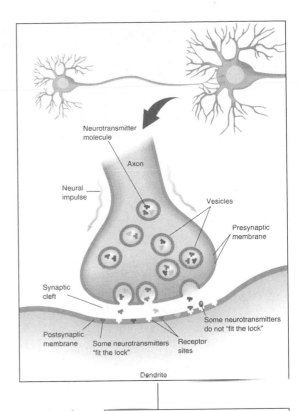

A synapse.

Cleanup at the Synapse

After a neurotransmitter has been released by a neuron and the chemical molecules either are in the synaptic gap or have been received by the receptors of another neuron, the whole mess must be cleaned up so that another message can come through. There are two ways in which cleanup at the synapse occurs:

1. There are **enzymes** in the body that are housekeeping chemicals. They attach to the neurotransmitter chemicals that have been released from the vesicles, and they recycle them. Each neurotransmitter has a corresponding enzyme. For example, one common enzyme that recycles transmitters is monoamine oxydase, commonly referred to as **MAO.** This enzyme is important in recycling the neurotransmitter **serotonin,** for example. People suffering from psychological depression often do not have enough serotonin activity in their brains. Today there are many drugs that can increase serotonin activity. The first of these, developed in the 1950s, is a class of drugs known as **MAO inhibitors (MAOIs).** These drugs inhibit the enzyme MAO, so serotonin cannot be recycled as much. Therefore there will be more serotonin in the synapse to stimulate the dendritic receptors. One problem is that MAOIs affect other things in the body, so a patient must be warned not to eat certain foods or take certain medications while on an MAOI. The combination could cause a heart attack. People have died in this manner. Because people are notoriously bad at following directions, the MAOIs are not the first choice in treating depression today.

2. When a vesicle releases a neurotransmitter, the vesicle then closes and sucks some of the transmitter chemical back inside the sending cell, the presynaptic neuron. This process is called **reuptake.** A transmitter chemical is squirted out into the gap, some of the molecules attach to the receptor chemicals on the receiving dendrite, some of the molecules are recycled by an enzyme, and some of the chemicals get pulled back inside the sending cell (reuptake occurs). There are medicines today that inhibit the reuptake process so that less transmitter chemical will get sucked back into the presynaptic cell, leaving more transmitter chemicals in the gap to signal the receiving receptors. People with depression can take these medicines, **reuptake inhibitors,** to increase the transmitter chemical activity in their brains. The best known of these drugs is Prozac, which is one of a group of drugs known as **selective serotonin**

Connecting Concepts

Alzheimer's disease, Parkinson's disease, and schizophrenia are discussed in Chapter 9 along with other mental disorders.

reuptake inhibitors (SSRIs). They work by decreasing the reuptake of serotonin, thereby allowing more serotonin to cross to the postsynaptic cell. For many people, this improves their mood.

Neurotransmitters

One of the most common neurotransmitters in the brain is **acetylcholine.** This chemical is used in many pathways of the brain and body and therefore influences many behaviors and mental states. For example, muscle movements depend on acetylcholine. So do memories and thoughts.

People with **Alzheimer's disease** have decreased levels of acetylcholine. Sometimes a certain kind of medicine can improve cognitive processes in patients with Alzheimer's. Drugs such as Aricept, Exelon, and Reminyl can improve cognition by slowing the breakdown of acetylcholine. Though the results are only modest and temporary, such medicines are effective because they increase the amount of acetylcholine in the brain and therefore help cognitive processes, such as memory. Unfortunately, side effects, such as liver damage, can occur because acetylcholine is active in parts of the body other than the brain.

Another important neurotransmitter is **dopamine.** Dopamine is also involved in a number of brain pathways and therefore influences many psychological qualities. In **Parkinson's disease,** the brain cannot make enough dopamine. The brain region that manufactures this chemical (the **substantia nigra**) has been damaged. The damage can occur in a number of ways; heredity is sometimes involved, and exposure to toxins, such as pesticides and herbicides, is often a cause. Both Alzheimer's and Parkinson's occur more often in older people. Alzheimer's patients show cognitive problems, such as memory impairment. The first symptoms of Parkinson's are tremor, uncontrollable shaking (particularly of the hands in the early stages), and other muscle movement problems. Patients with Parkinson's can take a medicine, such as L-dopa, that is a precursor of dopamine and therefore helps the brain make more dopamine. This will work for a while, but the brain will eventually become so damaged that it cannot make dopamine even with the precursor chemical.

Today there are no cures for Alzheimer's or Parkinson's, but electrodes placed into the brain, surgery, and brain cell transplants are having some limited success. In one case, adult stem cells were removed from a patient's brain, they were grown into neurons in the laboratory, then were implanted into the man's brain. His Parkinsonian tremors largely disappeared (Levesque, 2002). We can hope that science will uncover effective cures for these serious diseases in the near future.

When L-dopa was first used in treating Parkinson's, it was discovered that patients who took too much of the medicine began to show symptoms similar to those of the very severe psychotic disorder **schizophrenia.** This disorder will be discussed later, but for now, let's just say that it is not split personality but a serious brain disorder that causes people to have hallucinations and abnormal thinking. Since Parkinson's patients exhibited these symptoms when they took excessive amounts of L-dopa, scientists theorized that schizophrenia was linked to excess dopamine. This view became known as the **dopamine hypothesis.** Autopsies were made of the brains of people with schizophrenia who had passed away, but no excess amounts of dopamine were found. Then scientists got a bright idea.

Because dopamine is a neurotransmitter, it must pass the synaptic gap and make contact with receptor chemicals on the dendrites of a receiving cell. Scientists guessed that people with schizophrenia might have excessive amounts of dopamine receptors. This proved to be correct for many people with schizophrenia. Medicines that are used to treat schizophrenia work by blocking dopamine receptors. These drugs are called **neuroleptics** (literally, "grasping the neuron"). These medicines help to reduce symptoms in about 80% of patients with schizophrenia. Unfortunately, long-term use of neuroleptic drugs can cause impairment in the dopamine system. The result is **tardive dyskinesia,** a disorder in which patients have uncontrollable muscle twitches. Fortunately, there are a number of new medicines that act more narrowly on the various dopamine receptors in the brain and hence do not cause tardive dyskinesia.

Understanding how neurons work is important not only for scientists who want to find cures for problems, but also in helping us to explain the mind and behavior. It is impossible to imagine all of the startling discoveries and ideas that will undoubtedly arise as scientists discover even more about the intricate workings of the beautiful butterflies of our souls.

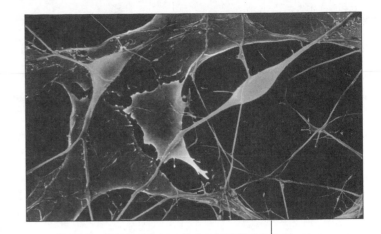

A glial cell.

Other Brain Cells

Neurons have been much studied by a lot by scientists, because they are the cells that transmit information throughout the nervous system. However, neurons are not the only kinds of cells in a brain. Another kind of brain cell is called a glial cell. In fact, about 90% of the human brain is composed of glial cells.

For years, neuroscientists have known that glia are important for normal brain functioning. These cells surround the neurons and provide support, sources of nutrition, and a sort of waste-disposal mechanism for the brain. You could think of the glia as the scaffolding and housekeeping cells of the brain.

New research indicates that glial cells are important for more than simple support and housekeeping. In 1997, researcher Ben Barres reported that one type of glial cells, known as **astrocytes,** were able to boost the growth of synapses in a cell culture. Synapses, of course, are the places where neurons communicate with each other chemically. Most experts believe that they are the key element in the processes of learning, memory, and cognitive functions. Barres reported in 1999 that astrocytes could be used to generate neurons. Scientists working in Barres's laboratory later found that astrocytes are necessary for the development of normal, mature synapses (Ullian, 2001).

Recap

— Neurons are brain cells that communicate by electrical and chemical processes.

— A signal travels from the dendrites and soma of the neuron, down the axon, to the terminal branches that will release a chemical message.

— An action potential (firing) occurs when gates on the neuron's axon open to allow positively charged sodium ions to enter the cell. The inside of the cell becomes more positively charged, thus sending the signal from the cell body (soma) to the terminals.

— One neuron communicates with another at a synapse, where a chemical (neurotransmitter) from the terminals of one cell is received by chemicals (receptors) on the dendrites of another cell.

— The synapse is cleaned up by enzymes and by reuptake (some of the neurotransmitter is sucked back into the sending cell).

HEREDITY

"Heredity matters. Choose your parents carefully."
—ANONYMOUS

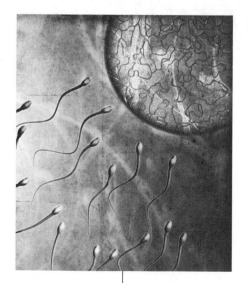

The 46 human chromosomes.

Now you have learned a great deal about the brain. But a biological understanding of psychology would not be complete without a discussion of heredity, the recipe for the formation of the brain and other parts of our bodies. Certainly, you've heard of the **Human Genome Project.** The goal of this project is to map the complete genetic recipe of human beings. A preliminary map of all the human genes, the human genome, was presented in 2000. In February 2001, the two groups of scientists working on this project presented the complete findings. Surprisingly, although experts had predicted that about 100,000 genes make up the human genome, closer to 30,000 seems to be the correct number. The next steps are to determine what all these genes do and then to devise ways either to trigger genes to express their recipes, or to stop genes from doing what they are programmed to do. Gene therapy has already been performed on humans on a very limited scale, and in the future, there undoubtedly will be significant and astounding progress in this important and amazing endeavor.

Reproduction

Heredity begins with a sperm and an egg. You were created by the union of a sperm cell from your father and an egg from your mother. The egg is called an **ovum** (plural = ova) and normally contains 23 chemical strands called **chromosomes.** These chromosomes were selected into the egg by a biological process (**meiosis**) that sorted a woman's 46 chromosomes into two ova. The **sperm cell** likewise contains 23 chromosomes, selected by meiosis from the father's 46.

Chromosomes come in pairs, and one from each pair of a woman's is selected into an ovum, and one from each pair of a man's is selected into a sperm cell. Scientists number the chromosome pairs according to their size, number 1 being the largest pair, number 2 the second-largest pair, and so on, to pair 22. A final pair are the sex chromosomes described below. If we take any cell from your body (other than sperm or ovum), we can look at it under a powerful microscope and see your 46 chromosomes.

When a sperm cell and egg unite, the fertilized egg is called a **zygote.** You were once a zygote, a long time ago, journeying down your mother's fallopian tube.

Zygotes develop by copying and dividing, a process called **mitosis.** One cell becomes two, two cells become four, four become eight, and so on. Therefore,

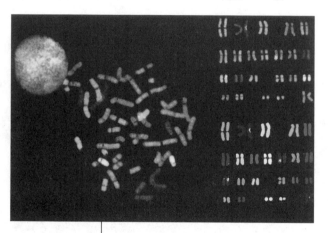

A normal sperm cell from a man contains 23 chromosomes, and a normal ovum from a woman has 23, in each case one selected randomly from each of their 23 chromosome pairs (by the process of meiosis). The resulting union of sperm and egg, called a zygote, has 46 chromosomes. These 46 will copy themselves (by the process of mitosis) so that each body cell will contain copies of the original 46 chromosomes.

each cell in the body has a copy of the original 46 chromosomes that were in the zygote (union of sperm and egg). Eventually (after a few days), a zygote implants in the mother's uterus, where further development occurs, and the basic stem cells begin to differentiate into particular kinds of cells.

Sometimes two zygotes develop in a uterus at the same time; these are twins. Twins are divided into two types. If a woman produces two different ova at around the same time and if two different sperm cells then fertilize those two eggs (resulting in two zygotes), the zygotes will develop into fraternal twins, which scientifically are called **dizygotic twins** ("two-egg" twins).

On the other hand, if a single zygote should separate into two, then identical twins will result. They are called **monozygotic twins** ("one-egg" twins). Identical twins are virtually identical in their genetic recipes, since they came from one egg and one sperm cell, while fraternal twins have somewhat different genes. In science, we abbreviate these two different kinds of twins as DZ and MZ.

DZ twins result when two different eggs are fertilized by two different sperm cells. The sperm cells don't even need to come from the same man (although of course they nearly always do). Also, the fertilization could take place in a laboratory, and the fertilized eggs (the zygotes) could then be implanted into a carrier woman. DZ twins need not be very much alike in genetic inheritance. Of course, DZ twins normally have the same parents and therefore share 25% of their chromosomes on the average.

FYI

Some people did not make the journey down a fallopian tube because their conception took place in a laboratory petri dish. In test-tube fertilization, also known as *in vitro* ("in glass") fertilization, mature eggs from the mother are mixed with sperm from the father in a laboratory. The zygote is then implanted into the mother's womb, where it begins to divide and grow. The first test-tube baby was Louise Brown, born on July 25, 1978. Today this is a common procedure at fertility clinics around the world. A more controversial procedure is cytoplasmic transfer, in which the cytoplasm that surrounds the nucleus of an egg is taken from a healthy donor and injected into the egg of an infertile woman before the egg is fertilized. Because cytoplasm has genetic material called mitochondria DNA, the resulting baby technically has three parents! A number of problems have been reported in using this procedure.

THINK TANK

In preimplantation genetic diagnosis (PGD), a woman's eggs are withdrawn and examined to choose those with certain genes.

The selected eggs are then fertilized in the lab and implanted in the woman's womb.

In 2002, a woman used such a procedure to ensure that her baby would not inherit the Alzheimer's gene she was carrying.

PGD is now able to screen only for certain rare genes, but it is becoming more common and has been used to select the gender of the baby.

Suppose genetic research develops to the point at which people can choose many characteristics of their children, such as intelligence, appearance, and personality.

Would such a thing be desirable?

Would it be better to leave such things to chance?

Why?

FYI

Many more males are conceived than females because the sperm cells that carry a Y chromosome (androsperm) on the average swim faster and have more pointed heads than the sperm cells that carry an X chromosome (gynosperm). However, males die more often than females at every stage of development, including prenatal. By birth, there are about 105 boys for every 100 girls; by young adulthood, there are about equal numbers; and by old age, there are many more women than men. This creates a social problem in old age.

MZ twins result from one fertilized egg—one ovum is fertilized by one sperm cell. Then, after copying the 46 chromosomes, the single fertilized cell splits into two zygotes that have the same chromosomes. Notice that MZ twins therefore have the exact same chromosomes as each other (except for biological variations and errors that occur).

DZ twins can be of different genders, but MZ twins must be the same gender, since they have the same chromosomes. Genetic sex is determined by two chromosomes known as **sex chromosomes.** Women have two sex chromosomes of the same type, called **X chromosomes.** Women get one X chromosome each from mother and father. Women get 23 chromosomes from their mother, one of which is an X chromosome. Women also get 23 chromosomes from their father, and one of them is an X chromosome. Men also get 23 chromosomes from their mother, including one X chromosome. But from their father, men get 23 chromosomes that include a much smaller chromosome called a **Y chromosome.** So, men have one X and one Y, while women have X and X.

The Gene

If we look at chromosomes up close, we see that they are long strands of a chemical called deoxyribonucleic acid (**DNA**). This chemical is often called the molecule of life. It is shaped like a **double helix,** two spirals wound around each other like a twisted ladder (or two intertwined Slinkys). Connecting the two spirals (like the rungs of a ladder) are pairs of chemicals hooked together called **base pairs.** There are only four chemical bases in the DNA molecule: adenine (A), thymine (T), cytosine (C), and guanine (G). These base chemicals always pair up a certain way. A always goes with T, and C always goes with G. (Remember: Always Together, and Closely Glued). This arrangement allows for easy reproduction. When the long chromosome divides (unzips down its middle), the DNA sequence can easily be replicated by replacing the appropriate chemicals in each case. Where there is an A, put a T. Where there is a T, put an A. Where there is a C, put a G. Where there is a G, put a C. Because of this copying process, all the cells in your body contain chromosomes that have the same sequence of base pairs as in the original chromosomes you received from your parents. The sequence of bases (A, T, C, and G) that is in your chromosomes is the genetic recipe for you—your genome.

A particular sequence of base pairs on a chromosome might have a biological job to do. That sequence is then called a **gene.** Genes, then, are segments of chromosomes that consist of a particular sequence of bases that represents a recipe for the body. A gene sequence will be something like ACGGGTCAATTCAGCAGCAGC . . . but very, very long. Combinations of three base pairs

A chromosome is made of DNA, which consists of four bases arranged in pairs in a certain sequence. A gene is a segment of a chromosome that has a certain sequence (chemical recipe).

(for example, CAG) are recipes for certain body proteins and often come in long repeating chains. When chromosomes are passed from generation to generation and are replicated, mistakes often happen. These mistakes are called **mutations.**

One common mutation is for a triplicate to be repeated too often. If CAG appears a small number of times, a person is normal; if CAG repeats a large number of times, the person has a mutation that produces a disease. As men age, their sperm cells divide many times, increasing the risk of mutations. For example, men over 50 have a three times higher chance of having a baby with schizophrenia than younger men do (Malaspina et al., 2001). Women's eggs are more likely to develop chromosome abnormalities, as described below. An interesting example: The most common form of inherited mental retardation is **fragile X syndrome.** Usually affecting boys, it is the result of a mutated gene on the X chromosome in which the trinucleotide CGG repeats more than 200 times. A gene with between 50 and 200 CGG repeats is called a permutation, and carriers will not have the full range of symptoms. However, such men may develop symptoms in old age, such as tremors, loss of balance, and diminished IQs (Hagerman, 2002).

Genes can be either dominant or recessive. Because we receive genes from both parents, sometimes there is a conflict in the recipes. One gene says brown eyes, and the other says blue, for instance. When this happens, normally our bodies follow one genetic recipe and ignore the other. The gene that is expressed is called **dominant.** The gene that is ignored is called **recessive.** To have a recessive trait, you would need to inherit a recessive gene from each parent, since if you got a dominant gene from either parent, you would have the dominant trait. **Huntington's disease,** a fatal brain disease that shows up late in life, is caused by a dominant gene on chromosome 4 (it is the most common CAG repeat disorder). Therefore, we need only inherit the gene for Huntington's from one parent to get this disease. By contrast, albinism and blue eyes are recessive traits. To have albinism or blue eyes requires that we inherit the respective genes from both parents.

An exception involves genes on the X chromosome, since men get only one. A recessive gene on the X chromosome will not be expressed in women who have a dominant gene on their other X chromosome. However, a recessive gene on the X chromosome in a man will always be expressed because he does not have another X chromosome with the possibility of a dominant gene. Such traits are more common in men; they inherit the genes from their mothers, who usually do not have the trait. For a woman to have such a recessive trait, she would need to inherit the recessive gene from both her parents (meaning her father has the trait). Such traits are called **sex-linked,** and include red-green color blindness, hemophilia, and baldness.

Chromosome Abnormalities

Sometimes errors occur in the number of chromosomes that are selected into the **germ cells,** the ovum or the sperm. Most of these errors do not develop to maturity, but some do. The most common error is when an extra chromosome 21 is selected. The **fetus** then has three chromosome 21s, for a total of 47 chromosomes. This condition is called **Down syndrome,** or Trisomy 21, and it causes mental retardation and a number of other physical problems. This mistake in chromosome selection becomes more likely as people age, so the newborns of older men and women have a higher risk of having Down syndrome. There are tests that can be done during pregnancy, such as removing cells from the fetus and looking at them under a microscope, that can detect Down syndrome far in advance of birth.

Another chromosome error involves the sex chromosomes. When a woman has too many sex chromosomes, the condition is called **superfemale.** When a man has too many Y chromosomes, the condition is called **supermale.** If a woman only has one X chromosome, the condition is called **Turner's syndrome,** and if a person has two X chromosomes and a Y chromosome, the condition is called **Klinefelter's syndrome.** Each of these chromosome errors results in physical and psychological problems. In chromosome land, more is not better; 46 is the right number. Any other number is a problem. For example, in Klinefelter's syndrome, a person has a mix of male and female characteristics. Women with Turner's syndrome are short, do not develop sexually, and have heart and kidney problems. Typically today, babies who are **transgender** are identified at birth and given surgical and hormonal procedures to correct their conditions. Sometimes this is even done without the parents' knowledge or consent. This practice, as you can imagine, is quite controversial.

Nature versus Nurture

As was mentioned earlier, one of the common issues in psychology is the extent to which we are shaped by our heredity and the extent to which we are shaped by experience. This is the **nature-nurture** issue that was a major question in the early days of psychology and continues to be debated today, though less intensely. As was indicated earlier, this is something of a false, or at least misleading, question. It is silly to deny that either nature or nurture is a significant contributor to our psychological lives. It is equally silly to try to divide them. Should we ask to what extent the images on our computer screen are due to hardware and to what extent to software? Should we ask whether the taste of our food is due to the recipe or the ingredients? Would it be helpful to know how much is contributed by ink and how much by paper in the reading of this book?

What's important is that these two things—heredity and experience—both affect us and that they are intertwined. In their analysis of language acquisition, for example, Karmiloff and Karmiloff-Smith (2001) argue that nature and nurture are so intertwined and dependent on each other that debate about their relative influences is not worthwhile. We are not born with everything we will have. Things develop. We are born with a recipe, a potential. The genes we inherit will express themselves at different times and to different degrees. Often we carry a gene for a trait that will never be expressed (for example, recessive genes). Also, experiences might provide for genetic expression, or they might not. A genetic predisposition might not be fulfilled because of the lack of environmental stimuli.

Nature and nurture are interdependent. Deprivation is not good for animals, whether they have "good" genes or not. For example, babies are genetically programmed to see a certain way—to see colors, shapes, forms, movement, and so on. However, if deprived of light and visual experiences, the cells of the eye and brain will not develop normally, and vision will not manifest its genetic destiny. There are tons of other examples of how deprivation can interfere with genetic potential. But experiences in the world also influence learning. Brains are genetically designed to learn—to change with experience. It is futile to try to separate the influences of genetics and of learning, since they are intricately interwoven.

Heredity gives us a blueprint for development. But experience influences how we develop. This interaction is often easiest to describe with examples of how experience interferes with heredity's recipe. For instance, **teratogens** (Greek for "causes monsters") are substances that disturb normal prenatal development. Alcohol is one; it can cross the placental barrier and damage fetal development, causing **fetal alcohol syndrome.** Thalidomide is an infamous teratogen that caused many birth deformities in the 1960s. Women who took this drug during the first trimester of pregnancy gave birth to babies who were missing arms or ears or fingers, depending on precisely when the drug interfered with development. Each characteristic has a time when it is most susceptible to things in the environment (a critical or sensitive period).

Every bit of us is the result of the dance between these two inseparable forces. We develop. I leave you with this thought: Heredity matters, but so does experience. These two forces interact in ways that can seldom be untangled in any meaningful way. We are the sum of our parts—and more: We are the interactions of our parts.

Recap

— Neurotransmitters are chemicals that pass signals from one neuron to another. There are over 50 different types of neurotransmitters in your brain.

— Many different diseases result from problems with neurotransmitters. For example, Parkinson's disease results when damage to a certain brain area reduces the amount of dopamine that is produced. Drugs such as L-dopa can help.

— Schizophrenia is associated with excessive dopamine activity. Neuroleptic drugs block dopamine receptors in the brain. A side effect is tardive dyskinesia.

— Glial cells nourish neurons and perhaps help to stimulate their growth.

— People normally inherit 23 pairs of chromosomes, long strands of DNA that consist of genes (arrangements of base pairs made up of the four chemicals A, T, C, and G). Abnormalities may occur when a person inherits the wrong number of chromosomes, as in Down syndrome, in which there are 47.

— Identical twins come from one fertilized egg and are called monozygotic (MZ); fraternal twins result from two fertilized eggs and are called dizygotic (DZ).

— Teratogens are substances that can harm prenatal development. For example, the use of alcohol by a pregnant woman can lead to fetal alcohol syndrome.

— Heredity and environment cannot easily be separated into two completely disconnected categories. Each depends on the other; they are interwoven, nearly inseparable forces.

I Link, Therefore I Am

There are many Web sites about Phineas Gage including
http://www.deakin.edu.au/hbs/GAGEPAGE/

There are many fascinating Web sites about brain anatomy. They allow you to see amazing pictures of brains and also provide information and resources. Here are some of the best:
http://www.brain.com/   http://www.med.harvard.edu/AANLIB/home.html
http://www.dana.org/brainweb/   http://lcweb.loc.gov/loc/brain/
http://thalamus.wustl.edu/course/
http://www.vh.org/Providers/Textbooks/BrainAnatomy/BrainAnatomy.html
http://www.brainconnection.com/   http://www.brainsource.com/
http://www.neurosurgery.org/cybermuseum/   http://www.loni.ucla.edu/data/rat/
http://brainmuseum.org/   http://uta.marymt.edu/~psychol/brain.html
http://www.neuroskills.com/index.html?main=tbi/brain.html
http://medlib.med.utah.edu/kw/brain_atlas/
http://medlib.med.utah.edu/WebPath/HISTHTML/NEURANAT/NEURANCA.html

If you'd like another explanation of neurons and axonal transmission, go to
http://www.csuchico.edu/psy/BioPsych/neurotransmission.html

For a good explanation of the biochemistry of neurotransmitters, go to
http://web.indstate.edu/thcme/mwking/nerves.html

A primer on heredity can be found on the Internet at http://vector.cshl.org/dnaftb/

STUDY GUIDE FOR CHAPTER 3:
BRAIN AND HEREDITY

Key terms and names (Make flash cards.)

neuron
hippocampus
neurogenesis
Hermann Helmholtz
efficiency theory
cerebrum
fissures (sulci)
gyri
longitudinal fissure
hemispheres
contralateral
spinal cord
nerve
afferent (sensory) nerves
efferent (motor) nerves
cranial nerves
tracts
corpus callosum
epilepsy
seizure
split-brain surgery
lateralized
optic chiasm
field of vision
confabulation
cortex
cerebral cortex
central fissure (fissure of Rolando)
lateral fissure (fissure of Sylvius)
frontal lobe
parietal lobe
occipital lobe
temporal lobe
Phineas Gage
pseudoscience
phrenology
localization of function
what pathway
where pathway
prosopagnosia
fusiform face area
auditory cortex
motor cortex
somatosensory cortex
multisensory (multimodel) neuron
McGurk effect
syntax
Paul Broca

Broca's area
stroke
Broca's (expressive) aphasia
Carl Wernicke
Wernicke's area
Wernicke's (receptive) aphasia
grammar
semantics
overgeneralization
psycholinguistics
Noam Chomsky
language acquisition device
nativism
cognitivist
instinct
circadian rhythms
superchiasmatic nucleus
plasticity
critical peroid
phantom limb
electroencephalogram (EEG)
brain waves
beta waves
delta waves
alpha waves
computerized axial tomography
    (CAT scan)
position emission tomography
    (PET scan)
localization of function
magnetic resonance imaging (MRI)
functional magnetic resonance
    imaging (fMRI)
transcranial magnetic stimulation
    (TMS)
subcortical
thalamus
olfactory bulb
hypothalamus
Prader-Willi syndrome
pleasure center
pain center
pituitary gland
endocrine system
hormones
master gland
hippocampus
amygdala

limbic system
brainstem
nuclei
medulla
pons
reticular formation
reticular activating system (RAS)
cerebellum
central nervous system (CNS)
peripheral nervous system (PNS)
somatic nervous system (SNS)
autonomic nervous system (ANS)
sympathetic division
parasympathetic division
neuron
glial cell
Santiago Ramón y Cajal
soma
nucleus
chromosomes
dendrites
axon
terminals
ion
axonal transmission
synapse
membrane
gates (channels)
semipermeable
resting potential
polarized
depolarization
action potential
all-or-none law
myelin
nodes of Ranvier
multiple sclerosis
synaptic transmission
terminals
buttons
vesicles
neurotransmitters
synaptic cleft
presynaptic
postsynaptic
receptors
excitatory
inhibitory

more-or-less process
enzymes
MAO
serotonin
MAO inhibitors (MAOIs)
reuptake
reuptake inhibitors
selective serotonin reuptake
   inhibitors (SSRIs)
acetylcholine
Alzheimer's disease
dopamine
Parkinson's disease
substantia nigra
L-dopa
schizophrenia
dopamine hypothesis
neuroleptics

tardive dyskinesia
Human Genome Project
astrocytes
ovum
chromosomes
meiosis
sperm cell
zygote
mitosis
dizygotic twins
monozygotic twins
sex chromosomes
X chromosome
Y chromosome
DNA
double helix
base pairs
gene

mutation
fragile X syndrome
dominant gene
recessive gene
Huntington's disease
sex-linked
germ cell
Down syndrome
supermale
superfemale
Turner's syndrome
Klinefelter's syndrome
transgender
nature-nurture
teratogens
fetal alcohol syndrome

Fill in the blank

1. The wrinkly part on the top of the brain is called the
   _____.

2. The wrinkles on the cerebrum are called
   _____, and the bumps
   that are formed by the wrinkling of the cerebrum are
   called _____.

3. The crossover point for the contralateral wiring is in
   the _____ _____.

4. The brain region that connects the hemispheres is
   called the _____,

5. An operation that is separates the hemispheres is
   called _____.

6. When a particular ability is processed more in one
   hemisphere than in the other, it is called

   _____.

7. The point where the optic nerves meet is called the
   _____.

8. Objects in the right field of vision are processed in
   the _____ hemisphere.

9. When people give explanations for their behavior, it
   is called _____.

10. The outer surface layer of the cerebrum is called the
    _____.

11. One large fissure extends down from the top center
    almost vertically. It is called the _____ fissure
    or fissure of _____; another large fissure that
    extends horizontally from the middle front of the
    cerebral cortex toward the back is called the
    _____ fissure or the fissure of _____.

12. Each hemispheric cortex is divided into four regions
    called _____.

13. Language (grammar) in most people is processed in
    the _____ hemisphere.

14. The idea that certain mental states and behaviors are
    controlled by a specific location in the brain is called
    _____ of _____.

15. Vision is perceived by cells in the
    _____ lobe.

16. Hearing is perceived by cells in the
    _____ lobe.

17. Damage to any section of the motor strip will cause
    _____.

18. A person who is injured in the _____
    strip will have numbness.

19. An area in the left frontal lobe that is important for
    pronunciation and grammar is called
    _____ area.

20. The brain region involved in processing the meaning
    of words and sentences is called
    _____ area.

21. When brain injury gives patients difficulty in using or
    understanding language, it is called
    _____.

22. The brain's ability to change is called
    _____.

23. A person whose leg has been amputated will still feel
    touch and pain in his or her leg. This is called
    _____ _____.

24. Electrodes record the electrical firing of cells in
    regions of the cerebral cortex in the procedure known
    as _____.

25. The _____ scan is essentially a very
    sophisticated X-ray device.

26. Both the _____ scan and
    _____ allow researchers to
    make an image of a living brain in action.

27. The _____ is a relay center for the senses.
28. The smell receptors in the nose send electrical signals to a brain area just at the bottom of the frontal lobe known as the _____ bulb.
29. The _____ acts as a regulator or control center for a number of motivations, such as hunger and thirst.
30. The pituitary gland is part of the _____ system.
31. The pituitary has been called the _____ gland.
32. The _____ (Greek for "seahorse") bends around in the middle of the inside of the temporal lobe. This brain region is important for the formation and storage of _____.
33. The _____ is a center for emotions, such as fear and anger.
34. The _____ _____ is at the top of the spinal cord. It is the place where the brain and spinal cord meet.
35. A brain network that keeps one awake and attentive to things in the environment is called the _____ activating system.
36. The _____ stores the programs for coordinated body movements.
37. The brain and the spinal cord together are known as the _____ nervous system.
38. The _____ nervous system works mostly automatically in the control of body organs and basic life functions.
39. The divisions of the autonomic nervous system are the _____ and the _____.
40. The fundamental unit of the communication process in the nervous system is the nerve cell, which is known as a _____.
41. Another type of nerve cell is called a _____ cell (Greek for "glue").
42. The part of the neuron that receives signals is the _____.
43. The part of the neuron that sends signals to a muscle, an organ, or another neuron is called the _____.
44. The resting potential of a neuron measures precisely _____.
45. As sodium ions enter the neuron, the inside of the cell becomes more _____ charged. We say that the cell is experiencing _____.
46. When a neuron has fired, it is called an _____ potential.
47. A neural signal cannot go part way or be only partial in strength. The signal goes all the way and at full strength. This is called the _____ law.

48. Mature neurons are covered with an insulating, fatty substance called _____.
49. The openings in the myelin sheath are called _____ of _____.
50. Inside the vesicles are chemical molecules known as _____.
51. The transmitter chemicals that cause channels to open are called _____, and the transmitters that close channels are called _____.
52. The body uses _____ (such as MAO) to recycle neurotransmitters.
53. When a vesicle releases a neurotransmitter, the vesicle then closes and sucks some of the transmitter chemical back inside the sending cell, the _____ neuron. This process is called _____.
54. In _____ disease, the brain cannot make enough dopamine. Such patients can take a medicine known as _____ that is a precursor of dopamine.
55. Medicines that are used to treat schizophrenia work by blocking dopamine receptors. These drugs are called _____.
56. The egg is called an _____, and normally contains 23 chemical strands called _____.
57. When a sperm cell and egg unite, the fertilized egg is called a _____.
58. Fraternal twins are scientifically called _____ twins; identical twins are called _____ twins.
59. Women have two sex chromosomes: _____ and _____, while men have _____ and _____.
60. _____ is often called the molecule of life.
61. A particular sequence of base pairs on a chromosome that has a biological job is called a _____.
62. _____ disease is caused by a dominant gene on chromosome 4.
63. The most common chromosome error is when an extra chromosome number _____ is selected, and the condition is called _____ syndrome.
64. The condition in which a person hash two X chromosomes and one Y chromosome is called _____ syndrome.
65. Substances that interfere with normal prenatal development are called _____.
66. The _____ _____ issue is about the relative contributions of heredity and experience.

Matching

1. pituitary _____
2. cerebellum _____
3. thalamus _____
4. corpus callosum _____
5. MZ _____
6. glial cell _____
7. white matter _____
8. cerebrum _____
9. Broca's area _____
10. DZ _____
11. dendrite _____
12. reuptake _____
13. Parkinson's disease _____
14. Klinefelter's syndrome _____
15. Wernicke's area _____
16. hippocampus _____
17. hypothalamus _____
18. zygote _____
19. DNA _____
20. serotonin _____
21. nodes of Ranvier _____

a. fraternal twins
b. XXY chromosomes
c. wrinkly top
d. meaning of language
e. neurotransmitter
f. regulating center for hunger
g. identical twins
h. master gland
i. fertilized egg
j. grammar
k. receiving part of neuron
l. dopamine
m. myelin
n. openings in the myelin
o. formation of memories
p. molecule of heredity
q. relay center for the senses
r. communication between hemispheres
s. synapse
t. glue
u. back of the brainstem

Multiple choice

1. Your uncle had a stroke in his left frontal lobe. Which of these symptoms would he likely experience?
   a. loss of vision on the right
   b. loss of hearing in both ears
   c. paralysis on the right side
   d. difficulty understanding language
2. A scientist finds that a certain toxic substance reduces myelin. What effect will this have
   a. numbness in the face
   b. aphasia
   c. endocrine system overload
   d. slower nerve signals
3. A person goes to the doctor complaining that his feelings of thirst are abnormal. Which part of the brain is most likely involved?
   a. cerebellum
   b. hypothalamus
   c. parietal lobe
   d. amygdala
4. A person with aphasia has
   a. numbness
   b. paralysis
   c. language difficulty
   d. difficulty recognizing objects

5. When a neuron fires, its inside becomes
   a. positively charged
   b. negatively charged
   c. densely packed with neurotransmitters
   d. broadly spaced
6. Damage to the somatosensory area of the brain results in
   a. numbness
   b. paralysis
   c. aphasia
   d. motor uncoordination
7. What is it called when a neurotransmitter is reabsorbed by the sending neuron?
   a. dopamine absorption
   b. myelin nodding
   c. enzyme release
   d. reuptake
8. Images from the left field of vision are processed in which hemisphere
   a. left
   b. right
   c. half in each
   d. both

9. If a split-brain patient holds a spoon in her left hand and a button in her right hand, what will she say she is holding?
   a. spoon
   b. button
   c. both
   d. she doesn't know

10. Damage to the temporal lobe would likely result in problems with
   a. vision
   b. feeling
   b. hunger
   d. hearing

11. Which of these is NOT a neurotransmitter?
   a. dopamine
   b. serotonin
   c. glia
   d. acetylcholine

12. A patient is having hallucinations involving seeing, hearing, and tasting. What part of the patient's brain is most likely involved?
   a. thalamus
   b. motor area
   c. brainstem
   d. pituitary gland

13. A patient had a stroke that damaged cells in the right parietal lobe. What problem is this patient likely experiencing?
   a. numbness on the left side of the body
   b. movement of the muscles of the face
   c. understanding the meanings of sentences
   d. visual blindness on the right

14. A new drug stops pain by blocking ion gates. This means that
   a. neurotransmitters cannot be created by cells
   b. action potentials cannot be created
   c. receptors are blocked
   d. myelin will be destroyed

15. What happens when the terminal of a neuron becomes positively charged?
   a. It becomes myelinated.
   b. It releases myelin.
   c. The nodes close.
   d. A neurotransmitter is released.

16. The openings in the myelin sheath allow
   a. neurotransmitters to enter the neuron
   b. positively charged sodium ions to enter the neuron
   c. calcium ions to exit the neuron
   d. neurotransmitters to be released

17. If a person has damage to the cerebellum, it will likely result in problems with
   a. language
   b. vision
   c. coordinated movements
   d. smell

18. How are the sex chromosomes of a woman designated?
   a. XX
   b. YY
   c. XY
   d. XXY

19. How many chromosomes are in a normal human sperm cell?
   a. 2
   b. 21
   c. 23
   d. 46

20. Which of these is NOT one of the chemicals in the base pairs that make up genes?
   a. A
   b. C
   c. Y
   d. T

21. Which of these statements is true?
   a. People use only about 10% of their brains.
   b. Adult brains make new brain cells.
   c. Some people can read minds.
   d. A brain is nothing like a computer.

22. The left hemisphere makes up reasons for a person's behaviors, a process called
   a. confabulation
   b. dissociation
   c. synesthesia
   d. olfaction

23. A stroke patient cannot see things on his left. His brain is likely damaged in the
   a. corpus callosum
   b. right occipital lobe
   c. cerebellum
   d. left temporal lobe

24. A person with damage to the somatosensory area will complain of
   a. hearing loss
   b. paralysis
   c. numbness
   d. memory loss

25. A new drug slows the reuptake of a neurotransmitter called GABA. This means there will be
   a. a decrease in the amount of GABA produced by the brain
   b. more GABA receptors
   c. more GABA in the synapses
   d. blockage of ion channels

26. A patient has damage in one place in her optic track that decreases her vision in both eyes. Where is the damage?
   a. in front of the retina
   b. in the retina
   c. in front of the optic chiasm
   d. behind the chiasm

27. The lobe at the top back of the brain is called
    - a. parietal
    - b. Rolando
    - c. occipital
    - d. temporal
28. If a neuron did not have any dendrites, then it would have difficulty
    - a. sending signals to other neurons
    - b. carrying an electrical charge to the terminals
    - c. creating glial cells
    - d. receiving chemical signals from other neurons
29. You are listening to a piece of music when suddenly the violin gets very loud. What change will occur in the neural signals from your ears to your brain?
    - a. The amount of chemicals released will increase.
    - b. The cells will fire at a faster rate of frequency.
    - c. The terminals will block the neurotransmitters.
    - d. Neurotransmitters will accumulate in the gates.
30. John was in a car accident. He was hit on the head and temporarily saw "stars" as his vision was disrupted. Which part of his head was likely hit
    - a. the top
    - b. the front
    - c. the back
    - d. the side
31. Phineas Gage is famous because he
    - a. discovered the lateral fissure
    - b. operated on people with epilepsy
    - c. was the first diagnosed case of aphasia
    - d. suffered a brain accident
32. The brain-imaging technique that measures brain waves is the
    - a. MRI
    - b. PET scan
    - c. EEG
    - d. fMRI
33. Which brain-imaging technique would be best for identifying the location of a brain tumor?
    - a. CAT scan
    - b. EEG
    - c. fMRI
    - d. PET scan

34. The pleasure and pain centers are found in the
    - a. endocrine system
    - b. pituitary gland
    - c. thalamus
    - d. hypothalamus
35. A central part of the limbic system is a small almond-shaped piece of brain called the
    - a. hippocampus
    - b. cerebellum
    - c. amygdala
    - d. reticular formation
36. Which system of nerves keeps us alert and paying attention?
    - a. endocrine system
    - b. reticular activating system
    - c. peripheral nervous system
    - d. cerebellum
37. The drug Novocain prevents neural signals from traveling to the brain by
    - a. blocking sodium channels on the axons
    - c. blocking the synaptic release of chemicals
    - b. blocking receptor sites on the dendrites
    - d. interfering with the neuron's threshold
38. Fraternal twins are known as
    - a. DZ
    - b. MZ
    - c. MZA
    - d. MZT
39. Which of these is a transgender problem?
    - a. Down syndrome
    - b. Huntington's disease
    - c. Klinefelter's syndrome
    - d. epilepsy
40. A woman's use of alcohol during pregnancy can harm the fetus. Alcohol is called a
    - a. genetic effector
    - b. channel blocker
    - c. chemical stamina
    - d. teratogen

Short answer and critical thinking

1. Name a common myth about the brain, and give the correction.
2. What is efficiency theory?
3. Describe what is meant by *contralateral*, giving examples.
4. What behaviors of a newborn baby might lead you to think that the baby has an underdeveloped corpus callosum?
5. What does *lateralized* mean? Give some examples.
6. What is confabulation?
7. What are the functions of the motor area and somatosensory area?
8. What does *plasticity* mean?
9. What is "phantom limb," and why does it occur?
10. Name two brain imaging techniques, and state what they are used for.
11. What is the problem in Parkinson's disease?
12. Describe how axonal and synaptic transmission work.
13. What are chromosomes, and how are they passed from parent to offspring?
14. What are genes? What information do they provide?

Chapter 4

Sensation, Perception, and Consciousness

PLAN AHEAD...

- How many senses do we have, and how do they work?
- How sensitive are the human senses?
- How do we see things? Do we see with our eyes or our brains?
- How do we see color? What causes color blindness?
- How does perception work? Are we born with perception, or does it develop?
- How do psychologists study the physiology of perception?

"To be conscious that we are perceiving or thinking is to be conscious of our own existence."
—ARISTOTLE

Do you wear glasses? A student once told me she didn't think people looked cool in glasses. I said that I have never felt that way and that, in fact, I leaned toward thinking that glasses made people look interesting or intelligent. What do you think? Later, I thought about how it is so common to correct vision but not the other senses. No one wears a device to improve their sense of balance, touch, or smell, for example. That same day, as I headed home, I happened to walk out with a foreign language professor. She asked me if I had had a good day, and I replied that I had because I very much enjoy talking about the physiology of vision. She then said, "I thought you taught psychology." Once again, I was reminded that the general public has a different idea of what psychology is than do psychologists. Yes, psychologists study the senses.

Our senses are our windows on the world, our microphones on our surroundings, our means of attaining information. We see, hear, smell, taste, we feel temperature, pain, and pressure on our skin; and we feel the position and movement of our own bodies. Our senses provide the information that our brains use and hence are the bases for our mental, emotional, and cognitive world of consciousness. It's obvious that psychology needs to pay attention to how the senses work.

In fact, the earliest questions about psychology were questions about sensation and perception. How do we see? Why does an apple look red and why does an orange look, well, orange? Why does an oboe sound so oboe-ish and a guitar so guitar-twangy? What causes an onion to taste so unlike chocolate? Why does the feeling of sandpaper seem so different from the sight of a yellow bird? How could anyone confuse those two perceptions?

The ancient Greek philosophers wondered about such things. For example, when we eat something, it is gone—consumed. But when we see something, the object seems to still be there. Why doesn't a thing that is seen get consumed by the process of seeing? Some ancient thinkers believed that seeing worked because tiny bits of objects broke off and entered our eyes. No? Then, do we really see the object? Or do we see the light that reflects from the object? What do we see—object or light? Is there a difference between seeing an object and seeing the light from an object? What do we mean by seeing? How do we see?

THE PROCESS OF SENSING

"It's not an optical illusion, it just looks that way."
—Anonymous

The sensory system consists of the parts of the body that bring information to the brain. The information that the brain receives originates from different forms of physical energy. Our bodies cannot sense all forms of physical energy or all qualities of the physical energy that we can sense. We cannot sense microwaves, ultraviolet light, barometric pressure, muons, neptons, very high- or low-pitched sounds, or lots of other stimuli. The human eye can detect only a small portion of the total spectrum of light. Our senses can detect only certain kinds and levels of physical energy in our surroundings.

Translation, Please!

The kinds of physical energy to which humans are sensitive include light, sound waves, molecules dissolved on the tongue, pressure on the skin, and temperature. Of course, a brain does not use these forms of energy to do its business. A brain uses neural energy, which involves both electrical and chemical communication. For example, the occipital lobe of the brain processes vision. But if you open someone's skull and shine a flashlight on the cells of the occipital lobe, the person will see nothing! The cells in the visual processing area of the brain do not use light. They use neural energy. Therefore, the human body must have some way of converting light energy into neural energy. The same thing is true of all the senses. The first step in sensing is to convert physical energy into neural energy.

The conversion of one form of energy to another is called **transduction.** Humans (and other animals, of course) have specialized receptors in their bodies that transduce energy. These are called **sensory receptors.** For example, in your eye are specialized cells that contain chemicals that undergo a chemical reaction when they are exposed to light. When light enters your eyes, chemical reactions occur in the cells in the back of your eyes, because those cells have chemicals that are sensitive to light. Those cells in the back of the eyes are the transducers of light. The chemical reaction causes light to be converted to a neural signal. Thus, those cells in the back of the eyes are responsible for the transduction that is necessary for your brain to process light.

Did You See That?

The sensory process begins with physical energy impressing on our bodies. Next, special receptor cells in our body convert (transduce) that energy into neural signals. These signals are sent to the brain. Then the brain produces a mental experience called a **sensation.** You see a red balloon. You smell rubber burning. You feel a bug crawling on your leg. You taste peanut butter. You hear a fire siren. Sensations are the experiences that we get when our brain processes the neural signals sent from our sensory receptors.

Do people have the same sensations? When I see red, do you also see red? There is no way to answer such questions empirically, since sensations are personal, subjective events. Only you know what is in your mental experience. However, because your sensory receptors are just like mine, the physical energy that stimulates your sensory receptors is the same as the physical energy that stimulates mine, and your brain is organized the same as mine, it is reasonable to assume that we have the same sensations. That is, when I see red, I believe that you do too. However, I cannot prove it empirically.

The final step in this process is called **perception.** Brains give meaning to sensations; that is, they interpret the incoming sensory signals. We don't see just blobs of color; we see objects and people and other stimuli. The brain is a pattern-seeking organ. Brains look for patterns and create meaning out of sensory experiences. Two people can see or hear the same thing but have very different interpretations or perceptions. Sensation refers to the mental experience of sensing, the feeling you get when your sensory receptors are stimulated. Perception refers to your interpretation of those sensations, the meaning it has for you. A baby listening to Mozart will hear the same thing that we hear but will not perceive what we perceive. A baby listening to a lecture on psychology will have the same exact sensations as will a college student listening to that lecture. But the college student (we hope!) will have an enormously different perception of the lecture than will the baby.

Here is a summary of the sensory process using vision as an example:

Physical energy   →   **Sensory receptor**   →   **Sensation**   →   **Perception**

(light)   (cells in the eye)   (see color, shape, etc.)   (it's a red bird)

THE HUMAN SENSES

"Nothing is more indisputable than the existence of our senses."
—Jean LeRond d'Alenbert

It is often said that humans have five senses. But this is ludicrous—humans have many more than five senses! How many? The exact number of senses we have depends on how one defines a sense. We could define senses on the basis of any of the four processes mentioned above. That is, we could classify senses according to the form of physical energy that stimulates them, according to the types of sensory receptors in our bodies, according to the different sensations we experience, or according to our different perceptions. Vision, for example, could be thought of as one sense, the sense that responds to light. Or it could be four senses, since there are four different kinds of receptors in the human eye. Or it could be as many senses as there are visual experiences: one sense for seeing blue, one for seeing red, one for seeing movement, and so on, since each is a different sensation. Finally, we could define vision according to our perceptions; for example, seeing a computer on a desk is different from seeing a car drive across a bridge. Are these different senses?

Here is one common way of classifying the human senses.

LONG-RANGE SENSES

1. *Vision:* The sense of seeing arises when light enters the eyes and strikes chemicals in the very back of the eye. The chemical reactions that take place stimulate the cells, causing them to fire and send electrical signals to other cells in the back of the eye. Eventually, the signals reach the occipital lobe of the brain, where they are processed. Vision has been studied more than any other sense, and some people say that it is the most important of the senses. Vision takes up much more brain area than any of the other senses. It will be discussed in greater detail later in this chapter.

2. *Hearing:* Scientifically, this sense is known as **audition,** or the auditory sense. Hearing is the brain's processing of incoming sound waves. When a person talks, for example, waves are created in the air. These waves enter your ears, cause a vibration of the eardrum, which causes a corresponding vibration of three small bones in the inner ear, which causes a vibration inside an organ called the **cochlea.** Inside the cochlea are tiny hair cells aligned on the **basilar membrane** that transduce sound waves into neural energy, which is then sent to the brain. Thus, you hear. The hair cells in the cochlea are arranged in order of their sensitivity to pitch, like the keys on a piano. The cells respond to different pitches (vibrations, known as frequencies) and fire at a faster or slower rate depending on the loudness of the sound. Loudness is measured in **decibels,** and very loud sounds can cause permanent damage to the cells of the cochlea, a fact that is well known by rock stars such as Ted Nugent, Alice Cooper, Bruce Springsteen, and Pete Townsend, all of whom have suffered hearing loss.

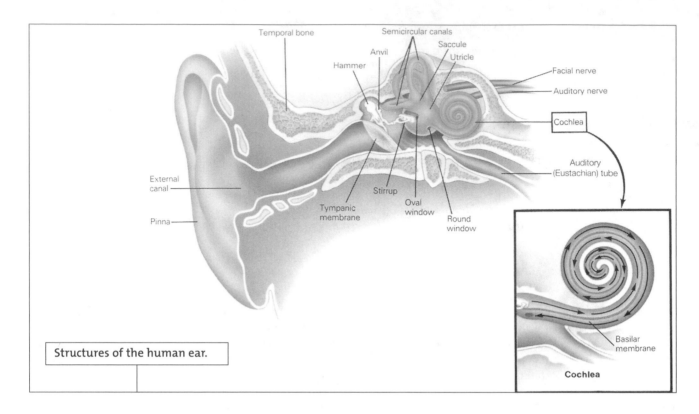

Structures of the human ear.

Some deaf people can gain hearing by getting a cochlear implant. Surgeons place electrodes into the damaged cochlea. A microphone worn behind the ear sends signals to a processor, which sends electrical signals to the electrodes, which in turn stimulate the auditory nerve. Amazingly, such implants not only increase activity in the auditory area of the brain, but also cause an increase in the visual area—brains, after all, are plastic, they can organize in creative ways to interpret incoming information. Also, scientists have now developed an alternative approach: a brainstem implant that bypasses the auditory nerve and sends signals directly to the auditory cortex (Rauschecker and Shannon, 2002). Interestingly, many people in the deaf community feel that being deaf is not a disability but is simply a difference, such as being short or having a big nose. They believe that cochlear implants could bring about the end of a valuable culture, that of deaf people who use sign language to communicate.

CHEMICAL SENSES

3. *Taste:* This sense is scientifically called **gustation** or the gustatory sense. On the tongue are **taste buds,** which contain receptors (proteins) that respond to different chemicals. The taste receptors are sensitive to molecules that are dissolved on the tongue. For a long time, scientists have recognized four major tastes: salt, sweet, sour, and bitter. Recently, a fifth was added: **umami,** the taste of monosodium glutamate (Chaudhari et al., 2000). The umami flavor is found in foods such as mushrooms, Parmesan cheese, seaweed, and meat.

Taste has been difficult to study, and scientists have thus far identified only the receptors for umami and bitter. In fact, there are several different types of receptors for the bitter taste, which allow us to experience and tell the difference between different kinds of bitter tastes. Textbooks often state that particular receptors are located only in certain areas of the tongue, but this is not correct. All five receptors are spread over the tongue and are even found in other regions of the mouth, with only minor differences in concentration (Lindemann, 2001). Some animals have taste receptors outside their mouths; fish, for example even have taste receptors on their skin.

Taste receptors evolved because they helped animals and people to survive. The bitter receptors help to detect poisons, salt helps us to get required minerals into our bodies, sour detects unripe fruits and spoiled foods, and sweet guides the intake of calories (Caicedo & Roper, 2001; Lindemann, 2001). However, when we say that food tastes a certain way, we are using more than just our gustatory sense. The taste of food depends on smell to a large extent (try holding your nose while eating) and on temperature, pressure, and even sometimes pain (do you like spicy foods?). Taste buds are always dying and reproducing. However, when people get older, they lose some of their taste buds. Hence, they lose some of their sensations of taste.

4. *Smell:* Scientists call this sense **olfaction** or the olfactory sense. Cells in the upper nose are sensitive to the shapes of molecules in the air. The molecules enter the nose and stimulate the olfactory receptors in the manner of a key fitting into a lock. It is the shape of the molecule that is important. Scientists believe that there are eight different receptors for smell. Smell is the only sense that is directly connected to the cerebral cortex. The other senses pass through the thalamus (the relay center for the senses) first. Smell is a very important sense in lower animals. Ants, for example, find their way home by using their sense of smell. It is unlikely that you will find a person who finds his or her way home by smelling. From an evolutionary perspective, humans use smell for two general purposes: sexual attraction (body scents and also perfumes, colognes, and deodorants) and detecting danger (smelling food before eating it, smelling smoke, etc.).

FYI The term *umami* was derived from the Japanese word *umai,* which means "yummy" or "delicious."

FYI Peppers contain a substance called capsaicin that stimulates the receptors for hot temperatures. Onions and radishes have similar compounds. Long-term use of capsaicin can reduce the sensitivity of the receptors, so, yes, people can develop a tolerance for hot, spicy foods. Mints, on the other hand, stimulate the nerve endings for cold temperatures. But when this substance is strong, as in menthol, there is stimulation of pain also, producing a stinging or burning sensation—hence the term *peppermint* for a type of mint that creates illusions of both heat and cold.

SKIN SENSES

5. *Light touch:* This sense is stimulated by gentle contact with the skin. Some areas of the skin, as you know, have more touch receptors than others and therefore are more sensitive to touch. You can demonstrate this sense by gently touching the hairs on your wrist or forearm. It will feel like a bug crawling on your arm and will probably give you an urge to scratch it. This demonstration will give you the idea of why we have such a sense. It is important in our environment to be able to sense when something is lightly touching us.

6. *Pressure:* When the skin is pushed down, certain receptors are bent, and they send a neural signal to the brain. This then gives us the sensation that something is pushing or pressing on our skin. This feeling is different from the sensation of light touch, as you can demonstrate by first lightly touching your arm and then pushing down hard on your arm. The two sensations are different. Pressure receptors stop sending signals if the pressure is constant. That's a good thing, since we would not want to constantly feel the pressure of our clothes, wristwatches, and eyeglasses on our bodies.

7. *Warm:* We do not have one sense of temperature. There is no thermometer in your skin. Instead, there are two kinds of receptors that react to temperature. Some sensory receptors, known as **Ruffini cylinders,** become active when something warm touches them. If you step into a warm shower or go outside on a warm day, your Ruffini cylinders send a signal to your brain, and you get the sensation of warmth. This is a very adaptable sense; the receptors change their threshold on the basis of the surrounding temperature. Therefore, a shower that seems very warm at first might soon feel a bit cooler. This is known as **sensory adaptation.** The warm and cold receptors are very adaptable, while other senses, such as pain, are not.

8. *Cold:* Another set of skin receptors is involved in our sense of temperature; these are called **Krause end bulbs,** and they are stimulated by things that are cold. When you go outside on a winter day, the cold air on your skin will stimulate the Krause end bulbs, which will send a neural signal to your brain. Brrrrrr! These cells, like the warm receptors, are subject to sensory adaptation. For example, a cold swimming pool will not seem so bad after a few minutes of adapting to it. Interestingly, both the warm and cold receptors are stimulated by things that are hot. We do not have separate receptors for sensing hot. We get the sensation that something is hot because both warm and cold receptors are sending signals to the brain at the same time. Therefore, you can fool your brain about temperature. Put a bowl of sand in the refrigerator and another bowl of sand in the hot sun. Later, quickly mix them together and grab a handful of the mixture. The warm and cold receptors in your hand will both be stimulated, and your brain will be tricked into sensing a hot stimulus. This is a temperature illusion.

9. *Pain:* There are receptors in your skin that are stimulated when your skin is damaged. You get the feeling of pain when discomfort or injury stimulates one or more of three different kinds of nerves. You can feel a sharp pain, a dull pain, or a combination. Pain signals are sent to the brain through a series of **gates** that chemically control the degree to which the signal reaches the brain. Therefore, pain can be regulated chemically. Also, pain can be affected by other methods, such as shifting your attention (put on headphones at the dentist), acupuncture (which attenuates the pain gates on the nerves), or meditation or relaxation exercises. Although they are most highly concentrated in the skin, pain receptors also exist inside the body; you can feel pain in your muscles, for example. When the stimulus for a sensation is coming from inside the body, the sense is called **proprioceptive.** So in addition to being a skin sense, pain is a proprioceptive sense.

PROPRIOCEPTIVE SENSES

10. *Kinesthetic:* **Kinesthesis** is the sense of body position and body movement. Lift your arm above your head. Do you feel the movement? Hold your arm up in the air. Feel it? Close your eyes, and try to touch your nose with your fingertip. This is fairly easy because your brain can tell where your arm is as you move it through space. Now close your eyes, extend both your arms to the sides, and try to touch your index fingertips together in front of you. That's a bit harder. Your fingertips are smaller than your nose, and they are moving. The kinesthetic sense is a proprioceptive sense because the physical energy that is being sensed is originating within the body. There are sensory receptors in the muscles, joints, and tendons of the body that are stimulated by movement. These signals are sent to the brain, where they are processed. We get a sensation, a feeling, of body position in space. You know where your arm is. You can feel it. That is the kinesthetic sense.

11. *Vestibular:* The **vestibular organ** is in the inner ear but has nothing to do with hearing. It is shaped like three curved tubes, called **semicircular canals,** that are each oriented in one of the directions: up-down, front-back, and left-right. Inside the organ is a fluid that moves as you move your head in three-dimensional space. The fluid stimulates hair cells inside the semicircular canals, and they send electrical signals to the brain. If you spin around fast, the fluid will move quickly through the vestibular organ, tickling many cells. If you stop suddenly, the fluid keeps moving for a moment, and you experience dizziness. Ear infections sometimes affect the vestibular nerve and therefore also cause dizziness.

So you can see that by a conservative method of defining the senses, humans have at least eleven. We could, of course, use a more liberal definition of the senses, and there would consequently be many more. You might have noticed that no extrasensory

TABLE 4.1   **The Human Senses**

Long-Range	Chemical	Skin	Proprioceptive
Seeing (vision)	Taste (gustation)	Light touch	Kinesthetic
Hearing (audition)	Smell (olfaction)	Pressure	Vestibular
		Warm	
		Cold	
		Pain	

sense, or so-called sixth sense, is listed. There are no sensory receptors for detecting the thoughts of others, for receiving signals coming from the future, for hearing messages from dead people, or for any other similarly weird thing. No one's brain or body has such receptors. Human brains and human sensory systems are all essentially the same. There are no special people who have different kinds of sensory abilities. No one has psychic abilities. Perhaps life would be easier if such things were real. On the other hand, perhaps people would use their psychic abilities for evil. What would you use yours for?

Some people experience a sensation in one sense when another sense is stimulated. For example, they might see a color when listening to music, or a word might conjure up a certain smell. This phenomenon is called *synesthesia*. Some psychologists believe that synesthesia is more common in young children than in adults (Dann, 1999; Harrison, 2001). Everyone has some crossover between the senses; for example, the touch area of the brain communicates with the visual area, so a touch on the hand can improve vision near that hand (Macaluso et al., 2000). Other cross-modal information has been found in the brain too (de Gelder, 2000).

THINK TANK

There are many different kinds of physical energy that humans can sense, such as light, sound waves, and touch.

Why do you think those senses evolved?

Can you think of some ways in which they gave early humans a survival advantage?

Can you think of some forms of physical energy that humans cannot sense?

Which sense do you prize the most?

Which do you value the least?

PSYCHOPHYSICS

"There are things that seem incredible to most people

who have not studied mathematics."
—ARISTOTLE

Now that you have learned about the senses, it is time to look at the branch of psychology that studies the senses. **Psychophysics** was founded by **Gustav Theodor Fechner** (1801–1887), who was a German professor of physics. As the term *psychophysics* indicates, this field of study is a combination of psychology and physics. If you enjoy both of those disciplines, then we have a career for you!

Fechner's father, grandfather, and uncle were all Lutheran ministers, and they instilled in the young Gustav an intense interest in religion. In adulthood, Fechner was troubled by the contradiction between his religious views (particularly the concept of free will) and the rule-bound laws of the universe. He became obsessed with the question "Does nature or the world have a soul?" Fechner wrote a series of works under the name Dr. Mises in which he attempted to resolve the contradiction between scientific laws and free will. Then, in 1839, Fechner suffered a mental and physical breakdown, partly caused by an eye injury he suffered from looking too long at the sun. Somewhat inexplicably, he became a complete invalid and resigned his job. One day in 1850, while lying in bed, Fechner had a revelation. He realized that the contradiction he struggled with could be solved by merging the mental and the physical in a scientific way. In 1860, he published his groundbreaking book on psychophysics.

Psychophysics is the study of how physical energy is related to the mind's experience of it. That is, psychophysicists seek to discover which sensations occur when we sense things and how strong those sensations are relative to the strengths of the physical stimuli. Psychophysics, then, is the study of the relationship between the physical world and our sensory experience of it. Psychophysicists seek mathematical laws, called psychophysical laws, that describe the relation between physical energy and our sensation of it. Gustav Fechner proposed a psychophysical law that today is known as **Fechner's law.** This mathematical law states that the subjective intensity of a stimulus (the feeling that a person reports) is equal to the logarithm of the physical intensity of the stimulus multiplied by a constant. It is written like this:

$$S = \log I \times k$$

In mathematics, the letter k is used to represent a constant number. In Fechner's law, I represents the intensity or level of the physical stimulus. What excited Fechner was that this law (and other psychophysical laws) allowed him to find a source of harmony between the physical world and the mental. Psychophysical laws prove that the mind can be studied scientifically, that mental experiences can be described mathematically, and that psychology can be an exact science. Our bodies and our minds respond predictably, mathematically, to physical stimuli.

You're So Sensitive

One of the common subjects of study in psychophysics is **sensitivity.** This is the attempt to discover how responsive the sensory system is to various levels of intensity

Connecting Concepts

If you recall the discussion of neurons in Chapter 3, you might be able to see why our senses work in a mathematical way. Neurons are electrochemical switches that convey signals according to chemical processes. Those processes function in a quantitative way. Remember the pyramid of sciences in Chapter 1? Psychology is based on biology, which is based on chemistry, which is based on physics. All of the sciences use mathematics.

of a stimulus. For example, how bright must a light be to be seen? How loud must a sound be to be heard? Psychophysics is an important field of study not only for providing specific information about how our bodies and minds are related to the world of experience, but also for practical applications, such as designing machines for efficient use by humans.

The term *sensitivity* has two meanings. We are not referring here to emotional sensitivity. Instead, we mean the extent to which sensory receptors are able to detect various types and levels of physical energy. Sensitivity is the study of how the mind reacts to physical energy, that is, the extent to which a person can detect different forms and intensities of physical stimuli.

The first type of sensitivity is called the **absolute threshold.** This is the simple idea of testing the sensory receptors to discover what level of energy is just enough to turn them on. In other words, the absolute threshold is the smallest amount of energy it takes to stimulate a sensation. What is the smallest amount of light you can see? What is the lowest number of decibels you can hear? What is the smallest number of molecules dissolved on your tongue that you can taste? What is the smallest number of molecules of vinegar in the air that you can smell? What is the smallest amount of touch on your skin that you can feel? Each of these smallest amounts is called the absolute threshold for the corresponding sense.

To determine absolute thresholds, large numbers of people are tested ("Look at the screen, and tell me when you see a dot of light on it"), and their scores are averaged. This gives the absolute threshold for people in general. Some absolute thresholds, for instance, are 10 quanta of light energy for vision, 0.0002 dyne/cm^2 for hearing, 1 teaspoon of sugar in 2 gallons of water for taste, and 1 part per 500 million for smell. Of course, people vary in their ability to sense stimuli. Another problem is that two people might just barely sense the same thing (for example, a very dim light), but one person might decide to say that he sees it, while the other decides that he needs to be more certain—he needs a slightly brighter light before he'll say that he sees it. In other words, not only do these experiments measure sensation, they also measure the cognitive process of decision making. Included in psychophysics is the study of why people detect a stimulus in some situations but not in others. This area of study is called **signal detection theory.** One simple reason that people may differ in their report of a sensation is whether or not they were expecting it. For example, if you were told that a stimulus was going to appear, you would more likely notice it than if it was a surprise. More complex issues are also included in signal detection theory, such as the amount of background "noise" (the surrounding signals) and the complexity of the stimulus field.

Sense Modality	Detection Threshold
Light	A candle flame seen at 30 miles on a dark, clear night
Sound	The tick of a watch under quiet conditions at 20 feet
Taste	One teaspoon of sugar in 2 gallons of water
Smell	One drop of perfume diffused into the entire volume of a three-room apartment
Touch	The wing of a bee falling on your cheek from a distance of 1 centimeter

Absolute thresholds of familiar events.

What's the Difference?

The second type of sensitivity is called the **difference threshold.** This concept refers to the amount of change in the intensity of a stimulus that is required for people to notice that the level has changed. How much brighter does a light have to get for you to notice that it got brighter? How much louder does a sound have to get for you to notice that it is louder? The difference or change that is required is called a **just-noticeable difference (JND).** Aren't you glad that scientists sometimes make up easy names for things?

The difference threshold was studied by Fechner's friend and colleague **Ernst Heinrich Weber** (1795–1878), a scientist from Leipzig, Germany. (Weber's name is pronounced "VAY-ber.") The JND is determined by measuring subjects' subjective judgments of the intensities of different stimuli. Weber found, for example, that if people lift small objects of varying weights, they could notice the difference between two weights only if the weights were at least a certain amount different from each other. This amount is called the JND. Weber found that the JND was not an absolute number but that it varied depending on how strong the stimuli were. For instance, an average person can tell the difference between a 50-ounce weight and a 51-ounce weight but cannot tell the difference between a 100-ounce weight and a 101-ounce weight. Similarly, an average person notices a change of 1 decibel in a sound of 20 decibels but does not notice when a 30 decibel sound increases to 31 decibels. Weber found that there is a constant ratio between the JND and the intensity of the stimulus. This mathematical relationship is expressed as **Weber's law:**

$$JND/I = k$$

Weber's law says that there is a constant (k) relationship between JND and the intensity of a stimulus (I). The constant (k) is different for each sense and is known as the **Weber fraction.** For instance, the Weber fraction for lifting weights is about 1/50. This means that an average person can notice 1 change for every 50 units of weight. If something weighs 100 pounds, how much heavier must it get for people on the average to notice that it got heavier? The answer is 2 pounds, because the ratio 1/50 is equal to 2/100.

Here's another example, see whether you can get the answer: The Weber fraction for the taste of salt is about 1/7. A chef has made a big pot of soup. She put into the soup 35 grams of salt. She tasted it and found that it wasn't salty enough. If salt is added in whole grams, how many grams must be added to make the soup saltier?

I'll bet I tricked you! The answer is 1. I asked how many grams would make it saltier, not how many grams would make it *taste* saltier. Remember, psychophysical laws are about the connection between the physical world and our subjective, mental experience of it. Weber's law is needed if we ask this question: How many grams of salt must the chef add to the soup for the soup to taste saltier to the average person? The Weber fraction is 1/7. The intensity of the stimulus is 35 grams. What's the answer?

Did you say 5 grams? You are so smart! The answer is 5, because 1/7 = 5/35.

Weber's law shows us that there is a mathematical relationship between our sensation of something and the physical measurement of it. This law is used any time we want to calculate how much a stimulus must change for people to notice that it changed. When a car's taillights are on and the driver applies the brake, how much brighter must the taillight get for people to notice that it got brighter? How much must a sound engineer increase the volume of a musical instrument on a recording for listeners to notice that it got louder? How much must a dial move on an airplane's instrument panel for the pilot to notice that it moved? The answer to each question depends on the intensity of the stimulus. The louder the musical instrument is playing, the more the volume must be increased for people to notice that it got louder. Weber discovered that this is true for almost all intensities of stimuli. However, for very small or very large intensities, the straight-line ratio is no longer adequate, and a more complicated mathematical formula is necessary. I'll assume you can look that up in the library if you're interested. Let's go on.

THINK TANK

People differ in sensitivity.

What do you think are some reasons for this?

To what extent, and in what ways, should society make accommodations for the differences between people in how well they can sense things?

What occupations require a person to have a very sensitive sense?

Recap

— The senses bring information to the brain. This requires receptors that transduce physical energy into neural energy.

— The awareness of sensing is called a sensation, but its interpretation or meaning is called perception.

— Eleven human senses were listed. Many more could be listed if the term *sense* was defined more liberally.

— Psychophysics (founded by Fechner) is the branch of psychology that attempts to find mathematical relationships between physical stimuli and human sensations of them.

There are two types of sensitivity: Absolute threshold is the smallest amount of stimulus that can be noticed, and difference threshold is the smallest change in the intensity of a stimulus that can be noticed (the JND).

— Weber's law says there is a constant ratio between the JND and the intensity of a stimulus. The constants (different for each sense) are called Weber fractions.

VISION

"We are as much as we see."
—HENRY DAVID THOREAU

The sense of vision has been studied more than any other; consequently, it is the sense that scientists know the most about. In addition, many people feel that it is the most important sense, the one they would least like to lose. (Pain is often chosen first!) Also, all the senses function similarly, so if you learn the details of vision you will have a good overall understanding of how sensory systems function in general. Those are some of the reasons that we will now take a very close look at vision (pun intended!).

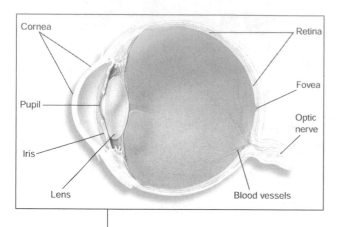

Anatomy of the eye.

Eye Anatomy

An eye is an organ that evolved for the purpose of bringing focused light to the cells in the back. Here are descriptions of the eye's most important structures that help accomplish that goal:

The **cornea** is the front of the eye, the window on the world. It is the part of the eye that contact lenses rest on. It is the part that bumps out; you can see it pushing out the eyelid when you look at a person whose eyes are closed. Because of this, we can watch the rapid eye movements that occur during sleep. The cornea is curved to bend incoming rays of light toward the opening in the eye. A cornea should be clear because light must pass through it to get to the inside of the eye. As people age, their corneas become less smooth and regular, which interferes with vision. For example, older eyes are more sensitive to glare. Also, corneas become yellowed with age, which interferes with color vision.

Behind the cornea is the **iris.** This structure is shaped like a doughnut or inner tube. The hole in the middle is the **pupil.** The word pupil means a "small person." If you look into someone's eye, you will see in the pupil a reflection of yourself, a small you—hence, the name. Light enters the eye through the pupil. Notice that the pupil is not a physical structure; it is the opening in the center of the iris. It is the donut hole.

The iris is colored (the word *iris* means "rainbow") by pigmentation. The amount of pigment in the iris is regulated mostly by heredity. A person with very little pigmentation has light-blue eyes. More pigmentation produces dark-blue eyes. Even more results in green eyes. With still more pigment in the iris, you get hazel eyes. Lots of pigmentation gives a brown iris, and still more results in dark brown or even a black iris. The purpose of the pigment is to block light from getting in. Too much light is harmful. The irises are natural sunglasses. People with blue eyes should wear sunglasses when in bright sunlight, since they do not have much natural protection. Otherwise, eye diseases are more likely to occur.

The pupil is black, because that is where light enters the eye. It is the opening into the inside of the eyeball. The pupil can change size by expansion and contraction of the iris. The iris is elastic and is pulled by muscles in the eye. When the iris expands, that is, when it increases in size, the pupil gets smaller. This happens in bright light to reduce the amount of light entering the eye. When the iris contracts, that is, pulls back, the pupil gets larger. This happens in dim light to let more light into the eye. Interestingly, when people get older, all parts of their bodies become less elastic, including the iris. Therefore, older people have a more fixed-size pupil. They need more light for reading than a younger person. Also, when moving from a bright space to a dark space, for example, when old people in a nursing home go from a social room into a hallway or stairwell, their pupils do not enlarge enough for good vision. Lots of accidents happen that way. Brighter lights should be put into hallways and stairwells in nursing homes. Can you think of other practical examples of such information?

For some reason, people find someone more attractive if his or her pupils are larger. When a person's pupils are large, he or she is more often perceived as good-looking, soft, kind, understanding, and warm. Perhaps this is because people's pupils increase in size when they are interested in you! You can make your pupils larger simply by being in a darker environment. Just tell your prospective partner to meet you in a dark place. Your pupils will be larger, and he or she will be more likely to find you attractive!

Behind the iris is the **lens.** The lens focuses the incoming light onto the back of the eye. Therefore, the lens must also be elastic, getting thicker or thinner depending on how near objects are to the person. Muscles in the eye pull on the lens, changing its thickness. This process is called **accommodation.** Newborn babies have poor visual accommodation; they have a fixed focus of about 8 inches for the first couple months. This is a handy distance for focusing on Mommy's face during breast-feeding and is probably the evolutionary significance of this fact. As people age, the lens becomes less flexible. By the age of 45 or 50, the lens of the eye is not able to get thick enough to see things up close. In middle age, adults need to hold reading material far away to focus on it. An old joke says that when your arms aren't long enough, you need glasses. This condition is called **presbyopia,** which literally means "old eyes." Make a note on your calendar to get reading glasses when you hit about 45.

The lens should be clear, since light must pass through it. Sometimes the lens develops patchy white spots called **cataracts** (the word means "waterfall," which refers to the fact that the spots in the lens look like the white water that occurs when water is rushing). Cataracts interfere with incoming light. Cataract surgery is the most common medical operation in old age. Put it on your calendar. You can decrease your risk of developing cataracts by wearing sunglasses and by taking antioxidants (vitamins C and E and beta-carotene).

There are two fluids inside the eye that help maintain the shape of the eyeball and do biological housekeeping functions. One fluid lies in the front of the eye between the cornea and the lens. It is called the **aqueous humor** ("watery fluid"). This fluid regularly drains out through a tube and is replenished. If the drainage system should become blocked and the aqueous humor cannot drain out, pressure builds up in the eyeball. This condition is called **glaucoma.**

Another fluid in the eye lies between the lens and the back of the eye. It is called the **vitreous humor** ("glassy or jellylike fluid"). This fluid does not drain out. It is of gel-like consistency and helps to maintain the spherical shape of the eyeball. Sometimes tiny bits of matter break off the inside wall of the eye and float around in the vitreous humor. A person then will see black spots floating in her vision. These are simply called **floaters** and often will go away.

In the very back of the eye, the inside back layer, is the **retina.** Here are located the sensory receptors for vision. Because they are responsive to light, the receptors in the back of the eye are called **photoreceptors** (*photo* means "light"). They come in two types and are named after their shapes: **rods** and **cones.** (How would you like to be named after your shape? What would your name be: Pear, Banana, Telephone Pole, Triangle?) Rods give us night vision, and cones are used for color and bright light. (Chickens have very few rods in their eyes, so they go home when it is dark. In the morning, they are very excited to be able to see again. Watch out for blind chickens at night.)

A photograph of the rods and cones in the retina at the back of the eye.

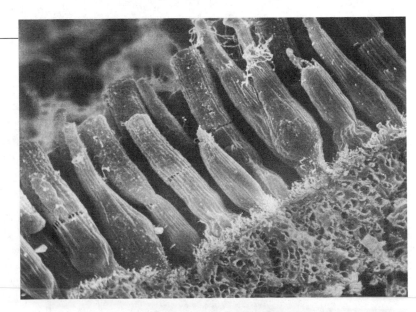

Recall the discussion of circadian rhythms in Chapter 3.

Connecting Concepts

Actually, it's wrong to say that there are only two types of photoreceptors, rods and cones. They have been known since 1850, but another type of retinal cell that responds to light was found in 1998. These cells do not help with vision; instead, they set the body's clockwork. Recall the discussion of circadian rhythms in Chapter 3.

The area of best vision is where the cones are most densely packed together, an area in the middle of the retina known as the **fovea**. When you look right at something, you are focusing the light onto your fovea. In bright light, vision is best when using the fovea, because the highest concentration of cones is there. In very dim light, when we are using rod vision, it is best to look a little to the side of an object, since the rods are found to the side of the fovea, on the periphery of the retina.

The lens focuses light on the retina in the very back of the eye. This process involves turning the light upside down and backward. In other words, light coming from an object down low is projected to cells near the top of the retina. Objects on our right project light to the left of the retina. The retina receives light information that is upside down and backward. Sometimes people with dyslexia say that they see things backward. For fun, I tell them that they don't; we all see things backward, so they must see them forward!

It doesn't matter that the retina receives information that is upside down and backward because the brain creates a coherent perception from the electrical signals it receives. Brains create vision from electrical and chemical actions. But what happens if the information coming to the brain is distorted? Way back in 1896, psychologist George Stratton wore goggles with prisms in them that made the world look upside down. At first, he was confused and had difficulty moving around. But after a while, his brain adapted to the upside-down signals, and he was able to function in the environment, even though things did not appear normal. After removing the goggles, he quickly readapted. Modern experiments have found that people can adapt to an upside-down world and function quite well.

To simulate alcohol intoxication, educators use goggles that make the world look as if it is skewed to one side. People wearing such goggles at first find it very difficult to move about and reach for things. But with experience, they learn to adapt to the distortion and reach for things accurately. I borrowed a pair of such goggles from a friend, and when I put them on, the world visually shifted to the right. Walking felt funny, and I immediately bumped into things. I asked my friend to shake hands. When I reached for his hand, I was way off—I reached to the right. Of course, I could see that my hand was not meeting his. My kinesthetic sense was telling me that my arm was in the right place, but my vision showed me that I was off. I knew that seeing my arm and hand before reaching would help (Redding & Wallace, 2001). At first, I had to constantly remind myself to reach slightly to the left of where his hand appeared to be, but with experience, my reach became almost automatic. Of course, a baby has to learn to coordinate the kinesthetic sense (hand and arm position in space) with vision. Distorting goggles help adults feel what this is like—to learn to coordinate movement with vision. After I removed the goggles, my reach readapted almost right away. I wondered what would happen if I wore the goggles for a long period of time. Researchers found that people could ride a motorcycle, ski, and even fly a plane while wearing upside-down goggles after they had a good bit of practice (Kohler, 1962; Dolezal, 1982). Apparently, people's brains are quite adaptive.

Rods and Cones

The rods and cones are the receptors of light; they transduce light into neural energy using light-sensitive chemicals they manufacture. Rods are very sensitive to light; they have a low absolute threshold. Only a small amount of light is necessary to fire rods. Cones, on the other hand, are not very sensitive to light; they have a higher absolute threshold. It takes more light to fire a cone than a rod.

FYI

Owls have been studied to see what effect experience has on the brain. The owls are fitted with little goggles that contain prisms that distort the visual world to the right. These owls must then visually locate sounds in space. (The delay between signals from the right and left ears is the key information in locating the source of a sound.) At first, they get it wrong—they look to the right of a sound's true location. But with experience, the neurons in the auditory cortex change, so the owls adapt. There is a critical period (see Chapter 1) when this adaptation is possible, from about 70 to 200 days of age (Brainard & Knudsen, 1998). When the prisms are removed, the owls quickly readapt and return to normal.

Rods contain a chemical called **rhodopsin** that is very sensitive to light. In an environment with a lot of light, the rhodopsin is used up faster than it can be replenished. Therefore, in bright-light conditions, you see with your cones. If you go from a well-lit room into a dark room, there won't be enough light for the cones, so they won't work, and the rhodopsin has been used up in the rods, so they won't work—you are blind! But only temporarily. Rhodopsin is being manufactured in the rods, and in time, you will have rod vision. The process takes about 30 minutes total, but you can see pretty well after only five to ten minutes in the dark. This process is called **dark adaptation.** Try it. Go from a bright room to a very dark room. Wait a while. Your rods are manufacturing rhodopsin, so you will be able to see shortly. Incidentally, rhodopsin requires vitamin A to be manufactured; therefore, people with vitamin A deficiency will lose their night vision.

Here's another fun fact about rod vision: Go into a dark room and wait for your rods to adapt (about 30 minutes). Then close one eye and turn on a light. Your open eye will be exposed to the light, and it will lose its rod vision (the rhodopsin will be used up). But the eye you keep closed will not lose its rod vision, since its rhodopsin will be spared. Next turn off the light. You will discover that you can see fine with the eye you protected but not with the open eye that used up its rhodopsin. This shows that dark adaptation occurs in the eyes, not in the brain. This trick might come in handy when you get up at night to go to the bathroom. Just be sure to close one eye when you turn on the bathroom light!

Dark adaptation is a problem because it takes so long. For our prehistoric ancestors, it didn't matter that it took 30 minutes to adapt to the dark, since the sun went down slowly. Because we have artificial lighting, it is often a problem to go from a well-lit room to a dimly lit one. This is particularly a problem for people who work in emergency occupations that require them to rush into the darkness of night after being in a bright room. Firefighters, Air Force pilots, paramedics, and others in these circumstances will not have very good vision when rushing into the dark. Wearing a patch over one eye would be a solution to this problem, but one-eyed vision is not as good as two. There is another solution. Rods do not respond to red light. Therefore, people can work in rooms that are lit with red light, and when they rush into the dark, they will not have used up the rhodopsin in their rods. This is the solution that many occupations have chosen.

Here's another interesting fact about the photoreceptors as mentioned above: Rods and cones are located in different areas of the retina (the back inside layer of the eye). The cones are more centrally located (the highest concentration is in the fovea), whereas rods are found more in the periphery, the outer regions of the retina. In bright light, we can look right at

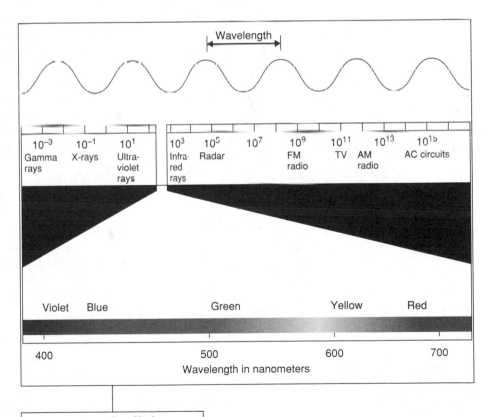

Most wavelengths of light cannot be detected by the cells of the eye. The wavelengths that can be seen are interpreted by the brain as colors.

objects and focus the light on the center of the retina where there are dense concentrations of cones. The funny thing is, a very dim light cannot be seen by looking directly at it. If you focus a dim light on the fovea (the center of the retina), the light is striking only *cones*, which are not sensitive enough to respond to the light (they have a higher absolute threshold than the rods). A very dim light can be seen only if you look a bit to the side of it because rods are most dense about 15 degrees to the side of the center of the fovea. So on a very dark evening, after you have adapted to the dark, you will see the dimmest stars in the sky if you look a bit to the side of them!

Rods and cones differ in one other important respect. Cones respond differently to different wavelengths of light, while rods do not. Light is a wave form of energy. If you throw a rock into a pond, ripples occur on the surface water. A big rock makes long waves, while a pebble makes short waves. Light comes in different intensities, which we perceive as brightness. But light also comes in different wavelengths—long, medium, short, and everything in between. For example, some light has waves that are far apart—a long wavelength. Other light has waves that are scrunched close together—a short wavelength. Our brains perceive these different wavelengths as different colors. Here's an amazing fact: Color is created in our brains on the basis of the wavelength of the incoming light. Color is not in objects. Color is our brain's perception of the wavelengths of light. This is possible because cones respond differentially to different wavelengths (just remember <u>c</u>ones = <u>c</u>olor).

Kinds of Cones

There are three kinds of cones in the normal human eye. One type of cone fires most rapidly when it is stimulated by a long wavelength of light. Let's call those cones the **long-wavelength cones.** These cones do respond to other wavelengths, but they react most vigorously to long wavelengths. The second type of cone gives the most rapid firing response to a medium wavelength of light. Let's call those cones the **medium-wavelength cones.** I bet you've guessed the third type of cone. The **short-wavelength cones** fire most rapidly when struck by short-wavelength light. This system is called **trichromatic** (tri = three, and chrom = color) and helps to produce normal color vision in humans.

A bumblebee sees a flower and zooms toward it. The color of the flower might look dull to us. But the bumblebee has different sensory receptors in its eyes than we do. So the flower looks different to the bee than it does to a human. Some people do not have all three types of cones in their eyes. This condition is called **color blindness.** Notice that the term should not be taken literally. These individuals are not blind; nor are they blind to all colors. However, they are unable to distinguish some differences between colors because they do not have all three types of cones in the retinas of their eyes. The most common form of color blindness is red-green, in which a person has difficulty recognizing the difference between those two colors. Red-green color blindness is caused by a recessive gene on the X chromosome, so men have this condition about 10 times more often than women. A similar condition is blue-yellow color blindness. In each of these cases the individual is called a **dichromat,** since he has only two kinds of cones. A **monochromat** has only one type of cone in the eyes and therefore sees the world in black and white and shades of gray. Of course, most people are trichromats.

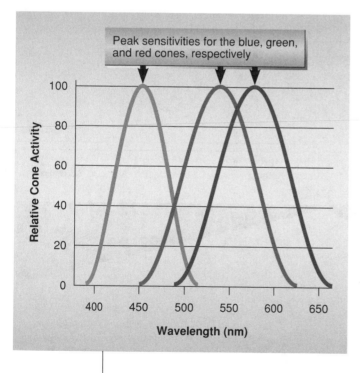

Peak sensitivities for the blue, green, and red cones, respectively

The normal human eye has three different kinds of cones that respond somewhat differently to different wavelengths of light. The brain uses this information—the different firing intensities of the cones—to help create the perception of color.

Many species have color vision, but a trichromatic process is relatively rare. Only humans and a few kinds of primates have three types of cones. Mammals in general are dichromats; that is, they have two kinds of cones in addition to rods. In some species, the females are trichromats, and the males are dichromats. An evolutionary psychologist might be able to tell us why there is a survival advantage for the females to be able to differentiate more colors than the males. Could it be because the males use color to attract the females? Tetrachromatic vision (four kinds of cones) is common in birds and fish. What does the world of color look like to them? The record for the greatest number of different kinds of photoreceptors goes to the mantis shrimp, which has ten! Do you wish you had ten kinds of cones? We can only imagine what the world looks like to a mantis shrimp.

The cells of the retina, like all cells, get their instructions, their recipes, from genes. As has been mentioned, the gene for red-green color blindness is on the X chromosome. Men have only one X, which they got from their mother. So a man cannot have a dominant gene on another X chromosome, as a woman can. A man with this gene will be color-blind (a dichromat), while his mother probably is not; she is most likely a carrier.

About 150,000 people in the United States have a type of blindness that is due to deterioration of the cells of the retina. A similar condition has recently been cured in dogs by the use of gene therapy. The dogs were born blind. University of Pennsylvania scientists injected a certain gene (rpe65) into the dogs' retinas. That gene provided the instructions for creating properly functioning retinal cells, and subsequently the dogs were able to see. Obviously, such genetic therapy offers great hope to human sufferers.

THINK TANK

Compare and contrast rods and cones.

How are they alike and how are they different in their functions, absolute threshold, position in retina, and sensing wavelengths?

Teamwork

Scientists have discovered that many cells in the nervous system have specialized jobs. For example, **David Hubel** and **Torsten Wiesel** received the Nobel Prize in Medicine for their research on cats' vision. They showed that certain cells in a cat's eye fire differentially to different stimuli. For example, a certain cell fires most rapidly when it sees a line at a particular angle. Another type of cell is most sensitive to a moving horizontal line. Still another cell fires most vigorously when exposed to a vertical line. Such cells are called **feature detectors.** These cells are specialized to respond to certain features of the visual environment.

Another interesting thing about sensory cells is that they work in teams. Cells do not do their jobs independently; rather, they receive signals from other cells that modulate what they do. That is, how vigorously a cell fires depends to some extent on whether other cells are firing vigorously. For example, some cells work in opposition to each other. Color vision is a good example of this process, known as the **opponent process.** If a bright red light is flashed into your eyes, the cells that see red will be temporarily "tired out." Those red-seeing cells work in opposition with green-seeing cells. Red and green are opponents, or complements. Because the red-seeing cells are tired, the green-seeing cells will fire more rapidly. Hence, you will see a green spot in front of your face for a little while. Soon the red-seeing cells will be back to full strength and the green spot disappears. This phenomenon is called an **afterimage.** It is the result of cells working according to the opponent process. A famous painting by Jasper Johns depicts an American flag in the colors green, black, and yellow (the opponents of red, white, and blue). If you stare at such a flag for a while and then look at a white surface, you will see a temporary image of a normal American flag. This is not hallucinating. This is a **negative color afterimage.**

Layers of the Retina

The retina has three layers of cells. The layer farthest back in the eye contains the photoreceptors, the rods and the cones. Light must pass through the other two layers, which are in front, to get to the rods and cones. In front of the rods and cones is a layer of cells called **bipolar cells.** They receive signals from the rods and cones and send signals to cells in front of them, in the front layer of the retina. These cells in the very front of the retina are called **ganglion cells.** Their axons come together and form a nerve that extends out of the back of the eye. That is the **optic nerve.** Each eye has one. The place where the axons of the ganglion cells exit out of the back of the eye cannot, naturally, have any rods or cones at that very point. Therefore, you cannot see anything that focuses light on that area of the retina. That place in the eye is called the **optic disk,** and its field of vision is known as the **blind spot.**

FYI

Certain ganglion cells in the back of the eye (front of the retina) are sensitive to the amount of light entering the eye. These cells contain a chemical called melanopsin that scientists believe is necessary for setting the biological clock. This subset of ganglion cells send axons to the superchiasmatic nucleus in the brain, the center for adjusting circadian rhythms. This is how the brain adjusts the body's clock (Berson et al., 2002).

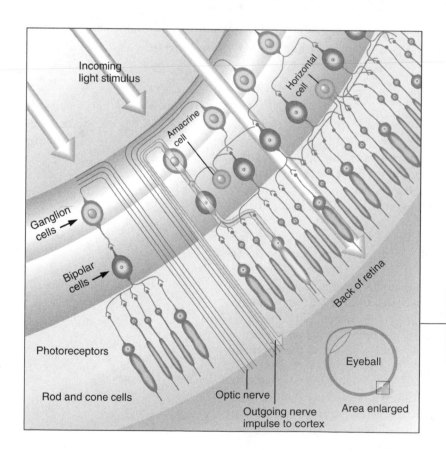

Incoming light stimulus

Horizontal cell

Amacrine cell

Ganglion cells →

Bipolar cells →

Back of retina

Photoreceptors

Rod and cone cells

Optic nerve

Outgoing nerve impulse to cortex

Eyeball

Area enlarged

The retina contains a number of different kinds of cells. Visual information has already been processed somewhat by the time it gets to the brain.

Close your right eye and put the image in front of your left eye. Move the book away from your face (about 10 inches) until the X disappears.

THINK TANK

Think about the fact that you have a blind spot in each eye.

Why can't you see your blind spot?

What does *blind* mean?

If you close your eyes, are you blind or just "seeing" blackness?

Could one have a "deaf spot" in hearing?

What if you couldn't feel pain in a certain area?

What if you couldn't smell things coming from a certain direction?

Could you have a smell-less spot?

To summarize: The rods and cones are all the way in the back of the retina. They are stimulated by light (chemical reactions occur), and then they send neural signals to the bipolar cells in front of them. Incidentally, there are far more rods and cones than there are bipolar cells, so visual information is being narrowed down inside the eye. An eye is not only like a camera; it is also like a computer. The cells of the retina are computing the light information before it goes to the brain.

The bipolar cells then send neural signals to ganglion cells in the front layer of the retina. There is more narrowing of information in that exchange. By the way, there are other cells in the retina that send signals back and forth between similar kinds of cells, so the cells communicate across to one another. The ganglion cells then send electrical signals out the back of the eye via the optic nerves. The two optic nerves (one from each eye) meet at the optic chiasm. There, signals that came from the left field of vision are sent to the right hemisphere of the brain, and light originating from the right visual field is sent to the left hemisphere. The left hemisphere sees things on the right, and the right hemisphere sees things on the left.

Of course, before reaching the hemispheres in the occipital lobe, visual information first passes through the thalamus, the relay center for the senses. A particular region of the thalamus specializes in visual information. It is called the **lateral geniculate nucleus (LGN)**. What a great name! Visual information from the eye passes into the LGN and then eventually to the occipital lobe, where it is processed, and we see! The system of cells that accomplishes this task is often described as a network. This network has three things going for it:

1. The forward-moving signal is being sent from one set of cells to another (called **feedforward**). The information is being computed as it moves downstream through various layers and specialized areas of the brain. For example, the occipital lobe has

Several research groups are attempting to create electrical implants that can be attached to the retina and will take the place of damaged rods and cones for patients who are blind because of retinal damage (Zrenner, 2002). Also, some scientists are using the tongue to help blind people see! A flexible cable with electrodes is placed against the tongue, which receives a pattern of electrical pulses from a camera. Using this device, blind people are able to recognize shapes and track motion visually. One woman was able to see a candle flame for the first time (Weiss, 2001). Dr. Bach-y-Rita explained how plastic and adaptable the brain is: "You don't see with the eyes. You see with the brain."

cells with special jobs in layers V1, V2, V3, and so on. Each layer of cells computes certain properties of vision, such as movement, color, and shape.

2. The cells that send signals downstream to other cells also receive signals back from the receiving cells (called **feedback**). For example, the cells of the lateral geniculate nucleus send signals to the occipital lobe, but they also receive messages back from the occipital lobe. This feedback enables the sending cells to modulate (adjust) their signals downstream. Many scientists believe that this is a necessary condition to create awareness of our senses. Stimulating the cells of the visual area in a person who is unconscious will not cause him or her to "see"—to have conscious vision. However, research has shown that people can accurately guess where an image is on a computer screen although they have no awareness of having seen it. Our brains apparently see things that we do not.

3. Finally, the various areas of visual processing are able to communicate with each other and with brain areas that are responsible for processing other functions, such as hearing. If you see a word, not only do you "see" it, but

Recap

— The part of the eye that contains the photo-receptors, the retina, is farthest in the back.

— The front of the eye, the cornea, bends light so it will pass through the pupil, the opening in the colored part, the iris. Behind the iris, the lens focuses light onto the retina, where the rods and cones (photoreceptors) will be stimulated.

— Rods are very sensitive to light; cones need much more light to be stimulated.

— When going from light to dark, one is temporarily blind while the rods manufacture more rhodopsin, which was used up by the bright light.

— Rods are not sensitive to wavelengths of light, but cones are. The mind perceives wavelengths of light as color. Therefore, cones = color.

— Humans have three kinds of cones (trichromatic): those most sensitive to short, medium, and long wavelengths. People who are missing one or more kinds of cones are color blind.

— The rods and cones send signals forward in the retina to bipolar cells, which send signals forward to ganglion cells, which send signals to the brain.

— The visual cells are specialized to respond to certain stimuli, and often work in teams. For example, in the opponent process, one group of cells fires while the opponents do not.

— A negative afterimage can be created by staring at a color (thus tiring the cells that see it), then looking at white. You will see the complementary color.

— Visual signals from the eye pass to the LGN of the thalamus and then to the occipital lobe where they are processed in layers of cells V1, V2, V3, and so on.

— Feedforward and feedback signals create a neural network that gives us conscious awareness of vision.

your brain connects the sight of the word with its sound, its meaning, its spelling, and memories that are stored in your brain that are associated with that word. The whole process is more than a network; it is multiple, interacting networks. Do you see?

Vision is a good example of a sensory system. All the senses work in essentially the same way. A sensory organ, such as the eye, ear, nose, tongue, or skin, contains receptors that transduce physical energy into neural signals that travel through a network of cells to a certain region of the brain. There a sensation is produced—a mental awareness, or feeling, of something—a sight, sound, smell, or taste. Complicated networks of cells connect the incoming signals with other brain regions. These brain networks use feedforward and feedback to produce sensations and interpret the incoming signals, giving them meaning. This is the process of perception.

PERCEPTION

"Beauty in things exists in the mind which contemplates them."
—DAVID HUME

The first questions that ancient thinkers pondered about psychology were issues of perception. How do we see and hear? How do objects in the world, things outside of our bodies, come to be represented in our minds? How can a mind perceive an apple, a bird, a face, or a mountain?

Perception is more than sensation. Perception involves interpretation. Two people can *sense* the same thing but *perceive* different things. Sensing and perceiving are not the same thing. For example, look at this stimulus:

B

Is it the letter B or the number 13? The same exact physical stimulus, the same sensation, can be interpreted in different ways. Do you know the funny childhood phrase "I scream for ice cream?" Say it fast. The sounds of "I scream" and "ice cream" can be exactly the same but be interpreted differently. In a scene in the Marx Brothers' film *A Night at the Opera*, Groucho and Chico are discussing a contract. Groucho explains a particular section: "It's all right, that's in every contract. It's what they call a sanity clause." Chico answers with a laugh, "You can't fool me. There ain't no Sanity Claus." Perception refers to the brain's process of interpreting sensory stimuli. The same sensations can be perceived with different meanings and interpretations.

Drawings can be made that are **impossible figures** that can't exist in reality. These drawings use principles of perception to trick us into perceiving things in an odd way. The artist **M. C. Escher** is best known for works of this nature. His books are widely available and make great gifts, especially for teens and young adults who are fascinated with these manipulations of the world of perception.

Perhaps you are familiar with drawings known as **magic eye** pictures, or **stereograms.** Although these pictures enjoy remarkable popularity today, the idea was discovered over a hundred years ago by a Scottish physicist named David Brewster. The pictures look 3-D because of how our brains create the perception of depth. In these pictures, the same image is repeated but separated by a small bit so that each eye can focus on it and our brains fuse them together and perceive them as if they are floating

FYI Gestalt psychology began with the problem of how a series of musical notes played in different keys can be recognized as the same melody. How do we do that?

in space. This illusion depends on the fact that our brains have stereo vision, a depth cue that is described below. For a complete description of how stereograms work, see Steven Pinker's book *How the Mind Works* (1997).

Basic Principles

Questions about perception go back thousands of years. However, the first people to study perception *scientifically* were the **Gestalt psychologists** of Germany, who worked primarily in the early twentieth century. They identified many psychological principles by which people perceive the world. Because of these principles a person could perceive an illusion. In fact, the study of illusions is one of the methods used by the Gestalt psychologists to identify the principles that brains use to form percepts.

Why do we perceive one thing rather than another? Why does the brain form a particular percept of a stimulus? One of the important cues that a brain uses to fashion a particular percept is the context of a stimulus. The surroundings matter. For example, in these two illustrations, the center figure is the same but is perceived differently because of the surrounding stimuli.

A I3 C   I2 I3 I4

A simple Gestalt principle is called **figure-ground.** This principle simply states that our brains organize the world of sensations into figures and backgrounds. That is, we pay attention to a certain stimulus (something sticks out), and we treat the surrounding stimuli as background elements. For instance, when you listen to someone who is talking to you at a noisy party, you concentrate on that person's voice and block out the other voices and noises. This is called the cocktail party effect. If you then hear someone else say your name, you shift your attention, making the other person's voice the figure (the thing you attend to), and the voice of the first person becomes part of the background. The figure-ground principle tells us that we pay attention to one thing at a time. That is why it is not good to daydream during class. It is best to keep your professor's voice as the figure and your own musings as ground!

Figures are perceived a certain way depending on the arrangement of elements. Things that are arranged close to one another are perceived as belonging together. This Gestalt principle is called **proximity.** Also, if things are similar to one another, our brains assume that they go together, and we perceive them as a group. This principle is called **similarity.** In other words, brains come with built-in perceptual mechanisms for grouping stimuli together to create a percept. **Closure** is another Gestalt principle. When we sense only partial information about a stimulus, such as a partial image, or part of a sentence, our brains fill in the gaps, or close the figure, so that we perceive it as a whole. That is, given slightly incomplete information a brain creates a complete perception; this is the

Some Gestalt principles of perception.

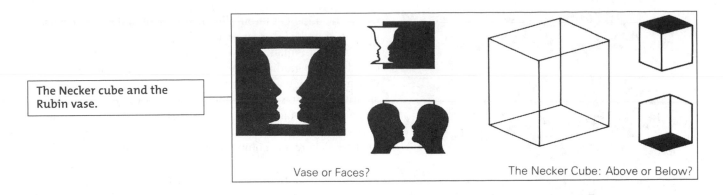

The Necker cube and the Rubin vase.

Vase or Faces?

The Necker Cube: Above or Below?

The old woman, young woman reversible figure.

principle of closure. Proximity, similarity, and closure are but three of the many Gestalt principles that brains use to perceptually organize our world of sensations.

Sometimes figures and grounds are ambiguous and can be perceived in more than one way. These instances are called **reversible figures.** In such cases, the brain determines that more than one perception is possible and therefore flips back and forth between the two. The **Necker cube** and the **Rubin vase** are the best-known examples.

Another example of figure-ground ambiguity is the drawing originally titled "My wife and my mother-in-law." This illustration is now usually called **old woman, young woman.** In this case it is possible to perceive two different faces, an old woman and a young woman.

These examples are fun, but they also make an important point: It is possible that two people will get two different perceptions from the same stimulus. During eyewitness testimony in a courtroom, for example, it is very possible for two people to report two very different observations of the same event. They each will say, "I saw it with my own eyes." But a bright psychology student will remind them that you *perceive* with your brain! Seeing and perceiving are not the same thing. You may see with your eyes, but you perceive with your brain. Perception refers to the interpretation that is given to a stimulus. Seeing or sensing means that we are aware of a stimulus, that it has stimulated our sensory system. You see, but what do you perceive? Get it? Do you see what I mean? Okay, perceive you later!

How Deep Is It?

One of the main acts of perception that brains perform, and one of the most studied aspects of perception, is **depth perception.** We don't call this process "depth seeing," because depth is a phenomenon that is created in our brains. We don't see in depth; we see the world flat. The retina of the eye receives two-dimensional information. It does not see in 3-D. Therefore, the brain must create the world of three dimensions. Brains

Connecting Concepts

Projective tests will be discussed in Chapter 7. These tests consist of ambiguous stimuli (such as inkblots) to which people respond. It is theorized that the responses tell something about the person's personality. Of course, different people can perceive the same stimulus in different ways. Do you think the perception that a person has is in any way a reflection of her or his personality?

We don't see depth, we perceive depth. Our brains use cues, such as texture, to determine what is near and what is far. Which depth perception cues can you find in this photo?

do this by using cues from the environment to determine what is close to us and what is far away.

One of the many cues that brains use to determine depth is called **texture gradient.** The change in texture as objects get farther from us signals a change in distance. **Linear perspective** is another depth cue. Parallel lines seem to converge in the distance; therefore, our brains are able to perceive the distance of objects relative to their positions with regard to those imaginary converging lines. There are a number of optical illusions that take advantage of the fact that our brains interpret the world a certain way; that is, our brains use predictable principles to make sense of incoming sensory information.

Another depth perception cue is the obvious fact that objects that are nearer to us seem larger; that is, they make a larger image on the retina than do objects that are farther away. When a person walks away from you, the image the person makes on your retina gets smaller, but your brain assumes that the decrease in **apparent size** is the result of distance from you, not because this person is shrinking. In fact, researcher Allan Dobbins and colleagues (1998) recently reported finding "nearness cells" and "farness cells" in the brains of monkeys. There is no doubt that human brains have similar cells. These cells help the brain to perceive depth by using incoming cues. Interestingly, people who were blind from birth but were given operations later in life that allowed them to see did not show this **size constancy.** They thought that the cars they saw from their hospital room windows were toy cars that they could reach out and pick up! Apparently, size constancy is something that develops in infancy.

One method that psychologists have used to measure depth perception in babies and in lower animals is known as a **visual cliff.** A clear glass tabletop has a checkerboard below it, but the sizes of the squares vary in a manner that makes it appear that there is a drop-off—a cliff—in one place. Will a baby or a lower animal cross the visual cliff? If they do, it means that they do not have the ability to perceive depth. By the time they can crawl, about six months, babies will not cross the deep side of the visual cliff, meaning that babies at this young age apparently can perceive depth, at least in this circumstance.

The Funny Room

A psychologist (and former painter) named Adelbert Ames built an oddly shaped room that takes advantage of depth perception cues and, in fact, looks normal. The back of the **Ames room** is shaped like a trapezoid: One side is much taller than the other, and the edges of the ceiling and floor are not horizontal, they slope down from the tall side to the short side. However, the short side is placed just close enough to an observer to be the same apparent size (makes the same size image on the retina) as the long side. The room appears to be a normal room because the brain is receiving cues that resemble a normal room. The funny thing is that when objects are placed in the two back corners of the room, one looks much smaller than the other. The room seems like a normal room; therefore, the observer assumes that the two objects are the same distance from him or her. In fact, one object is much closer than the other. Because the observer's brain assumes that the objects are equidistant, the closer object is perceived as much larger, and the more distant object is perceived as much smaller. Some movies use such optical tricks. For example, an Ames room appears in the Dutch film *The Sea That Thinks* (2000) by Gert de Graaff.

Some depth perception cues require having only one eye, such as texture, linear perspective, and size constancy. Those cues are called **monocular.** Another monocular cue is **motion parallax.** When you turn your head, you will notice that things that are close to you seem to move in a wider arc than do things that are far away from you. Put your finger in front of your face, and move your head back and forth. Your finger appears to move much more than do objects that are far away. That is motion parallax. This fact is used by your brain to help determine how far away something is. If you turn your head while viewing an object and its image moves a great distance, it must be close to you, and vice versa.

We also get information about depth because we have two eyes placed apart from each other on our faces. Such **binocular cues** include **binocular disparity,** the fact that each eye sees a slightly different image of an object than the other eye. Put your finger near your face and look at it alternately with each eye. You get two different views of your finger because your eyes are located in different places. **Convergence** is another binocular cue. Your eyes swivel inward a good deal more when focusing on something near than they do when focusing on something far. The extent to which the muscles need to turn the eyes inward is a cue your brain uses to determine how far away something is. This is known as **stereoscopic vision,** or simply **stereo vision.**

In fact, newborns do not have stereo vision; that is something that develops after three or four months of age. Brains need time to develop, and neurons are still forming networks far after birth. The cells in the visual cortex of the brain gradually come to respond to one eye or the other, a physiological necessity for stereo vision. Early experiences, of course, can interfere with this process. A baby who has the vision in one eye blocked early in life may develop permanent stereoblindness.

The Physiology of Perception

Certain regions of the brain are devoted to processing information about each of the senses. Visual information, for example, is processed by cells in the occipital lobe. Some cells receive information from the left eye, some from the right, and some from both (binocular cells). The various layers of cells in the visual area of the brain interpret the incoming signals. Auditory processing, on the other hand, occurs in the temporal lobe. However, there are brain cells that coordinate the various sensory

Psychologists use a visual cliff to study the development of depth perception.

The Ames room is a trapezoid shape, but appears normal from a point directly in front. The person in the left corner appears smaller because he is actually much farther away from the viewer.

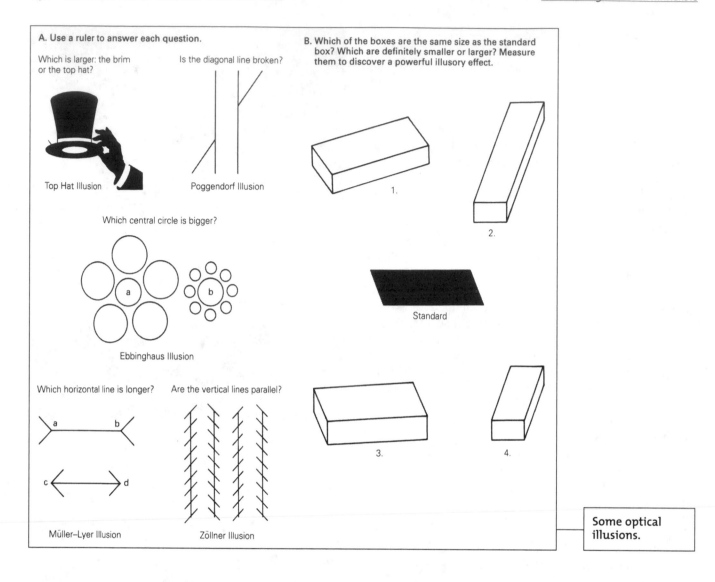

A. Use a ruler to answer each question.

Which is larger: the brim or the top hat?

Top Hat Illusion

Is the diagonal line broken?

Poggendorf Illusion

Which central circle is bigger?

Ebbinghaus Illusion

Which horizontal line is longer?

Müller–Lyer Illusion

Are the vertical lines parallel?

Zöllner Illusion

B. Which of the boxes are the same size as the standard box? Which are definitely smaller or larger? Measure them to discover a powerful illusory effect.

1.

2.

Standard

3.

4.

Some optical illusions.

areas, and there even are cells that receive information from more than one sense (multisensory cells). The frontal lobe is a major brain area in determining which cells get our attention.

Researchers have found that if each eye is presented with a different stimulus, the brain will flip back and forth between the two perceptions. This is similar to what happens with reversible figures, as described above. For example, if an image of a dog is shown to the right eye and the image of a cat is shown to the left eye, the person's perception will not be some weird hybrid animal but will shift back and forth between a dog and a cat.

Scientists have recorded brain cell activity during such **binocular rivalry** to determine which brain cells are responsible for the shift in perception (Logothetis, 1999). Brain cells in many regions of the visual pathway were found to change their firing when the perception changed. However, the cells that were most often associated with a change in perception were located far downstream in the medial temporal lobe, in the layer of cells called V5. On the other hand, cells that perceive depth are more concentrated in the V3 layer.

So apparently what is happening is that the brain uses certain cells, predominantly those in layer V3, to figure out depth perception. However, when there is conflict between two perceptions, other brain cell networks are involved, particularly those in region V5. These cells help to determine what we pay attention to. Perception is accomplished by teams of brain cells working together in networks. Communication between cells is essential. Our perceptions are created by the teamwork of various cells located in various layers of our brains' structures.

Recap

— Perception is the brain's act of interpreting or making sense out of sensory information. For example, the same stimulus can be perceived differently depending on factors such as the context or surroundings.

— The Gestalt psychologists attempted to find the basic principles of perception. Some Gestalt principles are figure-ground, proximity, similarity, closure, and reversible figures.

— Depth is a good example of perception. Our eyes see the world flat, but our brains use cues to create a 3-D percept.

— Some monocular depth perception cues are texture, linear perspective, apparent size, and motion parallax. Some binocular cues are binocular disparity and convergence.

— Psychologists use the Ames room (a distorted room) and the visual cliff to study depth perception.

— During binocular rivalry, brains switch percepts. Brain cell activity can be recorded to determine which cells are responsible for perception.

STATES OF CONSCIOUSNESS

"When I woke up this morning my girlfriend asked me, 'Did you sleep good?' I said, 'No, I made a few mistakes.'"
—STEVEN WRIGHT

Sensations and perceptions are the elements of our conscious awareness of our surroundings, and naturally, psychologists study the various states of consciousness that people experience. In the movie *Altered States* (1980), a researcher enters a sensory deprivation tank to see what will go through his mind if all sensory information is blocked. In fact, some psychologists once did such a thing. In the film, the man devolves into an ape—I'm pretty sure this part of the movie is fiction. But it's not fiction that some psychologists are very interested in studying **altered states of consciousness:** ways in which our consciousness is modified or unusual.

Have you ever been driving for a long time and suddenly became aware that you hadn't been paying attention for quite a while, that you had to look around to figure out where you were, that your mind had been off in some trancelike, inattentive, daydreaming world? Yet, remarkably, you didn't drive off the road. What you experienced was an alteration in your consciousness called **divided consciousness.** There are many such examples.

Blinded by the Light

There are people who are blind and don't know it! This is called **Anton's syndrome** or **blindness denial.** Brain damage deep in the visual pathway, but not in the primary visual cortex (the outer surface of the occipital lobe), causes this bizarre condition. Patients have consciousness of vision but lack the ability to process visual information entirely. They overestimate their ability to see. "What am I wearing?" the doctor asks. "A blue shirt with a red striped tie," the patient replies. "No," the doctor says, "I have a white shirt and no tie." The patient says, "Oh, I see that now. The reflection from the light fooled me."

Other people have the opposite problem—they can see but don't know it! Damage to an area of the primary visual cortex combined with no damage to the cells further along the visual pathway causes such patients to lack awareness of vision in a certain region of their visual field, yet they can respond to stimuli in that area. This condition has the paradoxical name, **blindsight.** While looking at a screen where images are projected, they say they can't see anything in one specific area. However, when asked to guess what is in that area, amazingly, they usually get it right. Visual information is getting to the deeper cells of the visual processing area of the brain, but the person is unaware of it. In fact, all normal people have such a thing, it is just very minor. We all see things that we are unaware of.

There are other people with damage to specific areas of their brains that causes them to ignore certain visual information, for example, things on the left or even parts of their bodies. This is called **neglect.** One woman tried to throw her leg out of bed because she thought it was a foreign object. Another patient thought she was hallucinating when her friends were speaking to her because they were standing on her left and she was visually unaware of them. In **alien hand syndrome,** a patient is unaware of the movements of one of his hands and finds it doing things unexpectedly. A man riding a bus felt a tug on his pant leg. He looked down and was surprised to find that it was his own hand doing the pulling.

There are many other examples of disconnections between behavior and consciousness. By **consciousness,** we mean awareness; that is, your conscious mind is your personal, private, subjective awareness of sensations, perceptions, memories, thoughts, and identity. But you are not conscious of everything happening in your brain. There are many things that are unconscious, as the strange examples above demonstrate.

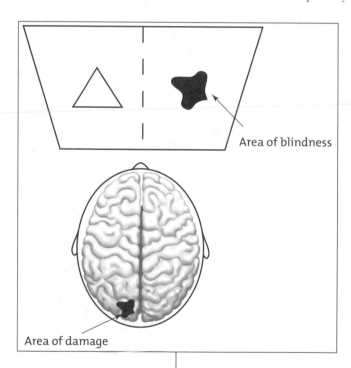

Area of blindness

Area of damage

In blindsight, a person has damage in his or her visual processing area. The person has no awareness of information that is in the visual field corresponding to the area of damage in the brain. However, some of that information does reach the brain through other pathways and the person can respond to it, though is visually unaware of it.

Somehow, some things a brain does become conscious. It's a little like a computer. The electrical actions in the hardware of the computer perform many computations. But only some information appears on the monitor screen. The images on the screen are illusions of the happenings in the computer. In this analogy, the computer is your brain and the monitor screen is your conscious mind (Norretranders, 1998). A brain does not contain images, sounds, or feelings. A brain consists of electrical and chemical happenings. Sometimes our brains make us conscious of things, and sometimes they don't. Consciousness is only one of many brain states and, in fact, consists of many different states itself.

How does consciousness arise? There is no one part of the brain that produces consciousness—there is no consciousness center. Rather, awareness is a multifaceted condition that arises when a brain is in a certain physiological state or states. Researchers do not yet know all the details of the physiology of consciousness, but they are gradually untangling this mystery (Hinrichs, 2000, 2002). For example, studies on binocular rivalry (mentioned above) are pinpointing cells that are active when an animal's awareness of a perception changes.

Consciousness lies on a continuum; it is not a uniform state. One can be drowsy, daydreaming, in a trance, or one can be alert, hyperattentive, concentrating—or anyplace in between. But conscious states differ not only in intensity; they also vary in quality. That is, different states of consciousness feel qualitatively different to us. Psychologists have traditionally divided consciousness into these various states, such as sleep, dreaming, hypnosis, and those produced by drugs. Let's look at each of these.

A British neurologist during World War I noticed that soldiers who had been wounded in the back of the head were able to react to objects in front of them yet denied being able to see them. Psychologist Larry Weisenkrantz studied this phenomenon in the 1970s and gave it the name *blindsight*. The same dissociation can occur in other senses. For example, people can have "deaf hearing" or "numb touch."

Perchance to Sleep

The amount that people sleep varies tremendously: Babies sleep 16 hours a day, while there are rare adults who seem to get along on only 15 minutes per night. The record for going without sleep is 11 days. In fact, sleep deprivation is a common problem, and research shows that average adults who got only six hours of sleep a night for two weeks performed poorly on tests of brain functioning.

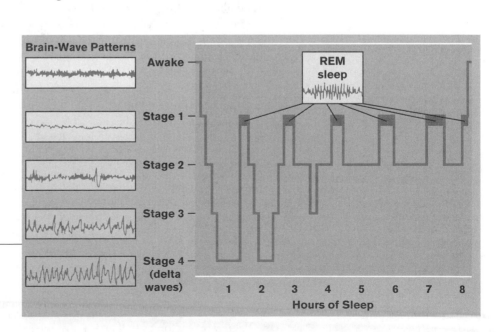

Brain waves during stages of sleep and the typical occurrence of the stages during a night of sleep.

Researchers divide sleep into stages based on brain waves (the electrical patterns measured by EEG). **Alpha waves** occur when a person is awake and relaxed with eyes closed; **beta waves** occur when a person is alert and aroused. The transition from awake to sleep is sometimes known as **hypnogogic sleep. Delta waves** are the slowest, most regular waves and occur most frequently during deepest sleep.

When a person falls asleep, brain waves get slower and slower. But eventually, brain waves get very active, almost as if the person is awake, and the sleeper's eyes dart around rapidly. This is **REM** (rapid eye movement; pronounced "rem") sleep. Other sleep is called **NREM** (pronounced "non-rem"). NREM sleep is divided into four stages, simply called 1, 2, 3, and 4, with 4 being the deepest, that is, having the slowest, most regular brain waves. People cycle through these stages four or five times during a typical night, passing from NREM 1 to 2 to 3 to 4, then to REM. Each stage lasts about 10 to 20 minutes, and a cycle through the stages lasts about 90 minutes on the average, though REM periods increase in length later in the sleep cycle as time spent in stages 3 and 4 decreases. A typical night might include two hours of REM sleep. Babies have more. In fact, the amount of both REM and NREM declines with age.

Because brain waves are active during REM, they look as they would if the person was awake. Therefore, REM is also called **paradoxical sleep** (a paradox is a contradiction). Also, during REM, a sleeper's autonomic nervous system is very active. One of the most interesting physiological events during REM is **atonia**—the sleeper's large, voluntary muscles are paralyzed! A switch in the brainstem stops electrical signals from going to the skeletal muscles, apparently so that the sleeper won't get up and act out his or her dreams. Only the eyes follow the dream. This means that sleepwalking occurs during NREM sleep. Sometimes **myoclonia** occurs when the brainstem switch is reconnecting—the person's body suddenly jerks. A sudden electrical signal is sent from the brain to the muscles. Has that happened to you? Or have you perhaps seen your father falling asleep in his chair when he had myoclonia?

When people are awakened during REM, they often report that they were dreaming, so REM is often thought of as dream sleep. However, people often report dreaming when awakened from NREM sleep too. But those dreams seem to be less vivid and storylike. No one knows why we dream, though there are several theories. Psychoanalysts (Freud) believe that dreams are clues to the content of the unconscious mind. That is, dreams have certain disguised meanings. There is not good evidence for this theory, though dreams do seem to reflect things a person is worried or concerned about or things that have happened recently.

Some theorists believe that dreams are just meaningless junk that results when the brain is doing its biological stuff. That is, dreaming is just the brain's way of dumping stuff, of cleaning out brain connections. However, most psychologists today think that sleep and dreaming play a role in learning and memory, that dreams result from the brain's processing and storing of information. There is some evidence linking sleep and dreaming to learning and memory, but there are also studies that do not support this theory (Maquet, 2001; Stickgold et al., 2001; Siegel, 2001). For example, when people are taught a task and then allowed to have REM sleep, they remember the skill better than if they were not allowed REM sleep. Rats that learned to run a maze showed the same brain activity while in REM sleep as when they were running the maze (Louie & Wilson, 2001). Another study found that people who had REM, even during a nap, had better memory of visual material (Mednick et al., 2003). On the other hand, certain medications that inhibit REM sleep do not affect people's memories at all. At present, the facts are somewhat contradictory. Sleep and dreaming likely do contribute to the physiology of learning and memory for certain activities or in certain as yet unknown ways.

Hypnosis

An interesting state of consciousness that is sometimes confused with sleep is hypnosis. There are few topics that are as misunderstood or misrepresented as hypnosis. For instance, movies often portray hypnosis as a magical means of controlling people. But this is not correct.

Hypnosis is a trancelike state of consciousness in which a person is very much awake but becomes highly suggestible. People differ in how easily they will follow suggestions. Some people are readily hypnotizable, others cannot be hypnotized at all, and most fall somewhere in between. Hypnotized people have different brain images than do people who are pretending to be hypnotized, so hypnosis seems to be different than faking or role-playing. Also, contrary to popular belief, people who are hypnotized are aware of what they are doing and will not do something awful (unless they would normally do it).

Hypnosis can help people control pain but in general is not a good method of helping people with disorders, particularly serious problems such as schizophrenia, drug addictions, and depression. Here is a table that corrects the major myths about hypnosis (Nash, 2001).

> ***Connecting Concepts***
>
> The history of how hypnosis was developed and became a technique used in psychotherapy is discussed in Chapter 10.

TABLE 4.2 Facts about Hypnosis

1. People vary widely in their ability to be hypnotized—some very easily, others not at all.
2. Hypnosis has nothing to do with sleep; the subjects are awake.
3. Hypnosis is *not* the result of faking, simple relaxation, good imagination, or the placebo effect.
4. It *cannot* help people relive the past, make them do immoral things, or improve their strength or abilities.

   Hypnosis is *not* a good treatment for most problems, though it can sometimes relieve pain.
5. Subjects do *not* lose control of themselves; it is not dangerous.
6. Hypnosis does *not* improve memory, and may, instead, cause false memories.
7. Hypnotists do *not* have special powers or skills, and people who are hypnotizable do *not* have certain kinds of personalities.

Psychoactive Drugs

There are a number of substances that influence and alter consciousness. These **psychoactive drugs** affect consciousness because they affect the brain. They affect the brain in a number of ways, such as by mimicking natural neurotransmitters, interfering with the reuptake of neurotransmitters, or changing brain cell function. It appears that all psychoactive drugs activate a series of brain areas known as the **pleasure pathway**. These areas are located in the middle of the brain, the hypothalamus, and the prefrontal cortex. All drugs and experiences that produce pleasure act on this pathway.

Psychoactive substances are so commonly used by people around the world that they obviously have some rewarding or pleasurable effects. However, such substances also can cause damage and addiction. The problems associated with drug use include (a) side effects, such as impaired judgment, increased aggression, and memory difficulties; (b) damage to body organs; (c) tolerance, that is, needing more drugs to get the same effect; and (d) dependence, that is, needing or craving the drug.

Here is how tolerance and dependence work: When drugs alter neurotransmitter balances in the brain, cells then adjust and change their normal proportions of chemicals. It then takes more of the drug to get the same effect (the brain has gotten used to having the drug), and in the absence of the drug, brain cells are deficient and need the drug to function properly. For example, cocaine slows the reuptake of dopamine. Therefore, there is more dopamine in the synapse than normal. Brain cells then adjust by making less dopamine. So without cocaine, a person feels down. Scientists distinguish **physical dependence** (need for the drug) from **psychological dependence** (craving for the drug).

Despite the fact that drugs alter consciousness in ways that many people seek out, drugs can potentially have very dangerous consequences. Nicotine is a stimulant that is highly addictive and dangerous. In the United States, about 1,000 people die each day from diseases caused by smoking. About two-thirds of fatal auto accidents, spouse beatings, and murders and half of child abuse cases involve alcohol. About 10% of adults in the United States are dependent on alcohol. The cost of drugs in human lives and suffering is enormous. The pleasurable effects of drugs are immediate, but the damage they do often is long-term.

Now we present a brief description of the most commonly used psychoactive drugs.

Alcohol

Probably the most commonly used drug in the world, alcohol is mostly a nervous system **depressant**; that is, it slows down the nervous system. In fact, large quantities of alcohol can kill by slowing body functions too much. People think of alcohol as a stimulant because it reduces inhibitions, making users more likely to do things they normally would not. Alcohol affects many parts of the body and brain, so its effects on mind and behavior are widespread. Alcohol affects motor control, memory, depth perception, spatial perception, ability to tell rhythm and pitch, smell, taste, time perception, night vision, and emotional stability. Because it reduces inhibitions, alcohol users often show increased aggression, violence, abuse, and hostility and tend to be less concerned about harmful consequences.

Alcohol has a global effect on the brain, influencing regions such as the frontal lobe (judgment and decision making), cerebellum (balance and motor control), and brainstem (breathing, body temperature, etc.). The amount of alcohol necessary to cause problems varies from person to person and depends on a number of biological factors. Women generally attain a higher level of alcohol in the blood than do men when they drink the same amount of alcohol. Digestive enzymes influence how much alcohol enters the bloodstream. Because enzymes and other physiological processes are highly influenced by heredity, there is a genetic component to alcoholism. That is, some people are more likely to become dependent on alcohol because of their physiological makeup (Gordis, 1996; Foroud, 1999). Of course, social situations and family and cultural factors play a huge role in alcohol abuse. For instance, binge drinking is a serious problem among young people in the United States, one that is called an "epidemic" by the National Center on Addiction and Substance Abuse (2002). Drinking large amounts of alcohol in a short period of time is very dangerous. A federal task force estimated that 1,400 college students are killed each year in alcohol-related accidents (Hingson, 2002).

Cocaine

Cocaine is one of a group of drugs known as **stimulants** because they stimulate, or speed up, the nervous system. Caffeine and nicotine are mild stimulants. Dependence on these substances is common. A more powerful stimulant is cocaine, which is derived from the leaves of the coca plant.

The main effect of cocaine on the brain is to interfere with the reuptake of certain neurotransmitters, primarily dopamine. Because reuptake is inhibited, there is more neurotransmitter chemical in the synapse to excite the receiving cell. The pleasure pathway is most affected; the result is feelings of euphoria, omnipotence, well-being, and energy (Brick & Erickson, 1998). As the drug wears off, a period of depression called a "crash" occurs. Heavy users may suffer personality changes, and addiction can readily occur.

Until 1914, cocaine was an ingredient in soft drinks such as Coca Cola. Though illegal, cocaine use in the United States today is very common, especially among teens and young adults; 10% report using cocaine at least once, and 5% report using cocaine monthly.

Marijuana

The active ingredient in marijuana is tetrahydrocannabinol (THC), a mild hallucinogen. This chemical works on the brain by stimulating THC receptors. But why are there THC receptors in the brain? There must be a natural substance in the brain for which those receptors are designed. In 1992, that chemical was found and dubbed *anandamide*. The THC molecule has a shape very similar to anandamide and therefore binds to anandamide receptors in the brain, causing an alteration in consciousness that is pleasurable because it increases dopamine activity.

Two common effects of THC, impairment of memory and an increase in hunger (the "munchies"), are produced because marijuana acts primarily on the brain area involved in learning and memory (the hippocampus) and because it influences the hormone leptin, which is involved in hunger (Wilson & Nicoll, 2002).

Marijuana has been known for nearly 5,000 years and is common in many cultures of the world but was outlawed in the United States in 1937. Some side effects of marijuana include problems in attention, memory, and perception; impaired immune system; lung disease; interference with hormones; and difficulty in judging time and distance. A small percentage of marijuana users, about 10% to 15%, become addicted to the substance. Nearly 100,000 Americans each year go to clinics to try to quit using marijuana (Blakeslee, 1997).

FYI

The term *anandamide* comes from the Sanskrit word *ananda*, which means "bliss." Brain chemicals that are mimicked by marijuana are called cannabinoids or endocannabinoids. They are involved in brain systems for appetite, memory, and pain. Chemicals that resemble anandamide were found in dark chocolate in 1996, causing the media to suggest that eating chocolate might stimulate the brain in the same way that marijuana does. Scientists say that not only are the concentrations vastly different, but also the compounds in chocolate do not have the same effect on the brain as marijuana.

Opiates

An **opiate** (also called a narcotic) is a drug derived from opium, the juice of a poppy plant. The main active ingredient in opium is morphine, a chemical that is a powerful pain reliever. Heroin is a version of morphine that is much more potent (it acts faster on the brain). Like marijuana, opiates influences consciousness by mimicking natural brain chemicals. The natural substances are known as **endorphins** (literally, "inner morphines"). So opiates influence the brain by binding to chemical receptors that exist for the natural relief of pain.

Opiates, particularly morphine and codeine, are used around the world as pain relievers. These drugs are also used to alter consciousness because they give a feeling of pleasure and euphoria in most users. Heroin is highly addictive, and withdrawal symptoms are quite severe.

Hallucinogens

Certain drugs cause such severe alterations in consciousness that they are known as **hallucinogens.** These drugs produce shifts in perception that result in illusions, hallucinations, and similar experiences. LSD (lysergic acid diethylamide, or acid) is the most notorious of these drugs.

LSD is an artificially produced substance (it does not exist in nature) that acts on the brain primarily by binding to serotonin receptors. Because LSD floods the serotonin synapses, its precise effects vary from person to person and are unpredictable for any individual. For example, both pleasant and unpleasant experiences can occur (what are called "good trips" and "bad trips"). During a bad trip, a person may experience fear of going insane,

FYI

GHB is being used in a new drug, Xyrem, for the treatment of narcolepsy, a sleep disorder that causes people to have "sleep attacks" in which they suddenly lose muscle tone. The person might fall down when he or she laughs or feels a strong emotion. This is called cataplexy and is similar to the atonia of REM sleep. People with narcolepsy have low levels of a brain chemical called hypocretin.

paranoia, a sense of unreality, disturbing hallucinations, and distortions of body parts. Deaths have occurred from bad trips, for example, from jumping out of a window.

One of the most disturbing side effects of LSD is a **flashback,** in which users later experience hallucinations without the drug. These can occur weeks or months after drug use and may be stimulated by darkness, going to sleep, stress, or driving.

LSD is one of the club drugs, a group of drugs so called because they are used by teens and young adults at dance parties such as "raves" or "trances," at bars, and at dance clubs. One of the most common, ecstasy (MDMA), is a stimulant and hallucinogen that can damage brain cells as well as cause serious body organ damage and sometimes death. It was found to be toxic to both dopamine and serotonin neurons in monkeys (Ricaurte et al., 2002), though the findings are controversial (Mithoefer et al., 2003). Despite the fact that ecstasy impairs memory, teens see it as a safe drug. Twelve percent of teens say that they have tried it, ranking third behind alcohol (53%) and marijuana (41%). In fact, although use of most drugs has declined among teens, ecstasy use has increased. GHB (G, liquid ecstasy) is often manufactured in homes from recipes found on the Internet. It is a depressant, is often mixed with alcohol, and in high doses can cause coma or death. It is sometimes known as a "date rape" drug.

Rohypnol is a relatively new club drug, a type of antianxiety drug similar to Valium. Taken with alcohol, rohypnol can cause severe amnesia and is therefore known as the "forget me" pill. It is reportedly used in date rapes and sexual assaults. Ketamine (K, Special K) is an anesthetic used primarily by veterinarians. It can be smoked, injected, or drunk. Its effects include high blood pressure, amnesia, depression, and impaired attention, learning, memory, motor ability, and breathing.

Club drugs are used for their intoxicating effects or for relaxation or stimulation. They are all potentially dangerous, can cause brain damage and death. Unfortunately, many club drugs are colorless, odorless, and tasteless and therefore can be used to secretly sedate others.

Recap

— Consciousness refers to our awareness of things. Altered states of consciousness include sleep, dreaming, hypnosis, and drug-induced states.

— Divided consciousness occurs when a person's awareness is separated in some way. Examples are Anton's syndrome, in which a person is aware of vision that is not there; blindsight, in which a person has no awareness of vision that is there; and neglect, in which a person has no awareness of certain sights or even parts of the body.

— Consciousness arises from certain brain states; it is a continuum consisting of many different states that vary in quality.

— Sleep is divided into stages based on brain waves. During REM sleep, brain waves are active, muscles are paralyzed, and people often report dreaming. NREM is divided into stages 1, 2, 3, and 4, each progressively deeper.

— Many psychologists believe that sleep and dreaming are important for learning and memory, though current data are contradictory on this question.

— Hypnosis is a trance state in which people become very open to suggestions. It is not a type of sleep, cannot control people, and is not very useful for helping treat disorders, other than in pain control.

— Psychoactive drugs alter consciousness by affecting brain chemicals; they act on the brain's pleasure pathway.

— Alcohol is a depressant that has widespread effects on the brain. Cocaine is a stimulant that increases dopamine activity. Marijuana mimics a natural brain chemical (anandamide), as do opiates, such as heroin (endorphins). Hallucinogens affect serotonin and produce marked shifts in perception.

STUDY GUIDE FOR CHAPTER 4:
SENSATION, PERCEPTION, AND CONSCIOUSNESS

Key terms and names (Make flash cards.)

transduction
sensory receptors
sensation
perception
audition
cochlea
basilar membrane
decibel
gustation
taste bud
umami
olfaction
Ruffini cylinders
sensory adaptation
Krause end bulbs
gates
proprioceptive
kinesthesis
vestibular organ
semicircular canals
psychophysics
Gustav Theodor Fechner
Fechner's law
sensitivity
absolute threshold
signal detection theory
difference threshold
just-noticeable difference (JND)
Ernst Heinrich Weber
Weber's law
Weber fraction
cornea
iris
pupil
lens
accommodation
presbyopia
cataracts
aqueous humor
glaucoma
vitreous humor

floaters
retina
photoreceptors
rods
cones
fovea
rhodopsin
dark adaptation
long-wavelength cone
medium-wavelength cone
short-wavelength cone
trichromatic
color blindness
dichromat
monochromat
David Hubel
Torsten Wiesel
feature detectors
opponent process
afterimage
negative color afterimage
bipolar cells
ganglion cells
optic nerve
optic disk
blind spot
lateral geniculate nucleus (LGN)
feedforward
feedback
impossible figures
M. C. Escher
magic eye (stereograms)
Gestalt psychologists
figure-ground
proximity
similarity
closure
reversible figures
Necker cube
Rubin vase
old woman, young woman

depth perception
texture gradient
linear perspective
apparent size
size constancy
visual cliff
Ames room
monocular cue
motion parallax
binocular cue
binocular disparity
convergence
stereoscopic (stereo) vision
binocular rivalry
altered states of consciousness
divided consciousness
Anton's syndrome (blindness denial)
blindsight
neglect
alien hand syndrome
consciousness
alpha wave
beta wave
hypnogogic sleep
delta wave
REM
NREM
paradoxical sleep
atonia
myoclonia
hypnosis
psychoactive drugs
pleasure pathway
physical dependence
psychological dependence
depressant
stimulant
opiate
endorphin
hallucinogen
flashback

Fill in the blank

1. The conversion of one form of energy to another is called _____.

2. The mental experience produced by the brain when we sense something is called a _____.

3. Brains give meaning to sensations. Brains interpret the incoming sensory signals. This is called _____.

4. Hearing is accomplished by cells in the _____ that are aligned along a membrane called the _____ membrane.

5. Taste is scientifically called _____.

6. _____ is the only sense that is directly connected to the cerebral cortex. The other senses pass through the _____.

7. When both the warm and cold receptors are stimulated, we experience the sensation of _____.

8. _____ signals are sent to the brain through a series of "gates" that chemically control the degree to which the signal reaches the brain.

9. When the stimulus for a sensation is coming from inside the body, the sense is called _____.

10. The _____ sense is the sense of body position and body movement.

11. The _____ organ is in the inner ear but has nothing to do with hearing. It is shaped like three curved tubes, called _____ canals.

12. The branch of psychology that studies the senses is called _____. This subfield was founded by Gustav Theodor _____.

13. The _____ threshold is the level of energy that is just enough to stimulate a sensory receptor.

14. Included in psychophysics is the study of why people detect a stimulus in some situations but not in others. This area of study is called _____ theory.

15. The _____ threshold refers to the amount of change in the intensity of a stimulus that is required for people to notice that the level has changed. The difference or change that is required is called a _____ difference or _____.

16. Weber's law is written: _____.

17. The _____ is the front of the eye, the window on the world.

18. Behind the cornea is the _____, which is shaped like a doughnut or inner tube. The hole in the middle is the _____.

19. The lens must also be elastic. Muscles in the eye pull on the lens, making it change in thickness. This process is called _____.

20. An old joke says that when your arms aren't long enough, you need glasses. This condition is called _____, which literally means "old eyes."

21. Sometimes the lens develops patchy white spots called _____.

22. The fluid that lies in the front of the eye between the cornea and the lens is called the _____ _____.

23. Another fluid in the eye lies between the lens and the back of the eye. It is called the _____ _____.

24. The very back of the eye, the inside back layer, is the _____.

25. The cells in the back of the eye that respond to light are called _____. They come in two types, _____ and _____.

26. The area of best vision is where the cones are most densely packed together, an area in the middle of the retina known as the _____.

27. Rods contain a chemical called _____ that is very sensitive to light.

28. There are _____ kinds of cones in the normal human eye. This system is called _____.

29. A _____ has only one type of cone in the eyes and therefore sees the world in black and white and shades of gray.

30. Scientists have discovered that many cells in the nervous system have specialized jobs. For example, certain cells in a cat's eye fire differentially to different stimuli. Such cells are called _____ _____.

31. Some cells work against each other. Color vision is a good example of this process, known as the _____ process.

32. In front of the rods and cones is a layer of cells called _____ cells. They receive signals from the rods and cones.

33. The cells in the very front of the retina are called _____ cells. Their axons come together and form the _____ nerve.

34. The place in the eye is called the _____ disk has a field of vision known as the _____ _____.

35. A particular region of the thalamus specializes in visual information. It is called the _____ _____.

36. The first people to study perception *scientifically* were the _____ psychologists.

37. Things that are arranged close to one another are perceived as belonging together. This Gestalt principle is called _____.

38. The Necker cube and the Rubin vase are the best-known examples of _____ figures.
39. Parallel lines seem to converge in the distance, a depth cue known as _____.
40. One method that psychologists use to measure depth perception in babies and in lower animals has a clear glass tabletop with a checkerboard below it. This is called the _____.
41. The back of the _____ room is shaped like a trapezoid; one side is much taller than the other and the edges of the ceiling and floor are not horizontal, they slope down from the tall side to the short side.
42. Two binocular cues are _____ _____ and _____.
43. In _____ _____ _____, a different image is presented to each eye.
44. When consciousness is changed in some way, it is called an _____ state.

45. Specific damage to the visual part of the brain can affect the awareness of vision, but some visual information can still be processed by the brain in the strange case of _____.
46. REM is also called _____ sleep because brain waves make the person seem _____.
47. Less storylike dreams occur during _____ sleep.
48. _____ is a trancelike state of consciousness in which people are very _____.
49. Alcohol is a nervous system _____, while cocaine is a _____ that increases activity of the brain chemical _____.
50. Marijuana and opiates act on the brain by _____ neurotransmitters.

Matching

1. cornea _____
2. Fechner _____
3. lens _____
4. retina _____
5. Weber _____
6. JND _____
7. cones _____
8. absolute threshold _____
9. gustation _____
10. ganglion cells _____
11. Rubin vase _____
12. convergence _____
13. gates _____
14. cochlea _____
15. presbyopia _____
16. perception _____
17. olfaction _____
18. blindsight _____
19. opiate _____
20. cocaine _____

a. optic nerve
b. depth perception cue
c. heroin
d. difference that is noticeable
e. old eyes
f. pain
g. psychophysics
h. difference threshold fractions
i. cataracts
j. figure-ground reversible
k. trichromatic
l. increase dopamine activity
m. taste
n. hearing
o. divided consciousness
p. smell
q. interpretation of sensations
r. front of eye
s. back of eye
t. smallest noticeable stimulus

Multiple choice

1. A book designer wants to add the illusion of depth to some illustrations. Which principle might be used?
   a. Weber's law
   b. linear perspective
   c. absolute threshold
   d. size constancy
2. In an Ames room, person A seems smaller than person B because person A is
   a. farther away from the viewer
   b. lower on the horizon
   c. partially blocked from view
   d. an illusion
3. An engineer designing the dials on an instrument panel needs to calculate how much the needles must move for users to notice the movement. Which principle will be used?
   a. binocular disparity
   b. difference threshold
   c. opponent process
   d. stereotaxic vision
4. The optic nerve is made up of _____ from the ganglion cells.
   a. neurotransmitters
   b. myelin
   c. dendrites
   d. axons

5. The opening into the eye is the
   a. pupil   b. lens
   c. retina   d. blind spot

6. Weber's law is about
   a. difference thresholds
   b. absolute thresholds
   c. depth perception
   d. visual illusions

7. A person watching a bird flying does not perceive a flat landscape in which everything is equally noticed. Instead, the bird stands out against the sky; its movements appear smooth and flowing. This perception is called
   a. focused attention
   b. figure-ground
   c. binocular rivalry
   d. magic eye

8. Because our sense of cold is subject to _____, jumping into a lake seems worse when we first go out in it than after a few minutes.
   a. sensory adaptation
   b. Gestalt closure
   c. Weber's law
   d. sensory constancy

9. The process of transduction takes place at the
   a. sensory receptors
   b. thalamus
   c. optic nerve
   d. axon divergence

10. If the Weber fraction for brightness is 1/60, what is the JND for a light that is 30 photons bright?
    a. 4 photons
    b. 1/2 photon
    c. 2 photons
    d. 120 photons

11. The basilar membrane is used for the sense of
    a. hearing   b. balance
    c. smell   d. kinesthesis

12. Which cells in the eye respond to different wavelengths of light?
    a. bipolar   b. ganglion
    c. retinal   d. cones

13. The sense that something is hot occurs because of the firing of which cells?
    a. warm
    b. olfactory
    c. vestibular
    d. both warm and cold

14. The lateral geniculate nucleus is found in the
    a. eye   b. optic nerve
    c. thalamus   d. cerebellum

15. The sense of smell responds to the _____ of molecules.
    a. position   b. shape
    c. distribution   d. energy

16. Which sense is called vestibular?
    a. smell   b. kinesthetic
    c. balance   d. ESP

17. The distorted room is known as the _____ room.
    a. Ames   b. perceptual
    c. visual illusion   d. Rubin

18. Which depth perception cue is binocular?
    a. linear perspective b. convergence
    c. visual   d. ambivalence

19. Which of these is a famous reversible figure?
    a. old woman and young woman
    b. visual cliff
    c. Ames room
    d. moon illusion

20. A baby is learning to reach for a cup, thus coordinating vision with _____.
    a. touch   b. vestibular sense
    c. kinesthesis   d. perception

21. The place where the optic nerve forms in the back of the eye creates the
    a. opponent process   b. blind spot
    c. optic chiasm   d. bipolar cells

22. Because of the opponent process, a person will perceive
    a. depth
    b. optical illusions
    c. negative afterimages
    d. multiple sensations

23. The semicircular canals are important for the _____ sense.
    a. vestibular   b. kinesthetic
    c. olfactory   d. auditory

24. The Weber fraction for lifting weights is about 1/50. How many ounces must be added to a weight of 400 ounces for the average person to notice that it is heavier?
    a. 50   b. 1
    c. 18   d. 8

25. Your friend says, "This food is delicious! It has such a nice, meaty flavor." You say, "It must be stimulating your _____."
    a. basilar membrane
    b. umami receptors
    c. bitter receptors
    d. vestibular organ

26. Two people are arguing about what they heard. One says it was "threesome," and the other says it was "trees hum." This reminds us of the principles of
    a. figure-ground
    b. opponent process
    c. reversible figure
    d. binocular cues
27. When sensing incomplete stimuli, brains fill in the gaps in a perceptual process called
    a. proximity
    b. figure-ground
    c. closure
    d. reversible figures
28. While your professor is lecturing, a student comes to class late and everyone stares at him as he makes his way to a chair. Of course, the professor's words were not perceived by anyone! This is an example of
    a. figure-ground
    b. retinal disparity
    c. umami
    d. Weber's law
29. Which of these is an example of divided consciousness?
    a. You switch back and forth between two TV channels.
    b. You manage to wash the dishes while thinking about your homework assignments.
    c. While dreaming, you are aware that you are dreaming.
    d. You are just falling asleep when you suddenly awaken at the sound of a door slamming.
30. Which type of drug acts similarly to endorphins?
    a. marijuana
    b. alcohol
    c. opiates
    d. LSD
31. Your uncle suffered a stroke that damaged the deeper layers of his visual processing area. Now he has lost a bit of his vision but acts as if he can still see perfectly fine. This appears to be an example of
    a. blindsight
    b. myoclonia
    c. retinal disparity
    d. Anton's syndrome
32. Which of these is true about hypnosis?
    a. It is similar to sleep in brain wave activity.
    b. It is a useful way to help people quit smoking.
    c. Anyone can be hypnotized.
    d. It is not the same thing as relaxation.
33. During REM sleep
    a. muscles are active
    b. a person is conscious
    c. atonia occurs
    d. brain waves are slow and regular
34. As people get older, the amount of REM sleep
    a. decreases
    b. increases
    c. stays the same
    d. converts to NREM sleep
35. Drug dependence occurs because drugs influence and change
    a. brain chemistry
    b. the pineal gland
    c. adrenal hormones
    d. the number of neurons

Short answer and critical thinking

1. What is meant by *transduction*? Give an example.
2. What philosophical problem bothered Gustav Fechner?
3. Compare and contrast absolute threshold and difference threshold.
4. Describe what Weber's law is about. What does it tell us?
5. Compare and contrast rods and cones.
6. What is a *dichromat*?
7. Describe how dark adaptation occurs.
8. What is a negative color afterimage and why does it occur?
9. Describe a Gestalt principle. Describe either the Necker cube, the Rubin vase, or the old woman, young woman picture.
10. Why do we see depth if the images on our retinas are flat?
11. What is binocular rivalry? How do researchers use it to study perception and consciousness?
12. How does drug dependence come about?
13. Give some examples of altered states of consciousness. What is consciousness, and why do psychologists refer to "states" of consciousness?
14. Describe some types of psychoactive drugs and how they affect consciousness.

UNIT
3
COGNITION

The discipline of psychology is centered on principles of learning. Learning is the study of how we change with experience or practice. The study of learning is perhaps the most important and influential subfield of psychology. And, of course, learning has practical as well as theoretical importance; that is, knowledge of the principles of learning can be very useful in daily life. In addition, the topic of learning is the backbone, the fundamental basis, for the understanding of many psychological phenomena. It is easier to understand mental disorders, for example, if you understand how people learn—how we are affected by our experiences.

On the other hand, memory is the flip side of learning. We remember what we have learned. Our brains store the physiological representations of our experiences—our memories. These two subjects—learning and memory—are part of what is called cognitive psychology, a most exciting, influential, and popular field of study within the world of psychology.

This unit includes two chapters:

Chapter 5 Learning—a detailed and complete discussion of classical conditioning and operant conditioning, the processes by which we change through experience. The various parameters of both types of conditioning are explained and accompanied by many examples. Other forms of learning, such as cognitive maps and incidental learning, are also included.

Chapter 6 Memory—a discussion of the many types of memories that psychologists define and a clear explanation of the processes of memory storage and retrieval. This chapter also includes a discussion of the physiology of memory and practical advice on how to improve memory.

Learning

PLAN AHEAD...

- What do psychologists mean by *learning* and *conditioning*?
- What did Pavlov discover in his research with dogs?
- How are emotional responses learned and unlearned?
- How are actions learned? Can they be unlearned? If so, how?
- What are reinforcers? What are positive and negative reinforcement?
- What is a Skinner box, and how is it used in psychology?
- How can the principles of learning be applied?
- What is a cognitive map?
- What is physically happening in the brain during learning?

WHY DOES MY BROTHER ACT SO ODD? HOW CAN I MAKE myself study more? Why did my sister suddenly start disliking school? How come my mom doesn't like riding in the car? Why do I find myself gambling more and more? How can I overcome my fear of the dark? Why are some people afraid of flying? Where did my dad pick up those weird habits of his?

Each of these questions and others like them can be answered by using the principles that will be covered in this chapter. Principles of learning are the fundamental laws of behavior; they explain why behaviors occur. These principles explain how behaviors develop, how they are maintained, and why they occur when they do and as often as they do. Principles of learning also demonstrate how we can change behaviors; in fact, change is the main component of learning.

No issue is more central to psychology than **learning.** Learning is what psychology is all about. No issue in psychology is more important for explaining behavior. In addition, no topic in psychology is more practical than the one you will now encounter. You will get many good, practical ideas from the topics included in this chapter. Finally, principles of learning are the basis for a large number of other topics. It is difficult to fully understand topics such as mental disorders, socialization, human development, educational psychology, interpersonal communication, motivation, and many others without an awareness of the fundamental ideas that will be included here. As you can see, the subject of learning is crucial within the discipline of psychology. Take heed, this is a good chapter to learn well!

LEARNING DEFINED

"I have but one lamp by which my feet are guided,

and that is the lamp of experience."
—PATRICK HENRY

We learn to feed ourselves. We learn how to walk. We learn to like our mothers. We might learn to be afraid of spiders. We learn to speak and understand a language, perhaps more than one. Some of us learn to play piano. We learn to dislike bullies. We learn to read and to write. We learn to drive a car. We might learn to smoke or to swear. We learn to be kind and compassionate. But we also sometimes learn how to cheat and how to get away with it. We learn to work hard and efficiently. We also learn how to get out of doing our assignments and jobs. We learn to love. We learn facts. We learn self-control. We sometimes learn compromise and cooperation and sometimes learn stubbornness and competitiveness. Each of us learns a multitude of things. Just what is learning?

Changes

Learning means change. You are different after you learn something than you were before. The agent of change is an experience in the environment. During learning, something about you is changed because of an experience. But this change comes about not because of brain damage. If you suffer injury to your brain, you definitely will change—but that is not learning. Learning involves changes that come about through some experience, some practice, other than injury to the brain. Somehow, experiences change you. That is learning. But what is the procedure for learning?

For learning to occur, one must have a certain, specific kind of experience. Learning does not occur randomly or haphazardly. Learning occurs by means of a very definite process. We can study that process scientifically; and we can take advantage of the principles of learning, applying them in the service of our goals. Psychologists who study learning perform experiments in an attempt to uncover the specific details of the experiences that produce learning.

Conditioning means about the same thing as learning. Sometimes we use the term *learning* when we are speaking broadly and the term *conditioning* when we are referring to simple cases or laboratory experiments. However, the two terms both refer to the process of change resulting from experience. You have an experience, and you change because of it. That is learning. That is conditioning.

Notice in the above examples that we can learn good things or bad, desirable things or undesirable ones. Learning is a neutral process, separate from value judgments about *what* we learn. We can learn to be nice or to be mean. We can learn to act in healthy ways or unhealthy ones. We can learn to be cooperative or competitive. We can learn to be ethical or to cheat. Learning is a process. *What* is learned is a different matter.

Learning occurs through certain kinds of experiences. Psychologists scientifically study the learning process to determine its main features.

Here, then, is our official definition of learning: *Learning is a relatively permanent change in behavior that occurs as a result of some experience or practice.*

Two Types of Behavior

We can divide behaviors into two groups. Some behaviors involve the somatic nervous system, moving us around in the world. We walk, talk, move our arms, our legs, and so on. These actions are called <u>operant behaviors</u> because they are ways in which we operate on the world. On the other hand, some of our behaviors involve the autonomic nervous system. Our heartbeat increases, adrenaline flows, our blood pressure increases, our pupils dilate, and so on. These are reflexive reactions to things in the world. A loud noise startles you, for example. Since these reactions are responses to stimuli in the world, they are called <u>respondent behaviors.</u>

Operant behaviors are movements that we make in the environment. Talking, walking, and doing things are operant behaviors. An operant behavior is an action on the environment—you do something to the world. You pick up a glass, you throw a football, you kick a stone, you talk to a person, you study your math, and so on.

Respondent behaviors are not actions, they are reactions. You don't act on the world; rather, something in the world causes you to respond. A sudden movement frightens you, pollen in your nose makes you sneeze, a gust of wind in your eyes makes you blink, a piece of food in your mouth causes saliva to be released from your salivary glands, the sight of a mouse scares you, and so on. Respondent behaviors are reflexes or reflexlike reactions. A stimulus in the world causes you to react.

The somatic and autonomic nervous systems do overlap and communicate with each other. Therefore, there is not a total separation between these two kinds of behaviors. However, it is best to begin the study of learning by first making this distinction between respondent and operant behaviors. This way, you will learn the fundamental principles that determine how behaviors are learned.

Two Types of Learning

The experience that is required to change a respondent behavior is different from the experience that is required to change an operant behavior. Therefore, there are two types of learning or two processes (procedures) by which change can occur. The two types of learning (or two procedures) are called classical conditioning (for learning respondent behaviors) and operant conditioning (for learning operant behaviors).

Respondent behaviors are reactions. They can be learned (in other words, conditioned). The process by which this happens is called **classical conditioning**. (Some people call it *respondent conditioning*, but that is less common, so we will use the more common term.) Classical conditioning is the process by which we learn reflexlike responses, such as fearful reactions. In classical conditioning, a person (or animal) is exposed to two things (stimuli) in the environment at about the same time. One of those stimuli already is capable of producing a certain reaction. The process of association between the two stimuli causes the other stimulus to produce the same reaction. Classical conditioning occurs when stimuli are associated with one another in our experience and one stimulus comes to cause (elicit) the same reaction as did the other stimulus. Having an unpleasant experience (first stimulus) at school (second stimulus) may make a child feel uncomfortable at school.

Operant behaviors, on the other hand, are changed according to a process called **operant conditioning**. Operant conditioning is the process by which we learn to act a certain way, such as to say a certain word, or move our arms. This process is based on consequences. Behaviors that are followed by desirable consequences are learned. If we do something that results in a pleasant feeling or a satisfying result, we are more likely to do that again.

Notice that in classical conditioning, the association between stimuli occurs *before* the behavior, while in operant conditioning, the important thing is the consequence, which comes *after* the behavior. Classical conditioning is the process by which we learn reflexive reactions, such as fears. Operant conditioning, on the other hand, affects our movements within the environment.

Let's summarize: There are two kinds of behaviors. *Respondent behaviors* are reflexes or reflexlike reactions to stimuli (you are startled by a loud noise), and *operant behaviors* are actions taken on the world (you pour milk into a glass). Respondent behaviors involve the autonomic nervous system, which controls physiological ("gut") responses such as heartbeat and blood pressure. Operant behaviors involve the somatic nervous system, which controls the skeletal muscles of the body, moving you about. These two types of behaviors are learned (changed) by two processes: *Classical conditioning* affects respondent behaviors (you learn a fear), *and operant conditioning* affects operant behaviors (you learn to play piano). Classical conditioning depends on experiencing *associations* between stimuli. Operant conditioning depends on the *consequences* of behaviors. Got that? Now, the details!

CLASSICAL CONDITIONING

"Once I had recognized the taste of the crumb of madeleine . . . immediately the old gray house upon the street rose up like the scenery of a theater."
—MARCEL PROUST

Classical conditioning is the process by which respondent behaviors are learned. The process is sometimes referred to as **association learning,** because an association (or pairing) of stimuli is required. By *stimuli,* we mean things in the environment that can be sensed. A **stimulus** is anything that you can see, hear, taste, smell, or feel. In classical conditioning, two stimuli are paired together. That is, they come together in your experience at about the same time. One of the stimuli causes you to have a reaction. For example, a tap below your knee causes your leg to jerk out. This is called a **reflex.** With enough associations or pairings between that stimulus (a tap below the knee) and another one (say, a bright flash of light), eventually the new stimulus (the flash of light) will cause a similar reaction (the leg jerk).

Essential Ingredients

Classical conditioning begins with a reflex. For example, a puff of air in your eye will make you blink. This reflex is natural; it is not learned. Therefore, it is called **uncond-itioned.** It helps to remember that *unconditioned* means "not learned" or natural. Any stimulus that causes an automatic reaction (in this case, the puff of air) is called an **unconditioned stimulus (US),** and the reaction (blinking) is called an **unconditioned response (UR).** We can make a diagram, called a **paradigm** (a drawing or model that shows the essential features of something), to illustrate a reflex:

$$US \rightarrow UR$$

The US is the unconditioned stimulus; it naturally causes (elicits) a response (for example, the puff of air). The UR is the unconditioned response (the blinking), the reaction that occurs naturally to the US. The arrow indicates that the relationship is natural, reflexive. It is not learned. The "U" tells us that.

Next in classical conditioning, a new stimulus is paired close together in time with the US. For example, I could say your name just as I blow a puff of air into your eye. The sound of your name in this case is called a **conditioned stimulus (CS).** Remember, *conditioned* means "learned," so a conditioned stimulus is a *learned* stimulus, one that you do not have a natural, reflex response to (humans do not naturally blink when they hear their name spoken). If I pair the conditioned stimulus together with the unconditioned stimulus, the cells in your nervous system will eventually make a connection between these two stimuli, and you will blink when I say your name (without the puff of air). In other words, you will react to the new stimulus (the CS) similarly as you did to the old stimulus (the US). Learning will occur. The reaction is now learned, so it is known as a **conditioned response (CR).**

Remember, learning means that a change takes place because of an experience. The experience in this case is the association (or, pairing together) of the two stimuli. The change is that you will now blink when you hear your name, whereas before you did not.

We can represent the essential features of classical conditioning in this paradigm:

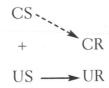

$$CS \dashrightarrow$$
$$+ \qquad CR$$
$$US \longrightarrow UR$$

All instances of classical conditioning fit this model, this paradigm. Let's take this simple example: A person attacked in a parking garage might become very afraid of parking garages. A conditioned stimulus (the CS is the parking garage) is paired with (+) an unconditioned stimulus (the US is the attack). The US automatically brings about, or elicits (→), an unconditioned response (the UR is the upset caused by the attack). With enough associations, the CS will elicit a conditioned response (the CR is the learned fear of parking garages). A CR is a learned response to a new stimulus; a UR is a natural (not learned) response to a stimulus. The UR is an *unlearned* automatic response, and the CR is a *learned* automatic response. Of course, the CR and UR will differ in intensity. If you are attacked by a dog, your nervous system will react quite strongly (a UR). Later, when you see the dog, your nervous system will react similarly (a CR) but less intensely than it did when you were being attacked. One more example: A person might learn to like the odor of a particular perfume or cologne because his or her partner wears it. What are the CS, US, UR, and CR in this case?

The Scientist Pavlov

Classical conditioning was first extensively studied by a Russian physiologist named Ivan Petrovich Pavlov (1849–1936). Pavlov studied dogs to learn about the digestive system. In fact, even today in medical schools students learn the essential features of digestion that Pavlov discovered. In 1905, the Nobel Prize in Physiology or Medicine was awarded to Pavlov for his research.

Pavlov put his dogs into a harness and surgically implanted a tube into their salivary glands so that he could scientifically study the salivation that occurred as the first step in the digestion of food. Pavlov or his assistants would put food in the mouth of each dog and then measure the amount of saliva released. This was done day after day. Soon Pavlov noticed a funny thing, something that many pet owners have likely noticed but thought nothing of. Pavlov noticed that the experienced dogs would begin to salivate *before* food was placed into their mouths. He wondered what could be causing this, and he spent the rest of his life studying the details of the process that we now call classical conditioning.

In Pavlov's most famous experiments, he used a bell as a conditioned stimulus, associating it with food (the unconditioned stimulus) placed into a dog's mouth. He found that with enough pairings of the bell and food, eventually a dog would salivate when the bell was sounded. In this example, the sound of the bell is the CS, the food placed into the dog's mouth is the US, and salivation is both the UR and the CR. Let's explain this

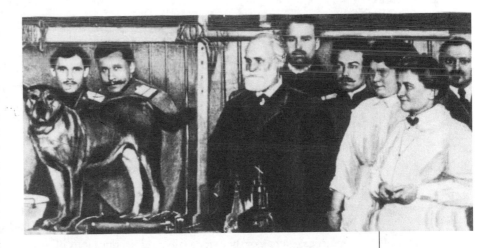

Ivan Pavlov defined classical conditioning.

If it is learned, a response is labeled *conditioned*. If a response is not learned, it is called *unconditioned*. So when a dog salivates in response to food, that response is labeled a UR, because it is not learned. But when a dog salivates in response to the sound of the bell, that response is called a CR, because it is learned. The UR and the CR are the same response, but they can (and do) vary in intensity. For example, a dog that experiences only a few pairings of bell and food will elicit only a small amount of salivation to the bell (CR) but will salivate much more in response to the food (UR).

Pavlov found that learning occurs at a particular rate. After only one pairing of the CS and US, there is only a small CR. That is, if we pair the bell and food only one time, a dog will release only a small amount of salivation to the bell—only a small amount of learning will have occurred. However, if we provide the dog with two pairings of bell and food, there will be more salivation to the sound of the bell, and three pairings will result in even more salivation to the bell, and so on. More pairings result in a stronger CR.

But the rate of learning is not a straight line. The strength of the CR (the amount of salivating to the bell, for instance) increases quickly in the beginning and then gradually tapers off. This is sometimes called **diminishing returns,** since each additional pairing of the CS and US results in a smaller gain than did previous pairings. Look at this graph. It is called the **learning curve.**

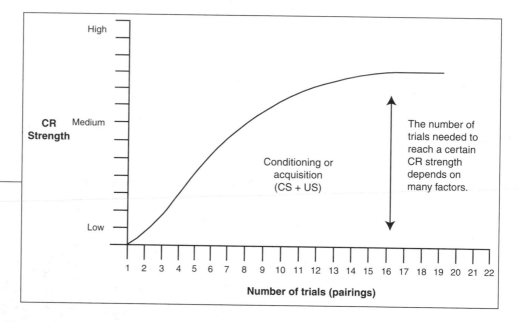

The learning curve increases fast in the beginning then gradually tapers off.

It Depends

Pavlov performed many experiments to determine the parameters of classical conditioning. One of the main questions he studied was how long it would take for classical conditioning to occur. Pavlov discovered that the answer depended on a number of variables.

The Timing between the CS and the US

There are a number of variations of the classical conditioning paradigm that alter the timing involved in the presentation of the conditioned and unconditioned stimuli. The most common procedure is for the CS to be presented and then the US to be presented while the CS is still present. For example, you could turn on a bell, then

> ## Recap
>
> — Learning is a change in behavior due to experience.
>
> — There are two kinds of behaviors, and two kinds of learning: Operant behaviors are actions that are learned by operant conditioning (via consequences), and respondent behaviors are reflexive reactions that are learned by classical conditioning (via associations between stimuli).
>
> — In classical conditioning, a reflexlike response is learned to a new stimulus because that stimulus (CS) is paired close in time with the original stimulus (US).
>
> — Pavlov studied salivation in dogs and discovered that the salivation reflex (UR) could be conditioned to a new stimulus, such as a bell (CS), and that dogs would eventually salivate when they heard the bell (CR).
>
> — Learning occurs at a certain rate, known as the learning curve.

place food in a dog's mouth while the bell is still sounding. This procedure is called **delay conditioning.**

Pavlov discovered that the rate of learning depended on the amount of time between the CS and the US. This amount of time is called the **CS-US interval.** If the interval is too long, learning is slow. The fastest learning occurs when the interval is about half a second. That is, if the CS is presented 1/2 second before the US, the fastest learning will occur. If the interval is one second, it will take more pairings to get to the same level of CR. In addition, if the interval is a negative number, that is, if the US is presented before the CS, then learning may never occur, or at least will be extremely slow. This is called **backward conditioning.**

Another variation is to present the CS, then turn off the CS, then present the US. This is called **trace conditioning,** because the animal must maintain a trace memory of the CS during the period of time between the two stimuli. Recent research (Clark & Squire, 1998) indicates that for learning to occur using trace conditioning, a person must be conscious. Perhaps this could be one way of testing whether animals have consciousness. If an animal can learn a CR via trace conditioning, it is evidence that the animal has consciousness. In trace conditioning, the longer the CS-US interval, the more difficult it is to condition the response. If the interval is too long, conditioning will not occur. You can't ring a bell, wait a week, and then put food in a dog's mouth and expect the dog to later salivate to the bell.

Delay conditioning: CS _____
                                       US _____

Backward conditioning: US _____
                                         CS _____

Trace Conditioning: CS ___   US ___

The Type of Response

Another variable that determines how long classical conditioning will take is the type of response that is being conditioned. Certain responses are learned more easily and more quickly than other responses. For example, suppose someone is driving in his car, listening to a song on the radio, has a head-on collision, and suffers major injuries.

Later, he will likely respond with anxiety when he hears that same song, or even when he gets into his car, or when he drives down the street where the accident occurred. All of those things—the song, the car, and the street—are CSs that were associated with the severe injuries suffered. An intense, life-threatening response is easily learned, even with just one pairing of CS and US.

Other responses are not so easily learned. If I say your name and then tap you below the knee, your leg will jerk out. After one pairing, I could test to see whether any learning had occurred. When I say your name, your leg will not jerk out. One association between the CS and US is not enough in this case. It would take hundreds of pairings, maybe a thousand, before I would get a leg jerk response to the sound of your name. This is because the leg jerk response is not important for survival and therefore is not learned very quickly. The more a response is linked to survival, the more easily it can be conditioned. Responses that keep us alive are learned quickly (only one pairing); responses that are not necessary for survival are more difficult to learn (it takes more pairings). Nearly any reflexive response can be conditioned to any stimulus. However, they will not all be learned as quickly. What varies is how many associations it will take.

One response that is learned very easily is **taste aversion.** If you eat a certain food and then later get sick, you learn an aversion, a feeling of disgust, toward that certain food. Have you ever experienced that? It takes only one pairing between food and sickness to condition a taste aversion. Of course, there need not be a cause-effect relationship between the food and the sickness. No matter why you get sick, your brain learns not to like the taste of the food you ate when you got sick. It is important to remember that classical conditioning is based on pairings or associations between stimuli, not on what you are thinking. Of course, *what you are thinking* is also a stimulus and can be associated with other stimuli. That is, you could learn a response to certain thoughts. If you are thinking a certain thought when something unpleasant happens, you may develop an aversion to that thought. A pleasant feeling may also be learned.

The Type of CS

Brains evolved over long periods of time; consequently, they are organized a particular way on the basis of which stimuli or behaviors allowed for survival over those many years. You are not born with a blank brain, a **tabula rasa** (Latin for "blank slate"), as many people assume. Brains come with instinctive organizations that allow for learning some things faster than others.

The rate at which classical conditioning occurs depends not only on the response being elicited, but also on the stimulus (the CS). A brain will quickly learn a response to a stimulus that was important for survival in our evolutionary past. Taste aversion is a good example. Suppose a person eats a pizza, then sits down in her favorite chair to watch TV, and after ten minutes gets very sick. That person's brain does *not* learn to feel sick when she is sitting in her favorite chair (that would take many more pairings), and her brain does not learn to feel sick when she is watching TV (again, that would take more associations) but *does* learn a sick reaction to the taste of pizza. The same response (feeling sick) is learned fast or slow depending on the CS. A CS that is linked to survival (food) is learned easily. A reaction to other CSs (chair or TV) is learned much more slowly.

Here is another example from recent research. Laboratory-reared monkeys were shown a film in which they saw and heard monkeys who were frightened by a snake. The monkeys that watched the film were frightened by the screeching that they heard from the monkeys in the film. In this case, the snake is the CS, the monkeys' screeching is the US, and the fearful response of the viewing monkeys is the UR. Did it take? Did the laboratory-reared monkeys learn a fear response to a snake after only one pairing—and while watching a film? To determine whether classical conditioning had occurred in this case, a snake similar to the one in the film was brought into the room.

What did the laboratory-reared monkeys do? Well, it did work: The monkeys screeched and ran away from the snake. The monkeys learned a fear of snakes with just one experience. Classical conditioning had occurred with just one pairing, one association—and from viewing a film!

Next comes the interesting part. The researchers modified the film using a computer to remove the image of the snake and replace it with an image of a flower. Another group of laboratory-reared monkeys were then shown the modified film. In this version of the film, monkeys saw the flower and ran away screeching. The laboratory-reared monkeys who saw the film were frightened (after all, it's the same film as before except for the flower replacing the snake). Then the monkeys who had viewed this modified film were tested to see whether classical conditioning had occurred. A flower was brought into the room. Surprise—the monkeys did *not* show fear!

When the CS was a snake, conditioning occurred with only one pairing. When the CS was a flower, conditioning did not occur with one pairing. To condition monkeys to be afraid of a flower, many more pairings would be necessary. A monkey's brain is wired (because of evolutionary experience) to learn some things more easily than others. It is easy for a monkey to learn a fear of snakes (and that's a good thing, because a snake bite could be fatal), but it is difficult for a monkey to learn a fear of flowers. It is easier to learn a reaction to some CSs than to others. Brains are wired to learn certain reactions to certain things very quickly.

Here's an example from developmental psychology (Blass & Camp, 2001): After nine-week-old babies were given sugar water while looking at a person's face for 3 1/2 minutes, they later stared longer at that face than at others. They had learned to recognize and prefer that person's face through classical conditioning—the association of the face with sugar. This shows that (1) very young babies can learn through classical conditioning, (2) babies' brains are prepared to recognize and remember human faces very quickly, and (3) the state of the person matters, because crying babies did not learn the association! Nature and nurture work together!

In another example, wolves and grizzly bears were recently reintroduced into the ecosystem of Yellowstone National Park after being absent for 50 years. At first, the moose in the park did not react with fear to these predators, and many moose were killed. But after one season, the moose quickly learned to fear the wolves and grizzlies (Berger, 2001). They became alert and wary, quickly moving away when they sensed danger. Some environmentalists had worried that the moose would become extinct because of the reintroduction of wolves and grizzlies, but this is a real-life example of how learning can occur very fast to some stimuli.

Variations on a Theme

Next let's look at a number of important variations that occur with classical conditioning.

Extinction

The removal of a conditioned response is called **extinction.** When a learned response has been eliminated, we say that it was extinguished. How could we get Pavlov's dog to stop salivating when the dog hears the bell? In classical conditioning, extinction is done by repeatedly presenting the CS without the US. In the case of Pavlov's dogs, it is necessary for a dog to repeatedly hear the sound of the bell *without* any food placed in the dog's mouth in order to extinguish the CR. A dog hearing a bell over and over again that is *not* paired with food will salivate less and less each time. Over a period of time, the salivation will eventually be reduced back to normal. The respondent behavior will be extinguished. Interestingly, just as conditioning depends on timing, so does extinction. Massing doses of extinction works better than does pacing it with long pauses between trials (Cain et al., 2003). This finding is important for therapists who want to help clients reduce or eliminate their unwanted CRs.

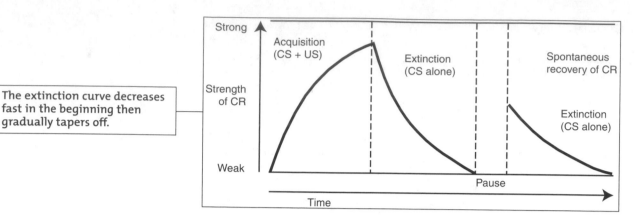

The extinction curve decreases fast in the beginning then gradually tapers off.

Psychotherapists often use extinction to help people extinguish classically conditioned responses. Of course, people do not go to therapists complaining about salivation. The sad news for therapists is that people do not seek them out to *learn* responses either. Being a therapist would be a lot more fun if clients came in requesting that they be taught pleasant responses to stimuli. "Could you help me to like my wife?" "I would like to feel better about my job." "Is it possible you could help me to like where I live?" These are not things that clients say to therapists. They say things like "Can you help me to get rid of this rotten feeling?" In other words, therapists are asked to extinguish unpleasant emotional responses. Clients want to get rid of their bad feelings—their fear, anger, jealousy, anxiety, and other undesirable reactions. This is a problem that calls for extinction.

Remember, to extinguish a response requires that the CS be presented over and over again without the US. Extinguishing salivation is a simple thing; but there is a wrinkle when it comes to extinguishing unpleasant responses. The problem is that when we present the CS, clients will have unpleasant responses and will want to discontinue their therapy. Even worse, they won't want to pay their bills! For instance, if a woman was raped (US) in a parking lot (CS) and now is deathly afraid of going into parking lots (CR), what will cure her is to go into parking lots *without* having anything bad happen to her. But if she goes into a parking lot, something bad *will* happen to her—she will freak out! In therapy, therefore, we need a method of sneaking up on the CS.

The most successful therapy for extinguishing unwanted responses is called **systematic desensitization,** which was developed by Joseph Wolpe (1973). This therapy is one way of sneaking up on a CS. The first step in this process is to teach the client to relax. When we later present the CS, we don't want the person to freak out (remember, extinction occurs when the CS is presented *without the* US). If we present the CS and the client then freaks out, classical conditioning will reoccur, and the client will continue to be afraid of the CS. Unfortunately, the client also will now be afraid of the therapist. So first the client learns relaxation techniques because that is incompatible with freaking out.

The second step in systematic desensitization is to make a **fear hierarchy,** a list of things that produce fear in order of strength. We need a list of stimuli that the client is frightened of. Most important, this list must be ordered according to how much fear is produced by each item. At the top of the list is the stimulus, situation, or variation that causes the most fear. For example, with a person who is afraid of snakes, the top item might be having a live snake wrapped around her neck. The second item might be a live snake on her lap. The third item might be a live snake on the floor in front of her. Far down the hierarchy is a rubber snake in her lap. Even farther down the list is a picture of a snake. Perhaps even lower would be a rubber hose on the floor in front of her or just the thought of a snake. It is important, too, to have small steps between each of the items on the fear hierarchy.

The final step in this process is extinction. This is accomplished by having the client relax and then presenting CSs, starting at the bottom of the hierarchy and moving up. So first, just think about a snake. If you get nervous, stop thinking about a snake and relax. Think about a snake again. And so on. Eventually, thinking about a snake will not produce any fear (it is extinguished). Then we move to the next item on the list. Look at this rubber hose. Nervous? Okay, take away the rubber hose. Relaxed? Okay, look at this rubber hose. And so on—to the top of the hierarchy. It sounds impossible, but after several months the client can have a live snake around her neck without any fear. Systematic desensitization is a remarkably successful therapy.

One more issue: When a response is being extinguished, the person's nervous system gets tired. Therefore, the person shows less response than he or she normally would. During systematic desensitization, for example, a client's response to a particular item (rubber snake) seems extinguished. But if we give her a rest period (she goes home and comes back next week), she will show an increase in her response to that stimulus. That is, she will be more afraid of the rubber snake at the next session. Similarly, if we are extinguishing a dog's salivation response to a bell, and part way through the extinction we give the dog a rest, when the dog returns there will be more salivation than before. This increase in response strength following a rest period is called **spontaneous recovery.** Therapists need to be aware of this phenomenon and plan accordingly. For example, when the client returns, extinction must be redone for some of the items that seemed extinguished at the last session.

Generalization

Once a response has been conditioned to a particular stimulus (a dog salivates to a bell), that response will also be elicited by other, similar stimuli. For instance, the dog will salivate when he hears other bells that are similar to the bell that was used in the conditioning. If you are bitten by a dog and learn to be afraid of that dog, you will also exhibit fear around other dogs. Someone who is conditioned to feel happy around a certain person will also feel happy around people who are similar to that person. This phenomenon is called **generalization.** We say that the response generalizes to other stimuli.

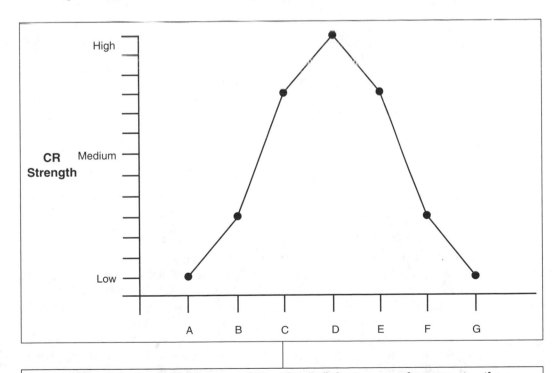

Generalization. A response has been conditioned to "D." The response also occurs to other stimuli, however, the less similar to "D," the less the response.

A generalized reaction will not necessarily be as strong or as intense as the original conditioned response, but the strength of the generalized response is predictable. The more similar a new stimulus is to the original CS, the more intense will be the response to it. For example, if a dog is conditioned to salivate to a bell that has a certain pitch, say, D (the CS), the dog will also salivate to a bell with a pitch of E, but the amount of saliva will be less. However, the amount of salivation to a bell in E will be the same as that to a bell in C, because the two stimuli are equally different from the original CS, the bell in D. However, the dog will salivate even less to a bell in F, since it is less similar to the original CS. A bell in the key of G will elicit even less saliva, and so on. The less similar the new stimulus is to the original CS, the less intense the response will be.

If a boy is bitten (US) by a St. Bernard dog (CS), in the future the boy will show the most fear (CR) to St. Bernards, less fear to huskies, still less to German shepherds, and even less to poodles. If a young girl gets a shot (US) from a nurse (CS) and the shot is painful (UR), the girl will later feel afraid of nurses (CR). The more similar a nurse is to the original nurse, the more fear the girl will feel. If a person is hurt at the dentist's office, in the future, the more similar a situation is to that dentist's office, the more fear the person will feel. Those are examples of the principle of generalization.

Discrimination

It is possible to learn a response to one stimulus but not to other stimuli that are similar. That is, we could condition a dog to salivate to one sound but not to another, similar sound. This is called **discrimination**. In this case, an animal or person learns to discriminate—to tell the difference—between one stimulus and another. How would you train a dog to respond to one sound but not to another?

Discrimination learning requires that only one stimulus be paired with the US. For instance, if we want a dog to salivate to a bell with a pitch of D but not to salivate to a bell in the key of E, we must pair food only with the bell in D. When the bell in E is sounded, at first the dog will salivate. But each time that bell is rung, the amount of salivation will decrease (extinction will occur). If we continue to pair food with the bell in D, then conditioning will continue to that stimulus. Eventually, the dog will salivate to one bell but not to the other. That is discrimination learning. It is how we learn to react differently to different stimuli, even though they may be very similar to each other. The more similar they are, of course, the longer it takes to learn to react to them differently.

Pavlov demonstrated discrimination conditioning by teaching dogs to salivate to the sight of a circle but not to an ellipse. He accomplished this by presenting the circle paired with food over and over again and presenting the ellipse without any food over and over again. Eventually, the dogs learned to discriminate between the two stimuli. They salivated when they saw a circle but not when they saw an ellipse. In our lives, discrimination learning happens all the time. We regularly learn to respond to one stimulus but not to another, even if they are similar. For example, we learn to respond one way to one person and quite differently to someone else. We might react with happiness to one person and with anger or fear to another.

Higher-Order Conditioning

Remember that classical conditioning begins with a stimulus and a reaction. A reflex is symbolized as US → UR. In classical conditioning, a neutral stimulus (a CS) is then paired with (is presented at about the same time as) the US, and eventually the animal learns to give an anticipatory response (now a learned response, so symbolized CR) in the presence of the CS. So classical conditioning is a kind of stimulus substitution. In classical conditioning, one stimulus comes to substitute for another. That is, the CS comes to elicit an anticipatory response similar to the US. This comes about because of the pairing (or associating) of the CS and US in time. Timing is important.

Classical conditioning can begin with a conditioned reaction. That is, if a response has been learned to some stimulus (if a dog learns to salivate to the sound of a bell), that learned stimulus-response can be used to condition the response to another stimulus. For example, once a dog has learned to salivate to a bell, the dog can then learn to salivate to the sight of a triangle by pairing the triangle with the bell. This is known as **second-order conditioning.** In this case, the bell is symbolized as CS_1, and the triangle is symbolized as CS_2. We could then condition the dog to salivate to a third stimulus, say, when we touch his paw. We do this by pairing together a touch of the paw (CS_3) with the triangle (CS_2). Eventually, the dog will salivate when touched on the paw. This is **third-order conditioning.** And so on. This procedure is called **higher-order conditioning.** Humans, as you would expect, are capable of more levels of higher-order conditioning than are lower animals. In fact, third- and fourth-order conditioning are rare among animals.

As you might expect, the amount of saliva that is elicited by higher-order CSs is typically smaller than that elicited by the US or the original CS. However, the number of pairings is the crucial variable. One major problem is that extinction will occur if the conditioning is stretched too far from the US. If the dog never gets food while we pair one stimulus after another, the response strength (the CR) will get weaker, and eventually the response will extinguish.

Higher-order conditioning is a part of our natural lives; it happens all the time simply by circumstances. People learn a fear of one stimulus, and then that stimulus is paired with something else, and soon they are afraid of the second one. Also, higher-order conditioning is a regular part of the planned world of persuasion. Advertising and political messages make frequent use of higher-order conditioning. A certain kind of soap is paired with a person or other stimulus that makes us feel good, or a politician is paired with an American flag. The advertisers are hoping that we will learn to feel good about the soap or proud about the politician.

THINK TANK

Describe some examples of classical conditioning from your experience—things that have happened to you or to others whom you know or that you have heard about.

Give examples of classical conditioning from literature, TV, or movies.

How could classical conditioning be used in advertising, or in other ways, to help people and society?

Developing Pavlov's Idea

Pavlov's work on animals was expanded to human beings by **John B. Watson** (1978–1958), an American psychologist who is known as the founder of the school of psychology known as **behaviorism.** In one case, Watson used classical conditioning on an infant (known as **Little Albert**) to demonstrate that emotions could be learned. Eleven-month-old Little Albert was conditioned to be afraid of a furry rat by Watson, who made a loud, frightening noise just as Albert reached for the rat. Watson found that Little Albert's fear response generalized to other small white animals, such as rabbits. Unfortunately, Little Albert was returned to his mother without receiving any extinction training. This experiment would not be allowed by today's ethical standards.

Watson's book *Behaviorism* detailed his idea that psychology could be revolutionized by concentrating on the scientific study of learning. Watson was convinced that (1) there are laws of behavior to be uncovered, (2) those laws have profound theoretical and practical implications, (3) psychology must abandon study of the mind and focus on observable behavior, and (4) human behavior is much more influenced by the environment, by experience, than it is by inherited factors.

Mary Cover Jones was the first behavior therapist because she used principles of classical conditioning to help her patients.

Watson eventually was forced to resign from Johns Hopkins University because he had a relationship with his graduate assistant—which would still be unethical today—that led to a scandalous divorce. He then took a job in advertising, where his starting pay was four times his teaching salary. Watson applied his knowledge of psychology to his new career and was immensely successful. Unfortunately, his second wife died unexpectedly, and Watson was devastated. He subsequently put his two children into boarding school and had little contact with them for the rest of his life. Both his sons grew up to regret their lack of an emotional relationship with their father, although they loved and respected him. One of them became a psychiatrist and later committed suicide; the other became an industrial psychologist.

Pavlovian conditioning, naturally, has important practical advantages. **Mary Cover Jones** (1896–1987) was a psychologist who recognized this fact and developed a therapeutic technique using the principles of classical conditioning. This technique is known as **counterconditioning**. As the name implies, this treatment attempts to undo a classically conditioned response by forming an incompatible one. If a person is afraid of wood paneling, for example, we can condition him to like wood paneling by associating it with very pleasant things. The fear response will eventually be overcome by the stronger pleasant feelings elicited by the pleasant circumstances used in the therapy.

In fact, Mary Cover Jones was the first behavior therapist. In 1924, she cured a three-year-old boy of his fear of rabbits by gradually bringing a small rabbit closer and closer to him as he ate his meals. Counterconditioning is similar to systematic desensitization (described above; Wolpe gave credit to Cover Jones). These are both types of behavior therapy, which is today one of the most successful approaches that mental health workers have for helping people with behavioral problems. Such therapies will be discussed more in Chapter 10.

Recap

— Classical conditioning depends on the timing between the US and CS (1/2 second is the fastest), the type of response (those with survival value are learned fastest), and the type of stimulus (again, survival value).

— Conditioned responses can be unlearned through extinction: presenting the CS without the US.

— Conditioned responses can generalize to similar stimuli, but discrimination can also be learned.

— A CS can be used to condition another CS in higher-order conditioning.

— Many applications of classical conditioning have been developed, including therapies for people who want to unlearn conditioned responses.

OPERANT CONDITIONING

"Cats and monkeys, monkeys and cats—all human life is there."

—HENRY JAMES

Classical conditioning is one type of learning. It involves respondent (automatic) behaviors and associations between stimuli. But there is another kind of learning. Operant conditioning involves operant behaviors (actions) and the consequences of those actions.

The Law of Effect

Edward Lee Thorndike (1874–1949) was a brilliant man who became a leader of educational psychology and who early in the twentieth century replaced William James as the most important American in the emerging field of psychology. Thorndike had studied with William James at Harvard but completed his Ph.D. with the leading psychologists of the day at Columbia University in New York.

While most psychologists were interested in research on humans, Thorndike was fascinated with animal research. For his Ph.D. dissertation, he studied the behaviors of chickens. Columbia, however, would not provide laboratory space for the pens Thorndike built for his chickens, so William James offered his house for Thorndike's experiments. James's children loved it! Thorndike built enclosures that separated some chickens from the flock. He then timed how long it took for a chicken to find its way out of its pen and back to the flock. Thorndike noticed that the amount of time it took decreased with experience. At first, the chickens displayed a kind of random (trial-and-error) behavior. But after some success, the chickens found their way to the flock with more deliberate actions, requiring less and less time to escape from their individual pens.

Next, Thorndike turned to cats as his subjects. He built elaborate **puzzle boxes,** the likes of which had never been seen in psychology. A hungry cat was placed into a puzzle box, and food was placed just outside a door in the box. The door could be opened if the cat would perform some behavior, such as stepping on a treadle, pulling a loop, or sliding a latch; sometimes the cat had to perform two such behaviors to get out of the puzzle box. Thorndike found that the cats acted similarly to the chickens. That is, they initially displayed trial-and-error behaviors, acting randomly. But once they stumbled on the behavior that opened the door, their behaviors became much more orderly. The time required to escape from a puzzle box got progressively shorter. Thorndike said that the animal's behavior became "stamped in" with experience. From these experiments, Thorndike proposed the **law of effect:** *A behavior followed by something pleasant will become more common, and a behavior followed by something unpleasant will become less common.*

Thorndike had uncovered the significant fact that operant behaviors are shaped and maintained *by their consequences.* Thorndike, however, did not use the term *operant.* This type of learning was known as **instrumental conditioning,** because an animal's behavior was viewed as an "instrument" that led to success. Thorndike emphasized the consequence of *satisfaction* as the key component in this kind of learning. Behaviors that led to satisfying results were learned.

Edward Thorndike defined the law of effect which states that the consequences of behavior influence their rate of occurrence.

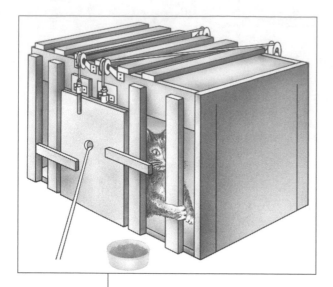

An example of the puzzle boxes used by Thorndike to study instrumental conditioning.

Mr. Skinner

Thorndike's important discovery that the consequences of a behavior are essential to learning was further advanced by Burrhus Frederic Skinner (1904–1990), who is known in the field of psychology as **B. F. Skinner,** and was called Fred by his friends. Skinner had studied English literature in college, but soon afterward found that he had nothing to write about. He read about Pavlov in an article by H. G. Wells and also read John B. Watson's *Behaviorism* because the famed philosopher Bertrand Russell had written that he believed there was much truth in it and behaviorism should be developed to the fullest extent possible. Skinner enrolled in the psychology program at Harvard University and began his work on operant conditioning, which would eventually make him one of the most influential psychologists in history.

Skinner's first academic appointment was at the University of Minnesota. There he began studying animals in very careful, detailed ways. Skinner was quite a tinkerer, and he loved to create and build things. He built boxes similar to Thorndike's puzzle boxes, but they were more elaborate and were designed to measure behaviors very accurately. Skinner called this experimental device an *operant conditioning apparatus*, but we call it a **Skinner box.**

Skinner found that the behaviors of his laboratory animals were intricately related to the consequences of those behaviors. Skinner believed that the animals' behaviors were strengthened by the consequences, and hence he called the consequences that influenced behaviors *reinforcing stimuli,* or more simply, **reinforcers.** *To reinforce* means to strengthen. Because behaviors depended on these reinforcers, Skinner wrote about **"contingencies of reinforcement,"** by which he meant that the rate of a particular behavior was determined by how often that behavior was followed by a reinforcer. For example, a hungry rat in a Skinner box receives food each time it pushes a metal bar. The rat's frequency of bar pushing is recorded. If the rate of bar pushing increases, the food is called a reinforcer, and the process of learning is called reinforcement.

Students sometimes mistakenly believe that the feeling that an animal gets (a pleasant or unpleasant feeling) is the reinforcer for their behavior. But this is not correct. Instead, the thing (the stimulus) that produces the feeling is the reinforcer—or, more correctly, the stimulus that increases or decreases the animal's behavior is the reinforcer.

To Operate

Skinner defined an operant behavior as any behavior whose frequency (or probability) was determined by its consequences. If a thirsty rat turns to the left and water appears, the rat will turn to the left more frequently. If a hungry pigeon pecks a red circle and a food pellet appears, the pigeon will peck the circle more often in the future. This is the essence of operant conditioning. In a Skinner box, a rat pushes a bar and receives a food pellet. The rat pushes the bar more frequently. The rate of bar pressing increases according to the learning curve in the case of classical conditioning. At first the rate increases rapidly, then it slowly declines or levels out until it reaches a certain maximum.

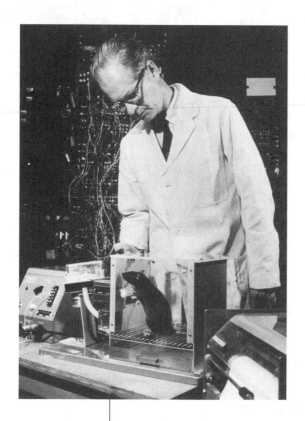

B. F. Skinner defined operant conditioning and all its variations.

An operant behavior is an action on the world. An operant behavior causes something to happen. If the result is satisfying, the behavior becomes more common. This is called *reinforcement*. If the result is unsatisfying, the behavior becomes less common. This is called **punishment.** Now, a couple of warnings: An operant behavior is *not* a specific set of muscle movements. It is a behavior that affects the environment. For instance, it doesn't matter by what means a rat in a Skinner box presses a lever, it only matters that the lever goes down. The rat can use his nose, his front paw, or his rear paw, or he can sit on the lever. An operant behavior is really a class of behaviors that accomplishes a certain effect on the environment—we operate on the world. Second, reinforcement and punishment refer to the operant behavior, not to the animal. It is incorrect to say that a rat is reinforced or punished. Rather, we should say the rat's *behavior* is reinforced or punished. A behavior that is reinforced is strengthened; that is, it is more likely to occur again. A behavior that is punished is weakened; it is less likely to occur again.

In operant conditioning, we do not use our opinions or theories about what is or is not a reinforcer or a punisher. In operant conditioning, we define things by the effect they have—we try them out! If a monkey is swinging on a rope, we can count how often he does this. The normal rate at which the monkey swings on the rope is called the **operant level.** The operant level of a behavior is the frequency at which it normally occurs without any reinforcement. Operant level means how often something happens naturally. Next we give the monkey a raisin each time he swings on the rope. Then we count to see whether the rate of rope swinging changes. If the monkey swings more often, the raisin is called a **positive reinforcer.** *Positive* means that behavior is reinforced if a stimulus is *added*. If the monkey receives a mild shock and when he swings on the rope the shock is reduced, he might swing more. The shock is then called a **negative reinforcer** because we need to *subtract* it to reinforce (strengthen) the behavior. Let's look at this in more detail.

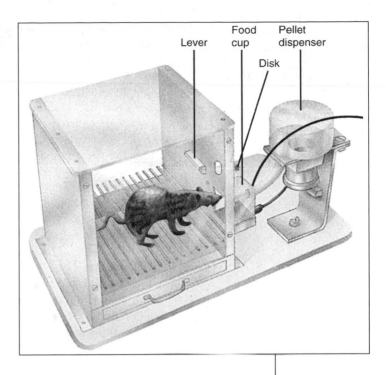

A typical Skinner box used in the study of operant conditioning.

The U.S. military asked B. F. Skinner to train pigeons to guide bomb-carrying missiles to their targets in a secret World War II project.

To Reinforce

Now for a difficult issue: The use of the terms *positive* and *negative.* Many students have difficulty with this. Think of it as in math class: *Positive* and *negative* do not mean good and bad, pleasant and unpleasant, or right and wrong. *Positive* means that something was added, and *negative* means that something was subtracted. (In math we don't say, "Oh, that bad 5," when the answer is negative 5.)

A reinforcer is a stimulus that can strengthen behavior. If we need to add a stimulus to strengthen a behavior, then that stimulus is called a *positive reinforcer* (an addition strengthener). If we need to subtract a reinforcer to strengthen a behavior, then that stimulus is called a *negative reinforcer* (a subtraction strengthener). If a rat pushes a bar more often when he receives food, then food is a positive reinforcer. If a rat will push a bar more often when his bar pushing is followed by the removal of an electric shock, then the electric shock is called a negative reinforcer.

Reinforcers are called positive or negative according to what effect they have. Some of Skinner's students once complained that their laboratory rats were not behaving as they should. Skinner replied, "The rat is always right." He meant that what the rat does is what we need to explain. If our predictions are wrong, we need new ideas.

Here is a general paradigm for operant conditioning:

$$S^D \rightarrow R \rightarrow S^R$$

In the paradigm, S^D stands for a **discriminative stimulus.** All behaviors occur in some situation or in the presence of some cue. A behavior does not occur around the clock. The things in the environment that cue or trigger an operant behavior are the S^Ds. An S^D is any stimulus that will signal a person or animal to engage in a behavior. It is the salient feature that is present when a behavior occurs. A red traffic light is an S^D that signals us to step on the brake pedal. All behaviors have discriminative stimuli that cue them.

The R in the paradigm simply means "response." This is the operant behavior. This is the action that is taken that will have an effect on the environment. The normal rate of a behavior (its operant level) can be measured, and we can determine under what conditions the rate changes.

The thing that influences the rate of an operant behavior comes after the behavior and is termed an S^R, which stands for "reinforcing stimulus." This is the thing we call a **reinforcer.** Reinforcers can strengthen behaviors that they follow, but the timing is very important. The reinforcer should come immediately after the behavior. The longer the interval between the response and the reinforcer, the more difficult learning will be. Humans can tolerate a longer delay than can lower animals. Even so, the sooner the reinforcer follows the behavior, the faster the learning.

Some reinforcers have strengthening power because of natural biology. Things like food, water, warmth, and sex are known as **primary reinforcers.** But some things reinforce behavior because they were learned through classical conditioning. We learn to like some things and not like some other things through associations with stimuli we already have reactions to. These learned things are called **secondary reinforcers,** and are abbreviated S^r. Sometimes they are called **conditioned reinforcers** because they are learned. Through experience, we learn to like attention, praise, money, and so on. We also learn through experience not to like criticism, embarrassment, guilt, and other things. Things that we *learn* to like or not like are called secondary reinforcers (S^r). Things that we *naturally* like or don't like are called primary reinforcers (S^R).

TABLE 5.1   Important Reminders about Reinforcers

1. Reinforcers are stimuli, not feelings. If a behavior leads to a pleasant (or unpleasant) feeling, we need to determine *what* is causing the feeling. That thing is the reinforcer.

2. Animals aren't reinforced; *behaviors* are reinforced. To reinforce means to strengthen. The behavior (not the animal) becomes stronger (it will occur more often).

3. Similarly, animals aren't punished; *behaviors* are punished. To punish means to weaken.

4. Reinforcers are called *positive* if they strengthen behavior when they are added. Reinforcers are called *negative* if they strengthen behavior when subtracted.

5. Reinforcers are called *primary* if they have their reinforcing value naturally, without experience. Reinforcers are called *secondary* or *conditioned* if their value has been learned (through classical conditioning).

Extinction

Each behavior (R) has a certain probability of occurring in a given situation (S^D). If a behavior is reinforced, then that behavior becomes more probable in that situation. We can simply count the frequency of a behavior to determine its probability. If a behavior is reinforced (if it is not successful), its frequency will decrease to its normal operant level. Behaviors will only occur more often than natural if they are reinforced. If they are not reinforced, they will return to their natural operant levels. Just as you can increase the frequency of a behavior by reinforcing it, you can decrease the frequency of a learned behavior by removing its reinforcement. This process is called extinction. We say that we *extinguish* a behavior.

To extinguish an operant behavior, it is necessary to stop reinforcing it. Suppose a rat has learned to push a bar in a Skinner box because bar pushing was followed by food. To extinguish that response, we need to stop giving food for bar pushing.

When extinction first begins, that is, when the reinforcer is removed from a behavior that was being maintained by the reinforcer, the immediate response is somewhat surprising. The first effect of extinction is an *increase* in the rate of the behavior. Can you believe it? The first effect of extinction is an increase in the behavior! If a rat's bar-pushing behavior has been reinforced by food and we then stop giving food for bar pushing, the immediate result is that the rat pushes the bar faster than ever. The rat's bar pushing was followed by food. He was pushing the bar at a high rate. Then suddenly the food does not appear when he pushes the bar. So he pushes it even faster than before; he is pushing it like crazy. It is as if the rat's brain is saying, "Hey, where's the food?"

This initial increase in the rate of the R is known as **extinction bursting**. There is a **burst,** or a temporary flurry, of the behavior when the reinforcer is first removed. Think about this: If you step on the brake pedal, your car stops. The stopping of the car is the reinforcer for stepping on the brake pedal. If one day your car doesn't stop when you step on the brake pedal, of course, you rapidly pump the brake pedal. If you are used to turning a doorknob to open a door and then one time the door doesn't open, you will rapidly turn the knob many times. Similarly, if a child is used to getting

> The extinction curve showing bursting, a temporary increase in the rate of behavior when reinforcement is stopped.

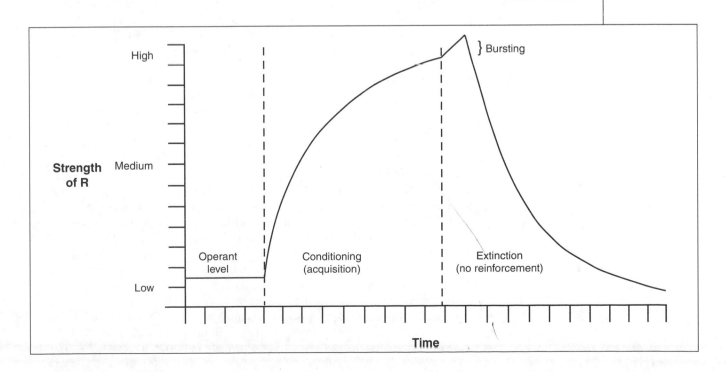

her way by whining, then suddenly she does not get her way, she whines even more vigorously. These are examples of extinction bursting.

After bursting, if the reinforcer is still withheld, the response will gradually diminish in frequency. That is, when we first start extinction (remove the reinforcer), the rate of the behavior skyrockets (bursting), but this increase is temporary. The rate of the behavior will soon begin to decline. The decrease in behavior will be relatively rapid in the beginning and then will taper off and eventually return to the natural operant level. The **extinction** curve on page 181 shows the rate of a behavior over time during extinction.

Types of Operant Conditioning

An operant behavior may be followed by any of four general consequences:

1. A positive reinforcer may be added (**positive reinforcement**)
2. A negative reinforcer may be added (**positive punishment**)
3. A positive reinforcer may be removed (**negative punishment**)
4. A negative reinforcer may be removed (**negative reinforcement**)

	Positive Reinforcer	Negative Reinforcer
Add	**Positive reinforcement** (rate of behavior increases)	**Positive punishment** (rate of behavior decreases)
Remove	**Negative punishment** (rate of behavior decreases)	**Negative reinforcement** **(escape or avoidance)** (rate of behavior decreases)

Notice that when a reinforcer of any kind is added (following a behavior), the process of learning is called *positive*, and when a reinforcer is subtracted, the learning process is called *negative*. A rat pushes a bar. If we then add something, the process is called positive; if we subtract something, it is called negative. Next we see what happens to the rate of the bar pushing. If the behavior increases in frequency, the process of learning is called *reinforcement*, while if the behavior becomes less common, the process is called *punishment*.

Here are some examples of each type of operant conditioning:

- **Positive Reinforcement** (Getting something pleasant): A student is praised for asking a question in class and subsequently asks more questions. A child who receives a smile from Mommy when he says "please" begins to say "please" more often. A dog comes when called because she receives a tasty treat. An animal in the forest returns to a place where it previously found food. A baby learns to feed himself because when the spoon hits his mouth, the food goes in.
- **Negative Reinforcement** (Escaping from something unpleasant or learning to avoid something unpleasant): A student learns to look the other way when the teacher is going to call on someone because then she does not get called on. (It works!) A driver turns a block before his exit to get out of a traffic jam because it worked once before. A child learns to say "I'm sorry" when her mother gives her a stern look because in the past when the child said "I'm sorry," her mother stopped looking at her sternly. A man scratches an itch and it stops irritating him. A child doesn't want to eat her spinach, and says, "Mom, I love you," and her mother then says that she doesn't have to eat her spinach.
- **Positive Punishment** (Getting something unpleasant): An animal in the forest bites an electric wire, gets a shock, and later will not go near electric wires. A woman leaned on a hot radiator and was burned, and now she stands far away

from radiators. A student asked a question in class, was laughed at by other students, and now asks fewer questions. A worker who was late for work was reprimanded and now does not come late.

- **Negative Punishment** (Something pleasant is removed): A child's TV privileges were taken away when he hit his sister, and now he waits until his parents are out of the room before he hits his sister. A man was docked pay for being late, and now he is always punctual at his job. A woman had to pay $100 for speeding on highway 101 and now slows down when driving on highway 101. A child's dessert was removed when she said a bad word, and now she does not say bad words when it is time for dessert.

Notice that punishment is one type of learning. It is not the same as unlearning (extinction). Many people make the mistake of thinking that punishment will cause a behavior to be permanently unlearned. However, a behavior that is punished will often continue at a high rate under different circumstances; it will not be gone. A child who is punished at home for aggression might be a bully at school. In addition, many new behaviors are learned during punishment, because it is an unpleasant experience. Remember classical conditioning? The person whose behavior is punished will feel upset in the circumstances in which he or she was punished, including in the presence of the person who did the punishing. Not only will unpleasant responses be learned, escape behavior also will be learned. A person wants to escape from a situation that is unpleasant, and escape behavior is reinforced by negative reinforcement.

Also, a person whose behavior is punished will feel nervous and upset; that is not conducive to learning. Therefore, punishment makes the learning of appropriate behaviors more difficult. (For example, it is hard to learn to drive a car if someone is yelling at you.) Because of all of these undesirable side effects of punishment, psychologists do not recommend its use. Instead, reinforcing of appropriate behaviors and extinguishing inappropriate behaviors are recomended. If extinction is not possible, then try to reinforce behaviors that are incompatible with the undesirable behavior. For instance, if a child likes to write on the wall, attach a large piece of paper to a wall

Recap

— Edward Thorndike studied cats in puzzle boxes and discovered the law of effect—that behaviors will increase or decrease if followed by pleasant or unpleasant consequences.

— B. F. Skinner used Skinner boxes to study animal behavior and discovered the principles of operant conditioning; behaviors that are reinforced will occur more often, and behaviors that are punished will occur less often.

— A discriminative stimulus (S^D) is a cue that signals when a behavior will be reinforced.

— Primary reinforcers are naturally pleasant or unpleasant; secondary (conditioned) reinforcers are learned through classical conditioning.

— Operant behaviors can be extinguished by removing their reinforcement.

— There are four types of operant conditioning: positive reinforcement adds something good; negative reinforcement removes something bad; positive punishment adds something bad; and negative punishment removes something good.

— Punishment is a type of learning that does not extinguish behavior and causes many bad side effects. Therefore, it is not recommended.

and reinforce writing on it. If a child runs around the room too much, reinforce sitting still. If a person acts impolitely, reinforce polite behaviors.

Variations of Operant Conditioning

We can increase the rate of learning by using a technique called **shaping.** Using shaping, a behavior is learned by the reinforcement of successive approximations. In fact, most things in life are learned by shaping. We do not teach children to read by waiting for them to read Shakespeare and then reinforcing that behavior. We teach reading in small, successive increments. That is the point of shaping. Let's take an example.

Suppose we want a rat in a Skinner box to push a bar at a high rate. The operant level of bar pushing among rats is low—that is, rats in Skinner boxes have other things to do besides push bars. They are busy sniffing, licking themselves, reaching their paws up on the side of the Skinner box, and so on. Bar pushing has a low operant level. Because it doesn't occur very often, we will have to wait a long time to reinforce that behavior. We can speed up the process by reinforcing behaviors that come closer and closer to bar pushing. We begin by giving the rat a food pellet every time he moves toward the bar. Soon he will be spending most of his time near the bar. Then we demand more. Now the rat must be near the bar and be looking at the bar to receive food. Soon the rat will be doing that. Next, the rat must be near the bar, facing it, and must lift a paw in order to receive food. When that behavior becomes frequent, we then reinforce only the behavior of touching the bar. It won't be long before the rat will push the bar. We then reinforce each bar press. Shaping can significantly speed up the process of learning.

Another variation of operant conditioning is similar to that described above for classical conditioning: **generalization.** A behavior that is reinforced in the presence of an S^D not only will increase in frequency under that condition, but also will increase in frequency in similar situations. The response *generalizes* to other situations. The more similar the new situation is to the one in which reinforcement occurred, the more the behavior will generalize. For example, if a student learns to ask questions in her psychology classroom because her questions are followed by satisfying results, she will also ask more questions in other classrooms. The more similar a classroom is to the psychology classroom, the more her question-asking behavior will increase.

We also have **discrimination** in operant conditioning, just as in classical conditioning. For example, we can put a light bulb into a Skinner box and reinforce a rat's bar-pushing behavior only when the light is on. When the light is off, extinction is in effect. When the light is on, reinforcement is in effect. Eventually, the rat will push the bar only when the light is on.

The light turned on (the stimulus that is present when behavior is reinforced) is called an S^D (pronounced "ess-dee"), and the light turned off (the stimulus that is present when behavior is not reinforced) is called an S^Δ (pronounced "ess-delta"). If we wanted, we could make a sign that says "PUSH BAR" and reinforce the rat's bar pushing only when we show him the sign. We could make another sign that says "TURN" and use shaping to condition the rat to turn in a circle when he sees this sign. We could do several similar things and then show our friends a rat that can "read." The rat will learn to respond appropriately to the signs in the same way that a child learns to say the appropriate sounds when she sees words. The rat and the child both learn to discriminate. This means that they learn to make different responses to different stimuli. That, of course, is a basic function of learning.

Sometimes the S^D can be used to control behavior. An S^D is present when a behavior occurs. Most behaviors have a number of discriminative stimuli—a number of different conditions under which the behavior will occur. When it is difficult to control the reinforcer for a behavior, sometimes it is easier to control the S^D. This is called **stimulus control.** For example, if a person wants to quit smoking, it is difficult to do because the reinforcer is physiological. Normally, we cannot control the reinforcer for smoking. However, we might list the conditions under which the person smokes the most and then recommend that she decrease the amount of time in these situations.

Perhaps she smokes a lot when she drinks coffee, for instance. We then recommend that she spend less time drinking coffee. This stimulus control technique is also appropriate when it is difficult to determine what is reinforcing a behavior.

THINK TANK

Give some examples of operant conditioning from your experience.

Give examples from TV or movies.

Name some occupations in which knowledge of operant conditioning would be useful.

Schedules of Reinforcement

Skinner discovered that behaviors have certain frequencies depending on how often they are reinforced. In daily life, only rarely is a behavior always reinforced or never reinforced. Typically, a behavior is reinforced sometimes when it occurs and not at other times. Skinner studied the effects of these different **schedules of reinforcement** and found that they had systematic and predictable effects on behavior.

If a behavior is reinforced every single time it occurs, the schedule of reinforcement is called **continuous**. If a child is praised every single time she says "please," that is called a continuous schedule. If a rat in a Skinner box receives food every single time he pushes a bar, the bar pushing is said to be on a continuous schedule of reinforcement. A continuous schedule results in the fastest possible learning. If we want someone to learn a behavior fast, then the behavior needs to be reinforced every time it occurs. However, if we stop reinforcing a behavior that is on a continuous schedule, it will extinguish at the fastest rate possible.

If a learned behavior is no longer reinforced, that is called extinction. We explained that term earlier. It simply means that the behavior will diminish in frequency. A behavior that is no longer reinforced will return to its natural, operant level.

In between the two extremes of always reinforcing a behavior (continuous schedule) and never reinforcing a behavior (extinction) is a **partial** or **intermittent schedule**. This means that a behavior is reinforced sometimes when it occurs, but not every time. Most of our behaviors—gambling, asking questions, saying things to people, moving around, and so on—are reinforced sometimes but not always. A partial schedule results in a slow rate of learning. In other words, it will take a long time to learn a behavior that is reinforced only once in a while. Remember, a continuous schedule will result in the fastest learning. A partial schedule results in slower learning. However, once learned, behaviors that are maintained on a partial schedule of reinforcement will extinguish very slowly. Partially reinforced behaviors are resistant to extinction. They are persistent and hard to get rid of. This phenomenon is called the **partial reinforcement effect**. Gambling is a good example. If a person wins at gambling just often enough to keep the behavior going, then gambling becomes very hard to get rid of. Even if the person loses and loses and loses, he or she keeps trying. It is as if the brain is used to not being reinforced and so becomes persistent. If you want a behavior to be persistent, to be hard to extinguish, then you should put that behavior on a partial schedule of reinforcement. Before people are released from institutions, their behaviors should be weaned from continuous schedules (the fastest learning) to partial schedules (the slowest extinction) so that they won't be back in so soon.

Ratios and Intervals

Psychologists divide partial schedules into different types. <u>Ratio schedules</u> involve a ratio: one reinforcer for every *n* instances of the behavior (*n* can be any number); the behavior must occur a number of times before it is reinforced. For example, perhaps a rat must push a bar ten times before bar pushing is reinforced. On the other hand, <u>interval schedules</u> are based on time passing. A behavior will be reinforced after an interval of time but not before the time has passed. For example, perhaps bar pushing will be reinforced if it occurs (even once!) only after two minutes.

A schedule is called *fixed* if the criterion for reinforcement does not change; for example: bar pushing is reinforced every tenth time it occurs (ratio), or bar pushing is reinforced every two minutes (interval). On the other hand, a schedule is called *variable* if the criterion for reinforcement changes. For instance, bar pushing is reinforced every ten times it occurs, *on the average*; sometimes three bar pushes will be reinforced, sometimes fifteen bar pushes, sometimes eight bar pushes, and so on—but on the average, every ten bar pushes will get one reinforcer. Similarly, bar pushes may be reinforced every two minutes on the average but with the amount of time varying.

Here are descriptions and examples of the four basic types of partial schedules:

Fixed Ratio (FR)

In case of a **fixed ratio**, a behavior must occur a certain number of times before it is reinforced. The number of times that is required stays the same. If bar pressing is on an FR (5) schedule, it means that when a rat presses the bar five times, then the behavior is reinforced, another five presses, and another reinforcer, another five, another reinforcer; and so on. If the rat presses four times, there is no reinforcer. The behavior must occur five times. For example, if I hire you to assemble clocks and I pay you one dollar for every three clocks you assemble, this is an FR (3) schedule. A salesperson who receives payment for every twenty phone calls is on an FR (20) schedule.

Behavior on a fixed ratio schedule occurs at a very high rate. This makes sense, because the faster one performs some behavior, the more reinforcers one receives. If you want a behavior to occur at a high rate, a fixed ratio schedule is a good choice. If the ratio is *lean*, the behavior must occur many times before it is reinforced. For example, Skinner conditioned a pigeon to peck a disk 1,000 times for a food pellet. That is a very lean schedule! In these cases, the rate of behaving increases as it approaches the reinforcement—the pigeon pecks faster and faster as it is nearing one thousand pecks. However, once the reinforcer is attained, the animal will take a pause before beginning the next round. This is called a **post-reinforcement pause.** The leaner the schedule, the longer the pause. Humans do this too when they must accomplish a lot of work for a reinforcer. Once we reach our goal, we take a pause before beginning the next round. Sometimes the schedule is too lean, and extinction occurs. This is because the reinforcer does not come often enough if the ratio is too lean. This phenomenon is called **ratio strain.** It sometimes happens to people who are studying for their Ph.D. and must complete a very long dissertation without any reinforcement. Many people put off their dissertation work forever. The behavior is extinguished—and they get no Ph.D. So watch out for ratio strain!

Variable Ratio (VR)

The post-reinforcement pause can be eliminated by using a schedule that varies the ratio. A **variable ratio** schedule still reinforces behavior based on its number of occurrences, but the number keeps changing. What we get is a ratio *on the average*. If pushing a bar is reinforced every ten times, *on the average*, that would be a VR (10) schedule. A good example is gambling. Let's say that a slot machine is adjusted to pay out 90% of what it takes in. In the long run, the house makes a profit. But the machine does pay out sometimes: For every one hundred dollars that go into the machine, ninety dollars come out. But they do not come out on a regular basis. The ratio keeps changing, but in the long run, it is one hundred dollars in and ninety dollars out.

Another example of a variable ratio schedule is salespeople who are paid on commission; that is, they get paid only when they make a sale. To make a sale, the salesperson must call on many people. Let's say that on the average, every twentieth person who hears a pitch will make a purchase. So a salesperson must call on twenty people *on the average* to make money. This is a VR (20) schedule. There is no pause in behavior with a variable ratio schedule because the ratio keeps changing. A salesperson who makes a sale will still call on the next person right away because it could be another sale. A rat on a VR schedule will work very fast without pause. Some labor unions prohibit such pay systems because people overwork. A VR schedule will produce the fastest work for the pay.

Fixed Interval (FI)

Fixed interval schedules are based not on the number of instances of a behavior, but on time passing. After a certain period of time, a behavior will be reinforced. Then, after a period of time, the behavior will be reinforced again. No matter how often it occurs, the behavior will not be reinforced until the time is up. For example, a rat's bar pushing may be on an FI (30 seconds). This means that every 30 seconds, the reinforcer will be available. If the rat pushes the bar, a food pellet will be given. Once the reinforcer is given, the clock starts again. Thirty seconds must pass before the reinforcer is available. What happens? The rat learns to tell time. After receiving a food pellet, the rat goes about other business and stays away from the bar. But as time passes, the rat begins to push the bar more and more rapidly. After 25 seconds, the rat is pushing the bar at a very rapid rate. Then, after 30 seconds, the next bar push is reinforced. The rat eats the food and goes back to other business, and the cycle begins again.

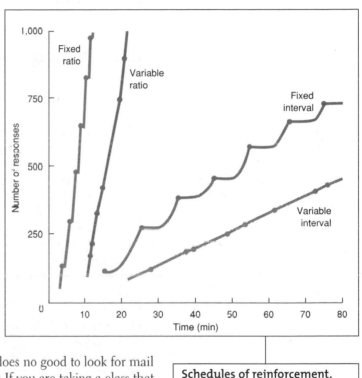

Schedules of reinforcement.

Mail delivery is done on a fixed interval schedule. It does no good to look for mail 10 minutes after it was delivered. Here's another example: If you are taking a class that gives a test every week, say, on Friday, then your study behavior is on a fixed interval schedule. What happens? You don't study at all on Saturday, and almost no studying occurs on Sunday. On Monday, you might look at the cover of your book. On Tuesday, maybe you do a little reading. On Wednesday, you do more reading, and on Thursday, you are cramming. You are just like the rat! The rat crams just before 30 seconds are up, and you cram just before your exam. A fixed interval schedule results in a rate of behavior that is extremely low just after the reinforcement and then progressively increases at a geometric rate, reaching a very high rate (cramming) just before the next reinforcer. Most schools in the United States use fixed interval schedules of reinforcement. This is not very effective for learning but is effective for cramming.

Variable Interval (VI)

A **variable interval** schedule is also based on time passing, but the time period keeps changing. We could, for example, reinforce a rat's bar pushing every five minutes *on the average*. This would be a VI (5 minutes) schedule. A food pellet would be given when the rat pushes the bar after four minutes, then seven minutes, then two minutes, then six minutes, then one minute, then eight minutes, then three minutes, and so on. It would average out to every five minutes.

Suppose you are taking a class in which you have pop quizzes. For example, in this class, 30 quizzes will be given in 16 weeks, but exactly when the quizzes will come varies. Quizzes could be given two days in a row, for example. How often would you study? Experiments show that behavior on a variable interval schedule occurs at a consistent low rate. That is, a rat will push a bar steadily but not very fast. Why push fast? The reinforcer does not come any sooner. But if a reinforcer does come, there could be another one right behind, so keep pushing. Students do the same thing. In a class with pop quizzes, students study a little each day but not very much. How much they study depends on how often the quizzes are given. If the quizzes come far apart on the average, then studying will be at a low rate because the probability of a quiz being given on a particular day is low. If the probability is high (quizzes come very often), then studying occurs at a higher rate.

Applications of Conditioning

Principles of classical and operant conditioning have had tremendous practical value. There are many ways in which institutions and individuals have used these two types of learning. Perhaps the first applications of operant conditioning were in the education of mentally retarded children and in the therapeutic treatment of the mentally ill. Today, behavioral programs are common and very successful.

Practical applications of *operant conditioning* are based on two procedures: reinforcing appropriate behaviors and extinguishing inappropriate behaviors. A kind word, a smile, a gold star on the refrigerator, a check mark on a piece of paper, and simply paying attention to someone are powerful reinforcers. However, what is a reinforcer for one person might not be for another, and what is a reinforcer in one situation might not be in another situation. For example, attention is normally a positive reinforcer, but not usually if a person is embarrassed or doing something wrong.

Sometimes reinforcement is given in symbolic form. In a **token economy,** for example, people are given the equivalent of tokens or check marks for appropriate behaviors. These tokens can be traded in later for various things, such as time off, access to toys, candy, books, and so on. Their main advantage is that they can be delivered immediately when an appropriate behavior occurs. Token economies and other operant conditioning programs have had great success.

Classical conditioning can be used when we want to either condition or extinguish behaviors that are reflexive. For example, wolves can be taught taste aversion by giving them sheep meat that is tainted with a pill that will make them sick. The wolves will later avoid sheep because of their smell. People can be conditioned to respond to certain stimuli also. Smell and taste are the best sensations to use as conditioned stimuli. For instance, people who need medicine to boost their immune systems can be given a sniff of a distinctive odor each time they take their medicine. After a few pairings, the odor itself will produce a boost in their immune systems.

Phobias are the best example of learned responses that can be extinguished in psychotherapy. If a person has an unpleasant reaction to some stimulus, the person can be trained to relax and then be exposed to the feared stimulus a little at a time. **Exposure therapies** (so called because the patient is exposed to the fearful stimuli), such as systematic desensitization described earlier in the chapter, are extremely successful at extinguishing classically conditioned responses.

Finally, classical and operant conditioning are also widely used in experimental research. When scientists plan experiments, often a person or an animal must first be taught some response. This is when principles of learning are applied. Much research in psychology depends on the principles described in this chapter.

THINK TANK | Describe some ways in which the principles of classical and operant conditioning could be used to help people or animals.

COGNITION

"To think is to differ."
—CLARENCE DARROW

Cognition is a general term for the processes by which people and animals gain and store information. Cognition includes paying attention, thinking, making decisions, problem solving, and memory. Cognitive processes may be conscious or unconscious. That is, your brain is learning and analyzing information, usually without your mind's awareness. Conditioning as described above does not involve complicated cognition. Humans and some other animals are capable of learning at a higher level than by simple conditioning. People learn to solve puzzles, work calculus problems, and do complex reasoning. Next we will look at two ways in which learning occurs in more complicated ways than those described above.

Observational Learning

It is not necessary for people or animals to have directly reinforced personal experiences in order to learn. Learning also occurs by witnessing someone else have an experience. This is known as **observational learning.** For example Bandura, Ross, and Ross (1961) found that children who watched a film showing adults beating on a Bobo-the-clown doll later imitated the adult's behavior very closely. There is a physiological basis for observational learning. Brain scientists have found cells, known as **mirror cells,** that fire when people perform an action but also fire when the people observe someone else perform the same action. We can learn how to bowl, golf, relate to others, use certain vocabulary, and many other behaviors via observation.

Observational learning is so common and so powerful that examples are innumerable. One of the most important is the effect that watching violent media has on aggressive behavior. To date, over 3,000 studies have found an increase in aggression and a decrease in sensitivity to aggression among people who watch violence on TV, in movies, and in video games (Anderson & Bushman, 2002). A study of 707 individuals over 17 years found that aggressive acts jumped 29% among teens who watched TV three hours or more daily (Johnson et al., 2002). Prime-time TV programs contain three to five violent acts an hour, and children's shows contain 20 to 25 per hour. Unfortunately, this correlation is downplayed by the media and is not firmly in public awareness (Bushman & Anderson, 2001).

Of course, not everyone who watches violent media commits an aggressive act. However, the effect is undeniable. For example, recently, we have seen gun shootings in high schools that were likely due in part to observational learning. Also, after terrorists crashed planes into the World Trade Center, a teenager flew a small plane into a building in Florida.

Even suicide and homicide are influenced by observational learning. During and shortly after a war, homicide rates increase in all the countries involved. Also, when a prominent person's suicide is widely publicized (for example, Kurt Cobain's some years ago), the suicide rate increases about 40% for a few months and then returns to normal. The suicide rate increases even after broadcast of a TV special or movie about suicide. A suicide intervention program in New Jersey (with all good intentions of course) informed teens about the high number of suicides among people their age. The result? Health researchers found that participating teens became much more likely to view suicide as a solution to their problems.

Look at yourself—your language, hairstyle, clothing choices, favored foods, values, habits, tastes, and nearly all of your behaviors have been caused or influenced by witnessing others. Advertisers count on it. Observational learning is undeniably important in our lives. TV and movies play a role, but our daily experiences with family, friends, and others likely contribute even more in shaping our behaviors, and most of this influence goes unnoticed. We normally are unaware of the power of observational learning. For example, when a child uses a profanity, and his parent might say, "Where the hell does he learn that kind of language?" Or a parent spanking a child might unwittingly utter a profound truth by saying, "This will teach you to hit your sister." Yes, that's often exactly what it is teaching him. We are normally unaware of the effects of observation, either as models or as observers.

Edward Tolman defined cognitive maps.

Cognitive Maps

In the 1930s, an American psychologist named **Edward Tolman** (1886–1959) performed a series of experiments that seemed to show that animals not only learned specific behaviors through experience, but also learned broader concepts. Tolman put rats in mazes with food as a reinforcer for finding the correct route through the maze. Just as Thorndike had found with his puzzle boxes, the rats got progressively faster at finding their way through the maze. Next Tolman did something clever. He rearranged the maze. Tolman discovered that the rats still could find their way to the goal box. He concluded that the rats had learned a mental idea of the maze, which he called a **cognitive map**. Apparently, the rats had learned not only the correct turns to make to reach the goal box, but also the general scheme—the layout—of the maze. When the maze was modified, the rats were still able to get to the goal box quickly because of their knowledge of its general layout. Can't you find your way around a familiar environment? You, too, have cognitive maps.

Cognitive maps are formed in the brain by interactions of cells in a region called the hippocampus and its surrounding areas. (These brain regions will also be discussed in the next chapter on memory.) The cells of the hippocampus that are dedicated to a certain space or orientation in our world are called place cells. Those cells provide the internal map that we conceptualize. Researchers have placed electrodes into the brains of mice and watched those cells fire as the mice move about their environment. Mice with impairments in certain genes have difficulty forming cognitive maps, indicating that this learning and memory process is dependent on genetic factors. The hippocampus is the region of the brain where new cell growth occurs. In fact, researchers have found a good deal of plasticity in this brain area. Interestingly, brain scans of taxi drivers in London found that their hippocampi were larger than average, apparently the result of learning vast cognitive maps of the city. The same thing has been found in a range of animals: A larger hippocampus is correlated with better spatial learning and memory (Biegler, 2001).

When we are learning something, often our brains are learning other things too. One thing we may learn is a mental idea of the situation—a cognitive map. But we may learn other things also. In fact, we usually do. This kind of learning, when extraneous things are learned almost as a side effect, is called **latent learning** or **incidental learning.** When we go about learning a specific thing, other things that perhaps are incidental or not intended to be learned are also being learned. Our memories are storehouses of many things that we learned incidentally to what was planned. As you read this textbook, for example, you are likely learning vocabulary terms, something about grammar, organization of information, and many other things that are incidental to learning the facts of the science of psychology.

> *FYI*
>
> Tolman was very charismatic and had many avid followers who called themselves "Tolmaniacs."

THE PHYSIOLOGY OF LEARNING

"Learning is a grim and serious business."
—MICHAEL R. BEST

When you learn, a change occurs in your brain. If you have an experience and you are different afterward, that's learning. Your behavior has changed because there was a change in your brain. The experience—classical conditioning or operant conditioning—produced a change in the cells of your brain. Many scientists are attempting to discover the precise biochemical details of the changes in the brain that represent learning.

One thing that research on this topic shows is that learning occurs at the synapses—the connections between brain cells. In addition, changes are often found in the hippocampus, the area of the brain that curls around in the middle of the temporal lobe. The physiological change that has been studied the most is called **long-term potentiation (LTP).** LTP has been found in the hippocampus during learning.

When a chemical signal is repeatedly passed from one cell to another at a synapse, changes take place in the structure of the cells so that the signal can be passed more efficiently. Usually, these changes are very short lived, and the cells return to their normal states. However, with repeated firing of cells, sometimes a long-term change takes place. The anatomical structure of the receiving cell changes in a manner that allows the signal to pass more easily. It's almost as if the cells get fused together into a network. This is the LTP process that many scientists believe is at the center of learning. The brain networks that are formed are like computer programs for the behaviors and mental phenomena associated with learning.

The details of LTP and other biochemical brain events that are involved in the process of learning will be discussed in the next chapter after a detailed description of the process that is the result of learning: the process of memory.

Recap

— An operant behavior can be learned faster by using shaping—reinforcement by successive approximations.

— Operant behaviors can generalize to other stimuli, but discrimination can occur if one stimulus is present when behavior is reinforced and the other during extinction.

— Schedules of reinforcement control how often a behavior is reinforced. Partial reinforcement results in behavior that is difficult to extinguish.

— There are four schedules: fixed ratio, variable ratio, fixed interval, and variable interval. Each results in a different rate of responding.

— Token economies use reinforcements that are abstract and can be used with groups. Exposure therapies are used to treat people with undesirable conditioned responses.

— Observational learning is the very common method of learning by seeing or hearing—similar to imitation.

— Tolman discovered cognitive maps: internal (mental) models of the environment that are learned through experience, such as with rats in a maze.

— Incidental or latent learning occurs when something is learned accidentally or unintentionally.

— The physiology of learning involves processes that occur at the synapse, such as long-term potentiation. These various processes theoretically strengthen and weaken the connections between neurons, thus influencing neural networks.

I Link, Therefore I Am

There are a number of Web sites that describe various types of learning including http://www.as.wvu.edu/~sbb/comm221/chapters/pavlov.htm on classical conditioning, http://www.brembs.net/operant/operant.html on operant conditioning, and http://www.pigeon.psy.tufts.edu/psych26/default.htm on animal Learning and Cognition.

The B. F. Skinner Foundation home page is at http://www.bfskinner.org/

The Exploratorium in San Francisco has an interesting Web site, including this feature on memory: http://www.exploratorium.edu/memory/index.html

STUDY GUIDE FOR CHAPTER 5:
LEARNING

Key terms and names (Make flash cards.)

learning
conditioning
operant behavior
respondent behavior
classical conditioning
operant conditioning
association learning
stimulus
reflex
unconditioned
unconditioned stimulus (US)
unconditioned response (UR)
paradigm
conditioned stimulus (CS)
conditioned response (CR)
Ivan Petrovich Pavlov
diminishing returns
learning curve
delay conditioning
CS-US interval
backward conditioning
trace conditioning
taste aversion
tabula rasa
extinction
systematic desensitization
fear hierarchy
spontaneous recovery
generalization

discrimination
discrimination learning
second-order conditioning
third-order conditioning
higher-order conditioning
John B. Watson
behaviorism
Little Albert
Mary Cover Jones
counterconditioning
Edward Lee Thorndike
puzzle boxes
law of effect
instrumental conditioning
B. F. Skinner
Skinner box
reinforcers
contingencies of reinforcement
punishment
operant level
positive reinforcer
negative reinforcer
discriminative stimulus
reinforcer
primary reinforcers
secondary reinforcers
conditional reinforcers
extinction
extinction bursting

extinction curve
positive reinforcement
positive punishment
negative punishment
negative reinforcement
shaping
generalization
discrimination
stimulus control
schedules of reinforcement
continuous reinforcement
partial (intermittent) schedule
partial reinforcement effect
ratio schedule
interval schedule
fixed ratio
postreinforcement pause
ratio strain
variable ratio
fixed interval
variable interval
token economy
exposure therapies
observational learning
mirror cells
Edward Tolman
cognitive map
latent (incidental) learning
long-term potentiation (LTP)

Fill in the blank

1. Learning means the same thing as _____.
2. Learning is defined as the process of _____ due to _____.
3. We walk, talk, move our arms, and so on. These actions are called _____ behaviors because they are ways in which we operate on the world.
4. Automatic, reflexive reactions to things are called _____ behaviors.
5. The two types of learning are called _____ conditioning and _____ conditioning.
6. Any stimulus that causes an automatic reaction is called an _____ stimulus.

7. Classical conditioning was first extensively studied by a Russian physician named _____ _____.
8. In Pavlov's most famous experiments, he used a _____ as a conditioned stimulus.
9. The fastest learning occurs when the CS-US interval is about _____.
10. If the US is presented before the CS, it is called _____ conditioning.
11. Recent research indicates that for learning to occur using _____ conditioning, the animal must be conscious.
12. One response that is learned very easily is _____ aversion.

13. The term _____ _____ means "blank slate."

14. The unlearning of a response is called

_____.

15. The most successful therapy for extinguishing unwanted responses is called _____

_____. In this therapy, the feared stimuli are paired with _____.

16. A dog will salivate when he hears other bells that are similar to a bell that was used in the conditioning. This phenomenon is called _____.

17. It is possible to learn a response to one stimulus but not to other stimuli that are similar. That is, we could condition a dog to salivate to one sound but not to another similar sound. This is called

_____.

18. John B. Watson was an American psychologist who is known as the founder of the school of psychology known as _____. Watson used classical conditioning on an infant known as

_____ to demonstrate that emotions could be learned.

19. A treatment that attempts to undo a classically conditioned response by forming an incompatible one is called _____.

20. The law of effect was discovered by a psychologist named Edward Lee _____.

21. Thorndike built elaborate _____

_____, in which he studied the behavior of _____.

22. Thorndike discovered the Law of _____, which states that a behavior followed by something _____ will become _____

_____ and a behavior followed by something _____ will become

_____ _____.

23. B. F. _____ built an experimental device that he called an *operant conditioning apparatus*, but we call it a _____

_____.

24. The consequences that strengthen behaviors are called _____.

25. The natural, normal rate at which a behavior occurs is called the _____ _____.

26. Some reinforcers have strengthening power because of our natural biology. Things like food, water, warmth, and sex are known as _____ reinforcers. But most things that reinforce behavior have been learned and are called _____ reinforcers.

27. The initial increase in the rate of a behavior at the beginning of extinction is called _____.

28. Escaping from something unpleasant is known as

_____ _____.

29. When something pleasant is removed, the process is called _____ _____.

30. We can increase the rate of learning by using a technique in which we reinforce behaviors that come gradually closer to the goal. This is called

_____.

31. If a behavior is reinforced every single time it occurs, the schedule of reinforcement is called

_____.

32. With _____ schedules of reinforcement, a behavior must occur a number of times before it is reinforced, while _____ schedules are based on time passing.

33. The behaviors of many people can be reinforced by using a _____ economy.

34. It is possible to learn by witnessing someone else have an experience. This is known as _____

_____.

35. When extraneous things are learned almost as a side effect, it's called _____ learning or _____ learning.

36. The physiological change in the brain that occurs during learning is called _____

_____.

Matching

1. Thorndike _____
2. Pavlov _____
3. Skinner _____
4. token economy _____
5. bursting _____
6. respondent behavior _____
7. S^D _____
8. S^r _____
9. S^R _____
10. operant behavior _____
11. imitation _____
12. partial reinforcement _____
13. LTP _____
14. extinction _____
15. FR _____
16. VI _____
17. Tolman _____

a. secondary reinforcer
b. reflexive reaction
c. puzzle boxes
d. cognitive maps
e. discrimination
f. ratio schedule
g. increase in response
h. an action
i. classical conditioning
j. interval schedule
k. physiology of learning
l. primary reinforcer
m. observational learning
n. resists extinction
o. unlearning
p. operant conditioning
q. operant conditioning for groups

Multiple choice

1. Your niece has learned to be nervous around fire-works because of the loud noise they make. What type of learning was involved?
   a. negative reinforcement
   b. classical conditioning
   c. latent
   d. cognitive maps
2. A psychologist says that he used operant conditioning to help a patient develop better social skills. This means that the psychologist used
   a. reinforcers
   b. cognitive maps
   c. compliments
   d. observational learning
3. If *negative reinforcement* causes a person to make more excuses, it means that the person is getting
   a. something pleasant when making excuses
   b. punishment when making excuses
   c. away from something unpleasant when making excuses
   d. classical conditioning
4. An ad for chewing gum uses upbeat music that makes listeners feel happy. What principle is at work here?
   a. shaping
   b. positive reinforcement
   c. higher-order conditioning
   d. discrimination
5. What principle is involved when a worker tends to repeat old habits during a new task?
   a. observational learning
   b. extinction
   c. schedules of reinforcement
   d. generalization

6. Mike's dog barks every time the doorbell rings. One day when they were out for a walk, Mike's pager rang, and his dog began to bark. What kind of response is barking, and what principle was demonstrated?
   a. classical conditioning; shaping
   b. operant; generalization
   c. negative punishment; discrimination
   d. CR; higher-order conditioning
7. Partial schedules of reinforcement result in
   a. fast learning
   b. less generalization
   c. resistance to extinction
   d. classical conditioning
8. A consequence that has an effect on an operant behavior is called a
   a. conditioned stimulus
   b. discriminative stimulus
   c. reinforcing stimulus
   d. partial schedule
9. If a flash of light is followed by a loud, unexpected noise, a person might later react to the flash of light. The flash of light is then called
   a. a conditioned reaction
   b. a conditioned stimulus
   c. a discriminative stimulus
   d. an unconditioned stimulus
10. If a student asks a question only when the student is with a certain friend, then the friend is known as a
    a. conditioned stimulus
    b. unconditioned stimulus
    c. discriminative stimulus
    d. reinforcing stimulus

11. If a dog learns to salivate when she sees a triangle but not when she sees a circle, this is called
    a. operant conditioning
    b. generalization
    c. discrimination
    d. backward conditioning

12. If a child learns to say "I'm sorry" to stop his mother from yelling at him, the process of learning is called
    a. classical conditioning
    b. positive reinforcement
    c. negative reinforcement
    d. negative punishment

13. A behavior may be operantly conditioned if a negative reinforcer is
    a. paired with the CS
    b. paired with the US
    c. added, following the behavior
    d. removed, following the behavior

14. A rat pushes a bar and receives a reduction in a painful stimulus. The rat's bar pushing increases in frequency. This procedure is called
    a. positive reinforcement
    b. classical conditioning
    c. discrimination learning
    d. negative reinforcement

15. Each time a rat pushes a bar, he is shown a red triangle. He pushes the bar less and less. What do we call this procedure?
    a. negative reinforcement
    b. negative punishment
    c. avoidance conditioning
    d. positive punishment

16. If a salesperson is paid only when she makes a sale, she is on a _____ schedule of reinforcement.
    a. continuous   b. discrimination
    c. ratio   d. interval

17. Partial schedules of reinforcement make extinction
    a. occur more easily   b. more difficult
    c. impossible   d. classical conditioning

18. A sales manager tells his staff that they will get paid each time they make a sale. But, of course, they must call a number of people to make a sale. What type of schedule is this?
    a. FR   b. VR
    c. FI   d. VI

19. Nikki took a new route through her neighborhood on her way to school, but she knew which way to turn at each point because she had formed a
    a. higher-order
    b. generalization
    c. schedule of reinforcement
    d. cognitive map

20. Your uncle had an accident on a train, and now he is too nervous to ride one again. A psychologist would recommend therapy focused on
    a. negative reinforcement
    b. extinction
    c. generalization
    d. avoidance conditioning

21. A student runs around the room when it is time to do arithmetic. The S^D is
    a. the teacher
    b. time to do arithmetic
    c. running around the room
    d. getting out of doing arithmetic

22. If a person learns fear of butterflies because people scream when they see a butterfly, then what is the CS?
    a. the screaming
    b. the butterfly
    c. the fear
    d. the situation the person is in

23. In Question #22, what is the CR?
    a. fear from the screaming
    b. fear from the butterflies
    c. screaming
    d. the butterfly

24. If a child swears only when Dad is around, then what is the R?
    a. Dad
    b. swearing
    c. the attention the child gets
    d. making Dad upset

25. In Question #24, what is Dad?
    a. the R   b. the CS
    c. the SD   d. the SR

26. Each time Frank scores a basket, his coach says that he can do two fewer push-ups after practice. What type of learning is this?
    a. classical conditioning
    b. positive reinforcement
    c. negative reinforcement
    d. punishment

27. Susan is learning to play the violin and finds the fingering easy because she already plays guitar. What principle is involved here?
    a. generalization
    b. classical conditioning
    c. discrimination
    d. shaping

28. When talking to one sister, Mark has learned not to mention babies, but he talks about babies with his other sister all the time. What principle is involved here?
    a. shaping   b. negative reinforcement
    c. generalization   d. discrimination

29. Which of these is an example of classical conditioning?
    a. Mary gets nervous when it's time to do math.
    b. His puppy barks every time Jimmy slams the door.
    c. A cat runs from the room when the TV comes on.
    d. A student opens his book in class.
30. A little girl was startled by a loud noise just as she reached for an ice cream cone, and now she is frightened of ice cream cones. What type of learning is this?
    a. classical conditioning
    b. operant conditioning
    c. observational learning
    d. incidental learning
31. In the above question, what is the CS?
    a. the ice cream cone
    b. the startled reaction
    c. whatever startled her
    d. the learned fear
32. Where on the learning curve does learning occur at the fastest rate?
    a. the beginning
    b. the middle
    c. the end
    d. it is consistent throughout
33. In backwards conditioning
    a. the CR comes before the US
    b. the CS comes before the US
    c. the R is not reinforced
    d. the US comes before the CS
34. In trace conditioning, the CS
    a. is not presented
    b. is left on when the US is presented
    c. is followed by a discriminative stimulus
    d. is off when the US comes on
35. If a rat learns to dislike a certain food because it make him sick, this is called
    a. negative reinforcement
    b. latent learning
    c. Skinnerian
    d. taste aversion

36. If an American flag is used as a stimulus to condition people to like a politician, this is an example of
    a. negative punishment
    b. negative reinforcement
    c. discrimination learning
    d. higher-order conditioning
37. A professor pauses, opens her eyes wide, and raises her eyebrows when she expects students to write something in their notes. These gestures serve as
    a. reinforcers
    b. unconditioned stimuli
    c. discriminative stimuli
    d. hierarchy elements
38. Psychologists usually do not recommend
    a. negative reinforcement
    b. systematic desensitization
    c. counterconditioning
    d. punishment
39. Stimulus control is sometimes used to change behavior. This involves using the
    a. reinforcing stimulus
    b. discriminative stimulus
    c. generalization gradient
    d. fear hierarchy
40. Which of the following is an example of negative reinforcement?
    a. A woman becomes afraid of driving because of an accident she had.
    b. A man stops eating tuna sandwiches after getting sick.
    c. A student takes a different route to school to avoid a bully.
    d. A dog comes running when he hears his master come to the door.

Short answer and critical thinking

1. What are respondent and operant behaviors? Give an example of each.
2. Describe and give examples of classical and operant conditioning.
3. What are generalization and discrimination?
4. Define higher-order conditioning. Give an example from advertising.
5. Describe a Skinner box and how it is used to investigate learning.
6. Contrast positive and negative reinforcement. Give an example of each.
7. What are some reasons that punishment is not recommended?
8. What is partial reinforcement? What effect does it have on the rate of learning and extinction?
9. What is the difference between ratio and interval schedules?
10. Describe the Bobo-the-clown doll experiment. What did it show?
11. What are cognitive maps? How were they discovered?
12. What is latent learning?

Memory

PLAN AHEAD...

• How does memory work? Are there different kinds of memory? •

• What causes amnesia?

• Where are memories stored in the brain, and how does this happen?

• What are short-term and long-term memories? How much information do they hold, and how long do they last?

• What causes forgetting?

• How can people improve their memories?

Do you have a good memory? Most people answer that question with an emphatic "No!" Why do so many people believe that they have a bad memory? I think it's because most people have the wrong concept of memory. They compare their memories to some near-perfect system, such as a copy machine. If you think that your memory is supposed to effortlessly copy things that you sense and then store those exact replicas in some perfect system for later retrieval, no wonder you think you have a bad memory! No one can do that. That is not how memory works. Memory is a funny, tricky process that does not work like a video camera, tape recorder, or computer. Memory is a *process* more than a storage system. The process is sloppy and easily influenced. It often fails to reproduce things accurately, and it often fails to store or retrieve things correctly. You probably don't have a bad memory at all. Your memory is probably perfectly normal. Now if you can only remember that I told you so!

THE ESSENCE OF MEMORY

"You have to begin to lose your memory, if only in bits and pieces, to realize that memory is what makes our lives. Our memory is our coherence, our reason, our feeling, even our action. Without it, we are nothing."
LUIS BUÑUEL, SPANISH FILMMAKER

Before getting into the sticky details of human memory, it's a good idea to get an overall picture, a conceptual understanding of memory. Here are some of the most important ideas for an accurate concept of the complicated process of human memory:

1. Memory is the flip side of learning. Learning refers to the process through which changes are made in the brain that lead to changes in behavior. Memory is the process that maintains changes in the brain over a period of time. Memory and learning are just two ways of looking at the same thing. Experiences cause physiological changes in the brain, changes that are manifested as changes in behavior. When those changes persist, we call it memory.
2. Memory is not one process. There are many different types of memory, each of which involves a number of different elements or steps. In this chapter, you will learn how psychologists divide memory into different categories and the steps involved in each different type of memory. As you will see, when someone asks if you have a good memory, a good answer would be "Which kind?"
3. Memory is a tricky thing—complex and difficult to talk about. We do not have the right words in our vocabularies to talk about the different types of memory and its intricacies, so in many cases, psychologists have had to create new terms. Still, that's often not good enough because the topic is very complicated, with many twists, turns, and parameters. For instance, recent research

has demonstrated that false memories can be implanted. If people are interviewed many times and each time they are asked whether a certain event happened to them in their childhood, somewhat surprisingly, many people eventually start remembering the event, although it was purely an invention of the interviewer. The more often a person is asked about it, the surer he or she becomes that it happened and the more details about the false memory the person recalls.

4. As was noted above, memory generally is not a photocopy or recording process. We do not simply record events precisely as they occur and then store them in our brains to be retrieved in the same form later. Memory is much more like perception or like a creative, problem-solving process. When we want to remember something from our past (what did you eat for lunch last Tuesday?), we do not merely reach into a memory bin and open the file for "Tuesday" or "lunch" and read what's on it. We recreate our memory working from landmarks: "Let's see, on Tuesday I was at Ted's house, and we were working on some writing, oh, yeah, then we ordered some Chinese take-out; I think I had fried rice, no, wait, I was going to get fried rice, but instead I ordered egg rolls." Memory is like solving a puzzle. It is also like perception in the sense that it is a process of creation and interpretation that is easily influenced. Memories often change over time.

5. Memory is a process of brain changes that are stored for future access. Those brain changes are physiological events. We do not know the precise nature of those events, although scientists have recently unraveled a good deal of the memory puzzle. The change in the brain that represents a memory is known as an **engram**. For many years, researchers have been attempting to uncover the secrets of the engram, and the search is nearing an end.

THINK TANK

In your experience, what are the most common ideas that people have about memory?

What are the most common questions or concerns that people have about memory?

The Search for the Engram

A neuropsychologist named **Karl Lashley** (1890–1959) is best known for his attempts to find the precise location of a memory in the brain. Lashley studied with the founder of behaviorism, John B. Watson. In his research, Lashley used laboratory rats in an attempt to find the precise location of a memory engram in the rats' brains.

Where is a memory stored in the brain? How could we find out? Lashley's approach to this problem was simple. First he taught a rat to do something, such as run a maze. The rat learned the task to the level at which it was firmly stored in the rat's memory. Then Lashley destroyed a tiny section of the rat's brain. The rat was then tested to determine whether the memory was still there. If it was, Lashley destroyed another small area of the rat's brain and tested the rat in the maze again. He continued this procedure until the rat could not remember how to run the maze. Then he assumed that he had found the engram—the last brain area that was destroyed before the rat failed to run the maze must have held the memory.

Lashley's simple plan did not work. He found that rats still remembered how to run the maze even when many areas of their brains had been destroyed. Lashley found that it was necessary to destroy practically the whole brain of a rat before the damage interfered with the rat's memory of the maze. For some reason, his method did not work. What went wrong?

The problem with Lashley's method is that it assumed that a specific memory was located in one small, specific area of the brain. But most memories are made of vast networks of cells that extend throughout many areas of the brain. For an analogy, suppose that you wanted to stop people from driving from Minneapolis to Chicago. You could destroy a section of a highway between the two cities, but drivers would just take another route. You could destroy a section of that second route, but drivers would take still another route. And so on. There are many routes from Minneapolis to Chicago. Similarly, memory in a brain is not located in one tiny area; it is spread through **neural networks**.

The brain stores and computes information in neural networks, similar to a spiderweb or highway system, except with feedback loops.

Though Lashley did not discover the location of a memory engram for a particular memory, more recent research has found that one area of the brain is critically important for memory formation.

Riding the Seahorse

In the middle of the brain's temporal lobe is a structure known as the **hippocampus** (Greek for "seahorse"), so named because it is has a curved shape. There is one hippocampal structure in each hemisphere of the brain, left and right, deep within the temporal lobes. The hippocampi are located in the medial temporal lobes of the brain, tucked under the cerebral cortex. The hippocampi are interconnected with a number of other structures of the medial temporal lobe, all of which are involved in the formation of memories. Damage to these areas results in severe problems in creating new memories, that is, in making the physical engrams that represent memories in the networks of the brain.

In 1954, in Montreal, a man with epilepsy underwent a brain operation to remove the abnormal tissue causing his seizures. The doctor removed the hippocampi in both hemispheres of the patient, who is now known in psychological literature by his initials, **H. M.** Following his recovery, it was noticed that H. M. no longer was able to retain information in memory. Amazingly, he could not form any new memory engrams. He still had all his old memories, that is, the engrams that had formed in his brain before his surgery were still in place. But now H. M. could not retain anything new. Removal of his hippocampi destroyed his ability to form any new memories.

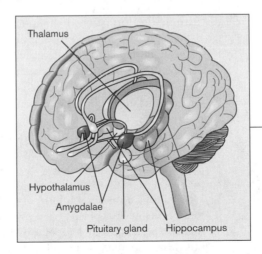

Thalamus

Hypothalamus

Amygdalae

Pituitary gland   Hippocampus

The hippocampus and its surrounding areas are important for storing declarative memories. The amygdala is where emotional memories are stored. The cerebellum stores memories for procedural memories involving muscle movements that are fast and automatic, that do not require thinking.

This fact—that the hippocampus helps create memories and damage to it results in a person with no ability to form new memory engrams—has seeped into the popular culture. Such a person can retain old memories but lose the ability to form new ones. This fact has been parodied on *Saturday Night Live* in a sketch called "Mr. Short-Term Memory" and has been portrayed in such films as *Winter Sleepers* (1997) and *Memento* (2001).

H. M.'s inability to form new memory engrams was studied by psychologist **Brenda Milner,** who in 1997 was inducted into the Canadian Medical Hall of Fame. Milner's research gave scientists fresh ideas about where to look in the brain for the seat of memory. Apparently, the hippocampal region is essential for creating memory engrams. This is where long-term potentiation (the physiological process associated with learning and memory) occurs and also is the area that recently has been found to make new brain cells. But the hippocampal area can be damaged in a number of ways, which thereby interferes with memory. Alzheimer's disease, stroke, alcohol, marijuana, and even stress can damage cells in that critical memory area.

Three Types of Amnesia

There are three types of amnesia, or memory difficulty:

1. **Anterograde amnesia** is what H. M. has. In this type of amnesia, a person has damage to the hippocampus or surrounding regions of the medial temporal lobe and hence is unable to form new memory engrams. People with anterograde amnesia have all of their previously stored memories but have no memories of events that occurred after damage to their hippocampi. A person with anterograde amnesia cannot form new memories. **Korsakoff's syndrome** is a type of memory loss that mostly involves anterograde amnesia. Korsakoff's occurs in people who use alcohol so heavily that it impairs their intake of vitamin B_1 (thiamine). Thiamine deficiency harms the neurons in areas of the brain required for memory formation.

2. In **retrograde amnesia,** a person has experienced a blow to the head or other injury or disruption that interferes with the formation of memories. The memories that were being processed when the injury occurred were not stored as memory engrams—they are permanently lost. Therefore, the person with retrograde amnesia will have no memory of events that happened *before* the injury; those memories did not get stored. Usually, retrograde amnesia causes a disturbance in memory formation for events up to about one hour before the disruption. An example is shock treatment, a medical therapy for depression that is discussed in Chapter 10. A patient who has this procedure will have retrograde amnesia because the brain seizure that is induced by electric shock disrupts the formation of memories. Another example is Princess Diana's bodyguard who survived the car crash that killed her. The bodyguard has no memory of the accident—he has retrograde amnesia. Attempts were made to use hypnosis and other means to help him recover memories of the accident and events that occurred just before. These attempts failed, and such attempts will always fail, because the engrams of the accident and events just before are not in his brain. The memory of those experiences was not formed because the accident (the blow to his head) stopped the physiological process by which his brain stores memories. He will never remember those events that happened about one hour before the car accident. In retrograde amnesia, the process of storing memories is disrupted, and the memories are lost.

3. **Dissociative amnesia** is a form of repression, a blocking of memory retrieval, that occurs when a person has a psychological shock. A person who has a traumatic experience may temporarily lose his or her memory of important, obvious things, such as name and address. This is a type of psychological disorder (discussed in Chapter 9) that results from extremely stressful circumstances. In this case, the amnesia is for things that are already stored in the brain, so this is a problem of memory retrieval. People with dissociative amnesia will later recover their memories. In dissociative amnesia, the memory engrams are in the brain and are only temporarily inaccessible because of psychological shock.

TWO KINDS OF MEMORY

"It's like déjà vu all over again."
—YOGI BERRA

People with damage to the medial temporal lobe, like H. M., who have anterograde amnesia, have difficulty forming new memories. But this is true only for one type of memory. The hippocampal area of the brain is necessary for what is called **declarative memory.** One could think of it as "conscious" or "aware" memory. This is the memory that allows you to declare things. For example, you declare your name, your phone number, where you live, the capital of France, the day of the week, and so on. Declarative memory includes your memory of things from your past and facts that you have learned. Declarative memory is what everyone thinks of when we talk about memory. It includes all of the memories that are in our minds or can be brought to mind.

The hippocampus and surrounding areas of the brain are necessary for helping to form the engrams for declarative memory. In fact, some researchers have placed electrodes into those areas of the human brain and recorded the firing of cells as a declarative memory is being formed (Fernández et al., 1999). The findings showed that different areas of the hippocampal region were involved and that declarative memory can be divided into even smaller processes. Of course, damage to that region of the brain interferes with forming declarative memories. However, there is one kind of memory that people with hippocampal damage have no trouble forming.

The second kind of memory is called **procedural memory** because it involves storing information in the brain about procedures for moving our bodies in certain learned ways. Procedural memories include things like remembering to feel afraid when you see a snake, to feel happy when you see a cute puppy, to be nervous when asked to speak in front of the class, and how to ride a bike, type, swim, walk, drink from a glass, reach for a pencil, and write. You do not "declare" them; you "proceed" on the basis of them. *Declarative memories* are in your conscious mind; *procedural memories* are your brain's automatic reactions to things. Procedural memories are a type of **implicit memory,** memories that are unconscious, automatic reactions that are implied or not readily apparent as memories. In this sense, declarative memories are sometimes called *explicit memories* because they are apparent, obvious, clear-cut memories.

Damage to the hippocampus and other areas in the medial temporal lobe of the brain interferes with the formation of declarative memories but not of procedural memories. H. M., for example, although he cannot form any new declarative memories, can retain procedural memories. For instance, if H. M. took piano lessons for six months, he would have no memory of having had the lessons, but he would be a better piano player—his brain would remember how to play piano, though his mind would have no memory of the lessons. Similarly, if you visited with H. M. every day and he had a pleasant time talking with you, later he would have no memory of ever having met you, but he would be happy to see you when you arrived. His brain would remember to react to you, but his mind wouldn't know why.

The existence of these two memories in the brain can help to explain many things. We might, for instance, have no memory of a certain event yet have feelings or reactions about it. We can have a **déjà vu experience,** for example. We could have a procedural memory of something (a feeling, a body reaction) but no declarative memory.

In a certain setting, a stimulus might trigger a body response or feeling, a procedural memory, but it might not be enough or might not be the right type of stimulus to activate the declarative system. Hence, you have a feeling but don't know why. The brain, to some extent, separates these two kinds of memory. Also, declarative and procedural memories are divided into subtypes.

THINK TANK

Have you ever had a procedural memory—a body reaction or feeling—without a corresponding declarative memory—the conscious awareness of where and when it came from?

What are some skills and habits you've learned that you can do without thinking?

What about emotional reactions—do you have some that you can't explain?

Types of Declarative Memory

The brain divides declarative memory into two types of memory storage. One is known as **semantic memory.** This refers to memory of general facts. Semantic memory stores information about the general world, facts that are not dependent on personal experience. Semantic memory includes things like the following: The past tense of "run" is "ran," the capital of Minnesota is St. Paul, the director of *Psycho* was Alfred Hitchcock, the sum of three and four is seven, the plural of "mouse" is "mice," and other general facts. What were the first names of the Beatles? Do you remember? That information is stored in your semantic memory.

The other type of declarative memory is called **episodic memory.** This is the storehouse of episodes that have happened to you. The episodes in your life are different from general facts because they are stored in your brain together with a place and a time—events happen in a particular setting and at a specific time. The brain stores these events in the parietal lobe, which is the brain region for time and place. Episodic memory includes the name of your sixth-grade teacher, what you did on your last birthday, how you get from your bedroom to your kitchen, what you ate for lunch yesterday, and where you put the batteries you recently bought. Episodic memory tends to decrease with age more than does semantic memory. An old person will still remember the capital of Minnesota but might not remember where he put his glasses a few minutes ago.

The episodic memory system uses somewhat different brain circuits and brain anatomy than does the semantic memory system. They are both declarative memories because they are both conscious (in the mind) memories. But a person could be better at one than the other because they use different brain pathways. Which one of your declarative memory systems is better: semantic or episodic?

In one interesting example, three schoolchildren with damage to their hippocampi were able to attend mainstream schools because their brain damage left their semantic memory systems relatively normal (Vargha-Khadem et al., 1997). These children can learn general facts; however, the injuries to their hippocampi have affected their episodic memories. The result is that these three children cannot recall the episodes that they experience in their daily lives. Time and space dimensions are not being stored in their brains. They can learn the names of countries, languages, and general facts, but they don't remember whether they ate lunch.

In another example, researchers using the EEG found different brain wave patterns associated with episodic memory than with semantic memory (Klimesch et al., 1997). They concluded that cognitive functions associated with attention, such as episodic memory, use lower-frequency brain waves than do functions that deal with general facts, such as semantic memory.

Interestingly, two sets of research in 1998 (Wagner et al. and Brewer et al.) showed that the amount of information that a person later remembered could be predicted by the amount and location of brain activity that occurred during learning. In other words, by looking at the brain activity that occurs when a person is learning something, we can then predict how well that person will later remember the information. The areas of the brain that were shown to be involved were the hippocampal area and the prefrontal lobes. Perhaps schools of the future will measure students' brain activity during learning to see whether their lessons have stuck in their memories.

Although the hippocampus and surrounding areas of the brain are necessary for the formation of declarative memories, those areas are not necessarily where declarative memories are stored. Studies have found that declarative memories eventually get stored into neural circuits in the brain's cortex (Bontempi et al., 1999). So the hippocampal region has cells that help somehow in creating declarative memories, but these memories are later stored in cortical networks. A person with damage to the hippocampus still has his or her old memories (stored in the cortex) but cannot form new ones because the hippocampus is required for that.

The hippocampus is the area of the brain that creates new brain cells (**neurogenesis**). Up to 5,000 new cells are generated every day, but most of them die; the number that survive depends on learning, that is, when we learn, more cells survive (Shors, 2001). After time, the memory gets stored in the neocortex. Researcher Tracey Shors said, "Learning did not generate new cells but rather enhanced the survival of cells that were generated prior to learning . . . the vast majority die within weeks, but there's something about hippocampus-dependent learning that rescues them from death."

Also, as mentioned in Chapter 5, the hippocampus and surrounding areas are important for forming memories of our position in the environment; for making cognitive maps. Certain cells in this brain area (place cells) fire when a person or animal is in a certain place or location within the surroundings (Maguire et al., 1998) and other cells (head direction cells) fire when we look in a certain direction (Sharp et al., 2001). Recall from Chapter 5 that people and animals with larger hippocampal areas are better at spatial learning and memory (Biegler et al., 2001).

Types of Procedural Memory

There are three subtypes of procedural memory, memories that are implicit, automatic body reactions:

First are skills and habits. These are the automatic ways in which our body moves in performing coordinated actions. You walk, brush your teeth, drink from a glass, use a fork to bring food to your mouth, sign your name, throw a ball, and so on. Memories of skills and habits are stored in circuits of nerve cells in the **cerebellum** of the brain. These circuits are created by practice. Each time you make a successful body movement, a network of cells in the cerebellum gets stronger or more tightly fused together. When you practice playing piano, you are gradually creating memory circuits in your cerebellum. Each practice of a body movement makes a stronger connection within the cerebellum's circuits.

A second form of procedural memory is classical conditioning. This process was described in Chapter 5. Classical conditioning involves learning an automatic, reflexive reaction to a new stimulus through an association or pairing of the new stimulus with a stimulus that already causes the reaction. Responses that are emotional in nature are stored in the brain's **limbic system,** particularly in the **amygdala.** For example, if a person learns to be afraid of something, or learns to react pleasantly to some stimulus, or learns to feel angry, in each case the emotional memory is stored in the circuits of the amygdala (LeDoux, 1996; Seidenbecher et al., 2003).

On the other hand, classically conditioned muscle movements are stored in the cerebellum, just as are skills and habits. If a person is conditioned to blink when he hears a bell, that response is "wired" into the cells of the cerebellum. These procedural memories are stored without the use of the hippocampal area. People with damage to their hippocampi, such as H. M., can learn and remember skills and habits and can be classically conditioned to react to stimuli. However, they will have no memory of the learning process. Several animal studies have shown that damage to the hippocampus does not prevent learning a fear response through classical conditioning but does interfere with learning an association to the situation or circumstances under which the learning occurs. A hippocampus is necessary for some kinds of memory, but not for others.

The third form of procedural memory is called **priming.** This is a physiological event that happens at the synapse, the connection between brain cells, and is the beginning of the learning and memory process. Each time a signal passes through a synapse, the cells change in such a way as to make it a little easier for the signal to pass again. This is called priming. We can measure it by how fast a person responds to a stimulus. With each presentation of a stimulus, the person will respond faster than before. For example, we could ask H. M. to look at words projected on a screen. If a word has only one syllable, we ask H. M. to push a button on the left. If a word has more than one syllable, he is to push a button on the right. We then measure how long it takes him to push a button. If we present a particular word to H. M. a second time, he will make the decision and push the button faster than he did the first time he saw the word. That is, his brain will process the word faster the second time. This is priming. Note, however, that H. M. will have no memory of having seen the word two times. The second time he sees the word, he has no declarative (conscious) memory of having seen it before. Although his mind doesn't remember having seen the word before, his brain cells remember it.

Here is a summary of the types of memory we have covered so far.

TABLE 6.1   Types of Memory

Declarative (Explicit)	Procedural (Implicit)
Semantic (facts)	Skills and habits
Episodic (personal events)	Classical conditioning
	Priming

Recap

— Memory is the flip side of learning; it is a tricky process with many different parameters. It is not a photocopy machine but is more like perception or problem solving.

— Lashley couldn't find the engram because he assumed that it was in one small place. Memories are stored all over the brain in neural networks, vast connections of brain cells.

— The hippocampus and its surrounding areas help to create memory engrams, the physiological representations of memory in the brain. Damage to these brain areas results in an inability to create new declarative memories. H. M. is a classic example.

— There are three types of amnesia: retrograde (brain disruption causes failure of recent information to be stored), anterograde (damage to hippocampus causes inability to form new memories), and dissociative (psychological shock temporarily blocks retrieval of personal memories).

— Memory is divided into two basic types: declarative (semantic and episodic) and procedural (skills and habits, classical conditioning, and priming). Declarative memory is our conscious "mind" memory; procedural memory is body memory.

THREE BASIC STEPS OF MEMORY

"Memory, the warder of the brain."
—Shakespeare (Macbeth)

To remember something requires that three things happen. Failure in any of these three will interfere with memory. If a person has a bad memory, it is because there is something going wrong with one or more of these three basic steps. All three are necessary for memory.

Encoding

The first step in memory is to get things into the brain. This process is simply called **encoding,** which literally means "coding in." You can't remember something if you don't first encode it. It won't be in there later if you don't put it in in the first place.

Encoding is related to several things. First, encoding obviously depends on paying attention. While you listen to a lecture, for example, if your attention is on something else, you will not encode the concepts being presented. Do you daydream during class? This interferes with memory because it does not allow information to be encoded—you are not focusing on the lecture. In a sense, brains can pay attention to (hold in the conscious mind) only one thing at a time. If you don't pay attention to certain information, it won't be encoded, and you won't recall it later. If you are introduced to someone and you are thinking about something else when the person's name is said, you will not recall that person's name later. You did not encode it.

You can significantly improve your memory merely by developing your ability to pay attention to the things that you later want to recall. You can use the principles of operant conditioning—reinforce your "paying attention" behaviors. For instance, when you meet people, get into the habit of saying their names back to them: "This is Sheila." "Hello, Sheila, it's nice to meet you." Having a good memory begins with paying attention to salient things. Fortunately, paying attention is a skill that can be improved.

When we encounter information, there are other stimuli present that get encoded with the information. When you listen to a lecture by a professor, the facts that are encoded into your brain are not separate from the situation. Encoded with the information are **cues** in the environment, such as the professor, the features of the classroom, the overhead screen, the blackboard, and your classmates. Therefore, memories can be triggered by cues that were encoded with them. During a test, if you come to a difficult question, try looking at the professor, the screen, or the blackboard to try to trigger the memory.

Memories are also encoded together with stimuli from your body and mind that are present when the information is experienced. If you are always hungry when you attend psychology lectures, then being hungry can be a trigger for recalling psychology information. The **state** that we are in when we encode something is also encoded and therefore can later be a trigger. A person who suffered a period of depression years ago might have forgotten about the things that happened then. But if that person experiences another period of depression, then many of the memories from the previous depression will come flooding back. In summary, memory depends on both cues (external stimuli) and states (internal body conditions). Therefore we say that memory is **cue dependent** and **state dependent.**

Finally, encoding can be done all at once or gradually over time. Psychologists refer to these two memorizing conditions as **massed** and **spaced** (also known as **distributed**). Decades' worth of research has consistently shown that spacing out your learning is much better than cramming all at once (Willingham, 2002). It is almost always better to learn something a little at a time than to spend hours in a single session. Spaced practice nearly always results in more material remembered and for a longer time.

Storage

The second step in the memory process is to store information, that is, to put information into the networks of the brain. This is a physiological process that is often called **consolidation.** As has already been pointed out, for declarative memory, storage depends on the hippocampal region of the brain. For procedural memories, the amygdala and cerebellum are important storage sites in the brain.

Memories are stored in networks of cells. Consolidation is a biological process that takes some time. If the storage process is interrupted, consolidation might not get completed, in which case the information will be lost. For example, if a person suffers an injury to her brain that disrupts the process of consolidation, she will not store any of the information that she recently encountered. A physical injury to the head impairs the physiological process of consolidation. The person will have retrograde amnesia for the information that did not get stored—information that she encountered about one hour before the brain disruption.

You can influence the storage process by learning information a certain way. Psychologists have a concept called **depth of processing.** This idea says that the deeper you process information, the better you will later remember it and understand it. Depth of processing is attained by thinking through material in rich and various ways. When you memorize information, the more mental operations you use (the more thinking and associating) and the more complex they are, the better you will remember the material. Presumably, by thinking deeply, you are creating more neural networks, more connections between different brain areas, and this helps to store the memory *deeper*. That is one reason why you should consider the "Think Tank" questions and other similar material in this textbook.

Consolidation is a physical event that takes time. Some research shows that sleep, particularly REM sleep, is important for helping memory consolidation to occur (Mednick et al., 2003). For example, subjects who learned a task performed poorly when they were tested only a few hours later but performed much better after a night's sleep. Also, subjects who had experienced REM sleep, even during a nap, had better visual memory. Much anecdotal evidence has suggested that problems can be solved by sleep and dreaming. All cultures seem to have the concept of "sleeping on a problem." A suggestive study found that rats that ran a maze showed the exact brain activity in their hippocampi during REM sleep as they had while learning the maze (Louie & Wilson, 2001). Apparently, brains use REM sleep as a means of replaying or recapitulating events that are being remembered. Our dreams might be vestiges of the brain's storage of memories. Take note: Students should not skip sleep when studying for a test!

Retrieval

The final step in the memory process is to get information out of storage when you want it. This process is called **retrieval.** Psychologists divide retrieval into three categories:

Free recall is a type of retrieval that requires you to find something in your memory without any help—you must freely recall things from memory. An essay exam is a good example of free recall retrieval. What is the capital of Wisconsin? You must retrieve the answer from your brain without any help. As you probably know, this is the most difficult type of retrieval because you must search through your stored memories without any outside help for where to look. Free recall, therefore, takes longer than other kinds of retrieval. Knowing something about what you're looking for helps to narrow the search. Free recall is hard because we have to look everywhere!

Cued recall is a bit easier because in this type of retrieval, you are given a cue to help you retrieve the information from your brain. The cue narrows the search. For example, the capital of Wisconsin is the name of a former president. What is it? Did you get it? If not, here's another cue: The capital of Wisconsin begins with the letter "M." Did you get it now?

You can improve your memory by converting free recall problems into cued recall problems. You do this by purposely encoding cues with the information you want to learn. For example, if you meet someone named Maggie, try to associate some distinctive feature of her face with the name Maggie. Perhaps you can see the letter "M" in her hairline or eyebrows. Or maybe the name Maggie reminds you of that old song "Maggie May" ("Wake up, Maggie, I think I've got something to say to you. / It's late September and I really should be back in school."), and you can find something in this woman's face or hair that reminds you of the singer Rod Stewart (maybe she has a rooster-style hairdo!). It also helps to use rhymes as cues. Perhaps you know someone named Larry whom you'd like to bury, or someone named Kate who's always late, or a man named Ted whose face is red, or a guy named Jim who likes to swim, or someone called Mike who should take a hike.

FYI

James McConnell trained flatworms (*Planaria*) to run mazes, then cut them in half (*Planaria* can regenerate body parts) to see whether the head or the tail would remember how to run the maze. They both did! He even chopped them up and fed them to other worms (*Planaria* are cannibals) to see whether memory would transfer chemically. He claimed that it did. Psychology professors got nervous. This research was so popular in the 1960s that a journal was created called the *Worm Runner's Digest*.

Last names can be rhymed too. Try it. Cues help us to retrieve information from memory storage.

The easiest type of memory retrieval is called **recognition.** In this case, you must merely recognize information that is stored in your brain. Recognizing someone's face is an example. This is why people are better with faces than with names. Recalling a name is a free recall problem (very hard), whereas recalling a face is a recognition problem (much easier). A multiple-choice question is also an example of the recognition type of retrieval. This is why most people prefer multiple choice: It is much easier to recognize an answer than to recall it with no help. Which of these is the capital of Wisconsin: Milwaukee, Madison, Montpelier, or Monroe?

Retrieval is dependent on encoding. That is, the manner in which you retrieve something from your memory depends on how you put it in (encoded it) in the first place. If you encode things in a sloppy way, you will retrieve them in a sloppy way. If you encode things in an organized way, then you will recall them in an organized way (hint, hint). When you want to remember something, you should encode it in the manner in which you later want to retrieve it. Use organization, outlines, rhymes, groupings, cues, alphabetical order, associations, and other practices that will encode information in a format other than randomly. Randomly stored memories are hard to retrieve.

Have you ever seen a question that you knew the answer to but you couldn't think of it? Have you ever experienced the **tip-of-the-tongue phenomenon?** These are problems of retrieval. You can't have a good memory just by encoding and storing information. You have to be able to find it when you want it. Encoding it properly will help. When you encode information, encode it in an organized way, associating it with cues that will later help you to find it and retrieve it from storage.

Another interesting feature of retrieval is called the **serial position effect.** When you want to learn a number of things in a particular order, such as the lines of a poem, it is later much easier to recall things from the beginning or end of the order than from the middle. Things in the middle of a list are hardest to remember. Things at the beginning of a list are the first ones to get into the brain. There is nothing before them to interfere with their encoding; the beginning of the list has the advantage of the **primacy effect.** Things at the end of the list, because they have nothing after them to interfere, have the advantage of the **recency effect;** they are the most recently encoded. However, things in the middle are at a disadvantage, being interfered with from both the front and the back. This is what is called the serial position effect. Therefore, you need to spend more time studying the middle of a chapter than the beginning or the end. The same thing is true for memorizing a poem or any other material that is to be learned in a certain order. The items in the middle of the list will be most difficult to recall.

THINK TANK   Give some examples from your experience of memory being cue dependent or state dependent, and also of the tip-of-the-tongue phenomenon.

What are some ways in which memory can be aided by encoding cues?

Recap

— The three steps of memory are encoding, storage, and retrieval.

— Encoding depends on paying attention. Also, memories are encoded with cues (external stimuli that are present) and with states (internal body conditions).

— Storage involves physiological events in the brain that create stronger connections between brain cells. This process is called consolidation. Depth of processing influences memory. Sleep, particularly REM sleep, also seems to be important for this process.

— Retrieval includes free recall, cued recall, and recognition, in order of ease.

— Information is retrieved from memory in the same manner that it was encoded. That is, retrieval depends on encoding. So, to get things out easily, encode them in a well-organized way.

— The tip-of-the-tongue phenomenon is a common retrieval problem.

— The serial position effect predicts that items in the middle of a list will be the most difficult to later recall.

A MODEL OF DECLARATIVE MEMORY

"A memory is what is left when something happens and does not completely unhappen."
—EDWARD DE BONO

You have certainly heard of short-term and long-term memory. These terms are part of a model of memory that psychologists have used for decades. This model divides declarative (conscious) memory into three separate components or storage systems. Here is a diagram that illustrates the model.

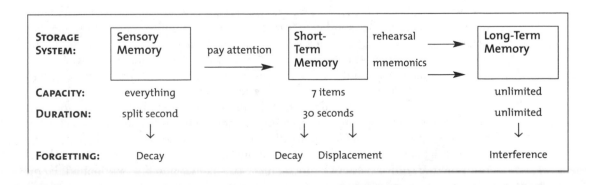

STORAGE SYSTEM:	Sensory Memory	pay attention	Short-Term Memory	rehearsal / mnemonics	Long-Term Memory
CAPACITY:	everything		7 items		unlimited
DURATION:	split second		30 seconds		unlimited
	↓		↓ ↓		↓
FORGETTING:	Decay		Decay Displacement		Interference

Sensory Memory

The first type of memory in this model is the very brief memory that is stored in our sensory systems when we sense something. When you look at something, the cells in your eyes are stimulated and send signals to other cells, which in turn send signals to other cells, and so on, throughout the visual pathway in your brain. For a split second, while the cells in the visual pathway are sending signals, the memory of what you have seen is stored in the networks of your brain. Everything that you have seen is now in your sensory pathways. This is called **sensory memory,** although the memory in each of the senses has its own terminology. For instance, visual information that is stored for a split second is called **iconic memory,** and auditory information that is stored for a brief moment is termed **echoic memory** (echoic lasts a bit longer than iconic). Both are part of sensory memory.

The information in sensory memory rapidly fades away, a process called **decay.** The cells of our sensory systems hold incoming information for only about a split second, then return to their resting state to receive more information. Wave a pencil in front of your face. If you move it fast enough, you will see more than one pencil. This is your sensory memory. Your brain retains the information for a split second, but it quickly decays. If information is to be retained for longer than a split second, it must be moved into another of the brain's memory systems: short-term memory. More about this in a minute.

Sensory memory was first studied by a psychologist named **George Sperling** (1960), who studied iconic memory. Sperling had people look at a screen on which he projected some letters of the alphabet, similar to the illustration shown here:

G   Z   P
B   D   K
H   M   F

The letters were on the screen for only 1/20 second, not long enough for subjects to rehearse them. (Look at them quickly.) Sperling then turned off the projector and asked the participants to recall as many of the letters as they could. (Go ahead—I'll wait.) He found that the average number recalled was about four of the letters.

Then Sperling did something interesting. Again he projected the letters onto the screen, and again he turned off the projector. But while the screen was blank, he sounded a tone indicating that one of the rows of letters should be recalled (a high, medium, or low tone). We would expect the participants to recall only a fraction of the letters in a particular row, but Sperling found that they got it right every time. You see, *all* of the letters were in their sensory memories, and if the tone occurred soon enough, they could "read" the visual information that had been retained for a split second. If the tone came too late, the information had decayed, because iconic memory fades away after only a split second.

Some people have remarkably strong iconic memories. They can look at a picture and later recall very precise details about it. This rare ability is known as **eidetic imagery.** It is probably what people mean by "photographic memory." A well-known case was described by the famous Russian psychologist **Alexander Luria.** The patient's name was Shereshevski, and he appeared to have an unlimited ability to remember details. He could repeat complex information, even backwards, after hearing it only once, even after many years. This seems like an ability that would be very useful, but in fact this man reported that all the details in his memory interfered with his attention. Apparently, it is possible to remember too much. The purpose of memory is to focus on what is important and to forget the unimportant details. Of course, for most of us, information drops out of our sensory memory very easily and rapidly. But what about when we want to retain information for a longer period of time?

To get information from sensory memory into the next memory system, **short-term memory,** it is necessary for the brain to pay attention to the information. If you are not paying attention when your professor says something important, that information will enter your sensory system and then fade away (decay) and be lost. Paying attention allows information to be encoded into the short-term memory system. We must mentally attend to information that we want to remember for more than a split second. Everything in our sensory fields enters our nervous system. However, almost all of it will stay there for only a split second. Only the information that we pay attention to will last; that information goes into the second memory system: short-term memory.

Short-Term Memory

Short-term memory is something of a buffer (protector) zone, because it holds information in memory long enough (it protects it) for us to decide whether we want to retain it. The sensory system holds *everything* that you sense. Everything is there for a split second. However, the short-term memory system holds only selected items—those that your brain pays attention to.

When you pay attention to something, that information is stored in your short-term memory. But the short-term system is a bit of a bottleneck because it can hold only a very limited amount of information. Whereas sensory memory holds *everything* that you sense, short-term memory has a very limited capacity. Psychologist George Miller (1956) called the capacity of short-term memory "the magic number seven, plus or minus two." On the average, short-term memory will hold only about seven bits of information. There is some variation between different people, of course, and depending on what types of items are to be remembered. But for almost all adults, short-term memory has a capacity of seven plus or minus two—in other words, a range of five to nine items.

Miller called short-term memory capacity a "magic number" because for all normal adults, the capacity is about seven items. Only seven items can be stored at once in short-term memory. If you try to put more in, some others will fall out. This process of dislodging items with new information is called **displacement.** Let's try it: Remember these numbers: 3, 7, 2, 8, 4. Close your eyes and repeat them. Can you do it? I bet you can, since five items is well within your short-term memory capacity. How about these: 6, 3, 2, 7, 9, 5, 8? Look away and try to say them. Did you get it? That is about the capacity of short-term memory, so you should have felt "filled up." Now remember these numbers: 4, 9, 2, 7, 8, 3, 2, 4, 6, 3, 9, 7. I bet you had great difficulty with those, since twelve items will not comfortably fit into short-term memory.

The items in short-term memory are called *chunks*, because they are not limited by their size. That is, you can fit more than seven items into your short-term memory if you put them into meaningful chunks. Remember these numbers: 2, 4, 6, 8, 1, 3, 5, 7, 2, 4, 6, 8. I bet you can do it. When we say that short-term memory will hold seven items, we mean seven completely separate items. This list of numbers is not really twelve separate items. The capacity of short-term memory is seven *chunks*, and each chunk can contain any number of items as long as they are grouped together as one unit. This means that many items can be squeezed into short-term memory by creating meaningful groupings. This process is called **chunking.** The numbers in the above paragraph, for instance, could be chunked like this: 4, 9, 2, 7 (49 is two 7s, or 7×7), 8, 3, 2, 4 (eight times three is 24), and 6, 3, 9, 7 (63 is nine times seven). In this way, twelve items are squeezed into three chunks. Similarly, the sequence of letters FBIUCLACIAJFK is hard to remember unless you chunk it into these four: FBI UCLA CIA JFK. When you need to squeeze a lot of material into memory very rapidly, then chunking is for you.

Short-term memory is not only limited in capacity, it is also limited in duration. Items in short-term memory will decay (fade away) after a period of time, unless you move them into **long-term memory.** The duration of short-term memory is measured by giving information to people, then distracting them so that they cannot hold the information in mind, then after a bit of time asking them to recall as much as they can. For example, I will show you a list of nonsense syllables, then ask you to count backwards by threes starting with 100, then after some time I will ask you to recall the nonsense syllables. Here: NES, TOF, YAJ, RUK, PYD, NAL, KEC. Now count backward, starting at 100, by threes: 100, 97, 94, 91, 88, 85. . . . Keep going. . . . After a while, I will ask you to recall as many of the nonsense syllables as you can. This kind of experiment has been done millions of times using many different types of information to be recalled. Results show that, on the average, information is retained in short-term memory for about 15 to 30 seconds for a normal adult. More meaningful information is retained longer than nonsense items, of course, and some people can hold information longer than others. But short-term memory does have a limited duration: less than a minute in most cases and for most people.

Short-term memory is much more limited in children and in people with brain diseases, such as Alzheimer's disease. For example, a young child might be able to hold only three items, rather than seven, in short-term memory. A person in the later stages of Alzheimer's disease might only be able to hold one or two items in short-term memory.

Long-Term Memory

Long-term memory is what most people think of when they talk about memory. It includes information that has been stored long ago and is available in a nearly unlimited way. That is, long-term memory is the brain's process of consolidating information into neural networks that can hold a virtually unlimited amount of information for practically one's whole life. Long-term memory, for practical purposes, is unlimited in capacity and duration. Once you learn your name, where you grew up, where you went to school, and so on, you will never forget—as long as the brain cell networks that hold that information are not interfered with. Of course, Alzheimer's disease and other brain diseases can impair long-term memory. The brain's frontal lobe is mostly responsible for long-term memory, and it begins its development between the ages of one and two (Liston & Kagan, 2002). That's why you don't remember being a baby.

Everyone believes that information decays (fades away) from long-term memory after long periods of time. Isn't that why we can't remember details from things that happened many years ago? No, this is usually not correct. The neural networks that store information in long-term memory may decay somewhat over time, but the loss of memory from long-term storage is more commonly caused by other factors. As we go through life and encounter new experiences and information, we use brain cell networks for storing new information. This process is called **interference.** You can't recall the details of events that happened years ago because the brain cells that once stored that information are now busy with new things. The memory loss is not primarily because of the time that passed, but because of the new information being stored. If you had an experience, stored it into your long-term memory, and then went into a coma for 30 years, you would still recall that experience when you awoke. Time passage (decay) is normally not the reason that information is lost from long-term memory. Interference is typically the culprit.

We say that long-term memory is unlimited, but perhaps you can see that this is not entirely true. Because of interference, items stored in long-term memory can be lost. This is because we do not have an unlimited number of brain cells with which to store information. However, the number of brain cells we have is so large that for practical purposes, one can always fit more things into long-term memory. Don't worry—you will never reach the point at which your memory is full and you have to tell your professor that you just can't learn any more. There is a limit to memory, of course. But that limit is so large that it does not have practical implications. More important than the limitations of brain cells is the process of forgetting, which will be discussed later in this chapter. But first, more about how long-term memories are stored.

There are two ways to move information from short-term memory into long-term memory. One is **rehearsal**: going over and over material. Because going over information again and again helps to *maintain* it in memory, psychologists call this process **maintenance rehearsal.** Going over information again and again changes the involved brain cells and synapses, thus strengthening the memory. Eventually, a change occurs in the structure of the synapses that makes the network of cells relatively permanent. The information is now stored in long-term memory. Maintenance rehearsal is like writing your name in wet cement. If you write it only once, the wet cement will ooze, flow, and fill it in. It will be gone. However, if you write your name again and again in the same place as the cement is drying, eventually it will stick.

Although maintenance rehearsal will transfer information into long-term memory, there are a number of problems with this approach. It is slow, boring, and tedious and makes for difficult retrieval because the information is put into the brain disconnected from cues that will later make it easy to find. If you memorize something by going over it again and again, it will eventually stick in long-term memory, but there is little motivation for such a boring process, and retrieval later will be difficult. There is a second way to transfer information from short-term memory to long-term memory that is more efficient. This second method involves connecting the new information (what you want to learn) with things that are already stored in memory. This process is called **mnemonics,** and it makes the transfer faster and the information easier to retrieve, because the new information will be associated with something already in long-term storage.

MNEMONICS

"The more you use your brain, the more brain you will have to use."
—GEORGE A. DORSEY

A **mnemonic device** is a gimmick, trick, or aid that helps to store information into memory. The term *mnemonic* (pronounced "nih-MAH-nik") comes from the Greek word for "memory capability." There are many different mnemonic devices that you can use. However, it is important to understand that in most cases, it is no good to use the exact details of someone else's mnemonic device; for maximum advantage, you must create your own. This is because a mnemonic device works by the cognitive process of making a connection between the new information and something meaningful that is already in storage. So in most cases, each person must determine what is meaningful to him or her and what items already in the person's long-term memory can properly (meaningfully) be associated with the new thing.

A common mnemonic that serves as a good illustration is to take the first letters of a list of things and make a meaningful word from them (an acronym). For instance, HOMES is a mnemonic for the names of the five Great Lakes (Huron, Ontario, Michigan, Erie, and Superior). ROY G BIV is a mnemonic used to recall the colors of the spectrum in order (red, orange, yellow, green, blue, indigo, and violet). CANU is an acronym for the four states that come together at one point in the Southwest United States (Colorado, Arizona, New Mexico, and Utah). A similar mnemonic device creates a sentence from the letters representing what we want to remember. For example, the lines of the music staff can be remembered with "Every Good Boy Does Fine."

Another mnemonic device is called the **pegword method.** In this technique, certain words are used as association "pegs" for the new information you want to remember. A simple example of a pegword system is called **one is a bun.** Take each digit from one to ten and associate a word with each: One is a bun, two is a shoe, three is a tree, four is a door, five is a beehive, six is sticks, seven is heaven, eight is a gate, nine is fine, ten is a hen. You memorize these pegwords, and then when you want to learn a list of things, simply associate each thing with the appropriate pegword. Let's try it.

Here is a list of 10 words to memorize: vacation, chair, stumble, create, math, bottle, truck, book, computer, microphone. Now associate each word with its pegword. Think of some crazy, wild connection between "vacation" and "bun" (one is a bun). Perhaps you took a ride on a bun for your vacation. Or for your next vacation, you are planning to go inside a bun and spend a lot of dough. Next, think of a weird, funny association between "chair" and "shoe" (two is a shoe). You put a chair on your foot, or you sit down on a big shoe. (Remember, you must make your own mnemonics—the association must be formed in *your* brain, not in mine. The examples I'm giving will not be as helpful as the ones you create yourself.) Now make an association between "stumble" and "tree." Got one? Mine is that I see a tree walking down the street, and it stumbles on a pebble. Next associate "create" and "door." Maybe you "created" a door in your mind that allows you to escape from this silly game! (Visual imagery is very helpful.) Next, associate "math" with "beehive." I know—you're stung by your math homework, or the π (pi) symbol is flying out of a beehive. Next, connect "bottle" with "sticks." Did you see that guy in the Guinness Book of World Records who sticks bottles in his mouth? "Truck" must be associated with "heaven." Got it? Now, "book" and "gate." Was that too easy? Remember, make the associations unusual, funny, or weird (not just a gate made of a book); otherwise, they will be hard to recall because they won't stick out from other items. Next, "computer" and "fine" (nine is fine). If you use your computer too much, you will be charged a fine. Making images in your mind will help you later recall the items. Finally, "microphone" and "hen" (ten is a hen). Did you see that standup comic who looked like a rooster doing jokes? The microphone laid an egg.

Okay, let's see how you did. What was the fifth word in the list? Five is beehive—what stung you? What was the ninth word? Nine is fine—so the answer is . . . What was the second word? Two is a shoe. What was the tenth word? How about the fourth? Four is a door. The first word went with bun. What was it? Do you remember the seventh word (seven is heaven)? Well, how did you do? Notice that this system allows you to recall the words in any order, not just the way they were presented. Psychologists have found that the pegword system is one of the best ways for people to quickly memorize a list of items. Of course, if this was your first try with it, you will improve immensely with practice (you're on the front end of the learning curve). So keep at it.

Still another mnemonic device that you might find helpful is called the **method of loci.** The term *loci* (pronounced "LOW-sigh") means "places"; it is the plural of *locus.* This system is similar to the pegword system, except that instead of using words as the pegs for making associations, you use places. First think of a series of places that are very familiar to you—for instance, the things that you see or encounter in your house when you get up in the morning: the bed, the nightstand, the hallway, the staircase, the dining room table, and so on. Or think about the things you pass when you drive from your home to school: gas station, shopping mall, big corporation, hotel, pink house, Evergreen Boulevard, elementary school, and so on. Then when you want to learn a list of things, you merely place each one into those loci in your mind, in the order in which you want to remember them. You make weird associations just as with the pegword method, except that here, each item is associated with a place—a locus.

Mnemonic devices are part of what psychologists call **deep processing.** If you simply go over and over some material (maintenance rehearsal), that information will be stored in a shallow way, difficult to retrieve and easy to forget. It is better to use **elaborative rehearsal** by connecting new information to material that you already know. Connecting new information in different ways to many different ideas that are already stored will help to make the new material be deeper, easier to retrieve, and less likely to be forgotten.

THINK TANK

Did you find the discussion of mnemonics helpful?

Can you think of other memory tricks?

In what areas of your life will these be most useful?

What social or educational policies or practices would you recommend in order to help people improve their memories?

Recap

— Declarative memory is divided into three types: sensory, short-term, and long-term.

— Sensory memory holds everything you sense but lasts only about a split second, short-term holds about seven items (plus or minus two) for about 15 to 30 seconds, and long-term memory is relatively unlimited but is affected by interference.

— Short-term memory is a bottleneck in the system because it can hold only about seven items. That information will fade away (decay) unless it is rehearsed or connected to things in long-term memory.

— Long-term memory is relatively unlimited in capacity and duration.

— Information can be moved into long-term memory by maintenance rehearsal (a tedious process) or by memory aids (mnemonics) that will associate new information with old.

— Mnemonic devices, such as the pegword system and the method of loci, help to connect new material to things already in memory and therefore aid the encoding, storage, and retrieval processes. This is part of deep processing.

— There are many mnemonic devices, including rhymes, stories, acronyms, the pegword method, and the method of loci.

FORGETTING

"The horror of that moment, the King went on, I shall never, never forget. You will,

though, the Queen said, if you don't make a memorandum of it."
—LEWIS CARROLL (THROUGH THE LOOKING GLASS)

Long-term memory is relatively unlimited in its capacity and duration, but that doesn't mean that we don't forget things. Items from *sensory memory* decay (fade away) in a very brief period of time—only a split second. Items from *short-term memory* will decay after

Hermann Ebbinghaus was the first psychologist to experimentally study forgetting.

about 30 seconds, and they also will be displaced if we try to remember more than our brains can hold (about seven items). Long-term memory is somewhat subject to decay, but is more often influenced by other types of forgetting. Interference is the major cause of forgetting from long-term memory, but other factors are also involved.

Early Research on Forgetting

The first psychologist to experimentally study forgetting was **Hermann Ebbinghaus** (1850–1909). Ebbinghaus received degrees in history and philosophy from the University of Bonn, fought in the Franco-Prussian War, and traveled for several years, earning his way by tutoring. In the 1870s, he read a book by Wilhelm Wundt (the first experimental psychologist) in which Wundt claimed that higher mental processes such as memory could not be studied experimentally. Ebbinghaus took this as a challenge. He also had recently read a book on psychophysics by Fechner (see Chapter 4) that showed how mathematics could be used to investigate sensations. Consequently, Ebbinghaus decided that math could also be used to study memory.

The initial method that Ebbinghaus used is very simple. He used himself as a subject, studied a list of items, timed how long it took to learn the whole list, waited for a period of time, then learned the list again, timing how long it took. If he could learn it faster the second time than the first, then he must have remembered something. The difference between the times was called the **savings score** because it indicated how much had been "saved" in memory.

What did Ebbinghaus memorize? Because stimuli differ greatly in their ease of memorization, Ebbinghaus invented **nonsense syllables** to use in his research. He created hundreds of consonant-vowel-consonant (CVC) combinations, such as TEJ, NAR, LEF, PUX, and GIR. He divided these CVC nonsense syllables into lists of 16. He learned a list perfectly, waited a period of time, and then memorized the list a second time. Of course, he carefully measured the amount of time it took to memorize a list the first and second times. Ebbinghaus also varied the amount of time (the delay) between the first and second memorizations.

Naturally, Ebbinghaus discovered that his average savings scores (the difference in the amount of time it took for perfect memorization between the first and second attempts) got smaller the longer the delay between the memorizations. The more time that passed, the less was saved in memory. For example, suppose it took 20 minutes to learn a list the first time and only four minutes the second time, with a delay of one hour. Then the savings score for a one-hour delay was 16 minutes. But if Ebbinghaus waited two hours, suppose it took him 14 minutes to relearn the list perfectly—a savings score of only six minutes. The longer the delay, the less the savings.

When Ebbinghaus mathematically graphed his results, he was astonished and delighted to find not only that savings scores decreased with delay times, but also that the pattern was consistent. Ebbinghaus's results fell on a **forgetting curve,** a sloping pattern that looks very much like the extinction curve shown in Chapter 5. Ebbinghaus discovered that memory fell off rapidly immediately after learning but then gradually subsided and almost leveled off. Here is a typical forgetting curve.

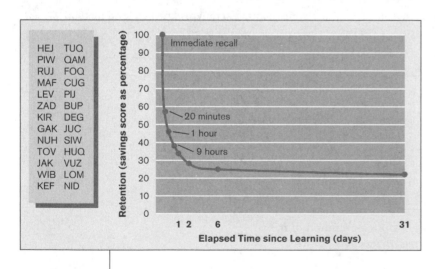

The forgetting curve. Information is forgotten most rapidly in the beginning.

Ebbinghaus's report of his findings, *On Memory* (1885), became one of the most highly regarded works in experimental psychology and proved that Wundt had been wrong in his belief that memory could not be experimentally studied. Ebbinghaus wrote this inscription on the title page of his book: "From the most ancient subject we shall produce the newest science." Of course, he was right; the scientific study of memory is today one of the most active fields within psychology.

Causes of Forgetting

There are many reasons why we forget. First, there are biological functions that can interfere with memory—injury and diseases that can cause permanent impairment of memory, as well as traumas and shock that can cause temporary amnesia. People with dementias, strokes, head injuries, substance abuse problems, medical conditions, and other biological impairments often have memory failure.

Second, remember that memory requires three processes: encoding, storage, and retrieval. Failure of any of these three steps will result in memory problems. For example, a common memory difficulty occurs not because information is lost from storage, but because it is difficult to retrieve. Certainly, you have had the experience of not being able to recall something at a particular moment but then being able to recall it later. Retrieval problems are common causes of forgetting.

Sigmund Freud proposed that sometimes memory retrieval is blocked by **repression**. That is, a person might be unable to remember something because the experience of remembering is traumatic or stressful. Freud said that our minds can protect us from the anxiety of remembering certain things by blocking those things from our consciousness. Repression is seen in cases of people who have had terrible traumas such as war experiences, imprisonment in a concentration camp, rape, incest, or physical abuse. Repression is a retrieval problem.

False Memories

Today a very controversial debate is raging over the idea of **repressed memories.** On the one hand, some psychologists argue that traumatic experiences in childhood, such as sexual abuse, can be repressed for long periods of time and can precipitate various psychological problems, such as anxiety, depression, and nightmares. Psychotherapists have stated that some of their patients have recovered repressed memories of childhood traumas during the process of therapy.

On the other hand, many psychologists believe that the evidence for repressed memories is overblown and that repressed memories are often **false memories** that were planted in the patients' minds. Some psychologists argue that many of the repressed memories of traumatic experiences that are recovered during psychotherapy are false memories that were induced by the treatment process and reinforced by the therapists. As you can imagine, this is a contentious and important issue and one that will likely inspire heated discussion for years to come.

Psychologist **Elizabeth Loftus** has been in the forefront of the view that false memories are common and easily planted in the minds of unsuspecting people. Her research has shown that 25% of participants believed that they had been lost in a shopping mall as a child after it was suggested to them. In another experiment, children were presented with various experiences and asked to "think really hard about each event and try to remember if it really happened." In this case, 44% of children aged three to four, and 25% of children aged five to six remembered at least one false event as if it were real. Two similar studies (Hyman & Billings, 1998) using college students as participants found between 20% and 25% of the participants came to believe that a false event was real. Loftus has planted false memories in more than 20,000 volunteers

Connecting Concepts

Memory is the flip side of learning. Do you remember studying conditioning in the previous chapter? If you look back at the extinction curve, you will find that it has the same shape as the forgetting curve.

(Woods, 2003). As was stated earlier, memory is a tricky business; not a filing cabinet, but a process that changes over time. Loftus described the process this way:

> As new bits and pieces of information are added into long-term memory, the old memories are removed, replaced, crumpled up, or shoved into corners. Memories don't just fade, they also grow. What fades is the initial perception, the actual experience of the events. But every time we recall an event, we must reconstruct the memory, and with each recollection the memory may be changed—colored by succeeding events, other people's recollections or suggestions. . . . Truth and reality, when seen through the filter of our memories, are not objective facts but subjective, interpretative realities. (Loftus & Ketcham, 1991)

Another study (Pezdek et al., 1997) found that some memories are more easily planted by suggestion than are others. The key factor in this study was the extent to which the memory was plausible. Children aged 5 to 12 were presented with two true events and two false events that supposedly happened to them when they were four years old. The plausible false event was that the child was lost in a mall while shopping. The implausible event was that the child had a rectal enema for constipation. This event was chosen by the researchers because it is similar to sexual abuse in that it is embarrassing and involves touch. An earlier study had shown that it was more difficult to plant a false memory that involved touch. The researchers found that many more of the children remembered the plausible event than the implausible event. Of 39 children, 17 recalled being lost in the mall, and four recalled the rectal enema. Research has found that adults also will recall plausible events more readily. However, it is important to realize that what is plausible to one person might not be plausible to another. A child who was sexually abused will likely be more susceptible to false memories about abuse than was a child who was not. Also, it is significant that four of the 39 children recalled the false implausible event as a real event. Such research findings will undoubtedly spur even more debate and research.

THINK TANK

Try to remember something from the distant past that can be verified with a photograph—for example, people from your high school class that you can look up in your yearbook.

Before doing any verification, create a distinct visual memory.

Then check it with your source.

How accurate were you?

In what ways did false memories creep in?

Say Cheese

Another kind of memory is **flashbulb memory** (Brown & Kulik, 1977). This funny term refers to memories of events that were surprising and important, such as remembering when you first heard about the terrorist attacks September 11, 2001. (I was in my office talking on the phone with my daughter. Where were you?) Flashbulb memory is a type of episodic memory, because it involves a time and a place. Like a flashbulb, these memories are vivid, quick, bright, and intense and stick in the mind like a photo. Flashbulb memories that have been studied are typically of upsetting events, such as assassinations or tragedies, but they could be of pleasant things too, as long as the event is a surprise and of major importance (Tekcan, 2001).

People's memories of the details of such events are very good; they recall as much as 90%, even two weeks after. A year later, subjects can recall more than 50% of the details of such things as where they were, what they were doing, how they found out about the event, and how they reacted. This is one type of memory that sticks in the mind very well. However, people often overestimate the accuracy of flashbulb memories; although they are often more accurate than memories of daily experiences, they are not perfect.

Interference

The most common cause of forgetting information from long-term storage is interference. Because we are constantly bombarded with new information, previously stored memory engrams are interfered with. If Ebbinghaus had gone to sleep between his first and second memorizations, his savings scores would have been much higher!

Psychologists divide interference into two types depending on whether our forgetting is being caused by something that happened before or after the event we want to recall. If you are having difficulty remembering the things you learned in your sociology course last semester because of the courses you are taking this semester, that is called **retroactive interference.** (It helps to remember that *retroactive* means to "move backward.") The other kind of interference occurs when you want to remember something now but are having difficulty because of things you learned in the past. This is called **proactive interference** (*proactive* means to "move forward"). Perhaps at work you have a new routine to learn, but you are having difficulty remembering it because the old routine is such a habit (so ingrained into long-term memory) that it gets in the way.

Everyday Forgetting

Psychologist Daniel Schacter has studied and written extensively about memory. He has summarized the normal ways our memories fail us in daily life and calls them the *Seven Sins of Memory* (2001). Here is his list of seven ways of forgetting:

1. *Transience:* Decreasing accessibility to information over time
2. *Absent-mindedness:* Lapses of attention and forgetting to do things
3. *Blocking:* Temporary inaccessibility to stored memories
4. *Misattribution:* Connecting memories to the wrong sources
5. *Suggestibility:* Implanted or false memories
6. *Bias:* Distortions of information based on knowledge and beliefs
7. *Persistence:* Unwanted memories that the person cannot forget

Connecting Concepts

As was noted earlier, emotional memories are stored when the amygdala interacts with hormones to strengthen neural networks. A flashbulb memory is probably vivid and long-lasting because it involves an emotional response. Of course, there is survival value in remembering such things.

THINK TANK

In what ways do you agree or disagree with Schacter's list?

What connections can you make between his seven types of forgetting and the information that was presented in this chapter?

Is he forgetting anything?

THE BIOLOGY OF MEMORY

"Seen it all, done it all, can't remember most of it."
—ANONYMOUS

Contemporary brain research has given scientists a good start in understanding the biological factors involved in memory. In the past, memory was conceived as simply an element of our intellectual and cognitive abilities. Today, scientists are more likely to think of memory as a series of complicated biochemical functions that are spread throughout the brain and, as has already been described, as occurring in different forms and guises.

Storage

Although the hippocampal region of the brain is critical for the formation of declarative memories, it should not be considered the filing cabinet or storage location of memories. The hippocampus and surrounding brain areas are necessary for the consolidation of declarative memory (making the brain changes necessary for a conscious memory to be stored for a long period of time), but memories are stored in networks throughout the brain.

Many of our conscious memories are stored in the cerebral cortex. There is no "memory center," however. Memories are distributed throughout the cortex in neural networks, complicated webs of interconnected brain cells. The components of a memory are stored in localized areas: Visual memories are in the back, in the occipital lobe; auditory memories are on the side, in the temporal lobe; spatial location memories are in the parietal lobe, and so on. Individual sensory "bits" of a memory are stored in localized areas of the brain and are then brought together by interconnecting neural circuits. The sensory bits are stored in the same areas where the sensory signals are processed. A complete, complicated memory is produced by connections between various localized areas. The organization of memories in the brain often does not follow intuition or logic. For example, I was once trying to recall a student's first name, and all I remembered was that it had three letters in it. I thought: How odd that the memory of a name is stored in my brain according to how many letters are in it!

The localized memory areas are scattered throughout the cerebral cortex. They store certain details about a memory and are interconnected to relevant other localized areas via neural networks in the cortex, thus producing a whole memory. These cortical areas are also connected to subcortical (below the cortex) regions of the brain. In fact, subcortical areas such as the amygdala and other areas of the limbic system are important regions for the consolidation and storage of emotional memories and procedural memories, such as habits and classically conditioned responses. The physiological storage of memory is not a static process. Memories are constantly changing as brains perform their dynamic biological events.

The process of consolidation takes time. The hippocampus works together with networks of cells in the cortex to permanently store declarative memories. In one study, it was found that the brain required six hours to create a permanent storage site for the memory of a newly learned skill (Shadmehr & Holcomb, 1997). The researchers measured blood flow in the brain and noted the movement of the memory from a temporary storage site in the front of the brain to long-term storage in the back of the brain. This consolidation could be interfered with by activities in which a person engaged within that six-hour window of time. Consolidation takes time, and as was mentioned above, some psychologists believe that one of the functions of sleep and dreaming is for this process to be performed more efficiently. Have you ever heard the phrase "sleep on it"? Studies show that sleeping not only helps us to solve problems and recall things, but also helps to store information into brain networks. Once again, be sure to sleep before a test!

As you know, people vary in their memory abilities. Many factors contribute to the variation; one of them is heredity. A gene known as BDNF is one of the many genetic factors that make one's memory better or worse than another's. BDNF affects hippocampal functioning and is also involved in fetal brain development and learning (Egan et al., 2003).

Working Memory

Contemporary brain-imaging research has focused on **working memory** (holding things in mind, thinking about something) because subjects can be asked to perform a task while their brains are being imaged, and researchers can then determine which brain areas are most active. Such research shows that working memory is a complex task that involves a number of brain regions, what scientists call a "distributed neural system." However, several brain-imaging studies show that the prefrontal cortex plays a central role in holding the contents of memory in mind. Several studies have identified a particular area of the prefrontal cortex, just in front of Broca's area, that is critical to the process of working memory (Courtney, 1998).

One of the major chemicals the brain uses for memory processing is the neurotransmitter acetylcholine. In Alzheimer's disease, for instance, the patient's brain is damaged in such a way that acetylcholine levels are decreased. There are medications (e.g., Aricept, Exelon, and Reminyl) that slow the breakdown of acetylcholine and thereby offer some memory improvement in some Alzheimer's patients. The improvement is only modest and is helpful for only a few years, however, and there are side effects.

Researchers have recently used the drug physostigmine, which blocks the breakdown of acetylcholine, in research on working memory involving visual stimuli. Participants were given the drug and then were tested on a visual memory task (look at a human face, then hold it in mind) while their brains were imaged (Furey, 2000). The participants showed a marked improvement in working memory. Interestingly, the part of the brain where increased activity occurred was not the prefrontal cortex, but the visual processing area in the occipital lobe. Memory is a distributed process, after all.

In addition, research has shown that increasing the activity of other brain transmitters, such as dopamine and norepinephrine, also results in improvements in memory (Mehta, 2000). Perhaps we will soon have a pill for memory improvement. For now, students can only hope.

Hebbian Physiology

In 1949, psychologist **Donald Hebb** theorized that memory must be stored in what he called **cell assemblies** (what we now call *neural networks*). In his book *The Organization of Behavior*, Hebb proposed that some biochemical events in the brain must be necessary to strengthen the connection between brain cells and thereby create the cell assemblies that represent the biology of memory. This process is sometimes referred to as *Hebbian*, but it is what we now call *consolidation*. The consolidation of memories involves one or more biochemical events in the brain.

The details of one molecular process, called **long-term potentiation (LTP)**, which occurs in the cells of the hippocampus, have been studied intently in recent years. In

---

Connecting Concepts

As you can see, the study of memory is intricately linked to biology. Look back to Chapter 3 to refresh your memory about how brain cells communicate with each other at the synapse. This process is at the root of learning and storing memories. A neuron releases a chemical—a neurotransmitter—that binds with a receptor chemical on the receiving neuron. Each time this happens, physiological changes take place that make the connection between those neurons stronger—a memory is forming!

LTP, a neurotransmitter chemical (glutamate) released from one neuron is received by another neuron. If the receiving neuron has a particular voltage, then a chemical receptor called the **NMDA receptor** is activated. This activation causes the receiving neuron to change in such a way that less chemical neurotransmitter is required to stimulate it. Thus, the connection between sending and receiving neurons is strengthened. LTP is a process by which the link between brain cells can be strengthened and remain strong over long periods of time. Learning and memory are based on such links between brain cells. That is why one researcher quipped, "I link, therefore I am."

Just as brain cell connections can be strengthened, they can also be weakened by physiological events. This process is called **long-term depression (LTD).** When a low-voltage charge is applied to certain synapses in the hippocampus, the cells weaken their connection. That is, in LTP, the connection between cells is strengthened, so it takes only a small amount of neurotransmitter chemical from the sending cell to stimulate the receiving cell. This Hebbian bond between cells lasts for a long time. In LTD, by contrast, the connection between cells is weakened, meaning that it will then take more neurotransmitter substance to stimulate the postsynaptic cell. These two processes appear to represent at least one part of the brain's physiological mechanisms that provide for the gaining and losing of memories.

In the late 1990s, scientists discovered another physiological process that occurs in the hippocampus and in the cerebellum, two brain regions that are important for creating memory engrams. This process was dubbed depolarization-induced suppression of inhibition (DSI). What a mouthful! This physiological process is essentially a means of fine-tuning synapses. It works on the inhibitory synapses by means of a chemical known as a cannabinoid—the same molecule as the active ingredient in marijuana. Scientists have identified a corresponding process that fine-tunes excitatory synapses, known as DSE, that also uses endogenous (inside the body) cannabinoids. Most scientists suspect that the DSI and DSE processes occur in many areas of the brain and are physiological mechanisms that help to modulate or adjust the strength of neural connections—they are part of the LTP process. Strengthening synapses is what a brain must do to remember something. Memory, after all, is the result of networks of brain cells.

The findings regarding DSI and DSE help to explain why marijuana use can interfere with memory. The endogenous cannabinoids work only in small, selected regions of the brain. Marijuana, by contrast, floods the brain with its active ingredient, THC, causing an overload of the LTP process. In fact, laboratory research shows that THC-treated rats perform on memory tests as if they have no hippocampus! Incidentally, in related research, neuroscientists have found that the endogenous cannabinoids also work in the hypothalamus to stimulate appetite. This explains why marijuana users get the "munchies." It also offers a possible idea for treating obesity: Block the actions of the natural cannabinoids or their receptors.

Snails and Mice

Three brain scientists won the Nobel Prize in Physiology or Medicine 2000 for their research on the physiology of neural connections. One of them, **Eric Kandel,** a professor at Columbia University, studies the neurons of the sea snail *Aplysia* and has uncovered some of the key ingredients of the physiological processes involved in learning and memory. Kandel has emphasized the role of a protein called **kinase.** His research shows that certain biochemical events at the synapse involving the kinase protein can produce the LTP effect.

Research at other laboratories has confirmed the importance of the NMDA receptor in both LTP and LTD. The NMDA receptor is a molecule that consists of four proteins and is positioned on the postsynaptic cells. NMDA receptors control the amount of calcium ions that can enter the cell. In this way, the NMDA molecule is a key component in controlling the extent to which the cell fires.

NMDA receptors are influenced by the incoming neurotransmitter substance and by the depolarization (increase in positive charge) of the cell. In a sense, the NMDA molecule is a switch that regulates the connection between two stimuli. Scientists have recently begun to investigate the NMDA molecule to discover how it can be manipulated.

For example, scientists have recently discovered certain genes that influence the LTP process, typically by influencing the NMDA receptor chemical. One such gene is known as **CREB.** Researchers have created mice that are missing the CREB gene (so-called **knockout mice**), and these mice show deficits in long-term memory. It seems reasonable that if we could find a way to increase the activity of the CREB gene or the NMDA receptors, we likely could improve the consolidation of memories. Just such a thing was recently accomplished.

Joe Tsien of Princeton University was able to genetically engineer mice so that their NMDA receptors would stay open just a bit longer than normal. This allows calcium ions to enter receiving neurons for a longer period of time than is typical, thereby strengthening the synaptic connections between cells. Tsien call these mice "Doogie" (after the adolescent TV doctor Doogie Howser) or, more commonly, **smart mice.** When tested on several learning and memory tasks, the smart mice outperformed normal mice by a significant margin. This research was so stunning that it even caught the attention of the popular media. For example, David Letterman presented a comedic list of "Top Ten Term Paper Topics Written by Genius Mice." (They included "Our Pearl Harbor: The Day Glue Traps Were Invented" and "Outsmarting the Mousetrap: Just Take the Cheese Off Really, Really Fast.")

If we can create smart mice, can we create smart people?

Where will genetic engineering lead? Where *should* it lead? Both Wisconsin and Oregon scientists reported in 2001 that they had successfully transferred a foreign gene into a rhesus monkey (News @ UWMADISON). The adverse consequences, if any, of genetically manipulating NMDA receptors are not known. We do not know what side effects may result in mice or other animals that are engineered to be smart. Learning is a neutral process; mice that learn fast can learn bad things as well as good. Tsien's smart mice, for instance, learned a classically conditioned fear reaction faster than did normal mice. In addition, it was recently reported that the Doogie mice are more sensitive to pain than are other mice (Zhou, 2001). It is possible, also, that manipulating NMDA receptors will affect the health, even perhaps the life span, of the mice. But, obviously, the big question is not what the side effects are of such genetic manipulation. The big question, of course, is: If we can build smart mice, can we build smart humans? Should we?

Recap

— Ebbinghaus was the first to study forgetting scientifically. He used himself as a subject, learning and relearning lists of nonsense syllables (CVCs), and graphing his savings scores.

— The forgetting curve swoops down rapidly, then gradually levels off, just like an extinction curve.

— Forgetting occurs because of decay, displacement, repression, or interference.

— Researchers have found that false memories can be implanted in some people.

— The physiology of memory is being researched. The key process appears to be long-term potentiation, in which a physiological change occurs at the synapse between brain cells.

I Link, Therefore I Am

The Exploratorium in San Francisco has an interesting web site, including this feature on memory: www.exploratorium.edu/memory/index.html Researcher Joseph E. Le Doux has traced the memory of fear to the amygdala in the brain. You can visit his web site at www.cns.nyu.edu/home/ledoux/

There are many web sites devoted to memory, particularly to ways of improving memory. Try some of these: The Memory page—information, activities and mnemonic devices, at www.premiumhealth.com/memory/ or the Cognitive Psychology Online Lab at http://coglab.psych.purdue.edu/ or descriptions of types of memory, a test, and suggestions for improving memory at www.epub.org.br/cm/n01/memo/memory.htm or more articles and mnemonic techniques at www.mindtools.com/memory.html

There is a support group called the False Memory Syndrome Foundation, whose web site is at www.fmsfonline.org/

You can read about the latest news in genetic engineering at www.genengnews.com/current.asp

STUDY GUIDE FOR CHAPTER 6:
MEMORY

Key terms and names (Make flash cards.)

engram	consolidation	one is a bun
Karl Lashley	depth of processing	method of loci
neural network	retrieval	deep processing
hippocampus	free recall	elaborative rehearsal
H. M.	cued recall	Hermann Ebbinghaus
Brenda Milner	recognition	savings score
anterograde amnesia	tip-of-the-tongue phenomenon	nonsense syllables
Korsakoff's syndrome	serial position effect	forgetting curve
retrograde amnesia	primacy effect	repression
dissociative amnesia	recency effect	repressed memories
declarative memory	sensory memory	false memories
procedural memory	iconic memory	Elizabeth Loftus
implicit memory	echoic memory	flashbulb memory
déjà vu experience	decay	retroactive interference
semantic memory	George Sperling	proactive interference
episodic memory	eidetic imagery	working memory
cerebellum	Alexander Luria	Donald Hebb
limbic system	short-term memory	cell assemblies
amygdala	displacement	long-term potentiation (LTP)
priming	chunking	NMDA receptor
encoding	long term memory	long term depression (LTD)
cue	interference	Eric Kandel
state	rehearsal	kinase
cue dependent	maintenance rehearsal	CREB gene
state dependent	mnemonics	knockout mice
massed practice	mnemonic device	Joe Tsien
spaced (distributed) practice	pegword method	smart mice

Fill in the blank

1. Memory is the flip side of _____.
2. The physiological change in the brain that represents a memory is known as an _____.
3. Memory in a brain is not located in one tiny area; it is spread through _____ _____.
4. In 1954, in Montreal, a man with epilepsy underwent a brain operation to remove the abnormal tissue causing his seizures. His _____ was destroyed, and therefore he has _____ amnesia. This man is known as _____.
5. In _____ amnesia, a person has experienced a blow to the head or other injury that interferes with the formation of memories.
6. The hippocampal area of the brain is necessary for what is called _____ memory.
7. A second kind of memory involves storing information in the brain about moving our bodies in certain learned ways. This is called _____ memory.

8. Memory of general facts is known as _____ memory.
9. The storehouse of things that have happened to you, events in a particular setting and at a specific time, is called _____ memory.
10. Memories of skills and habits are stored in circuits of nerve cells in the _____ of the brain.
11. Responses that are emotional in nature are stored in the brain's _____ system, particularly in the _____.
12. The first step in memory is to get things into the brain. This process is simply called _____.
13. Memory depends on both cues (_____ stimuli) and states (_____ body conditions).
14. The physiological process of storing memories is called _____.

15. The final step in the memory process is to get information out of storage when you want it. This process is called _____.

16. _____ is a type of retrieval that requires you to find something in your memory without any help.

17. The easiest type of memory retrieval is called _____.

18. When you want to learn a number of things in a particular order, it is most difficult to recall things from the _____. This is called the _____ effect.

19. The information in sensory memory rapidly fades away—a process called _____.

20. Some people are able to look at a picture and later recall very precise details about it. This rare ability is known as _____ _____.

21. Psychologist George Miller called the capacity of short-term memory "_____."

22. The process of dislodging items with new information is called _____.

23. The items in short-term memory are called _____, because they are not limited by their size.

24. There are two ways to move information from short-term memory into long-term memory: _____ and _____.

25. A _____ device is a gimmick, trick, or aid that helps to store information into memory.

26. "One is a bun" is a _____ _____ method.

27. Mentally putting things in places in order to remember them is called the method of _____.

28. The first psychologist to experimentally study forgetting was Hermann _____.

29. Sigmund Freud proposed that sometimes memory retrieval is blocked by _____.

30. Some psychologists argue that many of the repressed memories of traumatic events are actually _____ memories.

31. Psychologist Elizabeth _____ has been in the forefront of the view that false memories can be _____.

32. Events that are surprising and important, such as disasters and assassinations, are remembered as _____ memories. Typically, people remember the _____ of such events very well.

33. The most common cause of forgetting information from long-term storage is _____.

34. In 1949, psychologist Donald _____ theorized that memory must be stored in what he called _____ _____.

35. LTP occurs because of a chemical receptor called the _____ receptor.

36. Just as brain cell connections can be strengthened, they can be weakened by physiological events. This process is called _____ _____.

37. Long-term potentiation (LTP) occurs in the cells of the _____.

38. "Doogie" mice, or _____ mice, are the result of _____ engineering.

Matching

1. smart mice _____
2. H. M. _____
3. head trauma _____
4. LTP _____
5. short-term memory capacity _____
6. temporal lobe _____
7. snails (*Aplysia*) _____
8. procedural memory _____
9. loci _____
10. Donald Hebb _____
11. episodic memory _____
12. fade away _____
13. semantic memory _____
14. Ebbinghaus _____
15. eidetic imagery _____
16. iconic memory _____
17. mnemonics _____
18. one is a bun _____

a. cell assemblies
b. hippocampus
c. general facts
d. anterograde amnesia
e. seven plus or minus two
f. NMDA receptor
g. places
h. a pegword technique
i. photographic memory
j. genetic engineering
k. retrograde amnesia
l. kinase protein
m. study of forgetting
n. sensory memory
o. time and space
p. body memory
q. decay
r. memory aids

Multiple choice

1. Your friend is studying physics and creates a mnemonic device to help remember Newton's laws. This will aid her _____ memory of the material.
   a. sensory
   b. iconic
   c. eidetic
   d. semantic

2. Larry had a stroke and suffered retrograde amnesia. This means that Larry lost his memory for everything that happened
   a. within an hour before his stroke
   b. the day after the stroke
   c. in the future, after his stroke
   d. for a few minutes after his stroke

3. A waiter remembers customers' orders by grouping them into categories such as fish, veggies, pasta, and so on. What principle is being used?
   a. priming
   b. chunking
   c. retroactive interference
   d. phonics

4. Jenna uses the method of loci to memorize facts in her literature class. Which of these might she be doing?
   a. making rhymes
   b. making sentences from initials of words
   c. mentally putting a book in his kitchen
   d. alphabetizing authors' names

5. Who did the first scientific studies of forgetting?
   a. Tolman
   b. Kandel
   c. Milner
   d. Ebbinghaus

6. What kind of amnesia does H. M. have?
   a. anterograde
   b. retrograde
   c. dissociative
   d. episodic

7. You remember that Spain is a country. This fact is stored in your _____ memory.
   a. semantic
   b. eidetic
   c. implicit
   d. episodic

8. Your mother runs up to you at school and tells you that you won the lottery. Years later, you remember the details of this event very well. This is an example of _____ memory.
   a. dissociative
   b. procedural
   c. flashbulb
   d. eidetic

9. What kind of memory is it when you remember how to ride a bike?
   a. practice
   b. sensory
   c. procedural
   d. semantic

10. What kind of memory is it when you remember your first-grade classroom?
    a. iconic
    b. episodic
    c. semantic
    d. procedural

11. Memories are stored in the brain in
    a. the temporal lobe
    b. the occipital lobe
    c. the brain stem
    d. neural networks

12. Karl Lashley is known for his search for the
    a. hippocampal region
    b. engram
    c. mnemonic
    d. icon

13. A type of amnesia that results from psychological shock is called
    a. dissociative
    b. retrograde
    c. anterograde
    d. mnemonic

14. Princess Diana's bodyguard suffered a blow to his head in the car accident that killed her. His memories of the incident
    a. are repressed
    b. are stored in his hippocampus
    c. are permanently lost because they were not stored
    d. will be regained after a long rest period

15. Our conscious memories, those that we think about mentally, are called
    a. implicit
    b. sensory
    c. declarative
    d. semantic

16. I remember that the plural of "mouse" is "mice." This is an example of _____ memory.
    a. implicit
    b. eidetic
    c. semantic
    d. episodic

17. You are hired to work with a patient who has anterograde amnesia. You know that this person can learn using
    a. semantic memory
    b. eidetic imagery
    c. mnemonics
    d. classical conditioning

18. A memory stored in the amygdala is likely to involve
    a. places
    b. a certain time period
    c. a general fact
    d. emotions

19. A type of procedural memory is
    a. priming
    b. semantic
    c. episodic
    d. eidetic

20. Your memory of personal facts that happened to you is called
    a. episodic
    b. semantic
    c. implicit
    d. procedural

21. Which of these would be most typical for a flashbulb memory?
    a. You met your friend at a favorite restaurant.
    b. A major disaster occurred unexpectedly.
    c. A computer company called you for an interview.
    d. You found a quarter in the parking lot.

22. The most difficult type of retrieval is
    a. free recall
    b. recognition
    c. cued recall

23. TOT stands for
    a. total of trials   b. top of the theme
    c. tip of the tongue   d. trials of tests
24. Things at the beginning of a list are easy to remember because of the _____ effect.
    a. recency   b. mnemonic
    c. state   d. primacy
25. The serial position effect says that you should spend more time studying the _____ of a chapter.
    a. beginning   b. middle
    c. end   d. summary
26. How long does sensory memory last?
    a. split second   b. about 10 seconds
    c. about 30 seconds   d. It is unlimited
27. How long does short-term memory last?
    a. split second   b. about 10 seconds
    c. about 30 seconds   d. It is unlimited
28. How long does long-term memory last?
    a. split second   b. about 10 seconds
    c. about 30 seconds   d. It is unlimited
29. Alexander Luria wrote about a person with a kind of photographic memory called
    a. eidetic imagery
    b. echoic memory
    c. iconic memory
    d. tip-of-the-tongue phenomenon
30. Making groupings in order to squeeze more into short-term memory is called
    a. consolidation
    b. proactive interference
    c. capacity booming
    d. chunking
31. Displacement occurs in
    a. long-term memory   b. sensory memory
    c. procedural memory   d. short-term memory

32. The pegword method is a _____ device.
    a. TOT   b. mnemonic
    c. procedural   d. consolidation
33. HOMES is a mnemonic for
    a. the colors of the rainbow
    b. the Great Lakes
    c. the provinces of Canada
    d. a list of words to be recalled
34. Hermann Ebbinghaus used _____ in his studies of forgetting.
    a. TOT   b. mnemonics
    c. nonsense syllables   d. short-term memory
35. The forgetting curve has the same shape as the _____ curve.
    a. learning   b. extinction
    c. memorizing   d. consolidation
36. Some psychologists have argued that repressed memories are actually _____ memories.
    a. mnemonic   b. false
    c. interpreted   d. advanced
37. The two types of interference are proactive and
    a. retrieval   b. response
    c. recognition   d. retroactive
38. The NMDA receptors is involved in the process of
    a. mnemonics
    b. free recall
    c. recognition
    d. long-term potentiation
39. Eric Kandel studied snails and found that learning and memory were dependent on which protein?
    a. adrenaline   b. RNA
    c. DNA   d. kinase
40. Joe Tsien created smart mice using
    a. mnemonic devices
    b. long-term depression
    c. injection of RNA
    d. genetic engineering

Short answer and critical thinking

1. If a friend of yours said that she had a bad memory, what would you say?
2. Why did Lashley's attempt to find the engram fail?
3. Describe the difference between declarative and procedural memory, and give an example of each.
4. What do these brain regions have to do with memory: hippocampus, frontal lobe, cerebellum, and amygdala?
5. What would you do to remember things if you had anterograde amnesia?
6. What is the difference between decay and displacement?
7. What are some reasons that information is lost from memory?

8. What are false memories? Why are they important?
9. A researcher recently measured a physiological brain event and said that it probably was not "Hebbian." What did he mean?
10. Compare and contrast short-term and long-term memory.
11. Many metaphors and analogies are used to describe and explain memory, such as computer, filing cabinet, neural network. Create your own analogy or metaphor for a type of memory, amnesia, or other concept from this chapter.

UNIT
4
PERSONALITY

"New opinions are always suspected, and usually opposed, without any other reason but because they are not already common."
—JOHN LOCKE

In this fourth unit, we discuss the concept of personality, how psychologists measure personality (including IQ tests), and what major theories have been proposed by psychologists to describe and explain human personality and its course of development.

The two chapters included in this unit are as follows:

Chapter 7 Personality Approaches, Social Psychology, and Assessment—a description of three approaches to defining personality (types, traits, and behaviors), an introduction to the five-trait model, a description of the most important research and theories in social psychology, and a discussion of the many tests used to assess personality, including IQ tests, the 16PF, the MMPI, inkblot tests, and the TAT. This chapter provides a very complete introduction to the idea of personality as it has been approached historically by psychologists, including the concepts of how individuals are influenced by situations and groups, the development and use of IQ tests, modern ideas of intelligence, and the most frequently used personality tests.

Chapter 8 Personality Theories—a description of the major theories of personality that have been advanced by prominent theorists such as Freud, Jung, Skinner, and Maslow. This chapter includes detailed accounts of psychoanalytic theory and neo-Freudian theories, behaviorism and social learning theory, and humanistic theories. Also included are discussions of emotions and motivation as components of personality.

Personality Approaches, Social Psychology, and Assessment

PLAN AHEAD...

- What are some different ways of describing and classifying people's personalities?
- Are there certain personality dimensions or traits that can be used to describe anyone?
- Do a person's personality traits last throughout life, or do they change?
- Are people consistent in their personalities from one situation to another? How much are people influenced by the situations they are in?
- How do psychologists measure personality?
- How do psychologists define intelligence? How do IQ tests work? Are they accurate?
- What is the MMPI test, and how does it work?
- What is an inkblot test? Are there similar tests?

"What a chimera then is man! What a novelty! What a monster, what a chaos, what a contradiction, what a prodigy!"
—BLAISE PASCAL

A YOUNG MAN I KNOW, NAMED BARRY, WHILE UNDER A lot of stress, had a bad reaction to the drug ecstasy. In pouring rain, he tore off his clothes and ran down the middle of a busy city street screaming at people in their cars. He was taken to the psychiatric ward of a hospital, where I helped him deal with his problems. Later I wondered what bystanders might have thought about Barry's personality. I would describe him as intelligent, kind, very creative, witty, and outgoing. But how would others rate him? What is personality, and where do we get our ideas about it? This is one of the most diverse and fascinating topics in psychology. In this chapter are included descriptions of (1) three different approaches to the concept of personality (how should we describe Barry?); (2) research on social psychology that shows how behavior is influenced by situations (how did stress and drugs influence Barry?); and (3) psychological assessment—the testing that psychologists do to measure personality and intelligence (what tests could we give to Barry?).

How would you describe your own personality? What about someone else's personality—your mother's, your best friend's, your science teacher's, perhaps your neighbor's, a famous person's, or a classmate's? Okay, let's try it! Choose someone, and describe that person's personality right now. Go ahead, I'll wait.

Are you finished? Good. Now think about the description you gave. Don't focus so much on the content of your description; instead, think about what kind of description you used. This will give an idea of what the concept "personality" means to you. You see, people have different notions about what "personality" means and about what it includes. Let's look at some notions of personality.

THREE APPROACHES

"It seems that the analysis of character is the highest human entertainment."
—ISAAC BASHEVIS SINGER

There are three approaches that represent the envelope, the package, for concepts of personality. Each of these three approaches conceptualizes personality in a particular way, in a specific manner or form, and each, of course, has its advantages and disadvantages. In your description of personality, did you refer to the person as a *type* of personality, such as the jock type, the impulsive type, the chauvinistic type, the party type, the fun type, and so on? Or did you list certain qualities or *traits* that you believe the person has, such as shy, funny, generous, kind, deliberate, and so on? Perhaps you tended more to include some of the person's *behaviors*, for example, how he or she acts in certain situations, such as clumsy, dependent, back-stabbing, cautious, helpful, and so on. Did you? The three major approaches that are commonly used in the study of personality are types, traits, and behaviors.

Grouping by Type

One of the most common ways to describe personality, and one of the oldest, is to divide people into various **types** or categories. How often do we hear that someone is a "certain type of person"? The type approach to personality looks for similarities between people and attempts to place people into one of a certain number of pigeon-holes, or types. For example, it is common to divide people into two types: those who are **extraverted** (outgoing, friendly, gregarious, enjoy parties) and those who are **intro-verted** (quiet, shy, like to be alone). A type approach does not focus on differences between individuals, but tries to find patterns of similarity, and then groups people together on the basis of those shared characteristics. A type approach distributes people into a finite number of categories based on their similarities.

Examples of the type approach can be found far back in history. For example, early Greek physicians believed that the human body had four major fluids that were known as **humors**. People were divided into four personality types based on the abundance of a certain humor (body fluid). According to this reasoning, there were only four personality types. People were choleric (yellow bile = bad-tempered and angry), melancholic (black bile = sad and thoughtful), sanguine (blood = passionate, temperamental, and optimistic), or phlegmatic (phlegm = calm and unemotional). This idea was accepted for thousands of years. Even now, we have remnants of this once-popular type theory. For instance, we commonly use the term **melancholy** to describe someone who is sad. The term literally means "black bile" (melan + chol), which refers to one of the theorized four body humors. The next time you are feeling down and someone asks you how you are, just say you're feeling a bit black bile-ish today! In addition, the theory of humors proposed that a person whose body fluids were all in a good, proper balance had a good personality—he or she was said to have a good sense of humor. Believe it or not, that is the derivation of that common phrase. Do you have a good sense of body fluids?

Connecting Concepts

The belief that body humors influence personality led to some weird treatments for psychological disorders. For example, bloodletting was a common procedure for many years, based on the belief that too much blood made a person excitable and nervous. Such unusual treatments, along with modern approaches, are discussed in Chapter 10.

Judging Bods

In the 1940s, a psychologist at the University of Wisconsin named **William Sheldon** proposed a type theory of personality that resulted in a great deal of research and a bit of controversy because it was about physical appearance. Sheldon suggested that personality might be related to body physique. His idea, which became known as a theory of **somatotypes** (body types) divided people into three types. Sheldon thought that people who had a lot of fat on their bodies (**endomorphs**) were happy and easygoing; that skinny people (**ectomorphs**) were quiet, shy, and thoughtful; and that muscular individuals (**mesomorphs**) had personalities that were outgoing, athletic, aggressive, and assertive. Sheldon and other researchers took photos of scantily clad people and then had raters give scores to their physiques. These scores were then compared to personality descriptions of the individuals and correlation coefficients were calculated.

FYI

Some people included in Sheldon's research later became quite famous—a first lady and Supreme Court justice, for example—and their photos were a bit of an embarrassment.

Perhaps many people today still believe that you can accurately judge someone's personality by looking at his or her physical features. It turns out that this is not so. Sheldon's correlations were small. Apparently, any relationships that do exist between looks and personality are minor at best, and theories that attempt to connect personality with appearance do not make for good, precise science.

THINK TANK

What are some ways in which people are judged by their looks?

Have you ever been so judged?

Have you ever done it to others?

Is there anything good about such a thing?

Answer Me This

A more recent type approach to personality is the very popular and often-used test known as the **Myers-Briggs Type Indicator.** This test attempts to divide people into 16 categories based on their answers to items on a paper-and-pencil test. Right away, this seems suspicious. It is curious that people love to take personality tests, and after receiving their scores, revel in proclaiming whether the test results are accurate or not. Of course, if people already know what their personality is, why do they need the test?

Such tests might be fun to take and to discuss, but they are at best of only limited usefulness in a scientific enterprise that aims for a high degree of precision and accuracy. The Myers-Briggs might be fun and might generate discussion that is useful, but mostly such tests produce overgeneralizations that come close to what is called the **Barnum effect.**

P. T. Barnum was a circus owner who said, "There's a sucker born every minute." People have a remarkably agile ability to perceive things in so many ways that most anyone will accept a personality description if it is general enough. One fun demonstration of this is to pass out horoscopes to a classroom of students and ask how accurate they are. A large number of the students will rate them as mostly correct. The trick is to give the same horoscope to everyone. It is full of overly general statements such as "You often like to be with other people, but at times you feel a need to be by yourself," or "Others will rely on your common sense today." Nearly everyone feels that statements like this are accurate. This is an example of the Barnum effect.

Once, a student of mine read aloud a description of my personality from a book of birth dates. The other students were amazed. Everyone said that it was an uncannily good description of me. Then I gave them the bad news: I had lied about my birth date and simply picked one at random. I asked her to try again with my real birth date. Again, everyone was amazed how the second personality description seemed to fit me so well. Then came the bad news: I had lied again! My point was that every description in that book could be interpreted as fitting me if a person were predisposed to see it that way.

Another example of the Barnum effect is how we tend to explain a person's actions on the basis of something we know about that person. If we believe that someone is paranoid, then everything she does is interpreted as an example of her paranoia. Astrology is a good example. A person who tries to guess your astrological sign has a 1 in 12 chance to be right because there is no correlation between sign and personal characteristics. However, if you tell the person your sign, then he or she will interpret your personality and behaviors as indications of your sign. Nearly everything you do confirms your sign. This is the Barnum effect at work. That is why people ask you your sign rather than simply determining it from your characteristics. This idea will be further pursued when we discuss attribution theory, the study of what people believe causes behavior, and also will be mentioned in Chapter 9 on psychological disorders, since it is very common for people with mental illnesses to be victims of this kind of stereotyping.

Types of Problems

All type approaches are faulty. The first problem is deciding how many categories to divide people into. Many people say two—men and women! How often do we hear, "Men are like this, and women are like that"? Isn't it obvious that such approaches are terribly oversimplified and subject to numerous overgeneralizations? Although it seems apparent to many people, it is not true that men's and women's personalities are significantly different from each other. Even when consistent differences are found between men and women, these show only slight differences in the *averages*. There is tremendous overlap between the two groups. Would that it were so simple that there were only two types of personalities in the world! On the other hand, wouldn't that get a bit boring?

Another type idea, as noted above, is astrology. Besides the fallacious notion that personality is influenced by the positions of the stars in the sky thousands of years ago, this approach, like the men versus women one, has the problem of trying to squeeze people into a small number of categories; all people on earth are neatly divided into only twelve categories. Believe me, I know more than twelve types of people myself! It seems that we need a much larger number of pigeonholes to accurately represent all the various personality nuances that exist among people, which might be why the more sophisticated forms of astrology include things like "moon signs" as well as "sun signs." But if we attempted to construct a type approach that included a huge number of categories in order to represent the wide range of personalities that people have, then we would end up with a system that is impossible to use because we cannot accurately decide which box to put someone in—the categories will be too similar. What is the right number of personality boxes—types—to put people into? Can such a scheme ever be accurate?

Second, and even worse, type approaches to personality often lead to stereotyping—the unfair categorizing of people on the basis of one or a few of their qualities—for example, all jocks are the same, all Jewish people are the same, all college students are the same, or all women (men) are the same, and so on. Friends, we want science here, not silliness! Type approaches lead us down paths that not only are scientifically tenuous, but that also can lead to reaching harmful conclusions. Instead of categorizing (focusing on the similarities among people), how about using an approach that concentrates on the differences between people?

THINK TANK

Listen to yourself and others when you talk about people.

What types are used to describe or to define people's personalities?

For example, do people say, "Men are like this, and women are like that"?

Do you use terms like *jocks* and *geeks*?

What are some examples of stereotypes that are used to describe people?

Recap

— Three approaches to personality will be explained in this chapter: types, traits, and behaviors.

— Type approaches to personality divide people into categories. For example, William Sheldon divided people according to their body shapes.

— In the distant past, it was believed that four types of personality were caused by body fluids (humors). This approach gave us the terms *melancholy* and *good sense of humor*.

— A test known as the Myers-Briggs Type Indicator is a popular type approach to personality that is used today.

— All type approaches are faulty because there is no good number of categories to place people into on the basis of personality. Having too few types leads to gross overgeneralizations; having too many causes problems with the reliability of classification.

— Type approaches can lead to the Barnum effect (accepting overly general statements) or to stereotypes.

Rating by Traits

Most people don't like to be put into a category with others. Who wants to be pigeon-holed? Instead of grouping people into types, the **trait** approach rates people on a number of characteristics and a person's personality is described as the total pattern of ratings. A trait is defined as a relatively enduring or lasting characteristic of a person.

A trait approach to personality first identifies a number of characteristics or traits, then rates people (say, on a scale of 1 to 10) on the extent to which they exhibit those traits. Try it on yourself: Rate yourself on the following dimensions by placing a checkmark on each scale:

```
                    1  2  3  4  5  6  7  8  9  10
  extraversion  --- \ ----------------------- introversion
        happy  -------- \ ------------------ sad
    dependent  ------------------------ \ ------ independent
     friendly  --- \ ----------------------- cold
       mature  ------ \ --------------------- immature
 open to ideas  ------ \ --------------------- closed to ideas
good sense of humor  -------- \ ----------------- poor sense of humor
    impulsive  ------------------- \ --------- contemplative
```

Notice that each trait has two extremes. A trait is on a continuum, a scale. For example, if you are among the most extraverted people, you get a score of 1 on extraversion–introversion; if you are extremely sad, you get a score of 10 on happy–sad; and so on. Get the idea? Next look at your pattern of scores. Here are mine: 3, 6, 9, 2, 4, 2, 1, 8. What did you get? The pattern of scores is known as **a profile**.

Using a trait approach, we rate people on various psychological characteristics, then define their personalities as their total patterns of scores—their profiles. Note that this approach does not group people into categories (types), but allows people to be unique—each person can have his or her own profile.

How Many Traits?

An early psychologist who favored the trait approach was **Gordon Allport** (1897–1967). Allport asked his graduate students to look through dictionaries and find all the words that could be used to describe psychological traits. They found over 8,000. Many of the words, however, were synonyms or near synonyms of each other that described the same, or very similar, traits. After narrowing those down, Allport still had nearly a thousand traits. He realized, as I suppose we all do, that it is unreasonable to describe someone's personality using a thousand traits. What number of traits would be reasonable?

Allport also realized that certain traits are much more descriptive of people than are other traits. Research proved this to be true. For example, if we say that someone is cold instead of warm, that likely will change our opinion of him or her very much—particularly the idea of whether we will like that person. But changing a trait from flappable to unflappable probably will have less effect on our judgment. Allport decided to divide traits into three groups based on how descriptive the traits were.

If a person has one trait that describes him very accurately and completely (one trait that nearly totally represents his personality), it is called a **cardinal trait.** A cardinal trait is one that nearly completely colors a person's life—it sums up that person perfectly. Perhaps we could say that Mohandas Gandhi's cardinal trait was being self-sacrificing or that Abraham Lincoln's cardinal trait was being honest.

Most of us do not have one cardinal trait that defines our personality. For most of us, it takes maybe five or six or seven traits to give a fairly complete description of our personality. Allport called those **central traits.** If you were writing a short description of yourself, which five or six traits would you list? Funny, warm, outgoing, talkative, moody, or nice? Those are called your central traits. According to this approach, each of us has central traits that give a somewhat complete description of our personality. The other traits that we have, those that are not very complete in describing us, are called **secondary traits.** They include descriptions of us that are not very important in our personality, such as that you like chocolate ice cream.

THINK TANK

Do you have a cardinal trait?

Do you know anyone who does?

Name people from history or from fiction who have cardinal traits.

What are your central traits?

Do you have any traits now that you didn't have in the past?

Which of your traits would you most like to change?

Which traits do you most wish you had?

Figuring Factors

A problem with Allport's idea is that it does not adequately take into account the fact that certain traits overlap with each other. For example, if I measure both introversion and shyness in a group of people, I'm certain that there will be overlap between these two traits because they measure very similar things. A different way to think about personality is to propose that traits such as introversion and shyness are not our true personality, but are merely behaviors that reflect our inner personality. This is a common idea. The idea is that people have something in them—a personality—and that their behaviors, moods, thoughts, and emotions are just *reflections* of their personality, not personality itself. This idea suggests that personality is something internal and invisible, like a ghost or an abstract concept, and that actions, emotions, and thoughts are not personality characteristics in and of themselves, but merely conditions produced by personality. This is the common belief that we have an inner personality that guides us and how we act is merely a manifestation or representation of that internal thing.

A psychologist named **Raymond Cattell** (1905–1998) had this idea. He called the traits that we observe and measure in a person **surface traits**. The underlying causes (the personality) of these surface traits, he called **source traits**. Cattell theorized that he could determine the source traits by measuring numerous surface traits in a large number of people and then using mathematical analysis to find patterns of overlap and similarity. The statistical procedure he used is called **factor analysis**. In a sense, this calculation provides correlation coefficients for all pairs of traits that are measured. The mathematical analysis of test scores results in a number of **personality factors** that theoretically are the source traits for the surface traits measured. Using factor analysis, we can find the exact amount of overlap between introversion and shyness, for example. We can also find how much, if at all, other traits overlap with these two traits; in fact, factor analysis allows us to find all degrees of overlap among all the traits measured. The results are interesting because they are based not on opinion, but on empirical study and mathematical analysis.

A profile from the 16PF personality test.

Factor		1 2 3 4 5 6 7 8 9 10	
Warmth	More Emotionally Distant from People		Attentive and Warm to Others
Reasoning	Fewer Reasoning Items Correct		More Reasoning Items Correct
Emotional Stability	Reactive		Emotionally Stable
Dominance	Deferential		Dominant
Liveliness	Serious		Lively
Rule–Consciousness	Expedient		Rule–Conscious
Social Boldness	Shy		Socially Bold
Sensitivity	Objective		Subjective
Vigilance	Trusting		Vigilant
Abstractedness	Grounded		Abstracted
Privateness	Forthright		Private
Apprehension	Self–Assured		Apprehensive
Openness to Change	Traditional		Open to Change
Self–Reliance	Group–Oriented		Self–Reliant
Perfectionism	Tolerates Disorder		Perfectionist
Tension	Relax		Tense
	Low	Average	High

Cattell did the necessary research, measured a host of traits in a large number of people, put the numbers into a computer, and completed the factor analysis. His computation resulted in 16 personality factors. That is, Cattell found that to completely describe a person's personality, one would need to measure these 16 traits. If you measure 15 of these traits or fewer, you will not have a complete picture of a person's personality; something will be missing. If you measure 17 traits or more, you have measured more than you need to; some of your traits will overlap. Cattell's analysis demonstrates that if you take a trait approach, then personality can be completely described by a profile on 16 particular traits. Cattell devised a personality test to measure those 16 traits. The test is still widely used and is known as the **16PF** (personality factors). Naturally, there are other tests that measure personality traits too.

More Correlations

Another important personality theorist, **Hans Eysenck** (1916–1997), took a similar approach to that of Cattell. Eysenck was born in Germany but left at the age of 18 when the Nazis came into power. He moved to England, completed a Ph.D. in psychology, and served as a psychologist during World War II. It was during that service that Eysenck noted the tremendous subjectivity that psychologists used in diagnosing disorders. That realization led him to a career of research on the reliability of psychological diagnosis. Eysenck became a major critic of mainstream clinical psychology (he often attacked established opinions), wrote 75 books and over 700 articles, and developed a theory of personality based on the mathematical analysis of traits. Eysenck felt that only a strict scientific approach would give an accurate understanding of personality. Therefore, he used factor analysis to look at correlations among dozens of traits, and he identified three traits that he felt were statistically central to human personality.

Early in his research, Eysenck found two main dimensions of temperament, which he called **neuroticism** and **extraversion–introversion.** Neuroticism is an indication of the degree to which a person is calm or nervous. Extraversion–introversion is a scale with outgoing on one end and shy and quiet on the other. Eysenck created a four-quadrant graph in which he examined traits that fell at the intersection of these two dimensions. He argued, for example, that introverted people were more likely to develop phobias, while extraverts were more likely to show symptoms of hysteria (conversion disorder).

Eysenck later added a third dimension that he called **psychoticism,** a trait that borders on the extreme characteristics of the severely mentally ill. This scale was meant to denote such traits as recklessness, disregard for conventions, and inappropriate emotional expression. Eysenck believed that these three traits were predominantly caused by heredity, and his theory became one of the main catalysts for the discussion of nature and nurture. A test to measure these is the Eysenck Personality Questionnaire.

TABLE 7.1 Trait Ideas So Far

Gordon Allport—Cardinal, central, and secondary traits (based on how descriptive they are of a person)

Raymond Cattell—16 factors (source traits), determined by factor analysis, will completely describe a person's personality; the 16PF test

Hans Eysenck—Three inherited traits: neuroticism, extraversion-introversion, and psychoticism

Stability of Traits

If we accept a trait approach to personality, then one of our important questions is whether traits are stable, that is, whether people's scores on tests of traits will stay relatively the same over periods of time. For example, if people take the 16PF when they are 25 years old, then again when they are 35 years old, will their scores remain roughly the same?

This question has inspired a great deal of interest and research among contemporary scientists. A number of fascinating findings and theories have been generated in the attempt to uncover how much stability personality traits show over long periods of time. One particular set of studies has been of foremost importance in instigating the current interest in this subject. Those research results were reported by psychologists Costa and McCrae (1988, 1997).

There are two kinds of studies for determining how much change occurs over long periods of time. A **cross-sectional study** measures two or more groups of people of different ages and then compares them. For example, we could measure 25-year-olds and 50-year-olds at the same time and see how their scores compare. However, those different age groups had different experiences growing up (because they grew up at different times!) and hence any differences we find in their scores might be due not to age, but to differing experiences. A second kind of research, called a **longitudinal study,** eliminates this problem by measuring the same group of people at two different times. In this case, we measure some 25-year-olds, then wait 25 years, then measure them again when they are 50 years old. Naturally, a major drawback with a longitudinal study is the length of time it requires.

Another not-so-obvious problem with longitudinal research is that some of the people who are measured at an early age will not be available (they moved, quit the study, died, or for some other reason cannot be measured) at a later age. These people are called **dropouts,** and they are not randomly divided among various traits. That is, people with certain traits are more likely to drop out than are those who have other traits. This problem, known as the **dropout effect**, will affect the results of the longitudinal study. Therefore, researchers need to make adjustments to their final data to account for the dropout effect. There are a number of ways to do this, including statistical manipulations and changing the design of the study. For example, most researchers today use a research design known as a **sequential study** that combines cross-sectional and longitudinal designs.

Sailing the Ocean

Now back to Costa and McCrae. These two researchers conducted a longitudinal study of personality traits, following people from age 25 to 75. They reported that the scores on most personality traits changed a good deal as people went through various stages of life. However, there were five traits that showed some stability. These five traits are known by the amusingly simple name, the **Big Five.** (Students who complain that scientists are always creating complicated names should be pleased with this term.)

Costa and McCrae measured traits in a group of people who were 25 years old and then measured them every few years until they were 75 years old. Adjustments were made to counter the dropout effect. The researchers discovered that most people had very consistent scores on five of the traits—the Big Five. They found that one out of every three people had scores that changed a lot but that two out of three people stayed the same. Will your trait scores on the 16PF change over time? We do not know. But if you are like the people that Costa and McCrae studied, then most of your scores will change; however, there is a good chance that five of your scores will be the same in the future as they are now. If you scored high on "expedient–conscientious" at age 25, there is a high probability (2 out of 3) that you will continue to score high on this trait when you are older. If you scored in the middle on "conservative–experimenting" at age 25, you will likely still score in the middle when you are 75. Additional research has mostly confirmed Costa and McCrae's results. Some recent studies are finding this to be true in other cultures as well. Perhaps there are some traits that are stable—or at least, mostly stable. So what are they?

The Big Five traits can easily be remembered by using the acronym OCEAN (just remember that an ocean is a big, stable thing):

1. **Openness to experience:** This dimension can be described as imaginative versus down to earth, original versus conventional, creative versus uncreative, broad versus narrow interests, or witty versus simple. Of course, remember that using a trait approach to personality means that you can have a score anywhere along a continuum, from one end to the other. This is not a type approach in which you have to be an either-or. People who are low in this trait might always want to eat at the same restaurant; those who are high in openness will want to try new cuisines.

2. **Conscientiousness:** This trait can be described as including characteristics such as hardworking versus lazy, punctual versus late, orderly versus disorderly, neat versus messy, responsible versus careless, self-disciplined versus undependable, and so on. High scorers like things neat and tidy; low scorers are not bothered by messiness. Of course, a person can have a score anywhere along the continuum from one extreme to the other. Where do you fall?

3. **Extraversion:** The opposite end of this dimension is introversion. This trait measures whether people are outgoing or reserved, sociable or inclined to keep to themselves, talkative or quiet, joiners or loners, energetic or retiring, enthusiastic or sober, and affectionate or restrained. High scorers love parties and socializing; low scorers prefer being alone.

4. **Agreeableness:** Examples of traits included in this dimension are the degree to which people are trusting or suspicious, good-natured or irritable, cooperative or uncooperative, helpful or reluctant to help, and softhearted or ruthless. When a telemarketer calls on the phone, people who score high on this trait will be more likely to talk to them agreeably; low scorers might slam down the phone.

5. **Neuroticism:** This trait is often known as **emotional stability** and includes dimensions such as how emotional people are, whether they are more calm or worrying, high-strung or poised, self-conscious or comfortable with themselves, anxious or composed, neurotic or stable, compulsive or patient, and nervous or emotionally steady.

Remember, whatever your scores on these traits when you're young, the **five factor theory** proposes that you will likely have similar scores when you're older.

In Other Cultures

A number of tests have been devised to measure the Big Five traits; the **NEO-Personality Inventory (NEO-PI)** is the main one. The NEO-PI has been used in many different cultures, and researchers have found these traits to generally be stable in other cultures too. However, cultures often have different ideas about traits. For instance, an anthropologist studying the Big Five among the Shuar Indians of Amazonian Ecuador tried to find words in the Shuar language for "neuroticism" and got many different responses but nothing consistent. So he tried asking for synonyms of "worried." When he asked the Shuar people to rate themselves and others on this trait ("worried"), he found that they all said they were very worried. He then realized that to them, it meant that they were concerned about the welfare of themselves, their families, and of others. They considered "worried" to be a favorable trait (Roach, 2002).

Though the Big Five model has been widely accepted and has generated a great deal of interest and research, it is not universally recognized and accepted by psychologists. Some dispute the concept that there are five basic traits of personality. In addition, even if we accept these research findings, there is still a good bit of room for argument, since only two out of three people show consistent scores on these traits over time. That means that one out of three people change a good deal in these dimensions. In fact, data from over 100,000 adults showed a good deal of change in the Big Five traits; agreeableness and conscientiousness increased, while neuroticism and openness declined, starting when people were in their twenties and thirties (Srivastave et al., 2003). In addition, one can find plenty wrong with the trait approach itself. Therefore, let's turn next to a third approach to personality that attempts to counter some of the weaknesses of the trait approach.

THINK TANK

Compare and contrast the "type" and "trait" approaches—how are they alike and how are they different?

What are their advantages and disadvantages?

When describing human nature, is it better to stress certain qualities, such as the Big Five, or is it better to say that it is human nature to change over time and to be adaptive in different situations?

Are people's personalities more set in stone or more variable and constantly changing?

Behaviors in Situations

A trait approach to personality assumes that personality is consistent, that it is somehow inside of us, that we carry it around with us and exhibit it in essentially the same way even in varying situations, that our personality profile is a consistent part of us. The trait approach is founded on the idea that traits are our personality and that our behaviors are simply reflections of those inner traits. A trait theory is based on the idea that if you get a score of 9 on suspiciousness, then you are a very suspicious person and we can expect your behavior to reflect suspiciousness across the board—you will act suspicious nearly all the time.

But is this really accurate? Are personality traits consistent? If a person gets the highest possible score on a scale of introversion, can we expect that he or she will always act introverted in every situation? When I think about various people whom I know (including myself), I realize that sometimes they are extraverted, but in other circumstances, they are introverted. It depends. The same thing seems to be true about intelligence. Sometimes a person can say the most brilliant thing, and then at another time, in a different situation, the same person will say something wildly stupid. Likewise, I can think of people who are at times clumsy but just as often (in different circumstances) unbelievably graceful. Here is a true-life example: One day, a colleague of mine told me that my problem was that I always agreed to do everything that people asked me to do. (Don't you love it when people tell you what your problem is?) The very same day, another colleague told me that my problem was that I always said "no" when people asked me to do favors. Which colleague was right? I think they both were. People are often inconsistent in their behaviors because of differences in situations. Perhaps I am in a good mood when around the first person and I am grouchy and don't feel like doing things when around the second. Or perhaps around the second person, I feel a need to be authoritative.

We see snapshots of people, and from those snapshots we assume consistency. If a woman is acting extraverted every time we see her, we assume that she has an

THINK TANK

Name some ways in which your behavior has been inconsistent from one situation to another.

What are some traits that people have assumed you have because they saw you act a certain way in one situation?

Walter Mischel, who proposed the idea of situationism.

Connecting Concepts

In Chapter 5, you learned about discrimination learning. This explains why we might act differently from one situation to another. The same behavior might or might not be reinforced, depending on the circumstances and the people we are with. You can be extraverted with one person or in one situation and introverted with someone else or in a different situation.

"extraverted personality" and always acts that way. We assume that personality is "inside" a person and that it guides behavior. But should we assume that people carry their personality around with them, that personality traits are consistent and unaffected by circumstances? Students who see me in class (when I am nearly always extraverted) wrongly assume that I always act extraverted, even outside of class, when I am often introverted. How much do situations affect our personalities? Let's look at what the research tells us.

In 1968, a psychologist named **Walter Mischel** published a book titled *Personality and Assessment* in which he introduced a controversial idea that shocked the world of psychology. Mischel wrote that he had looked at the research on traits and behavior and discovered that what a person does in a given situation is only mildly influenced by personality. Behavior, Mischel said, is greatly influenced by the variables in the situation. This view is known as **situationism,** and many people took Mischel's notion to mean the end of personality! Even today this view is regularly denounced by psychologists who cling to the idea that personality is a consistent quality inside of us that we carry with us and express in every situation.

Situationists, on the other hand, argue that human behavior in any circumstance is determined mainly by the characteristics of the situation, not by the characteristics of the person. That is, how people will behave in a situation (what they will do) can be predicted more accurately by looking at the features of the situation than by looking at personality traits. This approach redefines personality as consisting not of types or traits, but of our various behaviors in different situations. Don't think of personality as something inside a person; think of it as simply the generalization that we make on the basis of a person's pattern of behaviors.

TABLE 7.2   **Three Approaches to Personality**

1. Types = similarities between people, categories, pigeonholes.
   Body humors, Sheldon's somatotypes, Myers-Briggs test.

2. Traits = dimensions, scales, profiles.
   Allport's cardinal, central, and secondary traits;
   Cattell's 16PF; Eysenck's three traits; Big Five.

3. Behaviors = situations are important, behavior can be inconsistent.
   Mischel's situationism.

Recap

— Trait approaches rate people on scales, such as introversion–extraversion.

— Traits are defined as relatively permanent characteristics. A set of scores on different traits is called a profile.

— Allport divided traits into cardinal, central, and secondary, based on their descriptive power.

— Cattell used statistics to derive 16 basic traits. The 16PF is a personality test that measures those 16 personality factors—theoretically a complete description of a person's personality.

— Eysenck suggested three inherited traits: neuroticism, extraversion–introversion, and psychoticism.

— Longitudinal research, which measures the same people over a long period of time, found that The Big Five traits (OCEAN) were relatively stable.

— A third approach to personality focuses on behavior rather than on something inside the person.

— Situationism (Walter Mischel) proposes that a person's behavior is determined primarily by the situation, not by personality.

SOCIAL PSYCHOLOGY

"Man is a social animal."
—SPINOZA

What causes a person to act a certain way? Are we guided by our personalities (something inside of us, such as traits), or are our behaviors more influenced by the situations we are in? One of the subfields of psychology—**social psychology**—can provide some scientific answers to this question. Social psychologists study how the behavior of an individual is influenced by others, by groups of people. Such research provides information about the extent to which behavior is influenced by personality factors (as personality psychologists believe) or by variables within the situation (as situationists believe).

To Lie or Not to Lie

Here is one experiment that situationists use to argue their point: People are told to play a pinball game and then to report their scores to the experimenter. Half the participants—the control group—are told that the experimenter is recording their scores (which they indeed are) and can verify whether they report the true score. On the other hand, half the participants—the experimental group—are told that there is no way for the experimenter to know their scores, so they must report them accurately. The independent variable in this experiment is the situation: whether or not participants are told that the experimenter knows their scores. The dependent variable is whether the participants lie about their scores. This is a measure of *behavior* (lying or truth-telling), and the situationists' hypothesis is that personality traits are not as relevant in influencing lying as is the situation.

If personality traits are the most important factor in determining how people act, then the two groups should have about the same amount of lying (since random assignment of participants ensures approximately equal personality traits in each group). On the other hand, if the situation is important in determining how people act, then the two groups should show very different amounts of lying.

This study and others like it have been done thousands of times. The results always support situationism. The participants in the experimental group typically lie at a rate of about 80%, and those in the control group lie at a rate of about 10%. Notice these numbers. By changing one factor, by telling the participants that we cannot verify their scores, we can increase the percentage of people who lie by 70 percentage points (from 10% to 80%). Obviously, the situation is powerful in determining this behavior.

Perhaps you find these percentages to be awfully high. However, they are correct; numerous psychological studies have confirmed that behavior is mostly a function of the situation. If you are a trusting soul, note that 20% of participants told the truth even when they thought they could get away with fibbing. If you are a cynic, I'm sure you have noticed the 10% who lied even when they knew they would be found out. If you are thinking like this, please note that you have missed the point of situationism.

Here's the point: If behavior is mostly influenced by circumstances, then we can change the circumstances and get nearly any percentage of lying that we want. The amount of lying is not a reflection of the people; it is a reflection of the situation. For example, if we tell people that they will receive a million dollars if they get a high score, I'm certain that we can expect the amount of lying to increase. Similarly, if we tell people that they will receive a million dollars if they report their correct score, I'm convinced that we can get the percentage of lying down to near zero. What do you think?

Stanley Milgram.

To Shock or Not to Shock

A multitude of other research in social psychology supports the situationist view. In 1964, for instance, **Stanley Milgram** (1933–1984) found that people would give an intense electric shock to a stranger if they were asked to do so as part of an experiment. In fact, no shocks were given in this famous series of studies, but the participants believed that they were giving as much as a 450-volt shock to a stranger in another room as a punishment for responding incorrectly to a word-pair problem.

Participants sat in front of a box, a so-called shock generator, that had switches starting at 15 volts and increasing in increments of 15 volts all the way to 450 volts. Participants were told that the shocks would be painful but would cause no permanent damage. If the stranger in the other room (supposedly another volunteer, but really an actor) indicated the wrong answer to a problem, the participant was told to push a

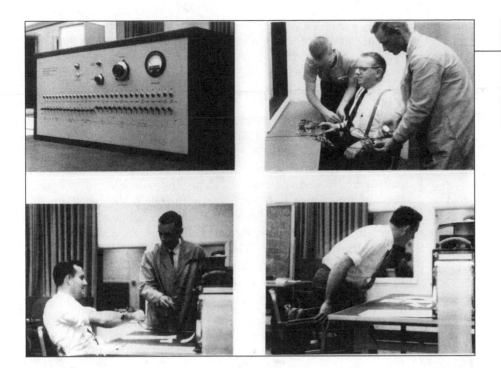

The shock generator used in the Milgram experiment. Do you think you would give a 450-volt shock to a stranger? Here we also see the actor playing the victim and a participant that refuses to continue.

switch that delivered a shock. Each mistake was followed by a shock that was 15 volts higher than the last. The real question was "At what point would the participants refuse to continue?"

Milgram discovered that nearly everyone he tested continued to the maximum, 450 volts. Even when he told participants that the stranger had a heart condition and also had the stranger screaming and pleading to quit, 65% went all the way to 450 volts. Shocking! The participants were emotionally upset, but they continued to push the switches. This experiment shows not that people are cruel, but that situations are terribly influential in determining human behavior.

Milgram found that certain variables influenced how soon participants would refuse to continue giving shocks. Participants were more likely to quit if the victim was in the same room with them or if the experimenter (Milgram) was in a different room. That is, to put it the other way around, people are more likely to obey if the victim is far away and the authority is near. Notice that this shows again that changes in the situation resulted in changes in the participants' behavior. Interestingly, Milgram found that the most influential variable was having another person quit. In a room full of participants pushing switches, if one participant (an actor) refused to continue, nearly everyone else quickly quit too. Behavior was influenced by the situation. In these classic experiments, Stanley Milgram showed that the demands of a situation could even overpower our consciences.

Incidentally, before conducting his experiments, Milgram asked some of his students, some psychologists, and some psychiatrists what they thought the participants would do. They all guessed that only a small percentage, only a fringe group of weirdoes, would go all the way to 450 volts. This is one more bit of evidence that people are not good predictors of human behavior. Even psychologists and psychiatrists were not good predictors in this case. In this case, the problem is that we believe personality traits are more

Connecting Concepts

Recall the discussion of research methods and ethics in Chapter 2. Milgram's experiment placed participants in a good deal of emotional stress. Today's ethics code would not allow an experiment such as this. Why not?

FYI

Milgram's shock experiment was so interesting that a TV-movie was made dramatizing it and starred William Shatner, *Star Trek*'s Captain Kirk, as Stanley Milgram.

powerful than they are. We give too much importance to personality, and we do not give enough importance to variables within the situation. This is the point that situationists make.

To Conform or Not to Conform

Even before Milgram's research was demonstrating the influence of situations regarding obedience, a social psychologist named **Solomon Asch** conducted a series of classic experiments in the 1950s, the results of which were eye-opening. Asch asked a group of people to visually judge the lengths of lines. The participants looked at a card on which there was a standard vertical line and three other lines to choose from. The participants, one at a time, simply said which of the three lines they believed was the same length as the standard line. But, as is often the case with experiments in social psychology, Asch was not measuring what he said he was. Asch's dependent variable was not the participants' ability to visually judge the lengths of lines. Asch was measuring conformity.

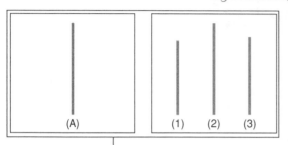

Solomon Asch found that people would often conform to a group that gave an obviously wrong answer to a simple question about the length of lines. Person number 6 has heard five people give the wrong answer. The look on his face shows his confusion—and the pressure he feels.

> "Where all men think alike, no man thinks very much."
> —WALTER LIPPMANN

Only one of the participants was a real subject; the others were actors who occasionally gave wrong answers so that Asch could determine what the one real participant would do. Would the real participant give the right answer or conform and go along with the group? Imagine: You can see that the correct answer is obviously line 2. The first person says line 3, the next person says line 3, the next says 3, the next says 3, and the next says 3. Then it's your turn. Do you stick to your guns and say line 2, or do you go along with the group and say line 3?

When asked what they would do in such a case, nearly everyone insists that they would stick to their guns and not go along with the group. But again, people are bad predictors of human behavior. In fact, Asch found that a significantly large percentage of people conformed and gave the wrong answer under these conditions. Only about 25% never gave in and conformed to the group answer. That means that even in this simple situation, three out of four people (75%) succumbed to conformity at least once. These results surprised nearly everyone. Asch found similar results under different conditions, but he also found that the amount of conformity was drastically reduced if just one other person gave the correct answer before it was the real participants' turn to respond. If one of the actors gave the right answer, the real participant almost always gave the right answer too, refusing to conform to the majority. Will people conform? It seems to depend more on the circumstances than on personality.

THINK TANK

Why do you think conformity evolved as a human characteristic?

Was there survival value in conforming?

What are the advantages and disadvantages of conformity in modern society?

Playing Prison

Perhaps you have noticed that deception was common in social psychology experiments in the past. In 1972, psychologist **Philip Zimbardo** wondered what would happen if people were not misled but were simply asked to role-play. Zimbardo set up a simulated prison in the basement of the Stanford University psychology building and asked volunteers to act as guards and prisoners. The participants were randomly assigned to the groups and were given uniforms and prison props. But the situation soon got out of hand as the "guards" became degrading and cruel while the "prisoners" rebelled or became depressively submissive. Zimbardo had to stop the experiment after only six days because the simulation was so out of control that the emotional and behavioral disruption was alarming (Zimbardo, 1972). Situations apparently are powerful enough to modify people's behavior even when they are aware that they are role-playing.

FYI A 2001 German film called *Das Experiment* was based on Zimbardo's Stanford Prison Experiment. Some people believe the experiment helps us better understand the abuse and torture of Iraqi prisoners by U.S. military that was discovered in 2004.

To Help or Not to Help

One evening in 1964, a woman named **Kitty Genovese** was attacked outside her New York apartment. The attack lasted over 30 minutes, and many people witnessed it; some even called out at the attacker to stop. But no one did anything to help Ms. Genovese, and no one even called the police. Kitty Genovese died on the steps of her apartment building. Why didn't people help? The newspapers said that it was because New Yorkers are apathetic, that they don't care about other people's problems. Two psychologists, **John Darley** and **Bibb Latané,** decided to conduct a series of controlled studies to discover the conditions under which people will help a stranger in trouble. These experiments became known as studies on **bystander apathy.**

Darley and Latané invented a number of situations in which people witnessed an emergency or a person was supposedly in trouble. For example, people in a room saw smoke coming under a door, people on a bus saw a passenger fall to the floor, people driving down the highway saw a motorist with a flat tire, people in a store saw a stranger steal something while the clerk wasn't looking, and college students heard someone on the phone who was having an epileptic seizure. In each case, the psychologists measured variables within the situations to determine which ones were related to helping behavior, known as **altruistic** or **prosocial behavior.**

The results were surprising. The most significant variable that determined whether someone in trouble would get help was the number of people present, and the results were in the opposite direction from what most people would have expected. It turned out that people in trouble were far more likely to be helped if they were seen by only one person rather than by a group. In fact, the more people witnessed the danger, the less likely anyone was to help. This finding is known as the **bystander effect**. For example, in cases in which only one person was in a room in which smoke was coming under a door, he or she went for help 100% of the time. But if three people were in the room, only 30% of the time did anyone go for help. The same thing was found in each experimental condition: The more people who were present to witness the emergency, the less likely they were to help. The fewer people were present, the more likely help was to be offered. Can you believe it? What could cause the bystander effect?

Darley and Latané suggested two important reasons why this might be true: First, to help a person in trouble, we must define the situation as an emergency that requires help. The first step in altruism is to recognize an emergency. However, the more people we see standing around doing nothing, the more likely it is that we will conclude that it is not an emergency. In one case, for example, a woman was raped on the street on a Monday morning. No one helped or called the police. When workers who had witnessed the event were later questioned about it, they said that they did not help because they thought it was just two people having sex. This seems terribly unreasonable! But that is because of our tendency to underestimate the power of situations to influence people. Because many people saw the rape and because they also saw many other people doing nothing about it, the watchers drew the conclusion that it must not be an emergency.

If a large number of people sitting in a theater hear someone yell "Fire!" they will not get up and run out. They will look around to see what others are doing. This is because no one wants to look stupid and run out first. If the people in the theater don't see anyone running out, they will conclude that it is not an emergency. They will not run out. In the case of people in a room in which smoke is entering from beneath a door, individuals who were alone in the room later said that they believed the smoke was from a fire or a broken hose that needed attention. That is, the people who were alone in the room did define it as an emergency. On the other hand, people who had been in the room with a group of others later said that they thought the smoke was just some innocent vapor that did not require attention. They did not think it was an emergency. Notice the important point here: The cognition, the interpretation, or the conclusion that a person reaches about an event is influenced by how many other people are present. In these situations, personality is only a minor component. The situation is most important in determining what people will do and even what they will think.

Second, Darley and Latané theorized that for people to help in an emergency, they must not only recognize the emergency, but also feel a sense of responsibility to help. However, the more people are present, the less responsible each person will feel. When there is a large group, each person reasons that someone else will call the police. This is called **diffusion of responsibility**. If we see a motorist stranded on an infrequently used road, we feel a much greater sense of responsibility to help than if we see a motorist stranded on a busy road. This is likely what happened in the Kitty Genovese case. People *did* recognize it as an emergency—they yelled at the attacker and later told the police that they knew Kitty was in danger. But they also knew that a large number of people were watching. Therefore, each person felt only a small amount of responsibility, and so no one took any action. Not only are behavior and cognition influenced by the number of people present, but the feeling of duty to do something is also influenced.

Amazingly, prosocial behavior is often influenced by elements of a situation that one would never expect to be influential and that people might not even notice. Several studies, for instance, have found that when pleasant odors are present, people are more helpful. Perfume, food odors, and the smell of lavender or vanilla have been found to be associated with increased prosocial behavior (Guéguen, 2001). Does this give you some ideas about how to make the world a better place?

TABLE 7.3   A Summary of the Findings of Social Psychology Research That
Show the Influence of a Situation on a Person's Behavior

1. The extent to which people will lie varies greatly depending on whether they believe
   they will be caught.

2. Stanley Milgram's research on obedience shows that circumstances can overcome
   even principles of conscience.

3. Solomon Asch's research on conformity shows that group pressure is very powerful.

4. The bystander effect shows that the number of people witnessing an emergency can
   influence whether a person helps.

THINK TANK   What are some ways in which you have been influenced by a situation you
were in?

Can you think of behaviors of other people that you believe were influenced by
the situation they were in?

Were you ever judged to be a certain kind of person because of the circumstance,
who you were with, what you were wearing, or how you looked?

How accurate are other people's ideas of your personality?

Who is the "real" you?

Consistency Theories

Some social psychologists have suggested that humans have a driving force to be consistent in their beliefs, attitudes, and behaviors. Such suggestions in social psychology are called **consistency theories.** Social psychologists have provided convincing experimental evidence, for example, that people will change their attitudes to bring them into line—to make them consistent—with their behaviors. In a given situation, a person might act a certain way because of the variables within that situation (dishonesty, conformity, obedience, altruism, etc.), then later may modify his or her attitudes or beliefs to make them consistent with the behavior exhibited. The granddaddy of these consistency theories is called **cognitive dissonance theory,** which was proposed by famed social psychologist **Leon Festinger** (1959).

When a person's cognitions and behaviors are not consistent with one another, Festinger argued, that person feels a sense of anxiety or uneasiness called **dissonance.** The person is then motivated to reduce the dissonance. Sometimes the easiest way to reduce dissonance, Festinger claimed, is to change one's attitudes or beliefs. Festinger conducted a number of ingenious experiments to demonstrate his theory.

In a typical study, Festinger paid participants to perform a very boring task. Some were paid 50 cents, and others were paid $20. After the task was completed and the participants were paid, Festinger asked them to fill out a questionnaire in which they were asked how interesting they thought the task was and whether they would be willing to volunteer for a similar experiment. The findings were incredible but exactly what Festinger's theory had predicted. Contrary to what nearly everyone expects, Festinger found that those who were paid 50 cents were much more likely to rate the task as interesting and were more willing to volunteer for similar tasks. One might naturally have expected the opposite results. But cognitive dissonance theory says those who were paid $20 did not experience any dissonance (their cognitions and behaviors were consistent with one another), since they could reason that they performed the boring task for the money. The participants who were paid only 50 cents had dissonance. The fact that they had done a boring task was inconsistent with the tiny payment they received. Therefore, they could reduce their dissonance by changing their attitudes about the task—by viewing it as interesting. That would then be consistent with the fact that they did the task for so little pay.

Festinger's theory of cognitive dissonance suggests that people want to be consistent. If we find ourselves doing something that is contrary to our beliefs or attitudes, we might come to change our beliefs or attitudes. Please note that this theory could have practical value. If we want people to change their prejudices, for example, we could place them into situations in which their behavior would be inconsistent with their prejudice—for example, helping someone whom they feel prejudice toward. The idea is to create a situation in which a person will act a certain way that is inconsistent with his or her cognitions. According to cognitive dissonance theory, this will produce a sense of dissonance in the person that could be relieved by changing his or her attitude. The person may then come to change his or her prejudicial ideas.

Attribution Theory

One of the most fascinating areas of research in social psychology is **attribution theory.** In this case, researchers are not trying to determine the actual causes of behavior; instead, they are attempting to discover what people *believe* causes behavior. A person's idea about the cause of a specific behavior is called an **attribution.** (It helps to think of the phrase "What do you attribute that to?")

Attributions are divided into two general categories: (1) Sometimes we believe that a person's action is caused by some characteristic within the person, such as his character, ability, or personality (a **personal** or **internal attribution**), or (2) we might conclude that a person's behavior is caused by something about the situation (a **situational** or **external attribution**). I might conclude that a person got an F on a test because he is not very smart (personal attribution) or because he was busy or had problems that kept him from studying (situational attribution).

Experimental studies of attribution theory show that people generally make an error in forming attributions. We tend to see behaviors as caused by personal attributions much more than they actually are. This mistake we make in attributing behaviors to personality variables more than they deserve is called **fundamental attribution error.** When someone acts a particular way, we are likely to attribute that action to his or her personality. A person who drops something is clumsy. A student who gets an "A" on a test is highly intelligent. A person who speaks up in class is an extravert. Someone who tells us a joke has a good sense of humor. We are not likely to look at the situation for the causes of the behavior. Instead, we look inside the person.

Why do people do what they do? Sometimes we believe a behavior is due to circumstances in the situation, but more often we believe that behaviors are caused by personality characteristics. This is fundamental attribution error. The results of empirical research show that people have a strong tendency to overestimate the influence of personal attributions and tend to underestimate the influence of situational attributions. We are more likely to find causes of behavior inside people than in the situation. We underestimate how powerful situations are in influencing what people do.

When we attempt to understand why others have certain behaviors, we look to their personality for the explanation. But when we seek explanations for our own behaviors, we are more likely to look at the situation for the causes. This is called the **actor-observer effect.** For example, if the guy in front of me drops his coffee, I conclude that he is clumsy (a personal attribution). But if I drop my coffee, I conclude that the cup was hot or slippery (a situational attribution). Because I know that I don't always drop my coffee, I correctly look to the situation for an explanation for why I dropped it this time. We get it right more often when explaining our own behaviors.

Similarly, fundamental attribution error (looking for personal attributions) is also less likely when we attempt to explain the behaviors of people whom we like or know very well. If a player on the opposing team drops a ball, he is clumsy. But if a player on my favorite team drops a ball, the sun got in his eyes.

There is one exception to the actor-observer effect. When attributing causes to our *own* behaviors, we are likely to use situational attributions more when explaining failures, and we are more likely to use personal attributions when explaining our successes. Doesn't that sound normal? This tendency is called **self-serving bias.** (A good name, too!) That is, if we are successful at something, we are likely to conclude that our success was due to our personal characteristics. "I did so well on the test because I am so smart!" On the other hand, when we fail at something, we are more likely to see the cause in the circumstances. "I didn't have time to study for that test because of all the work I had to do on my job, and that's why I got such a low score."

THINK TANK

Give examples of attributions that you and others have used to explain the behavior of yourself or of others.

Divide them into personal and situational attributions.

How do you think this kind of thinking is useful or harmful?

Why do we try to understand the reasons for someone's behavior, including our own?

Across Cultures

To a large extent, people in the United States are socialized by the culture to give credit and to find blame in individuals, not in circumstances. We believe that *people* are responsible for their behaviors rather than finding causes of behavior in the variables that inhabit situations. Perhaps that is why we are so amazed by the findings of research in social psychology that show how influential situations are. We do not expect situations to matter so much.

This is not true in other societies in the world. Cross-cultural studies show that adults in the United States are the most likely to use *personal attributions* to explain behavior and the most likely to underestimate the influence of situations (Miller, 1984). Also, in the United States, the use of personal attributions to explain the behavior of others increases as people grow from childhood into adulthood. Children in the United States will consider many situational variables as possible causes of someone's behavior, but adults are far more likely to see personal characteristics as the causes.

For example, the majority of adults in the United States believe that if you do well in school, it is because you are intelligent. By contrast, Asians tend to think that a student who does well is one who has the time to study, works hard, receives affirmation, and so on. The result is that if a student does poorly in the United States, there is a tendency for him or her to stop trying and to drop out of school. But in fact, Asians are correct: Circumstances, such as the amount of time spent studying, are more important than personality in most cases.

Similarly, in the United States, it is commonly believed that poor people are poor because they are lazy, unintelligent, or otherwise deficient in whatever it takes to succeed. But in fact, success depends much more on circumstances than Americans understand. One more example: Crime and immoral behavior are also blamed on individuals. The circumstances that lead to these behaviors are largely ignored. Therefore, it is very difficult to motivate people in the United States to change circumstances to reduce crime and unethical behavior (for example, the unemployment rate is directly related to the crime rate).

Here is but one of many examples from our culture: Every year, motorists are struck by trains at crossings that do not have a crossbar blocking the train tracks when a train is approaching. After a driver was killed in such an accident, a government representative said, "This should be a reminder that motorists should be careful." The clear assumption is that the person, not the situation, is responsible for the accident. What the representative should have said is that this is a reminder that we live in a society that is unwilling to spend the money to put crossbars up at every rail crossing. Obviously, people make mistakes. No one is infallible. Such accidents are a regular occurrence. But public policy assumes that people are at fault. The vast majority of the public insists on blaming the victims rather than changing the situation.

Another example that has been in the news recently: It has been noticed that crime rates decrease in neighborhoods in which broken windows are repaired and other minor problems are tended to. The neighborhood becomes a place that is less inviting to crime and vandalism. Most of us believe that crime is in the mind or personality of the criminal. But situations matter.

One final example: Recall the experiment on lying behavior. If people believe that they will be caught, lying is much less likely. The circumstances are very influential in determining whether a person will lie. But everyone has lied at some time. In spite of this fact, the overwhelming stereotype in the United States (and in most cultures) is that some people are liars and others are not. Lying behavior is attributed to personality variables. This is why in every political contest, candidates try to find examples of deception by their opponents. They can then tag the opponents with the label "liars," knowing that the public believes that a liar is a person who is predisposed to lie. The fact that lying behavior is predominantly a situational variable is apparently unknown or unaccepted by the public.

Social psychology is not only fun, it is relevant and practical. Many problems can be addressed by using the facts and principles from this enticing field of study. For instance, social psychologist Elliot Aronson studied the Columbine school massacre and described solutions to such situations in his book *Nobody Left to Hate* (2000). He suggests that we create atmospheres in which empathy, compassion, and cooperation dominate. This is good advice for all situations, and social psychology can help.

Recap

— Social psychology studies how an individual is influenced by others.

— A number of interesting experiments show that a person's behavior is influenced a great deal by variables within the situation.

— Lying about a score, giving shocks to a stranger, conforming to others' answers, and helping people in danger were all found to be behaviors that were greatly influenced by the situation.

— Milgram studied obedience and found that most people will give an intense electric shock to a stranger in an experimental situation.

— Asch studied conformity and found that many people will go along with a group even when they know that the answer is wrong.

— People in danger are more likely to be helped if fewer people are present. This is called the bystander effect.

Cognitive dissonance theory says that people will change their perceptions or attitudes to bring them into consistency with their other cognitions or actions.

— According to attribution theory, people typically overvalue personal attributions, such as personality traits, and undervalue the ability of the situation to influence people's actions.

So Far...

How should we describe people's personalities? Psychologists have taken three approaches: types, traits, and behaviors. Which is best? Here's an analogy: Suppose astronauts have landed on a planet that has many different flowers. How should those flowers be described? We might divide them into categories, such as those that are open and those that are closed. That would be a type approach. But what if some flowers are partially open? We might then make a rating scale so that each flower can be given a score on a dimension of openness. This would be a trait approach. However, we might notice that some flowers are more open when the light is bright and more closed when the light is dim. This would be a behavioral approach that stresses the situation. Are there types of people? Do people really have traits? Famous trait theorist Gordon Allport wrote, "A trait has more than nominal existence: it is independent of the observer, it is really there" (Hall & Lindzey, 1957). Is that correct? Or is the concept of personality simply a hypothetical construct that we have invented to describe people's behaviors? Are we like the flowers that are open more under some conditions than others?

Types, traits, and behaviors in situations are the three most common approaches that are used to try to understand personality. They are all fascinating approaches that have led to wonderfully provocative and intriguing research findings and theories. Each has its own advantages and disadvantages in helping us to better understand the concept of personality. Our overall understanding of the human mind and human behavior can rightly incorporate many of the ideas that are provided by these different approaches. But next we might ask, "How can personality be measured?" Let's turn now to a very common and important subfield of psychology: psychological testing, or assessment.

ASSESSMENT

"Man is the measure of all things."
—PROTAGORAS

Thousands of psychological tests are published for use by licensed psychologists and by researchers. The field of psychology that creates and studies tests is called **psychometrics.** Different categories of tests include those for measuring intelligence, achievement, aptitude, interests, skills and abilities, brain damage, dyslexia, and values, as well as a multitude of tests that attempt to assess personality.

The development of the modern discipline of psychology is heavily based on the process and study of assessment—measuring the characteristics of people. The history of psychology is in many ways a story of tests. There is undoubtedly no category of tests that is better known, more discussed, more misunderstood, or more controversial than **intelligence tests.** Let's learn about them first, and then we'll learn about personality tests.

Intelligence Testing

The attempt to measure intelligence goes back hundreds of years to times when scientists measured the sizes of people's heads to get an indication of how much they knew and how good they were at thinking. This seems silly to us today, partly because we know that there is no relationship between head size and intelligence and also because the concept of intelligence has changed over time. If you ask 50 people to define intelligence, you will probably get 50 different definitions. Each person has his or her own meaning of the term. But how do psychologists define and measure intelligence?

THINK TANK

What is your definition of intelligence?

Ask some people for their definitions, and then compare and contrast them. Do the definitions have anything in common?

Why do you think people value intelligence so much?

What human qualities do you think we should value?

Parisian Schools

The intelligence tests that are widely used today were developed early in the twentieth century. The concept was a simple one, but I'm afraid that it is not exactly what you are expecting. What psychologists call *intelligence* (in the context of intelligence tests) is not the same as the concept that the general public means by the term. Psychology should probably have another term for what intelligence tests are intended to measure—something like scholastic ability, academic aptitude, or school skills. That's because intelligence tests were originally designed to measure students' abilities to succeed at school-related tasks, such as reading, arithmetic, solving problems, and memory. So when you read or hear the term *intelligence test*, you should think "school ability test," because, for the most part, that is what intelligence tests attempt to measure.

The first modern intelligence test was designed by a French psychologist named **Alfred Binet** (1859–1911). Binet had been asked by the Paris school officials to help solve a problem. Many new students were entering the public schools of Paris (it was a popular destination), and they were typically placed in a grade based on **chronological age (CA)**, which is common even today. But some children were overly challenged because their abilities were significantly below those of their age-cohorts. Therefore, Binet was asked to devise a test that would allow proper placement of low-ability children.

Alfred Binet, creator of the modern IQ test.

Binet had a simple but elegant idea. He constructed a test that consisted of the kinds of problems, skills, and mental abilities that are used in schools. He then gave these test items to large numbers of children of various chronological ages. He was doing what we call **standardizing** the test, or developing **norms**. He wanted to know which items could be solved by children of various ages and what the range of abilities was. He was developing standards to which other children could be compared. Binet published his test in 1905 with the help of a colleague named **Theodore Simon.**

To construct their test, Binet and Simon selected a set of problems that they had demonstrated could be solved by average five-year-old children, another group of items that could be solved by average six-year-olds, another by average seven-year-olds, and so on. The complete test, then, consisted of sets of problems that it had been demonstrated children of various chronological ages could solve. When this test was given to a certain child, if the child could solve all of the average five-year-old problems but none at the higher ages, for example, that child was said to have a **mental age (MA)** of five years. A child who could solve all the seven-year-old problems, had an MA of seven. If a child could solve all of the problems that an average 10-year-old could solve, that child's mental age was 10. If a child could solve all of the six-year-old problems and half of the seven-year-old problems and no more, that child was said to have a mental age of 6 1/2. If a child could solve all of the problems that an average 12-year-old could solve and also one-fourth of the problems that average 13-year-olds could solve, the mental age was calculated to be 12 years and 3 months. In other words, the mental age was the person's score on the test and indicated how well the person did in comparison to a standard group of children of various chronological ages.

Calculating IQ

Another psychologist suggested that it would be useful to calculate an **intelligence quotient** or **IQ score** by comparing the mental age and chronological age of a child. Suppose a 10-year-old girl scores equal to an average eight-year-old on the test. Then this child has an MA (score on the test) of 8 and a CA (how old she is) of 10. The ratio between the MA and CA is 8/10 or 0.80. To eliminate fractions and decimals, the ratio is multiplied by 100, the result being an IQ of 80. When we divide one number by another number, the result is called a quotient; therefore, this fraction, or ratio, is

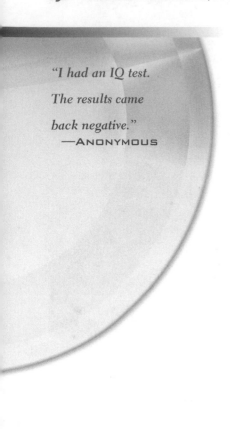

*"I had an IQ test.
The results came
back negative."*
—ANONYMOUS

called an intelligence quotient or IQ. If a child's MA is 6 and her CA is 8, then her IQ = 6/8 × 100, or 75. If a child is eight but scores as an average 10-year-old, his IQ is 10/8 × 100, or 125. A child of seven whose test score is 9 has an IQ of 9/7 × 100, or 129. A five-year-old child who scores equal to an average eight-year-old has an IQ of 8/5 × 100, or 160.

$$IQ = MA/CA \times 100$$

Notice that if a child's MA and CA are the same number (in other words, the child is average on this test), then the child's IQ will be 100. That is true for every chronological age. A child of five who scores a mental age of five will have an IQ of 100; a child of eight who scores an MA of 8 will have an IQ of 100, and a child of 12 whose MA is 12 will have an IQ of 100. Please notice that these three children definitely do *not* have the same abilities, although their IQ scores are the same. IQ does not tell how smart someone is; it tells how fast he or she is developing. The 12-year-old has much better school abilities than does the eight-year-old, who in turn has much better abilities than does the five-year-old. But each has an IQ of 100.

The IQ score is a quotient, a ratio. It does not tell how far developed a child is; instead, it tells how fast a child is progressing (in school abilities only, of course; the IQ tells us nothing about the child's other qualities). The IQ score is just like miles per hour: It tells how fast a car is going, not how far it has gone. The CA is how old a child is (how long he or she has been developing), the MA is his or her ability compared to average children (how far he or she has developed), and the IQ is the rate of development.

An IQ of 100 means that a child (of any chronological age) is developing at an average rate for children that age (in the ability to solve these specific problems). Similarly, an IQ of 150 means that a child is developing one and a half times as fast as the average child his or her age. For example, an eight-year-old child with an IQ of 150 can solve problems equal to an average 12-year-old (12/8 × 100 = 150). An IQ of 200 means the child's MA is twice his or her CA; for example, a child of five who can solve problems equal to an average 10-year-old has an IQ of 200.

Notice again that Binet did not use his personal opinion about the appropriate levels of intellectual development in establishing the norms for this test. That is, Binet did not use his opinion to determine what problems a six-year-old should be able to solve; instead, he measured six-year-olds and found out what they could and could not do. In other words, the items on the Binet test were chosen by **empirical scoring** or **criterion scoring.** The comparison groups (the criterion groups) for the test are the scores of average children of various chronological ages.

Terman and Wechsler

**Lewis Terman, who brought the
Binet test to the United States.**

Binet's test was brought to the United States by a psychologist at Stanford University named **Lewis Terman** (1877–1956). Terman translated the test into English, revised the problems on the test to fit American society, and re-standardized the items by testing American children. The result was titled the **Stanford-Binet IQ test** (Terman was modest; it should have been named after him, not after his university). The Stanford-Binet was first published in 1916 and has been revised many times over the years.

The Stanford-Binet IQ test was meant to measure school abilities and therefore was originally designed for children. Tests of *adult* intelligence originated with a psychologist named **David Wechsler** (1896–1981) at Bellevue Psychiatric Hospital in New York. In the 1940s, Wechsler had many patients who had suffered from brain damage, and he wanted to measure the progress of their intellectual abilities. He began developing tests similar to the Stanford-Binet, except using problems aimed at adults rather than at children.

Today there are three Wechsler tests: one for adults known as the **Wechsler Adult Intelligence Scale,** one for children called the **Wechsler Intelligence Scale for Children,** and one for very young children known as the **Wechsler Preschool and Primary Scale of Intelligence.** These tests are referred to by their acronyms: **WAIS, WISC,** and **WPPSI.** Each of these tests, as you can imagine, has different levels of questions. The WPPSI requires following simple instructions, solving sensory-motor tasks such as standing on one foot, and certain low-level memory problems. The WISC contains problems that are appropriate for school-aged children. The WAIS has problems aimed at adults, problems that range from easy to very difficult.

Wechsler tests consist of a number of subtests that measure different intellectual abilities. Until recently, the subtests were divided into two broad categories: Those that use words or demand verbal ability make up the **verbal scale,** and those that do not use words, that are mostly nonverbal, make up the **performance scale.** Three IQ scores are calculated: verbal IQ, performance IQ, and full-scale IQ (an average of verbal and performance).

Here are the subtests that were traditionally used on the WAIS:

David Wechsler, creator of adult IQ testing.

The Verbal Scale:

1. *Vocabulary:* Define words such as *nepotism.*
2. *Similarities:* Explain how two concepts are similar, such as piano and harmonica.
3. *Arithmetic:* Solve word problems involving simple arithmetic, such as how long it will take a train to go 120 miles if it is traveling at 30 mph.
4. *Digit span:* Repeat a series of digits (from two to nine digits long) after hearing them, such as 9, 3, 5, 2, 7. Sometimes the test taker must repeat the digits in backward order.
5. *Information:* Answer general knowledge questions from history, literature, and science, such as who wrote *Hamlet.*
6. *Comprehension:* Give detailed answers (showing the understanding of concepts) about why something is so, such as why clothing is sometimes made of cotton.

The Performance Scale:

1. *Picture completion:* Identify what is missing in a picture of a common scene, such as a picture of a house that is missing the front door.
2. *Digit symbol:* Learn a series of coded symbols that are associated with numbers, then write the appropriate symbols in a series of boxes, such as 1 = +, 2 = #, 3 = ↑, 4 = ⊕, and so on.
3. *Block design:* Duplicate a red and white pattern shown in a picture by arranging cubes that have red, white, or half red and half white on each of their sides. For example, create a red cross on a white background by placing the cubes in the correct pattern.
4. *Picture arrangement:* Arrange a series of pictures (similar to cartoon panels) in the correct order to make a story, such as (1) a bird building a nest, (2) the bird sitting on an egg, and (3) the egg hatching.
5. *Object assembly:* Put pieces of a jigsaw puzzle together to form a recognizable object.

The most recent editions of the Stanford-Binet and Wechsler are more complicated, measuring multiple abilities. The latest Wechsler test uses four indices: verbal comprehension, perceptual reasoning, working memory, and processing speed. New editions of the Stanford-Binet have become more like the Wechsler, now having norms for ages 2 to 85, measuring both verbal and nonverbal IQs, and using a number of different subtests, including mathematical reasoning and memory.

Deviation Scores

The IQ score is no longer calculated according to the **ratio formula** described above, since that method does not allow us to compare IQ scores across chronological ages (for instance, the spread of scores for 12-year-olds is greater than that of six-year-olds and IQs calculated by the ratio MA/CA will not mean the same thing across the two ages). In addition, the concept of mental age is inappropriate for adults. Obviously we cannot say that a 38-year-old is as intelligent as an average 41-year-old. Therefore, IQ today is calculated by using a statistic known as **standard deviation.**

Any set of scores has an average score that can be calculated by adding all the scores and dividing by how many scores there are. I'm sure you are familiar with this idea. The statistic calculated this way is known as the **mean.** Other averages include the **mode** (the most often occurring score) and the **median** (the score that is exactly in the middle of a range of scores).

In addition to having an average, a set of scores also has a certain amount of spread; that is, the scores might be widely spread out, they might be close together, or they might be anywhere in between. Besides calculating the mean, we can calculate a number that tells us how much spread there is, which is known as the standard deviation. It helps to think of this number as the normal or average (standard) amount of spread or variation (deviation). Think of it this way: Not all the scores are average. Some are higher than the mean, and some are lower. But how far above and below are they? The standard deviation is a number that essentially tells us the average amount that scores are different from the mean—the average amount of variability in scores. If a score is one standard deviation above average, it means that the score is an average amount higher than the average score. If the standard deviation for a set of scores is a *small* number, it means that the scores don't vary (spread out) much. If the standard deviation is *large*, it means that there is a great deal of variation among people on this ability.

On an IQ test, the average score is 100, and the standard deviation is 15 points (previous editions of the Stanford-Binet had a standard deviation of 16). So if a child gets a score of 115, that score is above the average. But by how much? Is it only a little above average, is it a great deal above average, or is it a medium amount above average? Because the average is 100 and the standard deviation is 15, a score of 115 is a medium amount above average; in fact, it is exactly the average amount above average! In other words, of all the scores that are above the average score (100), this score is the average. Similarly, a score of 85 is an average amount below average. A score of 130 is very high, two standard deviation units above average, and a score of 70 is very low, two standard deviations below the average. For every IQ score, we can determine its place in the distribution of IQ scores, and we can determine the percentage of test takers who get higher or lower scores. Sometimes **percentile** scores are used; the percentile tells the percentage of scores that are lower than a given score.

A graph that shows how commonly scores occur is known as a **frequency distribution.** Look at the example. The percentage of scores that fall between standard deviations is indicated. Note, for example, that about 34% of scores are between average and one standard deviation above or below average. This means that about two out of three people (about 68%) score within one standard deviation of average. Similarly, scores above 130 are in the upper 3% of scores, and scores below 70 are in the lower 3% of scores. Extreme scores, naturally, are less common than are scores near 100. In fact, it is common to say that scores between 85 and 115 are "normal" or "average."

Today, IQs are determined by using graphs like this one. Instead of the ratio method described above, a **deviation method** is now used to compute IQ. A score of 115, for example, means that the score is one standard deviation above average, or is at the 84th percentile (84% of the scores are lower). A score of 100 is at the 50th percentile, a score of 85 is at the 16th percentile, a score of 70 is at the 3rd percentile, and a score of 145 is at the 99th percentile. With the proper statistical table, we can convert back and forth between IQ scores and percentiles anyplace on the frequency distribution.

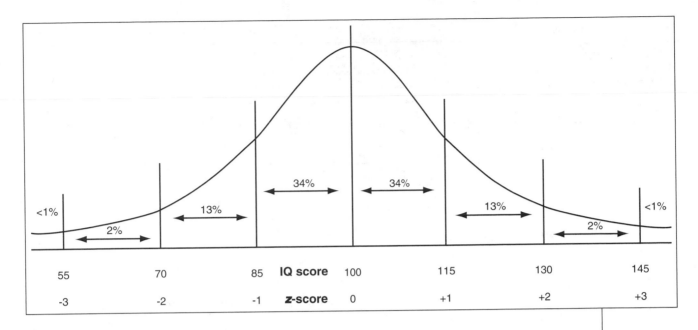

This frequency distribution shows the scores on the Stanford-Binet and Wechsler IQ tests, approximately what percent of people fall within each standard deviation, and z-scores.

Sometimes a set of scores is converted to standard deviation units so that comparisons can be made across different scoring systems. These are called **z-scores**. For example, a z-score of 0 would be average. A z-score of +1.00 would be one standard deviation above the average. A z-score of −2.00 would be two standard deviations below average, equal to the third percentile. IQ scores are also a type of standard score, based on standard deviation units. It is easy to convert z-scores to IQ scores and vice versa. As you can see from the graph, a z-score of +2.00 is the same as an IQ of 130.

Culture-Fair Tests

One of the most common things said about IQ tests is that they are biased. Perhaps at times they are, but we must think about this concept for a minute. Because an individual or a group scores low on a test does not necessarily mean that the test is biased. If a test measures what it is attempting to measure and the scores on that test accurately predict some criterion, then the test is not biased. IQ tests are meant to measure success at solving scholastic, academic problems, the kinds of skills that are used by students in schools. An IQ test is a measure of the ability to perform well in a specific situation, such as a classroom, on a specific set of problems. If a group of people do poorly (on the average) in school, then their IQ scores should be low to reflect this fact. Similarly, if a group of people do well (on the average) on an IQ test, then they should do well in school. Don't blame the tests for pointing out differences in schools and in society. Bias means that people will get scores that are not indicative of the criterion, that their scores are based on something other than what the test is attempting to measure. Of course, people from different cultures or backgrounds will likely get different scores on IQ tests. But do the tests accurately measure their ability to do well in academic situations?

Some years ago, psychologists attempted to construct **culture-fair IQ tests**. The idea was that there might be some intellectual ability that was independent of culture, that we could measure intelligence in the very same way for all kinds of people from different cultures around the globe. The culture-fair tests included problems such as solving mazes or visual tasks that supposedly did not depend on language. But the results were not good. It seems that every intellectual ability, even visual skill, is connected to culture and upbringing. Knowledge is not empty of experience. Ability does not exist in a vacuum. Culture is very important in influencing how people think about problems and what kind of thinking (or intelligence) is valued.

A typical problem found on a culture-fair intelligence test. Such "culture-fair" tests attempt to test intellectual ability separate from any cultural factors. Is this really possible?

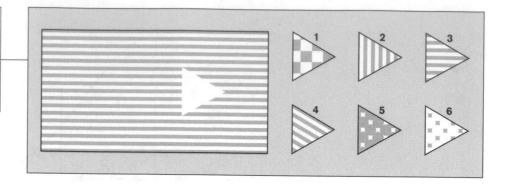

THINK TANK

The state of California has decided not to use standardized college entrance test scores (such as the SAT or ACT) to help determine which students to admit to its colleges.

What are the pros and cons of such a policy?

Extreme IQs

People whose IQs are very high are sometimes called **gifted.** That term can be used in many different ways, however. It might refer to students who have high aptitude in a particular discipline such as music, people with high motivation, students who get high grades in certain subjects in school, or people with high IQs. There is no official definition of the term *gifted* or even of the term *genius,* for that matter, so these terms are used in any way people see fit. Perhaps it is best simply to use the term *high IQ* for people who have high IQ scores.

Lewis Terman, who was responsible for developing the Stanford-Binet IQ test, began a longitudinal study of high IQ children in the 1920s. The results showed that people with high IQs were more successful on the average at most things than were people with normal or low IQs. However, Terman's findings are tainted because he did not use a random sample of high IQ children; he purposely chose those who were popular, physically capable, and had a desire to excel. A high IQ score tells us a very limited amount about a person. IQ tests measure analytical and verbal abilities.

People whose IQ scores are significantly below average have traditionally been termed **mentally retarded,** and this term is still used, although, as you know, it often has unpleasant connotations. Mental retardation is defined as including IQ scores more than two standard deviations below average (below 70 on the most recent Stanford-Binet or Wechsler). About 3% of people have such scores. Mental retardation is often divided into the categories **mild, moderate, severe,** and **profound,** one for each standard deviation group starting at two standard deviations below average.

Schools today often use the term **mentally handicapped,** and in the past the mentally retarded were divided into two groups: **educable** and **trainable.** These terms are not used much anymore. Nor do we use the original terms for categories of mental retardation: idiot, imbecile, and moron. These terms were selected by scientists long ago because they believed them to be so foreign-sounding that people would not use them in derogatory ways. Well, that didn't work out!

There are many different causes of mental retardation, including prenatal conditions, birth defects, genetic factors, deprivation in childhood, and poor learning environments. The most common cause of mental retardation is the lack of good nutrition among pregnant women. A common hereditary factor is called **Down syndrome.** In this case, a child inherits 47 chromosomes instead of 46. Because the child looks different, typically with upslanted eyes, this was initially called *mongolism*, and children with this condition were said to be mongoloid idiots. Well, need we be reminded that it is not polite to name mental retardation after races of people? Besides, this condition has nothing whatsoever to do with race. It occurs in children born to women of all races, although the risk increases as the women age. A woman in her forties has a much higher risk that her fetus will inherit 47 chromosomes than does a woman in her twenties. However, many more women in their twenties have babies than do women in their forties, so the absolute number of children with Down syndrome is higher for the younger women.

It is possible to diagnose Down syndrome early in a pregnancy, giving the parents the opportunity to have an abortion or to prepare for a mentally retarded child. People with Down syndrome are often happy and loved, of course. However, they do experience physical problems other than retardation, and if they live long enough, they typically develop Alzheimer's disease.

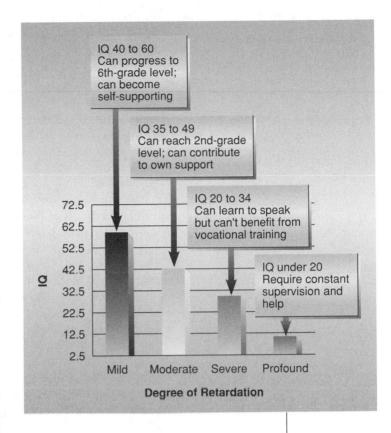

IQ 40 to 60
Can progress to 6th-grade level; can become self-supporting

IQ 35 to 49
Can reach 2nd-grade level; can contribute to own support

IQ 20 to 34
Can learn to speak but can't benefit from vocational training

IQ under 20
Require constant supervision and help

The terminology used for different categories of mental retardation.

New Ideas

Traditional IQ tests have been around for nearly one hundred years and are based on the idea that intelligence is equal to academic abilities. Many psychologists believe that this narrow definition of intelligence is an advantage both theoretically and in practice—that it has predictive value. However, some psychologists believe that this approach is too narrow and that the concept of intelligence should be broadened to include a wider range of skills, even including emotions. A number of studies have shown that ideas about intelligence, and even cognitive styles, differ markedly around the world (Nisbett, 2003; Benson, 2003). For example, people in Eastern cultures tend to see intelligence as "A way for members of a community to recognize contradiction and complexity and to play their roles successfully" (Benson, 2003). Of course, we must be careful not to overgeneralize; people of a culture do not all think alike. Still, research is increasingly showing the importance of culture and the different views of intelligence that exist around the world. Regarding culture-fair tests, for example, the new view is that even nonverbal or visual tests are significantly culture-bound (Greenfield, 1997).

New ideas about intelligence have resulted in the creation of new tests, such as the Kaufman Assessment Battery for Children (K-ABC), the Woodcock-Johnson Tests of Cognitive Ability, Differential Ability Scales, and the Cognitive Assessment System (CAS). These tests have not yet caught on in the world of psychometrics; still, there is excitement about new theories of intelligence, and we will discuss a few of them here.

Defining Intelligence

IQ tests are but one way to define the elusive quality that we call *intelligence*. Psychologists have offered many definitions for this complicated concept. In 1904, English psychologist **Charles Spearman** (1863–1945) argued that intelligence is a single ability, which he abbreviated **g** (for *general* intelligence). Spearman believed that intelligence is one mental factor—a single, overall capacity. This idea is still argued today and is part of what is now called the **theory of general intelligence,** the idea that intellect is best conceptualized as a single, overall ability.

Other psychologists have argued that intelligence is made up of many specific intellectual abilities in various areas of study. These specialized kinds of intelligence are abbreviated **s** (for *specific* factors). This notion is popular today and is referred to as a **multifactor theory of intelligence.** Some psychologists accept both views and argue that solving problems requires the use of both g and s, although a particular task might depend more on one than the other.

L. L. Thurstone (1887–1955) used factor analysis to determine what he called **primary mental abilities,** theoretically the fundamental sources of intelligence. People were measured on a wide variety of intellectual abilities, and a mathematical analysis of their scores found that there were seven basic abilities: (1) verbal ability, (2) word fluency (thinking of words), (3) number ability, (4) memory, (5) perception (speed at recognizing similarities and differences), (6) reasoning, and (7) spatial visualization. Tests were devised to measure each of these intellectual abilities.

Cattell (1963) and others divided intelligence into two types: **crystallized intelligence,** a person's knowledge of facts and the ability to use them, and **fluid intelligence,** a person's ability to think quickly and agilely, to figure out original solutions, and to shift gears nimbly. Crystallized intelligence is a measure of how much you know; fluid intelligence is a measure of how good you are at reasoning about things in general. It has been demonstrated that crystallized intelligence increases with age, while fluid intelligence seems to decrease. We see examples of this on TV shows such as *Jeopardy*. Young contestants are quick on the buzzer, clever and intellectually adroit, but have not stored as much information into memory. Older contestants have lots of facts and knowledge but require a bit more time to respond and to think in novel ways. Of course, this is true only as a generalization for people on the average; it does not apply to each individual.

One multifactor theory of intelligence was proposed by **Howard Gardner** of Harvard University (1983). His ideas are known as the **theory of multiple intelligences.** Gardner argues that there are eight fundamental forms of intelligence: (1) linguistic (use of language), (2) spatial, (3) musical, (4) logical-mathematical, (5) body, (6) intrapersonal (ability to understand oneself), (7) interpersonal (ability to understand others in social situations), and (8) naturalistic (ability to observe carefully). Recently Gardner has suggested a ninth basic form: existential intelligence, the ability to contemplate deep philosophical questions of our existence. Several schools are now using Gardner's theory in their curricula, teaching methods, and testing of students.

Another recent multifactor theory has been proposed by **Robert Sternberg** of Yale University (1990). His approach includes only three fundamental types of intelligence and hence is known as the **triarchic theory of intelligence.** The three abilities are (1) analytic, (2) practical, and (3) creative.

Does intelligence consist of one ability or many? Brain researcher John Duncan and his team in Cambridge, England, reasoned that if intelligence consists of one ability, then a person solving different kinds of problems would use the same area of the brain, whereas if intelligence consists of many different abilities, then different brain regions would be used to solve different kinds of problems. Duncan took brain images of people solving various problems and found (in Spearman's favor) that one brain area—the lateral prefrontal lobe—was active when people solved different problems (Duncan, 2000). Naturally, Sternberg is critical of these results and persists in arguing that success in life depends more on practical intelligence than on a general factor.

Several contemporary psychologists have argued that to succeed in modern life, intellectual ability might not be as important as **emotional intelligence**—the ability to deal socially with oneself and others. As Teddy Roosevelt said, "The most important single ingredient in the formula of success is knowing how to get along with people." The idea of emotional intelligence was first proposed by Yale University psychology professor Peter Salovey (Salovey & Mayer, 1990). The concept has been popularized by **Daniel Goleman** (1995), who has argued that skills such as caring about the emotions of others (empathy), knowing your own emotions, managing your feelings, recognizing emotions in others, and handling relationships are crucial attributes of people who succeed. Supposedly, having a high **EQ (emotional quotient)** not only helps people to deal with others, but also might help people to reason better by keeping their emotions in place. A test, the Emotional Intelligence Inventory, has been devised to measure these abilities (Tapia, 2001).

TABLE 7.4   **Summary of Theories of Intelligence**

1. Spearman	One kind of intelligence	g = general intelligence versus s = specific factors
2. Thurstone	Many basic factors	Seven primary mental abilities
3. Cattell	Two categories	Crystallized versus fluid intelligence
4. Gardner	Multiple intelligences	Nine fundamental types of intelligence
5. Sternberg	Triarchic theory	Three basic kinds: analytic, practical, and creative
6. Salovey and Goleman		Emotional intelligence

Connecting Concepts

Empathy is the ability to identify with someone else's feelings. Empathy is at the center of the idea of emotional intelligence. Brain imaging (Chapter 3) shows that when people see an expression of disgust on someone else's face, the "disgust" area of their brain becomes active. This kind of empathy is a physiological, emotional response (Chapter 8). There are cells in the brain called mirror cells that fire both when people perform an action and when they see someone else perform the same action; this is the basis of observational learning, a kind of empathy (Chapter 5). Psychiatrists use the term antisocial personality disorder for people who have a deficiency in the ability to show empathy for the feelings of others (Chapter 9).

THINK TANK

Match careers (engineer, nurse, artist, teacher, etc.) with kinds of intelligences.

Which kinds of intelligence do you value the most?

Why?

Which ones are most important for success?

Does it matter what the success is in?

Which is more important for getting along with people and having good relationships?

Are money and material goods the most important things in life?

What about values and lifestyle?

What kinds of intelligence should we encourage and try to develop in ourselves and other people?

Recap

— Psychometrics is the branch of psychology that focuses on assessment.

— Alfred Binet developed the first modern IQ test, which was revised by Lewis Terman and named the Stanford-Binet IQ test.

— David Wechsler developed the first adult IQ test, which gave three IQ scores: verbal, performance, and full-scale.

— The most recent Stanford-Binet and Wechsler IQ tests use an average of 100 and a standard deviation of 15. Both measure a number of different abilities including verbal, mathematical, perceptual, and memory.

— IQ was originally a measure of how fast intellectual development was occurring in a child. Today, it is a score on a distribution of scores, thus comparing a person's score to the scores of a large group of people.

— Mental retardation is defined by IQ scores lower than 70; categories are mild, moderate, severe, and profound. There is no official definition of genius or gifted.

— Psychologists have theorized many different kinds of intelligence. Some theories emphasize a single trait, g; others define specific kinds or factors of intelligence, s.

— Crystallized intelligence is the sum of knowledge a person has; fluid intelligence is a person's ability to think quickly and agilely.

— Modern theories that emphasize multiple intelligences have been proposed by Howard Gardner (nine kinds) and Robert Sternberg (triarchic = three kinds).

— A new idea is emotional intelligence (EQ), which focuses on a person's ability to handle emotions, show empathy, relate with others, and be understanding.

PERSONALITY TESTS

"Personality is the gland of creativity."
—SHOLEM ASCH

In a sense, intelligence tests are personality tests because they measure particular traits. However, not all psychologists would say that what is measured by typical IQ tests (school abilities) should be defined as components of personality. Personality tests typically measure traits that are emotional, social, or psychological rather than intellectual.

Personality tests are divided into two large categories: **structured tests** and **projective tests.** A structured test is like a multiple-choice test or true-false test; it has a structure and requires that you select from the answers given. You cannot give any answer you want. A structured test can be objectively scored, by a computer, for example. A projective test, on the other hand, encourages the test taker to give any possible answer, in the hopes that the answers will be a projection of the person's personality. A projective test is like a fill-in-the-blank test. The answers given cannot be objectively scored; they must be subjectively evaluated to see what they might reveal about the person who gave them. A projective test assumes that the responses given will project something about the test takers' personalities.

The MMPI

The most commonly used personality test in the world is the well-known **Minnesota Multiphasic Personality Inventory,** which is generally referred to as the **MMPI.** (A personality inventory is any test that asks people to mark things that are true about themselves.) The MMPI was constructed in the 1930s at the University of Minnesota by a psychologist and a psychiatrist. Their goal was to devise a test that would accurately diagnose mental disorders in patients, thereby saving time and money; psychiatrists would be free to work on therapy instead of diagnosis.

The MMPI is empirically scored, or criterion scored (just as IQ tests are). This means that the scoring is not subjective; it is not based on someone's opinion about how a mentally ill person will answer questions. Instead, the MMPI compares test takers' responses to those of known groups—criterion groups. A criterion is an outside standard that we can use for comparison. On the MMPI, responses by certain criterion groups are known, and test takers' responses are compared to them.

For example, if all people with the disorder schizophrenia responded the same way to a set of items and people who did not have schizophrenia did not respond that way, we could then use those items as a perfect diagnosis for schizophrenia. However, I'm sure you know that people are different and that not all people with schizophrenia respond the same to anything. Nevertheless, there are patterns, ways in which people with schizophrenia are *more likely* to respond to certain items than are people who do not have schizophrenia. That is the basis for the MMPI.

Clinical Scales

The MMPI consists of hundreds of statements that test takers respond to with "yes" (the statement is true about them), "no" (the statement is not true about them), or "can't say." Here are some items similar to those found on the MMPI: I like to go to parties. As a child I was a loner. I am afraid of being alone. My friends are jealous of me. People think I'm smart. I often have pains in my body for no good reason. No one understands me.

A test taker marks true, false, or can't say to each item on the MMPI. The person's responses are then put into a computer that compares the pattern of responses to the patterns made by known criterion groups. The scores that are computed make up what are called the **clinical scales:**

1. *Hypochondriasis:* An abnormal, excessive concern and anxiety about illness and body complaints.
2. *Depression:* A severely low mood that interferes with daily life activities such as eating, sleeping, and motivation.
3. *Hysteria:* An old-fashioned term (now called *conversion disorder*) that refers to simulated physical impairments (pain, blindness, numbness, etc.) in the absence of any organic cause.
4. *Psychopathic deviate:* An old-fashioned term (now called *antisocial personality disorder*) that refers to people whose consciences are underdeveloped, who do not care about the consequences of their actions, and who are unable to care about the feelings of other people.

5. *Masculinity–femininity:* A measure of whether the test taker responds to items more as men do or more as women do. A high score indicates responses more like that of the opposite sex; a low score indicates responses that are more similar to those of members of one's own sex.

6. *Paranoia:* Excessive, unrealistic suspiciousness. This term is today often mistakenly used to mean nervousness. In fact, paranoia refers to suspicious feelings, not necessarily anxiety.

7. *Psychasthenia:* An old-fashioned term (now called *anxiety disorder*) for nervousness, worry, stress, obsessions and compulsions, fears, and feelings of guilt.

8. *Schizophrenia:* Often mistakenly used to mean "split personality," in fact this term refers to bizarre, unusual thinking and altered perceptions (for example, hearing voices or seeing things), a serious mental disorder in which a person is out of touch with reality.

9. *Hypomania:* This means a little mania (the opposite of depression), including overexcitement, impulsiveness, inability to pay attention, thoughts jumping from one thing to another, and hyperactivity.

10. *Social introversion:* Lack of interest in social activities, being a loner, quiet, shy, and reserved; the opposite of extraversion. A high score indicates that the test taker responded as introverts do; a low score indicates responses similar to those of extraverted people.

For each of the 10 clinical scales, the responses of the criterion groups are known in advance. For example, the MMPI creators knew that people with schizophrenia responded to certain items differently than did people who did not have schizophrenia. In fact, the items on the MMPI were selected precisely because they were answered differently by people in the criterion groups than by people who were not in the criterion groups. For instance, a large number of statements were given to people with schizophrenia and to people who did not have schizophrenia. The items that were answered differently by the two groups (the differences were big enough to be statistically significant—see Chapter 2) were put on the test.

Therefore, if you get a high score on the schizophrenia scale, it means that you answered items very much the same way that people with schizophrenia answered those items. If you get a high score on depression, it means you responded to certain items the way that depressed people respond to those items. People often ask what the MMPI items mean. The items do not have a meaning in the traditional sense. They are on the test because a criterion group responded to them differently than did a non-criterion "normal" group. The items were not selected because they have a certain meaning or because it was someone's opinion that the criterion group would answer these items a certain way. The items were selected purely because of their statistical ability to differentiate between people in the criterion group and people not in the criterion group. A high score on a particular scale means that the test taker responded to a set of items in a similar way to people in the criterion group.

Scoring the MMPI

The MMPI is scored by a computer, and a graph is made indicating the scores on each of the 10 clinical scales. It is the pattern of these scores that is most important. The pattern is called a profile, and it is known that groups of people with certain characteristics tend to attain certain MMPI profiles. For example, alcoholics often have a certain profile of scores on the MMPI. When a person takes the MMPI, her or his profile is compared to known profiles.

The MMPI uses a scoring system called **T-scores.** This is just another type of standard score, like *z*-scores or IQ scores. With T-scores, the average of each MMPI scale is converted to a score of 50 and a standard deviation (the average amount that the scores spread out) of 10 points. In other words, if you get a score of 50 on the paranoia scale, it means you responded exactly as the average person does to that set of items. If you get a score of 60, it means you are an average amount above average in responding to those items. A score of 70 is in the top 3% of the population, and therefore we begin to think that you might be in the criterion group. The higher the score, the more likely that the test taker is not in the "normal" group but rather in the criterion group for that scale. However, remember that the MMPI is interpreted by looking at the pattern of scores, the profile, not by looking at individual scales.

Besides the 10 clinical scales, the MMPI includes other scales known as **validity scales.** These are measures of whether the scores can be considered accurate or legitimate. For instance, the validity scales include items that will detect people who are faking—trying to look good or bad. For example, certain items typically are not marked true by anyone, and if a person marks many of these, we suspect that something is funny. If the scores on the validity scales are too high, it means that we cannot trust that the scores on the clinical scales are accurate. So we first look at the scores on the validity scales before interpreting the test. If the validity scale scores are high, the accuracy of the test is in doubt.

The MMPI was updated in 1989; the new version is known as the **MMPI-2.** Some items were dropped because of sexist or old-fashioned language, the clinical scales were restandardized, and some new validity scales were added. Of 567 items, 107 are new. Some psychologists prefer to use the old version, the MMPI, because so much data has been collected on it. Others like the newer version, the MMPI-2, although we have a long way to go to learn as much about it as we do the original MMPI. Perhaps the reason the MMPI is the most-used personality test is the large amount of research that has been done using it and therefore the enormous amount of information that we have about the scores that various groups attain on the test.

Psychologists are often asked whether the MMPI is a good test, whether it is accurate, whether it can be trusted. No test is perfect, particularly a paper and pencil test.

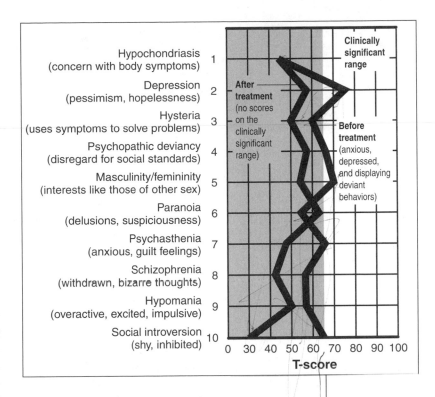

An MMPI profile showing a person's scores on the clinical scales both before and after psychotherapy.

THINK TANK

Under what conditions do you think psychological tests are appropriate? Should employers use them to select employees?

Should dating services use them?

Should schools use them to select students to admit?

Should courtrooms use them?

Why do we need to know someone's IQ score?

However, when it comes to personality tests, the MMPI is perhaps the most reliable and valid. These are the two measures of the quality of a test.

Testing Tests

Psychometrists use two statistical analyses to determine how good a test is. The first is called **reliability**. Essentially, this means the degree to which a test is consistent, trustworthy, or dependable. For example, if the scores on a test are easily influenced by extraneous, changeable factors, then the test is not very reliable. On the other hand, if people consistently get the same scores on a test, then it is reliable. For instance, if I measure your height with a tape measure and get a score of five feet six inches, then measure again with the same tape measure and get a score of eight feet two inches, we would say that the tape measure is not very reliable. This type of reliability is called **test-retest reliability**.

Psychometrists measure the reliability of a test in a number of ways, but roughly it boils down to determining whether the test gives the same score over and over again for the same people. Reliability is indicated by a **reliability coefficient**, a number between 0 and 1. The higher the number, the more reliable the test is. For example, the Stanford-Binet IQ test has a reliability of 0.97, while subtest reliabilities range in the 0.80s and 0.90s. In contrast, the MMPI reliabilities are in the range of 0.60s and 0.70s. Projective tests, described below, have much lower reliability coefficients.

A test can be reliable but still not be accurate. Suppose I have a tape measure and every time I use it to measure your height I get the same result: three feet, two inches. But you are six feet tall! Our tape measure is reliable, but it is not valid. The purpose of **validity** is to determine whether a test is actually measuring the thing that it claims to be measuring. If I invent a test of intelligence, give it repeatedly to a group of people, and find that their scores stay approximately the same, then my test is reliable. But does it measure intelligence? The problem is, it might be measuring something else. For example, tests that students take in college courses often are reliable but not valid. If a test depends a great deal on vocabulary and verbal skills (an essay test), then students who are good at those things will consistently do well, and students who are deficient in those areas will consistently do poorly. The test might not be measuring knowledge of history or literature; it might only appear to be doing so because students' scores are consistent. Perhaps the test is not valid—perhaps it is not measuring what it is intended to measure.

Psychometrists determine the validity of a test in a number of ways, including comparing the scores on the test with some criterion scores. That type of validity is called **criterion-related validity**. Another type is called **construct validity** because it attempts to assess how well a test measures the hypothetical idea or construct that it says it is measuring.

Just as with reliability, a statistic can be calculated, a **validity coefficient.** The higher the validity coefficient, the more valid the test is considered to be. Validity coefficients are always lower than reliability coefficients because a test must be reliable to be valid.

Both reliability coefficients and validity coefficients have been calculated for the many tests that psychologists use. These coefficients are never 1.00; no test is perfect. Therefore, psychologists should be cautious in interpreting test scores. If a psychologist makes a diagnosis or draws a conclusion solely on the basis of a test score, then that is a big mistake. But throwing out tests is also a big mistake. Test scores are one bit of information that can be combined with many other things to cautiously draw tentative conclusions about people. Naturally, we should be well aware of the possible errors and the consequences of being wrong. If a medical doctor made a diagnosis after taking your temperature, we would rightly consider that to be a huge mistake. But the solution is not to throw out thermometers! Psychological tests usually have a place if they are properly used, interpreted, and evaluated.

Projecting

The MMPI is a classic example of a structured test. However, as was mentioned above, there is another kind of personality test: the projective test. This kind of test does not require the test taker to select from a limited number of responses; you can give any answer you want. The idea of a projective test is to present a person with an unclear, ambiguous stimulus (something that has many possible interpretations or perceptions), then allow the test taker to give any response he or she chooses. The responses are analyzed with the assumption that they are projections of the person's personality characteristics. Again we look for patterns. If a person consistently gives responses that are sad, we might suspect that the person is feeling down or depressed.

An inkblot similar to those used on the Rorschach test.

The idea behind a projective test is obvious in this old joke: A psychiatrist shows a patient an inkblot, and the patient responds that it looks like two people having sex. To a second inkblot, the patient responds that it looks like four people having sex. To a third inkblot, the patient responds that it looks like a sex orgy. The psychiatrist stops the test and suggests that the patient seems to have sex on his mind. The patient replies, "Me? You're the one with the pictures!" Of course, the point is that psychiatrists assume that a person's responses tell not about the inkblots, but about the person.

The most commonly used projective test is an inkblot test devised in 1921 by a Swiss psychiatrist named **Hermann Rorschach.** This test is called the **Rorschach Inkblot Test.** It is said that Dr. Rorschach got the idea while listening to his two children describe clouds. Have you ever played that game, in which you say what a cloud looks like? Dr. Rorschach noticed that he could tell which child described a cloud by the kind of description given—that the perceptions and interpretations were reflections of the children's personalities. Hence, Dr. Rorschach developed the idea of having his patients respond to something ambiguous, like a cloud. He believed that analysis of the responses would provide personality diagnoses.

Dr. Rorschach created his test items by spilling black ink onto white paper, then folding the paper in half vertically. The inkblots that were formed were symmetrical left and right. The modern Rorschach Inkblot Test has five inkblots in black and white with shades of gray and five with some color (10 total inkblot cards). A person's responses to the inkblots are analyzed for content, style, emotional intensity, the portion of the inkblot the test taker focuses on, and other qualities. The scoring is typically rather subjective, although a computerized system is available, and other inkblot tests are available that are more objective. Still, projective tests, simply because of the type of test that they are, are not as objective as structured tests. Therefore, the Rorschach and other projective tests are not as reliable or valid as the MMPI or other structured tests. However, projective tests provide what some would call higher-quality information—richer, deeper, and more varied information than that available from a structured test. Those are some of the reasons that clinicians like using the Rorschach.

Tell Me a Story

Another projective test that has often been used in research is the **Thematic Apperception Test,** which is simply called the **TAT** (pronounced "tee-aay-tee"). The stimuli used in this test are drawings of people in various situations, drawings that are ambiguous (many possible interpretations are possible). Test takers are asked to tell or write a story

about each of the pictures saying what is happening, how it got to be like that, and how it will turn out. Because this is a projective test, the theory is that the stories will be projections of the writer's personality—the stories will be about the writer. The stories are analyzed in the search for themes that reveal the person's motivations, values, interests, goals, attitudes, and personality traits. Naturally, like the Rorschach Inkblot Test, because this test is subjectively scored, it is not as reliable or valid as are structured tests. Again, it is used because of the belief that it provides a quality of information that cannot be attained by computer-scored tests.

There are literally thousands of other personality tests available for use by clinicians and researchers. Each has its advantages and disadvantages. A wise test user will be aware of the need for caution in drawing conclusions and making diagnoses. Tests are not perfect, but they can add a bit of useful information to the total picture of an individual.

> A drawing similar to those used on the TAT. After I showed this in class, a student of mine asked, "You know the picture of the woman and her mother?" That is an example of projection—just what this test intends to measure.

Recap

— Personality tests are divided into two categories: structured tests, which require the test taker to choose from a set of responses, and projective tests, which allow any responses to be given to ambiguous stimuli.

— The MMPI is a criterion-scored test in which people's responses are compared to known groups such as those with schizophrenia, depression, or paranoia.

— The MMPI contains 10 clinical scales with an average of 50 and a standard deviation of 10. The sum of scores is called a profile.

— The MMPI also contains validity scales that help determine if the scores are accurate and should be interpreted.

— Tests are evaluated by measuring how reliable and how valid they are. Reliability refers to a test's dependableness, for example, getting the same score on repeated testings. Validity refers to a test's accuracy in measuring what it is attempting to measure.

— Projective tests (Rorschach Inkblot and TAT) present ambiguous stimuli to people, and their responses are interpreted on the assumption they are projections of their personalities.

I Link, Therefore I Am

Stanley Milgram's biography and a description of his famous experiment can be found at http://muskingum.edu/~psychology/psycweb/history/milgram.htm

A database for social psychology can be found at http://www.socialpsychology.org/

Find more information about personality theories and personality testing on the Web at http://www.learner.org/exhibits/personality/   http://www.wynja.com/personality/theorists.html http://www.ship.edu/~cgboeree/perscontents.html   http://assessments.ncs.com/

Learn more about these interesting scientists on the Internet.

Raymond Cattell at http://www.stanford.edu/~cattell/rbcmain.htm
Gordon Allport at http://www.ship.edu/~cgboeree/allport.html
Hans Eysenck at http://freespace.virgin.net/darrin.evans/apapres.htm
Walter Mischel at http://web.utk.edu/~wmorgan/psy470/mischel.htm

STUDY GUIDE FOR CHAPTER 7:

PERSONALITY APPROACHES, SOCIAL PSYCHOLOGY, AND ASSESSMENT

Key terms and names (Make flash cards.)

type
extraverted
introverted
humors
melancholy
William Sheldon
somatotypes
endomorphs
ectomorphs
mesomorphs
Myers-Briggs Type Indicator
Barnum effect
P. T. Barnum
trait
profile
Gordon Allport
cardinal trait
central traits
secondary traits
Raymond Cattell
surface traits
source traits
factor analysis
personality factors
16PF
Hans Eysenck
neuroticism
extraversion–introversion
psychoticism
cross-sectional study
longitudinal study
dropouts
dropout effect
sequential study
Big Five
openness to experience
conscientiousness
agreeableness
emotional stability
five factor theory
NEO-Personality Inventory (NEO-PI)
Walter Mischel
situationism
social psychology
Stanley Milgram
Solomon Asch
Philip Zimbardo

Kitty Genovese
John Darley and Bibb Latané
bystander apathy
altruistic or prosocial behavior
bystander effect
diffusion of responsibility
consistency theories
cognitive dissonance theory
Leon Festinger
dissonance
attribution theory
attribution
personal or internal attribution
situational or external attribution
fundamental attribution error
actor-observer effect
self-serving bias
psychometrics
Alfred Binet
chronological age (CA)
standardizing a test
norms
Theodore Simon
mental age (MA)
intelligence quotient (IQ)
empirical (criterion) scoring
Lewis Terman
Stanford-Binet IQ test
David Wechsler
Wechsler Adult Intelligence Scale (WAIS)
Wechsler Intelligence Scale for Children (WISC)
Wechsler Preschool and Primary Scale of Intelligence (WPPSI)
verbal scale
performance scale
ratio formula
standard deviation
mean
mode
median
percentile
frequency distribution
deviation method
z-score
culture-fair IQ tests

gifted
genius
mentally retarded
mild
moderate
severe
profound
mentally handicapped
educable
trainable
Down syndrome
Charles Spearman
g
theory of general intelligence
s
multifactor theory of intelligence
L. L. Thurstone
primary mental abilities
crystallized intelligence
fluid intelligence
Howard Gardner
theory of multiple intelligences
Robert Sternberg
triarchic theory of intelligence
emotional intelligence
Daniel Goleman
EQ (emotional quotient)
structured tests
projective tests
Minnesota Multiphasic Personality Inventory (MMPI)
clinical scales
validity scales
T-scores
MMPI-2
reliability
test-retest reliability
reliability coefficient
validity
criterion-related validity
construct validity
validity coefficient
Hermann Rorschach
Rorschach Inkblot Test
Thematic Apperception Test (TAT)

Fill in the blank

1. The three major approaches that have been commonly used in the study of personality are _____, _____, and _____.

2. Early thinkers believed that the human body had four major fluids that were known as _____.

3. William Sheldon suggested that personality might be related to _____. His idea became known as a theory of _____.

4. Wildly general statements about personality are readily accepted by nearly everyone. This is known as the _____ _____.

5. Type approaches to personality often lead to _____—the unfair categorizing of people on the basis of one or a few of their qualities.

6. A _____ is defined as an enduring or lasting characteristic of a person.

7. Raymond Cattell devised a personality test known as the _____.

8. Hans Eysenck found three main dimensions of temperament called _____, _____, and _____.

9. A _____ study measures the same group of people at two different times.

10. Researchers found five traits that showed some stability over aging. These five traits are known by the humorously simple name _____.

11. Walter Mischel said that behavior is greatly influenced by the variables in the _____. This view is known as _____.

12. Stanley Milgram found that people would give an _____ _____ to a stranger if they were asked to do so as part of an experiment.

13. A social psychologist named Solomon Asch conducted a series of classic experiments in the 1950s on _____.

14. The more people witnessing an emergency, the less likely anyone is to help. This finding is known as the _____ _____.

15. When there is a large group seeing an emergency, each person reasons that someone else will call the police. This is called _____ _____.

16. The granddaddy of the consistency theories is called _____ _____ and was proposed by famed social psychologist Leon _____.

17. In _____ theory researchers are not trying to determine the actual causes of behavior; instead, they are attempting to discover what people *believe* causes behavior.

18. In fundamental attribution error, people attribute behaviors to _____ variables more than they deserve.

19. The first modern intelligence test was designed by a French psychologist named Alfred _____.

20. The formula for IQ is _____.

21. A number that tells us how much spread there is in a distribution of scores is known as the _____ _____.

22. Lewis Terman developed the IQ test known as the _____.

23. The idea of adult intelligence testing originated with a psychologist at Bellevue Psychiatric Hospital in New York City named David _____.

24. The Wechsler tests are made up of subtests in two broad categories: _____ and _____.

25. People whose IQ scores are significantly below average have traditionally been termed _____ _____.

26. Psychologists use the terms _____, _____, and _____ for each standard deviation of mental retardation.

27. A common hereditary factor in which a child inherits 47 chromosomes is called _____ _____.

28. _____ intelligence is a person's knowledge of facts and the ability to use them; _____ intelligence is a person's ability to think quickly and agilely, to figure out original solutions, and to shift gears nimbly.

29. Personality tests are divided into two large categories: _____ tests and _____ tests.

30. The most commonly used personality test in the world is the _____ _____ _____.

31. Besides the 10 clinical scales, the MMPI also includes other scales known as _____ scales.

32. _____ means the degree to which a test is consistent, trustworthy, or dependable.

33. _____ is a measure of whether a test is actually measuring the thing that it claims to be measuring.

34. The most commonly used projective test is the _____ _____ test.

35. In the _____ test, people are asked to write stories about drawings.

Matching

1. Lewis Terman _____
2. TAT _____
3. inkblot test _____
4. William Sheldon _____
5. Myers-Briggs _____
6. 16PF _____
7. Walter Mischel _____
8. MMPI _____
9. WISC _____
10. humors _____
11. Down syndrome _____
12. Big Five _____
13. Stanley Milgram _____
14. conformity _____
15. bystander effect _____
16. MA _____

a. body fluids
b. write stories about drawings
c. judge lengths of lines
d. give electric shocks
e. score on an IQ test
f. Stanford-Binet IQ test
g. IQ test for children
h. 47 chromosomes
i. stability with aging
j. prosocial behavior
k. criterion scoring
l. factor analysis
m. somatotypes
n. situationism
o. Rorschach
p. test of personality types

Multiple choice

1. The teacher of your eight-year-old nephew thinks that he might be gifted. Which test should he be given to find out?
   a. MMPI
   b. WISC
   c. NEO-PI
   d. WAIS

2. Jim works at a factory that makes parts for computers. He divides the parts into five groups based on their shapes. This is similar to which personality approach?
   a. Big Five
   b. traits
   c. MMPI
   d. types

3. In a village in Vietnam, a platoon of U.S. soldiers were ordered to kill innocent women and children. They all did it. Which social psychology experiment comes closest to explaining this act?
   a. Asch's judging lines
   c. Festinger's cognitive dissonance
   b. Milgram's shocks
   d. bystander apathy

4. A psychologist is trying to determine whether birth order is related to how open people are to new experiences. Which test will she probably use?
   a. MMPI
   b. NEO-PI
   c. Rorschach
   d. Myers-Briggs

5. A company wants to hire people who can quickly match number codes with symbols. What test would help them the most?
   a. TAT
   b. Wechsler Performance Scale
   c. Stanford-Binet
   d. MMPI

6. What is wrong with a test that has a low validity coefficient?
   a. A person's score can vary greatly from one testing to another.
   b. It is not empirically scored.
   c. The average score will not be the mean.
   d. It is not measuring what it intends to.

7. Which test is based on the measurement of psychiatric traits?
   a. 16PF
   b. Big Five
   c. TAT
   d. MMPI

8. The idea that personality is related to body type was suggested by
   a. William James
   b. Raymond Cattell
   c. Lewis Terman
   d. William Sheldon

9. What is a key characteristic of situationism?
   a. It allows for inconsistency in behavior.
   b. It measures personality by traits.
   c. It says that traits will stay constant over long periods of time.
   d. It predicts that people are certain types of personalities.

10. If a test gives the same score each time it is given, it is called
    a. accurate
    b. valid
    c. reliable
    d. dependable

11. Zimbardo's prison experiment showed that situations could have a great effect on behavior even when the participants
    a. were all alone
    b. knew they were only role playing
    c. used a buddy system
    d. were in the presence of the experimenter

12. Which test resulted from longitudinal research?
    a. TAT   b. 16 PF
    c. Myers-Briggs   d. NEO-PI

13. Some people worry that if election results are predicted before the polls close everywhere, the reports will influence those who have not yet voted. Which experiment deals with this issue?
    a. cognitive dissonance
    b. Milgram's shock
    c. Asch's judging lines
    d. attribution

14. Your friend believes that personality can be mathematically reduced to fundamental elements. Her idea is closest to which test?
    a. 16 PF   b. MMPI
    c. Rorschach   d. WAIS

15. Being self-sacrificing was a _____ trait of Gandhi.
    a. cardinal   b. primary
    c. secondary   d. Big Five

16. The 16PF test was developed using
    a. a type approach   b. situationism
    c. criterion scoring   d. factor analysis

17. Dropout effects occur in which type of research?
    a. cross-sectional   b. longitudinal
    c. factor analysis   d. trait

18. If a person acts inconsistently from one situation to another, this is evidence of
    a. a trait
    b. the Big Five
    c. situationism
    d. diffusion of responsibility

19. Darley and Latané found that people were more likely to help someone in trouble if
    a. there were lots of people witnessing the person in trouble
    b. the witnesses had altruistic personality traits
    c. there were few people witnessing the person in trouble
    d. they were altruistic-type people

20. If you are among 100 people who see a problem, you might not report it because of
    a. the Big Five
    b. cognitive dissonance
    c. attribution theory
    d. diffusion of responsibility

21. According to attribution theory, in general, people do not give enough importance to
    a. source traits
    b. personal attributions
    c. situational attributions
    d. surface traits

22. If a child knows all the 10-year-old questions on an IQ test but is only five years old, what is her IQ score?
    a. 50   b. 100
    c. 150   d. 200

23. If a four-year-old child has an MA of 5, his IQ score is
    a. 80   b. 90
    c. 125   d. 145

24. What does MA stand for?
    a. mental age
    b. measured age
    c. mental assessment
    d. measured assessment

25. An eight-year-old has an IQ score of 100. What is her MA?
    a. 6   b. 8
    c. 10   d. 12

26. An eight-year-old has an IQ score of 75. What is his MA?
    a. 6   b. 8
    c. 11   d. 12

27. The Wechsler test has a verbal scale and a _____ scale.
    a. performance   b. practical
    c. practice   d. pragmatic

28. Which of these is found on the verbal scale?
    a. digit symbol
    b. object assembly
    c. vocabulary
    d. picture arrangement

29. What is the z-score for an IQ score of 116?
    a. 0   b. + 1
    c. − 1   d. + 2

30. At a restaurant, you notice that when people are in large groups, each person contributes a smaller amount to the tip than they would when they are alone. Social psychologists might say that this is due to
    a. actor-observer effect
    b. cognitive dissonance
    c. attribution error
    d. diffusion of responsibility

31. Suppose you are forced to do something that is against your beliefs. Festinger's theory of cognitive dissonance says that later you will
    a. make a personal attribution from it
    b. try to reduce your dissonance
    c. attempt to create dissonance in others
    d. arrange your cognitions to be more strict

32. The idea of an IQ test without any bias whatsoever is called a
    a. projective test   b. valid test
    c. culture-fair test   d. reliable test

33. The kind of intelligence that allows a person to think quickly and agilely is called
    a. fluid   b. crystallized
    c. primary   d. triarchic

34. How many primary mental abilities did Thurstone find using factor analysis?
    a. 5   b. 7
    c. 8   d. 12

35. The TAT is a _____ test.
    a. projective   b. structured
    c. crystallized   d. fluid

36. Validity scales are found on the
    a. MMY   b. TAT
    c. Rorschach   d. MMPI

37. A score of 50 on a clinical scale of the MMPI is
    a. average
    b. below average
    c. above average by a little
    d. far above average

38. The Myers-Briggs is a measure of personality _____.
    a. traits   b. profiles
    c. types   d. structures

39. The mentally retarded are divided into four categories including all of these EXCEPT:
    a. mild   b. moderate
    c. maligned   d. profound

40. Which approach to personality is represented by the MMPI?
    a. traits   b. the Big Five
    c. situationism   d. types

Short answer and critical thinking

1. What are the three approaches to personality described in the textbook? Give examples of each.
2. What is the Barnum effect?
3. What are the Big Five, what do they represent, and how were they determined?
4. Which approach to personality stresses the similarities between people, which emphasizes differences, which uses dichotomies, and which allows for people to be inconsistent?
5. Define situationism. What are its advantages and disadvantages?
6. Define longitudinal and cross-sectional types of research.
7. What similarities are there between the Milgram study and Asch's study of conformity?
8. What is meant by *diffusion of responsibility*?
9. What is the argument regarding g and s with regard to intelligence?
10. What is meant by *crystallized intelligence* and *fluid intelligence*?
11. What is the difference between structured and projective personality tests?
12. What is the difference between *reliable* and *valid*?
13. What is the assumption behind a projective test?

Chapter

8

Personality Theories

> "We all agree that your theory is crazy, but is it crazy enough?"
>
> —NIELS BOHR

PLAN AHEAD...

- How did Sigmund Freud explain personality development? Did he emphasize sexuality and the unconscious? What are id, ego, superego, and Oedipus complex?
- Who were some of Freud's followers, and how did they react to his theory?
- What is a collective unconscious? What are archetypes?
- How do behavioral and humanistic psychologists explain personality?
- Do we inherit our personalities? What is the nature-nurture controversy, and how do modern psychologists resolve it?
- What are the parts of an emotion? How do psychologists describe and explain emotional reactions?
- What motivates people to behave in a certain way?

SARA IS THE DAUGHTER OF MY GOOD FRIENDS, AND I watched her mature through adolescence and young adulthood. Throughout her teens, she was shy, cautious, and conservative in her political views and her approach to life. But in her twenties, Sara changed abruptly and dramatically, becoming animated, gregarious, and extremely liberal. Everything about her seemed to blossom and change. Do you know someone like that? As a psychologist, watching Sara made me wonder how any personality theory could adequately capture the nuances of the complex and changing thing we call personality.

Many psychologists have developed theories about personality—how to describe it, how it emerges, what influences it, how it changes, and what constitutes a healthy or an abnormal personality. Here you will learn about the three most important personality theories: psychoanalytic theory, behaviorism, and humanism. Do you remember reading about them in Chapter 1?

PSYCHOANALYTIC THEORY

"A Freudian slip is when you mean one thing and say your mother."
—ANONYMOUS

The first of the modern personality theories was developed by Sigmund Freud and is known as **psychoanalytic theory**. The psychiatric practice of this theory is called **psychoanalysis**. Freud's ideas were plentiful, profound, and often controversial. His theory about personality has had tremendous influence on societies around the world through many different disciplines. Not only psychology has been influenced and informed by the ideas of Freud, but also literature, art, philosophy, cultural studies, film theory, and many other academic subjects. Freud's theory represents one of the major intellectual ideas of the modern world. Right or wrong, these ideas have had a lasting and enormous impact.

Exploring the Unknown

To understand Freud's theory of personality, we must begin with the concept of the **unconscious**. This is the cornerstone idea in psychoanalytic theory. Freud believed that most behaviors are caused by thoughts, ideas, and wishes that are in a person's brain but are not easily accessible by the conscious part of the mind. In other words, your brain knows things that your mind doesn't. This reservoir of conceptions of which we are unaware is called the unconscious. Psychoanalytic theory proposes that personality characteristics are mostly a reflection of the contents of the unconscious part of the mind.

Sigmund Freud, founder of psychoanalytic theory and psychoanalysis.

FYI

Freud was named Sigismund Schlomo Freud by his parents. He never used his middle name and gradually switched his first to Sigmund during his university years. As a young man, Freud taught himself Spanish so that he could read *Don Quixote* in the original.

Freud's first book, *Studies in Hysteria*, was written with his colleague Dr. Joseph Breuer in 1896. The book consists of a series of case studies of people who had physical complaints in the absence of any organic cause, what was then known as **hysteria.** Most doctors at that time believed there was some organic cause for these symptoms and that research would eventually discover it. But Freud and Breuer believed that the cause of hysteria was in the unconscious—in the anxiety-provoking thoughts that lurked there, hidden from awareness.

Their first patient was a woman named Bertha Papenheim, who later went on to become a successful and important feminist leader. In the literature, she is known as Anna O. She began as a patient of Breuer, to whom she reported a large number of physical complaints, such as paralysis of her legs and right arm, that seemed to have no organic cause. In addition, after receiving hypnosis and therapy from Dr. Breuer for some time, Anna O. came to harbor the delusion that she was pregnant with Dr. Breuer's child (a type of delusion that is sometimes called hysterical pregnancy). This was tremendously upsetting to Dr. Breuer (and to his wife). Although Breuer had had great success in relieving many of her hysterical symptoms, he was terribly embarrassed by this turn of events and resigned as Anna O.'s therapist. Sigmund Freud took over and was able to complete Ms. Papenheim's cure by helping her to uncover the unconscious causes of her physical complaints. This case is presented in the 1962 film *Freud*.

Pushing Things Down

Freud believed that the unconscious is a part of our biological nature and that it operates naturally, just as do all our biological functions. Freud suggested that certain ideas and thoughts are **repressed,** that is, pushed out of awareness and into the unconscious. This happens, according to Freud's theory, when those ideas and thoughts are threatening to us. Repression works something like our immune system: It protects us from dangerous things. In the case of personality, dangerous things include anything that threatens self-esteem or feelings of comfort and pleasure. When we have thoughts or ideas that are threatening, they are pushed out of consciousness because awareness of them produces anxiety. They make us feel nervous. Thereby, through repression, our unconscious protects us from anxiety.

Here's an example from my personal life: I hate going to meetings. (That is a key fact in understanding this example.) One day, I had a meeting scheduled for 3 o'clock. I put the agenda of the meeting on my desk and wrote reminders to myself on my desk calendar and on my wall calendar. After returning to my office just before 3 o'clock, I looked at the meeting agenda on my desk, I looked at the meeting reminder on my desk calendar, and I looked at the reminder on my wall calendar. Then I put on my coat and went home! Three times I was reminded of the meeting, yet I did not go to the meeting. Although I looked at the agenda and the two reminders, I went home with no awareness that I was missing a meeting. I did not *forget* to go to the meeting. Forgetting and repressing are not the same thing. My unconscious was looking after me. It protected me from that horrible meeting by repressing it!

Of course, Freud wasn't talking about missing meetings. But this analogy might help you understand the idea of repression. Freud's theory is about how psychologically charged and threatening experiences, especially things that happen during childhood, can be repressed and later affect behavior and moods. Sexual abuse in childhood, for example, would be a very horrible experience that Freud theorized could affect one's personality through repression. Even sibling rivalry might be threatening enough to one's ego to be a source of repression.

Dreams and Slips

Although repression keeps undesirable information in the unconscious and out of awareness, that repressed information is influential and, according to Freudian theory, can seep out of the unconscious and express itself through behaviors, thoughts, and dreams. Unconscious thoughts express themselves in a disguised form so as not to overly disturb the conscious mind. It is as if the unconscious is a boiling cauldron of threatening and anxiety-producing ideas, but the steam from this boiling pot can filter up into our awareness and influence our behaviors and haunt our emotions and cognitions. Freud proposed that the best place to look for clues to the unconscious is in dreams. A dream, Freud said, is a disguised form of what we unconsciously wish for. Dreams are wish fulfillment. Through them, we get what our unconscious wants. But dreams are not obvious and direct mirrors of unconscious ideas. A dream must be analyzed and interpreted in order to understand the clues that it provides.

The things that are present and the events that happen in a dream are known as the **manifest content** of the dream. These are disguised versions of unconscious thoughts. The meanings of those dream elements are called the **latent content** of the dream. A dream about an Egyptian mummy (the manifest content) might be a dream about one's mother (mommy); or it might be a dream about frustration (being bound); or it might be about a desire for more freedom; or it might represent a wish to be hugged and cuddled or to feel possessed by someone; or it might be an expression of the death wish (**thanatos**, as opposed to the life wish, **eros**) that Freud used to explain suicides, war, and other circumstances; or it might represent a desire to go to heaven or to be warm or to be rested (all possible latent contents). The manifest content, the mummy, represents something in the unconscious, the latent content. Freud developed a number of counseling techniques (including dream interpretation) intended to help reveal what was in his patients' unconscious minds based on the belief that revealing the contents of the unconscious would cause the patient's symptoms to disappear.

Sometimes, according to Freud, a mistake is not a mistake. Just as dreams have hidden meanings, some mistakes have hidden meanings. When we make a mistake that is influenced by the unconscious (when a mistake is not a mistake, when a mistake has meaning) it is called a **Freudian slip,** for example, a slip of the tongue. If you accidentally call your boyfriend or girlfriend by the wrong name, it might just be a mistake; but it might be a Freudian slip. That is, it might be a mistake that reveals something about your unconscious thoughts and wishes. If a person has done something that he believes to be wrong (perhaps he told a lie earlier in the day) and this act has made him feel guilty, then perhaps later, while peeling potatoes, he might unintentionally cut himself. Freud said that sometimes such an act is no accident. The feelings of guilt in the unconscious might have directed the person to cut himself as a punishment for his lying.

Remember, it does no good to ask a person whether this is true. Freud's theory says that this information is in the unconscious—a person is not aware of it. In fact, during therapy, Freudian psychoanalysts believe that if a patient becomes overly upset when a therapist suggests that there is a particular thought or wish in the patient's unconscious, this might be evidence that the therapist is on the right track. In psychoanalytic theory, this is known as **resistance,** referring to the idea that patients will *resist* suggestions that probe the anxiety-producing contents of the unconscious. The unconscious wants to keep those thoughts from awareness and becomes upset when they are approached. One of the techniques used in psychoanalysis is to analyze the patient's resistance, to see what clues it might provide regarding the person's unconscious thoughts.

Theoretically, the stuff in the unconscious is there because it is bothersome to the person. The mind actively represses the information, whether that is rational or not. Freud's view is that repression might be harmful and might be the cause of a patient's mental or behavioral symptoms. Freud's "cure" is to reveal the unconscious information. If a therapist suggests that a patient's problems might be connected to his relationship with his mother and the patient screams, "Leave my mother out of this!" the psychoanalytic therapist views this response as indicative of repression and resistance and a signal that therapy should proceed in that direction.

Mental Protection

Psychoanalytic theory suggests that there are other ways in which our unconscious protects us besides by repression. These protective devices of the unconscious are known as **defense mechanisms.** Here are some examples.

- **Rationalization:** Sometimes our unconscious makes up a good-sounding reason to explain something we don't like. If we fail a test, we blame it on others. If our favorite candidate doesn't win the election, we say that it's for the best anyway. If we don't complete an assignment, we think the teacher was unfair to have given the assignment. "Sour grapes" is another example—if we don't get something we want, we find something wrong with it and convince ourselves we're better off without it. Rationalizing protects us from the anxiety of seeing ourselves as deficient. This is a common defense mechanism because of the importance placed on giving good reasons for things. However, this is not *rational*, it is *rationalizing*. Being rational means being objective. In rationalization, our mind protects us with a reason that only *sounds* good; it is not objective, it just seems to be. Our mind is trying to help us out!
- **Projection:** In this case, when we have some thoughts or feelings that we consider to be wrong or upsetting, we project them onto other people instead of on ourselves. If I believe that a certain attitude or feeling that I have is terribly wrong, I will claim that others have it. A person who wants to use illegal drugs but who believes that it would make him a horrible person might expect everyone else to want to use illegal drugs. This defense mechanism deflects the anxiety away from

us and onto others. Many of the predictions that a person makes about someone else are, in fact, true about the person making the prediction. Be careful what you say about others, it might be true about you! If a man says that he believes people lie on their resumes, perhaps it's an indication that he has an inclination to lie on his resume. Is he simply being objective? Or is he saying people lie because his unconscious knows he would act that way? That would be projection.

- **Sublimation:** We sublimate if we redirect or rechannel our undesirable emotions and thoughts into a socially acceptable activity. If I am full of rage and horrible thoughts, I might vigorously wash my car. Many people sublimate by pouring their emotions into works of art. The famous painter Vincent van Gogh is the example that is most often given. His mental and emotional distress seems evident in the vivid colors, thick paint, and forceful brushstrokes of his paintings. We can imagine van Gogh's moods merely by looking at his paintings. Many famous composers and poets also are good examples of this defense mechanism. Their mental anguish is redirected into wonderful works of art. There is a long list of composers and poets who suffered from depression and bipolar disorder. That is a tragedy, but one that provided us with a world of music and literature. Through sublimation, unpleasant mental energy is redirected into acceptable work.

- **Reaction formation:** Sometimes people's mental and emotional energy is so threatening that they adopt the reverse—the opposite—of what they really want. A person who believes that drinking alcohol is a terrible sin yet who has a desire to drink alcohol might be protected by reaction formation. In this case, the person's unconscious adopts a hatred of alcohol. The person might join groups that protest alcohol use and might attempt to pass laws against drinking alcohol. She becomes vociferous, wildly critical of alcohol. We might say, paraphrasing Shakespeare, that she *protests too much.* If a man believes that being gay is a horrible thing yet feels attracted to other men, he might express a deep hatred of gays and attempt to harm them. In reaction formation, a person's unconscious takes on the beliefs that are opposite of the true desires, those repressed in the unconscious. This protects the conscious part of the mind from what the unconscious considers to be awful.

- **Displacement:** Freud suggested this defense mechanism to explain how a person's unconscious wishes could appear in dreams but in disguise. A woman who is angry with her brother Tom might dream that she harms a noisy tomcat. Her conscious will not be aware of the connection between the names. Her anger is displaced onto a symbol of her brother. This defense mechanism is often used to explain behaviors outside of dreams; for instance, when a person's displeasure is directed toward some object other than the source of the displeasure (for example, if an employee displaces his anger toward his boss onto his wife, a subordinate, or his dog).

- **Denial:** This defense mechanism is a primitive form of repression. In this instance, a person simply denies things that produce anxiety. The term is often used today in referring to people who have obvious problems with alcohol, drugs, or relationships but refuse to accept that those problems exist.

- **Regression:** Under conditions of severe trauma or stress, a person might revert to developmentally earlier forms of behavior and thinking. This is known as regression. A person who is under significant stress, for example, might begin sucking his or her thumb. Freudian theory argues that regression provides a person with feelings of security and calm when under threatening conditions.

There are many other defense mechanisms that have been proposed by Freud and other psychoanalytic theorists, but these seven, together with repression, will give you a good understanding of the basic premise of Freud's ideas about where personality comes from. At the center is the unconscious and its biological drive to protect us from

---

Connecting Concepts

The projective tests (such as the Rorschach Inkblot Test) described in Chapter 7 are based on the concept of projection. That is, it is assumed that what a person sees in an ambiguous stimulus is a reflection of the person's personality—people project their characteristics (values, traits, ideas) into the stimulus.

"Denial ain't just a river in Egypt."
—MARK TWAIN

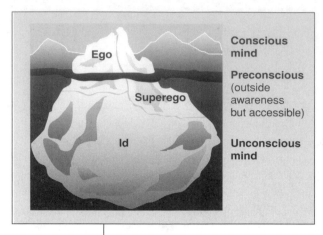

Freud theorized that personality contains three structures—the id, ego, and superego—and that the mind is like an iceberg, the unconscious making up 90% while the conscious (like the tip of the iceberg floating above water) makes only 10% of the mind.

what is threatening. Defense mechanisms protect us from anxiety and threats. In that sense, they are useful and good. However, they can go too far and take us into abnormality. When defense mechanisms become extreme, they cause more problems than they solve. A person might then develop symptoms of mental disturbance. Freud proposed a clinical therapy to deal with those instances, as noted above, a therapy known as psychoanalysis. The essence of this approach is to reveal the contents of the unconscious to the patient so that he or she can see that there is nothing to be afraid of. This, Freud said, will result in a disappearance of the symptoms. We will return to this issue later in Chapter 10. For now, more about psychoanalytic personality theory.

Personality Structures

Freud suggested an analogy about the mind. He said that the mind is like an iceberg in the ocean, floating 10% above the water and 90% below. The unconscious, Freud proposed, makes up the vast majority of our mind. In Freud's view, only about 10% of our behaviors are caused by conscious awareness—about 90% are produced by unconscious factors. According to psychoanalytic theory, most of what controls our behaviors, thoughts, and feelings is unknown to our aware minds. Normally, the unconscious guides us.

Freud said that the mind could be divided into three abstract categories. These are the **id**, the **ego**, and the **superego**. Although these are known as *structures*, do not take the term literally. Freud did not mean that these are physical parts of our bodies or our brains. He coined these terms and proposed this division of the mind as abstract ideas meant to help us understand how personality develops and works, and how mental illnesses can develop.

Connecting Concepts

Freud did not develop his theory on the basis of scientific experiments, such as correlation and controlled studies (see Chapter 2). He drew his conclusions mostly from the patients that he saw. He used the case study method. The therapy that he developed is discussed in Chapter 10.

1. *The id*: Latin for the term "it," this division of the mind includes our basic instincts, inborn dispositions, and animalistic urges. Freud said that the id is totally unconscious, that we are unaware of its workings. The id is not rational; it imagines, dreams, and invents things to get us what we want. Freud said that the id operates according to the **pleasure principle**—it aims toward pleasurable things and away from painful things. The id aims to satisfy our biological urges and drives. It includes feelings of hunger, thirst, sex, and other natural body desires aimed at deriving pleasure.

2. *The ego*: Greek and Latin for "I," this personality structure begins developing in childhood and can be interpreted as the "self." The ego is partly conscious and partly unconscious. The ego operates according to the **reality principle**; that is, it attempts to help the id get what it wants by judging the difference between real and imaginary. If a person is hungry, the id might begin to imagine food and even dream about food. (The id is not rational.) The ego, however, will try to determine how to get some real food. The ego helps a person satisfy needs through reality.

3. *The superego*: This term means "above the ego," and includes the moral ideas that a person learns within the family and society. The superego gives people feelings of pride when they do something correct (the **ego ideal**) and feelings of guilt when they do something they consider to be morally wrong (the **conscience**). The superego, like the ego, is partly conscious and partly unconscious. The superego is a child's moral barometer, and it creates feelings of pride and guilt according to the beliefs that have been learned within the family and the culture.

Freud theorized that healthy personality development requires a balance between the id and the superego. These two divisions of the mind are naturally at conflict with one another: The id attempts to satisfy animal, biological urges, while the superego preaches patience and restraint. The struggle between these two is an example of **intrapsychic conflict**—conflict within the mind. According to psychoanalytic theory, defense mechanisms are automatic (unconscious) reactions to the fear that the id's desires will overwhelm the ego. Freud believed that a healthy personality was one in which the id's demands are met but also the superego is satisfied in making the person feel proud and not overwhelmed by guilt. If the id is too strong, a person will be rude, overbearing, selfish, and animalistic. If the superego is too strong, a person is constantly worried, nervous, and full of guilt and anxiety and is always repressing the id's desires.

An overly strong id makes one a psychopath, lacking a conscience, or an ogre, selfishly meeting one's needs without concern for others. An overly strong superego, on the other hand, makes one a worrier, a neurotic, so overwhelmed by guilt that it is difficult to get satisfaction. Sometimes it is said that the ego is the mediator between the id and the superego, but this is not what Freud said. The ego does not help to find compromise; the ego helps the id to satisfy its desires by focusing on what is real.

Recap

— Sigmund Freud developed an intricate theory of personality known as psychoanalytic theory. The therapeutic practice is called psychoanalysis.

— This theory says that traumatic events are repressed into the unconscious part of the mind, where they can influence behavior and personality.

  Freud described hysteria as an example of repression.

— Freud taught that slips of the tongue and dreams could be analyzed to give clues as to what is in a person's unconscious. The elements of a dream are called the manifest content; the hidden meanings are called the latent content.

— In psychoanalytic theory, the mind protects itself from threats by using defense mechanisms such as repression, rationalization, and sublimation.

— Freud theorized three structures of personality: the id (seeks pleasure), the ego (judges reality), and the superego (morality, including conscience).

— Intrapsychic conflict can involve disputes between the id (which attempts to satisfy biological urges) and the superego (which represents morality).

The Stage Is Set

Freud theorized that personality traits evolve through a series of stages that occur during childhood and adolescence. These are called **psychosexual stages** because they focus on mental (psyche) ideas about sex. However, it is important to note that Freud's language was German, and not everything from German translates precisely into English. When we say that Freud's theory concentrates on "sex," we are using that term in an overly broad manner. There is no word in English for exactly what Freud was talking about. "Sensuality" might be closer than "sex" to the concept that Freud had in mind. Freud was referring to everything that gave a person bodily pleasure. In psychoanalytic theory, sucking your thumb is part of sex. Massaging your neck is also included. Freud believed that these pleasurable activities of the body were instinctually inborn and that they were often frowned on by society. The sexual activities that were most disapproved of were repressed into the unconscious and therefore were most likely to influence personality.

Freud proposed that personality traits arise at certain times of our lives. For instance, dependency is a personality trait that arises during childhood when the child is very dependent on others. In a sense, Freud suggested that the seeds of adult personality traits are planted during childhood. The particular things that happen to us, those things that were repressed because they were sexual or traumatic, are retained in our unconscious and thereby sprout up as adult personality characteristics. The seeds of our adult traits were planted during the psychosexual stages.

The adult personality, according to Freud, is a reflection of the contents of the unconscious. The unconscious is the reservoir of important things that happened to us in childhood. Biological urges, trauma, sexuality, aggression, and other incidents that were repressed provide the impetus for certain personality traits. According to Freud's psychoanalytic theory, an adult personality trait is a throwback to some unconscious urge, such as the urge to gain parental favor. If too much or too little satisfaction occurs during a childhood stage or if a traumatic event occurs during that stage, then a person will exhibit personality traits consistent with that stage. This is known as **fixation**. We say that a person with babyish traits such as dependency or biting his or her fingernails is fixated in the oral stage. According to psychoanalytic theory, the roots of personality are found in childhood.

The Psychosexual Stages

Freud's psychosexual stages are as follows:

1. *Oral:* The first stage in Freud's theory covers babies up to about the age of one and a half years. The driving force during this stage is interest and pleasure in activities involving the mouth (hence the term *oral*), such as sucking and biting. Adult oral personality traits that derive from the oral stage include anything to do with the mouth, such as smoking, overeating, or biting the nails, and anything that is babylike, such as being naïve ("swallowing" anything you are told) or being dependent on others.

2. *Anal:* This stage centers on toilet training, beginning around the age of 18 months or two years and extending up to preschool, about age three. The term *anal*, of course, refers to the anus, the rear end (the opposite end of oral), and one of the jokes in psychology is that you can't spell *analysis* without *anal*. This joke makes light of the fact that Freud believed this stage to be crucial in planting the seeds for a number of adult personality traits. In the anal stage the child is being toilet trained and is learning to hold in and to let out at appropriate times. Therefore, Freud proposed that personality traits related to either holding in or letting out were formed during the anal stage. The following traits are known as **anal-retentive** (finding pleasure from holding in): neatness, orderliness, punctuality, cleanliness, compulsiveness, perfectionism, and stinginess. The following are called **anal-expulsive** (finding pleasure from letting out): being undisciplined, messy, disorderly, late, impulsive, and overly generous.

3. *Phallic:* This stage occurs approximately during the preschool years. The term *phallic* means any representation of the penis, which, according to Freud, is the main occupation of the unconscious during the childhood years of about three to six among both boys and girls. It is at this time,

theoretically, that children become aware of whether or not they have a penis, and Freud believed that this causes a bit of anxiety in the unconscious parts of their minds. Boys, Freud reasoned, become protective of their penis and fear having it taken away. This is known as **castration anxiety** and might be manifested in a young boy's fear of knives, scissors, or being bitten by dogs. Girls, Freud thought, feel resentful that they do not have a penis and hence seek phallic things and activities that will provide them with feelings of power and possession. This is known as **penis envy** and might be seen when preschool girls develop a deep fondness for horses, unicorns, and other strong, masculine things or long, pointed objects.

Freud proposed an unconscious drama during this stage that he called his most important idea. It is called the **Oedipus complex** (sometimes referred to as the *Oedipal conflict*). This unconscious process is named after the Greek story of Oedipus, the man who was raised by foster parents and grew up to unwittingly kill his biological father and marry his biological mother. Freud said that a similar drama occurs in the unconscious minds of preschool boys, who favor their mothers and fear their fathers (castration anxiety). The child resents the father for getting all of the mother's attentions. Many psychoanalysts suggest a similar conflict for preschool girls, referred to as the **Electra complex**; it is essentially the reverse of the situation for boys: love and desire for father, resentment for mother.

According to psychoanalytic theory, these complexes become so severe and anxiety-producing that the child's unconscious must resolve them using a defense mechanism. The solution is for the child to begin to identify with the same-sexed parent. The child begins to internalize the personality of the same-sexed parent, thereby relieving the anxiety and vicariously winning the love of the opposite-sexed parent. For a little boy, being like daddy means no longer having to fear and resent him, and it also means getting mommy's love through daddy. For a little girl, it means winning daddy's love by being like mommy. This process is called **identification with the aggressor**; sometimes simply known as *identification*. The result is that children begin to internalize the values, morals (the superego), traits, attitudes, and behaviors of their parents.

In fact, in 1925, Freud concluded that he had been wrong about penis envy in young girls and theorized that the Oedipal struggle for girls, as well as for boys, centered on love for the mother. As you can imagine, this remains a controversial idea among psychoanalysts.

4. *Latency*: After resolving the Oedipal conflict through identification (at about the age of six), children enter a stage during which sexual urges are dormant or resting. The term *latent* means that something is present or has potential without being active or evident. During this stage, sexual urges are taking a recess; they are at a minimum. From about the ages of 6 to 12, boys typically stick together and say that they do not like girls, or they act squeamish around girls. Similarly, girls during this stage are highly critical of boys, are shy around them, and avoid them. Apparently, the demands of the previous stage and the Oedipal drama were so overwhelming that the unconscious needs a bit of a rest.

5. *Genital*: This final of the psychosexual stages arises during adolescence when teenagers begin again to show sexual interests. This stage leads to adult affection and love. If all has gone well in the previous stages, Freud theorized, interest during adolescence is on heterosexual relationships. This is a time of exploring pleasure through more mature love and affection.

TABLE 8.1 Freud's Psychosexual Stages

Stage	Approximate Ages	Main Features
1. Oral	Birth–1 1/2 or 2	Mouth, dependency
2. Anal	1 1/2–3	Toilet training, give and take
3. Phallic	3–6	Oedipus complex, identification, superego
4. Latency	6–12	Repression of sexuality
5. Genital	12–Adulthood	Development of normal sexuality

THINK TANK

Can you think of characters from literature or movies that represent psychoanalytic concepts?

Is it always good to know what is in one's unconscious?

Why or why not?

One should not think of Freud's psychoanalytic theory as a scientific theory, but more as a form of literature or storytelling. People often ask whether Freud's theory is right or wrong. This question is difficult to answer, perhaps impossible, because psychoanalytic theory is not totally a scientific or empirical theory that can be tested to determine its veracity. It is probably best to treat psychoanalytic theory as a series of interesting stories with plots and characters. Whether these stories are good or not depends on the extent to which they provide a deeper and better understanding of human personality development. Some of Freud's concepts have met that test—for example, the unconscious, repression, the importance of childhood sexuality, and the influence of parenting on the child's personality. It is hard to deny the basic tenets of psychoanalytic theory: The unconscious can influence our behaviors and our personality, things that happen in childhood plant the seeds for adult personality development, traumatic events in childhood can have lasting effects on our personalities, and the sexual drive is an important factor in our lives that can influence our personality.

On the other hand, many of Freud's ideas are not supported by research and observation. His theory provides some provocative ideas about the course of human development and the causes of behaviors, but these often fail when put to an empirical test. Perhaps a good way to conclude this discussion of Freud's ideas is to use a variation on Freud's remark about his cigar smoking: Sometimes a theory is just a theory.

Freud had great influence, particularly early in the twentieth century, and he had many followers who developed their own theories of personality development, often contradicting Freud's. Here are a few of the major ideas of some **neo-Freudians,** early followers of Freud who splintered off and formed their own theories.

Carl Jung

Freud's closest friend and dearest colleague was a psychiatrist from Switzerland named **Carl Gustav Jung** (1875–1961). (The name *Jung* is pronounced "yooung.") Freud selected Jung to be the first president of the International Psychoanalytic Association in

1910. However, Carl Jung later developed his own ideas that deviated from Freud's, and as a result, the two great thinkers grew distant toward each other and even stopped writing or talking to each other. By 1914, their friendship and communication had ceased, and they never saw each other again. Jung's personality theory is known as **analytic theory** or **analytical psychology.**

Jung placed a great deal of emphasis on the study of different cultures. He believed that the similarities between cultures were an indication of what it means to be human; that is, by looking at how we are all alike, we can determine the essence of humanity. Like all psychoanalysts, Jung looked for signs and symbols that for him were clues to understanding human personality.

Perhaps Jung's greatest contribution was that he expanded the notion of the unconscious. Freud used the term *unconscious* to apply to the hidden thoughts and ideas of one person. In Freud's view, each person has his or her own unconscious, and although they have some similarities (the structures and defense mechanisms, for example), what is in one person's unconscious might not be in another person's unconscious. This conception is known as the **personal unconscious.** Each of us has our own personal unconscious. However, Carl Jung proposed a broader idea. He suggested that all human beings share certain unconscious ideas because we are all human and were created from similar evolutionary circumstances and common ancestors. The unconscious that we all share is called the **collective unconscious.**

According to Jung, the collective unconscious is the storehouse of hidden memory traces that were inherited from our ancestral past. It is our minds' residue of human evolutionary development. Jung theorized that the components that make up the collective unconscious are universal types or propensities that we all share and that have a mythic, overarching quality. These elements (the content) of the collective unconscious are known as **archetypes.** They include the following:

1. *The self:* Our feelings of wholeness and unity, our sense of organization within our personality, our identity
2. *The persona:* The artificial, phony self that we show to others; our public self that conforms to societal standards, the personality "mask" that we wear in public
3. *The anima:* The feminine side of men
4. *The animus:* The masculine side of women
5. *The shadow:* The dark, cruel side of us that contains animal urges and feelings of inferiority. Jung considered the shadow to be a source of creativity.

Other of Jung's theoretical archetypes represent the universal themes of the human experience, things such as wise old man, mother, death, God, the sun, and the hero. Jung taught that the archetypes color our world of experience and express themselves within our personalities. The archetypes are manifested in our dreams, influence whom we are attracted to, and become part of our art, our folklore, and the symbols that we use in our cultures. The symbols for motherhood, for example, are the same from one culture to another, Jung argued.

Jung also proposed what he called *the attitudes:* two types of personalities—extraverts and introverts. The extraversion attitude orients a person toward the external world; the introversion attitude drives a person toward the inner, subjective world. Most people, he said, are a blend of both, ambiverts!

Carl Jung

Jung's theory remains very popular. In many ways, it does not seem like a psychological theory, because it leans so heavily on anthropology, spirituality, and myths. It is probably the most mystical of all the psychological personality theories.

THINK TANK

Try using Jung's archetypes on yourself.

Divide a piece of paper into three sections.

In the first, write PERSONA, and list things about yourself that you show to others.

In the second section, write ANIMA or ANIMUS, and list the qualities of the opposite sex that you have.

In the third section, write SHADOW, and list your personality qualities that you keep hidden, that might represent the "bad" part of you.

Erik Erikson

Erik Erikson

Sigmund Freud had a daughter named Anna, who also became a famous psychoanalyst. One of her star pupils was a teacher named **Erik Erikson** (1902–1994). He is one of very few people to become a psychoanalyst without being a psychiatrist. Erikson learned about Freudian psychology from Anna Freud, then moved to New York, where he took up the practice of psychoanalysis.

The funny thing is that Erikson noticed that most of his patients were not hung up on sexual problems, as the patients of Sigmund Freud reported, but instead talked about problems with understanding themselves and getting along with others. Erikson believed that Freud's theory needed to be updated. In 1950, he wrote a book entitled *Childhood and Society*, in which he proposed a theory of **psychosocial development.**

Erikson converted Freud's emphasis on sexuality to a focus on social relationships and then extended Freud's five *psychosexual* stages to eight *psychosocial* stages. These stages became known as the **Eight Ages of Man.** (As you know, at that time in history, the word *man* was used to apply to all human beings. No sexist discrimination was intended.) Each of Erikson's eight stages was described as a time of crisis—a time when the personality would go one way or the other. For example, you've likely heard of the identity crisis. Erikson theorized that during adolescence, we all face a crisis of figuring out who we are. Each of the stages has this either-or quality.

Karen Horney

Not all of Freud's disciples were men, and not all (though nearly all) concentrated on the personality development of men. The leader of the exceptions was a strong-willed woman named **Karen Horney** (1885–1952), who today is recognized as having proposed the most complete psychoanalytic theory of women's personality development. Whereas Freud had placed great importance on biological factors, Horney believed that the differences between men and women were mainly due to societal conditions. She argued that women felt inferior to men not because of an innate penis envy, but because of the way women were treated in society.

TABLE 8.2   Erikson's Psychosocial Stages

1. Infant	**Trust versus mistrust**	Babies whose needs are met develop a feeling of trust for the environment. If infants have frustration and deprivation, they learn a basic mistrust for the world that will stick throughout life.
2. Toddler	**Autonomy versus shame and doubt**	When toddlers learn to act independently and to control their bodies (toilet training, walking, etc.), they learn self-confidence and a feeling of autonomy. Failure leads to feelings of inadequacy and therefore a sense of basic shame and doubt.
3. Preschool	**Initiative versus guilt**	The preschooler is ready to take action—in play, in imagination, and in running his or her life. Success here leads to good self-esteem; problems lead to feelings of guilt.
4. Early school age	**Industry versus inferiority**	The school-aged child is ready for learning many new skills and, if successful, will develop a sense of industry—being good at things. Failures at this stage result in a deep sense of being no good, of being inferior to others—a feeling that might carry into adulthood.
5. Adolescent	**Identity versus role confusion**	An adolescent is beginning to think abstractly and can conceptualize his or her self-identity and personality. The adolescent begins to consider questions of identity such as: Who should I be? What should I value? And what interests should I have? The teen must answer these to develop a good sense of self-identity. Exploration of various roles and personalities is common in this stage.
6. Young adult	**Intimacy versus isolation**	A young adult faces the challenge of developing close emotional relationships with other people. Here the term *intimate* does not mean sexuality, but social and emotional connections with others. The opposite result, for those who do not develop a sense of intimacy, is to become isolated from social contact.
7. Middle-aged adult	**Generativity versus stagnation**	Middle-aged adults feel an urgency to leave a mark on the world, to generate something of lasting value and worth. Finding a purpose in life is a central theme. To fail at generating something significant means a person becomes stagnant and stops moving forward; this person may become selfish and self-absorbed.
8. Old adult	**Integrity versus despair**	In old age, it is common to look back on life and reflect on what was accomplished. People who feel good about what they have done build a sense of integrity. For those whose evaluations are not so good, there is despair, the feeling of regret and remorse for the life they led.

THINK TANK

What are some ways in which young adults show that they are dealing with the issue of intimacy versus isolation?

How does adolescent behavior represent a crisis in identity?

Give examples.

Karen Horney

In addition, Horney theorized that psychological disorders did not arise from fixation on psychosexual stages, as Freud taught, but from poor interpersonal relationships during childhood, particularly with parents. She stressed that certain parenting styles could influence the child's development of personality traits. Today, many contemporary thinkers are returning to the writings of Horney because of her emphasis on parent-child interactions and the role of society and culture in shaping personality.

Alfred Adler

Adlerian psychology still flourishes in certain parts of the United States. **Alfred Adler** (1870–1937) was an early follower of Freud who became a neo-Freudian because of his strong disagreement with Freud over a few issues. Adler's theory is known as **individual psychology.** First, Adler assumed that we are motivated not so much by sexuality as by social urges. He considered our interest in social relationships to be an inborn drive. Second, Adler theorized the **creative self,** a subjective experience by which we interpret and find meaning in our experiences.

Third and most important, Adler said that the primary motivation of humans was a **striving for superiority.** Because children are small and weak, Adler thought that they develop feelings of inferiority. If these feelings become overwhelming, a child develops an **inferiority complex,** which has to be overcome. The final goals toward which we all strive, according to Adler, are perfection, security, conquest, and being successful. Adler considered the striving for superiority to be the utmost drive of human beings and believed that it is inborn. When this striving goes too far, a person develops a **superiority complex** in which this drive is wrongly self-directed and aimed at selfish goals, such as power and self-esteem, whereas, according to Adler, a normal individual's goals should be manifested in the social arena.

Recap

— Personality evolves in stages, according to Freud's psychoanalytic theory. The psychosexual stages are oral, anal, phallic, latency, and genital. Events that happen during these stages influence the development of certain traits. For example, generosity is an anal trait.

— The Oedipus complex occurs in preschool children. In the unconscious part of their minds, they develop affectionate feelings for the opposite-sex parent and harbor ill feelings for the same-sex parent. This conflict is solved by identification with the same-sex parent.

— Freud had a number of followers who later developed their own theories of personality. They are known as neo-Freudians.

— Carl Jung was Freud's best-known follower. Jung developed a theory centered on the collective unconscious, which consists of universal archetypes.

— Erik Erikson developed a theory of psychosocial stages, consisting of eight crises, such as the identity crisis of adolescence, known as the Eight Ages of Man.

— Karen Horney was one of the few psychoanalysts to emphasize female personality development. Her theory stresses societal conditions and parental interactions.

— Alfred Adler stressed the drive for superiority, and the inferiority complex.

BEHAVIORISM

"The term Science should not be given to anything but

the aggregate of the recipes that are always successful."
—PAUL VALÉRY

Freud's psychoanalytic theory was the first modern theory of personality and, as was shown above, had great influence and many adherents. However, psychoanalytic theory also had numerous detractors. Chief among the critics of psychoanalytic theory was a young American psychologist named **John B. Watson** (1878–1958), who believed that psychology should eschew the subjective study of the mind and instead should embrace scientific methodology and empirical research. Watson initiated a revolution in thinking about psychology, creating a new school of thought called **behaviorism.** Watson was joined by a large number of psychologists who also believed that psychology should reject the mental and unconscious ideas of Freud and others and that psychology should focus on the scientific exploration of overt, observable behavior.

Searching for Laws

The behaviorists were like physicists attempting to uncover the fundamental natural laws of behavior, one experiment at a time, while ignoring the mind altogether. Their leader was **B. F. Skinner** (1904–1990), a brilliant experimentalist who eventually equaled, or even surpassed, Freud in influencing the course of psychology. Skinner performed many experiments on lower animals, discovering the basic laws of animal action, and wrote many books. He was an ethical person, a hard worker, a good husband and father, and a brilliant scientist. Unfortunately, because many people did not like the results that Skinner found in his experiments, they criticized him unfairly. Skinner suffered the same complaints that Socrates, Galileo, and Darwin did. Because their ideas challenged common views, people who didn't like the message often attacked the messengers.

Skinner was often asked whether he thought about himself the same way that he thought about his research animals. It's likely that this question was not meant in all fairness, because Skinner's research animals were lower animals such as rats and pigeons. But Skinner took the question seriously and in 1983 responded somewhat proudly and defiantly: "The answer is yes. So far as I know, my behavior at any given moment has been nothing more than the product of my genetic endowment, my personal history, and the current setting." This is a good summary of the behaviorist view of personality. Personality is defined as behavior, and behavior has three causes: genetics, personal history, and the current setting.

The Basics of Behaviorism

First, notice from Skinner's response that he answered the question with reference to behavior. A psychoanalyst, by contrast, would have responded to this question with reference to the unconscious. When questioned

B. F. Skinner, foremost proponent of behaviorism, with some of his common experimental subjects.

about personality, behaviorists think first of behavior. Second, notice that Skinner does not ignore genetics. It is often said that behaviorism does not give any regard to heredity. This quotation from the leading behaviorist shows that the suggestion is incorrect. Next, note that Skinner credits the current setting as a contributing factor. This portion of answer refers to situationism, the notion that circumstances around us at any given moment can influence how we act. Finally, Skinner mentions personal history. This needs some explanation.

When behaviorists speak of personal history, they are not referring to the kind of events that Freud and the psychoanalysts believed were important in personality formation, such as the traumatic, aggressive, and sexual events that become stored in a child's unconscious. When they speak of personal history, behaviorists are not referring to the mind at all. What they mean is that each person has experiences in his or her environment, most importantly experiences with people, experiences that by means of reinforcement and other laws of behavior influence the person's disposition to act a certain way. For instance, if a child's outgoing behavior is reinforced, then that behavior will become more common. Similarly, if a child has unpleasant experiences around animals, then that child may come to dislike animals. A child who consistently receives praise for acting cooperatively or generously will begin to act cooperatively or generously in similar situations in the future, depending on the circumstances and on hereditary variables. By personal history, behaviorists mean the reinforcing events that each of us has experienced in our pasts. Behaviorists theorize that personality is behavior and that behavior is shaped mostly by our experiences in the environment. Behaviors that are successful or that lead to pleasure will become more frequent. Behaviors that fail or that lead to unpleasantness will become less frequent. These considerations are modulated by the constraints of heredity and situationism.

The cornerstone idea of behaviorism is that behavior is learned and that behavior might or might not be consistent from one situation to another. If extraverted behavior is reinforced in one set of conditions but not in another, the person will come to demonstrate extraverted behavior in situations that are similar to the first but not in situations similar to the second. Skinner's answer provides us with the fundamental argument made by behaviorism: As far as we know, a person's *behavior* at any moment is the result of (1) his or her heredity, (2) the situation he or she is in, and (3) that person's previous experiences in the environment. Please note that one very optimistic thing about behaviorism is the idea that if behaviors are in fact learned, they can also be unlearned.

Social Learning Theory

Behaviorism is technically not so much a coherent theory of personality as it is a collection of experimental research findings that suggest certain principles of personality formation. Behaviorism is not so much a theory as it is an extrapolation of experimental findings. Its principal teachings are based on the results of scientific research. All behaviorist explanations of personality embrace situationism. The focus of behaviorism is not on the personal characteristics of people, but on how people behave in various situations. Behaviorists do not talk about traits; they talk about actions. Personality, in the context of behaviorism, is the sum of the actions a person takes in different circumstances.

Some followers of behaviorism have proposed theoretical models based on the experimental research findings that are at the core of this school of psychology. These theories are often called **social learning theories** because they emphasize the importance of social settings (interactions with people), and the significance of learning as the key component of personality development. Behaviorism defines personality as the different behaviors that a person engages in and argues that these behaviors have been learned, primarily through interactions with parents, family members, teachers, and others.

Observational Learning

One of the fundamental principles of social learning theory is that humans learn many of their behaviors not through their own direct experiences with the world, but by

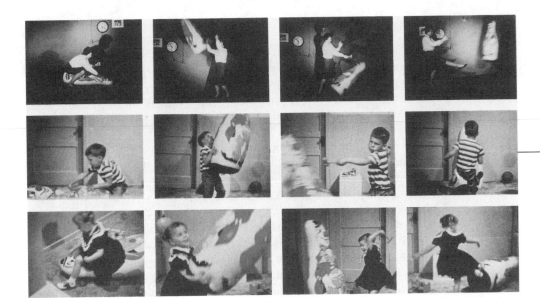

The famous Bobo-the-clown experiment by Bandura, Ross, and Ross (1961) found that children were very influenced by observational learning. After watching a movie in which adults hit a doll, children imitated the behavior very precisely.

observing others. Certainly, babies learn to speak and understand words not by any formal training, but by the constant, little by little, trial-and-error process of listening and pronouncing. When behaviors are learned via seeing or listening, this process is called **observational learning.** One of the leading social learning theorists, **Albert Bandura,** has proposed that observational learning is a key component of human personality development. Bandura was the lead researcher in an important and influential experiment that demonstrated that observational learning could affect even children watching movies.

Bandura, Ross, and Ross (1961) showed children a movie in which an adult hit and punched a blow-up Bobo-the-clown doll in rather distinctive ways. For example, the adult knelt atop the doll and hit it in the face with a wooden mallet. After the children watched the movie, they were sent to a room to play—a room full of many toys, including a Bobo-the-clown doll. Cameras recorded the children's behavior in the room. As you might have guessed, the children ran directly to the doll and began hitting it and punching it in precisely the same distinctive manner that the adult had used in the movie. The results were stunning—observational learning was far more powerful than anyone had imagined. Thousands of similar experiments have been done since that seminal study, and these studies have consistently shown the same results. For instance, Dutton (2000) reported that abusive adults were likely to have witnessed abuse as a child.

Behaviorist theories have incorporated the powerful influence of observational learning into their explanations of personality formation. On the basis of the extensive research on this topic, Albert Bandura expressed his belief that "Most human behavior is learned by observation through modeling."

THINK TANK   Name some behaviors of your own (or of others) that were influenced by observation.

Behaviorism's Tenets

The basic tenets of behaviorism are fairly simple, though the details may not be. Here are the fundamental theoretical beliefs of behaviorism:

1. Personality is an abstract, hypothetical concept that is best conceptualized as the sum of a person's behaviors in various situations. Personality should be viewed not as part of the mind, but as observable behavior.
2. Behaviors should be studied empirically to determine the precise variables within the world of experience (the environment) that influence and shape personalities. Psychology must be a scientific enterprise.
3. Mental variables (the mind) are not proper subjects of scientific inquiry and furthermore are not elements that influence behavior. Skinner said, "The practice of looking inside the organism for an explanation of behavior has tended to obscure the variables which are immediately available for a scientific analysis. These variables lie outside the organism, in its immediate environment and in its environmental history. The objection to inner states is not that they do not exist, but that they are not relevant" (Skinner, 1953).
4. People are born neither good nor bad, but are shaped by their experiences. Each person has hereditary factors that influence his or her development, but the primary forces of personality development are the events that happen to people in their lives.
5. Behaviors are developed predominantly via learning. Learning occurs mainly through the processes of reinforcement and observation. Behaviors that are learned under one set of conditions might not be learned under a different set of conditions; therefore, personality might be inconsistent from one situation to another.

Behaviorism had tremendous influence on the course of psychology, particularly during the first half of the twentieth century. Behaviorism influenced the kind of research that was done, the development of many theories and many practical applications that

Recap

— Behavior theorists shifted the focus away from the mind and onto observable, measurable behavior. They emphasize that personality is learned.

— John B. Watson was the founder of behaviorism, but B. F. Skinner was the most influential researcher and advocate of this school of psychology.

— Skinner stressed three factors as determiners of behavior: genetics, personal history, and the current setting.

— Behaviorism focuses on behavior, how it is learned within the environment, and how situations influence a person's actions.

— The behaviorist approach to personality sees a newborn as essentially neutral; behaviors are learned depending on experiences in the world.

— Social learning theories emphasize the role of human interaction in the development of personality.

— Behavioral theories also emphasize observational learning—learning behaviors by seeing or hearing others.

— Bandura, Ross, and Ross showed how children learn aggressive behaviors by viewing adults acting aggressively.

continue to be used in schools, mental hospitals, workplaces, and the home. In recent years, behaviorism has waned somewhat, and today is often tempered with doses of cognitive psychology and physiological psychology. Still, the remnants of this powerful school of psychology reverberate throughout the discipline. Many research studies that are conducted in contemporary psychology use methodology that would not have been possible without the progress and paradigms created by B. F. Skinner and his followers. In this sense, behaviorism will always be a part of psychology.

HUMANISM

"When the only tool you own is a hammer, every problem begins to resemble a nail."
—ABRAHAM MASLOW

Psychoanalytic theory and behaviorism were the first two major theories of personality development in the modern discipline of psychology. Both have had tremendous influence and have inspired practical endeavors as well as theoretical notions. But there is still another theoretical school in modern psychology. This third approach, called **humanism** or **humanistic psychology**, was initiated in the 1950s by an American psychologist named **Abraham Maslow** (1908–1970).

The Inner Drives

Maslow was critical of psychoanalytic theory because it focused on the abnormal personality and had little to say about the normal, healthy personality. Maslow argued that psychology should give more attention to the highest and most affirming of human personality qualities, things like love, self-esteem, and creativity. Maslow wrote, "It is as if Freud has supplied to us the sick half of psychology and we must now fill it out with the healthy half" (Maslow, 1998).

Additionally, Maslow believed that a personality theory should be centered on the conscious, not the unconscious, mind. He argued that human personality is primarily a matter of making conscious choices and rational decisions that are guided by our desire for excellence and fulfillment. Maslow wanted the aware mind to take center stage in a theory of personality.

Abraham Maslow, founder of humanistic psychology.

Just as he was critical of psychoanalytic theory, Maslow also criticized the basic tenets of behaviorism. Personality theories should emphasize human qualities, not the behavior of lower animals, he reasoned. Personality theories should focus on the inner life (feelings and thoughts) of the individual, not on a person's overt behaviors. Maslow did not believe that taking a scientific approach to personality was important. For him, personality should focus on the subjective mental life of people—emotions, thoughts, attitudes, and the conscious mind. Maslow carefully began to build a third approach to personality, the approach now known as humanism or humanistic psychology.

Maslow's ideas were similar to those of many philosophers who are collectively known as existentialists. It is not easy to define **existential philosophy,** because the topics covered in this broad field are very diverse and abstract.

FYI

While at the University of Wisconsin, Maslow longed to marry a girl from back home in Brooklyn (his first cousin) but was wary of asking her to join him. He asked a professor for advice and was told to follow his heart. He was happily married for years. Perhaps this personal incident influenced his ideas about psychology.

Fundamentally, existentialism is concerned with matters of existence. Humans are viewed as having free will and therefore being capable of making free choices in a world of possibilities. The main topic of interest in existentialism is the purpose of life—finding meaning in the world of experience. Humans are viewed as fallible, rational, suffering, and driven. Up against the many problems of life, a person must select the path that will take him or her to a place of inner satisfaction. A person must make the choices that will lead to fulfillment and meaning.

One of the shared characteristics of these two philosophies is the emphasis on **phenomenology.** In humanism, the focus is on how a person perceives the world. Scientific objectivity is useless, the humanistic psychologists argue, because what matters is the person and his or her perspective. What humanists care about is a person's private, personal, subjective view—his or her feelings, thoughts, perceptions, and concerns. This is what is real and important. It doesn't matter what the objective situation is. What matters is how the person perceives it and feels about it. The focus is on the person—the inner, conscious life of the person.

Remember, the central theme of psychoanalytic theory is the unconscious and the central theme of behaviorism is learning. For humanistic psychology, there is no more important idea than **self-actualization.** Theoretically, this is the highest human motivation, the most advanced drive of humans, the ultimate end of our inner personality and our attempt to understand ourselves. Self-actualization is a process of self-fulfillment, of finding our true inner self, of becoming true to our inner identity. Maslow said, "What a man can be, he must be" (Maslow, 1998). Erich Fromm said, "Man's main task in life is to give birth to himself, to become what he potentially is. The most important product of his effort is his own personality" (Fromm, 1962). For humanistic psychologists, self-actualization is the struggle of a lifetime that we all experience: the struggle to find a personality that fits, that is right and true to our inner desires and needs.

Maslow hypothesized that self-actualization, although the ultimate goal of the human personality, could not be satisfactorily achieved unless other drives and needs were mostly fulfilled first. These other needs are called **prepotent,** because they must be mostly fulfilled in order to concentrate on higher ones. Maslow placed human needs and motivations into five categories and then arranged them in a hierarchy that is often referred to as Maslow's **pyramid of needs.**

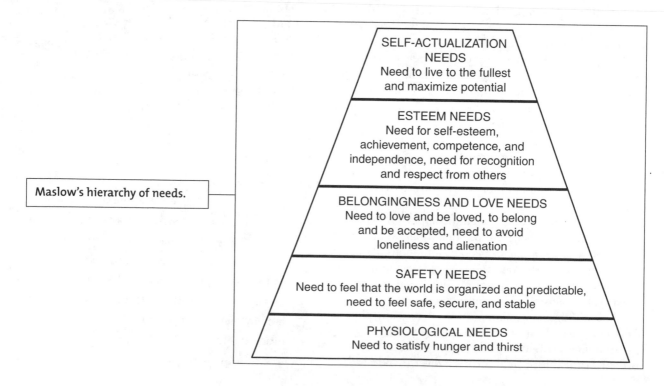

Maslow's hierarchy of needs.

SELF-ACTUALIZATION NEEDS
Need to live to the fullest and maximize potential

ESTEEM NEEDS
Need for self-esteem, achievement, competence, and independence, need for recognition and respect from others

BELONGINGNESS AND LOVE NEEDS
Need to love and be loved, to belong and be accepted, need to avoid loneliness and alienation

SAFETY NEEDS
Need to feel that the world is organized and predictable, need to feel safe, secure, and stable

PHYSIOLOGICAL NEEDS
Need to satisfy hunger and thirst

According to humanistic psychology, a person must fulfill the lower, prepotent needs to a certain level in order to move up the pyramid and work on satisfying the higher needs. We cannot become creative and intellectually fulfilled if we are starving to death. We must be accepted and loved and feel that we belong in order to develop a sense of healthy self-esteem. And, of course, we cannot make a successful journey of self-actualization unless all of our lower, prepotent needs are satisfactorily met.

FYI

Maslow studied with Harry Harlow, who worked with monkeys at the University of Wisconsin (remember from Chapter 1). Harlow's study of monkey dominance hierarchies likely influenced Maslow's ideas.

THINK TANK

Describe some situations in which needs higher on Maslow's hierarchy might take precedence over lower needs. For example, do people who are hungry always delay higher needs until they get food? Also, can you think of any human needs that Maslow did not include?

Focus on Self

One of Maslow's colleagues and collaborators in humanistic psychology was a counseling psychologist named **Carl Rogers** (1902–1987) who developed an influential theory of personality centered on the idea of self-concept. Rogers's theory is quite often known as **self theory.** This approach emphasizes conditions of worth, valuing people, and the self-actualizing tendency.

Rogers theorized that each person has an inner concept of what she or he ideally would like to be—an **ideal self.** This is your conception of what kind of person, what kind of personality, would be perfect for you. Also, it is theorized that each of us has an inner concept of what we are really like—a **real self.** This is your conception of what kind of person, what kind of personality, is actually true about you—what you are really like. The drive of self-actualization, then, is the striving to merge these two concepts. Self-actualization is the ongoing attempt to make your real self congruent with your ideal self, to bring the concept of what you are actually like (your real self) more and more into accord with what you think you should be like (your ideal self).

Rogers proposed a style of counseling that included many therapeutic techniques intended to help people along their journey of self-actualization. These counseling techniques are widely used today and are known by several terms, including **Rogerian, person-centered, client-centered,** and **nondirective.**

The essence of Rogers's counseling style is to help clients (notice that they are not called *patients*) with the process of self-discovery. That is, the counselor helps a client to become aware of his or her true inner self, the true personality of feelings and self-concept. Then the client must come to accept his or her true feelings and personality and to embrace the inner self. The client should then be ready to take the necessary steps to fulfill his or her inner needs and to bring the world of experience into line with the inner self-concept.

Carl Rogers

Connecting Concepts

Learn more about non-directive counseling (including a short example) in Chapter 10.

Humanism's Tenets

The fundamental tenets of humanism are as follows:

1. Every person exists in a continually changing world of experience of which he or she is the center. A person is the best source of information about himself or herself.
2. A person reacts to the world of experience according to his or her own perceptions, interpretations, and feelings.
3. A person acts as a whole, integrated organism, not with a series of simple stimulus-response reactions.
4. A person's one basic striving is to maintain and actualize the self. The self-concept is at the center of the personality.
5. The structure of the self is created by experiences in the world and through interactions with others. The self is the organized pattern of perceptions, values, and emotions that create the concept of "I" or "me."
6. Behavior is a goal-directed activity meant to satisfy needs. A person adopts ways of acting that are consistent with the concept of the self. Therefore, the best way to change behavior is to change the self-concept.
7. Experiences that are not consistent with the concept of self are threatening. Psychological maladjustment occurs if a person denies awareness to experiences and does not allow them into the self-concept. Humans seek congruence between their world of experience and their self-concepts. When there is **incongruence**, abnormality results. Self-actualization is the process of building **congruence** between our experiences in the world and our sense of self.

Humanism has made a lasting impression on psychology. It is widely popular among the general public and continues to have adherents within psychology, especially on the practical or applied side of the discipline in such fields as counseling. While psychology has become much more of a scientific discipline in recent years, humanistic psychology has been somewhat left behind, although a new subfield called **positive psychology** uses scientific methods to explore similar topics, such as happiness and optimism. Like those of psychoanalytic theory, the concepts of humanistic psychology are not easily placed into a scientific framework; still, humanistic psychology has been very influential, was founded and flourished during the "love and peace" era of the 1960s, and is at the root of the currently popular self-help movement.

Table 8.3 allows you to compare and contrast the three major theories of personality.

Now that we have looked at the most important personality theories, let's turn next to some research findings and speculations about where personality comes from.

THINK TANK Name some human characteristics, behaviors, or problems and state how they might be viewed or explained by psychoanalytic theory, behaviorism, and humanism.

TABLE 8.3 Summary of Personality Theories

	Psychoanalytic theory	Behaviorism	Humanism
Major leaders:	Sigmund Freud	John B. Watson, B. F. Skinner	Abraham Maslow
Important others:	Carl Jung, Erik Erikson, Karen Horney, Alfred Adler	Albert Bandura	Carl Rogers
Emphasis:	Unconscious mind	Observable behavior	Self-concept, subjective feelings and thoughts
View of people:	Animalistic, biological drives for sex and aggression	Behavior is subject to laws; depends on experience in the environment	Whole, unique, good, valuable, worthy of dignity and respect
Personality structure:	Id, ego, superego	Sum of behaviors in situations	Conscious, human qualities
Motivation:	Sex, defense mechanisms, intrapsychic conflict	Reinforcement, observational learning	Self-actualization; pyramid of needs
Development:	Psychosexual stages	Learning of behaviors through reinforcement and observation	Emergence of self-concept and self-esteem; congruence
Abnormality:	Fixations, unconscious conflicts	Maladaptive behaviors are learned	Incongruence, poor self-actualization
Example: Anorexia	Unconscious desire to avoid sex and pregnancy (food makes stomach big)	Learned behavior through attention and other reinforcements	Self esteem problem; inability to accept self

BIOLOGICAL SOURCES OF PERSONALITY

"Personality must be accepted for what it is."
—OSCAR WILDE

All personality theories stress the importance of experiences, particularly childhood experiences, in shaping and influencing personality. They differ, of course, in the precise dynamics of how experiences contribute to personality development and change. Whereas the effects of experience take center stage in personality theories, physiological factors are normally given only a secondary role. Though some theories mention heredity and other biological factors (Eysenck's theory in particular), the classic theories have mostly ignored biological sources as contributors to personality. However, in recent years, psychologists have shown much more interest in how personality may be influenced by biological factors, particularly heredity.

Nature and Nurture

For a hundred years or more, psychologists have debated and researched what has been called the **nature-nurture question**. To what extent are psychological characteristics a part of our innate, inherited nature, and to what extent are they influenced by our upbringing, our experiences, our nurturing? Psychologists of the past gave a great deal of attention to this issue. In addition, it has generated a tremendous amount of controversy, because the question typically gives rise to statements about race, gender, ethnicity, and other biological factors that many people get very upset about. How would you like it if some scientists said that people of your ethnic background are likely to have a certain kind of personality—particularly if the personality was something undesirable?

Although the nature-nurture question is still with us and many psychologists continue to research and discuss it, some of the most forward-thinking psychologists today now dismiss this issue as phony. Of course, they argue, everything about us is a result of both hereditary factors and experience; it is impossible and irrelevant to divide our qualities into certain percentages of each. Just like everything else in this world, they say, we are a mix of numerous influences. These contributing factors work together in ways that are inseparable. For example, cognitive psychologist Steven Pinker in *How the Mind Works* (1997) wrote:

> Framing the issue in such a way that innate structure and learning are pitted against each other is a colossal mistake. These statements are true but useless. Learning is not a surrounding gas or force field, it is made possible by innate machinery designed to do the learning. The metaphor of a mixture of two ingredients, like a martini, is wrongheaded. We need new ways of thinking.

It is silly to suggest that either nature or nurture makes us what we are or even to try to divide our psychological qualities into some proportion of these two interacting influences. It would be like asking what percent of a chocolate cake is the result of the recipe and what percent is the result of oven temperature? Or what percentage of a TV's reception is due to the receiving antenna and what percentage is due to the transmitter? Although the idea of dividing human qualities into some percentage of inborn and learned is not an accurate or even useful endeavor, most psychologists and most of the general public continue to try to untangle heredity from experience.

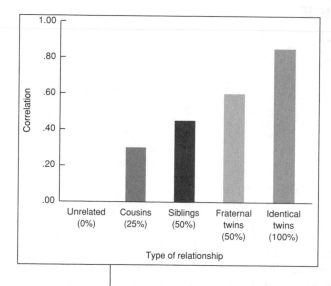

The more genetically related people are, the more similar they are in IQ scores. However, experience also influences IQs, of course.

The Heritability of Intelligence

The primary psychological trait that has been at the center of the nature-nurture debate is intelligence. Thousands of studies have been conducted in an attempt to ascertain what percentage of the variation in intelligence is caused by heredity and what percent by experience. People have different IQ scores. Why? If we all had the same heredity, by how much would the variation in scores shrink? If we could all be reared exactly the same—same food, same parents, same everything—we would end up more like one another in IQ. But by how much? Correlational studies give us some clues about the answers to these questions.

Many correlational studies have been done, and the results have been somewhat consistent, though not exactly the same. Predominantly, these studies show that IQ scores are most similar among identical twins raised together and that correlations get lower and lower as people get less and less similar in heredity and in environment. Identical twins raised together have IQs that correlate about +0.90, while identical twins raised apart have a correlation of about +0.75. Less similar environments result in less similar IQ scores. However, fraternal twins who are raised together have a correlation in IQ of about +0.65, lower than that for identical twins raised apart. This means that heredity is important. In fact, across the board, correlations decrease as genetic relatedness decreases. Again, this is evidence that heredity is important. Today most reasonable experts would say that the differences between people in IQ scores are due about 50% to heredity and 50% to environment. Notice that this applies to groups. For any one individual, we do not know whether this question even makes sense.

Many psychologists have suggested that a useful way to think about intelligence (as measured by IQ tests) is that the limits of what is possible are set by our heredity, but precisely where we end up is determined by our experiences. There is no doubt that heredity contributes to whatever it is that allows a person to score high on an IQ test. Certainly, we can imagine that things like brain anatomy and physiology are involved. However, there is also no doubt that IQ is heavily influenced by experience. Disadvantaged children who enroll in programs such as Head Start make significant gains in IQ scores. Even environmental experiences that we don't normally think of, such as diet, are critically important for a brain to do well intellectually. Children who live in older, poorly maintained neighborhoods often suffer from lead poisoning, a significant contributor to decreased mental abilities. There are many similar environmental conditions that affect IQ. Heredity may be a contributor, but it is only part of the story.

FYI

Sir Cyril Burt (1883–1971) was a famed British psychologist who argued that intelligence was mostly inherited. The schools of England placed children into tracks because of Burt's influential research. In 1976, Burt was accused of fabricating his data. This view was later refuted by other investigators. The whole affair was troubling, to say the least, but more important, it missed the main point. It is wrong to conclude that if something is influenced by heredity, it is not changeable. This is perhaps the greatest error of Burt and his followers, whether he cheated or not.

Double Your Pleasure

One of the common ways today to investigate the influences of heredity and environment are studies of twins. There are many such research efforts, including the **McArthur Longitudinal Twin Study** and the **Minnesota Study of Twins Reared Apart (MISTRA).** Psychologists at the University of Minnesota comb the world to find twins, particularly identical twins who were raised apart, then bring them to Minneapolis and put them through a weeklong series of tests. The results of these tests often indicate that heredity plays a large role in the formation of personality and other psychological qualities. For example, happiness has been discovered to be influenced by heredity (Lykken & Tellegen, 1996). Divorce, too, turns out to be affected by genetics (McGue & Lykken, 1992). Reciprocal social behavior, the extent to which children engage in social interaction with others, was recently found to be highly influenced by heredity (Constantino, 2000). There are many other examples; heredity plays a significant role in shaping personality.

MISTRA has studied 59 pairs of identical twins and 47 pairs of fraternal twins who were adopted into different families. Researchers have reported that correlation coefficients for the identical twins were much higher than for the fraternal twins in two traits: **extraversion** and **neuroticism.** The two traits appear to be highly influenced by heredity.

What must be surprising to personality theorists is that MISTRA found that the family environment in which one is reared contributes only modestly to personality. Family environment does not have the same effect on each child. Children respond differently to the same family event or experience. Perhaps how a child responds is influenced by his or her **temperament,** which has been shown to be a highly inherited quality. Temperament can be thought of as analogous to climate, something that is long-term and pervasive, rather than a moment-to-moment quality. Moods or emotions are more like weather in the sense that they are more immediate and related to the situation. More about emotions in a minute.

Temperament = climate   Mood or emotion = weather

Scientific research has identified a significant number of personality traits and behaviors that appear to be influenced by heredity. These include shyness, amount of time spent watching TV, religious attitudes, political attitudes, leisure time interests, and even the number of accidents a child has. Psychologists do not believe that these variables are directed by specific genes—rather, that certain overarching features, such as activity level, are highly influenced by heredity and that subsequently such general attributes influence specific behaviors and dimensions of personality. For example, a child with a certain temperament and activity level will be more likely to have accidents.

On the other hand, research has indicated that certain personality variables are less related to heredity and more the result of the family environment. These include the desire for social closeness and being actively engaged in the environment. Remember, however, that all psychological traits are the result of a complex blending of forces and that these studies apply to trait variability among *groups*, not in individuals. Everything about us is influenced to some extent by our genes. But of course, our experiences also contribute to what kind of person we become.

Recap

— Abraham Maslow founded a third theoretical school of psychology called humanistic psychology.

— Humanism is similar to existential philosophy and focuses on subjective, phenomenal experiences.

— Self-actualization is the key motivation in humanistic theory. Maslow's pyramid of needs puts it at the top, while prepotent needs are below.

— Self-actualization represents a drive to merge the real self with the ideal self.

— Carl Rogers developed self theory and a method of nondirective counseling aimed at helping people become more self-actualized and building congruence between experiences and the person's sense of self.

— Humanistic psychology has led to the self-help movement and a new subfield called positive psychology that scientifically studies good human qualities.

— The nature-nurture question asks to what extent our personalities are shaped by heredity or by experience. Contemporary thinkers believe that this question is oversimplified and misleading. All traits come from a complex interaction between those forces.

— The heritability of intelligence has been extensively studied. The current understanding is that variability between people in intelligence is due about 50-50 to heredity and to environmental variables.

— Studies of twins have found personality traits that are greatly influenced by heredity, including extraversion, neuroticism, and temperament.

EMOTIONS

"Emotional responses are the result of a long history of evolutionary fine-tuning. Emotions are part of the bioregulatory devices with which we come equipped to survive."
—ANTONIO DAMASIO

Emotions are a major component of personality and a critical feature of our lives. We love, we hate; we get angry, afraid, and surprised; we feel delighted, sad, and even disgusted. Emotions are typically triggered by some experience, such as seeing a snake, winning the lottery, or being cheated, but, of course, they are created by and connected to biological events in our brains and bodies. Emotions evolved because they helped people to adapt. For instance, anger is useful in helping people change how they react to a situation that was not satisfying in the past. Fear and happiness have obvious advantages. So our emotions help us to adapt. But just what are emotions, and how do they work?

Emotional Baggage

Emotions are more complicated than they seem at first. We can begin to understand emotions by dividing them into four components:

1. *Affect:* The subjective feeling that one experiences, such as happiness, fear, anger, disgust, or sadness
2. *Physiology:* The biological events that take place in one's body, such as increased blood pressure and heart rate, the release of adrenaline and other hormones, or dilation of the pupils
3. *Expression:* The facial reactions and nonverbal body movements a person makes, such as a smile, raised eyebrows, furrowed brow, wide-open mouth, stooped shoulders, or a hand slapped on the forehead
4. *Cognition:* The thinking and interpreting that one does during an emotion, such as "That guy's a jerk," "This is a scary situation," or "What a fun place."

So emotions consist of APEC! Let's briefly examine each of these four.

Affect

What are the various feelings that people experience, that is, what is the range of emotions? Some psychologists have theorized that our feelings arise from certain **basic** or **primary emotions**. The most commonly listed primary emotions are happiness, sadness, anger, fear, surprise, and disgust. Theoretically, other feelings (**secondary emotions**) result from combinations of these six primary emotions. For example, contempt is a combination of anger and disgust, remorse is a combination of disgust and sadness, and disappointment is a combination of sadness and surprise. Also, emotions vary in what is called *valence*, that is, whether the emotion is pleasant or unpleasant.

Do newborn infants experience emotions? Or do emotions develop as a part of socialization? Like the nature-nurture question, this is a bit unfair, because all human qualities are an interdependent blending of both forces. However, feelings of pleasure and pain seem evident in newborns, as does a startle or fear reaction (to a loud noise,

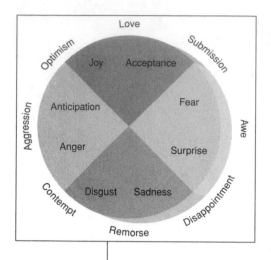

Psychologists have created many different models for defining and classifying emotions. One model proposes eight primary emotions that each can vary in intensity. Secondary emotions are a combination of basic emotions; for example, love is a combination of joy and acceptance (Plutchik & Kellerman, 1980).

Connecting Concepts

Learn more about stress and the body's reaction to it in Chapter 9 (Psychological Disorders).

a fall, or other stimuli). Also, people in all cultures show similar emotions and reactions. So the capacity for emotion and the range of emotions seem to be determined as part of our evolutionary heritage. But the nuances and particulars of emotions are obviously learned. An angry person might act aggressively, scream, talk it out, or merely pout, depending on his or her cultural and personal experiences.

Physiology

Our bodies react to emotional experiences in many ways, including the release of various hormones and changes in the cardiovascular system. These physiological events prepare the body for action, as in the **fight-or-flight response** to fear. Interestingly, these physiological changes are useful in the short run but can be harmful in the long run. For example, the hormones that are released during emotional distress help us by providing energy and strength but ultimately can damage body organs, including brain cells (Sapolsky, 1996). So a life of constant stress could, in fact, kill you.

Most people assume that physiological events in the body are caused by the awareness or feeling of an emotion. However, over one hundred years ago, American psychologist William James and Dutch psychologist Carl Lange separately proposed that this common view is exactly backward. How do we identify an emotion? The **James-Lange theory** said that physiological events come first and give rise to the emotion. That is, one becomes aware of an emotion because of the body's reactions. The James-Lange theory is playfully summarized by the statement. "I am running, therefore I must be afraid!" One fascinating fact in support of this theory is that people often do feel happier when they force a smile. Try it! This is called the **facial feedback hypothesis,** because it supposes that feedback from the muscles in your face influences your brain to feel a certain emotion (Izard, 1971).

Years ago, researchers Walter Cannon and Phillip Bard showed good evidence why the James-Lange theory cannot be completely correct. They showed that physiological responses are too slow—that emotions occur faster than body reactions. Cannon and Bard believed that the brain, not physiological responses, was the central factor. The **Cannon-Bard theory** said that the brain produces both the emotion and the body events at about the same time.

Subsequent research has shown that both of these early theories of emotion have some truth to them but that they are incomplete. Physiological events are different for different emotions and do provide a cue for emotions, as James and Lange argued. However, the brain is the main determiner of emotion, as Cannon and Bard pointed out. In fact, there are different brain pathways for the basic emotions. Unfortunately, it is difficult to embrace either of these theories entirely because they both exclude important features of emotions, such as the cognitive processes that accompany, and even help shape, an emotion. Take fear, for example. Neuroscientists have found that there are two pathways in the brain for this emotion: one that is quick, that produces a rapid body response, and one that is slower, using the thinking part of the brain. An emotion, it turns out, is a complicated tangle of many interacting events—in the mind, the body, and in the way the feeling is expressed.

Expression

People in all cultures of the world are remarkably consistent in their facial expressions of emotions and in their ability to judge another person's emotional state by that person's facial expression. Although there are some minor variations in body language and posture, it is amazing how similarly people react to emotional experiences. It is easy to notice when people are happy, sad, afraid, or angry simply on the basis of their expressions.

Look at your face in a mirror when you are thinking about (1) an awful, hideous odor (did you wrinkle your nose?); (2) a foul-tasting food (did you make the "yech" expression with your mouth?); (3) a big surprise (did you open your mouth and raise your eyebrows?). Humans have universal ways of signaling their emotions with their faces. Researchers found brain activity in the same emotional centers when people watched someone else show disgust in their face (Wicker et al., 2003). Also, people with damage to particular regions of their brains, such as the amygdala, experience difficulty in expressing emotions and judging the emotions of other people on the basis of their facial expressions (Damasio, 1999).

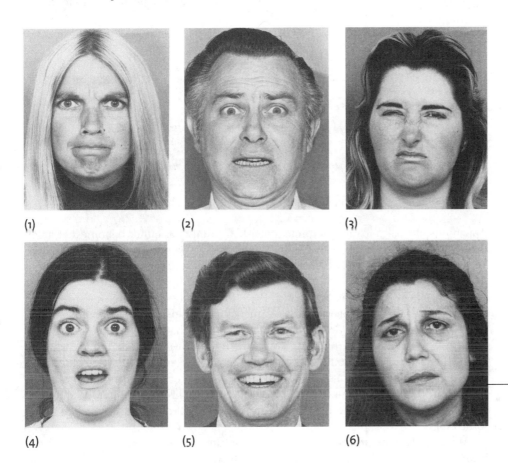

(1)   (2)   (3)

(4)   (5)   (6)

Can you tell what emotion is being expressed in each of these photos? Happy, sad, fear, anger, surprise, disgust? Answers on page 310.

Cognition

How do we determine which emotion we are feeling? In unclear situations, cognition—or mental interpretation—becomes an important part of creating or influencing an emotion. As was mentioned above, the brain has two pathways for emotions: one that quickly produces unconscious reactions and another that recruits the higher thinking areas of the brain. So cognition is also important.

A famous 1962 experiment by Stanley Schachter and Jerome Singer showed how people could be influenced to interpret their emotions a certain way. The participants were given injections of adrenaline. This aroused their physiology. They were then placed in a room where a stranger (an actor) was acting either happy or angry. The participants felt their bodies becoming aroused but didn't know why, because they were told that the injection was a vitamin (a control group was told the truth). The researchers found that the participants felt either happy or angry depending on how the stranger was acting.

THINK TANK

Anthropologists define an adaptation as a feature that was designed by natural selection to help individuals survive and ultimately reproduce.

How was it helpful for our ancestors to be able to identify emotions by people's expressions?

How could this ability have made the difference between life and death for an early human? Is it useful today?

In what ways?

How do you tell what someone else is feeling?

How certain are you that your judgment is right?

Do you ever get it wrong?

Connecting Concepts

The response of a person's amygdala (Chapter 3) depends on his or her personality. Canli and colleagues (2002) found that extraverts show strong amygdala activation when they see a happy face, but introverts do not. Apparently extraverts learn that a happy face is an important social stimulus to pay attention to, while introverts do not deem it relevant.

Apparently, the participants interpreted their body arousal as either happiness or anger depending on the situation. Those in the control group did not have the same response because they knew why their body was aroused. The idea that cognition is important in influencing our emotions is often called the **Schachter-Singer theory.**

In an earlier experiment, Schachter (1959) found that people who were frightened wanted to be with other people in the same situation, apparently to make comparisons to determine precisely what to feel. Schachter said that not only does misery love company, but misery loves miserable company! In other words, to determine what we are feeling and how we should act, especially in unclear situations, we often observe those around us who are in a similar situation. This is part of **social comparison theory**, the notion that our ideas about ourselves often come through comparing ourselves with others. How should we feel when it is not obvious? Look around at others to get some clues!

When people are aroused, they may look around at the circumstances or the surrounding people to determine what they are feeling. We may come to identify our aroused state as a certain emotion depending on the situation. For example, researchers found that if a hiker encountered an attractive woman while on a swaying bridge (an arousing situation), he was more likely to find her attractive and to call her for a date than if he encountered her on a hiking trail (not a very arousing situation) (Dutton & Aron, 1974).

Most people think that emotions are separate from intellect. Consider, for example, the character Mr. Spock on *Star Trek*. Mr. Spock supposedly maintains a high intellect by not allowing his emotions to interfere with his thinking. But current research suggests that this won't work. Some studies found that patients who had brain damage that made them unable to feel certain emotions also suffered from cognitive impairments, particularly in making judgments (Damasio, 1999). Also, researchers found that when people are making decisions, the emotional areas of their brains are active (Shibata, 2001). Apparently, emotions help us to direct our thinking and make value judgments, thereby helping us to make better decisions. So emotions and cognitive processes are linked in a give-and-take manner.

MOTIVATION

"We talk on principal, but act on motivation."
—WALTER SAVAGE LANDOR

Personality theories include explanations for what motivates people and animals. Motivation refers to what moves us to act a particular way. Psychoanalysts (led by Freud) found motivation for behavior in the unconscious; behaviorists (Watson and Skinner) emphasized incentives in the environment, such as reinforcers, as motivational forces; and humanistic psychologists (Maslow and Rogers) tended to look inside a person's feelings and conscious mind, at things such as self-actualization. Maslow, for instance, created the well-known pyramid of needs as one way to view motivation.

Naturally, some motivations are driven by survival needs. Hunger, thirst, and other internal **drives** are part of our biological makeup. Other motives are more social in origin. Things such as achievement motivation, thrill-seeking, and the needs for power, status, cognition (enjoying thinking), and affiliation (wanting to be with others) certainly are grounded in our evolutionary past but also are greatly shaped by our personal experiences in the world. These more social motives have been extensively studied by psychologists. For instance, the need for achievement was studied for more than 30 years by David McClelland.

Motivation has been described by using certain key ideas:

1. An **instinct** is an inherited tendency toward certain behavior. Evolutionary psychologists have explained a number of human behaviors on the basis of their survival value (and reproduction value, of course, since surviving isn't enough to pass on genes!) for our predecessors. The biological drives such as hunger and thirst have obvious value. But some psychologists have also pointed out that motives such as affiliation, aggression, and achievement have their roots in our evolutionary past. That is, these motives had reproduction value for our ancestors. For instance, people today have an instinct (a natural competency, a natural reaction) to avoid people who cheat in social situations. This is because affiliating with cheaters in the past, for our distant predecessors, reduced their ability to reproduce (Cosmides & Tooby, 1992).

2. **Intrinsic motivation** refers to an animal's tendency to perform a behavior for its own sake. For example, you might enjoy doodling, singing in the shower, or playing computer games just for fun, not because you get something for these activities. Intrinsic means the motivation is coming from within. Psychologists use the term **drive** to refer to a force inside of us that makes us do something.

   Extrinsic motivation, on the other hand, refers to behavior that is motivated by some payoff, something outside the body. For instance, you might agree to do some boring work to get money. The term *incentive* is used to refer to the payoff.

   One of the interesting debates in psychology is the extent to which people are motivated by drives or incentives. Interestingly, it has been found that if a person's behavior consistently leads to a tangible reward, the person may come to think of the behavior as one that is not interesting in its own right. That is, intrinsic motivation may in fact be decreased by receiving tangible rewards. If we want someone to enjoy a behavior, perhaps we should not make that behavior constantly dependent on an outside reward. Praise, compliments, and fun often increase intrinsic motivation more than do money, treats, or goodies. However, if a person has little or no intrinsic motivation to perform a task, then extrinsic, tangible rewards can increase motivation.

Almost always, intrinsic and extrinsic factors work together to motivate behavior. As an analogy, consider the fact that a plant will grow toward sunlight. What causes this: the internal nature of the plant or the effect of sunlight on the plant? Of course, it is the interaction between the two forces that gives rise to the actions of the plant. Similarly, humans and other animals have internal mechanisms that interact with things in the environment. It is this interaction that motivates us.

3. **Homeostasis** refers to a body's internal state of balance. For example, body temperature, hunger, and thirst are homeostatic motives. A person's body attempts to maintain a balance in those things. When the body state is too low, a person is motivated to increase it (eat or drink, for example), and when the body state is too high, the motivation is to lower it (stop eating or drinking).

An interesting example is **arousal.** Psychologists have found that people tend to strive for a medium level of stimulation. When a lecture is boring, students begin to swing their legs, tap their pencils, and fidget. They are motivated to become more aroused. But when people have too much stimulation, say, after a hard, stressful day at work, they tend to want relaxation and quiet.

Researchers found that people normally perform at their best when at a medium level of arousal. This is known as the **Yerkes-Dodson law.** If we need to perform some task and we are understimulated, we will be careless and sluggish. However, if we are overstimulated (too nervous, for example) then we will be tense and distracted and will make mistakes. That's why opposing coaches call a time-out when a player is to shoot a free throw or kick a field goal. The attempt is to increase that player's arousal so as to decrease performance. Think about the Yerkes-Dodson law when you take tests. Your best performance is likely to result when you are stimulated some but not too much.

Of course, the optimum level of arousal, though in the middle, does vary from one task to another. In general, tasks that require creativity are performed better at a lower level of arousal than are tasks that require tedious repetition. You will probably need a higher level of arousal to add a table of numbers than to solve a crossword puzzle.

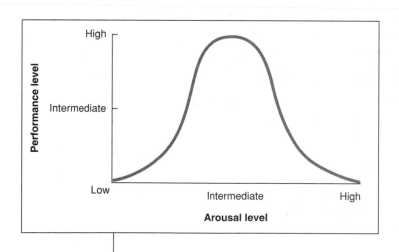

The Yerkes-Dodson law states that performance is best when motivation is medium, neither too high nor too low.

Answers from page 307

1. anger
2. fear
3. disgust
4. surprise
5. happy
6. sad

Recap

— Emotions can be divided into four components: affect, physiology, expression, and cognition.

— Emotions can be thought of as primary or secondary. The most commonly listed primary emotions are happiness, sadness, anger, fear, surprise, and disgust. Secondary emotions are a combination of these.

— The body reacts to emotions with physiological events such as the release of hormones. These events prepare the body for action in what is called the fight-or-flight response.

— Physiological responses to emotion, such as hormones, are helpful in the short run but can harm body organs in the long run. Stress is dangerous in the long run.

— The James-Lange theory says that we are aware of an emotion because of the physiological events that are happening in our bodies.

— The Cannon-Bard theory says that our brains both produce our emotional feeling and produce body changes at about the same time.

— The Schachter-Singer theory says that interpretation (cognition) is important in determining which emotion we feel.

— Social comparison theory says that our ideas about ourselves and how we feel and act are influenced by comparing ourselves with those around us.

— People are remarkably consistent in the facial expressions they make when experiencing a particular emotion. There are brain areas dedicated to this.

— Ideas of motivation include these concepts: instinct, intrinsic versus extrinsic, and homeostasis.

— Some motives, such as hunger, are based on survival. Others, such as status and achievement, are more social in nature.

— Motivation is almost always the result of an interaction between internal states and external conditions.

— The Yerkes-Dodson law states that behavior is best when arousal is at a medium level.

I Link, Therefore I Am

The Freud home page is at http://freudnet.tripod.com/ and the Freud archives are at http://users.rcn.com/brill/freudarc.html There are many other sites devoted to Freud including http://www.freudfile.org/ and http://freud.t0.or.at/ and http://www.mii.kurume-u.ac.jp/~leuers/Freud.htm

The B. F. Skinner Foundation home page is http://www.bfskinner.org/

Learn more about Maslow and his ideas at http://www.ship.edu/~cgboeree/maslow.html

The Association for Humanistic Psychology is at http://www.ahpweb.org/

Additional information about Carl Rogers can be found at http://www.oprf.com/Rogers

Information about Carl Jung can be found on many Web sites, including http://www.cgjungpage.org

For a description of Erikson's theory see http://snycorva.cortland.edu/~ANDERSMD/ERIK/

You can find some interesting data about temperament and personality at http://www.educ.drake.edu/doc/dissertations/TMPR/home.htm

STUDY GUIDE FOR CHAPTER 8: THEORIES

Key terms and names (Make flash cards.)

psychoanalytic theory
psychoanalysis
unconscious
hysteria
repression
manifest content
latent content
thanatos
eros
Freudian slip
resistance
defense mechanisms
rationalization
projection
sublimation
reaction formation
displacement
denial
regression
id
ego
superego
pleasure principle
reality principle
ego ideal
conscience

intrapsychic conflict
psychosexual stages
fixation
anal-retentive
anal-expulsive
castration anxiety
penis envy
Oedipus complex
Electra complex
identification with the
    aggressor
neo-Freudians
Carl Gustav Jung
analytic theory or
    analytical psychology
personal unconscious
collective unconscious
archetypes
Erik Erikson
psychosocial development
Eight Ages of Man
Karen Horney
Alfred Adler
individual psychology
creative self
striving for superiority

inferiority complex
superiority complex
John B. Watson
behaviorism
B. F. Skinner
social learning theories
observational learning
Albert Bandura
Humanism (humanistic
    psychology)
Abraham Maslow
existential philosophy
phenomenology
self-actualization
prepotent
pyramid of needs
Carl Rogers
self-concept
self theory
ideal self
real self
Rogerian
person-centered
client-centered
nondirective
incongruence

congruence
positive psychology
nature-nurture question
McArthur Longitudinal
    Twin Study
Minnesota Study of
    Twins Reared Apart
    (MISTRA)
temperament
affect
basic (primary) emotions
secondary emotions
fight-or-flight response
James-Lange theory
facial feedback hypothesis
Cannon-Bard theory
Schachter-Singer theory
social comparison theory
drive
instinct
intrinsic motivation
extrinsic motivation
incentive
homeostasis
arousal
Yerkes-Dodson law

Fill in the blank

1. The first of the modern personality theories was developed by _____ _____ and is known as _____ theory.

2. The cornerstone idea in psychoanalytic theory is the _____ mind.

3. When ideas and thoughts are pushed out of awareness and into the unconscious, it is called _____.

4. The things that are present and the events that happen in a dream are known as the _____ content of the dream, and the meanings of those dream elements are called the _____ content of the dream.

5. When a mistake is not a mistake, that is, when a mistake has meaning, it is called a _____ _____.

6. In psychoanalytic theory, when patients resist suggestions that probe the anxiety-producing contents of the unconscious, it is called _____.

7. Protective devices of the unconscious are known as _____ _____.

8. When the unconscious makes up a good-sounding reason to explain something we don't like, it is called _____.

9. Vincent van Gogh is often used as an example of the defense mechanism of _____.

10. Sometimes a person's mental and emotional energy is so threatening that the person adopts the reverse, the opposite, of what they really want. This is called

_____ _____.

11. Under conditions of severe trauma or stress, a person might revert to developmentally earlier forms of behavior and thinking. This is known as

_____.

12. Freud said that the id operates according to the

_____ principle.

13. The ego operates according to the _____ principle.

14. The _____ includes the moral ideas that a person has.

15. The struggle between the id and the superego is known as _____ _____.

16. If too much or too little satisfaction occurs during a childhood stage or if a traumatic event occurs during that stage, then _____ in a stage may occur.

17. The first stage in Freud's theory is the

_____ stage.

18. The following traits are known as _____: neatness, orderliness, punctuality, cleanliness, compulsive, perfectionism, and stinginess.

19. The unconscious process named after a Greek myth is called the _____

_____.

20. Carl Jung proposed an unconscious that we all share called the _____ unconscious.

21. The elements or content of the collective unconscious is known as _____.

22. The artificial, phony self that we show to others is called the _____.

23. A theory of psychosocial development was proposed by Erik _____.

24. Erikson's theory includes stages became known as the _____ Ages of _____.

25. The most complete psychoanalytic theory of women's personality development was proposed by

_____ _____.

26. Alfred _____ said that the primary motivation of humans was a striving for superiority.

27. John B. Watson initiated a revolution in thinking about psychology, creating a new school of thought called _____.

28. The behaviorists were like physicists attempting to uncover the fundamental natural laws of behavior, one experiment at a time while ignoring the mind altogether. Their leader was B. F. _____.

29. Skinner said that behavior at any given moment is a result of three things: _____, _____, and _____.

30. Behaviorism theory is also known as _____ _____ Theory.

31. When behaviors are learned via seeing or listening, this process is called _____ learning.

32. The Bobo-the-clown experiment was performed by Albert _____.

33. The third approach to personality was initiated by _____ _____ and is called _____.

34. Humanism's ideas are similar to those of _____ philosophy.

35. The focus on how a person perceives the world is called _____.

36. In humanistic psychology, there is no more important idea than _____ _____.

37. Maslow theorized a _____ of needs.

38. Carl Rogers developed an influential theory of personality centered on the idea of

_____ - _____.

39. Rogerian counseling is also known as _____.

40. For a hundred years or more, psychologists have debated and researched whether personality comes from _____ or _____.

41. Identical twins who are raised together have IQs that correlate about _____.

42. A major study of the effects of heredity is the Minnesota Study of _____

_____ _____.

43. Identical twins are more like one another than fraternal twins in two traits: _____ and

_____.

44. Temperament = _____ and mood or emotion = _____.

45. The four components of emotion are _____, _____, _____, and _____.

46. The body's reaction to a stressful situation is known as _____ or _____.

47. The _____ theory says that emotions are identified by the body's reaction.

48. The Cannon-Bard theory says that emotions and body reactions are both triggered by

_____.

49. Interpretation or cognition is important in the _____ theory.

50. Social comparison theory says that our behavior is often influenced by comparing ourselves with

_____.

51. Behavior that is driven by forces inside the person is called _____, and motivation arising from things in the environment is called _____.

52. The state of bodily equilibrium or balance is called

_____.

53. The _____ law says that behavior will be most efficient when arousal is at a _____ level.

Matching

1. Carl Jung _____
2. Karen Horney _____
3. B. F. Skinner _____
4. Oedipus complex _____
5. rationalization _____
6. Abraham Maslow _____
7. anal stage _____
8. homeostasis _____
9. repression _____
10. incentive _____
11. pleasure principle _____
12. superego _____
13. Cannon-Bard theory _____
14. reality principle _____
15. observational learning _____
16. self theory _____
17. Yerkes-Dodson law _____
18. identical twins _____
19. identity crisis _____
20. sublimation _____

a. push into unconscious
b. balance
c. id
d. second of Freud's stages
e. University of Minnesota study
f. feminist psychoanalytic theory
g. sounds logical
h. archetypes
i. conscience
j. extrinsic motivation
k. Vincent van Gogh
l. Carl Rogers
m. during phallic stage
n. brain is main factor
o. Erik Erikson
p. humanism
q. laws of behavior
r. arousal
s. ego
t. Bobo-the-clown

Multiple choice

1. Sheila's school counselor tells her to listen to her heart to decide what to do. Which personality theory does this advice remind one of?
   a. behaviorism
   b. humanism
   c. psychoanalytic
   d. social-learning
2. A new technique attempts to determine whether people are in love by measuring their eye movements. Which aspect of emotion is being studied?
   a. affect
   b. expression
   c. physiology
   d. cognition
3. At the movies, when the audience laughs at something on the screen, it makes me think that thing was funny. Which theory of emotion does this remind one of?
   a. James-Lange
   b. Cannon-Bard
   c. Schachter-Singer
   d. Yerkes-Dodson
4. Which theorist suggested the idea of a collective unconscious?
   a. Carl Rogers
   b. Carl Jung
   c. Karen Horney
   d. Erik Erikson
5. You are talking to a friend who is rocking back and forth, shifting her feet, and moving her arms. Your conclusion that she is bored is based on
   a. the Yerkes-Dodson law
   b. the power of incentives
   c. sublimation
   d. Maslow's hierarchy of needs

6. Suppose Freud and Skinner were talking about a person who washes his hands too much.
   a. Freud would mention the importance of the consequences of hand washing.
   b. Skinner would point out the unconscious mental suffering that must be causing this behavior.
   c. Freud would say the hand washing is just a symptom of some inner, unconscious problem.
   d. Skinner would be concerned about the person's inner mental state.
7. Your friend says that your generosity must be due to the praise and encouragement that you got from your parents. Which personality theory does this thinking best represent?
   a. psychoanalytic
   b. behaviorism
   c. humanism
   d. social comparison
8. Observational learning is part of the theory of
   a. humanistic psychology
   b. existentialism
   c. behaviorism
   d. psychoanalysis
9. The true meaning of a dream is called its
   a. latent content
   b. manifest content
   c. valid content
   d. thanatos content
10. The life instinct is called
    a. the id
    b. the superego
    c. eros
    d. sublimation

11. In which defense mechanism does a person "protest too much"?
    a. projection
    b. displacement
    c. reaction formation
    d. sublimation

12. If a person is nervous and curls up into a fetal position and starts to suck his or her thumb, this might be considered to be the defense mechanism of
    a. sublimation
    b. displacement
    c. regression
    d. reaction formation

13. Jehane failed her test and is blaming it on the fact that the teacher required too much reading and did not explain things very well, although these things are not really true. This is the defense mechanism called
    a. rationalization
    b. sublimation
    c. reaction formation
    d. displacement

14. A person who is very neat, clean, orderly, and obsessed with perfectionism might be said to be fixated in the _____ stage.
    a. Oedipal
    b. oral
    c. anal
    d. phallic

15. The Eight Ages of Man was theorized by
    a. Karen Horney
    b. Carl Rogers
    c. Erik Erikson
    d. Alfred Adler

16. A feminist psychoanalytic theory was suggested by
    a. Karen Horney
    b. Carl Rogers
    c. Anna Freud
    d. Alfred Adler

17. The most important element in the theory of Carl Rogers is the
    a. animus
    b. collective unconscious
    c. self-concept
    d. persona

18. For Alfred Adler, the most critical personality component is
    a. the archetypes
    b. the personal unconscious
    c. generativity
    d. striving for superiority

19. Erik Erikson suggested the identity crisis and a crisis in
    a. social conditions
    b. intrapsychic conflict
    c. self-actualization
    d. trust versus mistrust

20. A car's cruise control speeds up or slows down the car depending on road conditions. This is similar to the principle of
    a. homeostasis
    b. instincts
    c. the Yerkes-Dodson law
    d. observational learning

21. Your friend says that he didn't notice he was nervous during his exam until he saw his palms get sweaty. Which theory of emotions does this best exemplify?
    a. Schachter-Singer
    b. Cannon-Bard
    c. Yerkes-Dodson
    d. James-Lange

22. Which personality theory is based mostly on scientific research?
    a. psychoanalytic
    b. behaviorism
    c. humanism
    d. existentialism

23. Albert Bandura found that children _____ an adult who hit a Bobo-the-clown doll.
    a. criticized
    b. disliked
    c. wouldn't talk to
    d. imitated

24. Which theory says that the conscious mind is not a proper subject of scientific study?
    a. behaviorism
    b. humanism
    c. analytic psychology
    d. psychoanalytic

25. The founder of humanistic psychology was
    a. Albert Bandura
    b. B. F. Skinner
    c. Abraham Maslow
    d. Erik Erikson

26. Popeye says, "I am what I am." Which personality theory would Popeye probably like best?
    a. psychoanalytic
    b. behaviorism
    c. humanism
    d. social-learning

27. Phenomenology refers to
    a. the personal feelings and perspective of a person
    b. the archetypes manifested through behavior
    c. the scientific analysis of variables
    d. a personality crisis as seen by others

28. Existentialism is most closely related to which personality theory?
    a. psychoanalytic
    b. behaviorism
    c. humanism
    d. Personal psychology

29. At the top of the pyramid of needs is
    a. physiology
    b. self-esteem
    c. love
    d. self-actualization

30. The nature-nurture question asks how much of personality is influenced by
    a. heredity and environment
    b. unconscious mental processes
    c. memory and other cognitive processes
    d. internal biological functions

31. Identical twins raised together have IQ scores that correlate about
    a. +0.90
    b. +0.75
    c. +0.50
    d. −0.75

32. Studies have found that _____ is a highly inherited variable.
    a. desire for social closeness
    b. temperament
    c. striving for superiority
    d. being actively engaged in the environment

33. Alloys are complex metals that are combinations of elemental metals. This idea is similar to the idea of
    a. the id
    b. the Oedipus complex
    c. secondary emotions
    d. the MMPI

34. What was the point of Freud's analogy that the mind is like an iceberg?
    a. The mind is always melting and then refreezing as we change our opinions about things.
    b. You cannot know what's in someone's mind because it is so cold.
    c. The mind is cloudy, fuzzy, and difficult to see into, just like cloudy ice.
    d. Most of what controls us is below the surface, just as with a floating iceberg.
35. Which of these comparisons is most correct?
    a. Freud's approach is like a detective searching for clues.
    b. Maslow's approach is like a physicist studying and measuring variables.
    c. Jung's approach is like a good friend who listens carefully to you and does not make judgments.
    d. Skinner's approach is like a doctor doing an interview for a case study of an individual.
36. If a preschool boy begins to imitate his father, according to psychoanalytic theory
    a. there is a defect in his superego
    b. he is resolving the Oedipus complex
    c. his id has taken a prominent role in his life
    d. his intrapsychic conflict is entering his conscious mind

37. Your aunt believes that people are essentially good and that psychology should stress the worth of the normal individual. Which theory of personality would your aunt like best?
    a. Schachter-Singer
    b. psychoanalytic
    c. behaviorism
    d. humanism
38. Which of these most closely resembles the homeostatic concept?
    a. A refrigerator motor starts and stops to keep the inside temperature constant.
    b. A baseball pitcher throws pitches harder and harder throughout the game.
    c. A professor's voice tires as his lecture gets longer.
    d. A dog's tail wags very rapidly when she sees her owner approaching.

Short answer and critical thinking

1. Name two defense mechanisms, and give an example of each.
2. What is intrapsychic conflict?
3. What is the difference between the personal unconscious and the collective unconscious?
4. What is the meaning of Freud's iceberg metaphor?
5. Describe self-actualization with regard to the "ideal self" and the "real self."
6. Choose a personality trait or behavior and give a brief idea of how it would be viewed by (1) psychoanalytic theory, (2) behaviorism, and (3) humanism.

7. What is the nature-nurture question? Why does Steven Pinker call it "wrongheaded"?
8. Which personality theory appeals to you the most? Why? Which one do you think most accurately captures the truth about people? Why?
9. Name the four components of emotions, and give a general statement or example for each one.
10. Choose a motivation of some type, such as hunger or achievement, and describe some intrinsic and extrinsic variables that would influence it.

UNIT
5
DISORDERS

Now we turn to what many people believe psychology is all about: the study of psychological disorders and their treatments. What is mental illness, how are different disorders categorized, what are their symptoms and their causes, and how do psychologists help people who suffer from mental illnesses? This unit will explore in detail these questions and many more.

This unit includes two chapters:

Chapter 9 Psychological Disorders—a description of the wide range of mental illnesses as defined by psychologists and psychiatrists. This chapter includes detailed descriptions of schizophrenia, mood disorders, anxiety disorders, and many others. The causes of psychological disorders are also discussed.

Chapter 10 Therapies—a brief discussion of how mental illness has been viewed throughout history and therapies that were used in the past, along with a detailed list of the many therapies that are available today for treating psychological disorders. Medications, shock treatment, and talk therapies are described in detail, and a final section deals with community factors, such as hospitalization and legal issues.

Chapter
9

Psychological Disorders

PLAN AHEAD...

*   What is a mental illness? How are psychological disorders defined?
*   Who decides whether someone has a mental illness, and what are the different types of disorders?
*   What does *psychotic* mean? What is schizophrenia?
*   Is depression the most common mental illness? Why do people commit suicide? What are the statistics of suicide?
*   What are the main causes of psychological disorders?
*   Are there mental illnesses that are specific to certain cultures?

"Where does the violet tint end and the orange tint begin? Distinctly we see the difference of the colors, but where exactly does the one first blend into the other? So with sanity and insanity."
—HERMAN MELVILLE

Aғᴛᴇʀ I ʜᴀᴅ ɢɪᴠᴇɴ ᴀ ʟᴇᴄᴛᴜʀᴇ ᴏɴ IQ ᴛᴇsᴛɪɴɢ, ᴀ sᴛᴜᴅᴇɴᴛ approached me and angrily said, "I am sick and tired of you talking about me in class." I asked her what I had said that day, and she replied that I had told everyone about her dirty laundry. I suggested that she tell a school counselor about it. She looked at me warily and said, "I know you don't believe me and are trying to trick me into going to the counselor." A few days later, she was admitted to a mental hospital. What do you think about her?

Psychological disorders are commonly known as mental illnesses. The term **mental illness** was first popularized by mental health professionals in the 1950s for a very specific reason. One of the most intransigent problems we have in society is that people associate psychological disorders with shame and humiliation. On the other hand, most people do not associate *medical* illnesses with shame; rather, most people understand that a medical illness is caused by germs or injury and is not the fault of the sufferer. Therefore, mental health officials in the 1950s hoped that by calling psychological disorders *illnesses* the general public would stop blaming sufferers for their problems. They thought that it would reduce the embarrassment attached to psychological problems.

Hence the term *mental illness* was adopted in the hopes that the public would begin to think of psychological disorders the same way they thought about the flu, tuberculosis, a broken leg, asthma, hepatitis, or arthritis. In other words, it was hoped that the public would have more sympathy and concern for people with mental illnesses, that they would recognize psychological disorders as natural events with natural causes, and that sufferers would feel less shame and humiliation.

As you must already know, this strategy failed. Regrettably, there is still a stigma associated with mental illness. In addition, the public treats the issue of mental illness as a source of humor. This is most disconcerting because mental illnesses cause a good deal of suffering. Comedians no longer joke about cancer, but it is still common for them to make light of and poke fun at psychological problems. Needless to say, this is not helpful. Perhaps we can help to reduce the stigma associated with mental illness through education. The more we know about these problems, the less mysterious they will be, and perhaps the less comical and humiliating. You can help by learning about mental illnesses and spreading the word to others.

DEFINITIONS

"On the other hand, you have different fingers."
—Aɴᴏɴʏᴍᴏᴜs

Wʜat is a mental illness anyway? Is it really like a medical illness? Let's begin by defining what is included in the category we call *psychological disorders*. Perhaps you recall that earlier in this textbook, we defined psychology as the study of the ABCs: affect, behavior, and cognition. Therefore, psychological disorders are problems that people experience in their ABCs. Psychological disorders almost always include suffering, discomfort, or behavior that is significantly outside the typical human experience. A psychological disorder is a significant problem in affect, behavior, or cognition.

A, B, and C

By *affect*, we mean emotions or moods. Problems in this realm include phobias, nervousness and other anxiety disorders, depression and mania, and excessive or uncontrollable anger, jealousy, or other emotion. Such emotional problems are very common. Almost everyone has experienced a situation in which they were nervous, anxious, or worried to the point of being uncomfortable. Depression is also widely experienced. Besides being disorders themselves, problems in affect also occur in almost every other type of psychological disorder. Even when a person's main symptoms do not involve emotions, rarely is it true that the sufferer is not affected emotionally. Because affect is a crucial part of nearly every mental illness, sometimes the term *emotional disorder* is used as a synonym.

Problems in *behavior* include such things as excessive hand washing, exhibiting bizarre behaviors, the inability to interact socially in an appropriate way, alcohol and drug addictions, panic attacks (rapid heartbeat and breathing), ritualistic behaviors, uncontrollable impulses (such as shoplifting or starting fires), and hyperactivity. A significant difficulty is that observers often think that people with psychological disorders are capable of simply controlling their behaviors by concentrating, and they therefore conclude that the mentally ill can simply change their behaviors by trying after being told to do so. This, of course, is not at all the case. If one could change a behavior merely by concentrating, it would not be a mental illness. For example, a person who has a compulsion or an addiction might *want* to change but be unable to do so without psychotherapy or medical treatment of some sort. Everyone can think of certain behaviors that they have wanted to change but for some reason could not. Obviously, behaviors are not always under conscious control.

Cognition refers to brain information processing. Problems in cognition include complaints about memory, perception, and thinking—the kinds of difficulties that are seen in conditions such as Alzheimer's disease, schizophrenia, and mental retardation. Cognitive problems are often associated with brain diseases and injuries but are also common reactions to stressful situations. A person in shock might experience amnesia, for example. Memory difficulty is an especially common complaint in many psychological disorders and, as with problems in affect, might not be the main symptom, but an additional stress that a person with a psychological disorder suffers from.

Attitudes

The category of *psychological disorders* includes many different types of problems, and, of course, they have differing degrees of severity. A survey in 1990 asked people whether they had had any problems in their emotions, behavior, or thinking in the past year. An astonishingly high number—80%—said yes. A 2001 report by the World Health Organization found that other than infectious and parasitic diseases, which are extremely common in developing nations, neuropsychiatric disorders are the world's leading cause of disability. Depression is the most common cause of disability in the Americas and is projected to be the leading cause worldwide by 2020. More hospital beds are taken up by patients with psychological disorders than by those with non-ABC medical illnesses.

You can find estimates of the prevalence of various mental illnesses in the *Surgeon General's Report on Mental Illness*, which was published by the U.S. Department of Health and Human Services in 1999. The report includes these astonishing numbers:

During a 1-year period, 22 to 23 percent of the U.S. adult population have diagnosable mental disorders . . . about 28 to 30 percent of the population have either a mental or addictive disorder . . . 9 percent of all U.S. adults experience some significant functional impairment . . . a subpopulation of 5.4 percent of adults is considered to have a "serious" mental illness . . . about 20 percent of children are estimated to have mental disorders with at least mild functional impairment . . . 5 to 9 percent of children have serious emotional disturbance.

In the 1990 survey, individuals who reported that they had had problems in the past year were asked whether they had sought professional help for their problem. Quite a small number—only 20%—said yes. That means that 80% of the 80% who had problems did not seek help. They simply lived with their problems.

If we could reduce the shame that people feel about psychological problems, perhaps many more people would seek help. Also, many health insurance plans do not cover mental illnesses, and when they are covered, it is typically at a lower rate than for non-ABC medical illnesses. There is a very strange attitude in the United States: If something is wrong with your body, insurance will cover it. If something is wrong with your ABCs, that's your problem! In addition, a large number of people in the United States (particularly poor people) do not have *any* health insurance.

It is a major paradox that psychotherapies are quite successful at helping people with psychological problems, yet so many people do not seek them out. A 1995 study by the Consumers Union found that a high percentage of people who went for professional psychotherapy were very satisfied with the results. It's funny that word doesn't get out that psychotherapy can often be successful. Perhaps it's the shame thing again—people don't want to talk about their mental problems because they feel humiliated or embarrassed by them.

Subjectivity

Psychological disorders are hard to define because it is hard to say what is or is not a problem in the ABCs. Everyone has problems. Which types of problems are disorders, and which are not? How severe does a problem have to be before we call it a psychological disorder? There is no way to answer these questions objectively. The concept is a subjective one. Typically, it is up to the person to decide when his or her problem has reached the level of being bothersome or uncomfortable enough to be a psychological disorder. However, sometimes parents, spouses, relatives, or friends make the judgment that someone's problems have reached that critical point. When a problem in emotion, behavior, or cognition becomes so severe that it interferes with normal daily functioning, then a person may be said to have a psychological disorder. This is a subjective judgment. Which problems are mental illnesses and which are not is a matter of opinion.

For example, before 1973, homosexuality was considered a mental illness, but it is not today. In the 1950s, alcoholism was *not* called a mental illness; it was viewed simply as immoral behavior, and alcoholics could be thrown into jail. Today, of course, alcoholism is treated as an addictive behavior, and sufferers are treated with various therapies. Today, depression is considered a mental illness, but boredom is not. Washing your hands excessively is a mental illness, but compulsively overeating or driving too fast is not.

Just because mental illness is a subjective judgment does not mean that problems do not exist. Think about the taste of food. This is a subjective concept—what tastes good to one person does not to another. That doesn't mean that taste doesn't really exist.

Warnings

There is no clear dividing line between normal and abnormal. Most often, psychological disorders represent extremes of normal conditions rather than something entirely different. A person with a psychological disorder typically does not do anything differently than anyone else. Rather, people with mental illnesses have behaviors, emotions, and thoughts that either are inappropriate for the situation they are in or are different in quantity rather than quality. Because the concept is a subjective one, it is impossible to define clear criteria for what is normal and what is abnormal. In practice, abnormality is defined by psychiatrists, and everything that is not called "abnormal" is therefore "normal." Three criteria that are commonly used to define a psychological disorder are (1) statistically rare, (2) maladaptive, and (3) self-distressing. However, even these criteria are often subjective, and *normal* and *abnormal* can overlap a good deal.

Because there is no clear dividing line between normal and abnormal, you are likely to see yourself described many times as you study psychological disorders. Watch out for **medical school syndrome.** This is the tendency for people to imagine that they have the disorders that they are studying. Do not become an amateur psychiatrist and start diagnosing yourself or others. Remember the subjectivity of this field and the fact that psychological disorders are best thought of as complaints in the ABCs that a person has rather than as conditions that are imposed on people from the outside.

One more important warning: Do not mistake descriptions of disorders for explanations of their causes. It is one thing to describe a condition and to give it a label; it is quite another thing to explain how the condition came about. A common mistake is to conclude that the name of a disorder explains the condition. For example, we might ask a psychiatrist why a man is acting oddly. The psychiatrist might say it's because the man has schizophrenia. "How do you know he has schizophrenia?" we ask. The psychiatrist answers, "Well, look at how oddly he is acting." See the problem? It's a circle. We notice symptoms and give them a label. Then we use that label to explain why the symptoms exist. Watch out for this fallacious reasoning. Labeling a syndrome (a set of symptoms) "schizophrenia" does not explain why that syndrome occurs.

THINK TANK

Give examples from literature, TV, or movies of how mental illness is stereotyped or presented in an inaccurate way.

What are the most common attitudes about mental illness that are portrayed by the media?

What are the most common attitudes held by your family and friends?

THE DSM

"O, let me not be mad, not mad, sweet heaven."
—WILLIAM SHAKESPEARE

What is and what is not a mental illness (or what should or should not be called a mental illness) is a matter of opinion. However, the opinion that matters most comes from the **American Psychiatric Association.** Psychiatrists, who are medical doctors, with advice from psychologists and other mental health workers, prepare a book that lists the official mental illnesses. The **Diagnostic and Statistical Manual of Mental Disorders**

is known simply as the **DSM.** This book includes the definitions of mental illnesses that are important for medical, social, and legal purposes. If your symptoms are described in this book, then you are legally mentally ill. If not, then you are "normal." Weird but true.

The DSM has a number of problems that most psychologists and psychiatrists are aware of. First, it is based on a disease or medical model rather than on behavior or normalcy. Also, disorders are typically not categorized by their causes, since the causes are not known, but by symptoms. Third, there is sex bias in the DSM, which influences not only diagnosis, but also research and therefore our understanding of psychological problems. For instance, most studies of attention deficit disorder use only boys or a large majority of boys as participants, men are in the majority of 73% of studies on substance abuse, 75% of studies of schizophrenia use more men than women, and the DSM field studies of the body disorder known as somatization included only women (Widiger, 2002). Despite these concerns, the DSM is widely used around the world to diagnose psychological disorders; therefore, we will use it as our base in this chapter.

The Concept of Syndromes

The DSM was first published in 1952 and is now in the fourth edition. Hence, the current version is called **DSM-IV.** This is the official list of mental illnesses that is used around the world for classifying and diagnosing psychological disorders; over 1800 are listed! You can find a copy of this important book in any library. Just ask for the DSM-IV.

The purpose of the DSM is to make the definitions and diagnoses of mental illnesses standard around the world so that we will have consistency. However, psychiatrists are constantly changing what is and what is not included in the DSM and are regularly changing the criteria for mental illnesses. DSM-IV was published in 1994 and is due for a revision. DSM-V is currently being prepared and will likely be published in 2010. It will include some modifications in what are now considered to be mental illnesses.

The DSM classifies mental illnesses using a model based on the concept of **syndromes.** This is a medical idea. A syndrome is a group or cluster of symptoms (complaints) that are associated with a disorder. Typically, in the DSM, a disorder is defined by the presence of certain symptoms that tend to cluster together. For example, one disorder is called **major depression.** To be classified with this disorder, a person must have five or more of a list of nine symptoms for a period of two weeks or longer. The nine symptoms are (1) low mood, (2) loss of interest or pleasure in things (must have at least one of those first two), (3) change in appetite, (4) change in sleep patterns, (5) agitation or retardation in movement, (6) loss of energy, (7) feelings of guilt or worthlessness, (8) problems concentrating, and (9) thoughts of suicide. A person who is diagnosed with major depression does not necessarily have all of these symptoms; but

Connecting Concepts

Recall the personality approaches discussed in Chapter 7: type, trait, and behavior. The DSM uses a type approach. That is, in psychiatric diagnosis, people are placed into groups or categories based on some criteria in which they are similar. There are many drawbacks to a type system. What if psychiatry used a trait approach or classified disorders on the basis of behaviors in situations?

Recap

— Mental illness is a problem in the ABCs: affect, behavior, or cognition. Although disorders are very common, many people are ashamed of them and do not seek therapy.

— Mental illness is a subjective concept; what is called a mental illness changes from time to time and depends on circumstances.

— The official definition of psychological disorders is determined by psychiatrists and contained in the DSM.

— The DSM uses the concept of syndromes (groups of symptoms), just as is done with non-ABC illnesses.

he or she must have five or more of them (including one of the first two). Therefore, two people diagnosed with major depression could have quite different symptoms from each other, but each will have at least five of the nine. This is an example of the syndrome concept that is used by the DSM for diagnosing most psychological disorders.

Next we will discuss in detail a few of the most common and serious psychological disorders. There are five groups that will be included here.

TABLE 9.1   Psychological Disorders

Disorder	Prominent Symptoms	Incidence
1. Schizophrenia	Hallucinations, delusions, bizarre thinking, and often problems in perception, cognition, and movement	A very serious disorder that occurs about equally in men and women, mostly in young adulthood, about 1%
2. Mood disorders	Severe depression (unipolar) or mania (bipolar) with problems in eating, sleeping, and thinking	Very common, perhaps as many as 25% lifetime incidence; more women than men, seen throughout adulthood
3. Anxiety disorders	Nervousness, fear, obsessions, compulsions, or panic attacks	Perhaps the most common of all disorders; seen in all ages
4. Somatoform disorders	Body complaints without organic cause	Less common; more women than men
5. Dissociative disorders	Problems in consciousness, memory, or identity, such as amnesia for personal information	Rare; often the result of traumatic childhood experiences or extreme stress

SCHIZOPHRENIA

"Everyone is kneaded out of the same dough, but not

baked in the same oven."
—YIDDISH PROVERB

Perhaps the most serious and mysterious of the mental illnesses is schizophrenia. This is a vastly misunderstood disorder that presents major challenges to mental health professionals and to the families of its sufferers, and of course, to the individuals with this enigmatic disease. Psychotherapist **Fritz Perls,** the developer of Gestalt therapy, quipped that "Neurotics build dream castles in the sky, psychotics live in them, and psychiatrists collect the rent." **Psychotic disorders** are severe problems in which a person experiences perceptions and thoughts that are not real, that are out of touch with reality. Schizophrenia is the most common of the psychotic disorders. Contrary to the popular view, schizophrenia is not multiple personality. Multiple personality is now referred to as dissociative identity disorder (discussed later in the chapter), and its sufferers have varying personal identities. Schizophrenia, by contrast, is a severe brain disorder in which a person loses touch with reality and lives in a mental world full of confusion and delusions but is aware of his or her identity.

The vast majority of people with schizophrenia can lead happy and productive lives; some even fully recover from their illness. Most, however, need to take medications for long periods, even for a lifetime. Schizophrenia has been studied for nearly one hundred years, and scientists still do not have a definitive understanding of it. Before I describe this puzzling disorder, it is best to begin by saying what it is not—to dispel some myths about it.

Misconceptions

A common misconception is that **schizophrenia** is the same as split personality. The confusion comes from the literal meaning of the term (*schiz* means "split," and *phrenia* means "mind"). The word was coined in 1910 by **Eugen Bleuler,** a psychiatrist who later said he wished he hadn't invented the term because of the confusion it caused. His idea was that a person with schizophrenia has a separation between different components of the mind, such as emotion and behavior, not that the personality is split. Also, it is helpful to think of schizophrenia as a separation between a person's mind and reality rather than a split in identity. People with schizophrenia do *not* have a split personality.

A second misconception is that people with schizophrenia are mentally retarded. This idea probably arises because of the bizarre behaviors and odd things that are sometimes said by people with schizophrenia. However, there is no correlation between intelligence and schizophrenia. Sufferers of this disorder can have any level of intelligence, though many individuals with schizophrenia find it difficult to succeed in school because they can't concentrate and because they experience high levels of stress. Still, people with schizophrenia often have normal or high IQs. As an example, the book and film *A Beautiful Mind* relate the story of the brilliant mathematician John Nash, who has schizophrenia.

Another problem is that we often label people as if their diseases fully describe everything about them. A person with any illness is first and foremost a person. He or she has values, interests, needs, desires, abilities, longings, and so on. We should probably avoid terminology that makes us forget this. We should probably not name people after their illnesses. Let's try to avoid terms like alcoholic, diabetic, or schizophrenic. Otherwise, the next time you have a cold I'll call you a "coldic."

A final misconception is the belief that people with schizophrenia are dangerous. Although it is true that some people with schizophrenia are dangerous and do commit violent acts, the vast majority do not. Most sufferers of schizophrenia are meek, scared, and socially withdrawn. They are likely to stay away from other people. Individuals who are diagnosed with mental illnesses sometimes commit violent acts but in general have a *lower* rate of violence than do people who are not diagnosed as mentally ill.

> **FYI**
>
> Because of the stigma and misconceptions associated with the term *schizophrenia*, the Japanese Society of Psychiatry and Neurology voted at its 2002 meeting to change the name to *integration disorder*.

Describing Schizophrenia

It is difficult to describe schizophrenia with much precision because this illness is manifested in different ways by its sufferers. There are many symptoms that are typical, but no two people with schizophrenia suffer exactly the same ones. Remember the idea of a syndrome—a group of symptoms. In schizophrenia, there are problems in a wide range of psychological characteristics. These problems are not short-term difficulties. Schizophrenia is a long-term illness in which people must deal with dysfunctional affect, behavior, and cognition—in most cases, for all their lives. Schizophrenia is a severe disorder of thinking, perception, language, and movement.

The most common symptoms of schizophrenia are hallucinations and delusions. These are indications of **psychosis,** signs that a person is out of touch with reality.

A **hallucination** is a false perception. A person might see, hear, taste, smell, or feel something that is not there. A hallucination seems like reality to the person who is experiencing it. The most commonly reported hallucinations involve hearing voices talking to the person, often saying things that are horrible. A person with schizophrenia might hear his father, the president of the United States, or God telling him that he is a horrible person who needs to kill himself. Schizophrenia is not the fun or comical disease that is often depicted in Hollywood movies. Of course, the hallucinations are being produced by the sufferers' own brains. But people with schizophrenia are unable to tell that the voices they hear or the things they see are not real.

Delusions are false beliefs that are held despite clear evidence to the contrary. A person with schizophrenia might believe that he is Jesus, that he has a computer in his brain that can receive other people's thoughts, that he is dead, that he is being chased by aliens attempting to get his mathematical secrets, and so on. These ideas might seem wild or silly to us but are achingly real to the person with schizophrenia. No amount of logic or evidence to the contrary can shake these beliefs—that is the ultimate criterion of a delusion. A delusion is extreme and persistent. Here are some different types of delusions that are seen in schizophrenia.

TABLE 9.2   Types of Delusions

Type of Delusion	Description
1. Persecution	Others are trying to harm me.
2. Reference	Things that people do are aimed at me.
3. Control	My thoughts, feelings, and behaviors are being controlled by some external force.
4. Grandiosity	I have great powers, knowledge, or talent; or I am a famous person.
5. Thought broadcasting	Others can hear my thoughts.
6. Thought insertion	Others are putting thoughts into my mind.
7. Thought withdrawal	Others are removing thoughts from my mind.

FYI

People who claim to have been abducted by aliens might be lying or suffering from schizophrenia, but it is more likely that they have a sleep disorder called sleep paralysis, in which they awaken from deep sleep only partially conscious and can't move. Their sensations often are mistaken as alien encounters.

People with schizophrenia also have other symptoms. Cognitive problems are common, for instance. The person's perceptions, memory, intellectual abilities, and reasoning are often disturbed. Also in schizophrenia, language is often used in odd ways. A person with schizophrenia might have a **loosening of associations** (or **derailment**) in which he makes odd connections between ideas—connections that do not make sense to us. Many years ago, after I told a person with schizophrenia that I lived alone, he put a birdhouse in my backyard. He later explained in a very complicated way that the birdhouse has a very steep roof in the shape of the letter "A," the letter that begins the word "alone," the word that had stuck in his mind. This is an example of loosening of associations. Sometimes sufferers will talk in rhymes (**clanging**) or will make up words (**neologisms**). Often it is difficult to make sense of what people with schizophrenia are talking about, but at other times, they are lucid and normal in their conversations. The sum of problems involving disorganized thinking is often called **formal thought disorder.**

For many years, schizophrenia has been defined by its psychotic symptoms: hallucinations and delusions. But modern researchers are now focusing more on the cognitive impairments of this disease. Many studies are finding that problems with memory, thinking, making judgments, and processing information are at the heart of the difficulties that people with schizophrenia experience. Brain imaging studies have begun to pinpoint the abnormalities in cognition that occur in schizophrenia, and perhaps new therapies and new theories aren't far behind. Kim and colleagues (2003), for instance, found a disconnection between the frontal and parietal lobes in patients with schizophrenia, suggesting a biological cause for the cognitive problems, particularly working memory.

Some people with schizophrenia have symptoms that involve body movements. Sometimes a sufferer will stand perfectly still for hours and then suddenly will run wildly through the hospital hallways. This is called **catatonia.** In such cases, there is nothing wrong with the person's muscle system. The problem arises from the patient's disturbed thinking and perceptions.

The symptoms of schizophrenia are seen in different combinations and in different degrees of severity from one patient to another. The symptoms are divided into two categories: **Positive symptoms** are things such as hallucinations and delusions—symptoms that we want to reduce. Medications often help keep positive symptoms down. **Negative symptoms** are things that the patient does not do often enough—things that we want to increase. The most common negative symptom of schizophrenia is **social withdrawal.** The vast majority of patients with schizophrenia stay away from other people and keep to themselves. They seem to live in a world more of their own imaginations and thoughts than of reality. **Poverty of speech** means that people with schizophrenia are very quiet and, when they do speak, are not expressive or descriptive in their choice of words. Another negative symptom is **flat or blunted affect.** People with schizophrenia often do not respond emotionally as much as they should. Often, their emotional reactions are stunted, showing less than normal emotional response to stimuli. Their faces are sometimes masklike, with flat expressions, showing no emotion. Patients with schizophrenia who experience mostly negative symptoms are said to have **deficit schizophrenia.** Negative symptoms often do not respond to medications, but behavioral and cognitive therapies have had some success in treating them. Some recent research has shown that the newer atypical medicines (see Chapter 10) provide some help with negative symptoms.

As mentioned above, schizophrenia to a large extent involves disturbances in cognition. Perception, attention, thinking (formal thought disorder), language, and memory difficulties are common in patients with schizophrenia. An analysis of 54 factors of schizophrenia (Heinrichs, 2001) found more evidence for defective cognition than for defective biology. On the average, men experience cognitive problems more often and more seriously than do women (Goldstein et al., 1998).

TABLE 9.3 Symptoms of Schizophrenia

Positive Symptoms	Negative Symptoms
1. Hallucinations (false perceptions)	1. Social withdrawal
2. Delusions (false beliefs)	2. Poverty of speech
3. Cognitive problems (thinking, memory, and perception)	3. Flat or blunted affect
4. Bizarre thoughts and behaviors	
5. Loosening of associations	
6. Language problems, such as clanging and neologisms	

Subtypes

When people are diagnosed with schizophrenia, they are categorized into a subtype based on the dominant symptoms that they have. The DSM includes three major subtypes or categories of schizophrenia plus a miscellaneous category and a category for those people who are improving and exhibit only some of the symptoms they previously experienced. The total, then, is five.

Paranoid Type

The primary symptom of **paranoid schizophrenia** is **delusions of persecution.** The person irrationally believes that others are trying to harm him or her. The person might believe that aliens or some unsubstantiated thing is trying to harm him or her. Occasionally, the person believes that others are out to harm him or her because of some great power or knowledge that the person possesses. The person might believe that he or she knows the mathematical secrets of the universe, for example, and therefore certain people are trying to steal them, or some such thing. This is known as a **delusion of grandiosity.** Hallucinations are also common and often involve the delusional theme. This is the most common subtype diagnosis for people when they are first diagnosed with schizophrenia, probably because hallucinations and delusions are the most prominent features of this mental illness and are most likely to be noticed and emphasized on first hospitalization.

Disorganized Type

The person with **disorganized type** schizophrenia shows very disorganized speech and behavior. His or her behavior might be very juvenile and accompanied by silliness and excessive laughter. For that reason, this subtype was previously known as **hebephrenia,** a term that literally refers to a "childlike mind." There might be such severe disorganization of behavior that the person is unable to function independently, experiencing disruption of normal daily activities. This patient often exhibits grimacing, unusual mannerisms, strange and childish speech, and bizarre behaviors. This subtype often is diagnosed earlier than the others, and the **prognosis** (the expected course and outcome) is often worse.

Catatonic Type

The essential features in **catatonic type** schizophrenia include motor immobility, sometimes excessive motor activity, extreme negativism, mutism (doesn't talk), or peculiarities of voluntary movement. Often, this patient holds his or her body in a stiff, immovable position for hours at a time. The person seems to be in a trance, although after recovery, the catatonic patient often recalls events that transpired during his or her catatonia. Bizarre postures and grimacing are common. **Echolalia,** or parrotlike speech, is also a symptom of this subtype of schizophrenia. Sometimes the person's body can be repositioned, as if he or she was made of wax—a condition known as **waxy flexibility.**

Undifferentiated Type

The diagnosis of **undifferentiated type** schizophrenia is used for individuals who do not meet the qualifications for any of the above three subtypes yet do meet the criteria for schizophrenia. In other words, these individuals have a mix of the above symptoms or some other prominent symptoms that do not neatly fall into the three main subtypes. Undifferentiated is a miscellaneous or "other" category. In fact, this is a common diagnosis.

Residual Type

The designation of **residual type** schizophrenia is suitable for individuals with a prior episode of schizophrenia who are currently not experiencing any severe positive symptoms. The person still experiences negative symptoms, however, such as flat affect, poverty of speech, and social withdrawal. In other words, this classification is for people who are getting better but still have some residue of their illness.

TABLE 9.4   Subtypes of Schizophrenia

Subtype	Primary Symptoms
1. Paranoid	Delusions of persecution or grandiosity
2. Disorganized	Silly, bizarre behaviors, giggling, disorganized speech
3. Catatonic	Stiff, frozen motor behavior sometimes with excessive motor activity, mutism, or waxy flexibility
4. Undifferentiated	A mix of the above
5. Residual	Improvement with a few symptoms remaining

Statistics

Schizophrenia, unfortunately, is fairly common. Schizophrenia occurs at a rate of about 1% (the **lifetime incidence**). In other words, in one's lifetime, the odds of being diagnosed with schizophrenia are about 1%. About one in a hundred people will be diagnosed with this serious disorder in their lifetime.

The rate of schizophrenia varies in different places in the world, just as with any illness. For example, schizophrenia is more common in Ireland and Eastern Europe and less common in Africa and Asia. The rate of schizophrenia is about average in the United States, about 1%.

Most surveys find that schizophrenia occurs about equally in men and women, although some studies indicate that men get the disease earlier and have more severe symptoms than do women, and a recent meta-analysis found that men did have a higher rate in some countries in recent years (Aleman et al., 2003). Overall, this is not a disorder that shows significant gender differences, as do depression, eating disorders, and alcoholism. Gender differences appear in disorders that are linked to hormone differences, the sex chromosomes, or cultural factors that affect males and females differently.

Schizophrenia shows a very distinct pattern regarding age of onset. It is rarely first diagnosed in children or in adults beyond middle age. Schizophrenia typically begins when people are in adolescence or young adulthood. A common pattern is for a person to start showing odd symptoms, such as social withdrawal, during the teen years and then for the disorder to get progressively worse for many years. By middle adulthood, many sufferers have improved, and some are even free of symptoms.

About 25% of people with schizophrenia are free of symptoms 10 years after first diagnosis. Another 25% are much improved and can live independently. About 10% commit suicide because of the horrors of their illness. The rest are either mildly improved or reside in institutions, where they remain unimproved. About 15% are known as *very poor outcome* or **Kraepelinian.** (Kraepelin was a nineteenth-century psychiatrist who wrote the first important classification of mental disorders.) Such patients do not improve. In general, then, schizophrenia is not a progressive degenerative disorder in which patients get worse and worse (Goldstein et al., 1998).

One of the tragedies of the mental health system in the United States is that there are very few places that come between independent living and institutions. Some people with schizophrenia who need care find help from their relatives. Others live in institutions. But an amazing and depressingly large number of people with schizophrenia live on the streets. Cities with warm climates especially have large numbers of mentally ill homeless people. This is more than just an embarrassment to our society; it is a human tragedy. Who can be proud of the mental health system we have created?

Schizophrenia, like most serious illnesses, is linked to social class. People in lower social classes are much more likely to be diagnosed with schizophrenia. Part of this is probably due to the subjective nature of diagnosis—an upper-class person might be called "eccentric," while a poor person with the same symptoms is more likely to be labeled mentally ill. Also, people with schizophrenia often migrate down the social classes because of their difficulties in being successful in society. Finally, the conditions of lower-class living are more stressful and more likely to precipitate illnesses of all kinds. Poor medical care, limited education, poor living conditions, crowding—all of these contribute to illness.

THINK TANK

Many people with schizophrenia live on the streets and don't take their medicine.

Should laws be changed to force people to take medicine?

Wouldn't this be a violation of constitutional rights and a law that could be misused?

To what extent should society force people to get help?

Stages of Schizophrenia

Each person with schizophrenia is unique and likely has an idiosyncratic progression of the disorder. However, there is a simple pattern of development that is common in schizophrenia. Psychiatrists identify three stages as follows: **Prodromal** is a term that refers to the early signs of an illness. In schizophrenia, this typically occurs in adolescence or young adulthood and might last many months or even years. The first signs are things that might be perceived as someone merely "going through a stage" such as social withdrawal, odd behaviors, diminished affect, lack of motivation, peculiar speech, and retreat into a world of imagination. There is encouraging evidence that help during the prodrome can delay or reduce symptoms (Patterson, 2003).

The **active phase** is the term used when a person with schizophrenia begins to exhibit severe positive symptoms such as hallucinations and delusions. Speech is often incoherent or odd, social withdrawal is extreme, auditory hallucinations are common, and the person shows disorganized and unpredictable behavior. The active phase is when most people are diagnosed with schizophrenia, since the symptoms are too severe to ignore. This stage may last for many years.

The final stage of schizophrenia is known as the **residual phase.** Gradually, over many years' time, most people with schizophrenia find that their symptoms begin to ease and their life improves somewhat. In fact, as was mentioned above, more than half of people with schizophrenia will eventually be either free of symptoms or very much improved. Some, of course, chronically suffer the symptoms of this tragic disorder.

Causes of Schizophrenia

Researchers have studied schizophrenia for nearly one hundred years and still have not identified the specific cause or causes of this disorder. That should tell us something—and not that researchers don't know what they're doing! What it tells us is that this disorder is very complicated. Schizophrenia may, in fact, be a number of similar, overlapping disorders with multiple, interacting causes. In fact, a recent study of memory deficits in schizophrenia found at least three categories of patients (Turetsky et al., 2002).

One consistent finding is that heredity is a contributing factor in schizophrenia. Many studies of twins, families, and adopted children have shown a link between genetic relatedness and the incidence of schizophrenia. That is, the higher the genetic relatedness to a person with schizophrenia, the greater is the risk of schizophrenia. However, the genetic factor is not 100%. Identical twins, who have the same heredity, do not necessarily concur in having schizophrenia. The **concordance rate** for identical twins is about 50%. If one identical twin has schizophrenia, the other has the disorder half the time. The same rate applies when both parents have schizophrenia: Each child has a 50% risk. Adopted children show the same pattern: If their biological parents have schizophrenia, half of them will also have the disorder. Specific genes that contribute to schizophrenia have not been definitively identified, but several have been targeted as candidates, notably genes on chromosomes 1, 6, 8, and 22 (Sawa & Schneider, 2002). Remember, schizophrenia is a complex disorder that likely has numerous contributing causes.

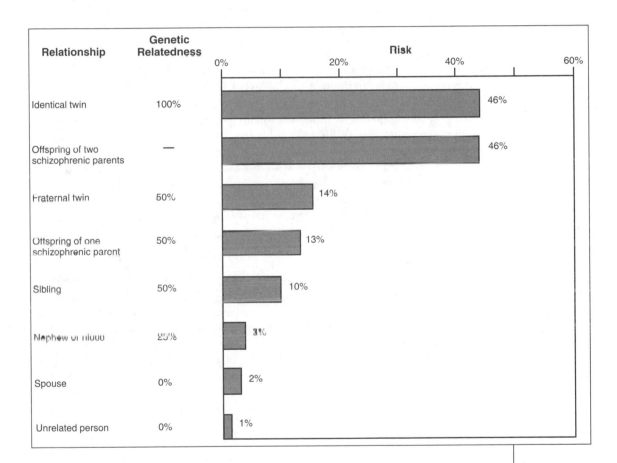

Relationship	Genetic Relatedness	Risk
Identical twin	100%	46%
Offspring of two schizophrenic parents	—	46%
Fraternal twin	50%	14%
Offspring of one schizophrenic parent	50%	13%
Sibling	50%	10%
Nephew or niece	25%	3%
Spouse	0%	2%
Unrelated person	0%	1%

The specific biological effect of genes in schizophrenia is not known. Still, many studies have found abnormalities in the brain's prefrontal lobes in patients and in their siblings (Callicott et al., 2003; Kim et al., 2003). These and similar findings support the new view that schizophrenia is mainly a cognitive disorder; they might also one day lead to the identification of biological risk factors for this disease.

Recent research (Malaspina, 2001) has found a link between the risk of a child's developing schizophrenia and the father's age. Men in their fifties or older have three times the risk of fathering a child with this disorder. As men age, their sperm cells go through repeated divisions. Each division is another opportunity for genetic mutations to occur. Of course, most elder men who have children have perfectly normal ones. But the risk does increase, showing the influence of genetics on schizophrenia.

Heredity is one contributing factor to schizophrenia but is not the only influence.

Connecting Concepts

Recall the discussion in Chapter 3 regarding heredity. Don't think of nature and nurture as two separate things; rather, think of them as existing on an interacting continuum. Environmental experiences conspire with genetic factors to give us the characteristics—and the disorders—that we have.

In the past, psychologists theorized that schizophrenia might be caused or influenced by the kind of parenting a child received. But there is no scientific evidence that parenting styles or child-rearing techniques contribute to the onset of schizophrenia. However, a stressful environment does make a person's symptoms worse. Therefore, a family situation with lots of criticism will often exacerbate the problems of a person with schizophrenia. Researchers call this family variable **emotional expression (EE)**. Families with high EE use lots of criticism and threats, a circumstance that causes schizophrenia symptoms to be more visible and more severe. People with schizophrenia living with family members who demonstrate high EE will have more severe symptoms and higher relapse rates. So although the family environment does not appear to be a causative factor in schizophrenia, it may contribute to the manifestation of symptoms because of the stress it produces.

Another factor that does not cause schizophrenia but can bring out its symptoms is the use of drugs. People often mistakenly conclude that their child developed schizophrenia from taking illegal drugs because that's when they first noticed the symptoms. Schizophrenia is not caused by using marijuana, cocaine, or any other illegal drug. However, such drugs often do precipitate symptoms. Amphetamines (stimulants) in particular can worsen the symptoms of schizophrenia, and patients should avoid these drugs.

It is common today to think of schizophrenia as a classic example of the **diathesis-stress theory.** This idea states that a disorder comes about through a combination of a genetic potential (a diathesis) and something in the person's experience (stress). It is as if certain people are genetically susceptible to schizophrenia but do not develop the disorder unless they experience certain stressful events. Just what these experiences are is unknown. One likely candidate is a virus. For example, some research has found that women who have the flu, herpes virus, or other infections during their pregnancies have babies who later are diagnosed with schizophrenia at a higher-than-average rate. Also, statistically, there is a slight increase in the number of people with schizophrenia who were born during the winter months, when viruses are more prevalent. Some researchers today are investigating the notion that schizophrenia may be, at least in part, a viral disorder.

Brain-imaging research has identified a number of abnormalities that occur in schizophrenia, although there is no universal marker, as in Alzheimer's disease, for instance. In schizophrenia, abnormalities have been found in the thalamus and other areas of the limbic system (Ettinger, 2001), the frontal lobe (Buchanan et al., 1998), the temporal lobe (Hirayasu et al., 1998), and the cerebellum (Tran et al., 1998). Schizophrenia is either a brain disease that is global, affecting many areas, or a number of diseases with overlapping symptoms. One study found underdeveloped olfactory bulbs in the brains of patients with schizophrenia, perhaps explaining why many such patients report smelling odd odors or have difficulty differentiating odors. Relatives of people with schizophrenia were also found to have abnormalities in their olfactory bulbs, probably implicating heredity as a contributing factor (Turetsky et al., 2003).

The most common finding is that the **ventricles** of the brain, the hollow cavities through which spinal fluid moves, are larger in the brains of people with schizophrenia. This means that the brain itself must be smaller. In fact, the brain cells themselves are reduced in size, and the volume of the brain decreases with age in people with schizophrenia. Also, the prefrontal cortex is smaller in patients with schizophrenia. Because the prefrontal cortex is so important in organizing complex cognitions and behaviors (Goldman-Rakic, 1987), it is not surprising that people with schizophrenia have such an assortment of problems.

Research using PET scan and fMRI shows that the brain of a person with schizophrenia processes information differently than the average brain. For example, one study found deficits in the functioning of the left prefrontal cortex (Russell, 2000). In fact, most patients with schizophrenia have cognitive impairments, or odd ways of thinking, perceiving, and remembering. During auditory hallucinations, for example, brain scans

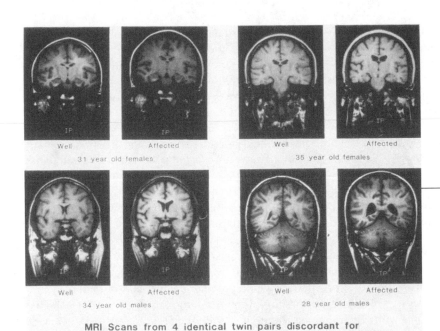

The brain's ventricles are sometimes enlarged in cases of schizophrenia, indicating that the brain volume has decreased.

MRI Scans from 4 identical twin pairs discordant for schizophrenia showing varying degrees of increased ventricular dilatation in the affected twin compared to the well twin.

show activity in the speech areas of patients' brains, indicating, of course, that the voices are coming from their own brains. Formal thought disorder, one of the core symptoms of schizophrenia, is associated with decreased activity in Wernicke's area of the brain, the region that is responsible for interpreting the meaning of language (Kircher, 2001).

Another idea about schizophrenia that has long been held by scientists is called the **dopamine hypothesis.** Many studies have indicated an abnormality in the activity of the brain chemical dopamine in people with schizophrenia. The most consistent finding is that the person's brain appears to have an increased number of dopamine receptors (the chemical receivers of dopamine that sit on the dendrites of brain cells). There are many different dopamine receptors in the brain, and the ones that appear to be involved in schizophrenia are known as D_2 and D_3 receptors. It is not possible to count the number of dopamine receptors in the brain of a living person. However, scientists recently suggested that a blood test could identify the amount of RNA molecules that convey the genetic message for making dopamine receptors in white blood cells (Fuchs & Ilani, 2001). In fact, these researchers found that people with schizophrenia had three times more RNA molecules in their blood than did healthy people. On the basis of this fact, perhaps in a few years we will have a relatively simple blood test for diagnosing schizophrenia.

A number of brain chemicals other than dopamine have recently been suggested as linked to schizophrenia. Glutamate receptors, for example, are related to the negative symptoms and cognitive impairments of the illness (Goff & Coyle, 2001). Also, new research found that genes suppressing myelin production occurred in both schizophrenia and bipolar disorder (Tkachev et al., 2003). So schizophrenia might be a white matter problem and might be linked to the mood disorders—a complex disorder, indeed.

Treatments for Schizophrenia

The most common and most effective treatments for schizophrenia are antipsychotic medicines, also known as **neuroleptic drugs.** These medicines block dopamine receptors, thereby reducing the amount of dopamine that can get from cell to cell. The result is typically a reduction in the positive symptoms, such as hallucinations, delusions, and disorganized speech. The neuroleptic drugs do not cure schizophrenia; they merely alleviate some of the symptoms. They also have side effects that can range from merely unpleasant to dangerous. Unfortunately, these drugs normally have very little effect on the negative symptoms of schizophrenia, such as social withdrawal, apathy, lack of affect, and poverty of speech. These symptoms typically require some form of psychotherapy, although newer **atypical antipsychotic drugs** seem to affect glutamate receptors and do help negative symptoms in some patients.

Some recent studies have found that a significant number of people with schizophrenia have low levels of fatty acids in their blood. It is well known that even small deficiencies of fatty acids can lead to cognitive impairments because of interference with neurotransmitters binding to receptors. Some psychiatrists have prescribed dietary intake of omega-3 fatty acids (fish oil) for schizophrenia. Time will tell whether this approach has any merit. But be warned that there have been numerous treatments for schizophrenia that have failed in the long run to deliver their promise.

Behavior therapies have had some success in treating certain symptoms of schizophrenia. These therapies typically rely on the principles of operant conditioning and extinction. That is, problem behaviors are extinguished by removing their reinforcement, and appropriate behaviors are strengthened by reinforcement. These are not cures by any means, but they do provide significant improvements in functioning for many patients.

Many people with schizophrenia require help with social skills and assistance with day-to-day functioning. This is one area in which there are often problems with our country's system of health care. Social workers provide some help, but there is little support from the public for such services. Most often, the job of caring for people with schizophrenia falls to their families. Two things that would help enormously would be better prevention of mental illnesses and better social and personal care assistance outside of a hospital—community care.

Recap

— Schizophrenia is a psychotic disorder (not split personality) with symptoms such as hallucinations, delusions, loosening of associations, and social withdrawal.

— Schizophrenia occurs in about 1% of the population, developing mostly during adolescence and young adulthood.

— There are five subtypes of schizophrenia: paranoid, catatonic, disorganized, undifferentiated, and residual.

— The progression of schizophrenia is divided into three stages: prodromal, active, and residual.

— The diathesis-stress theory is the most common idea about the cause of schizophrenia. Diathesis is the genetic predisposition. Heredity is important but is not the only cause; viruses are suspected of playing a role.

— Neuroleptic drugs block dopamine receptors and thereby reduce the positive symptoms of a person with schizophrenia.

MOOD DISORDERS

"Time cools, time clarifies; no mood can be maintained quite

unaltered through the course of hours."
—MARK TWAIN

Although schizophrenia is fairly common (1%) and is a terribly serious disorder, the mood disorders are nearly 10 times more common and cause perhaps more suffering than any other psychological disorder. Clinicians see more clients with mood disorders than any other mental illness. Many of the sufferers commit suicide; the rate is about 15% among those with mood disorders. In addition, the rate of mood disorders is increasing around the world. This is one of our most troubling problems. Fortunately, there are a number of treatments that help, and research continues to provide answers that offer help for people with these painful disorders.

Defining Mood Problems

It is normal for people to experience a fairly wide range of moods. When good things happen, we feel happy, cheerful, upbeat, excited, talkative, and joyful. When bad things happen, we naturally feel down, blue, sad, disappointed, and unhappy. Sometimes we wake up in a certain mood, and we don't know why. Moods vary. However, when moods get so high or so low for long periods of time that they interfere with people's lives, then that is a mood disorder.

This category of psychological disorders was once called **affective disorders.** However, the term *affect* refers to all emotions, not just moods. Anxiety disorders in that sense are affective disorders. This category was also once known as **manic-depressive disorders.** But over the years, people have come to use the term *manic-depressive* to refer to only one particular type of mood disorder, making this an inappropriate label for the whole category of mood disorders.

Mood disorders are frightfully common. One study found that nearly 25% of people at some time in their lives will have severe enough mood swings to be diagnosed with a mood disorder (Usten, 2001). By age 19, 35% of girls and 19% of boys report having had an episode of major depression (Duenwald, 2002). Because these disorders are so psychologically painful and disabling, many sufferers of mood disorders do seek professional treatment. It is difficult to simply "live with" a severe mood disorder. Therefore, therapists see many clients with mood problems. Also, mood disorders are increasing in frequency in every society that has been measured. We don't know why, but depression is reaching epidemic proportions. Contrary to some beliefs, depression increases with age. Already there is a tremendously high rate of depression among teens and young adults. If the trend continues, there will be a most troubling high rate of depression in older people in the future.

There is a clear gender difference in the mood disorders. Depression occurs at a rate three to four times higher in women than in men. Part of this difference might be due to biological differences between the sexes. For example, women's bodies in general are more sensitive to cyclical changes than are men's bodies. Depression is a cyclical disorder—it comes and goes episodically. Also, women seem in general to be more sensitive to changes in the amount of light, which is also a contributing factor to moods. There likely are also social factors that help to account for the gender difference. Women in general are more often encouraged to hold in their psychological problems, while men are encouraged to actively express them. Men have much higher rates of alcoholism, drug abuse, crime and vandalism, and other "acting out" disorders, while women have higher rates of anxiety, depression, and other "holding in" disorders.

Heredity also plays a role in mood disorders. Family and twin studies show good evidence that genetics is a contributing factor. In addition, brain-imaging research implies the influence of genetics (Kennedy et al., 1997). Also, a number of studies have found that people with type O blood have a slightly higher rate of depression, a finding that indicates that genetics is involved (Singg & Lewis, 2001). Of course, the most common influence on mood disorders is life experience. For instance, the rate of major depression is as high as 71% among sexually abused adolescents (Pillay & Schoubben-Hesk, 2001). Adults who were abused in childhood also have a higher rate of suicide attempt and aggression (Brodsky et al., 2001). Not surprisingly, depression is seen more commonly in children from dysfunctional families and in families with alcoholism. However, Caspi and colleagues (2003) found that genes can modulate the influence of experience. People with certain genes were more likely to develop depression when under stress than were people with different genes. Once again, we are reminded of the intricate relationship between nature and nurture.

Recent findings link depression to the hippocampus, a brain area that is connected to virtually every other part of the brain and is involved in learning and memory. Brain imaging shows a loss of volume in the hippocampus in people with depression; it appears to be the dendrites that are affected. But antidepressant medicines have a protective effect (Sheline et al., 2003). Also, as was mentioned in Chapter 3, the hippocampus produces new cells daily. This neurogenesis seems to be slowed in people with depression. Evidence in animals shows that antidepressant medicines stimulate neurogenesis and help relieve symptoms (Santarelli et al., 2003).

Moods in the DSM

The DSM divides the mood disorders into two distinctly different categories based on the presence or absence of mania. People who experience both low moods (depression) and high moods (mania) at various times in their lives are diagnosed with **bipolar disorder** (literally "two extremes"). There are three categories of bipolar disorder based on the severity of the person's symptoms. For example, mild manic episodes are known as **hypomania,** and when mood swings are mild, the diagnosis is **cyclothymia.**

On the other hand, people who never experience mania but who have periods of depression at times in their lives are diagnosed with **depressive disorder.** The DSM lists nine symptoms of depression, as listed earlier in the chapter. The symptoms include low mood, loss of interest, problems with appetite and sleep, and suicidal thoughts. If a person experiences at least five of these symptoms over a period of two weeks, the diagnosis is major depression (sometimes called **clinical depression**); if a person has at least two of these symptoms that persist for two years or more, the diagnosis is **dysthymia.**

TABLE 9.5   Mood Disorders

Depressive Disorders

1. **Major depressive disorder:** five or more symptoms for two weeks.
2. **Dysthymic disorder:** two or more symptoms for two years.
3. **Double depression:** both of the above at the same time.

Bipolar Disorders

1. **Bipolar I disorder:** severe manic and severe depressive episodes
2. **Bipolar II disorder:** depressive episodes and less severe manic episodes (hypomania)
3. **Cyclothymic disorder:** numerous mild depressive and hypomanic episodes for at least two years

In other words, there appear to be two separate types of mood disorders that are significantly different from one another, although some symptoms may overlap. In bipolar disorder, the person's moods go through a cycle, swinging from normal to high to low and back to normal. The public often uses the term *manic depression* for this disorder, though that is not an official diagnostic term. The mood cycles that are experienced in bipolar disorder may occur one or more times per year. People who have more than three cycles in a year are said to be **rapid cyclers**; others are known as slow cyclers.

The manic episodes experienced by people with bipolar disorder are typically shorter than the depressive episodes because they require more energy. During mania, a person cannot sit still, sleeps very little, is constantly on the go, has a **flight of ideas,** becomes very impulsive, often acts erratically and irresponsibly, may experience psychotic symptoms such as hallucinations and delusions, and often does things that the person later regrets. Manic episodes are nearly always followed by longer periods of depression. In other words, the person crashes into a severe low right after a manic high. After weeks, months, or sometimes years of depression, the person then returns to a normal mood, and the cycle continues.

Bipolar disorder is much less common than the depressive disorders, which are often referred to as **unipolar** (literally "one extreme"). That is, it is far more common for people to alternate between normal moods and low moods, never experiencing a manic episode. Unipolar depression in the United States occurs at a rate of about 17%, while bipolar disorders occur about 1% (Usten, 2001). The gender difference mentioned above is seen only in unipolar depression, not in bipolar disorder, which strikes men and women equally. Depressive disorders in the United States occur in women three or four times more often than in men. However, these large gender differences are not found in developing countries, where unipolar depression is seen about equally in men and women (Gater, 1998).

Some people meet the DSM criteria for both of these diagnostic categories: major depression (five or more symptoms for two weeks) and dysthymia (two or more symptoms for two years). The term **double depression** is used in such cases. Also, some people who are diagnosed with a depressive disorder experience only a single episode of depression, whereas others have recurrent depression. Unusual brain activity (a depression trait marker) occurs in an area of the frontal lobe where antidepressant medicines act in people who are at risk for recurrent depression (Liotti & Mayberg, 2002).

FYI

Several studies have found that bipolar disorder occurs at a very high rate among creative artists. In fact, the suicide rate is extremely high among twentieth-century poets and writers, as well as among composers of the past. Mood disorder sufferers included Handel, Beethoven, Charles Dickens, Sylvia Plath, William Styron, Edgar Allan Poe, and Sir Isaac Newton.

The occurrence of bipolar disorder follows very close to a genetic pattern. This so-called manic-depressive disorder apparently is influenced very little by social and familial events—it is primarily an inherited disorder. Unipolar depression, on the other hand, is highly influenced by both hereditary and experiential factors. Some people seem to have a genetic susceptibility to depression; more than a dozen genes have been identified that contribute, including some in women only and genes that interact with female hormones, perhaps helping to explain the gender difference (Carey, 2003). But genes aren't everything; family variables also play a role in the depressive disorders. For example, when a father suffers from alcoholism, it is common for his sons to have "acting out" problems, such as substance abuse or crime, while his daughters are more likely to develop symptoms of depression. Similarly, children who experience traumas or situations in which they are helpless are more likely to develop depression. A severe life event is a major trigger for depression but appears not to be a causative factor in bipolar disorder. The combination of heredity and family circumstances or the experience of severe life events seems to be the primary cause of depression. However, researchers suspect that there are many different routes one can take to reach depression. These include genetics, family experiences, traumas, biology (such as thyroid problems), vitamin B deficiency, and a host of others.

One well-known factor that influences moods is the amount of sunlight we experience. Several studies have documented that people who live in regions far from the equator, such as Iceland, Denmark, or Minnesota, where sunlight is rarer in the winter months, have higher rates of depression and suicide than do people who live in regions that get more sunlight. Certain individuals seem to be especially sensitive to fluctuations in the amount of light, and a diagnosis of **seasonal affective disorder (SAD)** is used when such people experience extreme depression during the winter months. Women suffer from SAD more than men do, perhaps because women's bodies are more sensitive to changes in the circadian rhythm. Sunlight is the main factor in adjusting the body's daily biological cycles. When there is a significant decrease in light, the result may be an upset in biochemical functioning that affects mood.

Suicide

Psychiatrist Kay Redfield Jamison is an expert on mood disorders and in 1995 revealed that she has suffered from bipolar disorder and attempted suicide at age twenty-eight. She is now a world-renowned advocate of suicide prevention programs and has summarized the facts about suicide in her 1999 book *Night Falls Fast*. Sometimes the term **psychache** is used to refer to the horrible psychological distress experienced by suicidal people (Shneidman, 1999). Perhaps the main ingredients of psychache are feelings of hopelessness and loneliness.

The suicide rate is very high among people with mental illnesses, particularly sufferers of mood disorders and schizophrenia. A 1970 study put the lifetime risk of suicide among depressed people at 15%. However, a more recent review found the lifetime rate of suicide among depressed people ranged from about 2% to 9% depending on degree of treatment intensity, whereas for nondepressed people the rate was about 0.5% (Bostwick & Pankratz, 2000). Though we don't know the precise number, we do know that the suicide rate is very high in the United States—higher than the homicide rate, which is so much higher than in any other developed country that it is an international embarrassment. A National Mental Health Association survey indicated that as many as 8.4 million Americans have contemplated suicide. Somewhere between 35,000 and 50,000 Americans kill themselves each year. That is about one every 20 minutes, on the average. This is a serious and heartbreaking problem.

It is important to distinguish between **suicide,** in which the person dies, and **suicide attempt,** in which the person lives. These two different events have very different demographic statistics. Of course, people who committed suicide *did* make an attempt—and succeeded. However, we use the term *attempt* only when people fail to kill themselves. In contrast to suicide attempts, suicides are sometimes called *completed* or *successful*, though here we will simply say *suicide* if the person died. Attempted suicides, similarly, are sometimes referred to as *unsuccessful*, though here we will use the standard term: *suicide attempt*. Remember, *attempt* means that the person did not die; *suicide* means that the person did die. Now for the statistics.

Men have higher suicide rates than women, while women have higher suicide attempt rates than men. Also, old people have higher suicide rates than teens and young adults, while teens and young adults have higher suicide attempt rates than old people. Both of these facts are primarily based on the method that is used by the suicidal person. In the United States, but not in most other countries, most suicides are by gunshot. Men and old people are more likely to use more lethal methods, such as guns, than are women and younger people, who more often use less lethal methods such as pills, cut wrists, and carbon monoxide. This fact, however, is changing. Women and young people in recent years have increased their use of guns, and if this trend continues, they will eventually have higher suicide rates than men and old people. People aged 15 to 24 once accounted for 5% of suicides but now make up 14%.

Suicide in the United States is more common among white people than among minorities. Black Americans, Mexican Americans, and Puerto Ricans, for example, have lower suicide rates than whites do (Oquendo et al., 2001). The reasons for this are unknown, although it is very likely that genetic and familial variables both contribute. Looking at suicide rates among various groups, you can see that the person who is most likely to commit suicide is an old white man. However, the person who is most likely to make a suicide attempt is a young white woman.

The suicide rate is slightly higher in the spring and lower in the winter. This is partly due to the increase in hormonal activity in the spring that is experienced by all animals, including humans. Your body is raging a little more in the spring. The most deadly suicide attempts are made by people with low serotonin activity in the prefrontal cortex (influenced by heredity as well as experience). Also, our moods are determined largely by comparison to surrounding conditions. In the spring, there are flowers, romance, sunshine, and other optimistic things. Low feelings may be exaggerated in those conditions. Poets knew that. T. S. Eliot wrote that "April is the cruelest month."

Following a suicide, psychologists sometimes conduct a **psychological autopsy** in which they seek to determine the causes of the person's suicide. Often a note is left that can give clues. Also, family members and friends are interviewed. I'm sure you will not be surprised to learn that such investigations reveal that as many as 75% of suicide victims were suffering from a mood disorder. In fact, roughly 30% of depressed people attempt suicide, and nearly half of those succeed.

The most significant way to reduce the suicide rate is to get effective treatment for people with mood disorders. In 2001, the U.S. Surgeon General announced a national suicide prevention plan modeled after a plan that had been successfully used by the Air Force. The Air Force had experienced an extremely high rate of suicide from 1990 to 1994. Health officials devised a program to lower the rate and by 1998 had cut the rate in half.

Treatments for Mood Disorders

There are a number of medicines, biological treatments, and behavioral and talk therapies that have had good success in treating people with depression or bipolar disorder. Most common today are **antidepressants** taken by many depression sufferers. Improvement typically occurs in 60% to 80% of patients who take such medications.

A controversial treatment that has some success with the mood disorders is **electroconvulsive therapy (ECT)**, which is commonly called *shock treatment*. Although it is frightening to most people, modern ECT is relatively safe and effective.

One of the most promising treatments for mood disorders is **cognitive-behavior (CB) therapy**. Patients learn to change their thinking and their behaviors, and these changes result in improved moods. Naturally, CB therapy may take longer and be more expensive than pills or ECT, but it is much less frightening and has many fewer side effects. Results typically last longer, too.

People suffering from SAD are often prescribed **light therapy (phototherapy)**, in which they sit in front of a bright light source for a few hours each day during the winter months. Recent research shows that light therapy can increase serotonin activity (Rosenthal, 1995). Just as researchers have focused on dopamine in the understanding and treatment of schizophrenia, the brain chemical serotonin has been of dominant interest for mood disorders. Antidepressant medications increase the brain's serotonin activity. A more detailed discussion of therapies is included in the following chapter.

Recap

— Mood disorders are divided into depressive and bipolar (includes mania).

— Depressive disorders are far more common than bipolar disorders. Women have depressive disorders more often than men do.

— Both hereditary and experiential factors contribute to mood disorders.

— Seasonal affective disorder (SAD) occurs in certain sensitive people who do not get enough sunlight.

— The suicide rate is high among people with schizophrenia and mood disorders.

— Suicide rates are higher among men and old people, while suicide attempts are higher among women and teens.

— Effective therapies for mood disorders include anti-depressant medicine, ECT (shock treatment), cognitive-behavioral therapy, and light (photo) therapy.

ANXIETY DISORDERS

"A crust eaten in peace is better than a banquet partaken in anxiety."
—AESOP

The anxiety disorders are likely the most common of all the psychological disorders. However, a clinical psychologist will not be overburdened by people with anxiety disorders, because most such sufferers do not seek treatment—they simply live with their problems. The irony is that mental health workers have devised some very effective treatments for anxiety disorders. Now if we could just get people to try them!

Anxiety Defined

Anxiety means nervousness. It is essentially the same thing as fear. People with anxiety disorders worry, feel stressed, **ruminate** (go over and over things in their mind), have daily life difficulties, such as problems with sleep and eating, and suffer from physiological upset, such as sweating, rapid heartbeat, and high blood pressure.

Everyone experiences anxiety sometimes. We call it a disorder when the anxiety is pervasive and disabling, that is, when it begins to interfere with a person's life. People are different, of course, and some are more sensitive to worry and nervousness than others. There likely is a genetic or biological susceptibility to anxiety that some people have to a greater degree than others. On the other hand, anyone will develop anxiety in extremely dangerous or traumatic situations. Therefore, although some people are more likely to develop these disorders, they can strike anyone unlucky enough to experience the wrong circumstances.

The anxiety disorders are divided into several categories in the DSM. Sometimes anxiety is connected to some object or situation, as when a person is afraid of heights. This is called **bound anxiety,** meaning the anxiety only occurs in certain conditions. Other times, people experience anxiety in general, not bound to anything. This is known as **free-floating anxiety**. Naturally, anxiety is often a component of other disorders. In fact, anxiety rarely exists in isolation; there is a high comorbidity of anxiety and mood disorders (Nemeroff, 2002). Unfortunately, this means that people with anxiety disorders are at high risk of suicide (Weissman et al., 1989).

DSM Classifications

The DSM includes six types of anxiety disorders:

1. **Generalized anxiety disorder (GAD)** is the term that is used when a person complains of experiencing anxiety at all times. There is nothing in particular that brings on the anxiety; the person is just always nervous. It is very likely that these people have nervous systems that are overly sensitive, although life conditions, of course, often play a role. About 5% of people have GAD (two-thirds of them are women), and more than half say that the symptoms began in childhood (Harvard Mental Health Letter, 2003). Such patients can take medications that will slow down their nervous systems or can learn various relaxation techniques that will help to reduce their sense of anxiety.

2. **Panic disorder (PD)** is the term that is used when a person has attacks of extreme anxiety that seem to come out of nowhere. The person might think he or she is having a heart attack because his or her heart and breathing are going so fast. The person might rush to the emergency room only to be told by the doctors that there is nothing wrong with the person's heart; it is merely beating fast. A person with PD has recurrent **panic attacks,** which are very unpleasant. The PD sufferer wants very much to avoid panic attacks and will therefore avoid situations in which he or she has previously experienced them.

   What causes panic attacks? First, people with PD have overly sensitive "alarm systems" in their brains, a condition that is apparently inherited. A part of the brain known as the **locus coeruleus** triggers the physiological reactions to danger. Many studies have documented the fact that patients with panic disorder are highly susceptible to CO_2-induced panic attacks (Kent, 2001). If you put a plastic bag over your head, you will experience the terror associated with panic attacks. The amount of carbon dioxide will increase inside the bag while the amount of oxygen decreases. This will lead the "alarm system" in your brain to increase your physiological responses—your brain is warning you that you are going to die. Some people have a very sensitive locus coeruleus. Their brains respond to nonemergencies as if they were life threatening. Hence, such people will have panic attacks in places such as a car, elevator, or classroom. Then classical conditioning occurs. The situation itself becomes a trigger for a panic attack. Eventually, the person has many panic attacks, and because these experiences are so unpleasant, the person begins to avoid circumstances that might cause panic.

   Panic disorder is seen in both men and women, though it is more common in women, and women have more severe symptoms. This may be due to gender differences in sensitivity to carbon dioxide (Sheikh et al., 2002). PD can be treated with a combination of medication and behavioral therapy. That is, certain medications can help to decrease the nervous system response, and behavioral therapy can help people to have more control over their thoughts and behaviors so that panic is less likely to occur.

3. A **phobia** is an irrational fear of something that is not harmful. A **specific phobia** is fear of a particular thing, such as snakes, heights, water, or flying. **Social phobias** are fears related to being around people, such as a fear of signing one's name in public. A social phobia is like excessive shyness in

which a person is terribly embarrassed around others. **Agoraphobia** is a very broad fear in which a person is nervous about going out in public. Some people who suffer from agoraphobia stay at home nearly all the time. A person with panic disorder might develop agoraphobia because of his or her fear of having a panic attack. Other people develop agoraphobia because of traumatic experiences they have had away from home that generalize. These people might feel safe only at home and stay there most of the time.

Phobias are extremely common. Everyone has some unreasonable fears, and the question often asked is "When does a fear become a phobia?" As was mentioned above, there is no clear dividing line between "normal" and "disordered," but a good criterion is the person's level of discomfort. If the fear gets in the way of living a normal life, if it incapacitates a person or prevents the person from doing the things he or she wants to do, then perhaps we should call it a phobia. Most people live with their fears and do not seek therapy. However, the phobias are among the most successfully treated psychological disorders. Many phobia clinics report nearly 100% success.

4. **Obsessive-compulsive disorder (OCD)** really involves two problems. An **obsession** is an idea or thought that intrudes uncontrollably into a person's mind. The thought is something horrible that causes a person great anxiety. For example, one woman told her psychiatrist that while driving in the car with her baby, she constantly thought about throwing the baby out of the moving car. She was very troubled by this obsession and wanted help. In another case, a man reported that every time he saw his five-year-old son, he couldn't help but think of hitting him in the head with a hammer. He said that he loved his son and must be going crazy to have such an awful thought. Obsessions are unpleasant thoughts that push their way into consciousness, unwelcome. If you have ever had an unwanted song go through your mind, you have an idea what an obsession is like.

Compulsions, on the other hand, are behaviors (not thoughts) that people feel they must perform lest something horrible happen. For example, a common compulsion is excessive hand washing. People with OCD often count things excessively, too. Many other ritualistic and perfectionist behaviors are common. Compulsive behaviors are maintained by negative reinforcement: By engaging in the compulsive activity, the person feels a sense of relief. For example, if a person has an obsession about germs, he finds relief by washing his hands. He touches a piece of paper and thinks, "Others have touched this paper, and there are germs on it," and then he washes. Soon afterward, he touches his mail and thinks, "There are germs on this from the post office," and washes again. And so on.

OCD is a fairly common disorder, with a lifetime incidence of about 2%. Both men and women have this disorder. About half the patients are diagnosed in childhood, and the other half are diagnosed during adulthood. Early-onset OCD is associated with more severe problems than is the adult-onset type (Rosario-Campos et al., 2001). People with OCD are usually perfectionists who are driven to engage in ritualistic behaviors. These might range from relatively minor patterns to very severe disorganization of behavior. In other words, there is a wide range in the level of impairment seen in patients with OCD. Therapies are quite successful and involve both medications and behavioral treatments that use principles of conditioning to change the person's behavior.

FYI

Lower animals have behaviors that resemble OCD. Some dogs, for example, will lick, scratch, and bite themselves excessively. This condition is called acral lick dermatitis. When such dogs are given antidepressant drugs, their symptoms decrease. Also, mice that were bred to be missing a gene called Hox8b, a gene that is important for embryonic development, groomed themselves excessively (Greer & Capecchi, 2002). Perhaps such findings will help us to locate genes that contribute to OCD in humans.

5. **Posttraumatic stress disorder (PTSD)** has been in the news in recent years. When people experience traumatic events, it is natural for them to suffer a bit of shock and psychological distress. This reaction typically lessens with time, and after a few weeks or months, people are much improved. However, occasionally, a person continues to experience significant problems many months and even years after experiencing a trauma. This is then called "posttraumatic" because the symptoms linger for so long.

   It is well known that men in war situations often have posttraumatic stress disorder for many years afterward. What is not as well known is that women experience PTSD at an even higher rate than men do (Zlotnick, 2001). For women, the trauma is more likely to be physical or sexual abuse or rape. Years after the trauma, such victims may continue to experience anxiety, nightmares, **flashbacks** (sudden memories of the trauma replayed in images and thoughts), panic attacks, and other psychological distress.

   Unfortunately, PTSD is among the most difficult disorders to treat. Brains are specially designed to remember traumatic events and resist forgetting such important things. However, many PTSD sufferers find help from medications, self-help groups (group discussions with other PTSD sufferers), and various talk therapies.

6. **Acute stress disorder (ASD)**, like PTSD, is a distressing reaction to a traumatic experience. The symptoms of ASD are similar to those of PTSD and include flashbacks, anxiety, emotional distress, and even dissociative states (a kind of trance, or feeling of being cut off from oneself, or other distortions of awareness). ASD is the diagnosis if these symptoms persist for about the first month after a trauma; if the symptoms persist for longer than that, the diagnosis is posttraumatic stress disorder. It is hoped that by diagnosing ASD, people who suffer traumatic experiences can be helped before they develop PTSD.

TABLE 9.6 Anxiety Disorders

1. Generalized anxiety disorder: nervous all the time
2. Panic disorder: sudden, severe panic attacks
3. Phobic disorder: irrational fears, including specific phobia, social phobia, and agoraphobia
4. Obsessive-compulsive disorder: uncontrollable thoughts (obsessions) and ritualistic, repetitive behaviors (compulsions)
5. Posttraumatic stress disorder: psychological distress long after a traumatic event
6. Acute stress disorder: psychological distress within four weeks of a traumatic event

THINK TANK

What phobias or other anxiety disorders are common among people you know?

Why do you think people are reluctant to seek help for anxiety problems?

What can be done to better educate people about mental illnesses?

BODY PROBLEMS

"There are two times I feel stress—day and night."
—ANONYMOUS

There are a number of psychological disorders that could be thought of as "body" problems. There are many situations in which people with mental illnesses experience physical symptoms, and often physical symptoms are brought on or worsened by psychological factors.

Stress

Sometimes a "real" physical symptom (a headache, for example) is caused or worsened by stress. For example, a person who is worried might develop constipation, high blood pressure, acne, or a stomach ulcer. In such a situation, the physical condition is really there. This is known as a **psychosomatic** illness (sometimes called **psychophysiologic**).

Many people mistakenly believe that the term *psychosomatic* implies that the problem is not real, that it is just "in the head." On the contrary, the terms *psychosomatic* and *psychophysiologic* technically mean that the person has a real physical problem that has been brought on by psychological factors. An ulcer caused by eating certain foods would not be psychosomatic, but an ulcer caused by constant worry and stress would be. Nearly any physical symptom can be either caused or worsened by stress.

A cure for a psychosomatic problem can be approached in three ways: (1) by treating the specific physical symptoms, (2) by relieving the stress, or (3) by teaching patients stress management techniques, such as relaxation, changing their ways of thinking, or getting social support. Of course, many psychosomatic problems disappear on their own if the psychological stress is removed. If not, physical problems can become quite severe, even resulting in death from heart attack or stroke.

Stress is defined as any demand on the body or anything that throws your body off balance, out of equilibrium. Think of a heavy truck putting stress on a small bridge. Anything that places a demand on your body is called a **stressor.** Jogging, worrying, having a cold, being overly tired, being threatened, trying to do too much, and working too hard are all stressful. Stressors come from the environment around us as well as from our emotional and cognitive states. As I'm sure you know, stressors are plentiful.

Canadian psychologist **Hans Selye** (1976) studied stress more than anyone. From his experiments, Selye concluded that stress affects the body in a general way (all stressors cause the same reaction) and that bodies adapt to stress. The body's reaction to stress is called the **general adaptation syndrome** (just remember that stress causes GAS!), which is divided into three phases:

1. *Alarm stage:* When first encountering a stressor, the body becomes aroused. Heart rate and blood pressure increase, digestion slows, and hormones are released from the endocrine glands. These body changes make you ready for **fight-or-flight.** In the short term, these body changes are helpful. But in the long run, they are harmful because they damage body organs, including the brain. Stress can harm you!

2. *Resistance stage:* Soon the body adapts to the stress. Symptoms, such as pains and body complaints, might even disappear. This is a dangerous phase

because a person might feel that he or she is not under stress, but in fact the person's body is working overtime to maintain this state of equilibrium.

3. *Exhaustion stage:* If the stress continues, the body cannot maintain equilibrium and will develop damage and illness. Excessive or continuous stress causes the immune system to be weakened, illnesses to occur, and even brain cells to be damaged (Newcomer, 1999).

Although stress is helpful in an immediate situation, in the long run, it is very damaging to the body. The immune system is weakened, the heart is strained, and brain cells are damaged by constant stress. Stress has been shown to reduce neurogenesis in the brain and can trigger depression and anxiety (Vogel, 2003). Meditation and a similar technique known as the relaxation response have been shown to help reduce the effects of stress.

Unconscious Body Problems

Somatoform disorders are not consciously controlled, nor are they real physical problems in the patient's body. Rather, they are unconscious brain problems in which a person's brain leads the person to believe that there is something wrong with his or her body. The patient really believes that he or she has a physical ailment but does not. It is not a psychosomatic disorder. A somatoform disorder is not created intentionally or purposely, as are factitious disorder and malingering (discussed later in the chapter). Instead, the somatoform sufferer unconsciously believes that there is a real physical problem in his or her body, such as blindness, deafness, paralysis, numbness, or pain.

Somatoform disorders have been observed and treated for thousands of years. Ancient doctors called this problem *hysteria* (literally "womb" or "uterus") because they believed that only women had such problems and that they were caused by the uterus moving around inside the woman's body yearning to become impregnated. Doctors often recommended that the woman become pregnant to keep the uterus in place. The term *hysteria* has been replaced with **conversion disorder**, a reference to the idea that a person's *psychological problems* have been *converted* into simulated *physical problems*.

When a person has many physical complaints (a dozen or more) without organic causes for them and these complaints persist for years, the condition is called **somatization disorder.** When there is one complaint of a dysfunction in movement or sensation, the condition is called conversion. Conversion disorder often is manifested as a sensory impairment, such as "hysterical" blindness or deafness. Often the physical symptoms that occur do not correspond to the anatomy of the body. For example, a person might complain that his hand has gone numb but that he still has feeling in his arm. This **glove anesthesia** was common among teenaged boys hundreds of years ago when they were taught that masturbation would cause horrible problems. In fact, the nerves of the arm do not allow for this condition to occur—part of the arm and part of the hand are served by one nerve, and the other parts are served by another nerve. It is not possible to have a numb hand and a feeling arm. Also, hysterically blind patients do not bump into things, and hysterically deaf patients sometimes react to sounds.

A person with conversion disorder is being tricked by his or her brain. The brain knows something that the mind doesn't. For example, a hysterically blind person does not bump into things because his or her brain can "see." However, the person's brain is blocking "seeing" from his or her mind. The person's seeing is unconscious. Conversion disorders are a type of unconscious defense mechanism in which the brain protects the mind from threatening ideas. A proper therapy would be aimed at helping the patient to discover and face the unconscious ideas that are causing the disorder.

Worry, Pain, and Ugliness

The best known of the somatoform disorders is **hypochondriasis.** Today, the term *hypochondriac* is often used to tease or insult a person who is worried about his or her health. With hypochondriasis, patients do show an intense fear and worry about developing many varied health problems. It is normal to worry about one's health, but in this case, the worry is serious, extended, and unfounded. The DSM requires at least six months of worry and that the preoccupation with illness is not alleviated by medical evaluations and assurance.

Often patients report feelings of lingering pain in various body parts that have no organic damage. These feelings of pain are not consistent with injury or disease and, as with conversion disorder, are often not even consistent with anatomical and physiological facts. In other words, the pain the patient is experiencing is not coming from the body but is being created in the person's brain. This is called **pain disorder.** The complaints that are given are often extreme and exaggerated and typically are motivated by psychological factors. It is important to remember that these complaints of pain are not being faked or intentionally feigned (as in factitious disorder and malingering, which are discussed later in the chapter). As in conversion disorder, psychological problems are at the root of these complaints.

One of the more puzzling psychological disorders is **body dysmorphic disorder (BDD),** in which people complain that they are extremely ugly and repugnant to others. These people are preoccupied with their appearance and believe that one of their physical characteristics is excessively unattractive. Sometimes the complaint is totally imagined; at other times, it is based on a slight physical anomaly the person has that has been exaggerated beyond reason. A person with a large nose, for example, might believe that his nose is hideously ugly, misshapen, or horrifyingly large. He might refuse to go out in public without something covering his face.

People with BDD often seek out plastic surgeons and request that unreasonable changes be made in their supposed defects. Some BDD sufferers have many operations to correct their imagined ugliness but still remain unsatisfied. It is common for people with BDD to constantly check their supposed defect in mirrors and to engage in excessive grooming behaviors. One young man, an identical twin, strongly believed that he was very ugly, though he found his brother to be very handsome. His distress was so great that he committed suicide. So, you see, BDD can be a very distressing disorder.

Demographics and Treatment of Somatoform Disorders

There has been little research on the **epidemiology** (frequency and distribution in a population), and the **etiology** (various causes and influences) of somatoform disorders. However, historical records indicate that these problems have been around for centuries. All indications are that the somatoform disorders are much more rare today than they were in the past, perhaps because people today are better informed about the true causes of physical body problems. Theorists have pointed to the roles of learning, cultural influences, cognitive misinterpretations, and unconscious processes in the development of these disorders.

Treatment for somatoform disorders has historically been psychoanalytic (Freudian), attempting to help patients understand the unconscious mechanisms that are at the core of their illnesses. However, in recent years, a number of other treatment modalities have had some success. One study, for example, found that hypochondriasis patients attained significant improvements in their worries about illnesses by use of the antidepressant drug Prozac. Behavior and cognitive therapists also have reported success in treating patients with conversion disorder and other somatoform disorders. The behavior therapist helps patients to gain control over their symptoms using principles of learning; the cognitive therapist helps patients to better understand and control their thinking and reasoning about their body and their complaints.

TABLE 9.7 Somatoform Disorders

1. Conversion disorder: simulated sensory or motor impairment, such as blindness or numbness
2. Somatization disorder: many physical complaints over several years
3. Hypochondriasis: fear of having or getting illnesses based on misinterpreting symptoms
4. Pain disorder: feeling pain due to psychological factors
5. Body dysmorphic disorder: imagined ugliness or defect in physical appearance

Recap

— Anxiety disorders are likely the most common mental illnesses, although most sufferers do not seek help for their problems.

— Panic disorder typically results when a person's "alarm system" is too sensitive. Agoraphobia can result from fear of fear.

— Phobias are extremely common and can be successfully treated.

— Obsessions are terrible thoughts a person can't control; compulsions are repetitive, ritualistic behaviors. These are the symptoms of OCD.

— Posttraumatic stress and acute stress are diagnoses given to people who are suffering the emotional effects of trauma.

— Psychosomatic illnesses are real body problems that are brought on by psychological factors such as stress.

— Stress refers to demands placed on the body. The body's reaction is called the general adaptation syndrome. It has three stages: alarm, resistance, and exhaustion. Although stress helps in the short run, it is harmful in the long run.

— Somatoform disorders, such as conversion and hypochondriasis, are unconscious problems in which a person believes there is something wrong with his body, but there is not.

DISSOCIATIVE DISORDERS

"You must always be puzzled by mental illness."
—LUDWIG WITTGENSTEIN

Some of the most curious psychological disorders involve alterations in a person's conscious awareness and sense of identity. These are known as **dissociative disorders.** The term *dissociative* implies a split or break in a person's consciousness. One might think of a dissociative episode as a kind of trance, or state of detachment, in which a person's awareness of himself is distorted and confused. Dissociative states are often experienced by people in a state of shock, by people using psychoactive drugs, and by sufferers of various mental illnesses. For example, dissociative episodes often occur in people with eating disorders, personality disorders, mood disorders, and schizophrenia.

When a dissociative state is the primary symptom that a person has, then four diagnoses are available in the DSM. In other words, the DSM includes four types of dissociative disorders. The first is **dissociative amnesia.** As you know, the term *amnesia* refers to a memory problem. In this case, a person has suffered an emotional or psychological shock that has temporarily blocked his memory of significant personal information, such as his or her identity and life situation. In dissociative amnesia, there are gaps in a person's memory that correspond to times of great emotional stress, such as violence, suicide attempts, self-mutilation, or traumatic experiences. There is no such thing as total amnesia, because such people do remember insignificant things. The memory loss is restricted to the events and facts that cause emotional upset.

A second classification is **dissociative fugue.** The term *fugue* literally means "flight," which is a handy thing to remember because this diagnosis requires that a person travel. We might say that this person has amnesia and doesn't know it. A person with *dissociative fugue* might suddenly and unexpectedly move to another city and mentally block out his or her past—in fact, might even assume a new identity.

For example, a man interviewed in Los Angeles was asked where he had lived before he moved there. He said that he didn't know. How could this be? He said that he just didn't think about it. When the question arose in conversations, he changed the subject. The police were able to trace him back to St. Paul, Minnesota, where his family lived. When he was reunited with his family, he did not recognize them.

In another case of fugue, a woman who had suffered a series of horrible life events suddenly moved to Cleveland and changed her name and career to those of a person she greatly admired (a piano teacher). A college professor who was told that his job was in jeopardy suddenly disappeared and was found three weeks later in another part of the country with no memory of how he got there or what he had done. A woman who was found in Florida had no idea who she was or how she got there. Her abandoned car was found at the Mall of America in Minnesota. Her family was found in Canada, and when reunited with them, the woman did not recognize them. These are cases of fugue.

The third form of dissociative disorder is the most rare, interesting, and mysterious. Formerly known as **multiple personality disorder,** this condition is now termed **dissociative identity disorder (DID)** in the DSM, although the public often calls it *split personality*. In this case, a person's identity seems at times to suddenly shift from one personality to another. The various identities the person experiences are known as **alternate personalities,** typically shortened to *alters*. This is a disorder that mental health experts disagree about more than any other. Some believe that it is not an actual disorder. People have faked it (and other dissociative disorders). Most experts believe that it is over-diagnosed. However, most experts also believe that it is a real, though rare, problem.

The most famous case of DID was that described in the book *The Three Faces of Eve* (Thigpen et al., 1957). A woman went to a doctor complaining of long blackouts for which she had no memory. After some counseling, a psychiatrist was able to determine that during these blackouts, the woman had adopted another identity and was engaging in behaviors (partying, drinking, etc.) that her "true" personality believed to be sinful. The psychiatrist wrote about this case and used the name "Eve White" to refer to the first alter and "Eve Black" for the second alter. Later, even more alters emerged. Interestingly, Eve Black knew about Eve White, but Eve White did not know about Eve Black. For example, Eve Black would say, "I go out drinking, and then she wakes up with a hangover!"

The woman in this case, Christine Sizemore, was eventually cured of her DID and later wrote a book about her experience titled *I'm Eve* (1977). Her story was put on film in 1957 (*The Three Faces of Eve*) and starred Joanne Woodward, who won an Academy Award for her portrayal of Ms. Sizemore.

A final category of dissociative disorder is **depersonalization disorder.** In this case, a person reports feelings of detachment or estrangement from himself or herself. Some sufferers report feeling like a robot or automaton or as if living in a dream. It is common for such people to report that they don't recognize their own bodies, or that they feel "out of their bodies," or that they are outside observers of their bodies. Other symptoms of depersonalization are complaints of sensory impairments, such as numbness, lack of control of one's actions (such as speaking), and lack of appropriate emotional responses or excessive apathy.

Studies indicate that certain aspects of depersonalization are common. For example, in one survey, 14% of people said they sometimes did not recognize themselves in a mirror. Because these symptoms apparently are fairly common, a diagnosis of depersonalization disorder is not made unless the symptoms are severe enough to cause significant distress or impaired functioning.

Most psychologists believe that dissociative disorders are a form of defense mechanism that emerges as a protection from the horrible thoughts of a traumatic experience. Amnesia certainly is a means of protecting one's mind from an awful experience. Also, DID may arise as a protective device by a child who is in a horrific situation from which she cannot escape, such as being sexually assaulted by a parent. By developing the feeling that she is someone else, she protects her mind from the stress of the trauma. In fact, most experts agree that DID nearly always is the result of traumatic events experienced in childhood. Of course, not everyone who experiences a traumatic event will develop a dissociative disorder. Other factors, such as heredity, learning, prior experiences, personality, and the details of the situation, might be contributing influences in determining who develops this type of defense mechanism.

TABLE 9.8   Dissociative Disorders

1. Dissociative amnesia: repression of important personal information caused by trauma or stress

2. Dissociative fugue: sudden, unexpected travel away from home with inability to recall one's past

3. Dissociative identity disorder: two or more distinct identities

4. Depersonalization disorder: feeling detached from, or as an outside observer of, one's mind or body

OTHER CLINICAL SYNDROMES

"No excellent soul is exempt from a mixture of madness."
—ARISTOTLE

Besides the five major categories discussed above, the DSM includes many other clinical syndromes. Here are some of them.

Disorders Usually First Diagnosed in Infancy, Childhood, or Adolescence

This is the only section of the DSM that classifies mental illnesses on the basis of the age of onset. Nearly all disorders are more common at certain ages than at others, but the DSM usually classifies disorders according to their symptoms rather than the age of onset. However, this section groups together disorders that typically strike people early in life, before reaching adulthood.

Autism is included here. This is a very serious disorder that causes debilitating symptoms, including bizarre behaviors, lack of language development, lack of social development, impaired nonverbal behavior (such as eye contact), impaired peer relationships, and lack of social reciprocity. Autism is strongly genetically determined (Romoz, 2004), and a number of studies have found brain abnormalities in children with autism, including a smaller cerebellum and temporal lobe dysfunction (Zilbovicius, 2000). There has been a large increase in autism in the last decade. Researchers guessed that childhood vaccinations were the cause, but this now seems unlikely; rather, the main reason seems to be awareness, identification, and funding for special education that have increased diagnosis (Harvard Mental Health Letter, 2003).

Attention deficit/hyperactivity disorder (ADHD) is also included in this section. Although this condition is sometimes diagnosed in adults, it is far more commonly first diagnosed in childhood. Children with ADHD have difficulty paying attention and sitting still. Researchers have found that heredity plays a strong role in ADHD but that nongenetic factors are also part of the etiology. For example, prenatal and birth complications (e.g., mother's nicotine use, low birth weight, premature birth, oxygen deprivation) are a common part of the history of children with ADHD. Signs of brain damage are found in only about 5% of ADHD cases. However, minor neurological problems, such as difficulties in fine motor coordination, are common. ADHD is often treated with Ritalin, but a nonstimulant drug called Strattera (atomoxetine) is now available.

Mental retardation is also classified in this section because it is typically diagnosed early in life. Other childhood problems described in this chapter are communication disorders, learning disorders, and developmental disorders. Also included are **conduct disorder** and **oppositional defiant disorder,** two categories that describe children whose behaviors represent a serious transgression of societal norms. Such children might be bullies, lose their temper easily, or be angry and resentful, or they might set fires, steal things, lie, and persistently violate rules.

Connecting Concepts

Look back to Chapter 7 to find the definition and categories of mental retardation.

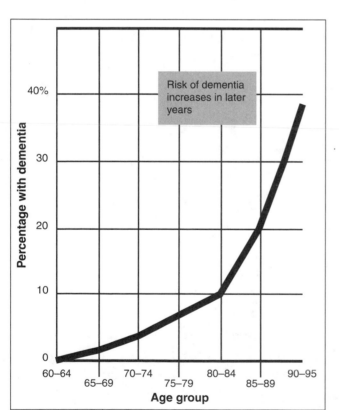

Rates of dementia increase drastically in older age.

Delirium, Dementia, Amnestic Disorders, and Other Cognitive Disorders

This section was once known more simply as "Organic Disorders," a name that implied that these problems were due to brain dysfunctions. However, in recent years, psychiatrists have rightly recognized that *all* psychological disorders arise from the brain. Therefore, the term *organic* wrongly implies that other disorders are not organic.

Included here are the **dementias**—injuries or diseases of the brain that decrease a person's cognitive abilities in the long term (*dement* means "decrease in mental functions"). Dementias are rare in young people and become strikingly more common with age. People over age 65 have by far the highest rates of dementia. In older people, this disorder is called **senile dementia;** in younger people, it is called **presenile dementia.** (Contrary to popular belief, *senile* does not mean "demented," it merely means "old.") There are more than seven million people in the United States with dementia; the rate among those over age 80 is nearly 50%. These are permanent degenerative problems that result in death. Therefore, they are tragic for the individual, family and friends, and society. Cures are desperately needed.

Alzheimer's disease (AD) is the most common of the dementias, affecting about four million people in the United States. It is normally diagnosed on the basis of the patient's symptoms (cognitive loss), but research now shows that PET scans can identify people in the early stages of AD (Silverman et al., 2001).

Although it can occur in younger people, the incidence of Alzheimer's skyrockets in older age. Alzheimer's is identified by specific damage to brain cells. It is caused by the buildup of proteins (particularly **beta amyloid**) that damage brain cells and result in brain cell clumps called **plaques,** and twisted, deformed cells called **tangles.** Such brain cell damage causes problems with memory, orientation in the environment, the recognition and naming of objects, other cognitive abilities, and eventually biological life functions. The term **mild cognitive impairment (MCI)** is used when people have some decline in memory and mental abilities that is not severe enough to be diagnosed as Alzheimer's. About eight million people have MCI, and about 15% develop AD every year. In fact, studies have found that elderly subjects with cognitive decline have smaller brain volume near the hippocampus (Pantel et al., 2003). However, some neurologists warn that we must be careful not to define normal age changes as disorders.

The exact causes of AD are not known; however, the concordance rate in identical twins is about 50%, so heredity is important, but it is not the only cause. Several genes have been identified that increase the risk of developing Alzheimer's, but identical twins do not have a 100% concordance rate. The environmental factors that contribute to Alzheimer's are not yet known, though stress is a likely influence. Some evidence implicates high blood pressure, high cholesterol, diabetes, and strokes as causative factors, meaning that diet, smoking, and other lifestyle factors probably contribute to AD. It also means that statins, cholesterol-lowering drugs, and antioxidants, such as vitamins C and E, may help to prevent or delay the onset of Alzheimer's disease. Eating fish and seafood appears to lower the risk (Barberger-Gateau, 2002), and estrogen treatment in postmenopausal women improves cognitive functions (Kugaya et al., 2003). Also, people who stay mentally active have lower rates of dementia; adults with hobbies that keep their intellect active, such as puzzles, chess, and reading, are more than twice as likely to avoid Alzheimer's (Friedland, 2001). So keep studying!

There is no cure for AD, though certain medicines, such as Aricept, that block the breakdown of acetylcholine can provide some help. A new medicine, memantine, which slows activity of both NMDA receptors (see end of Chapter 6) and the neurotransmitter glutamate, slows the decline in some people. Recently, lithium, the drug used to treat bipolar disorder, was found to inhibit the development of amyloid plaques, a very hopeful sign for effective treatment (Phiel et al., 2003). Also, an enzyme, Pin1, may help to prevent some brain damage (Lieberman, 2003). Scientists have developed a vaccine that can prevent and even reverse the development of amyloid plaques in mice and other animals, but the first trial studies on humans, begun in 2001, had to be halted because some of the patients showed adverse reactions.

Scientists also have reported the first gene therapy for Alzheimer's (Tuszynski, 2001). Cells were taken from the patient's skin and were then given a gene that produces a chemical known as **nerve growth factor,** a natural substance that promotes healthy brain cells. The cells were implanted into the patient's brain. Such a procedure won't cure Alzheimer's, but it might provide another treatment option for the millions of Americans who suffer from the disease.

Another common dementia is **Parkinson's disease (PD),** which causes muscle tremors (shaking) because of damage to the brain area that produces the neurotransmitter **dopamine.** About one of every 100 people over 60 has PD, men more often than women. A number of things can cause PD, including genetics and exposure to bacteria and toxins. So far, three genes have been identified that contribute to this dementia. However, environmental causes are more common among men because they are more likely to be exposed to pesticides, herbicides, industrial chemicals, and work-related head injuries that can damage the brain area that makes dopamine. As with Alzheimer's, there are no cures for PD, but medicines such as **L-dopa** (which helps the brain to make more dopamine) can reduce the symptoms in the early stages. A brain implant similar to a pacemaker (known as a deep-brain stimulator) sends electrical impulses into certain brain areas (in the thalamus) and may reduce symptoms. Two different types of brain surgery are also available, and gene therapy trials (implanting genes in the brain) have begun (Talan, 2003).

Scientists at Harvard University and the National Institutes of Health say that they have "cured" PD in mice and rats by implanting stem cells into the animals' brains (Isacson & McKay, 2001). The first cells that develop in a fertilized egg are not yet differentiated and are known as stem cells. Because such cells are taken from embryos, this line of research is controversial. Although some attempts at implanting embryonic cells into the brains of people with PD have had success, a recent controlled study of brain cell implants did not fare well (Freed, 2001). Some of the patients developed side effects involving severe, uncontrollable motor movements. The researchers reasoned that too many fetal cells had been implanted and too much dopamine was being produced in the patients' brains. Still, surgery is an option, though many experts warn that more research should be done before recommending this procedure. The latest news on this issue is that scientists have reported methods of extracting stem cells from placentas, from baby teeth, and even from corpses (Palmer, 2001). If these methods work, it will resolve the controversy about the source of embryonic cells.

Substance-Related Disorders

As you know, alcohol and drug addictions are very common problems around the world. There are many different substances, from marijuana to nicotine to heroin, that cause chemical changes in the brain resulting in addiction or dependency, but there are also other substances, such as medications and toxins that can cause psychological problems. Therefore, the DSM categorizes problems related to (1) taking a drug of abuse, (2) the side effects of medication, and (3) exposure to toxins.

The term *substance* can refer to anything that results in psychological difficulty, including alcohol, amphetamines, caffeine, cannabis (marijuana), hallucinogens, inhalants, nicotine, opioids (such as heroin), and sedatives. This chapter of the DSM includes criteria for disorders based on substance dependence, abuse, intoxication, and withdrawal. The most common problems involve alcohol, nicotine, and caffeine.

Alcoholism is one of the most common disorders in nearly every country in the world. In the United States, it is often rated near depression as the most common of all psychological disorders. Substance dependencies are often difficult to treat because of the significant changes that occur in brain chemistry. Therefore, it is wise to advise people not to begin using addictive substances. Unfortunately, this advice goes largely unheeded. There are a number of treatment options, and they do have some success. For example, about 25% of people who are treated for alcoholism will go alcohol-free during the first year after treatment (Miller et al., 2001). About 10% will be able to drink moderately. The others show substantial improvement, reducing their alcohol consumption. So although these problems are difficult to treat, there is significant promise if we can get people to go to treatment.

THINK TANK   What are some societal attitudes and policies about substance abuse that make this a difficult problem to solve?

How is substance abuse portrayed in movies, magazines, and TV shows, and by comedians?

Factitious Disorder

In **factitious disorder,** a person will purposely make himself or herself sick or pretend to be sick solely for the purpose of receiving medical attention. It is as if the person has an obsessive desire to go to the hospital and receive medical attention. This disorder is sometimes called **Munchausen syndrome,** named after Baron von Munchausen, who was a famous exaggerator and teller of tall tales. Factitious disorder is not the same as faking an illness, or **malingering,** because in malingering, the person has a clear external motivation. For example, a person might pretend to be sick to get out of work. In factitious disorder, there is no such motivation. This person just wants medical treatment. When caught, such people often admit their fakery, thus indicating that they were conscious of their actions; that is, factitious disorder does not occur during a trance or other unconscious state.

Sometimes a person will make someone else sick, typically his or her child, solely for the purpose of getting medical attention. This is commonly known as **Munchausen by proxy,** although the DSM refers to it as **factitious disorder by proxy.** This condition is not currently listed as a mental illness in DSM-IV but is included among a number of problems that are under study and therefore will likely be included in DSM-V as a psychological disorder. Currently, people with Munchausen by proxy are sent to jail rather than to treatment.

Now that the Internet is in such wide use, there are even instances of factitious disorder online. Sometimes people who have been communicating online suddenly report that they are ill, even dying. Their online acquaintances offer support and sympathy. Sometimes, these acquaintances eventually learn that the person did not die and maybe didn't even exist. Psychiatrist Marc Feldman has studied such cases and calls them *Munchausen by Internet.*

THINK TANK

To what extent should criminal behavior be viewed as mental illness or the result of mental illness?

How should a civilized society deal with problems such as Munchausen by proxy that are not official disorders but probably should be?

Sexual Disorders

The DSM includes three categories of sexual disorders. First are the **sexual dysfunctions,** which have been extensively studied by **Masters and Johnson.** William Masters, a doctor, and Virginia Johnson, a psychologist, work together in St. Louis and study problems that couples have with sexual performance. Masters and Johnson defined the **human sexual response cycle,** the normal physiological events that occur during sexual arousal (1966). The cycle is divided into four stages: excitement, plateau, orgasm, and resolution. Often sexual dysfunctions are categorized into these four domains.

Sexual dysfunctions include a man's inability or difficulty in achieving an erection (**erectile dysfunction**), when a man ejaculates too soon for a woman's pleasure (**premature ejaculation**), a woman's inability to achieve orgasm (**orgasmic dysfunction**), and when a woman's vaginal muscles tighten before sexual intercourse (**vaginismus**). These are mostly highly treatable disorders. For example, Masters and Johnson report a cure rate of 100% for vaginismus. They use a treatment similar to systematic desensitization (see Chapters 5 and 10) to condition the woman's muscles to relax. Similarly, premature ejaculation, the most common of the sexual dysfunctions, is easily treatable with a classical conditioning procedure called the **squeeze technique.** The problem is not discovering treatments for these disorders; it is that people feel shame about sexual dysfunctions and therefore are very reluctant to seek treatment. Masters and Johnson have estimated that nearly 50% of married couples have sexual dysfunctions, most of which go untreated.

A second type of sexual disorder is called **paraphilia**—unusual ways of achieving sexual gratification. This is an example of the subjective nature of mental illness. What is considered unusual varies from culture to culture and from time to time. What is a paraphilia in one society at one time is not in another. The paraphilias include a **fetish,** in which a person must use an object (e.g., a shoe, nylon stocking, or book) or a part of the body (e.g., a foot, an ear) to achieve sexual satisfaction. Other paraphilias include **exhibitionism** (a person exhibits his or her genitals to strangers) and **voyeurism** (a person secretly watches other people engaging in sexual activities). Treatment programs for paraphilias have been relatively successful. For example, Maletzky (1998) reports that cognitive behavioral treatments had success rates from 78% to 96% for various problems such as **pedophilia** (sexual attraction to children), exhibitionism, and fetish.

A third sexual disorder is **gender identity disorder.** This unfortunate circumstance arises when an individual's biological sexual characteristics do not match the person's mental idea of his or her gender. A person's mental (or psychological) concept of himself or herself as a man or a woman is called gender identity. This concept is at least partially developed early in life. By the age of two, children have a very strong concept of themselves as boys or girls. Normally, of course, gender identity is congruent with a person's biological status as male or female. However, in some cases, there is a mismatch between the biological and the psychological. In adults, this is called **transsexualism.**

Don't confuse this disorder with **transvestism,** which is a kind of fetish in which a man wears women's clothing to get sexual satisfaction, or with **homosexuality,** in which a person's gender identity is fine but he or she is sexually attracted to members of the same sex. Homosexuality is not considered a mental disorder. **Transsexuals** can have psychotherapy to try to convert their gender identity (a tough task), or they can have sex reassignment surgery (a so-called sex change operation) that will allow their bodies to match their minds. Thousands of people have had such an operation, and an overwhelming number of them are very pleased with the results. However, the number of such operations has decreased greatly in the past 20 years as transsexuals are turning more to counseling.

Recap

— Dissociative disorders, such as amnesia, fugue, and identity disorder, are problems in which a part of the mind is split off from the rest.

— *Fugue* means "flight." In this disorder, a person travels to another location and has amnesia about his or her previous life.

— Multiple personality disorder (as in *The Three Faces of Eve*) is now known as dissociative identity disorder. Most experts believe that this is a real problem, though rare, that begins because of childhood abuse.

— One category of disorders in the DSM includes problems that are usually first diagnosed in childhood or adolescence, such as autism, ADHD, mental retardation, and learning disorders.

— The dementias include Alzheimer's and Parkinson's diseases. These are much more common in old age and currently are not curable, though there are some treatments for symptoms.

— Substance-related disorders, such as alcoholism, are among the most common problems.

— In factitious disorder, people purposely fake illness or make themselves sick.

— Sexual disorders include sexual dysfunctions, which are performance difficulties; paraphilias, in which a person has an unusual way of attaining sexual satisfaction; and gender identity disorder, in which a person's idea of his or her gender is inconsistent with the person's physical body.

Eating Disorders

The two types of eating disorders are well known by the general public. In **anorexia nervosa,** a person does not eat enough. This person refuses to maintain a normal body weight, has an intense fear of becoming fat, and seemingly has a disturbance in his or her body image. People with anorexia often claim to be fat when in fact they are very thin. Women with anorexia also experience **amenorrhea,** the absence of a menstrual cycle. European researchers found that 11% of anorexics, compared to 4.5% of controls, carried a certain form of a gene for an appetite hormone (Harvard Mental Health Letter, 2003).

In **bulimia nervosa,** a person **binges** (eats a large amount at one time) and then **purges** (removes the food from his or her stomach by self-induced vomiting or the use of laxatives). As in anorexia, the patient with bulimia has a disordered view of his or her body and in self-evaluation is unduly influenced by his or her body shape and weight. These disorders are very serious and can result in permanent biological problems and even death.

Eating disorders are seen almost exclusively in adolescents and young adults and occur about 10 times more often in women than in men. This gender difference is believed to be due both to biological (hormonal) differences between the sexes and to our culture's insistence that the ideal woman's body should be very thin.

However, the desire to be thin is *not* seen in women everywhere in the world. In West Africa, for instance, women are encouraged to be overweight and often eat fatty foods and substances that will increase their body size. Being obese is a sign of wealth and high status for those women. A Nigerian doctor said, "The world is a funny place. In America you are rich, you have everything, and the women want to become so thin as if they had nothing. Here in Africa, we have nothing, the women who buy these products have nothing, but they want to become fat as if they had everything" (Harvard Mental Health Letter, 2003). A group of teenage girls in Niger was asked what they thought was the ideal body shape, and they unanimously picked an obese woman. This illustrates the effect of cultural attitudes on behavior and psychological disorders. Anorexia is unknown in many developing countries.

Eating disorders, like many other psychological disorders, often overlap with other syndromes. This is called **comorbidity** (*co* means "together"; *morbid* means "illness"). For example, many people with an eating disorder also suffer from perfectionism (obsessive-compulsive disorder) and depression (Anderluh et al., 2003). In fact, eating disorders are often treated with antidepressant psychotherapies. Perfectionist personality traits are risk factors for eating disorders. Also, mothers of patients with eating disorders had high levels of perfectionism (Woodside, 2002).

FYI The German word for anorexia is *Pubertätsmagersucht,* which means "craving for thinness at puberty."

Comorbidity often occurs with mental disorders because they are subjective categories that define mental illnesses on the basis of symptoms. But symptoms often overlap. It is wise to think of people with mental illnesses as people with problems. It is not wise to think that mental illnesses are fixed, concrete conditions that are the same from person to person. In fact, the terminology that we use often confuses this issue. We say that a person "has" anxiety, as if anxiety is a thing that people catch. When we say that a person has a mental illness, we simply mean that the person is reporting complaints about his or her ABCs.

Though difficult to treat, eating disorders do respond well to behavior therapy, cognitive behavior therapy, antidepressant medications, and other therapies (Peterson & Mitchell, 1999). Specifics on these treatments are provided in the next chapter. However, there is a relatively low rate of improvement with these problems, partially because only people with the most severe symptoms seek out help (Keel et al., 2002). Some new research has found that antiseizure medicines can help binge eaters (McElroy et al., 2003).

Sleep Disorders

Sleep disorders are fairly common. Most research and university hospitals have sleep laboratories where people can be appropriately diagnosed for such disorders. The most common of these is **insomnia** (difficulty sleeping that persists for at least one month), which almost all adults have had some experience with—haven't you? **Hypersomnia** (excessive sleepiness for at least one month), **sleepwalking** (repeated episodes), and **nightmare disorder** are also included.

The sleep-wake cycle is an example of a **circadian rhythm** ("circles around the day"), a biological cycle that revolves around approximately a 24-hour period. Body temperature, blood pressure, and other physiological functions follow a circadian rhythm set by the body's biological clock, which is primarily influenced by the actions of the brain's **pineal gland.** The sleep-wake cycle is regulated by a series of brain mechanisms and chemicals, particularly the hormone **melatonin.** Light entering through the eyes helps to adjust the cycle each day. People who work night shifts often have sleep problems because they are fighting against their natural brain regulations. Such sleep problems are known as **circadian rhythm sleep disorders.**

In 2001, scientists announced that they had identified one of the genes that controls the brain mechanisms involved in the sleep-wake cycle (Toh, 2001). The gene is located on chromosome 2 and was discovered by studying a family in which the gene caused the sleep-wake cycle to be adjusted earlier than normal by about six hours. Each family member grew very tired at about 5:00 in the evening, and woke up early every morning.

Narcolepsy is a neurological sleep disorder in which a person suffers from "sleep attacks," sudden losses of muscle tone. A person with narcolepsy can fall into REM sleep at any moment, particularly in the presence of a surprising stimulus, such as a flash of light or a loud noise, or even in response to an emotional reaction such as laughing. The person will fall to the ground during a sleep attack because the muscles of the body suddenly lose their tone. About 140,000 Americans have narcolepsy. The loss of muscle tone is caused by low levels of a brain chemical called hypocretin. Medications are taken to control the symptoms of narcolepsy.

Finally, a breathing-related sleep disorder, often known as **sleep apnea,** occurs in a relatively large number of people. In effect, the person with sleep apnea cannot sleep and breathe at the same time! The person might even be unaware of the problem and might complain about sleeplessness or snoring. There are several remedies for such a problem, including surgery or use of a device that blows air into the lungs during sleep.

PERSONALITY DISORDERS

"Personality is a mask you believe in."
—DR. WHITE

The **personality disorders** are markedly different from the disorders described above. They are conceptually different from the clinical syndromes because personality disorders are considered long-term qualities of a person rather than a problem that strikes them during their lives. Clinical disorders (those described above) are viewed as problems that temporarily affect a normal person. They represent a *change* in a person's usual pattern. A person might be stricken with depression or a phobia, for example, or a person might suddenly notice a change in his or her behavior, thinking, or emotions.

Personality disorders, by contrast, are significantly part of a person rather than something that happens to them. They are ingrained development problems that are relatively lifelong, inflexible, and enduring. It is as if a person has developed a personality that is troubling, problematic, or deviant. It isn't that something has gone awry with the person's behavior or thinking or emotions; rather, the person's personality itself is the problem. People with personality disorders often deny that they have a problem—rather, they typically cause severe problems for others who relate to them.

The DSM defines ten personality disorders and divides them into 3 clusters: Cluster A includes people who are odd or eccentric; Cluster B includes personalities that are dramatic, erratic, or emotional; and Cluster C includes people who are anxious, fearful, or nervous. It is common for people to have symptoms of more than one disorder, typically from the same cluster.

TABLE 9.9 Personality Disorders

Cluster A: Odd, eccentric

1. Paranoid—excessively suspicious.
2. Schizoid—isolated, withdrawn, cold, detached.
3. Schizotypal—odd beliefs; peculiar, magical thinking.

Cluster B: Dramatic, erratic, emotional

4. Antisocial—deceitful, impulsive, reckless, criminal, lack of remorse.
5. Borderline—unstable, feelings of emptiness, fear of abandonment, erratic emotions, disloyal, raging.
6. Histrionic—center of attention, seductive, disloyal, theatrical, role-playing.
7. Narcissistic—self-important, grandiose, selfish, arrogant, demanding.

Cluster C: Anxious, nervous, fearful

8. Avoidant—socially inhibited, fear of criticism.
9. Dependent—demands support, advice, and nurturance; needy.
10. Obsessive-Compulsive—preoccupied with details, lists, orderliness, perfectionism; inflexible, stubborn.

Here are brief descriptions of two of the more common and studied personality disorders included in the DSM:

1. People with **antisocial personality disorder (APD)** are unable to appreciate the feelings of others. They often act in ways that are cruel and thoughtless, though many have disarmingly charming but superficial personalities. This disorder was once known as *psychopathic*, but that term has been so distorted by TV and movies that it represents an overblown image of APD. People with this disorder often get into difficulties with friends, family, and the police. One very common characteristic is the inability to learn from mistakes. Lying and cheating are common behaviors, but more to the point, this person does not feel guilt or remorse for hurting or taking advantage of others, and his or her harmful behavior continues. This person might apologize profusely for taking your money and at the same time be taking your car keys. Antisocial personality disorder is seen much more often in men than in women, which may be partly due to biological factors, since this is true in all societies.

2. **Borderline personality disorder (BPD)** is marked by instability in personal relationships, unfaithfulness, problems with self-image and self-esteem, depression, dependency, and impulsive behaviors. The title of a book about BPD,

I Hate You, Don't Leave Me (Kreisman & Straus, 1991), neatly captures the needy, desperate, and helplessly dependent feelings experienced by a person with this disorder. It is common for people with this disorder to harm themselves, often by cutting their forearms with a knife or razor. This behavior is simply termed **cutting,** and people who regularly do it are called cutters. "Splitting" is also common—viewing people as all good or all bad, and suddenly switching. Some people with BPD attempt suicide, or make suicide gestures, and most suffer from depression. This person appears to have a personality that is not well grounded. Self-image problems are common, as are fears of being abandoned. Women suffer from this disorder more often than men do.

The personality disorders, perhaps because they are an integral, ingrained part of a person, are among the most difficult to treat effectively, although there has been some success with psychodynamic and cognitive-behavioral therapies. (See Chapter 10 for a discussion of specific therapies.) A six-year follow-up of BPD found more improvement than was expected and good prognosis for most patients (Zanarini et al., 2003). Most researchers think that the personality disorders develop over long periods of time and are integrated into the lifetime development of the person. In that sense, these disorders likely are influenced by genetic and other biological factors and particularly by family circumstances.

Children whose mothers have personality disorders are more likely to have personality disorders even if adopted. Patients with BPD often remember their childhoods as being awful, and recall their family members and others as trying to injure them. Childhood abuse, neglect, and severe punishment have been linked to personality disorders. Also, neurological examinations often show abnormalities in the nervous system's responses in people with personality disorders, particularly in APD. Brain abnormalities are likely.

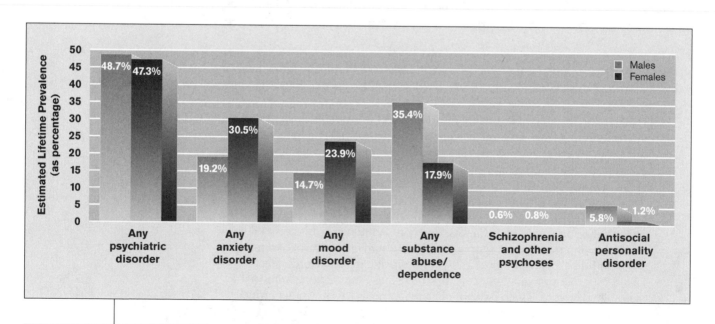

Lifetime prevalence of psychological disorders.

Recap

— Eating disorders include anorexia (failure to maintain weight) and bulimia (binging and purging).

— *Comorbidity* is the term used for the very common occurrence in which a person experiences more than one disorder at a time.

— Sleep disorders are very common and include insomnia, narcolepsy, circadian rhythm disorders, and sleep apnea.

— The personality disorders are different from the clinical syndromes in that they are lifelong, ingrained problems of personality.

— Personality disorders include antisocial (APD), in which a person lacks a conscience, and borderline (BPD), in which sufferers have numerous symptoms, including depression, instability in relationships, weak identity, and desperate dependency on others.

CAUSES OF PSYCHOLOGICAL DISORDERS

"The cause is hidden; the effect is visible to all."
—OVID, ROMAN POET

Mental illnesses are psychological disorders—meaning there is something *out of order* with the *psychology* of a person. Psychology includes the ABCs; therefore, a mental illness is an emotion, behavior, or cognition that is out of order. But those three things—emotions, behaviors, and cognitions—are all produced by the biological activities of brain circuitry. Therefore, mental illnesses are produced by actions of the brain.

The term *mental* is unfortunate, because it implies a distinction from physical. But mental *is* physical. That is, mental is a subset of physical. Not all physical things are mental, of course. But all mental things are, at their fundamental basis, physical. Emotions, behaviors, and cognitions are produced by the brain via biochemical events and neural networks. Psychological disorders are physically (biologically) caused.

Unfortunately, it is common to confuse this issue. The confusion arises for two reasons: (1) Because mental events are conscious, aware conditions, most people think of them as separate from the physical, biological world. However, conscious awareness results from the actions of the brain. Therefore, mental states are essentially physical (biological) events. (2) Most people assume that the brain is a static, unchanging thing. The prevailing popular view is that our brain is "set" at birth and continues essentially unchanged throughout life. For example, people often ask whether some psychological condition is "inborn"—apparently implying that certain things are "permanently in us" and other things "happen to us." This concept is terribly wrong.

Brains are dynamic, living organs that change with experience. For example, researcher Martin Teicher studies children who have been abused. He and many other researchers have found that the brains of abused children are markedly changed by the experience. Even verbal abuse has been shown to cause significant changes in children's brains. But, of course, why wouldn't it? A brain is a dynamic organ that responds to its experiences. Brain wiring and biological functioning are influenced by what we sense. Researchers who studied child abuse found changes in the victims' brains. They wrote, "The brain is fundamentally sculpted by our experiences. Adverse experience will sculpt our brain in a different way" (Teicher, 2000).

Because mental illnesses are produced by the brain, anything that influences the brain can potentially cause mental illness. The term *etiology* is used to refer to the causes or influences of a disorder. These include genetic factors, diet, bacteria and viruses, injuries, learning, and family and cultural experiences. In nearly all cases, it is impossible to pinpoint only one cause for any particular mental illness. Nearly all psychological disorders have multiple causes, and for most mental illnesses, it takes a combination of things to produce the condition. In other words, psychological disorders are complicated problems that can arise through various combinations of forces. Listed here are the major contributing factors; however, be sure to remember that for most disorders, a combination of these factors is required to cause the condition.

Heredity

Our brains develop and function according to the blueprints provided by our heredity. Over 1,000 genes have been identified that contribute to creating the anatomical structure of the brain. Other genes have been found that impair brain functioning. For example, **Huntington's disease** is a form of dementia that strikes late in life and eventually results in death due to destruction of major brain areas. Huntington's is caused by a dominant gene on chromosome 4. Alzheimer's disease is an example of a mental disorder that is not entirely caused by heredity but for which heredity plays a major role. Several genes have been identified that contribute to the brain destruction that is characteristic of Alzheimer's. Similarly, genes that contribute to both depression (Carey, 2003) and bipolar disorder (Shaw et al., 2003) have been identified. **Down syndrome,** which results in both mental retardation and Alzheimer's disease, is caused by an extra chromosome 21. Several genes have been found that likely contribute to schizophrenia (Ambrose, 2002). In fact, all mental illnesses are influenced at least to some extent by heredity—some more than others, of course, and perhaps hundreds or thousands of genes may predispose people toward certain problems.

Bacteria, Viruses, Traumas, and Toxins

Brains are not commonly influenced by germs because there is a blood-brain barrier that protects the brain from most foreign substances. However, a number of tiny microorganisms and toxic substances can invade the brain and cause impairments in emotions, behaviors, or thinking. Lead poisoning is a major cause of mental retardation and other neurological disorders. The National Academy of Science estimates that 60,000 children each year have neurological problems due to exposure to mercury in the womb. Solvents, such as alcohol, glue, and cement, also kill neurons.

As was mentioned above, it has been suggested that schizophrenia might be influenced by viruses or infections during the prenatal period or childhood. Bipolar disorder, too, is seen more often in people born during the winter or early spring. This indicates the possible influence of viruses, more common in winter months. Brain lesions are found more commonly in people born between January and March (Moore et al., 2001).

Parkinson's disease has been linked to bacteria and toxic substances, such as herbicides and pesticides. Many other dementias are also influenced by exposure to viruses and toxic substances. Two final examples: Strep germs and chorea are associated with obsessive-compulsive disorder (Asbahr et al., 1998), and the syphilis germ can cause a type of brain damage called **general paresis,** a condition that was common in the past but less so today because of the use of antibiotics to treat syphilis.

Prenatal complications and birth traumas, such as lack of oxygen, are likely causes of a wide range of neuropsychiatric disorders. The fetal brain is especially sensitive to traumas, toxic agents, and stress. New brain cells generate at a rate of 250,000 per minute at the peak of fetal development.

A rare brain disorder in humans is called **Creutzfeldt-Jakob disease** (CJD). Cattle have a similar disease that is popularly called *mad cow disease*. In sheep, it is called *scrapie*. When people get this disease from eating contaminated meat, it is called *new variant CJD*. This strange brain disorder is caused by a misshapen protein called a **prion.** Protein folding is a normal biological process. Proteins that are misfolded normally get recycled by the cells of the body. However, some misfolded proteins can survive, and problems can occur. When a protein folds in an unusual way, it becomes sticky and creates clumps in the brain that damage brain cells. This then spreads to other proteins in the brain. Some scientists believe that other diseases, such as type 2 diabetes, Alzheimer's disease, and Parkinson's disease, may also be affected by this process (Selkoe, 1999). When misfolded proteins were injected into rats' brains, the rats showed significant memory problems (Walsh et al., 2002). It is known that prions can occur spontaneously in rare cases and that they can be passed by blood contact and by eating. Cooking contaminated food does not destroy the misshaped proteins.

Childhood Experiences

The events that happen to us as children influence the wiring and functioning of our brains. When a child has traumatic experiences, for instance, brain development is changed and impaired. The result can be depression, dissociative disorder, anxiety disorder, substance abuse, or other problems in psychological adjustment. Childhood abuse and neglect have deleterious effects on the brain, even to the extent of interfering with anatomical development. For example, in abused children, the corpus callosum, the connecting fiber between the hemispheres, is smaller than average. In a general population sample, MacMillan and colleagues (2001) found significantly higher rates of psychological disorders among people who reported childhood physical or sexual abuse, particularly in women. The authors concluded: "A history of abuse in childhood increases the likelihood of lifetime psychopathology." Another study found that abused children were more likely to interpret faces as angry and would retreat or lash out as a consequence (Pollak & Kistler, 2000). The U.S. Department of Health and Human Services estimates that about 176,000 children are physically abused each year in the United States.

Of course, years ago, Sigmund Freud emphasized the effects of childhood experiences on the unconscious mind. Many psychological disorders involve problems of lack of awareness or unconsciousness. The dissociative disorders are the most obvious.

Connecting Concepts

Recall from Chapter 1 the discussion of contact comfort and attachment theory. Harry Harlow found that infant monkeys did not develop normally if denied good mothering, and non-securely attached children had worse social and cognitive development. Childhood experiences are often important in the development of psychological health.

Childhood traumas can trigger the development of unconscious processes meant to protect a person from the memories of such tragedies. These unconscious brain effects can then cause psychological distress that might be manifested in a variety of symptoms, including anxiety, depression, nightmares, and dissociative and somatoform disorders.

It is clear that childhood is an important period in the development of personality. Family experiences can have a dramatic effect on a child's psychological development. Abuse, alcoholism, traumas, and parental attitudes and behaviors are crucial ingredients in the etiology of psychological disorders. An ongoing federal study (Belsky, 2001) is tracking 1,300 children. Early results indicate that good childcare fosters school readiness, while time away from home, including day care, is associated with problems such as aggression and disobedience. Murray (2001) scanned children's brains as they watched violent media and found brain activity similar to that of people who experience traumatic events, such as war or rape. Also, children who spent more time playing violent video games got into more fights and did worse in school. Violent song lyrics can increase aggressive thoughts and hostile feelings according to another study (Anderson et al., 2003). Perhaps most disheartening, several of these studies found that parents typically are unaware of what their children are watching.

Now is the time to recall that nature and nurture work together. Not everyone who experiences stress or trauma develops a psychopathology. Not everyone who watches or listens to violent media becomes more aggressive. Why? Well, in some cases, scientists have identified genes that predispose a person toward resilience or disorder. For instance, researchers found that boys who were severely maltreated were much more likely to develop disorders. But boys with a gene for low levels of the enzyme MAO were two to three times *more* likely to have problems than boys with a gene for high MAO activity (Caspi et al., 2002). Nature and nurture interact in the development of all of our ABCs.

Learning

Throughout our lives, we are learning. This means that we change because of our experiences. We can learn new fears, anxieties, habits, or ways of thinking. We can even learn to be depressed. For example, studies on **learned helplessness** show that when an animal is in an unpleasant situation with no escape, the animal learns to give up trying to escape and develops the characteristics of depression. Psychologists believe that humans, too, can learn to be helpless by being in unpleasant situations with no means of escape. Such learning experiences often lead to depression.

Phobias are probably the clearest example of how a disorder can be caused by learning—in this case, classical conditioning. Similarly, troubling behaviors, such as compulsions, are learned by reinforcement. Eating disorders are taught by one girl to another in dormitories, on athletic teams, and in dance studios. Nearly every psychological disorder is likely influenced by conditioning, since this is the way that brains change through experience. Learning is a significant component in the etiology of many psychological disorders.

Psychological Traumas

Naturally, horrible experiences at any age will produce psychological consequences. People who are sexually assaulted, have traumatic experiences in war, or are accident victims or crime victims and others who experience trauma will normally exhibit short-term psychological distress and often develop long-term disorders because of their traumatic experience. The most obvious example is posttraumatic stress disorder, although many other disorders are at least somewhat influenced by traumas that people experience. Dissociative amnesia, somatoform disorder, anxiety, and mood disorders all could be influenced by trauma. The link between traumas early in life and depression in adulthood has been firmly established (Kendler et al., 2000).

Domestic violence is an all too common form of trauma. In the United States, it is the leading cause of injury among women. The problem is worldwide. In Russia, 14,500 women were killed and 56,000 were injured by their husbands in 1993. In Canada, 62% of women who are murdered die from domestic abuse. In Zimbabwe, one in every three women is physically assaulted; in South Africa, it is one out of four (Kuhn, 1994). Besides the physical injuries, posttraumatic stress, mood, and anxiety disorders are common results of such circumstances (Zlotnick, 2001).

Social and Cultural Factors

A number of psychological disorders are said to be **culture-bound** because they arise as part of the folklore, the superstitions, or the common beliefs of a particular culture. The DSM lists 25 culture-bound syndromes that might be encountered in clinical practice in North America.

Amok is a dissociative episode followed by a violent outburst that occurs primarily in men in southeastern Asia and the Pacific Islands. *Dhat* is a man's intense fear of the loss of semen during sleep or through the urine, supposedly resulting in a loss of natural energy. Dhat occurs primarily in India.

Ghost sickness is seen among American Indians and involves a preoccupation with the spirits of dead people. Sufferers have nightmares, anxiety, loss of appetite, and other symptoms. *Zar* is the term used in North Africa and the Middle East to describe possession by spirits. Symptoms include dissociative episodes, shouting, banging the head against the wall, laughing, and crying. Sufferers are often apathetic and withdrawn. *Locura* is a term used by Latinos in the United States and Latin America to describe a psychotic episode similar to schizophrenia, including incoherence, hallucinations, and unpredictability.

Brain fag is a term that originated in West Africa to describe the symptoms of "too much thinking," such as blurred vision, pain and tightness in the head and neck, and difficulty concentrating. (Uh, oh—I can see it now, a new excuse for doing poorly on a test!) *Koro* is seen primarily in Southeast Asia. In this case, people believe that their genitals will recede into their body, causing their death. *Susto* is a folk illness of Latinos consisting of unhappiness, no motivation, low self-esteem, and sickness resulting from the belief that the soul has left the body.

Naturally, cultural factors do not affect only the mental disorders of people from foreign lands. In the United States, there are many social and cultural beliefs that influence the development of symptoms. Eating disorders are influenced by our society's emphasis on the thin female body. Several cultures had a very low incidence of eating disorders until they were introduced to Western culture's ideas of female beauty, usually through TV programs. The incidence of eating disorders then skyrocketed. The kinds and peculiarities of the delusions of schizophrenia are also influenced by culture; for example, it is only recently that people with schizophrenia began complaining about extraterrestrial abductions and other delusions that include scientific and technological concepts. One hundred years ago, people with schizophrenia did not believe their thoughts were being stolen by computers. As you can see, mental illnesses are influenced in many ways by the social and cultural beliefs of the culture in which they occur.

Determining the etiology of a mental illness is a complicated and difficult process. Many varied factors influence a person's emotions, behaviors, and cognitions. In addition, it is important to realize that people do not neatly fit into the rigid categories defined in the DSM. The DSM is merely one tool, albeit an important and influential one. However, people rarely fit snugly into the categories that are described. People are complex, as are the multiple forces that contribute to feelings, actions, and mental states. Unraveling all of the interacting factors and their nuances is a mighty task. Still, a good deal is known about the causes of mental illnesses, and a number of therapies have found good success in helping people who experience psychological distress. In the next chapter, we turn to a discussion of those treatments.

Recap

— The term *etiology* refers to the causes or influences of a disorder.

— Behavior and mental states derive from the brain; however, the brain is a dynamic, ever-changing organ that is influenced by social and cultural experiences as well as by genetic and material factors.

— Mental illnesses often have a mix of complicated causes including heredity, bacteria, viruses, toxins, childhood experiences, learning, traumas, and social and cultural factors. While heredity plays a role in a great number of disorders, experience is often a key factor also.

— The DSM identifies a number of culture-bound disorders, such as amok, dhat, and koro, that occur because of the cultural beliefs of a group of people. Of course, social and cultural factors influence nearly every mental illness to some extent.

I Link, Therefore I Am

There are an extraordinarily large number of Web sites devoted to mental illnesses, probably because they are so common. To get started, try these, which are very thorough: http://www.mentalhealth.com/ or http://www.psychcentral.com/ or http://www.mhsanctuary.com or http://www.psyweb.com

There is a group devoted to criticizing the excessive use of medicines and shock treatment. Their Web site is http://www.antipsychiatry.org/

It seems that every psychological disorder has one or more Web sites devoted to it. Here are a few of the many that are available to you:

OCD at http://www.ocdawareness.com/ or http://www.ocfoundation.org

Borderline personality disorder at http://bpdcentral.com/

Eating disorders at http://www.edap.org or http://www.anred.com or http://www.acadeatdis.org or http://www.somethingfishy.org

Factitious disorder (Munchausen syndrome) at http://ourworld.compuserve.com/homepages/Marc_Feldman_2/

Anxiety disorders at http://www.adaa.org/ or http://www.nimh.nih.gov/anxiety/

Sleep disorders at http://www.nlm.nih.gov/medlineplus/sleepdisorders.html or http://www.asda.org/

Sex disorders at http://www.mastersandjohnson.com/

Disorders of childhood and adolescence at http://www.aacap.org/web/aacap/publications/factsfam/

Mood disorders at http://www.ndmda.org/ or http://www.mghmadi.org/home.html or http://www.walkers.org/ or http://www.bipolarhome.org/

There are many Web sites devoted to schizophrenia. Get started with these:
http://www.mentalhealth.com/dis/p20-ps01.html   http://www2.addr.com/~y/mn/   http://www.schizophrenia.com/
http://www.mentalhealth.com/book/p40-sc01.html   http://www.mhsource.com/narsad/

The Surgeon General's Report on Mental Illness can be found on the Internet at http://www.surgeongeneral.gov/library/mentalhealth/home.html

Here are some Web sites about depression and suicide:
http://www.afsp.org/   http://www.metanoia.org/suicide/index.html   http://www.suicideinfo.ca/
http://www.spanusa.org/   http://www.psycom.net/depression.central.html   http://www.depression-net.com/
http://www.depressiondepot.net/   http://www.bipolarhome.org/

STUDY GUIDE FOR CHAPTER 9:
PSYCHOLOGICAL DISORDERS

Key terms and names (Make flash cards.)

mental illness
medical school syndrome
American Psychiatric Association
Diagnostic and Statistical Manual
    of Mental Disorders (DSM)
DSM-IV
syndromes
major depression
Fritz Perls
psychotic disorder
schizophrenia
Eugen Bleuler
psychosis
hallucination
delusion
loosening of associations
    (derailment)
clanging neologism
formal thought disorder
catatonia
positive symptoms
negative symptoms
social withdrawal
poverty of speech
flat or blunted affect
deficit schizophrenia
paranoid schizophrenia
delusions of persecution
delusion of grandiosity
disorganized type
hebephrenia
prognosis
catatonic type
echolalia
waxy flexibility
undifferentiated type
residual type
lifetime incidence
Kraepelinian
prodromal
active phase
concordance rate
emotional expression (EE)
diathesis-stress theory
ventricles
dopamine hypothesis

neuroleptic drugs
atypical antipsychotic drugs
bipolar disorder
hypomania
cyclothymia
depressive disorder
clinical depression
dysthymia
rapid cycler
flight of ideas
affective disorders
manic-depressive disorders
unipolar
double depression
seasonal affective disorder (SAD)
psychache
suicide
suicide attempt
psychological autopsy
antidepressants
electroconvulsive therapy (ECT)
cognitive-behavior (CB) therapy
light therapy (phototherapy)
ruminate
bound anxiety
free-floating anxiety
generalized anxiety disorder
panic disorder (PD)
panic attack
locus coeruleus
phobia
specific phobia
social phobia
agoraphobia
obsessive-compulsive disorder
    (OCD)
obsession
compulsion
posttraumatic stress disorder (PTSD)
flashback
acute stress disorder (ASD)
psychosomatic (psychophysiologic)
stress
stressor
Hans Selye
general adaptation syndrome

fight or flight
somatoform disorders
conversion disorder
somatization disorder
glove anesthesia
hypochondriasis
pain disorder
body dysmorphic disorder (BDD)
epidemiology
etiology
dissociative disorders
dissociative amnesia
dissociative fugue
multiple personality disorder
dissociative identity disorder (DID)
alternate personalities
depersonalization disorder
autism
attention deficit/hyperactivity
    disorder (ADHD)
mental retardation
conduct disorder
oppositional defiant disorder
dementia
senile dementia
presenile dementia
Alzheimer's disease (AD)
beta amyloid
plaques
tangles
mild cognitive impairment
nerve growth factor
Parkinson's disease (PD)
dopamine
L-dopa
factitious disorder
Munchausen syndrome
malingering
Munchausen by proxy
    (factitious disorder by proxy)
sexual dysfunction
Masters and Johnson
human sexual response cycle
erectile dysfunction
premature ejaculation
orgasmic dysfunction

vaginismus
squeeze technique
paraphilia
fetish
voyeurism
exhibitionism
pedophilia
gender identity disorder
transsexualism
transvestism
homosexuality
anorexia nervosa
amenorrhea

bulimia nervosa
binge
purge
comorbidity
insomnia
hypersomnia
sleepwalking
nightmare disorder
circadian rhythm
pineal gland
melatonin
circadian rhythm sleep disorder
narcolepsy

sleep apnea
personality disorders
antisocial personality disorder (APD)
borderline personality disorder
    (BPD)
cutting
Huntington's disease
Down syndrome
Creutzfeld-Jakob disease (CJD)
general paresis
prion
learned helplessness
culture-bound disorders

Fill in the blank

1. Mental health officials in the 1950s hoped that if psychological disorders were called _____, the general public would stop blaming sufferers for their problems.

2. A survey in 1990 asked people whether they had any problems in their emotions, behavior, or thinking in the past year. An astonishingly high number, _____%, said yes.

3. It is likely that many people will not seek help because of the _____ that is associated with mental illness.

4. In the 1950s, _____ was considered a mental illness, whereas _____ was not.

5. The book that includes the definitions of mental illnesses is called the _____ and _____ _____ of Mental Disorders.

6. The DSM is based on the concept of _____.

7. _____ disease is the most common form of dementia.

8. In _____ disease, muscle tremors (shaking) are caused by damage to the part of the brain that produces dopamine.

9. Schizophrenia is the most common of the _____ disorders.

10. When a person has mania as well as depression, this condition is termed _____ disorder.

11. In _____ disorder, a person will purposely make himself or herself sick or pretend to be sick solely for the purpose of receiving medical attention. This disorder is sometimes called _____ syndrome.

12. _____ _____ have been extensively studied by Masters and Johnson.

13. Sexual problems in which a people have unusual way of achieving sexual gratification are called _____.

14. When an individual's biological sexual characteristics do not match the person's mental idea of his or her gender, it is called a _____ _____ disorder.

15. In _____ _____, a person binges (eats a large amount at one time) and then _____.

16. Many psychological disorders overlap with other syndromes. This is called _____.

17. The most common sleep disorder is _____.

18. The body's biological clock that revolves around the day is called a _____ _____.

19. The hormone that influences the sleep-wake cycle is _____.

20. _____ is a neurological sleep disorder in which a person suffers from "sleep attacks."

21. A breathing-related sleep disorder in which a person cannot sleep and breathe at the same time is known as sleep _____.

22. _____ disorders are considered to be inherent long-term qualities of a person rather than something different that strikes them during their lives.

23. People with _____ personality disorder are unable to appreciate the feelings of others.

24. Instability in personal relationships, problems with self-image, self-esteem, depression, dependency, and impulsive behaviors are seen in _____ personality disorder.

25. A common misconception is that schizophrenia is the same as _____ _____.

26. A _____ is a false perception.

27. _____ are false beliefs that are held despite clear evidence to the contrary.

28. A person with schizophrenia might have a _____ of _____ in which he makes odd connections between ideas—connections that do not make sense to us.

29. Sometimes a person will stand perfectly still for hours, which is called _____.

30. _____ symptoms are things like hallucinations and delusions—symptoms that we want to reduce; _____ symptoms are things that the patient does not do often enough—things that we want to increase.

31. _____ schizophrenia was previously known as hebephrenia.

32. In _____ schizophrenia, a person has delusions of persecution.

33. _____ is a miscellaneous or "other" category of schizophrenia.

34. The lifetime incidence of schizophrenia is about _____%.

35. _____ is a term that refers to the early signs of an illness.

36. The _____ phase is when a person with schizophrenia begins to exhibit severe positive symptoms such as hallucinations and delusions.

37. A family situation with lots of criticism will often exacerbate the problems of a person with schizophrenia. Researchers call this family variable _____.

38. A genetic potential is known as a _____.

39. In schizophrenia, it is common for the _____ of the brain to be larger than normal.

40. Many studies have indicated an abnormality in the activity of the brain chemical _____ in people with schizophrenia.

41. The most common and most effective treatments for schizophrenia are _____ medicines, also known as _____ drugs.

42. Depression occurs at a rate three to four times higher in _____.

43. Mild manic episodes are known as _____.

44. When mood swings are mild, the diagnosis is _____.

45. Some people meet the DSM criteria for both major depression and dysthymia. The diagnosis then is _____ depression.

46. Certain individuals are especially sensitive to fluctuations in the amount of light, and a diagnosis of _____ disorder is made.

47. It is very important to distinguish between suicide, in which the person dies, and suicide _____.

48. Old people have _____ suicide rates than teens and young adults.

49. Following a suicide, psychologists sometimes conduct a _____ _____, in which they seek to determine the causes of the person's suicide.

50. People suffering from SAD are often prescribed _____ therapy.

51. The most common treatments for depression are _____ medicines.

52. A controversial treatment that has some success with the mood disorders is _____ therapy (_____), which is commonly called _____ treatment.

53. In _____ therapy, patients learn to change their thinking and their behaviors, and these changes result in improved moods.

54. Sometimes anxiety is connected to some object or situation, as when a person is afraid of heights. This is called _____ anxiety. Other times, people experience anxiety in general, not bound to anything. This is known as _____ anxiety.

55. _____ anxiety disorder is the term used when a person complains of experiencing anxiety at all times.

56. _____ disorder is the term used when a person has attacks of extreme anxiety that seem to come out of nowhere.

57. _____ is a very broad fear in which a person is nervous about going out in public.

58. An _____ is an idea or thought that intrudes uncontrollably into a person's mind, while _____ are behaviors that people feel they must do lest something horrible happen.

59. Men in war situations often develop _____ stress disorder.

60. Sometimes a *real* physical symptom (a headache, for example) is caused or worsened by stress. This is called _____.

61. A demand placed on the body is called _____.

62. The things that place demands on the body are called _____.

63. The body's reaction to stress is called the _____ _____. It was defined by _____.

64. The three stages of GAS are _____, _____, and _____.
65. The term *hysteria* has been replaced by the term _____ disorder.
66. In _____ _____ disorder, people believe that they are extremely ugly and repugnant to others.
67. Psychological disorders that involve alterations in a person's conscious awareness and sense of identity are known as _____ disorders.
68. The psychiatric term _____ literally means "flight."
69. Multiple-personality disorder is now termed dissociative _____ disorder.
70. In _____ disorder, a person reports feelings of detachment or estrangement from himself or herself, as if out of his or her body.

71. The term _____ is used to refer to the causes or influences of a disorder.
72. _____ disease is caused by a dominant gene on chromosome 4.
73. Studies on _____ _____ show that when an animal is in an unpleasant situation with no escape, the animal learns to give up trying to escape and develops the characteristics of depression.
74. A number of psychological disorders are said to be _____ because they arise as part of the folklore, the superstitions, or simply the common beliefs of a particular culture of people.

Matching

1. comorbidity _____
2. etiology _____
3. syndrome _____
4. paraphilia _____
5. DSM _____
6. schizophrenia _____
7. SAD _____
8. fugue _____
9. agoraphobia _____
10. panic disorder _____
11. a somatoform disorder _____
12. dysthymia _____
13. delusion _____
14. hallucination _____
15. hysterical blindness _____
16. depersonalization _____
17. ADHD _____
18. narcolepsy _____
19. paranoia _____
20. hypochondriasis _____

a. classification manual
b. false belief
c. mild depression
d. cause
e. psychosis
f. excessive suspiciousness
g. winter depression
h. body dysmorphic disorder
i. sexual disorder
j. coexisting illnesses
k. out of body experience
l. fear of open spaces
m. fear of getting illnesses
n. group of symptoms
o. sleep disorder
p. carbon dioxide
q. false perception
r. a dissociative disorder
s. conversion disorder
t. hyperactivity

Multiple choice

1. Your English teacher has dysthymia. You know this means that he
   a. has hallucinations
   b. has a psychotic disorder
   c. feels many body symptoms
   d. is mildly depressed
2. A friend says that she is nervous all the time, without any apparent cause. What is the likely DSM diagnosis?
   a. agoraphobia
   b. OCD
   c. generalized anxiety disorder
   d. borderline personality disorder

3. Movies often show characters who lie and cheat and then seem indifferent to the suffering of other people. What DSM diagnosis does this best represent?
   a. disorganized schizophrenia
   b. APD
   c. Huntington's disease
   d. BDD
4. Cognitive impairments are common to all of these disorders EXCEPT:
   a. social phobia
   b. schizophrenia
   c. Alzheimer's disease
   d. MCI

5. About half of people who suffer from depression also have an anxiety disorder. Which concept best describes this fact?
   a. MCI
   b. formal thought disorder
   c. etiology
   d. comorbidity
6. Which of these is a dissociative disorder?
   a. schizophrenia
   b. amnesia
   c. posttraumatic stress disorder
   d. conversion disorder
7. Which of these is another name for Munchausen syndrome?
   a. fugue   b. conversion disorder
   c. cyclothymia   d. factitious disorder
8. Which of these is a psychosis?
   a. identity disorder
   b. generalized anxiety disorder
   c. bipolar disorder
   d. schizophrenia
9. What is the main symptom of body dysmorphic disorder?
   a. perceived ugliness
   b. panic attacks
   c. fear of illness
   d. simulated body dysfunctions
10. The suicide rate is highest for
    a. males
    b. females
    c. middle-aged adults
    d. pre-teens
11. Which of these is a dementia?
    a. somatoform disorder   b. Alzheimer's disease
    c. schizophrenia   d. paranoia
12. The causes or influences of an illness are known as its
    a. etiology
    b. epidemiology
    c. comorbidity
    d. incidence
13. What is the main symptom of a conversion disorder?
    a. fear of illness
    b. delusions
    c. simulated body dysfunctions
    d. amnesia
14. In which disorder does a person have an abnormal reaction to carbon dioxide?
    a. panic disorder
    b. schizophrenia
    c. dysthymia
    d. cyclothymia

15. In which disorder does a person experience loosening of associations?
    a. agoraphobia
    b. schizophrenia
    c. hypochondriasis
    d. dissociative identity disorder
16. Which sexual problems do Masters and Johnson study?
    a. sexual dysfunctions
    b. paraphilias
    c. gender identity disorders
    d. factitious disorders
17. Depersonalization is classified as a
    _____ disorder.
    a. dissociative
    b. delusional
    c. somatoform
    d. psychosomatic
18. An abnormal false belief is known as a
    a. hallucination
    b. fugue
    c. dementia
    d. delusion
19. Which subtype of schizophrenia includes mutism?
    a. genetic
    b. catatonic
    c. paranoid
    d. disorganized
20. Schizophrenia is diagnosed more often among
    a. lower-class individuals
    b. upper class individuals
    c. men
    d. women
21. Which of these disorders is seen much more commonly in men?
    a. antisocial personality disorder
    b. anorexia
    c. major depression
    d. OCD
22. In a movie, a character with schizophrenia is shown laughing loudly and acting very emotional and happy. This is misleading because people with schizophrenia
    a. are unable to laugh because of their medications
    b. are emotional only about their fantasies and fears
    c. experience only depression, not happiness
    d. have flattened emotions
23. The cause of Huntington's disease is
    a. a dominant gene
    b. childhood trauma
    c. a virus
    d. psychological repression

24. Which disorder involves travel?
    a. body dysmorphic
    b. narcolepsy
    c. paraphilias
    d. fugue
25. Amok is a type of
    a. schizophrenia
    b. dissociative disorder
    c. depressive disorder
    d. culture-bound disorder
26. A police officer was forced to shoot a suspect who later turned out to be innocent. The officer developed a feeling of numbness in his shooting hand. This is an example of which disorder?
    a. dysthymia
    b. hypochondriasis
    c. dissociative fugue
    d. conversion
27. A very serious childhood disorder that involves bizarre behaviors, lack of language development, and problems in social development is
    a. delirium
    b. autism
    c. pica
    d. malingering
28. In factitious disorder by proxy, parents may
    a. accidentally harm their children
    b. act indifferently toward their children
    c. never develop a bond with their children
    d. intentionally make their children sick
29. Voyeurism and exhibitionism are types of
    a. sexual dysfunctions
    b. sexual response cycles
    c. paraphilias
    d. gender identity disorders
30. People with sleep apnea have difficulty _____ while sleeping.
    a. dreaming
    b. moving
    c. resting
    d. breathing
31. People with schizophrenia
    a. have multiple alternate personalities
    b. experience unusual perceptions
    c. are dangerous
    d. are outgoing and have wild moods
32. A person with catatonic schizophrenia has problems with
    a. depression
    b. motor movement
    c. fear of illness
    d. perceived ugliness

33. Social withdrawal is a common _____ symptom of schizophrenia.
    a. delusional
    b. genetic
    c. proactive
    d. negative
34. The most common theory about the cause of schizophrenia is
    a. a dominant gene
    b. a virus
    c. diathesis-stress
    d. childhood trauma
35. Which of these is a unipolar disorder?
    a. major depression
    b. schizophrenia
    c. phobia
    d. fugue
36. The term *rapid cyclers* is used to refer to people who suffer from
    a. bipolar disorder
    b. dysthymia
    c. double depression
    d. recurrent depression
37. Severe winter depression is known as
    a. SAD
    b. double depression
    c. cyclothymia
    d. photodepression
38. A person who is nervous about going out in public would be diagnosed with
    a. cyclothymia
    b. agoraphobia
    c. bipolar disorder
    d. a specific phobia
39. "Glove anesthesia" is a type of
    a. hypochondriasis
    b. phobia
    c. malingering
    d. conversion disorder
40. The study of the frequency and distribution of disorders within various segments of the population is called
    a. epidemiology
    b. etiology
    c. prognosis
    d. statistical analysis
41. *The Three Faces of Eve* is an illustration of which disorder?
    a. dissociative identity disorder
    b. depersonalization disorder
    c. schizophrenia
    d. somatoform disorder

42. Parkinson's disease, general paresis, and perhaps schizophrenia can be caused by
    a. traumatic childhood experiences
    b. taking illegal drugs
    c. mental stress
    d. bacteria and viruses

43. Stress causes changes in the body known as the general _____ syndrome.
    a. awareness
    b. arousal
    c. exhaustion
    d. adaptation

44. Which stage of stress is a person in who has adapted to a continuous stressor?
    a. arousal
    b. equilibrium
    c. resistance
    d. alarm

45. The fight or flight response is most connected to which stage of stress?
    a. alarm
    b. arousal
    c. exhaustion
    d. endocrine

Short answer and critical thinking

1. What does it mean to say that the concept of mental illness is subjective?
2. What is a dementia? Give an example.
3. How is a personality disorder different from a clinical syndrome?
4. What is the difference between a delusion and an obsession?
5. What is meant by positive and negative symptoms of schizophrenia?
6. Compare schizophrenia and depression regarding (a) incidence, (b) gender differences, and (c) age of onset.
7. Define hallucinations and delusions.
8. Name and define two of the subtypes of schizophrenia.
9. What is the difference between unipolar and bipolar?
10. Compare and contrast psychosomatic, somatoform, and factitious disorder.
11. Name two causes of psychological disorders, and give examples of disorders that result from them.
12. What is the concept behind culture-bound disorders?
13. What is stress, what are some causes of stress, and what is the body's reaction to stress?
14. What are some different types of body problems that are psychological disorders?

Chapter 10

Therapies

PLAN AHEAD...

- What ideas did people have about mental illness in the past?
- When and where did mental hospitals originate? Why?
- What is hypnosis, and where did it come from?
- What are the current medical treatments that are used for mental illness?
- What kinds of talk therapies are used to treat mental illness?
- What is shock treatment, and what is it used for?
- What is a lobotomy, and why was it used?
- What is an insanity plea? What are some other legal issues involving psychological disorders?
- What kinds of community treatments are available for treating or preventing mental illness?

"Canst thou not minister to a mind diseased, pluck from the memory a rooted sorrow, raze out the written troubles of the brain, and with some sweet oblivious antidote cleanse the stuff'd bosom of that perilous stuff which weighs upon the heart?"
—SHAKESPEARE (MACBETH)

ONE DAY, MY FRIEND CAROL, WHILE SITTING AT A BUS stop, saw a little puppy playing at her feet. When she reached down to pet it, the puppy vanished into thin air. Later, when she saw the bus approaching, she got up to meet it, but as it got near—poof!—it too disappeared. Carol has schizophrenia. At one point in her life, she was so distraught that she poured gasoline on herself and tried to light it. Fortunately, the lighter failed. Today, Carol is doing very well. She receives treatments that allow her to be happy and to live independently. Carol takes medications, gets counseling from a psychologist, and sees a social worker, who helps to guide her through life's challenges. Many of the therapies that are available for people with psychological disorders are described in this chapter, together with a look at historical attitudes and treatments so that you can see what has been tried before and how we got where we are today.

HISTORICAL THERAPIES

"I proceed, Gentlemen, briefly to call your attention to the state of Insane Persons

confined within this Commonwealth, in cages, closets, cellars, stalls, pens:

Chained, naked, beaten with rods, and lashed into obedience."
—DOROTHEA DIX

It has been said that those who are ignorant of the past are forced to relive it. It is important to know about historical events not only for the intellectual value of such knowledge, but also for the practical reason that it helps us to better understand current attitudes and practices, and provides us with the impetus to move forward to better, more progressive and effective ideas.

Holes and Spirits

Skulls of some people who lived in prehistoric times have been discovered that had holes punched in them with a sharp rock. Some of these skulls show healing, meaning that the unfortunate "patient" lived through the experience. Drilling holes in people's heads was a fairly common practice in Europe hundreds of years ago. Without the use of any anesthetic (other than alcohol, we might presume), a metal tool was used to drill a hole in a person's forehead. This practice was called **trephining** or **trepanation** and was performed for the purpose of releasing "evil spirits" from the person. Naturally, most of the "patients" who received this procedure were suffering from mental illnesses. Why the evil spirits were in the person's head and why they couldn't go out the way they came in were never explained.

Apparently, it was a very common belief in the past, and continues to be a common belief today, that spirits can enter people's bodies and control thoughts, emotions, and behaviors. A number of creative methods other than trephining were invented to remove the evil spirits from people who were supposedly so inflicted. **Exorcism** is the general term used for such practices. People's heads were put into ovens, exorcists

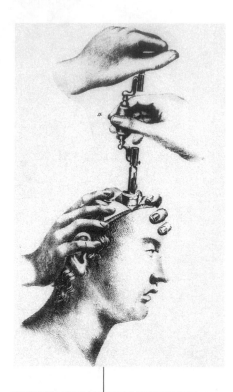

Trephining was used in the past to release evil spirits from a mentally ill person.

Connecting Concepts

Recall from Chapter 7 that the body humor theory of personality is a type approach. People with various kinds of problems were divided into categories based on four body fluids.

pulled marbles and stones from people's heads in fake surgical procedures, and various incantations and rituals were performed to force the spirits out. Even today, exorcism is sometimes performed.

In 1486, a book was published that told people how to recognize witches (evil people who had made a contract with the devil) and what to do with them. This book was titled **Malleus Malifecarum** ("Hammer of the Witch"), and was very popular. In the *Malleus*, it was written that witches were the cause of all bad things and that they were always women. Readers were told how to test for a witch—for example, by looking for red spots on her body or by determining whether she floats (tie a rope around her and throw her into a pond)—and then were instructed to torture and kill witches. Looking at the *Malleus* now, it seems very likely that most of the women described were suffering from schizophrenia or depression. A book with a similar attitude, *Demonologie*, was written by King James I of England in 1611.

As a result of such misconceptions, thousands of women were burned at the stake in Europe and were hanged in England and the United States. You have likely heard of the Salem witch-hunt of 1692 during which hundreds of people were accused and chained to prison walls, and more than 20 people were killed. These events represent a nearly unbelievable tragedy of such magnitude and acts of such great ignorance that it is important for every person to learn about them.

Humors and the Moon

Supernatural forces have been and continue to be among the most common causes suggested for strange behaviors. This is where we get phrases such as "What got into him?" It was commonly believed that "things" got inside people and caused their craziness. It was even thought that a person could turn into an animal (**lycanthropy**). Incredibly, this continues to be a common belief in the United States as well as in cultures around the world. Certain physical causes also have been proposed to explain aberrant behaviors. Astrology has been around for centuries. This nutty notion says that the positions of the stars in the sky when one is born can somehow guide and control one's life. The phases of the moon are also popularly believed to influence behavior. We still hear people make such absurd comments. The terms **lunacy** and *lunatic* derived from this notion.

For hundreds of years, it was believed that one's body fluids (**humors**) caused certain personality characteristics, moods, and odd behaviors. **Bloodletting** was a common treatment for people suffering from anxiety, mania, or psychological agitation and was practiced even into the twentieth century. The well-known red and white barber's pole was the sign that marked an establishment that would happily take out some of your blood.

Early psychiatrists did not have medications to treat mental illnesses and instead often relied on physical methods, such as spinning chairs, dunk tanks, salt baths, straightjackets, and isolation. Lobotomies (**prefrontal lobotomy**) were often performed in the 1930s and 1940s; the procedure destroyed a portion of a patient's brain. Patients became very subdued after these surgeries. Oddly, these brain operations were deemed a great success, and thousands of them were performed; Moniz, who introduced the lobotomy, even won a Nobel Prize. By the 1950s, people began to see that simply quieting a person was not necessarily a cure for his or her psychological disorder. Furthermore, medications and other treatments were gaining favor, so lobotomies gradually faded away.

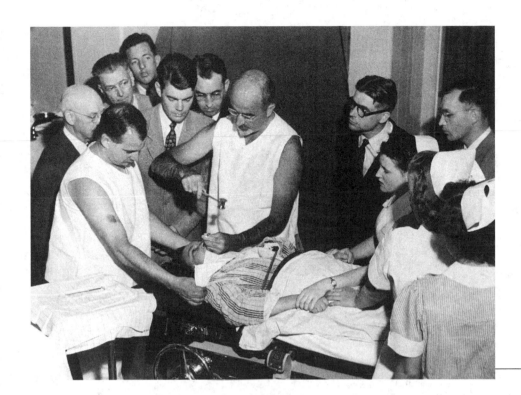

A person receiving a lobotomy. The surgery was sometimes performed through the eye socket, a so-called transorbital lobotomy.

THINK TANK

Why do you think that people did not react against the barbaric treatment of the mentally ill in the past?

Why did people allow witch burnings and asylums?

What practices and attitudes do we have today that future students might view as ignorant and barbaric?

How could education help?

How could the mass media be used to help change people's attitudes?

The Rise and Fall of Hospitals

In the eighteenth century, undesirable people, including the mentally ill, homeless, blind, and crippled, were placed into dungeons, where they were chained to the walls. Such facilities were called **hospitals,** the term implying a place where people would receive kind, hospitable treatment. It is amazing today—in fact, nearly unbelievable— to realize that such was the beginning concept of a hospital.

Such dungeons (hospitals) were used in many countries and were sometimes called **asylums.** In England, one of the first such places was called **Bethlehem Hospital.** In a Cockney accent, the name of this place was pronounced "**bedlam,**" which is now a word that means a riotous, out-of-order, chaotic situation. Such were the early mental asylums. These were not places of treatment or "hospitality"; they were filthy pits that housed indigent and unwanted people. Often, the public was invited to pay a fee to enter these asylums and observe and laugh at the people chained there.

Philippe Pinel releasing the chains from his patients.

Philippe Pinel (1745–1826) was a doctor who, in 1793, took charge of a large mental hospital, *La Bicêtre*, in Paris. Pinel put a stop to the harsh practices and was convinced by the inmates to release them from their chains. He argued that "madness is caused by physical illness" and stressed the need for sunshine and fresh air in treating mental disorders. Pinel's reforms are often noted as the beginning of modern psychiatry (*psyche* means "mind/soul"; *iatros* means "healer") and in particular the beginning of the **moral therapy** approach. This view promoted the idea that people with psychological disorders were not crazed animals who had "lost their minds (souls)," but were suffering individuals who could benefit from hospital care similar to that given to people with non-ABC medical illnesses. In the United States, moral therapy was promoted most effectively by **Dorothea Dix** (1802–1887), a schoolteacher who argued so persuasively that 32 mental hospitals were constructed because of her beliefs.

Benjamin Rush (1745–1813) is known as the "father of American psychiatry." In 1812, Rush wrote the first American textbook on psychiatry. He also was an advocate of **moral therapy;** in fact, the hospital he founded, Pennsylvania Hospital in Philadelphia, was the first to admit patients with psychological disorders. Rush advocated treating such patients with kindness and respect. Although he believed that mental illnesses were caused by too much blood in the brain and recommended the use of bloodletting, he also recommended more humane treatments, such as occupational therapy, relaxation, outside travel, and music therapy.

The moral therapy movement gradually faded in the late nineteenth century as people came to believe that mental illnesses could not be cured. As a result, mental hospitals became merely places of custodial care. By the mid-twentieth century, hundreds of such hospitals in the United States housed more than half a million patients. Mental hospitals had become appalling places—overcrowded, with deplorable conditions, so bad that they were often labeled "snakepits." Eventually, the discovery of medications, combined with an increased interest in the civil rights of mental patients, led to **deinstitutionalization** of the mental hospitals. Today, there are fewer than 100,000 individuals in mental hospitals. Unfortunately, because the United States provides very little care outside of hospitals, most of those who left ended

FYI

Dr. Benjamin Rush was one of the signers of the Declaration of Independence, and Dr. Philippe Pinel was a leader of the French Revolution.

up living in the care of relatives or, more commonly, on the streets as homeless people. This problem has reached the point of being a national disgrace. As the number of people in psychiatric hospitals has declined in the United States, the number of mentally ill people in jails and prisons has grown. The number of inmates with serious mental disorders in 1999 was 283,000. Unfortunately, many state officials incarcerate the mentally ill because it is cheaper than hospitalization.

A Magnetic Personality

Some early psychiatrists had the idea that mental illnesses were caused by conflicted or altered mental events rather than by things supernatural or physical. The notion of hypnosis, for example, was discussed among psychiatrists in the nineteenth century as a possible explanation, as well as a treatment, for various psychological disorders, particularly hysteria (conversion disorder). But hypnosis had its beginnings not from a "mental" theory, but from a rather strange idea about a physical cause of mental illness.

Franz Anton Mesmer (1734–1815) was a most curious fellow, a physician in Vienna who promoted the idea that animals had magnetic energy. Mesmer claimed that mental disorders were produced by disruptions or interference in a person's animal magnetism. He also claimed that he was specially gifted in that he could realign a person's disrupted magnetic field by moving his hands around the person's body.

Mesmer received his medical degree by plagiarizing a paper on the influence of the planets on the human body. In Vienna, he married a wealthy, older widow and played the role of high society patron, even commissioning 12-year-old Mozart to write an opera and perform it in Mesmer's large, lush gardens. Mesmer's medical practice consisted mostly of taking advantage of people, primarily the young women of Vienna. He had his patients swallow a medicine containing iron and then passed magnets over their bodies. Later, he used his hands in place of the magnets. Often his patients would fall into a sort of violent convulsion, what Mesmer called a **crisis**, after which their psychological symptoms would be gone. Today, we even have the official English word **mesmerism** to refer to such hypnotic appeal.

Mesmer's claims and treatments infuriated other physicians, and he was forced to leave Vienna. He moved to Paris, where he again took up the practice of animal magnetism. Soon he had so many patients that he invented a form of group therapy. Mesmer constructed a wooden tub known as a *baquet* (French for "tub") that was filled with water and magnetic iron filings. Metal handles protruded out of the *baquet*, which patients held as they sat around the tub. Mesmer then emerged wearing a flowing purple robe and began pointing at the metal rods or the supposedly diseased parts of the patients' bodies. Soon afterward, a patient would experience a crisis and would be cured. Mesmerism was a rousing success and a profitable enterprise.

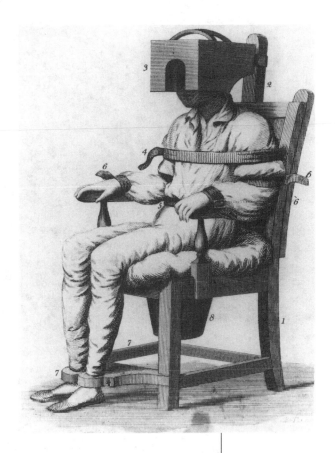

One of the early treatments for mental illness was this "tranquilizing chair." Could you imagine a person with depression, dementia, or schizophrenia receiving such a treatment?

THINK TANK

In the movie *M*A*S*H* (1970), a character says, "This isn't a hospital, it's an insane asylum."

Comment on the pros and cons of such a statement.

Mesmer creating a crisis in a patient by the use of "animal magnetism," the forerunner of hypnotism

A commission was formed to study this odd idea. Benjamin Franklin, the American ambassador to France (and an expert on electricity), served on this group, which also included Joseph Guillotin, the inventor of the guillotine (supposedly a humane device for executing people), and the chemist Antoine Levoisier, who ironically was a victim of the guillotine (along with many others whose heads were chopped off) during the French Revolution. The commission came to the inevitable conclusion that animals do not have any sort of magnetic energy or magnetic fields. Mesmer was forced out of business again and in 1784 disappeared into obscurity.

The Rise and Fall of Hypnosis

One of Mesmer's students suggested to a patient that the crisis state was too violent and he wanted the patient to be relaxed. Somewhat surprisingly, his patient acted relaxed. Thus was discovered the power of suggestibility. This idea soon spread to other magnetizers, who found that they too could make people behave as if something was true simply by asserting it. They had discovered what we now call **hypnosis.** Of course, the power of hypnosis has nothing to do with magnets. The "power" is the natural fact that many people are suggestible. There is no magic in the procedure. The person's belief is the powerful factor in this strange truth. Thus, those who do not want to be hypnotized cannot be.

The term *hypnosis* (meaning "sleeplike") was coined in 1843 by a Scottish physician, James Braid, because he erroneously believed that this state of suggestibility was like sleeping. This newfound curiosity became an important topic of debate among psychiatrists in Europe. The most influential teacher of psychiatry at that time was **Jean-Martin Charcot** (1825–1893) of France. Charcot (pronounced "Shar-COE") came to believe that hysteria could be caused by a kind of self-hypnosis and that hypnosis was an effective cure for such cases. His belief was fueled by the fact that his students had been paying actors to fake mental illnesses and then be "cured" by Charcot. When Charcot learned of this trickery, he was humiliated (after all, he had been the prime advocate of hypnosis), and that, together with a number of scientific studies that refuted his claims, forced Charcot to admit that his theories about hypnotism were wrong.

One of Charcot's students was a physician from Vienna named **Sigmund Freud** (1856–1939). After returning to his medical practice in Vienna, Freud tried hypnosis but discovered that it was not necessary to use magnets or even suggestibility to help his patients. Freud discovered the power of "talk" therapy. Just by talking and listening, Freud was able to "cure" nearly all his patients who had hysteria. Freud believed that hysterical symptoms were nearly always being caused by a repressed sexual idea. It is said that Charcot was once asked what caused mental illness and replied (of course, in French!), "Always, always, always, always, always sex." Perhaps Freud overheard this remark by his esteemed professor!

FYI

Alfred Binet, the inventor of modern IQ tests, learned hypnosis from Charcot.

On the basis of his experiences with hysterical patients, Freud developed one of history's most influential theories about mental illness. Freud, as you know by now, emphasized the power of the unconscious part of the mind. His approach, **psychoanalysis,** consisted of various techniques meant to analyze what was going on inside a patient's unconscious and then to aid the patient in becoming aware of those unconscious elements. Freud proposed that when the contents of the unconscious were revealed, the patient's hysterical symptoms would no longer be needed. Freud's ideas remain somewhat influential today, and his techniques are still used by many therapists and are effective in some instances.

Freud's ideas were dominant in the early twentieth century but have since been largely replaced by the ideas of behavioral and cognitive psychology as well as by the introduction of medications suitable for treating psychological disorders. Next we will look at the treatments that are commonly used today.

Recap

— Trephining or trepanation involved pounding or drilling a hole in a person's head for the purpose of releasing evil spirits.

— Exorcism is a ritual that is supposed to release evil spirits from a person.

— The *Malleus Malifecarum* was a popular book that told how to identify witches and how to get rid of them. Thousands of women were killed.

— People once believed that humans could turn into animals (lycanthropy), that body fluids (humors) influenced personality, and that the moon could make one crazy (lunacy).

— Thousands of lobotomies were performed in the 1940s and 1950s.

— Hundreds of years ago, undesirable people were put into dungeons that were called hospitals.

— Philippe Pinel was the first to release inmates from their chains in the early hospitals. This became known as the moral treatment.

— Mesmer taught that humans have magnetism and that it can be controlled to cure mental illnesses. This idea later proved to be the power of suggestion and was renamed *hypnosis*.

— Charcot was a famous teacher of psychiatry. One of his students was Sigmund Freud, who rejected hypnosis in favor of a "talking cure," called psychoanalysis, which emphasized the role of the unconscious.

THINK TANK

What do you think are the most common and most harmful myths that people have about mental illnesses? Which of the things discussed above are the most surprising to you?

If you could change one attitude that the general public has about mental illness and its treatment, what would you choose?

MODERN THERAPIES

"Healing is a matter of time,

but it is sometimes also a matter of opportunity."
—HIPPOCRATES

The various treatments for psychological disorders are known as **psychotherapies.** However, sometimes the term is limited to talk treatments, while other times, it includes behavioral treatments, such as the use of reinforcers to increase behaviors or relaxation training. Quite often, the term *psychotherapy* is used in a context that excludes "medical" treatments such as medications or shock therapy. In this textbook, the term *psychotherapy* is used to include all of the above types of treatments: Psychotherapy includes any approach to treating psychological disorders.

Medications

By far the most common treatments used today for mental illnesses are medical in nature. Nearly every person who is diagnosed with a psychological disorder is offered a medical treatment, typically medication. This undoubtedly springs from two reasons: First, our system of health insurance supports medical approaches over other types of treatments. Second, the major suppliers of psychotherapy are psychiatrists, who are medical doctors, educated and licensed to provide medical services.

Although medical therapies are often successful, nearly every mental health expert laments the fact that our society relies on them so extensively and to a large extent shuns more psychological, and even social, therapies that are often equally successful with longer-lasting results and causing fewer side effects. Although many studies have shown the efficacy of social treatments, such approaches to psychotherapy are not widely available because they are not financially supported by the United States health care system. Medical approaches are number one, and medications are by far the most common treatment for mental disorders. Medications can be divided into four categories.

Antipsychotic or Neuroleptic

This group of medications is used in the treatment of psychoses, particularly schizophrenia. These medications are sometimes referred to as *major tranquilizers*, though that term is problematic because it is easily confused with minor tranquilizers (described later). The first of the **neuroleptic drugs** was Thorazine or chlorpromazine (each medication has two names, the brand name given by the pharmaceutical company, and the chemical name), which was introduced in the 1950s.

Typical neuroleptic drugs block certain chemical receptors for the brain neurotransmitter **dopamine.** That is, these drugs bind with certain chemical receptors in the brain, thus decreasing dopamine activity at the synapses. Because the receptors are blocked, less dopamine can get through to stimulate the receiving cell. The result is that there is a reduction in the hallucinations, delusions, and other positive symptoms of schizophrenia.

Some of the commonly used antipsychotics today are Stelazine, Prolixin, Haldol, and Mellaril. A number of side effects can occur, including a serious condition called neuroleptic malignant syndrome. One of the side effects of neuroleptic drugs is permanent changes in the brain's dopamine receptor chemicals. These brain changes can result in involuntary muscle movements. The most severe of these side effects is called **tardive dyskinesia.** In this condition, a person's body writhes and twitches, his or her eyes blink, lips smack, and face, mouth, and limbs move uncontrollably. Sometimes the person's eyes move so erratically that the person is unable to read. About 30% of patients who take first-generation (typical) antipsychotic medications for extended periods of time will develop side effects involving body movement. There are few treatments for tardive dyskinesia, although vitamin B_6 seems to offer some help (Lerner et al., 2001).

Fortunately, some newly developed neuroleptic drugs do not seem to cause tardive dyskinesia. These are known as **atypical** (or **second-generation) antipsychotics.** They apparently work by affecting fewer and different types of dopamine receptors, and also block some serotonin and glutamate receptors (Tuma, 2003). The first of these was Clozaril (clozapine); recent additions are Risperdal (risperidone), Zyprexa (olanzapine), Seroquel (quetiapine), Geodon (ziprasidone), and Abilify (aripiprazole). These drugs are the first line of treatment for schizophrenia today, though Clozaril has the serious side effect of impairing white blood cells, and patients taking this medication need regular blood tests.

Not only do second-generation neuroleptics have fewer side effects, they also have been shown to provide help in reducing the negative symptoms of schizophrenia, such as social withdrawal, apathy, and lack of speech; to increase cognitive functioning; and to be effective in patients who do not respond to the typical medications, thus reducing the number of patients with chronic schizophrenia (Lohr & Braff, 2003). These new drugs are sometimes used to treat other disorders; for example, Zyprexa (olanzapine) is sometimes used in the treatment of bipolar disorder.

Antidepressants

The medicines known as **antidepressants** increase the activity of certain brain neurotransmitter chemicals, most notably **serotonin.** Also, new research shows that depression is associated with a decrease in new cell growth in the hippocampus and that antidepressants can stimulate such neurogenesis (Santarelli et al., 2003). Adults often have good responses to antidepressants, but these drugs are generally not recommended for children, because children's bodies do not absorb and eliminate the drugs as those of adults do, and the drugs can lead to serious symptoms, including suicide.

There are many varieties of antidepressants, based on several methods of increasing neurotransmitter activity. The first of these to be developed were the **MAO inhibitors** (MAOIs). MAO (monoamine oxidase) is an enzyme (a housekeeping chemical) in the brain that cleans up certain neurotransmitters. The MAOIs decrease the amount of MAO, thereby increasing the activity of neurotransmitters. Trade names include Marplan, Nardil, and Parnate. MAOI drugs do not interact well with certain foods and medications; therefore, patients taking these medicines must maintain strict care in avoiding foods and other substances that contain a chemical called tyramine, lest they have a heart attack. Some deaths have occurred among users of MAOI drugs—a serious side effect! The MAOI drugs are particularly effective in treating the less typical cases of depression—for example, when a person has an increase in appetite and sleep rather than a decrease, which is more common. For the typical symptoms of depression, there are two other types of antidepressants that are usually more effective. Therefore, MAOIs normally are not the first line of treatment for depressive disorders.

The second type of antidepressant drug that was discovered is named **tricyclic** because of the three rings in its chemical structure. A tricyclic antidepressant (TCA) medication is a **reuptake inhibitor;** that is, it inhibits, or decreases, the amount of neurotransmitter that is sucked back into the cell that releases it. The reuptake process occurs when a sending cell releases neurotransmitter molecules then pulls some of them back in. When the reuptake process is inhibited, fewer molecules are pulled back in; therefore, TCA drugs cause an increase in the amount of neurotransmitter chemicals present at the synapse, leaving more molecules to stimulate the receiving brain cell. Thus, there is an increase in neurotransmitter activity. Reuptake inhibitors do not increase the amount of neurotransmitter chemicals in the brain; they increase the activity of the available chemicals by reducing the amount that gets sucked back into the releasing cell.

Tricyclic medications are relatively safe (though some patients have used them to commit suicide) and have side effects that will disappear when the drug is discontinued. The most common of the TCAs are Elavil, Norpramin, Pamelor, Sinequan, Anafranil, and Tofranil. A similar medicine is Remeron, which is a tetracyclic (four rings). TCAs are especially effective in typical cases of depression, particularly if the patient also experiences anxiety.

The newest category of antidepressant medicines is **selective serotonin reuptake inhibitors (SSRIs),** sometimes called **second-generation antidepressants.** Like the tricyclics, these drugs are reuptake inhibitors. However, they are more selective than the TCAs, usually affecting only serotonin and not other neurotransmitter chemicals, as the tricyclics do. The first of the SSRIs was Prozac, which was introduced in 1988 and is today one of the first lines of treatment for depression as well as for other psychological disorders. A generic form of Prozac is now available, though the filler used in the pill is different and might cause some mild side effects in some patients. Other SSRIs include Zoloft, Paxil, Celexa (Lexapro), and Luvox. These medicines are among the safest of all drugs and have had as good success in treating depression as have the tricyclics. A patient must gradually build up to an effective dose of an antidepressant medicine and, when discontinuing treatment, must reduce the dosage gradually. Some patients have difficulties when reducing their dosage, and side effects may occur. Many other SSRIs have since been discovered, and a new category has recently been added—drugs that affect both serotonin and norepinephrine—called **serotonin/ norepinephrine reuptake inhibitors (SNRIs)** or *dual-action antidepressants.* Effexor is the most commonly prescribed drug in this category. Some drugs both inhibit reuptake of serotonin and block serotonin receptors (**SRIBs).** Deseryl (trazodone) works in this manner. Wellbutrin is a similar medicine that is prescribed for treating mood disorders, ADHD, cigarette smoking, and other drug addictions. All of these medicines have side effects; fortunately, most of them are mild and temporary. However, there have been complaints of liver damage (e.g., from Serzone) and other potentially serious side effects, so one should, as always, consult a medical professional when such drugs are used. New medications are approved each year, so it is impossible for textbooks such as this to keep completely up to date. You can check the Internet (try ePocrates, for example) for more current information, or check the Physicians Desk Reference (PDR) in a library.

Another group of drugs is currently under investigation. These drugs block the activity of a brain neurotransmitter called **substance P.** Preliminary research shows some success in the treatment of depression with these medicines. Finally, the herb **St. John's wort,** an extract from a flowering plant, is being studied as an antidepressant.

TABLE 10.1   Types of Antidepressants

Type of Antidepressant	Medication Brand Names	Neurotransmitter Affected
1. MAO Inhibitor	Marplan, Nardil, Parnate	Serotonin, dopamine, norepinephrine
2. Tricyclic	Elavil, Norpramin, Pamelor, Sinequan, Anafranil, Tofranil	Serotonin, norepinephrine
3. Tetracyclic	Remeron	Serotonin, norepinephrine
4. SSRI	Prozac, Zoloft, Paxil, Celexa (Lexapro), Luvox	Serotonin
5. SNRI	Effexor	Serotonin, norepinephrine
6. SRIB	Deseryl (trazodone)	Serotonin
7. Aminoketone	Wellbutrin	Norepinephrine, dopamine

This herb apparently acts as a reuptake inhibitor, although any dangerous side effects are not yet known. One problem is that herbs are not regulated by government agencies, as are medications; consequently, consumers cannot know exactly what they are getting in the herbal preparations they purchase. Also, St. John's wort interferes with body physiology and can cause problems, notably in women taking birth control pills. A large clinical study found that the herb was not effective in treating major depression (Davidson, 2002).

Although the term *antidepressant* implies that these medicines are appropriate only in treating depressive disorders, one should not take the name too literally. In fact, antidepressant drugs are often useful in treating many types of mental disorders other than depression, including eating disorders, panic disorder, and obsessive-compulsive disorder, because they increase neurotransmitter activity in the brain. The rate of improvement with such medicines is at least 60%. Because so many different antidepressant medications are available today, a patient can try a number of them (not all at once, of course!) thus increasing the odds of finding one that helps and also extending the person's hopefulness, which is one of the most significant problems in depression.

THINK TANK   Some psychologists think that medications merely treat the symptoms of a disorder and do nothing about the underlying causes, such things as poverty, social problems, unemployment, lack of education, and poor values.

They argue that mental illnesses will only increase until we deal with the deeper causes and that we should stop medicating people so that there will be motivation to change things in society and life.

What do you think about this idea?

Antimanic

The first line of treatment for bipolar disorder are drugs that contain **lithium**, such as Eskalith or Cibalith. These are called **antimanic** drugs. In fact, lithium is technically not a drug; it is a natural element (an alkalai metal, like sodium), number 3 on the periodic table. Although its exact method of action is not known, lithium is certainly not a cure for bipolar disorder; rather, it works as a mood stabilizer that prevents outbreaks of mania. Other mood-stabilizing drugs include Tegretol and Depakote, which are also used to control seizures.

Antimanic drugs are maintenance drugs. They are very successful in helping bipolar patients maintain a relatively even level of moods as long as they continue taking them. Perhaps as many as 80% of sufferers find improvement when taking such medications. Unfortunately, many patients stop taking their medication because they think it works like aspirin. But lithium must be taken continuously to prevent or inhibit mood swings.

Unfortunately, lithium is toxic to the body in large doses; it can damage internal body organs. Therefore, patients taking lithium must have regular blood tests to monitor the level in their bloodstreams.

Antianxiety

Antianxiety drugs are commonly known as *minor tranquilizers* and, as the name indicates, are used in the treatment of anxiety disorders. They slow down the nervous system and relax the muscles of the body. The most common subtype of antianxiety medicines is the **benzodiazepines**, which include Valium, one of the most prescribed drugs in the world. Librium, Xanax, Tranxene, Miltown, and Equanil are others. Antianxiety drugs can cause drowsiness and can even cause death when taken with alcohol, and users can develop tolerance, dependence, and withdrawal symptoms. Anxiety disorders are also often treated with antidepressants or nonmedical therapies.

TABLE 10.2   Categories of Psychotherapeutic Drugs

1. Antipsychotic or neuroleptic: block dopamine receptors (Thorazine)

2. Antidepressant: increase the activity of serotonin and other transmitters (Prozac)

3. Antimanic (lithium): stabilize mood swings (Eskalith)

4. Antianxiety (minor tranquilizer): slow down and relax the nervous system (Valium)

FYI Peter Breggin is a psychiatrist who is famous for arguing against the medical treatment of psychological disorders. He calls shock treatment "barbaric," and believes that medications not only do not help, but are harmful. He is part of a movement called *antipsychiatry*. One of their Web sites is http://www.antipsychiatry.org/

In addition to these four categories, there are medications available for the treatment of brain diseases and dementia. Patients with Parkinson's disease, for example, often find relief from their tremors (shaking) with the use of a drug called **L-dopa.** This drug is a precursor chemical for dopamine and thereby helps the brain to make more of the neurotransmitter that is being depleted by destruction of the brain cells that manufacture it. Similarly, patients with Alzheimer's disease sometimes find improvement in their cognitive abilities when taking medicines such as Aricept and others that slow the breakdown of **acetylcholine,** a brain neurotransmitter that is depleted by Alzheimer's disease.

Shock Treatment

Easily the most controversial and misunderstood treatment that is in common use today is **electroconvulsive therapy (ECT)**, which is often simply called *shock treatment*. Many years ago, it was noticed that epileptic seizures, in which the brain's electrical activity is grossly disturbed, resulted in improved moods in the people experiencing them. On the basis of this observation, early doctor/researchers tried inducing seizures in mental patients, at first using an overdose of insulin, in a procedure called **insulin coma therapy.** This method proved dangerous, and in 1939, an Italian psychiatrist, Ugo Cerletti, introduced the use of electricity, which he had observed being used on animals in slaughterhouses, to cause a brain convulsion. Cerletti had wrongly believed that convulsions would be effective in treating schizophrenia. ECT generally did not help alleviate the symptoms of schizophrenia, but many ECT patients reported an improvement in their moods following the convulsions, and today this treatment is applied almost exclusively to patients with mood disorders.

It is not known why ECT sometimes is beneficial, but as many as 80% of ECT patients report improvement in their moods following such treatment. The most commonly accepted theory is that convulsions cause a change in various brain chemicals, such as neurotransmitters and their receptors. Today the procedure is relatively safe, although most people view it as frightening. Therefore, ECT is nearly always recommended only after other appropriate therapies have been tried and failed.

ECT at one time was much more common than it is today. The development of medicines has reduced the need for this more expensive and discomforting procedure. However, ECT is today a relatively common treatment, given to as many as 200,000 patients a year in the United States. The patient is given a muscle relaxant and anesthesia before the procedure. Therefore, ECT is typically provided in hospitals. The patient is unconscious during ECT and therefore will likely experience a loss of memory for the events surrounding the actual procedure. More extensive memory loss has also been reported, though there is inconsistent evidence regarding the extent to which a patient's memory loss was caused by ECT or by other factors, such as lack of oxygen during the procedure, or by the mood disorder itself.

To produce a convulsion, or brain seizure, about 90 volts of electricity is applied to the brain by use of electrodes placed on the patient's skull. Often, the electrodes are applied only to the right side of the brain, avoiding the language-controlling left hemisphere. Such a procedure is called *unipolar ECT*. The ECT treatment is normally given two or three times a week over a period of several weeks. Some patients have *outpatient ECT*, in which they leave the hospital or clinic the day of the procedure; others remain in the hospital for the duration of the treatment. Some patients return for ECT every year or so, in what is called *maintenance ECT*, an attempt to prevent depression from recurring. When ECT is given within a few months of recovery as a means of preventing relapse, it is called *continuation ECT*. Several studies have found good success with such preventive treatments in comparison to subjects who took only antidepressant medicines (e.g., Gagné, 2000).

Many patients find significant relief from their depression following ECT. For example, TV personality Dick Cavett praised the treatment as a fast and efficient means of ending his horrible depression. Other patients found no relief in their symptoms from this treatment and became vocal critics of it. One prominent psychiatrist calls ECT a barbaric misuse of electricity. Obviously, there are varying opinions about this strange procedure.

Because ECT is viewed as an extreme, even last-ditch treatment, when it fails, it may cause patients to lose all hope in ever finding relief from their depression. The famed author Ernest Hemingway received ECT at the Mayo Clinic in Rochester,

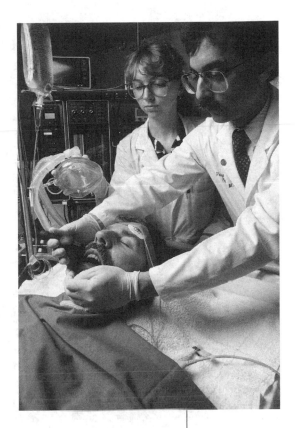

Although electroconvulsive therapy (ECT, or "shock treatment") was a more common procedure in the past, it is still a common and effective treatment for mood disorders today.

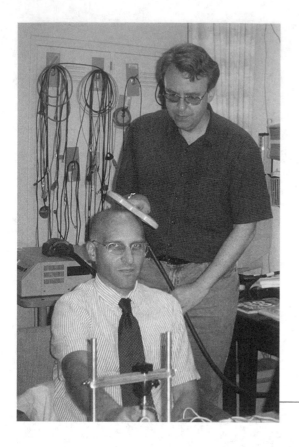

Minnesota, but found no relief and soon afterward committed suicide. One of my young students had tried many treatments for her depression, without relief. Therefore, she asked her doctor for ECT. After several weeks of treatment, she went home unchanged. Soon afterward, she killed herself. I believe she thought of ECT as the ultimate treatment—that if ECT didn't work, then nothing could work. I believe it is important for patients to view ECT as only one approach in an arsenal of therapies—that if it fails, they should continue trying and not give up hope.

Fortunately, a new treatment is being investigated that might help to reduce the number of ECT patients. In **transcranial magnetic stimulation (TMS),** an electromagnetic coil placed on the head transmits magnetic pulses to the brain. No anesthesia is required for this procedure, and early research indicates that about half of the depressed patients who are given this treatment experience enough improvement that ECT is not necessary. If continued research bears out the value of TMS, perhaps we can greatly reduce the number of patients who find it necessary to try ECT. Interestingly, TMS has also had some success in reducing auditory hallucinations in patients with schizophrenia (Hoffman et al., 2000). In that case, the magnetic energy is directed toward the left side of the brain, where language is processed, for about 15 minutes.

> Transcranial magnetic stimulation (TMS) is one of the newest medical approaches.

THINK TANK   If a friend of yours were severely depressed, would you recommend ECT?

Under what circumstances do you think it is appropriate?

Psychosurgery

In 1935, a Portuguese psychiatrist named Antonio Egas Moniz described a procedure in which he surgically severed the connections between the frontal lobes and the lower brain areas in some of his patients. This was called a prefrontal lobotomy, often shortened to *lobotomy*. Moniz claimed high rates of success with this radical treatment, and other doctors began performing lobotomies on their most difficult patients. Many thousands of such surgeries were performed, even as late as the 1980s. As you can imagine, although these patients did quiet down, they also experienced severe disruptions in their normal cognitive and emotional functions. The development of medications in the 1950s helped to reduce the number of people who were given lobotomies, and this procedure is no longer practiced.

Psychosurgery is the general term for brain operations that are performed to help people who suffer with psychological disorders. Lobotomies have been replaced by much more rare and more refined psychosurgeries. For example, two surgeries are available for treating Parkinson's disease. In one procedure, the brain region that produces tremors (the shaking of the hands) is destroyed. In another surgical procedure, called a deep brain stimulator, electrodes are placed into the thalamus, and an electrical stimulator is placed under the patient's skin below the collarbone. Stimulation stops the tremors.

There is also a brain operation that will help the most severe cases of obsessive-compulsive disorder that do not respond to more conventional therapies. This procedure is very precise, and the results are remarkably effective. Still, one might easily question the idea of destroying a part of someone's brain as a form of psychotherapy. This notion is highly controversial, and such procedures fortunately are rare.

Recap

— Medical treatments for mental illnesses are extremely common.

— Drugs include (1) neuroleptics (antipsychotics) for treating schizophrenia and other psychotic disorders, (2) antidepressants for depression and many other disorders, (3) antimanic drugs, used to treat bipolar disorder, and (4) antianxiety drugs (tranquilizers) for anxiety.

— The neuroleptic drugs, such as Thorazine, Haldol, Clozaril, and Risperdal, block dopamine receptors. A possible side effect is tardive dyskinesia.

— There are several categories of antidepressants, including MAO inhibitors, tricyclics, SSRIs, and SNRIs. In each case, these drugs cause an increase in the activity of certain brain neurotransmitters, particularly serotonin.

— ECT, also called shock treatment, is an effective therapy for mood disorders. Although common, it is very controversial.

— Psychosurgeries are rare today and not as damaging as were the lobotomies done in the past.

Psychodynamic Therapies

Sigmund Freud (1856–1939) introduced the idea that psychological disorders are sometimes caused by conflicts in the person's unconscious. Freud developed a therapy known as psychoanalysis, which consists of a number of techniques meant to help a person become aware of unconscious conflicts and thereby resolve them. Similar therapies are often grouped together under the term **psychodynamic.** Psychoanalytic or psychodynamic therapies are, of course, among the various **talk therapies,** in which the goal is to help patients gain insight into the causes and dynamics of their disorders. Sometimes such approaches to treatment are referred to as **insight therapies** because they help patients to gain insight into themselves and their problems. There are many different types of insight therapies; patients often get better when they develop an understanding of their situation.

The techniques of psychoanalysis involve interpreting various behaviors and mental phenomena of the patient in order to understand unconscious elements. **Dream interpretation** is one of these techniques. Freud believed that a dream is a disguised version of unconscious thoughts or feelings. For Freud, dream interpretation is the "royal road to the unconscious"; that is, it is the best way to find what's in the unconscious.

A **projective** technique originated by Carl Jung is **word association,** in which the patient quickly responds to words in the hopes that clues to the unconscious will be blurted out before they can be prevented. Sometimes **inkblot tests** or other projective assessment tools are used by psychoanalysts to gather information that can then be interpreted regarding unconscious ideas.

Psychoanalysts also use the analysis of two of a patient's behaviors: In **analysis of resistance,** the therapist assumes that if a patient resists talking about something, it is because that idea, thought, or feeling is being held in the unconscious. It is therefore

Psychoanalysis attempts to uncover and reveal what is in the patient's unconscious. The patient relaxes on a couch to help reduce defenses while the therapist uses dream interpretation, free association, and other techniques.

necessary to analyze the things that are resisted. **Analysis of transference** is a similar idea. Psychoanalysts assume that a patient will transfer some of the feelings that he has for significant people in his life to the therapist. A patient will unconsciously see the therapist as his father, for example. In psychoanalytic therapy, this transference is then analyzed to better understand the patient's unconscious ideas. Psychoanalysis was the most common therapy for psychological disorders early in the twentieth century. Today, it has been largely replaced by a number of other therapies and medical treatments; although it remains important, it no longer holds the high level of influence that it once enjoyed. Psychoanalysis is typically very time consuming and therefore not cost effective today. However, most talk (insight) therapists use some psychodynamic concepts. For example, a recent survey found that about 80% of therapists report using psychoanalytic techniques sometimes, but only about 10% call themselves psychoanalysts and stick strictly to this approach. New psychodynamic therapies that are short-term (often called **brief psychotherapies**) are being offered to patients who do not want to commit for long periods, and researchers have reported some success with this approach.

Because the emphasis in psychodynamic therapies is on the unconscious, this approach has its greatest success in the treatment of disorders that involve unconscious processes. For example, the dissociative and somatoform disorders respond fairly well to psychoanalytic treatment. In addition, some psychiatrists have found good success with psychoanalysis in the treatment of borderline personality disorder, a condition that is notoriously difficult to treat (Bateman & Fonagy, 2001). Conditions such as schizophrenia that are clearly related to significant disturbance of brain anatomy are not successfully treated by psychoanalysis. In fact, Freud recognized this and did not attempt to treat people with schizophrenia.

Humanistic Therapies

Another group of insight therapies are based on the theories of **humanistic psychology**, including the ideas of **Abraham Maslow** and **Carl Rogers**. These are talk therapies that

Carl Rogers, founder of client-centered therapy.

can be provided to individuals or to groups. The fundamental premise of these therapies is that psychological disorders are sometimes caused by disturbances in a person's **self-concept** and his or her drive toward **self-actualization**. These therapies, therefore, are aimed at helping people to understand themselves better and realign their behaviors, values, and ideas to better fit with their concepts of who they are. People seeking help are not called *patients*, a term that implies a medical approach, but are called *clients*, a term that empowers the person and provides a better environment for humanistic counseling, deemphasizing the medical model.

Carl Rogers, the originator of **client-centered therapy,** argued that some psychological disorders are caused by lack of a coherent and unified self-concept. This comes about because a person's internal, mental life has become **incongruent** with his or her experience. The person's desired and valued personality, his or her **ideal self,** has become incompatible with the way the person perceives himself or herself, the person's **real self.** Humanistic therapies consist of a number of techniques, primarily involving listening and asking probing questions, that are aimed at helping a person to correct this kind of incongruence and thereby form a more satisfying self-concept. Therefore, humanistic therapy, like psychoanalysis, is an insight therapy.

Humanistic therapy begins with the therapist providing **unconditional positive regard,** an attitude of respect and positive feelings for the client regardless of the client's behavior or personality—it is unconditional. Humanistic therapists believe that progress can be made only in a therapeutic environment that is warm, accepting, and comfortable. One exception is **Gestalt therapy,** which was pioneered by **Fritz Perls.** Perls believed that clients must be challenged to see their incongruities; therefore, he would often point out inconsistencies in their behaviors that would make them angry or uncomfortable. In those moments, Perls believed, his clients were achieving a kind of self-realization because they were facing up to their true selves—angry or uncomfortable as they were. However, Gestalt therapy is similar to all the humanistic therapies in that clients are encouraged to live in the present moment—what is commonly referred to as the **Here and Now.** Clients are encouraged to reject the past, to brush aside things that have happened to them, and also to ignore what might come in the future. The emphasis should be on living in the present moment.

Humanistic therapists also employ **empathy;** that is, they try to put themselves into the mind of their client. They believe that an empathetic attitude will help clients to find their true selves. Another common technique used in this approach is **reflection.** In this case, the therapist repeats back to the client what he or she has said. The purpose of reflection is for the client to consider what he or she has said, contemplating its truth and its value to him or her. Let's look at a short illustration.

Fritz Perls, founder of Gestalt therapy.

Client: "I don't know what to do."

Therapist: "You sound indecisive or confused."

Client: "Well, no, I can make decisions, but in this case I just don't know what would be best for me."

Therapist: "You don't know what's best for you?"

Client: "I know what's best usually, but in this case I don't know what I should do."

Therapist: "You see this case as different from others, and therefore you don't know what to do?"

Client: "Yes, I guess that could be. I wish I knew what would happen if I quit my job."

Therapist: "That might be handy, if we could see the future. What do you wish would happen?"

Client: "I don't know."

Therapist: "You are confused or uncertain about your goals in this situation?"

Client: "No, I guess I know what I want. I just don't know how to get there."

Therapist: "You want a guarantee that your goals will be met?"

Client: "Yes, that would be nice! Can you give me one?"

Therapist: "I can guarantee that the answer is inside you. You are the world's expert on your goals and what makes you satisfied. Let's explore what they are."

Humanistic therapies are often called **nondirective** because the therapist does not give directions to the client. It is believed that clients must find the answers within themselves. It is the *process* that is important. Therefore, it would do no good to give clients the answers, even if we knew them. The client is the world's expert on himself. Therefore, the therapist doesn't know the answer anyway. These approaches are also called *client-centered* because, as you can see, the therapy focuses on the client rather than on suggestions or directions from the therapist, as is common in some other therapies, such as psychoanalysis.

A variation of humanistic therapy is an attempt to help people who are struggling with philosophical ideas about existence. This approach is called **existential therapy.** A good example is **logotherapy** (literally "therapy for the spirit"), which concentrates on helping people find meaning in their lives. Issues that are raised involve living life to the fullest, finding purpose in the events of life, discovering spiritual feelings, and realigning one's personality and attitudes to better cope with modern life. One of the many techniques that are used in this form of counseling is **paradoxical intention.** In this method, a client is asked to try to *worsen* his or her symptoms. That's right—to worsen them. If a person complains that she washes her hands 30 times a day, the counselor suggests that she try for 40. The point is to show the client that she is in control of her behavior. If you can increase it, you can decrease it. Existential therapies, such as logotherapy, attempt to help clients find their own spiritual meaning and purpose in life and therefore focus on free will and making choices.

Humanistic therapies are not as common today as they were in the 1960s and 1970s, though the general principles of this approach are widely accepted and are used by therapists in all sorts of talk therapies and counseling sessions. Of course, such an approach is of little use in the treatment of brain dementias, schizophrenia, psychotic disturbances, or severe mental illnesses. Humanistic techniques are most effective with intelligent, verbal, insightful people who have relatively minor everyday problems—what we might think of as problems in living. Humanistic therapies can help people to explore their inner landscapes, clarify values, make satisfying choices, and learn more about themselves, including how to be more content and to live more meaningful lives.

THINK TANK

What kinds of problems do you think humanistic therapies are best at treating?

In what way are humanistic therapies different from just listening?

What side effects might result from humanistic therapies?

Behavior Therapies

Some of the most effective therapies for a wide range of psychological disorders are based on the principles of classical and operant conditioning (see Chapter 5). Because these therapies focus on changing observable behavior, they are simply known as **behavior therapies.** Treatment is not aimed at helping patients gain insight into their problems, as with psychoanalytic and humanistic therapies. Instead, behavior therapies aim at changing the problem behaviors that the patient experiences. This means that more than just talk is involved. The patient must take some action. Hence, these approaches to treatment are called **action therapies,** as opposed to insight therapies.

Freud believed that a psychological disorder has an underlying cause at the root of the disturbing symptoms. Therefore, Freud believed that a mental illness can be alleviated only by treating its underlying cause. He argued that if we were to treat only the symptoms and not the cause of a disorder, then new symptoms would arise in place of the old. This **symptom substitution,** however, was not discovered by early behavior therapists who treated only patients' symptoms. On the contrary, behavior therapists often found that improvement in one symptom was followed by a **generalization** effect—other symptoms also improved. Let's look at some examples.

Systematic desensitization (described in Chapter 5) is a behavior therapy that is used in the treatment of phobias and other similar disorders. First, the patient learns to relax; then the upsetting stimuli are presented very gradually over a period of time. Eventually, the person's nervous system comes to accept the stimuli and will not overreact. This treatment is highly successful, primarily because it involves the patient coming into contact with the upsetting stimuli while relaxed. A person who is afraid of shopping malls, for example, will eventually go to a shopping mall while relaxed but not until first going through a series of steps leading up to a visit to the mall. Systematic desensitization is one of a category of therapies known as **exposure therapies** because the patient is exposed to the stimuli that are upsetting to him or her.

A similar approach is called **flooding.** In this therapy, the patient is asked to imagine the upsetting stimuli in a very intense manner for a long period of time. A person who is afraid of spiders, for example, is asked to imagine spiders crawling all over his body, up and down his legs, over his head, onto his face, and so on. The idea is that experiencing the feared stimuli without anything unpleasant happening will result in extinction of the upset response. This therapy is often successful but is not as effective as systematic desensitization because the patient uses his or her imagination rather than encountering the stimuli directly and because something unpleasant often does happen during the presentation of the stimuli—the person gets upset. Therefore, there is a possibility that the conditioned reaction (fear) will continue and even strengthen rather than weaken.

Counterconditioning is a psychotherapy that also uses classical conditioning and is sometimes used with systematic desensitization. In this approach, a reaction is conditioned to a stimulus that is opposite from the current one. If a person has an unpleasant reaction to something, then counterconditioning attempts to condition a pleasant reaction to that thing. Or a pleasant reaction might be replaced by an unpleasant one. This therapy is often used in treating alcoholism and smoking. For example, a chemical (Antabuse) that will make the drinker sick is put into his or her alcohol. Or a person is subjected to a disgusting odor while smoking. The idea is to condition the person to react unpleasantly to the alcohol or cigarette smoke. These examples fall into the category of **aversive therapy,** because they involve putting a person into unpleasant or painful situations. Such therapy is also used to treat deviant sexual responses or self-injurious behaviors. In those instances, a mild but unpleasant electric shock might be used. More often, the behavior in question is paired with embarrassment or humiliation.

In **operant conditioning therapies,** a behavior is increased through **reinforcement.** The therapist uses something pleasant, such as a checkmark on a piece of paper, a smile, or a compliment, as a reinforcer for appropriate behavior. This procedure can be used with large groups of people in what is called a token economy. When his or her behavior is appropriate, a person receives a token of some sort that can later be traded for privileges or goodies. The tokens allow for immediate reinforcement and allow for the person to decide what it will be traded for. Behaviors can be decreased by removing their reinforcement. This is known as **extinction therapy.** For example, a

FYI

A new approach to exposure therapy is possible because of modern technology. In virtual reality therapy, patients wear goggles that allow them to experience fearful stimuli without leaving the clinic. The treatment is being used for phobias and PTSD. Also, brain researchers believe that success in getting over a fear depends on brain receptors receiving a certain protein and that this physiological event could be helped by a drug that is already used to treat tuberculosis. Subjects in virtual reality therapy improved much faster if they took the pill (Barad et al., 2003).

child's inappropriate behavior can be reduced by removing its reinforcer—attention, escape from homework, or whatever it is. Such operant conditioning therapies have been highly successful in the education of mentally retarded children and in treating sexual disorders, obsessive-compulsive disorders, and hypochondria.

Operant conditioning techniques also include **modeling,** in which the therapist uses imitation and reinforcement to teach a patient certain appropriate behaviors, and **social skills training,** in which a patient is taught effective skills for relating to other people, controlling anger, being more assertive, and acting appropriately in social situations. Such therapy has proven very helpful in the treatment of schizophrenia. Behavior therapies are highly successful and especially easy to conduct and measure the results of, because they focus on observable behaviors.

Cognitive Therapies

The fundamental assumption in cognitive therapies is that many psychological disorders are influenced by a patient's perceptions, illogical reasoning, irrational beliefs, and other inaccurate cognitive functions. As Hamlet said, "there is nothing either good or bad, but thinking makes it so." Therefore, this form of psychotherapy aims to change a patient's cognitive processes in the hopes of alleviating disturbances in emotion and behavior. In cognitive therapy, the emphasis is on changing the way a person thinks— hence, the term *cognitive.* The theory is that changes in thinking will result in changes in feeling and acting.

Perhaps the idea of changing the way a person thinks has been around since the beginning of civilization. However, modern cognitive therapies began in the 1950s with the ideas of **Albert Ellis.** Ellis believed that all emotional distress was caused by perception. He argued that an event, no matter how traumatic, could not *in itself* cause distress. It was the fact that a person *perceived and thought about* an event a certain way that caused emotional distress. Ellis reasoned that there was always an underlying cognitive thought or belief that was at the root of emotional distress. If a person gets divorced, it might be uncomfortable and inconvenient, but why would a person become severely depressed and suicidal? Ellis assumed that a person must be telling himself something unconsciously, something like "No one loves me, and I must be loved by everyone to be happy," or "I'll never be happy divorced," or "This is the end of the world for me because I cannot be happy with anyone else."

Ellis said that these are irrational beliefs. He concluded that any extreme emotional reaction must be caused by such internal cognitive statements. Therefore, Ellis developed a kind of psychotherapy, called **rational-emotive therapy (RET),** aimed at uncovering the irrational beliefs that the patient was telling himself and then correcting them. The notion was that if a person came to see his faulty reasoning and replaced it with rational thinking, then his extreme emotional reaction would be relieved. Today, this treatment is more commonly known as **rational emotive behavior therapy (REBT)** because of the current focus on behavioral elements.

A newer form of cognitive therapy was developed by **Aaron Beck** as a treatment for depression (Beck, 1979). It is called **cognitive behavior (CB) therapy.** This is one of the most common psychotherapies used today. Research has shown that CB is as effective as medications in the treatment of depression. Just as in REBT, the focus in CB therapy is on **cognitive restructuring,** changing faulty or dysfunctional ways of thinking into more realistic, rational ones. CB also incorporates techniques of behavior therapy, such as modeling and reinforcement. A review of psychology literature found more interest today in CB therapy than in any other treatment (Killgore, 2000). Aaron Beck and others also recommend CB as an effective treatment for personality disorders, which are notoriously difficult to treat (Beck, 1990).

Assessment is an important part of cognitive therapy because the therapist needs to determine which thoughts and behaviors are dysfunctional. Often, the patient is asked to keep a record of his activities, thoughts, and feelings throughout the day. This record

Connecting Concepts

Think back to Chapter 2 and the discussion of scientific methodology and ethics. Should mentally ill patients be participants in experiments on therapies? Under what conditions would it be okay?

will demonstrate that certain activities are associated with certain thoughts and feelings. The patient can then be advised to try alternative patterns of activity and new, more appropriate ways of thinking about the events that happen. When something goes wrong, for example, one need not think that it is the end of the world and that suicide is the only answer. Instead, a person can learn to think of unpleasant situations as learning experiences or as the source of interesting stories to tell to friends, for example.

Psychologist David Burns has written a book called *Feeling Good: The New Mood Therapies* (1980) that describes many of the techniques that are used in CB therapy. Research has shown not only that is CB therapy very effective in treating depression and similar psychological disorders, with improvement rates around 60% to 80%, but also that patients who simply read this book also show significant improvement in their symptoms.

Today, the most often recommended treatment for depression is a combination of antidepressant medication and CB therapy. Some people, of course, will improve with drugs, and some will not. The same is true of CB. But the combination of medication and CB therapy will effectively treat a larger percentage than either approach by itself. Both antidepressant drugs and CB therapy have success rates around 60%. But when patients are given both medicine and CB, the cure rate is about 80%. Though regularly attending CB therapy might be more inconvenient and more expensive than taking pills, the results have fewer side effects and longer-lasting results. A four-year follow-up found protective effects of CB on depression, though they faded after six years (Fava et al., 1998). Some researchers have found that CB is not more successful than other therapies as a general treatment for depression (in fact, behavior therapy did better) but should be targeted to certain patients, particularly those with personality disorders (Parker et al., 2003).

THINK TANK

Give examples of how your behavior or feelings were influenced by the way you thought about something—by your beliefs.

Give examples of times when you were able to change the way that you thought about something and it resulted in a change in your behavior or feelings.

Recap

— Psychodynamic therapies are insight therapies based on Freud's theory of psychoanalysis. These therapies attempt to reveal the contents of the unconscious.

— Humanistic therapies are also insight therapies, but they aim at conscious feelings in the attempt to help people toward self-actualization. The most common of these is the nondirective approach of Carl Rogers.

— Existential therapies are similar to humanistic approaches but concentrate on helping people to find meaning and purpose in life.

— Behavior therapies treat observable behaviors through procedures such as systematic desensitization, reinforcement, modeling, token economy, and social skills training.

— Cognitive therapies such as RET (Albert Ellis) and CB (Aaron Beck) attempt to change the way people think or how they perceive things in the belief that this change will help to improve their emotions and behaviors.

Trends

One of the newest approaches to treatment is called **narrative therapy.** The term *narrative* refers to telling a story or giving an account of something in a storylike fashion. This is a cognitive approach to treatment that does not try to change a client's way of thinking about things (as do CB therapy and RET), but instead encourages clients to develop narratives, or stories, that they find satisfying and useful in understanding themselves, their lives, and their relationships with others. Narrative approaches sometimes overlap with psychodynamic or Jungian therapies. However, the emphasis in a narrative approach is on helping a client find a story that brings a psychological understanding to his or her problems—an understanding that leads to insight, acceptance, and a deeper level of psychological awareness. Another new therapy is **dialectical behavior therapy,** also a variation of the cognitive approach. Designed to treat borderline personality disorder, this therapy relies on specific techniques for controlling emotions and regulating behaviors.

The majority of therapists do not fit neatly into any one of the various theoretical types described above. Most therapists are **eclectic;** that is, they pick and choose among various techniques that they feel comfortable with or that they think would be beneficial for an individual client with specific problems and personality. Therapists typically learn of new approaches through reading scientific research or participating in educational training and seminars. Although there are many specialists who only treat clients with certain problems or therapists who specialize in a certain type of treatment (psychoanalysis or systematic desensitization, for example), eclecticism today is the norm.

One of the problems that is inherent to contemporary therapy for psychological disorders is the reliance on **managed health care** in the United States. This is the system of health maintenance organizations (HMOs) that focus on cutting costs by treating only what is "medically necessary." Under this system, many mentally ill patients are not treated at all, and others are not provided with the best therapy because it is too expensive. Managed care has been much criticized for problems it creates in the treatment of non-ABC illnesses, but the system is especially unresponsive to the needs of the mentally ill.

TABLE 10.3 Some Modern Therapies

Medical	Psychodynamic	Humanistic	Behavioral	Cognitive
Medications	Psychoanalysis (Sigmund Freud)	Client-centered (Carl Rogers)	Systematic desensitization (exposure)	Rational-emotive (Albert Ellis)
ECT (shock)	Brief psychotherapy	Gestalt (Fritz Perls)	Flooding	Cognitive behavior (Aaron Beck)
TMS		Existential	Counterconditioning	Narrative
Psychosurgery			Aversive Token economy Extinction Modeling and social skills training	Dialectical behavior therapy

Outcome Studies

Naturally, mental health experts and mentally ill people are very much interested in which type of therapy has the highest success rate. A number of controlled experiments have been done in an attempt to determine which therapy is the best choice for patients. These studies are known as **outcome studies** because they attempt to assess the relative outcomes of different types of treatment. Because psychological disorders and therapies are complicated, as you might guess, the results of outcome studies are not clear-cut. Most experiments show that patients do better with therapy than without and that it doesn't especially matter which type of therapy is used. That is, different therapies show about the same success rate in helping people with mental illnesses (for example, Smith et al., 1980; Robinson et al., 1990). This finding is known as the **Dodo Bird verdict,** based on a line in *Alice in Wonderland* in which the Dodo Bird evaluates a race and concludes that "Everybody has won and all must have prizes."

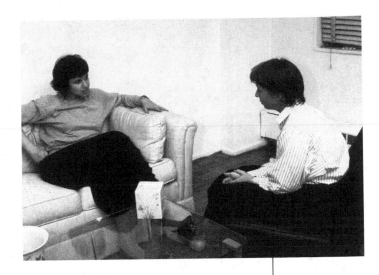

What kind of therapy do you think this person is receiving? Why? What cues are there?

On the other hand, a large number of therapists and psychologists believe that patient outcome is dependent on the characteristics of the patient and the therapist and that certain types of psychological disorder are better treated by certain types of therapies. Some research has supported this view (e.g., Beutler et al., 1994), and certainly a good deal of anecdotal evidence has been offered. Depression, for example, seems to respond best to antidepressants and cognitive therapies, while people with phobias find the highest cure rates with behavioral treatments, and psychoanalysis provides the best outcomes for people with somatoform or dissociative disorders. This is a widespread view among practicing therapists, who argue that research showing the Dodo Bird effect (all therapies are equally successful) is biased by a number of problems.

The Consumers Union, publishers of *Consumer Reports* magazine, completed a large-scale survey of its members in 1995 regarding their satisfaction with psychotherapeutic services they had received. As was mentioned earlier, a large number of those surveyed responded that they were satisfied with their therapy. The only type of therapy that received low ratings was marriage counseling. In general, all different types of therapies received about the same scores. People were generally satisfied with the therapy they received.

COMMUNITY

"Insanity—a perfectly rational adjustment to an insane world."
—R. D. LAING

Most psychotherapy occurs on an individual outpatient basis. However, there are a number of large-scale approaches to the treatment of psychological disorders. As a community, naturally we are concerned about mental illness. Efforts to deal with this issue range from mental hospitals to courtrooms.

Institutions

Of course, mental hospitals and asylums have been part of a community approach to dealing with mental illness for centuries. During the 1950s, the numbers of mental hospitals and inpatients reached a peak in the United States. However, since then, the advent of medications and the civil rights movement have together given impetus to the deinstitutionalization that continues today. Still, many people suffering from psychological disorders are today inpatients in various kinds of facilities.

During the 1970s, general hospitals in the United States overestimated the number of patients they would have; as a result, they were overbuilt. Finding many of their rooms unoccupied in the 1970s and 1980s, general hospitals began admitting mentally ill patients to their wards. Today in the United States, nearly all general hospitals have a wing or section of the hospital devoted to the treatment of psychological disorders. Of course, there remain institutions devoted solely to the treatment of patients with mental illnesses, some private and some government operated.

Psychiatric hospitals are not always especially therapeutic places. Often, the patients in such large, impersonal settings receive very little attention and care from professional staff members, such as psychiatrists. An interesting experiment was reported in 1973 by psychologist **David Rosenhan** and his friends. They admitted themselves to mental hospitals, claiming that they heard voices. Nearly all of them were diagnosed with schizophrenia. Once in a mental hospital, these normal people stopped pretending and acted as their true personalities. Rosenhan discovered that nearly everything the fake patients did was interpreted by the hospital staff as symptoms of their illness. None of the hospital staff seemed to notice that these patients were not ill. Some of the other mental patients noticed, however. They asked the fake patients why they were there and wondered whether they were news reporters. Rosenhan concluded that the mental hospital staff were unable to tell who was sick and who was not. Doctors rarely responded to simple questions asked by the fake patients. Only 6% of the time, for instance, did doctors answer a request for ground privileges. Rosenhan argues that labels are a dangerous thing that can lead to making overgeneralizations about people.

On the other hand, psychiatric hospitals have made some small improvements in recent years and some patients might find needed rest, information, and therapy in such institutions. General hospitals offer psychiatric services to people in crisis situations and other, more flexible institutions, such as halfway houses, sheltered workshops, and day care facilities, offer respite for some. There has been an attempt in the United States to move toward a *community mental health center* approach and away from large public hospitals that traditionally provided more warehousing of mental patients in the past. However, there still exist many deficiencies in the system, and while psychiatric hospitals can be helpful in some cases, there is a need for more services in between the hospital and individual treatment. Too many mentally ill people are on the streets or in our jails and prisons. A 2001 Department of Justice report found about 16 percent of the jail population had severe mental illnesses, and concluded that "jails and prisons have become the nation's new mental hospitals."

We still have the practice of **involuntary commitment** in the United States, which means that a person can be taken into custody for mental health care against his or her will. Such a practice is sometimes called **civil commitment** because the person has not committed a crime. Today, such commitment depends on judging a person to be dangerous. If a person is considered to be dangerous to himself or to others, he can legally be taken by the police to a hearing and potentially be placed into an institution, although he has committed no crime. Unfortunately, scientific studies show that judging dangerousness is very difficult, if not impossible. There are many instances of people who were judged to be dangerous who later did not engage in any violent acts whatsoever during or after their institutionalizations. Similarly, there have been many people who were

Connecting Concepts

Remember the Barnum effect discussed in Chapter 7? When people are labeled a certain type of person or are assigned a certain personality trait, it is common to judge all of their actions in light of that label. This is what Rosenhan discovered. It is a common mistake, similar to fundamental attribution error (also discussed in Chapter 7), which says that people often judge the behavior of others based on internal, personality variables rather than on the situation. Be careful out there.

judged to be nondangerous, were released from institutional care, and immediately engaged in violent acts toward themselves or others. This is a tricky business indeed. Adding to the problem is the fact that many experts believe that involuntary commitment is a violation of a person's constitutional right to freedom and that it should be abolished. Still, all 50 states allow involuntary commitment, as do most countries.

Large mental hospitals are not especially caring and supportive places for people. Some communities have smaller, more personal institutions that provide treatment for those with psychological disorders. A system of **community mental health centers (CMHC)** was created by an act of Congress in 1963. As a result, today there are more small, community-based alternatives to hospitalization than ever before—places such as halfway houses, group homes, social and recreational centers, and day- or night-care facilities. However, we still do not have nearly enough **aftercare** for people leaving mental hospitals, and unfortunately, many mentally ill people end up living as homeless people on the streets of our cities.

Organizations

The **National Alliance for the Mentally Ill (NAMI)** is one of the largest and most active organizations of many that have been created in recent years to help deal with issues of mental health. NAMI consists of former mental patients, psychologists, psychiatrists, and other mental health professionals, lawyers, teachers, and other interested people. Its goals include support for mentally ill people, educating the public about mental illnesses, and lobbying for appropriate legislation to help the mentally ill. NAMI has chapters in every state in the United States.

A number of **self-help organizations** exist today, groups of former and current sufferers who provide support and education to each other. Such groups exist for every psychological disorder, and they can be contacted through the Internet, by calling numbers found in the phone book, or by contacting NAMI. These groups include Borderline Personality Disorder Central, National Foundation for Depressive Illness, and the National Alliance on Schizophrenia and Depression.

Research on mental illness goes on in nearly every university and research center around the world, and resources are available in libraries and on the Internet. The **National Institutes of Health (NIH)**, with its main campus in Bethesda, Maryland, is a national center for medical research, including the study of mental illnesses. It is part of the U.S. Department of Health and Human Services.

Legal Issues

As you know, mental illness is often an issue in courtroom proceedings. A person who has committed a crime can offer a plea of **insanity.** Because this concept depends so much on mental illness, many people mistakenly believe that the term *insanity* refers to a psychological disorder of some sort. In fact, *insanity* is a legal term, not a psychiatric one, and is used when a person is not held accountable for a crime he or she has committed.

Typically, mental illness is the main criterion that is used to determine insanity in courtrooms, although some jurisdictions still use a variation of the older idea of judging whether a person knew the difference between right and wrong. This is called the **M'Naghten rule** after Daniel M'Naghten, who in 1843 in England shot and killed the Prime Minister's secretary in an attempt to kill the Prime Minister because "the voice of God" ordered him to. Although most jurisdictions have more complicated tests for defining insanity, the idea of knowing right from wrong continues to be influential.

Contrary to popular myth, the insanity plea is rarely used because it has a very low level of success. Fewer than 1% of insanity pleas are won in court. Most people do not like the idea of releasing a person who has committed a crime, regardless of the circumstances or the person's mental state. Juries believe that a person who is judged to be mentally ill will not be punished, will not suffer, for his or her bad behavior. A good example is Jeffrey Dahmer who engaged in the most outrageous behaviors, yet was judged by a jury to not be mentally ill. If he wasn't mentally ill, then who is? What in the world do we mean by mentally ill? In fact, a number of mental patients have pointed out that jail inmates have many services and accommodations that institutionalized mentally ill do not have. Perhaps imprisonment in a mental hospital is not a less severe punishment than a prison. But should the mentally ill be punished for their actions?

After John Hinckley shot President Ronald Reagan and his press secretary, James Brady, a jury found Hinckley not guilty by reason of insanity, partly owing to psychiatric testimony and pictures of Hinckley's brain that showed abnormalities. Many people were outraged that Hinckley was sent to a mental hospital instead of to a prison. As a result, some states changed their insanity laws to a verdict called **guilty but mentally ill (GBMI).** This weird idea says that a person was not responsible for his or her actions, but we're going to put him or her in prison anyway. The GBMI verdict was challenged but was found by the U.S. Supreme Court to be in accord with the Constitution.

There have been many court rulings that affect the treatment of people with mental illnesses. For example, **least restrictive environment** is a principle that prescribes that mental health providers must not restrict patients any more than is necessary. **Mainstreaming** requires that mentally retarded and other children with psychological disorders be placed in regular classrooms as much as possible. Also this was a reaction to the old practice of segregating such children in "special" classrooms. Also the right to treatment, right to refuse treatment, and informed consent have all been upheld and affirmed by court cases in the United States.

Prevention

One of the most significant problems we have in dealing with mental disorders is that not enough effort is given to prevention. Psychiatrists and other mental health experts sit in their offices and wait for people with disorders to come in with complaints. Wouldn't it be much better to create a system that prevented mental illnesses in the first place? Why wait until they have already occurred? Shouldn't we put our energy, money, and resources into the front end instead of the tail end?

Imagine if we treated non-ABC illnesses that way. What if we had no health department? Restaurants could serve anything under any conditions, and doctors would simply wait for people to get sick and come in for treatment. There would be no immunizations or inoculations against disease. There would be no consumer warnings about products. There would be no testing or inspections of conditions that might cause disease or injury. There would be no education or information about health issues. What kind of weird society would that be? Well, that's pretty much how it works with mental health.

One of the most interesting and promising recent movements by mental health professionals is called **community psychology.** This approach is not so much a set of practices as it is an attitude or way of thinking. The emphasis in community psychology is on prevention and **containment** (keeping mental problems from spreading). This idea includes TV and radio informational pieces, telephone hotlines that people who need help can call for immediate assistance, neighborhood crisis centers and clinics, and counseling for people in vulnerable situations. Psychologists can go into the community instead of sitting in their offices. They can get to know the people of a neighborhood, their personalities, concerns, and problems. The community psychologist provides education and information to help people cope with difficulties and resist psychological distress. Perhaps the idea of community psychology will spread, and in the future we will have fewer mental illnesses by means of prevention rather than via treatment. Let's hope so.

Recap

— A new trend in counseling is narrative therapy, which encourages patients to develop stories that will help them better understand themselves.

— Most therapists are eclectic—they pick and choose different approaches.

— Outcome studies often find that therapy is better than no therapy, but that all therapies are about equal in effectiveness. Not everyone agrees with this Dodo Bird verdict, however.

— Deinstitutionalization has continued since the mid-1950s, when therapeutic drugs became widely available.

— A number of organizations, including the National Alliance for the Mentally Ill, attempt to help the mentally ill.

— Involuntary commitment is based on how dangerous a person is to himself or herself or to others.

— The insanity plea is a legal procedure in which a person claims to not be responsible for a crime they have committed.

— Legal rulings have given mental patients a number of rights, such as least restrictive environment and right to refuse treatment.

— Community psychology is a modern approach that focuses on the prevention and containment of psychological disorders.

I Link, Therefore I Am

You can learn a lot more about history's witch killings and read excerpts from the Malleus Malifecarum on the Internet. For example, here are some links:

http://www.malleusmaleficarum.org
http://www.history.hanover.edu/early/wh.html
http://www.illusions.com/burning/burnwitc.htm
http://www.zpr.uni-kocln.de/~nix/hexen/e index.htm
http://www.geocities.com/Athens/2962/witch.html

You can find tons of information about psychotherapies on the Internet. For example, the Online Dictionary of Mental Health is at http://www.shef.ac.uk/~psysc/psychotherapy/index.html. A national database listing support groups by county and state can be found at http://www.grouptherapylist.com/

Also, try these: http://www.cybercouch.com or http://www.allaboutcounseling.com/ or http://www.aboutpsychotherapy.com/ or http://members.aol.com/lacillo/ or http://www.psynews.com/ or http://www.mentalhealth.org/

Information about Carl Rogers can be found at http://www.oprf.com/Rogers

Information about Fritz Perls and Gestalt therapy at http://psy1.clarion.edu/jms/Perls.html

Although psychotherapy is no joke, some cartoons demonstrating the lighter side of this topic can be found at http://www.palme.nu/comics

The NAMI Web site is http://www.nami.org. The NIMH Web site is http://www.nimh.nih.gov

The National Mental Health Association, a large nonprofit organization dealing with all issues related to psychological disorders and support, has its Web site at http://www.nmha.org

STUDY GUIDE FOR CHAPTER 10:
THERARIES

Key terms and names (Make flash cards.)

trephining (trepanation)
exorcism
Malleus Malifecarum
lycanthropy
lunacy
humors
bloodletting
prefrontal lobotomy
hospital
asylum
Bethlehem Hospital
bedlam
Philippe Pinel
moral therapy
Dorothea Dix
Benjamin Rush
deinstitutionalization
Franz Anton Mesmer
animal magnetism
crisis
mesmerism
hypnosis
Jean-Martin Charcot
Sigmund Freud
psychoanalysis
psychotherapies
psychiatrist
neuroleptic drugs
dopamine
tardive dyskinesia atypical (second-
    generation) antipsychotics
antidepressants
serotonin
MAO inhibitors (MAOIs)
tricyclic drugs
reuptake inhibitors
selective serotonin reuptake
    inhibitors (SSRIs)
serotonin/norepinephrine reuptake
    inhibitors (SNRIs)
SRIBs
substance P
St. John's wort

lithium
antimanic
antianxiety drugs
benzodiazepines
L-dopa
acetylcholine
electroconvulsive therapy (ECT)
insulin coma therapy
transcranial magnetic stimulation
    (TMS)
psychosurgery
psychodynamic
talk therapies
insight therapies
dream interpretation
projective
word association
inkblot test
analysis of resistance
analysis of transference
brief psychotherapies
humanistic psychology
Abraham Maslow
Carl Rogers
self-concept
self-actualization
client-centered therapy
incongruent
ideal self
real self
unconditional positive regard
Gestalt therapy
Fritz Perls
Here and Now
empathy
reflection
nondirective
existential therapy
logotherapy
paradoxical intention
behavior therapies
action therapies
symptom substitution

generalization
systematic desensitization
exposure therapies
flooding
counterconditioning
aversive therapy
operant conditioning therapies
reinforcement
token economy
extinction therapy
modeling
social skills training
cognitive therapies
Albert Ellis
rational-emotive therapy (RET)
rational emotive behavior therapy
    (REBT)
Aaron Beck
cognitive behavior (CB) therapy
cognitive restructuring
narrative therapy
dialectical behavior therapy
eclectic
managed health care
outcome studies
Dodo Bird verdict
David Rosenhan
involuntary (civil) commitment
community mental health centers
    (CMHC)
aftercare
National Alliance for the Mentally
    Ill (NAMI)
self-help organizations
National Institutes of Health (NIH)
insanity
M'Naghten rule
guilty but mentally ill (GBMI)
least restrictive environment
mainstreaming
community psychology
containment

Fill in the blank

1. In the past, holes were made in people's heads in a procedure called _____.
2. Drilling holes in people's heads was performed for the purpose of _____ _____ _____.
3. In 1486, a book called the _____ _____ was published that told people how to recognize witches.
4. The term _____ came from the idea that the moon could make people act crazy.
5. The term _____ derived from Bethlehem Hospital.
6. Philippe _____ was a French doctor who put a stop to the harsh practices of hospitals and released inmates from their chains. His approach became known as _____ therapy.
7. Franz Anton _____ taught that mental disorders were caused by a disturbance in a person's _____ _____. His practices led to the use of _____ as a therapeutic tool.
8. The most famous early teacher of psychiatry was Jean-Martin _____.
9. The medications used in the treatment of psychoses, particularly schizophrenia, are called _____ or _____. These medicines block the brain's receptors for _____.
10. New medicines for treating schizophrenia are called _____ antipsychotics.
11. The medicines known as *antidepressants* have the effect of increasing the activity of certain brain neurotransmitter chemicals, most notably _____.
12. A tricyclic antidepressant (TCA) medication is a _____ inhibitor.
13. Bipolar disorders are treated with the element _____.
14. The medicines commonly known as minor _____ are used in the treatment of anxiety disorders. Thus, they are also called _____ drugs.
15. Patients with Parkinson's disease often find relief from their tremors (shaking) with the use of a drug called _____.
16. _____ therapy is often simply called shock treatment.
17. In transcranial _____ stimulation (TMS), an electromagnetic coil placed on the head transmits magnetic pulses to the brain.
18. _____ is the general term for brain operations that are performed to help people who suffer with psychological disorders.
19. Sigmund Freud (1856–1939) introduced the idea that psychological disorders are sometimes caused by conflicts in the person's _____ mind. Freud developed a therapy known as _____.
20. Freud believed that a _____ is a disguised version of unconscious thoughts or feelings.
21. The fundamental notion of humanistic therapy is the idea that psychological disorders are sometimes caused by disturbances in a person's _____.
22. Humanistic therapy begins with the therapist providing _____ _____ regard.
23. The most common technique used in humanistic counseling is _____.
24. _____ therapy was pioneered by Fritz Perls.
25. Humanistic therapies are often called non-_____.
26. Humanistic therapies are also called _____-centered.
27. A variation of humanistic therapy is an attempt to help people who are struggling with philosophical ideas about existence. This approach is called _____ therapy.
28. _____ literally means "therapy for the spirit."
29. _____ approaches to treatment are called action therapies.
30. _____ is a behavior therapy that is used in the treatment of phobias and other conditioned disorders.
31. In _____, the patient is asked to imagine the upsetting stimuli in a very intense manner for a long period of time.
32. In _____, a reaction is conditioned to a stimulus that is opposite from the current one.
33. In operant conditioning therapies, a behavior is increased by use of _____.
34. Operant conditioning with large groups of people is called a _____ economy.
35. Albert Ellis developed a kind of psychotherapy called _____ therapy, which focuses on _____.
36. A newer form of cognitive therapy was developed by Aaron Beck as a treatment for depression. It is called _____ therapy.
37. In a new treatment approach called _____ therapy, clients are encouraged to create stories that will help them to understand and accept their situation.
38. Studies that compare the cure rates of various types of therapy are known as _____ studies.

39. The fact that many studies show that different types of therapy are about equal in their cure rates is called the _____ _____ _____ .

40. The advent of medications and the civil rights movement have together given impetus to the _____ of mental patients that continues today.

41. The _____ _____ for the Mentally Ill is one of the largest and most active organizations that have been created in recent years to help deal with issues of mental health.

42. _____ is a legal term, not a psychiatric one, and is used when a person is not held accountable for a crime he or she has committed.

43. The emphasis of _____ psychology is on prevention and containment

Matching

1. psychoanalysis _____
2. *Malleus Maleficarum* _____
3. lunatic _____
4. dementia _____
5. trephining _____
6. St. John's wort _____
7. bedlam _____
8. Fritz Perls _____
9. Mesmer _____
10. Pinel _____
11. ECT _____
12. systematic desensitization _____
13. neuroleptic drugs _____
14. bipolar disorder _____
15. logotherapy _____
16. token economy _____
17. community psychology _____
18. Carl Rogers _____
19. SSRI _____
20. Parkinson's disease _____

a. herb
b. Alzheimer's disease
c. exposure therapy
d. shock treatment
e. dream interpretation
f. prevention
g. Prozac
h. L-dopa
i. lithium
j. operant conditioning
k. unchaining of inmates
l. hole in head
m. nondirective therapy
n. existential therapy
o. antipsychotics
p. London hospital
q. Gestalt therapy
r. witches
s. moon
t. hypnosis

Multiple choice

1. Your friend is seeing a therapist and tells you that the therapist uses a different approach to treatment at each session. The therapist is
   a. a psychoanalyst
   b. a Gestalt therapist
   c. eclectic
   d. humanistic

2. A person with conversion disorder is seeing a therapist who asks her to sit back in her chair and say anything that comes to mind. Her therapist is using the techniques of
   a. narrative therapy
   b. psychoanalysis
   c. C-B therapy
   d. Gestalt

3. Which of these is an indication that a patient is showing resistance?
   a. He talks about his relationship with his mother.
   b. He wants to change the way he thinks about his situation.
   c. He talks about unimportant things.
   d. He talks only about his dreams.

4. In the Socratic method, a teacher uses discussion to gradually lead students to discover important truths about themselves. This is similar to which type of therapy?
   a. Rogerian
   b. Gestalt
   c. narrative
   d. C-B

5. Dream interpretation is a major part of which therapy?
   a. logotherapy
   b. psychoanalysis
   c. systematic desensitization
   d. nondirective therapy
6. Which type of therapy has been most recommended in the treatment of depression?
   a. Rogerian counseling
   b. psychoanalysis
   c. flooding
   d. cognitive behavior
7. Which of these types of medication is used in the treatment of depression?
   a. neuroleptics
   b. lithium
   c. SSRI
   d. minor tranquilizers
8. The *Malleus Maleficarum* said that witches were
   a. women
   b. men
   c. good spirits
   d. mentally ill
9. Psychoanalysis is an appropriate treatment for
   a. major depression
   b. schizophrenia
   c. bipolar disorder
   d. somatoform disorder
10. Systematic desensitization is a type of _____ therapy.
    a. client-centered
    b. existential
    c. aversive
    d. exposure
11. ECT is effective in the treatment of
    a. schizophrenia
    b. paranoia
    c. dementia
    d. mood disorders
12. Mesmer is known as the founder of
    a. psychodynamic therapy
    b. flooding
    c. hypnosis
    d. trephining
13. Neuroleptic drugs affect the brain by
    a. stimulating the release of neurotransmitters
    b. blocking the reuptake of neurotransmitters
    c. reducing the effects of enzymes
    d. blocking dopamine receptors
14. Flooding is a treatment that would be appropriate for
    a. phobias
    b. sexual disorders
    c. somatoform disorders
    d. dissociative disorders
15. Therapies that use punishment or painful stimuli are called _____ therapies.
    a. exposure
    b. action
    c. aversive
    d. existential
16. Tardive dyskinesia is a
    a. side effect of neuroleptics
    b. side effect of ECT
    c. behavior treatment
    d. type of shock treatment
17. The antidepressant drugs include the
    a. MAO inhibitors
    b. atypical antipsychotics
    c. neuroleptic medicines
    d. dopamine blockers
18. The SSRI drugs act by interfering with the process of
    a. reuptake
    b. enzyme synthesis
    c. calcium intake
    d. action potential
19. L-dopa is a drug that is used in the treatment of
    a. Alzheimer's disease
    b. Parkinson's disease
    c. schizophrenia
    d. major mood disorders
20. Which of these treatments would likely be used in the case of a severe mood disorder that does not respond to medications?
    a. psychosurgery
    b. ECT
    c. neuroleptics
    d. flooding
21. A token economy is a type of _____ therapy.
    a. operant conditioning
    b. psychoanalytic
    c. Gestalt
    d. counter
22. The use of transcranial magnetic stimulation might reduce the number of patients who are treated with
    a. antipsychotic drugs
    b. prefrontal lobotomies
    c. shock treatment
    d. insight therapies
23. Your aunt asked a clinical psychologist to give her a nonmedical treatment for depression. She will probably receive
    a. ECT
    b. psychoanalysis
    c. narrative therapy
    d. cognitive behavior therapy

24. Modeling and social skills training are important parts of _____ therapy.
    a. client-centered
    b. existential
    c. paradoxical
    d. operant conditioning

25. A friend is seeing a counselor who asks him to talk about his dreams and make word associations. The counselor would most likely be classified as
    a. Gestalt
    b. existential
    c. Rogerian
    d. psychoanalytic

26. Which of these approaches to therapy is cognitive?
    a. Mary is asked by her therapist to keep a dream diary.
    b. Sue is required to keep track of her thoughts during the day
    c. Bob is taught to relax and then to think about germs.
    d. Mick receives reinforcers for not washing his hands for a specified period of time.

27. Norm is helping a group of people with schizophrenia. He shows them how to engage in social interaction and gives them check marks when they perform correctly. Norm is using a technique known as
    a. Gestalt therapy
    b. client-centered therapy
    c. cognitive behavior therapy
    d. token economy

28. Empathy and reflection are important techniques in _____ therapy.
    a. action
    b. cognitive
    c. client-centered
    d. existential

29. Which type of therapy aims at helping people find spiritual meaning in life?
    a. token economy
    b. flooding
    c. systematic desensitization
    d. logotherapy

30. Instead of symptom substitution, behavior therapists often find a _____ effect when they treat a symptom.
    a. generalization
    b. placebo
    c. paradoxical
    d. counter

31. The technique of paradoxical intention asks patients to try to
    a. think more rationally
    b. keep a dream diary
    c. engage in observational behaviors
    d. increase their symptoms

32. Cognitive behavior therapy was developed by
    a. Fritz Perls
    b. Carl Rogers
    c. Aaron Beck
    d. B. F. Skinner

33. David Rosenhan and friends were admitted to mental hospitals and concluded that
    a. the staff were not good at determining who was mentally ill
    b. the psychiatrists mistreated the patients
    c. most of the patients were not mentally ill
    d. deinstitutionalization is not occurring

34. Involuntary commitment is
    a. not allowed in the United States
    b. based on dangerousness
    c. the same as deinstitutionalization
    d. used only when a crime was committed

35. You and a friend are both going for therapy, but one of you sees a psychoanalyst and the other sees a client-centered therapist. The therapists agree that it is important for both of you to
    a. gain insight into your problems
    b. treat the symptoms of your problem
    c. understand your unconscious
    d. find the answers on your own

36. A psychiatrist at a mental hospital notices a patient with schizophrenia is shaking, walking clumsily, and having difficulty moving her eyes, mouth, and hands. The psychiatrist concludes that the patient
    a. has taken antipsychotic medicine for a long time
    b. is developing symptoms of paranoia
    c. is in the residual phase of her disorder
    d. did not receive any medication for her disorder

37. "Guilty but mentally ill" is a form of
    a. insanity law
    b. self-help group
    c. least restrictive environment
    d. prevention

38. Prevention and containment are important parts of _____ psychology.
    a. legal
    b. community
    c. behavioral
    d. cognitive

39. Narrative therapy encourages patients to develop
    a. journals of their behaviors
    b. classical conditioning
    c. dream diaries
    d. personal stories

40. The Dodo Bird verdict refers to the results of
    a. deinstitutionalization
    b. outcome studies
    c. insanity pleas
    d. health management

Short answer and critical thinking

1. What were some of the reasons that so many mentally ill people were put into hospitals in the past, and why is deinstitutionalization occurring now?
2. Why do you think that Mesmer's ideas and practices had so much appeal to so many people?
3. What are some of the advantages and disadvantages of today's reliance on the use of medications to treat psychological disorders?
4. What is ECT, how is it done, and what is it used for?
5. Why do psychoanalysts interpret dreams?
6. What things do each of these therapies try to change: (a) psychoanalysis, (b) behavior therapy, (c) humanistic therapy, and (d) cognitive therapy?
7. What is the essential idea behind cognitive therapies?
8. What is the Dodo Bird verdict, and what are some criticisms of it?
9. Describe the 1973 Rosenhan experiment. Do you think the same results would occur today? Why or why not?
10. What is community psychology? What are its goals?

REFERENCES

Abel, T. (1998). Memory suppressor genes: Inhibitory constraints on the storage of long-term memory. *Science, 279,* 338–341.

Adams-Campbell, L. L., Wing, R., Ukoli, F. A., Janney, C. A., & Nwankwo, M. U. (1994). Obesity, body fat distribution, and blood pressure in Nigerian and African-American men and women. *Journal of the National Medical Association,* 86(1), 60.

Adolphs, R. (1996). Cortical systems for the recognition of emotion in facial expressions. *Journal of Neuroscience, 16,* 7678–7687.

Ainsworth, M. D. S. (1978). *Patterns of attachment: A psychological study of the strange situation.* Hillsdale, NJ: Erlbaum.

Aleman, A., et al. (2003). Sex differences in the risk of schizophrenia: Evidence from meta-analysis. *Archives of General Psychiatry,* 60(6), 565–571.

Allport, S. (1986). *Explorers of the black box: The search for the cellular basis of memory.* New York: Norton.

Aloia, M. S., Gourovitch, M. L., Missar, D., Pickar, D., Weinberger, D. R., & Goldberg, T. E. (1998). Cognitive substrates of thought disorder. II: Specifying a candidate cognitive mechanism. *American Journal of Psychiatry,* 155(12), 1671–1677.

Ambrose, S. G. (2002). Set up for schizophrenia. *The Dallas Morning News,* December 2, 2002.

American Psychiatric Association. (1994). *Diagnostic and statistical manual of mental disorders,* 4th ed. Washington, DC: American Psychiatric Association.

Anderluh, M. B., Tchanturia, K., Rabe-Hesketh, S., & Treasure, J. (2003). Childhood obsessive-compulsive personality traits in adult women with eating disorders: Defining a broader eating disorder phenotype. *American Journal of Psychiatry,* 160(2), 242–244.

Anderson, C. A., Carnagey, N. L., & Eubanks, J. (2003). Exposure to violent media: The effects of songs with violent lyrics on aggressive thoughts and feelings. *Journal of Personality and Social Psychology,* 84(5), 960–971.

Anderson, C. A., & Bushman, B. J. (2002). The effects of media violence on society. *Science, 295,* 2377–2379.

Anderson, J. R. (1990). *Cognitive psychology and its implications,* 3rd ed. San Francisco: Freeman.

Anderson, J. R. (1996). Working memory: Activation, limitations on retrieval. *Cognitive Psychology, 30,* 221–256.

Andreasen, N. C. (2001). *Brave new brain: Conquering mental illness in the era of the genome.* New York: Oxford Press.

Aronson, E. (2001). *Nobody left to hate.* New York: Henry Holt and Company.

Asbahr, F. R., et al. (1998). Obsessive-compulsive and related symptoms in children and adolescents with rheumatic fever with and without chorea: A prospective 6-month study. *American Journal of Psychiatry,* 155(8), 1122–1124.

Asch, S. E. (1951). Effects of group pressure upon the modification and distortion of judgment. In H. Guetzkow (Ed.), *Groups, leadership, and men.* Pittsburgh, PA: Carnegie.

Atkinson, R. C., & Shiffrin, R. M. (1968). Human memory: A proposed system and its control processes. In K. W. Spence & J. T. Spence (Ed.), *The psychology of learning and motivation: Advances in research and therapy.* New York: Academic Press.

Baddeley, A. D. (1976). *The psychology of human memory.* New York: Basic Books.

Baddeley, A. D. (1986). *Working memory.* Oxford, England: Clarendon Press.

Bailey, A. (1995). Autism as a strongly genetic disorder: Evidence from a British twin study. *Psychological Medicine, 25,* 63–77.

Bandura, A., Ross, D., & Ross, S. A. (1961). Transmission of aggression through imitation of aggressive models. *Journal of Abnormal and Social Psychology, 63,* 575–582.

Bandura, A., & Walters, R. (1963). *Social learning and personality development.* New York: Holt, Rinehart & Winston.

Barad, M. G., Davis, M., Quirk, G. J., & Phelps, E. A. (2003). Learning to feel safe: Extinction of conditioned fear. Paper presented at Society for Neuroscience meeting, November 10.

Barberger-Gateau, L. L., Deschamps, V., Peres, K., Dartiques, J.-F., & Renaud, S. (2002). Fish, meat, and risk of dementia: cohort study. *BMJ Journal, 325,* 932–933.

Barkow, J. H., Cosmides, L., & Tooby, J., (Eds.) (1992). *The adapted mind: Evolutionary psychology and the generation of culture.* New York: Oxford University Press.

Baron, J. (1988). *Thinking and deciding.* New York: Cambridge University Press.

Barres, B. A. (1999). A new role for glia: Generation of neurons! *Cell,* 97(6), 667–671.

Bateman, A., & Fonagy, P. (2001). Treatment of borderline personality disorder with psychoanalytically oriented partial hospitalization: An 18-month follow-up. *American Journal of Psychiatry,* 158(1), 36–42.

Baynes, K., Eliassen, J., Lutsep, H., & Gazzaniga, M. (1998). Modular organization of cognitive systems masked by interhemispheric integration. *Science,* 280(5365), 902–906.

Beck, A. T. (1961). An inventory for measuring depression. *Archives of General Psychiatry, 4,* 561–671.

Beck, A. T. (1967). *Depression: Causes and treatment.* Philadelphia: University of Pennsylvania Press.

Beck, A. T. (1976). *Cognitive therapy and emotional disorders.* New York: International University Press.

Beck, A. T. (1979). *Cognitive therapy of depression.* New York: Guilford Press.

Beck, A. T. (1990). *Cognitive therapy of personality disorders.* New York: Guilford Press.

Belsky, J. (2001). Effects of day care on children's behavior. Research report presented at the International Conference on Child Development, Minneapolis, MN.

Benson, E. (2003). Intelligent intelligence testing. *Monitor on Psychology,* Vol. 34, 2, pp. 3–4. American Psychological Association.

Berger, J. (2001). Recolonizing carnivores and naïve prey: Conservation lessons from Pleistocene extinctions. *Science,* 291(5506), 1036–1039.

Berson, D. M., Dunn, F. A., & Takao, M. (2002). Phototransduction by retinal ganglion cells that set the circadian clock. *Science, 295,* 1070–1072.

Bertram, L. (2000). Evidence for genetic linkage of Alzheimer's disease to chromosome 10q. *Science,* 290(5500), 2302.

Beutler, L. E. (1995). Integrative and eclectic therapies in practice. In B. Bongar & L. E. Beutler (Eds.), *Comprehensive textbook of psychotherapy.* New York: Oxford University Press.

Biegler, R., McGregor, A., Krebs, J. R., & Healy, S. D. (2001). A larger hippocampus is associated with longer-lasting spatial memory. *Proceedings of the National Academy of Sciences of the United States,* 98(12), 6941–6944.

Bisiach, E., & Luzzatti, C. (1978). Unilateral neglect of representational space. *Cortex, 14,* 129–133.

Black, C. B. (2000). Can observational practice facilitate error recognition and movement production? *Research Quarterly for Exercise and Sport,* 71(4), 331.

Blakeslee, S. (1997, June 27). Brain studies tie marijuana to other drugs. *New York Times,* p. A16.

Blandin, Y. (1999). Cognitive processes underlying observational learning of motor skills. *Quarterly Journal of Experimental Psychology,* 52(4), 957.

Blass, E. M., & Camp, C. A. (2001). The ontogeny of face recognition: Eye contact and sweet taste induce face preference in 9- and 12-week-old human infants. *Developmental Psychology, 37,* 6.

Bontempi, B., Laurent-Demir, C., Destrade, C., & Jaffard, R. (1999). Time-dependent reorganization of brain circuitry underlying long-term memory storage. *Nature, 400,* 671–675.

Borenstein Graves, A., Mortimer, J. A., Bowen, J. D., McCormick, W. C., McCurry, S. M., Schellenberg, G. D., & Larson, E. B. (2001). Head circumference and incident Alzheimer's disease: Modification by apolipoprotein E. *Neurology, 57,* 1453–1460.

Bostwick, J. M., & Pankratz, V. S. (2000). Affective disorders and suicide risk: A reexamination. *American Journal of Psychiatry,* 157(12), 1925–1932.

Bouchard, T. J., & McGue, M. (1981). Familial studies of intelligence: A review. *Science, 212,* 1055–1059.

Brain, L. (1965). *Speech disorders: Aphasia, apraxia, and agnosia.* London: Butterworth.

Brainard, M. S., & Knudsen, E. I. (1998). Experience affects brain development. *American Journal of Psychiatry, 155,* 8, 1000.

Brannon, E. M., & Terrace, H. S. (2000). Representation of the numerosities 1–9 by Rhesus macaques (Macaca mulatta). *Journal of Experimental Psychology: Animal Behavior Processes, 26*(1), 31–50.

Bremmer, F., Schlack, A., Shah, N. J., Zafiris, O., Kubishchik, M., Hoffmann, K.-P., Zilles, K., & Fink, G. R. (2001). Polymodal motion processing in posterior parietal and premotor cortex: A human fMRI study strongly implies equivalencies between humans and monkeys. *Neuron, 29,* 287.

Breuer, J., & Freud, S. (1937). *Studies in hysteria.* Boston: Beacon Press. (Originally published in 1896).

Breuer, J., & Freud, S. (1961). *Studies in hysteria.* Boston: Beacon Press.

Brewer, J. (1998). Making memories: Brain activity that predicts how well visual experience will be remembered. *Science, 281*(5380), 1185–1188.

Brick, J. & Erickson, C. K. (1998). *Drugs, the brain, and behavior: The pharmacology of abuse and dependence.* New York: The Haworth Medical Press.

Brodsky, B. S., Oquendo, M., Ellis, S. P., Haas, G. L., Malone, K. M., & Mann, J. J. (2001). The relationship of childhood abuse to impulsivity and suicidal behavior in adults with major depression. *American Journal of Psychiatry, 158*(11), 1871–1877.

Brown, J. W. (1989). The nature of voluntary action. *Brain and Cognition, 10,* 105–120.

Brown, R., & Kulik, J. (1977). Flashbulb memories. *Cognition, 5,* 73–99.

Buchanan, R. W., Vladar, K., Barta, P., & Pearlson, G. (1998). Structural evaluation of the prefrontal cortex in schizophrenia. *American Journal of Psychiatry, 155*(8), 1049–1056.

Burns, D. (1980). *Feeling good: The new mood therapies.* New York: Morrow.

Bushman, B. J., & Anderson, C. A. (2001). Media violence and the American public. *American Psychologist, 56*(6), 477–489.

Buss, D. M. (1999). *Evolutionary psychology.* Boston: Allyn & Bacon.

Caicedo, A., & Roper, S. D. (2001). Taste receptor cells that discriminate between bitter stimuli. *Science, 291,* 1557–1560.

Cain, C. K., Blouin, A. M., & Barad, M. (2003). Temporally massed CS presentations generate more fear extinction than spaced presentations. *Journal of Experimental Psychology: Animal Behavior Processes, 29*(4), 323–333.

Callicott, J. H., et al. (2003). Abnormal fMRI response of the dorsolateral prefrontal cortex in cognitively intact siblings of patients with schizophrenia. *American Journal of Psychiatry, 160*(4), 709–710.

Canli, T., Sivers, H. Whitfield, S. L., Gotlib, I. H., & Gabrieli, J. D. E. (2002). Amygdala response to happy faces as a function of extraversion. *Science, 296,* 2191.

Carey, B. (2003, July 7). DNA research links depression to family ties. *Los Angeles Times,* p. 3.

Carmena, J. M., Lebedev, M. A., Crist, R. E., O'Doherty, J. E., Santucci, D. M., Dimitrov, D. F., Patil, P. G., Henriquez, C. S., & Niolelis, M. A. L. (2003). Learning to control a brain-machine interface for reaching and grasping by primates. *Public Library of Science, 1*(2), E42.

Carmena, J. M., Lebedev, M. A., Crist, R. E., O'Doherty, J. E., Santuso, D. M., Dimitrov, D., Patil, P. G., Henriques, C. S., Nicolelis, M. A. (2003). Learning to control a brain-machine interface for reaching and grasping by primates. *PLoS Biology,* Nov. 1 (2), E42.

Carter, C. S., Perlstein, W., Ganguli, R., Brar, J., Mintun, M., & Cohen, J. D. (1998). Functional hypofrontality and working memory dysfunction in schizophrenia. *American Journal of Psychiatry, 155*(9), 1285–1287.

Caspi, A., McClay, J., Moffitt, T. E., Mill, J., Martin, J., Craig, I. W., Taylor, A., & Poulton, R. (2002). Role of genotype in the cycle of violence in maltreated children. *Science, 297*(5582), 851–854.

Caspi, A., et al. (2003). Influence of life stress on depression: Moderation by a polymorphism in the 5-HTT gene. *Science, 301,* 386–389.

Cattell, R. B. (1963). Theory of fluid and crystallized intelligence: A critical experiment. *Journal of Educational Psychology, 54,* 1–22.

Cattell, R. B., & Dreger, R. M. (Eds.). (1977). *Handbook of modern personality theory.* Washington, DC: Hemisphere.

Ceci, S. J. (1996). *A bioecological treatise on intellectual development.* Cambridge, MA: Harvard University Press.

Centorrino, F., Price, B. H., Tuttle, M., Bahk, W. M., Hennen, J., Albert, M. J., & Baldessarini, R. J. (2002). EEG abnormalities during treatment with typical and atypical antipsychotics. *American Journal of Psychiatry, 159*(1), 109–110.

Cervenakova, L., Goldfarb, L. G., Garruto, R., Lee, H.-S., Gajdusek, D. C., & Brown, P. (1998). Phenotype-genotype studies in kuru: Implications for new variant Creutzfeldt-Jakob disease. *Proceedings of the National Academy of Sciences of the United States, 95*(22), 13239–13242.

Chambless, D. L., & Gillis, M. M. (1993). Cognitive therapy of anxiety disorders. *Journal of Consulting and Clinical Psychology, 61,* 248–260.

Chang, E. F., & Merzenich, M. M. (2003). Environmental noise retards auditory cortical development. *Science, 300,* 498–499.

Chaudhari, N., Landin, A. M., & Roper, S. D. (2000). A metabotropic glutamate receptor variant functions as a taste receptor. *Nature Neuroscience, 3,* 113–119.

Chess, S., & Thomas, A. (1996). *Temperament: Theory and practice.* New York: Brunner/Mazel.

Chomsky, N. (1957). *Syntactic structures.* Mouton: The Hague.

Chomsky, N. (1965). *Aspects of a theory of syntax.* Cambridge, MA: MIT Press.

Chomsky, N. (1972). *Language and mind.* New York: Harcourt Brace.

Chomsky, N. (1975). *Reflections on language.* New York: Pantheon.

Churchland, P. S. (1986). *Neurophilosophy: Toward a unified science of the mind/brain.* Cambridge: MIT Press.

Clark, R., & Squire, L. (1998). Classical conditioning and brain systems: The role of awareness. *Science, 280*(3360), 77–82.

Constantino, J. N. (2000). Genetic structure of reciprocal social behavior. *American Journal of Psychiatry, 157*(12), 2043–2044.

Conway, M. (1995). *Flashbulb memories.* Hove, England: Lawrence Erlbaum Associates.

Cosmides, L., & Tooby, J. (1992). Cognitive adaptations for social exchange. In J. Barkow, L. Cosmides, & J. Tooby (Eds.), *The adapted mind.* New York: Oxford University Press.

Cosmides, L., & Tooby, J. (1996). Are humans good intuitive statisticians after all? Rethinking some conclusions from the literature on judgment under certainty. *Cognition, 58,* 1–73.

Costa, P. T., & McCrae, R. R. (1988). Personality in adulthood: A six-year longitudinal study of self-reports and spouse ratings on the NEO personality inventory. *Journal of Personality and Social Psychology, 54,* 853–863.

Costa, P. C., & McCrae, R. R. (1997). Longitudinal stability of adult personality. In R. Hogan, J. Johnson, & S. Briggs (Eds.), *Handbook of personality psychology,* pp. 269–290.

Courtney, S. M. (1998). An area specialized for spatial working memory in human frontal cortex. *Science, 279*(5355), 1347–1352.

Crair, M. C., Gillespie, D. C., & Stryker, M. P. (1998). The role of visual experience in the development of columns in cat visual cortex. *Science, 279*(5350), 566–571.

Crick, F. (1994). *The astonishing hypothesis.* New York: Charles Scribner's Sons.

Crick, F., & Koch, C. (1995). Are we aware of neural activity in primary visual cortex? *Nature, 375,* 121–123.

Crick, F. & Koch, C. (1998). Consciousness and neuroscience. *Cerebral Cortex, 8,* 97–107.

Crick, F., & Mitchison, G. (1995). REM sleep and neural nets. *Behavioral Brain Research, 69,* 147–155.

Crits-Christoph, P. (1992). The efficacy of brief dynamic psychotherapy: A meta-analysis. *American Journal of Psychiatry, 149,* 151–158.

Curtis, V. A., Bullmore, E., Brammer, M., Wright, I., Williams, S., Morris, R., Sharma, T., Murray, R., & McGuire, P. (1998). Attenuated frontal activation during a verbal fluency task in patients with schizophrenia. *American Journal of Psychiatry, 155*(8), 1056–1064.

Damasio, A. (1994). *Descartes' error.* New York: G. P. Putnam's Sons.

Damasio, A. (1999). *The feeling of what happens: Body and emotion in the making of consciousness.* New York: Harcourt Brace.

Dann, K. (1999). *Bright colors falsely seen: Synaesthesia and the search for transcendental knowledge.* New Haven, CT: Yale University Press.

Darley, J. M., & Latané, B. (1968). Bystander intervention in emergencies: Diffusion of responsibility. *Journal of Personality and Social Psychology, 10,* 202–214.

Darwin, C. (1859). *The origin of species.* Cambridge, MA: Harvard University Press.

Darwin, C. (1965). *The expression of emotions in man and animals.* Chicago, IL: University of Chicago Press. (Originally published in 1872)

Davidson, J. R. D. (2002). Effect of Hypericum perforatum (St. John's wort) in major depressive disorder. *Journal of the American Medical Association, 287,* 14.

Dawkins, R. (1976). *The selfish gene.* Oxford, England: Oxford University Press.

de Gelder, B. (2000). More to seeing than meets the eye. *Science, 289,* 5482, 1148–1149.

Denes, G. (1988). *Perspectives on cognitive neuropsychology.* London: Erlbaum.

Dennett, D. C. (1991). *Consciousness explained.* Boston: Little, Brown.

Desimone, R. (1991). Face-selective cells in the temporal cortex of monkeys. *Journal of Cognitive Neuroscience, 3,* 1–8.

D'Esposito, M. (1995). The neural basis of the central executive system of working memory. *Nature, 378,* 279–281.

Dimond, S. J., & Beaumont, J. G. (1974). *Hemisphere function in the human brain.* New York: Wiley.

Dobbins, A. C., Jeo, R., Fiser, J., & Allman, J. (1998). Distance modulation of neural activity in the visual cortex. *Science, 281*(5376), 552–556.

Dolezal, H. (1982). *Living in a world transformed: perceptual and performatory adaptation to visual distortion.* New York: Academic Press.

Dretske, F. (1988). *Explaining behavior.* Cambridge, MA: MIT Press.

Driver, J., & Spence, C. (1998). Attention and the crossmodal construction of space. *Trends in Cognitive Sciences, Vol. 2,* pp. 254–262.

Duenwald, M. (2002). "Lab monkeys may reveal secrets of childhood depression." *Brain in the News, 9,* 24.

Duncan, J. (2000). A neural basis for general intelligence. *Science, 289,* 5478, 457–463.

Dutton, D. G. (2000). Witnessing parental violence as a traumatic experience shaping the abusive personality. *Journal of Aggression, Maltreatment & Trauma, 3,* 59–67.

Dutton, D. G., & Aron, A. P. (1974). Some evidence for heightened sexual attraction under conditions of high anxiety. *Journal of Personality and Social Psychology, Vol. 30,* pp. 510–517.

Duzel, E., Vargha-Khadem, F., Heinze, H. J., & Mishkin, M. (2001). Brain activity evidence for recognition without recollection after early hippocampal damage. *Proceedings of the National Academy of Sciences of the United States, 98*(14), 8101.

Eaves, L J., Eysenck, H. J., & Margin, N. G. (1989). *Genes, culture, and personality: An empirical approach.* London: Academic Press.

Ebbinghaus, H. (1885). *Memory: A contribution to experimental psychology.* New York: Dover.

Edelman, G. M. (1992). *Bright air, brilliant fire: On the matter of the mind.* New York: Basic Books.

Egan, M. F., Kojima, M., Callicott, J. H., Goldberg, T. E., Kolachana, B. S., Bertolino, A., Zaitsev, E., Gold, B., Goldman, D., Dean, M., Lu, B., & Weinberger, D. R. (2003). The BDNF val66met polymorphism affects activity-dependent secretion of BDNF and human memory and hippocampal function. *Cell, 112,* 257–269.

Eichenbaum, H. (1997). How does the brain organize memories? *Science, 277*(5324), 330–332.

Ellenberger, H. F. (1970). *The discovery of the unconscious.* New York: Basic Books.

Ellis, A. (1958). Rational psychotherapy. *Journal of General Psychology, 59,* 35–49.

Ellis, A. W., & Young, A. W. (1987). *Human cognitive neuropsychology.* Hillsdale, NJ: Erlbaum.

Emde, R. N., & Hewitt, J. K. (2001). *Infancy to early childhood: Genetic and environmental influences on developmental change.* New York: Oxford Press.

Emery, P., So, W. V., Kaneko, M., Hall, J. C., & Rosbash, M. (1998). CRY, a *Drosophila* clock and light-regulated cryptochrome, is a major contributor to circadian rhythm resetting and photosensitivity. *Cell, Vol. 95,* pp. 669–679.

Erikson, E. H. (1950). *Childhood and society.* New York: Norton.

Ettinger, U. M. (2001). Magnetic resonance imaging of the thalamus in first-episode psychosis. *American Journal of Psychiatry, 158*(1), 116–118.

Evans, D. (2001). *Emotions: The science of sentiment.* New York: Oxford Press.

Evans, R. I. (1973). *Jean Piaget: The man and his ideas.* New York: Dutton.

Eysenck, H. J. (1967). The biological basis of personality. Springfield, IL: Charles C. Thomas.

Fancher, R. E. (1990). *Pioneers of psychology,* 2nd ed. New York: W. W. Norton.

Fava, G. A., Rafanelli, C., Grandi, S., Canestrari, R., & Morphy, M. A. (1998). Six-year outcome for cognitive behavioral treatment of residual symptoms in major depression. *American Journal of Psychiatry, 155*(10), 1443–1446.

Feigl, H. (1967). *The "mental" and the "physical."* Minneapolis: University of Minnesota Press.

Feng, R., & Tsien, J. (2001). Deficient neurogenesis in forebrain-specific presinilin-1 knockout mice is associated with reduced clearance of hippocampal memory traces. *Neuron, 32,* 911–926.

Fernández, G., Effern, A., Grunwald, T., Pezer, N., Lehnertz, K., Dümpelmann, M., Van Roost, D., & Elger, C. E. (1999). Real-time tracking of memory formation in the human rhinal cortex and hippocampus. *Science, 285*(5433), 1582–1585.

Festinger, L., & Carlsmith, J. M. (1959). Cognitive consequences of forced compliance. *Journal of Abnormal and Social Psychology, 58,* 203–210.

Fink, M. (Ed.) (1974). *Psychobiology of convulsive therapy.* Washington, DC: Winston.

Finney, E. M., Fine, I., & Dobkins, K. R. (2001). Visual stimuli activate auditory cortex in the deaf. *Nature Neuroscience, 4,* 1171–1173

Finocchiaro, M. A. (1989). *The Galileo affair.* Berkeley, CA: University of California Press.

Flavell, J. H. (1999). Cognitive development: Children's knowledge about the mind. *Annual Review of Psychology, 50,* 21–45.

Fodor, J. A. (2000). Why we are so good at catching cheaters? *Cognition, 75,* 29–32.

Foroud, T., & Li, T. K. (1999). Genetics of alcoholism: a review of recent studies in human and animal models. *Am J Addiction, 8*(4), 261–278.

Fouts, R. (1997). *Next of kin: what chimpanzees have taught me about who we are.* New York: William Morrow and Company.

Fox, P. T. (1986). Mapping human visual cortex with positron emission tomography. *Nature, 323,* 806–809.

Fox, S., & Spector, P. E. (2000). Relations of emotional intelligence, practical intelligence, general intelligence, and trait affectivity with interview outcomes: It's not all just 'G.' *Journal of Organizational Behavior, 21,* 203–220.

Fox, W. M. (1982). Why we should abandon Maslow's need hierarchy theory. *Journal of Humanistic Education and Development, 21,* 29–32.

Freed, C. R., Greene, P. E., Breeze, R. E., Tsai, W. Y., DuMouchel, W., Kao, R., Dillon, S., Winfield, H. C., Trojanowski, J. Q., Eidlelberg, D., & Fahn, S. (2001). Transplantation of embryonic dopamine neurons for severe Parkinson's disease. *New England Journal of Medicine, Vol. 344*(10), 710–719.

Freedman, A. M., Kaplan, H. I., & Sadock, B. J. (Eds.). (1975). *Comprehensive textbook of psychiatry,* vol. 1. Baltimore: Williams & Wilkins.

Freeman, H. (1994). Schizophrenia and city residence. *British Journal of Psychiatry, 164,* 39–50.

Freeman, W. J. (1991). The physiology of perception. *Scientific American, 264*(2), 78–85.

Freud, S. (1961). *The interpretation of dreams.* New York: Science Editions. (Originally published 1900)

Freud, S. (1910). The origin and development of psychoanalysis. *American Journal of Psychology, 21,* 181–218.

Freud, S. (1966). *The complete introductory lectures on psychoanalysis.* New York: Norton.

Fried, I. (1998). Electric current stimulates laughter. *Nature, 391*(6668), 650.

Friedland, R. P., Fritsch, T., Smyth, K. A., Koss, E., Lerner, A. J., Chen, C. H., Petot, G. J., & Debanne, S. M. (2001). Patients with Alzheimer's disease have reduced activities in midlife compared with healthy control group members. *Proceedings of the National Academy of Sciences, 98*(6), 3440–3445.

Fromm, E. (1962). *The art of loving.* New York: Harper and Row.

Fuchs, S., & Ilani, T. (2001). A blood test for detecting schizophrenia. *Proceedings of the Academy of Sciences.*

Furey, M. L. (2000). Cholinergic enhancement and increased selectivity of perceptual processing during working memory. *Science, 290*(5500), 2315–2319.

Furst, C. (1979). *Origins of the mind: Mind-brain connections.* Englewood Cliffs, NJ: Prentice-Hall.

Fuster, J. (1997). Network memory. *Trends in Neurosciences, 20,* 451–459.

Gage, F. H., & Kempermann, G. (1999). New nerve cells for the adult brain. *Scientific American, 280*(5), 48.

Gagné, G. G. (2000). Efficacy of continuation ECT and antidepressant drugs compared to long-term antidepressant alone in depressed people. *American Journal of Psychiatry, 157*(12), 1960–1965.

Gajdusek, D. C. (1977). Unconventional viruses and the origin and disappearance of kuru. *Science, 197,* 943–960.

Gardner, H. (1983). *Frames of mind: The theory of multiple intelligences.* New York: Basic Books.

Gardner, H. (1985). *The mind's new science: A history of the cognitive revolution.* New York: Basic Books.

Gardner, M. (1981). *Science: Good, bad and bogus.* Buffalo, NY: Prometheus Press.

Gardner, R. A., & Gardner, B. T. (1969). Teaching sign language to a chimpanzee. *Science, 165,* 664–672.

Gater, R., Tansella, M., Korten, A., Tiemens, B. G., Mavreas, V. G., & Olatawura, M. O. (1998). Sex differences in the prevalence and detection of depressive and anxiety disorders in general health care settings. *Archives of General Psychiatry, 55,* 405–413.

Gazzaniga, M. (1985). *The social brain: Discovering the networks of mind.* New York: Basic Books.

Gazzaniga, M. S. (1992). *Nature's Mind.* New York: Harper Collins.

Gazzaniga, M. S., & LeDoux, J. (1978). *The Integrated Mind.* New York: Plenum Press.

Geschwind, N. (1965). Disconnexion syndrome in animals and man. *Brain, 88,* 237–294, 585–644.

Geschwind, N. (1967). Wernicke's contribution to the study of aphasia. *Cortex, 3,* 448–463.

Gibson, J. J. (1966). *The senses considered as perceptual systems.* Boston, MA: Houghton Mifflin.

Gibson, J. J., & Walk, R. D. (1960). The visual cliff. *Scientific American, 202,* 64–71.

Giraud, A-L., Price, C. J., Graham, J. M., Truy, E., & Frackowiak, S. J. (2001). Cross-modal plasticity underpins language recovery after cochlear implantation. *Neuron, 30,* 657–663.

Globus, G. G., Maxwell, G., & Savodnik, I. (Eds.). (1976). *Consciousness and the brain.* New York: Plenum Press.

Goff, D. C., & Coyle, J. T. (2001). The emerging role of glutamate in the pathophysiology and treatment of schizophrenia. *American Journal of Psychiatry, 158*(9), 1367–1377.

Goldberg, T. E., Aloia, M. S., Gourovitch, M. L., Missar, D., Pickar, D., & Weinberger, D. R. (1998). Cognitive substrates of thought disorder. I: The semantic system. *American Journal of Psychiatry, 155*(12), 1671–1676.

Goldman-Rakic, P. S. (1987). Circuitry of primate prefrontal cortex and regulation of behaviour by representational memory. In: *Handbook of physiology, Vol 5* (Plum F, Mouncastle U, eds.), pp. 373–417. Washington, DC: The American Physiological Society.

Goldstein, G., Allen, D. N., & van Kammen, D. P. (1998). Individual differences in cognitive decline in schizophrenia. *American Journal of Psychiatry, 155*(8), 1117–1118.

Goldstein, J. M., et al. (1998). Are there sex differences in neuropsychological functions among patients with schizophrenia? *American Journal of Psychiatry, 155*(10), 1358–1359.

Goleman, D. (1995). *Emotional intelligence.* New York: Bantam Books.

Gopnik, A. (1996). The post-Piaget era. *Psychological Science, 7,* 221–225.

Gordis, E. (1996). Alcohol research and social policy: An overview. *Alcohol Health and Research World, 20*(4), 208–212.

Gould, E., Reeves, A. J., Graziano, M. S. A., & Gross, C. G. (1999). Neurogenesis in the neocortex of adult primates. *Science, 286,* 548–552.

Greenfield, P. M. (1997). You can't take it with you: why ability assessments don't cross cultures. *American Psychologist, 52*(10), 1115–1124.

Greenfield, P. M., & Savage-Rumbaugh, S. (1990). Grammatical combination in Pan paniscus: Processes of learning and invention in the evolution and development of language. In S. T. Parker & K. Gibson (Eds.), *Language and intelligence in monkeys and apes.* New York: Cambridge University Press.

Greenfield, S. A. (2001). Altered states of consciousness. *Social Research, 68*(3), 609–638.

Greenfield, S. A. (1995). *Journey to the centers of the mind.* New York: W. H. Freeman.

Greer, J., & Capecchi, M. (2002). Hoxb8 is required for normal grooming behavior in mice. *Neuron, 33,* 23–34.

Grigsby, J., & Stevens, D. (2000). *Neurodynamics of personality.* New York: Guilford Press.

Guéguen, N. (2001). Effect of a perfume on prosocial behavior of pedestrians. *Psychological Reports, 88,* 1046–1048.

Guyton, A. C. (1981). *Textbook of medical physiology.* Philadelphia: Saunders.

Hagerman, R. J. (2002). *Fragile X syndrome: Diagnosis, treatment, and research,* 3rd ed. Baltimore: Johns Hopkins University Press.

Hall, C. S., & Lindzey, G. (1957). *Theories of personality.* New York: John Wiley and Sons.

Halpern, D. F. (1992). *Sex differences in cognitive ability.* Hillsdale, NJ: Erlbaum.

Halpern, D. F. (1997). Sex differences in intelligence: Implications for education. *American Psychologist, 52,* 1091–1102.

Hardy, J., & Gwinn-Hardy, K. (1998). Genetic classification of primary neurodegenerative disease. *Science, 282.*

Harris, J. R. (1998). *The nurture assumption: Why children turn out the way they do.* New York: The Free Press.

Harris, M. (1974). *Cows, pigs, wars, and witches.* New York: Random House.

Harrison, J. (2001). *Synaesthesia: The strangest thing.* New York: Oxford Press.

Harvard Mental Health Letter (2003). Anorexia Nervosa. Harvard Medical School, *19*(8), 1–3.

Harvard Mental Health Letter (2003, December). Autism mysteries: New clues. Harvard Medical School, *20*(6), 3–4.

Hebb, D. O., & Penfield, W. (1940). Human behavior after extensive bilateral removals from the frontal lobes. *Archives of Neurology and Psychiatry, 44,* 421–438.

Hebb, D. O. (1949). *The organization of behavior.* New York: Wiley.

Heinrichs, R. W. (2001). *In search of madness: Schizophrenia and neuroscience.* New York: Oxford Press.

Heiser, J. F. (1979). Parry. *Journal of Psychiatric Research, 15*(3), 149–162.

Held, R., & Hein, A. (1963). Movement-produced stimulation in the development of visually guided behavior. *Journal of Comparative and Physiological Psychology, 56,* 872–876.

Hellige, J. B. (1993). *Hemispheric asymmetry: What's right and what's left.* Cambridge, MA: Harvard University Press.

Helmuth, L. (2002). Redrawing the brain's map of the body. *Science, 296,* 1587–1588.

Helmuth, L. (2003). Fear and trembling in the amygdala. *Science, 300,* 568–569.

Hilgard, E. R. (1977). *Divided consciousness.* New York: Wiley.

Hingson, R. W. (2002). Task force on college drinking. Bethesda, MD: National Institute on Alcohol Abuse and Alcoholism.

Hinrichs, B. H. (1991). What got into him?: On the causes of human behavior. *Communitas, 4,* 148–153.

Hinrichs, B. H. (1997). Brain research and folk psychology. *The Humanist, 57*(2), 26–31.

Hinrichs, B. H. (1998). Computing the mind. *The Humanist, 58*(2), 26–30.

Hinrichs, B. H. (1999a). Spiderwebs of silken threads: Memory and the brain. *Communitas, 11,* 10–25.

Hinrichs, B. H. (1999b). *Film & Art.* St. Paul, MN: J-Press.

Hinrichs, B. H. (2000). *Mind as mosaic: The robot in the machine.* St. Paul, Minnesota: J-Press.

Hinrichs, B. H. (2001). The science of reading minds. *The Humanist, 60,* 3.

Hinrichs, B. H. (2002). Never mind? *The Humanist, 62*(1), 36–38.

Hirayasu, Y., et al. (1998). Lower left temporal lobe MRI volumes in patients with first-episode schizophrenia compared with psychotic patients with first-episode affective disorder and normal subjects. *American Journal of Psychiatry, 155*(10), 1384–1386.

Hobson, J. A. (1994). *The chemistry of conscious states.* Boston: Little, Brown.

Hobson, J. A. (1995). *Sleep.* New York: Scientific American Library.

Hobson, J. A. (1996). How the brain goes out of its mind. *Endeavor, 20*(2), 86–89.

Hobson, J. A. (2000). Dreaming and the brain: Toward a cognitive neuroscience of conscious states. *Behavioral and Brain Sciences, 23*(6), 793.

Hoffman, R. E., Boutros, N. N., Hu, S., Berman, R. M., Krystal, J. H., & Charney, D. S. (2000). Transcranial magnetic stimulation and auditory hallucinations in schizophrenia. *The Lancet, 355*(9209), 1073–1075.

Hofstadter, D. R., & Dennett, D. (1981). *The mind's I: Fantasies and reflections on self and soul*. New York: Basic Books.

Holden, C. (1980). Identical twins reared apart. *Science, 207*, 1323–1328.

Holland, A. J. (1988). Anorexia nervosa: Evidence for a genetic basis. *Journal of Psychosomatic Research, 32*, 561–571.

Honderich, T. (1988). *A theory of determinism*. New York: Oxford University Press.

Horney, K. (1937). *Neurotic personality of our times*. New York: Norton.

Horowitz, M. J. (1998). Personality disorder diagnoses. *American Journal of Psychiatry, 155*, 1464.

Hothersall, D. (1984). *History of psychology*, 2nd ed. New York: McGraw-Hill.

Hróbjartsson, A., & Gotzsche, C. (2001). Is the placebo powerless? An analysis of clinical trials comparing placebo with no treatment. *The New England Journal of Medicine, 344*(21), 1594–1603.

Hubel, D. H., & Wiesel, T. N. (1962). Receptive fields, binocular interaction and functional architecture in the cat's visual cortex. *Journal of Physiology, 165*, 559–568.

Hubel, D. H., & Wiesel, T. N. (1965). Receptive fields of neurons in two nonstriate visual areas (18 and 19) of the cat. *Journal of Neurophysiology, 28*, 229–289.

Hubel, D. H., & Wiesel, T. N. (1979). Brain mechanisms of vision. *Scientific American, 241*, 150–162.

Hull, C. L. (1943). *Principles of behavior*. New York: Appleton-Century-Crofts.

Hunt, M. (1993). *The story of psychology*. New York: Doubleday.

Hyman, I. E., & Billings, F. J. (1998). Individual differences and the creation of false childhood memories. *Memory, 6*, 1–20.

Hyman, I. E., & Pentland, J. (1996). The role of mental imagery in the creation of false childhood memories. *Journal of Memory and Language, 35*, 101–117.

Isacson, O., & McKay, R. (2001). Report to the annual meeting of the American Association for the Advancement of Science.

Ismail, B., Cantor-Graae, E., & McNeil, T. F. (1998). Neurological abnormalities in schizophrenic patients and their siblings. *American Journal of Psychiatry, 155*(1), 84–90.

Ismail, B., Cantor-Graae, E., & McNeil, T. F. (1998). Minor physical anomalies in schizophrenic patients and their siblings. *American Journal of Psychiatry, 155*(12), 1695–1703.

Izard, C. E. (1971). *The face of emotion*. New York: Appleton-Century-Crofts.

Jacobsen, L. K., Giedd, J., Berquin, P., Krain, A., Hamburger, S., Kumra, S., & Rapoport, J. (1997). Quantitative morphology of the cerebellum and fourth ventricle in childhood-onset schizophrenia. *American Journal of Psychiatry, 154*(12), 1663–1670.

James, W. (1890). *Principles of psychology*. New York: Dover.

Jamison, K. R. (1995). *An unquiet mind: A memoir of moods and madness*. New York: Knopf.

Jamison, K. R. (1999). *Night falls fast: Understanding suicide*. New York: Knopf.

Jausovec, N. (2000). Differences in cognitive processes between gifted, intelligent, creative, and average individuals while solving complex problems: An EEG study. *Intelligence, 28*(3), 213.

Johnson, J. G., Cohen, P., Smailes, E. M., Kasen, S., & Brook, J. S. (2002). Television viewing and aggressive behavior during adolescence and adulthood. *Science, 295*, 2468–2471.

Jones, J. H. (1993). *Bad Blood: The Tuskegee Syphilis Experiment*, new and expanded ed. New York: Free Press.

Jonides, J. (1980). Toward a model of the mind's eye's movement. *Canadian Journal of Psychology, 34*, 103–112.

Jonides, J. (1983). Further toward a model of the mind's eye's movement. *Bulletin of the Psychonomic Society, 21*, 247–250.

Kagan, J. (1996). Three pleasing ideas. *American Psychologist, 51*, 901–908.

Kagan, J., & Snidman, N. (1991). Temperamental factors in human development. *American Psychologist, 46*, 856–862.

Kaplan, H. S. (1981). *The new sex therapy: Active treatment of sexual dysfunctions*. New York: Brunner/Mazel.

Karmiloff, K., & Karmiloff-Smith, A. (2001). *Pathways to language: From fetus to adolescent*. Boston: Harvard Press.

Kastner, S. (1998). Mechanisms of directed attention in the human extrastriate cortex as revealed by functional MRI. *Science, 282*, 108–111.

Keel, P. K., Dorer, D. J., Eddy, K. T., Delinsky, S. S., Franko, D. L., Blais, M. A., Keller, M. B., & Herzog, D. B. (2002). Predictors of treatment utilization among women with anorexia and bulimia nervosa. *American Journal of Psychiatry, 159*(1), 140–141.

Kelly, I. W., Rotton, J., & Culver, R. (1996). The moon was full and nothing happened: A review of studies on the moon and human behavior and human belief. In Nickell, B., & Genoni, T. (Eds.), *The outer edge*. Amherst, NY: CSICOP.

Kendler, K. S., & Diehl, S. R. (1993). The genetics of schizophrenia: A current genetic-epidemiologic perspective. *Schizophrenia Bulletin, 19*, 87–112.

Kendler, K. S., Thornton, L. M., & Gardner, C. O. (2000). Stressful life events and previous episodes in the etiology of major depression in women: An evaluation of the "kindling" hypothesis. *American Journal of Psychiatry, 157*, 1243–1251.

Kennedy, S. H., Javanmard, M., France, J., & Vaccarino, F. J. (1997). A review of functional neuroimaging in mood disorders: Positron emission tomography and depression. *Canadian Journal of Psychiatry, 42*, 467–475.

Kent, J. M. (2001). Specificity of panic response to CO_2 inhalation in panic disorder: A comparison with major depression and premenstrual dysphoric disorder. *American Journal of Psychiatry, 158*(1), 58–67.

Killgore, W. D. S. (2000). Academic and research interest in several approaches to psychotherapy: A computerized search of literature in the past 16 years. *Psychological Reports, 87*, 717–720.

Kim, J.-J., et al. (2003). Functional disconnection between the prefrontal and parietal cortices during working memory processing in schizophrenia. *American Journal of Psychiatry, 160*(5), 919–920.

Kircher, T. (2001). Neural correlates of formal thought disorder in schizophrenia. *Archives of General Psychiatry, 58*, 8.

Klein, D. B. (1970). *A history of scientific psychology*. New York: Basic Books.

Klimesch, W., Doppelmayr, M., Schimke, H., & Ripper, B. (1997). Theta synchronization and alpha desynchronization in a memory task. *Psychophysiology, 34*, 169–176.

Klitzman, R. (1998). *The trembling mountain: A personal account of kuru, cannibals, and mad cow disease*. New York: Plenum.

Knowlton, B. J., Mangels, J. A., & Squire, L. R. (1996). A neostriatal habit learning system in humans. *Science, 273*, 1399–1402.

Koch, C. (1997). Computation and the single neuron. *Nature, 385*(6613), 207–211.

Koffka, K. (1935). *Principles of Gestalt psychology*. New York: Harcourt Brace.

Kohlberg, L. (1981). *Essays on moral development*. San Francisco: Harper & Row.

Kohler, I. (1962). Experiments with goggles. *Scientific American, 206*(5), 62–86.

Kohler, W. (1947). *Gestalt psychology*. New York: Liveright.

Koren, G., Cohn, T., Chitayat, D., Kapur, B., Remington, G., Reid, D. M., & Zipursky, R. B. (2002). Use of atypical antipsychotics during pregnancy and the risk of neural tube defects in infants. *American Journal of Psychiatry, 159*(1), 136–137.

Kosslyn, S. M., & Koenig, O. (1992). *Wet mind: The new cognitive neuroscience*. New York: Free Press.

Kreisman, J. J., Straus, H. (1991). *I Hate You, Don't Leave Me*. New York: Avon Books.

Kugaya, A., et al. (2003). Increase in prefrontal cortex serotonin2A receptors following estrogen treatment in postmenopausal women. *American Journal of Psychiatry, 160*(8), 1522–1525.

Kuhn, E. K. (1994, December 3). Does freedom bring more violence against women? *The Daily Dispatch*, p. 3.

Kurzweil, R. (1990). *The age of intelligent machines*. Cambridge, MA: MIT Press.

Lai, C., Fisher, S. E., Hurst, J. A., Vargha-Khadem, F., Monaco, A. P. (2001). A forkhead-domain gene is mutated in a severe speech and language disorder. *Nature, 413*(6855), 519–523.

Lai, C. S., Fisher, S. E., Hurst, J. A., Vargha-Khadem, F., & Monaco, A. P. (2001). A forkhead-domain gene is mutated in a severe speech and language disorder. *Nature, 413*, 519–523.

Langleben, D. D. (2001). Functional magnetic resonance imaging of the brain during deception. Presentation at Society for Neuroscience annual conference, San Diego, CA.

Largie, S. (2001). Employment during adolescence is associated with depression, inferior relationships, lower grades, and smoking. *Adolescence, 36*(142), 395–401.

Lashley, K. S. (1950). In search of the engram. *Society of Experimental Biology Symposium*. New York: Cambridge University Press.

Latané, B., & Darley, J. M. (1968). Group inhibition of bystander intervention. *Journal of Personality and Social Psychology, 10*, 215–221.

Latané, B., & Darley, J. M. (1970). *The unresponsive bystander: Why doesn't he help?* New York: Appleton-Crofts.

Laver, A. R. (1972). Precursors of psychology in ancient Egypt. *Journal of the History of the Behavioral Sciences, 8*, 181–195.

LeDoux, J. E. (1994). Emotion, memory and the brain. *Scientific American, 270*(6), 50–57.

LeDoux, J. E. (1996). *The emotional brain: The mysterious underpinnings of emotional life*. New York: Simon & Schuster.

Lee, A. K., & Wilson, M. A. (2002). Memory of sequential experience in the hippocampus during slow wave sleep. *Neuron, 36*, December 19, 1183–1194.

Lerner, B., Miodownik, C., Kaptsan, A., Cohen, H., Matar, M., Lowewenthal, U., & Kotler, M. (2001). Vitamin B$_6$ in the treatment of tardive dyskinesia: A double-blind, placebo-controlled, crossover study. *American Journal of Psychiatry, 158*(9), 1511–1514.

Levenson, R. W. (1992). Autonomic nervous system differences among emotions. *Psychological Science, 3*, 23–27.

Leventhal, A. G., Wang, Y., Mingliang, P., Yifeng, Z, & Yuanye, M. (2003). GABA and its agonists improved visual cortical function in senescent monkeys. *Science, 300*, 812–814.

Levesque, M. (2002, April 8). Report to the American Association of Neurological Surgeons meeting, Chicago.

Levy, J. (1985). Right brain, left brain: Facts and fiction. *Psychology Today, 19*, 38–44.

Levy, J., Trevarthen, C., & Sperry, R. W. (1972). Perception of bilateral chimeric figures following hemispheric disconnexion. *Brain, 95*, 61–78.

Libet, B. (1985). Unconscious cerebral initiative and the role of conscious will in voluntary action. *Behavioral and Brain Sciences, 8*, 529–566.

Lieberman, B. (2003, August 3). Study finds enzyme can help prevent Alzheimer's. *The San Diego Union-Tribune*, p. B6.

Lindemann, B. (2001). Receptors and transduction in taste. *Nature, 413*, 219–225.

Liotti, M., & Mayberg, H. (2002). Unmasking disease-specific cerebral blood flow abnormalities: Mood challenge in patients with remitted unipolar depression. *American Journal of Psychiatry, 159*, 1830–1840.

Lisman, J. E., & Fallon, J. R. (1999). What maintains memories? *Science, 283*(5400), 339.

Liston, C., & Kagan, J. (2002). Brain development: Memory enhancement in early childhood. *Nature, 419*, 896.

Llinás, R. (1999). *The Squid Giant Synapse: A model for chemical transmission*. New York: Oxford University Press.

Llinás, R., & Churchland, P. S. (Eds.). (1998). *The mind-brain continuum: Sensory processes*. Cambridge, MA: MIT Press.

Loftus, E. F. (1993). The reality of repressed memories. *American Psychologist, 48*, 518–537.

Loftus, E. F. (1994). *The myth of repressed memory: False memories and the allegations of sexual abuse*. New York: St. Martin's Press.

Loftus, E. F., & Ketcham, K. (1991). *Witness for the defense: The accused, the eyewitnesses, and the expert who puts memory on trial*. New York: St. Martin's Press.

Loftus, E. F., & Hoffman, H. G. (1989). Misinformation and memory: The creation of new memories. *Journal of Experimental Psychology, 118*, 100–114.

Logothetis, N. K. (1999). Vision: a window on consciousness. *Scientific American, 281*, November, 68–76.

Lohr, J. B., & Braff, D. L. (2003). The value of referring to recently introduced antipsychotics as "second generation." *American Journal of Psychiatry, 160*(8), 1371–1372.

Louie, K., & Wilson, M. A. (2001). Temporally structured replay of awake hippocampal ensemble activity during rapid eye movement sleep. *Neuron, 29*, January, 145–156.

Lumer, E. D., Friston, K. J., & Rees, G. (1998). Neural correlates of perceptual rivalry in the human brain. *Science, 280*(5371), 1930–1935.

Lykken, D. (1993). Heritability of interests: A twin study. *Journal of Applied Psychology, 78*, 649–661.

Lykken, D., & Tellegen, A. (1996). Happiness is a stochastic phenomenon. *Psychological Science, 7*, 186–189.

Macaluso, E., Frith, C. D., & Driver, J. (2000). Modulation of human visual cortex by crossmodal spatial attention. *Science, 289*(5482), 1206–1208.

MacDonald, A. (2003). Images that last: the amygdala and emotional memory. *Brain Work, 13*, (5, September–October), 1–3.

MacMillan, H. L., Fleming, J. E., Streiner, D. L., Lin, E., Boyle, M. H., Jamieson, E., Duku, E. K., Walsh, C. A., Wong, M. Y.-Y., & Beardslee, W. R. (2001). Childhood abuse and lifetime psychopathology in a community sample. *American Journal of Psychiatry, 158*, 1878–1883.

Maess, B. Koelsch, S., Gunter, T. C., & Friederici, A. D. (2001). Musical syntax is processed in Broca's area: An MEG study. *Nature Neuroscience, 4*, 540–545.

Maguire, E. A., Burgess, N., Donnett, J., Frackowiak, S. J., Frith, C., & O'Keefe, J. (1998). Knowing where and getting there: a human navigation network. *Science, 280*, 5365, 921–925.

Mahowald, M. A., & Mead, C. (1991). The silicon retina. *Scientific American, 264*(5), 76–83.

Malaspina, D., Harlap, S., & Fennig, S. (2001). Risk of schizophrenia increased with increasing age. *Evidence Based Mental Health, 4*, 123.

Maletzky, B. M. (1998). The paraphilias: Research and treatment. In P. Nathan & J. Gorman (Eds.), *A guide to treatments that work*. New York: Oxford University Press.

Malone, K. M., Waternaux, C., Haas, G. L., Cooper, T. B., Shuhua, L, & Mann, J. J. (2003). Cigarette smoking, suicidal behavior, and serotonin function in major psychiatric disorders. *American Journal of Psychiatry, 160*(4), 773–779.

Maquet, P. (2001). The role of sleep in learning and memory. *Science, 294*, 1048–1052.

Marr, D. (1982). *Vision*. San Francisco: W. H. Freeman.

Maslow, A. (1968). *Toward a psychology of being*, 2nd ed. New York: Van Nostrand.

Maslow, A. (1970). *Motivation and personality*, 2nd ed. New York: Harper.

Maslow, A. (1998). *Toward a psychology of being*, 3rd ed. New York: Wiley.

Masters, W., & Johnson, V. (1966). *Human sexual response*. Boston: Little, Brown.

Maxwell, M. L., & Savage, C. W. (Eds.). (1989). *Science, mind, and psychology*. Lanham, MD: University Press of America.

Mayes, A. R. (1988). *Human organic memory disorders*. New York: Cambridge University Press.

McClelland, J. (1999). Research presented at meeting of the Cognitive Neuroscience Society, Washington, DC.

McCrae, R. H., & Costa, P. (1984). *Emerging lives, enduring dispositions: Personality in adulthood*. Boston: Little, Brown.

McCrae, R. H., & Costa, P. (1997). Personality trait structure as a human universal. *American Psychologist, 52*, 509–516.

McElroy, S. L., et al. (2003). Topiramate in the treatment of binge eating disorder. *American Journal of Psychiatry, 160*(2), 255–256.

McGue, M., & Lykken, D. T. (1992). Genetic influence on the risk of divorce. *Psychological Science, 3*, 368–373.

Mednick, S., Nakayama, K., & Stickgold, R. (2003). Sleep-dependent learning: A nap is as good as a night. *Nature Neuroscience, 6*, 697–698.

Mehta, M. A. (2000). Memory improvement. *Journal of Neuroscience, 20*, 65.

Merzenich, M. (1998). Long-term change of mind. *Science, 282*(5391), 1062.

Milgram, S. (1963). Behavioral study of obedience. *Journal of Abnormal and Social Psychology, 67*, 371–378.

Milgram, S. (1974). *Obedience to authority: An experimental view*. New York: Harper & Row.

Miller, G. (1956). The magic number seven, plus or minus two: Some limits on our capacity for processing information. *Psychological Review, 63*, 81–97.

Miller, J. G. (1984). Culture and the development of everyday social explanation. *Journal of Personality and Social Psychology, 46*(5), 961–978.

Miller, W. R., Walters, S. T., & Bennett, M. E. (2001). How effective is alcoholism treatment in the United States? *Journal of Studies of Alcohol, 62*(2), 211–220.

Milner, A. D., & Goodale, M. A. (1995). *The visual brain in action*. Oxford, England: Oxford University Press.

Milner, B. (1968). Further analysis of the hippocampal amnesic syndrome: 14-year follow-up study of H. M. *Neuropsychologia, 6*, 215–234.

Mischel, W. (1968). *Personality and assessment*. New York: Wiley & Sons.

Mischel, W. (1984). Convergences and challenges in the search for consistency. *American Psychologist, 39*, 351–364.

Mishkin, M., & Appenzeller, T. (1987). The anatomy of memory. *Scientific American, 256,* 80–89.

Mithoefer, M., Jerome, L., & Doblin, R. (2003). MDMA ("ecstasy") and neurotoxicity. *Science, 300,* 1504–1505.

Moore, P. B., El-Badri, S. M., Cousins, D., Shepherd, D. J., Young, A. H., McAllister, V. L., & Ferrier, I. N. (2001). White matter lesions and season of birth of patients with bipolar affective disorder. *American Journal of Psychiatry, 158*(9), 1521–1524.

Moulton, F. R., & Schifferes, J. J. (Eds.) (1960). *The autobiography of science.* Garden City, NY: Doubleday.

Murray, J. (2001). Brain scans of children watching violent media. Research report presented at the international conference on child development in Minneapolis, MN.

Mussa-Ivaldi, S. (2000). Real brains for real robots. *Nature, 408,* 305–307.

Nash, M. R. (2001). The truth and the hype of hypnosis. *Scientific American, 285*(1), 47–55.

National Center on Addiction and Substance Abuse at Columbia University. (2002, February 26). CASA report on underage drinking. New York: Author.

Neimeyer, R. A. (2001). *Meaning reconstruction and the experience of loss.* American Psychological Association.

Neisser, U. (1967). *Cognitive psychology.* New York: Appleton-Century-Crofts.

Neisser, U. (1982). *Memory observed.* San Francisco: Freeman.

Nelson, E. B. (1998). Attentional performance in patients with psychotic and nonpsychotic major depression and schizophrenia. *American Journal of Psychiatry, 155*(1), 137–140.

Nemeroff, C. B. (2002). Comorbidity of mood and anxiety disorders: The rule, not the exception? *American Journal of Psychiatry, 159*(1), 3–4.

Newcomer, J. W., Selke, G., Melson, A. K., Hershey, T., Craft, S., Richards, K., & Alderson, A. L. (1999). Decreased memory performance in healthy humans induced by stress-level cortisol treatment. *Archives of General Psychiatry, 56*(6) Jun 1999, 527–533.

News@UWMadison. http://www.news.wisc.edu/story. Posted September 11, 2001.

Nicolelis, M. A. (2001). Actions from thoughts. *Nature, 409,* 403–408.

Nicolelis, M. A., & Chapin, J. K. (2002). Controlling robots with the mind. *Scientific American, 7*(4), 46–53.

Nisbett, R. E. (1972). Hunger, obesity, and the ventromedial hypothalamus. *Psychological Review, 79,* 433–453.

Nisbett, R. E. (2003). *The geography of thought.* New York: The Free Press.

Norretranders, T. (1998). *The user illusion: Cutting consciousness down to size.* New York: Viking Press.

Ochsner, K. N., & Lieberman, M. D. (2001). The emergence of social cognitive neuroscience. *American Psychologist, 56*(9), 717–734.

O'Donohue, W., & Ferguson, K. E. (2001). *The psychology of B. F. Skinner.* Thousand Oaks, CA: Sage.

Olds, J. M., & Milner, P. M. (1954). Positive reinforcement produced by electrical stimulation of septal area and other regions of rat brain. *Journal of Comparative and Physiological Psychology, 47,* 419–427.

Olton, D.S. (1979). Mazes, maps and memory. *American Psychologist, 34,* 583–596.

Ona, V. O. (1999). Inhibition of caspase-1 slows disease progression in a mouse model of Huntington's disease. *Nature,* 263–268.

Oquendo, M. A., Ellis, S. P., Greenwald, S., Malone, K. M., Weissman, M. M., Mann, J. J. (2001). Ethnic and sex differences in suicide rates relative to major depression in the United States. *American Journal of Psychiatry, 158,* 1652.

Orton, S. (Ed.) (1934). *Localization of function in the cerebral cortex.* Baltimore: Williams & Wilkins.

Overmeier, J. B., & Seligman, M. (1967). Effects of inescapable shock upon subsequent escape and avoidance responding. *Journal of Comparative and Physiological Psychology, 63,* 28–33.

Palmer, T. D., Schwartz, P. H., Taupin, P., Kaspar, B., Stein, S. A., & Gage, F. H. (2001). Progenitor cells from human brain after death. *Nature, 411*(6833) May 3, 42–44.

Pantel, J., Kratz, B., Essig, M., & Schröder, J. (2003). Parahippocampal volume deficits in subjects with aging-associated cognitive decline. *American Journal of Psychiatry, 160,* 379–382.

Parker, G., Roy, K., & Eyers, K. (2003). Cognitive behavior therapy for depression?: Choose horses for courses. *American Journal of Psychiatry, 160*(5), 825–831.

Pascalis, O., de Haan, M., & Nelson, C. (2002). Is face processing species-specific during the first year of life? *Science, 296,* 1321–1323.

Patterson, K. (2003, August 11). Early warning system. *The Dallas Morning News,* p. E1.

Pavlov, I. P. (1917). *Conditioned reflexes.* London: Oxford University Press.

Pavlov, I. P. (1928). *Lectures on conditioned reflexes.* New York: International.

Penfield, W., & Perot, P. (1963). The brain's record of auditory and visual experience. *Brain, 86,* 595–696.

Penfield, W., & Rasmussen, T. (1950). *The cerebral cortex of man: A clinical study of localization of function.* New York: Macmillan.

Penfield, W., & Roberts, L. (1959). *Speech and brain-mechanisms.* Princeton, NJ: Princeton University Press.

Perls, F. S. (1969). *Gestalt therapy verbatim.* Lafayette, CA: Real People Press.

Peterson, C. B., & Mitchell, J. E. (1999). Psychological and pharmacological treatment of eating disorders: A review of research findings. *Journal of Clinical Psychology, 55,* 685–697.

Pezdek, K., Finger, K., & Hodge, D. (1997). Planting false childhood memories: The role of event plausibility. *Psychological Science, 8,* 437–441.

Phiel, C. J., Wilson, C. A., Lee, V. M.-Y., & Klein, P. S. GSK-3α regulates production of Alzheimer's disease amyloid-β peptides. *Nature, 423,* 435–439.

Piaget, J. (1962). *Play, dreams, and imitation in childhood.* New York: The Free Press.

Piaget, J. (1969). *The mechanisms of perception.* New York: Basic Books.

Pillay, A. L., & Schoubben-Hesk, S. (2001). Depression, anxiety, and hopelessness in sexually abused adolescent girls. *Psychological Reports, 88,* 727–733.

Pinker, S. (Ed.). (1985). *Visual cognition.* Cambridge, MA: MIT Press.

Pinker, S. (1994). *The language instinct: How the mind creates language.* New York: Penguin.

Pinker, S. (1997). *How the mind works.* New York: W. W. Norton.

Plomin, R. (1990). *Nature and nurture: An introduction to human behavioral genetics.* Pacific Grove, CA: Brooks/Cole.

Plutchik, R., & Kellerman, H. (1980). *Emotions: A psychoevolutionary synthesis.* New York: Harper & Row.

Pollak, S. D., & Kistler, D. J. (2000). Early experience is associated with the development of categorical representations for facial expressions of emotion. *Proceedings of the National Academy of Sciences, 99,* 9072–9076.

Posner, N. I., & Raichle, M. (1994). *Images of mind.* New York: Freeman.

Postman, L. (Ed.) (1962). *Psychology in the making.* New York: Knopf.

Pribram, K. (1971). *Languages of the brain.* Englewood Cliffs, NJ: Prentice-Hall.

Putnam, F. W. (1989). *Diagnosis and treatment of multiple personality disorder.* New York: Guilford Press.

Ramoz, N., Reichert, J. G., Smith, C. J., Silverman, J. M., Bespalova, I. N., Davis, K. L., & Buxbaum, D. (2004). Linkage and association of the mitochondrial apartate/glutamate carrier SLC25A12 gene with autism. *American Journal of Psychiatry, 161*(4), 662–669.

Randi, J. (1982). *Flim-flam!: Psychics, ESP, unicorns, and other delusions.* Buffalo, NY: Prometheus Books.

Rauschecker, J. P., & Shannon, R. V. (2002). Sending sound to the brain. *Science, 295,* 1025–1029.

Ray, O., & Ksir, C. (2002). *Drugs, society, and human behavior.* Boston: McGraw-Hill.

Redding, G. M., & Wallace, B. (2001). Calibration and alignment are separable: Evidence from prism adaptation. *Journal of Motor Behavior, 33*(4), 401–413.

Reed, S. K. (1982). *Cognition: Theory and applications.* Monterey, CA: Brooks/Cole.

Rest, J. R. (1986). *Moral development: Advances in research and theory.* New York: Praeger.

Ricaurte, G. A., Yuan, J., Hatzidimitriou, G., Cord, B. J., & McCann, U. D. (2002). Severe dopaminergic neurotoxicity in primates after a common recreational dose regimen of MDMA ("ecstasy"). *Science, 297,* 2260–2263.

Roach, P. (2002). *A cross-cultural test of birth order effects on personality.* Unpublished manuscript, University of Oregon at Eugene, Oregon.

Robbins, T. W. (1996). Refining the taxonomy of memory. *Science*, 273(5280), 1353–1355.

Roberts, J. P. (2004). Melanopsin lights the way. *The Scientist*, 18(8), 32.

Robinson, D. N. (1986). *An intellectual history of psychology*. Madison, WI: University of Wisconsin Press.

Robinson, L. A., Berman, J. A., & Neimeyer, R. A. (1990). Psychotherapy for the treatment of depression: A comprehensive review of controlled outcome research. *Psychological Bulletin*, 108, 30–49.

Rock, I. (1983). *The logic of perception*. Cambridge, MA: MIT Press.

Rodriquez, E., George, N., Lachaux, J., Marinerie, J., Renault, B., & Varela, F. (1999). Perception's shadow: Long-distance synchronization of human brain activity. *Nature*, 430, 4.

Rogers, C. R. (1961). *On becoming a person*. Boston: Houghton Mifflin.

Rogers, C. R. (1980). *A way of being*. Boston: Houghton Mifflin.

Rosario-Campos, M. C., Leckman, J. F., Mercadante, M. T., Shavitt, R. G., Prado, H. S., Zamignani, D., & Miguel, E. C. (2001). Adults with early-onset obsessive-compulsive disorder. *American Journal of Psychiatry*, 158(11), 1899–1903.

Rosenhan, D. L. (1973). On being sane in insane places. *Science*, 179, 250–258.

Rosenthal, N. E. (1993). *Winter blues: Seasonal affective disorder: What it is and how to overcome it*. New York: Guilford Press.

Rosenthal, N. E. (1995, October 9). The mechanism of action of light in the treatment of seasonal affective disorder. Paper presented at the conference on *Biological Effects of Light*, Atlanta, Georgia.

Rumelhart, D., & McClelland, J. L. (1986). *Parallel distributed processing: Explorations in the microstructure of cognition*, 2 vols. Cambridge, MA: MIT Press.

Russell, T. (2000). Exploring the social brain in schizophrenia: Left prefrontal underactivation during mental state attribution. *American Journal of Psychiatry*, 157(12), 2040–2042.

Ryle, G. (1949). *The concept of mind*. London: Hutchinson.

Sacks, O. (1987). *The man who mistook his wife for a hat*. New York: Harper & Row.

Sacks, O. (1995). *An anthropologist on Mars*. New York: Knopf.

Sagan, C. (1979). *Broca's brain*. New York: Random House.

Sagan, C. (1996). *The demon-haunted world*. New York: Random House.

Sahraie, A., Weiskrantz, L., Barbur, J. L., Simmons, A., Williams, S. C. R., & Brammer, M. J. (1997). Pattern of neuronal activity associated with conscious and unconscious processing of visual signals. *Proceedings of the National Academy of Sciences of the United States*, 94, 9406–9411.

Salovey, P., & Mayer, J. D. (1990). Emotional intelligence. *Imagination, Cognition, and Personality*, 9, 185–211.

Santarelli, L., Saxe, M., Gross, C., Surguet, A., Battaglia, F., Dulawa, S., Weisstaub, N., Lee, J., Duman, R., Arancio, O., Belzung, C., & Hen, R. (2003). Requirement of hippocampal neurogenesis for the behavioral effects of antidepressants. *Science*, 301, 805–809.

Sapolsky, R. M. (1992). *Stress, the aging brain, and the mechanisms of neuron death*. Cambridge, MA: MIT Press.

Sapolsky, R. M. (1996). Why stress is bad for your brain. *Science*, 273, 749–750.

Sapolsky, R. M. (1997). *Why zebras don't get ulcers*. New York: Freeman.

Sawa, A., & Snyder, S. H. (2002). Schizophrenia: Diverse approaches to a complex disease. *Science*, 296, 692–695.

Sayre, K. M. (1976). *Cybernetics and the philosophy of mind*. Atlantic Highlands, NJ: Humanities Press.

Schachter, S. (1959). *The psychology of affiliation*. Stanford: Stanford University Press.

Schachter, S., & Singer, J. (1962). Cognitive, social, and physiological determinants of emotional state. *Psychological Review*, 69, 379–399.

Schacter, D. L. (1987). Implicit memory: History and current status. *Journal of Experimental Psychology*, 13, 501–518.

Schacter, D. L. (Ed.). (1995). *Memory distortions*. Cambridge MA: Harvard University Press.

Schacter, D. L. (1996). *Searching for memory: The brain, the mind, and the past*. New York: Basic Books.

Schacter, D. L. (1998). Memory and awareness. *Science*, 280, 5360, 59–61.

Schacter, D. L. (2001). *The seven sins of memory: How the mind forgets and remembers*. Boston: Houghton Mifflin.

Schank, R. (1982). *Dynamic memory: A theory of reminding and learning in computers and people*. New York: Cambridge University Press.

Scharff, C. (2000). New neuronal growth in the zebra finch. *Neuron*.

Schlechter, T. M., & Toglia, M. P. (Eds.). (1985). *New directions in cognitive science*. Norwood, NJ: Ablex.

Scott, S. (2003). Brain images of Mandarin speakers. Science exhibit, British Royal Society, London.

Segal, N. L. (1999). *Entwined lives: Twins and what they tell us about human behavior*. New York: Dutton/Penguin Books.

Seidenbecher, T., Rao Laxmi, T., Stork, O., & Pape, H.-C. (2003). Amygdalar and hippocampal theta rhythm synchronization during fear memory retrieval. *Science*, 301, 846–850.

Seligman, M. (1995). The effectiveness of psychotherapy: The Consumer Reports study. *American Psychologist*, 50, 965–974.

Selkoe, D. J. (1999). Translating cell biology into therapeutic advances in Alzheimer's disease. *Nature*, 399(6738), A23.

Selye, H. (1976). *The stress of life*. New York: McGraw-Hill.

Senior, K. (2001). Brain plasticity allows recognition of transplanted hands. *Lancet*, 357(9274), 2108.

Shadmehr, R., & Holcomb, H. H. (1997). Neural correlates of motor memory consolidation. *Science*, 277(5327), 821–825.

Sharp, P. E., Cho, J., & Tinkelman, A. (2001). Angular velocity and head direction signals recorded from the dorsal tegmental nucleus of gudden in the rat: Implications for path integration in the head direction cell circuit. *Behavioral Neuroscience*, 115(3), 571.

Shaw, S. H., Mroczkowski-Parker, Z., Shekhtman, T., Alexander, M., Remick, R. A., Sadovnick, A. D., McElroy, S. L., Keck, P. E., Jr., & Kelsoe, J. R. (2003). Linkage of a bipolar disorder susceptibility locus to human chromosome 13q32 in a new pedigree series. *Molecular Psychiatry*, 8, 5.

Shean, G. (1978). *Schizophrenia: An introduction to research and theory*. Cambridge, MA: Winthrop.

Sheikh, J. I., Leskin, C. A., & Klein, D. F. (2002). Gender differences in panic disorder: Findings from the National Comorbidity Survey. *American Journal of Psychiatry*, 159(1), 55–58.

Sheline, Y. I., Gado, M. H., & Kraemer, H. C. (2003). Untreated depression and hippocampal volume loss. *American Journal of Psychiatry*, 160(8), 1516–1518.

Shermer, M. (1997). *Why people believe weird things*. New York: W. H. Freeman.

Shibata, D. K., & Zhong, J. (2001). A rational decision: don't bet on it. Paper presented at the 87th Scientific Assembly and Annual Meeting of the Radiological Society of North America, Nov. 26, Chicago, IL.

Shneidman, E. S. (1999). The psychological pain assessment scale. *Suicide & Life-Threatening Behavior*, 29, 287–294.

Shors, T. J. (2001). Neurogenesis in the adult is involved in the formation of trace memories. *Nature*, 410, 372–375.

Shorter, E. (1997). *A history of psychiatry*. New York: John Wiley.

Shreeve, J. (1995). The brain that misplaced its body. *Discover*, 16(5), 39–44.

Siegel, J. M. (2001). The REM sleep-memory consolidation hypothesis. *Science*, 294, 1058–1063.

Silverman, D. H. S., et al. (2001). Positron emission tomography in evaluation of dementia: Regional brain metabolism and long-term outcome. *Journal of the American Medical Association*, 286, 17, 2120.

Simon, H. A. (1981). *The sciences of the artificial*, 2nd ed. Cambridge, MA: MIT Press.

Simons, D. J. (1999). Current approaches to change blindness. *Visual Cognition*, 7, 1–15.

Singg, S., & Lewis, J. L. (2001). Depression and blood types. *Psychological Reports*, 88, 725–726.

Sizemore, C. C. (1978). *I'm Eve*. San Francisco: Berkley Publishing Group.

Skinner, B. F. (1938). *The behavior of organisms*. New York: Appleton-Century-Crofts.

Skinner, B. F. (1953). *Science and human behavior*. New York: Free Press.

Skinner, B. F. (1953). *Science and human behavior*. New York: Macmillan.

Skinner, B. F. (1957). *Verbal behavior*. New York: Appleton-Century-Crofts.

Skinner, B. F. (1961). *Cumulative record*. New York: Appleton-Century-Crofts.

Skinner, B. F. (1971). *Beyond freedom and dignity*. New York: Knopf.

Skinner, B. F. (1974). *About behaviorism*. New York: Knopf.

Skinner, B. F. (1983). *A matter of consequences*. New York: Knopf Publishing.

Smith, M. L., Glass, G. V., & Miller, T. I. (1980). *The benefits of psychotherapy*. Baltimore: Johns Hopkins University Press.

Sperling, G. (1960). The information available in brief visual presentation. *Psychological Monographs, 74*, 11.

Sperry, R. W. (1968). Hemisphere disconnection and unity of conscious experience. *American Psychologist, 29*, 723–733.

Springer, S. P., & Deutsch, G. (1998). *Left brain, right brain: Perspectives from cognitive neuroscience*, 5th ed. New York: Freeman.

Squire, L. (1987). *Memory and brain*. New York: Oxford University Press.

Srivastave, S., John, O. P., Gosling, S. D., & Potter, J. (2003). Development of personality in early and middle adulthood: Set like plaster or persistent change? *Journal of Personality and Social Psychology, 84*, 5.

Stephan, K. E., Marshall, J. C., Friston, K. J., Rowe, J. B., Ritzl, A., Zilles, K., & Fink, G. R. (2003). Lateralized cognitive processes and lateralized task control in the human brain. *Science, 301*, 384–386.

Stickgold, R., Hobson, J. A., Fosse, R., & Fosse, M. (2001). Sleep, learning, and dreams: Off-line memory reprocessing. *Science, 294*, 1052–1057.

Stoffregen, T. A., & Bardy, B. G. (2001). On specification and the senses. *Behavioral and Brain Sciences, 24*(2), 195–213.

Styron, W. (1990). *Darkness visible: A memoir of madness*. New York: Random House.

Sulloway, F. J. (1996). *Born to rebel: Birth order, family dynamics, and creative lives*. New York: Pantheon.

Suppes, P., & Han, B. (2000). Brain-wave representation of words by superposition of a few sine waves. *Proceedings of the National Academy of Sciences of the United States, 97*, 8739–8743.

Talan, J. (2003, August 19). A gene therapy for the brain. *Newsday (New York)*, p. A35.

Talwar, S. K., Xu, S., Hawley, E. S., Weiss, S. A., Moxon, K. A., & Chapin, J. K. (2002). Behavioural neuroscience: Rat navigation guided by remote control. *Nature 417*, 37–38.

Tapia, M. (2001). Measuring emotional intelligence. *Psychological Reports, 88*(2), 353–364.

Teicher, M. H. (2000). Wounds that time won't heal: the neurobiology of child abuse. *Cerebrum, 2*(4), 36–39.

Tekcan, A. (2001). Flashbulb memories for a negative and a positive event: News of Desert Storm and acceptance to college. *Psychological Reports, 88*(2), 323–331.

Tellegen, A. (1988). Personality similarity in twins reared apart and together. *Journal of Personality and Social Psychology, 54*, 1031–1039.

Terrace, H. M., & Brannon, E. (1998). Ordering of the numerosities 1 to 9 by monkeys. *Science, 282*(5389), 746.

Terrace, H., Pettito, L. A., & Bever, T. G. (1976). *Project Nim: Progress report I*. New York: Columbia University Press.

Terrace, H. S. (1979). How Nim Chimpsky changed my mind. *Psychology Today*, November, 23–28.

Terrace, H. S. (1986). *Nim: a chimpanzee who learned sign language*. New York: Columbia University Press.

Thiele, T. E., Marsh, D., Ste. Marie, L., Bernstein, I., & Palmiter, R. (1998). Ethanol consumption and resistance are inversely related to neuropeptide Y level. *Nature, 396*, 366–370.

Thigpen, C. H., & Cleckley, H. M. (1957). *The three faces of eve*. New York: McGraw-Hill.

Thompson, P. M., Cannon, T. D., Narr, K. L., van Erp, T., Poutanen, V.-P., Huttunen, M., Lönnqvist, J., Standertskjöld-Nordenstam, C.-G., Kaprio, J., Khaledy, M., Dail, R., Zoumalan, C. I., & Toga, A. W. (2001). Genetic influences on brain structure. *Nature Neuroscience, 4*, 1253–1258.

Thorndike, E. L. (1911). *Animal intelligence*. New York: Macmillan.

Thorndike, E. L. (1927). The law of effect. *American Journal of Psychology, 39*, 212–222.

Thorndike, E. L. (1933). A proof of the law of effect. *Science, 77*, 173–175.

Thurstone, L. L. (1938). *Primary mental abilities*. Chicago: University of Chicago Press.

Thurstone, L. L., & Thurstone, T. G. (1941). *Factorial studies of intelligence*. Chicago: University of Chicago Press.

Tiedge, H., Bloom, F. E., & Richter, D. (1999). RNA, whither goest thou? (nerve cell synaptic memory). *Science, 283*(5399), 186.

Tkachev, D., Mimmack, M. L., Ryan, M. M., Wayland, M., Freeman, T., Jones, P. B., Starkey, M., Webster, J. J., Yolken, R. H., & Bahn, S. (2003). Oligodendrocyte dysfunction in schizophrenia and bipolar disorder. *The Lancet, 362*(9386), 798.

Toh, K. L., Jones, C. R., & He, Y. (2001) Familial advanced sleep-phase syndrome: A short-period circadian rhythm variant in humans. *Science, 291*, 1040–1043.

Tolman, E. C. (1932). *Purposive behavior in animals and men*. New York: Century.

Torrey, E. F. (1988). *Nowhere to go: The tragic odyssey of the homeless mentally ill*. New York: Harper & Row.

Torrey, E. F. (1997). Seasonality of births in schizophrenia and bipolar disorder: A review of the literature. *Schizophrenia Research, 28*, 1–38.

Trachtenberg, J. T., Trepel, C., & Stryker, M. P. (2000). Rapid extragranular plasticity in the absence of thalamocortical plasticity in the developing primary visual cortex. *Science, 287*(5460), 2029–2032.

Tran, K. D., Smutzer, G. S., Doty, R. L., & Arnold, S. E. (1998). Reduced Purkinje cell size in the cerebellar vermis of elderly patients with schizophrenia. *American Journal of Psychiatry, 155*(9), 1288–1289.

Tulving, E. (1985). How many memory systems are there? *American Psychologist, 40*, 395–398.

Tuma, R. S. (2003). New drugs may add up to good news in schizophrenia. *Brain Work, 13*, 1.

Turetsky, B. I., et al. (2003). Low olfactory bulb volume in first-degree relatives of patients with schizophrenia. *American Journal of Psychiatry, 160*(4), 703–704.

Tuszynski, M. (2001). UCSD School of Medicine News, Retrieved May 7, 2004 from http://health.ucsd.edu/news/2001

Ullian, E. M. (2001). Control of synapse number by glia. *Science, 291*, 657–660.

Umilitá, M. A., Kohler, E., Gallese, V., Fogassi, L., Fadiga, L., Keysers, C., & Rizzolatti, G. (2001). I know what you are doing: A neurophysiological study. *Neuron, 31*(1), 155–165.

Ungerleider, L. G. (1995). Functional brain imaging studies of cortical mechanisms for memory. *Science, 270*, 769–775.

Ungerleider, L. G., & Haxby, J. V. (1994). What and where in the human brain. *Current Opinion in Neurology, 4*, 157–165.

Ungerstedt, U., & Ljungberg, T. (1974). Central dopamine neurons and sensory processing. *Journal of Psychiatric Research, 11*, 149–150.

Usten, T. B. (2001). The worldwide burden of depression in the 21st century. In M. M. Weismann (Ed.), *Treatment of depression: Bridging the 21st century*. Washington, DC: American Psychiatric Press.

U.S. Department of Health and Human Services. (1999). *Mental Health: A Report of the Surgeon General*. Rockville, MD: U.S. Department of Health and Human Services, Office of the Surgeon General.

U.S. Department of Justice. (1999). *Mental health and treatment of probationers*. Retrieved May 7, 2004, from http://www.ojp.usdoj.gov/bjs/abstract/mhtip.htm

van der Kolk, B. (1987). *Psychological trauma*. Washington, DC: American Psychiatric Press.

Van Turennout, M., Hagoort, P., & Brown, C. M. (1998). Brain activity during speaking: From syntax to phonology in 40 milliseconds. *Science, 280*(5363), 572–575.

Vargha-Khadem, F., Gadian, D. G., Watkins, K. E., Connelly, A., Van Paesschen, W., & Mishkin, M. (1997). Differential effects of early hippocampal pathology on episodic and semantic memory. *Science, 277*(5324), 376–381.

Vassar, R. (1999). Beta secretase cleavage of Alzheimer's amyloid precursor protein by the transmembrane aspartic protease BACE. *Science, 286*, 735–741.

Vaughan, S. C. (1997). *The talking cure: The science behind psychotherapy*. New York: Putnam & Sons.

Vogel, G. (2003). Depression drugs' powers may rest on new neurons. *Science, 301*(757), 203.

Von Neumann, J. (1958). *The computer and the brain*. New Haven, CT: Yale University Press.

Wagner, A. (1998). Building memories: Remembering and forgetting of verbal experiences as predicted by brain activity. *Science, 281*, 1188–1191.

Walsh, D. M., Klyubin, I., Fadeeva, J. V., Cullen, W. K., Anwyl, R., Wolfe, M. S., Rowan, M. J., & Selkoe, D. J. (2002). Naturally secreted oligomers of amyloid β protein potently inhibit hippocampal long-term potentiation in vivo. *Nature, 416*, 535–539.

Watson, J. B. (1903). *Animal education*. Chicago: University of Chicago Press.

Watson, J. B. (1913). Psychology as the behaviorist sees it. *Psychological Review, 20*, 158–177.

Watson, J. B. (1924). *Behaviorism*. New York: Norton.

Watson, J. B., & Raynor, R. (1920). Conditioned emotional reactions. *Journal of Experimental Psychology, 3*, 1–14.

Webb, J. (1980). *Mechanism, mentalism, and metamathematics*. Hingham, MA: D. Reidel.

Wechsler, D. (1958). *The measurement and appraisal of adult intelligence*, 5th ed. Baltimore: Williams & Wilkins.

Wegner, D. M. (2002). *The illusion of conscious will*. Cambridge, MA: MIT Press.

Wegner, D. M., Ansfield, M., & Pilloff, D. (1998). The putt and pendulum: Ironic effects of the mental control of action. *Psychological Science, 9*(3), 196.

Wegner, D. M., & Wheatley, T. (1999). Apparent mental causation: Sources of the experience of will. *American Psychologist, 54*(7), 480–492.

Weickert, T. W., Goldberg, T. E., Gold, J. M., Bigelow, L. B., Egan, M. F., & Weinberger, D. R. (2000). Cognitive impairments in patients with schizophrenia displaying preserved and compromised intellect. *Archives of General Psychiatry, 57*(9), 907.

Weinberg, R. A. (1989). Intelligence and IQ: Landmark issues and great debates. *American Psychologist, 44*, 98–104.

Weiss, P. (2001). The seeing tongue. *Science News, 160*, 140–141.

Weissman, M. M., Klerman, G. L., Markowitz, J. S., & Ouellette, R. (1989). Suicidal ideation and suicide attempts in panic disorder and attacks. *New England Journal of Medicine, 321*, 1209–1214.

Wicker, B., Keysers, C., Plailly, J., Royet, J.-P., Gallese, V., & Rizzolatti, G. (2003). Both of us disgusted in *my* insula: The common neural basis of seeing and feeling disgust. *Neuron, 40*, 655–664.

Widiger, T. A (2002). Values, politics, and science in the construction of the DSM. In J. Z. Sadler (Ed.), *Descriptions and prescriptions: Values, mental disorders, and the DSM*. Baltimore, MD: Johns Hopkins University Press, pp. 25–41.

Widman, L. E., Loparo, K. A., & Nielsen, N. R. (Eds.). (1989). *Artificial intelligence, simulation, and modeling*. New York: John Wiley & Sons.

Willingham, D. T. (2002). Allocating student study time. *American Educator*, Summer, 63–68.

Wilson, F. (1979). *The mental as physical*. London: Routledge & Kegan Paul.

Wilson, E. O. (1998). *Consilience: The unity of knowledge*. New York: Alfred Knopf.

Wilson, R., & Nicoll, R. A. (2002). Endocannabinoid signaling in the brain. *Science, 296*, 678–682.

Wolpe, J. (1973). *The practice of behavior therapy*, 2nd ed. New York: Pergamon.

Wolpe, J. (1997). Thirty years of behavior therapy. *Behavior Therapy, 28*, 633–635.

Woods, B. T. (1998). Is schizophrenia a progressive neurodevelopmental disorder?: Toward a unitary pathogenetic mechanism. *American Journal of Psychiatry, 155*(12), 1661.

Woods, M. (2003, February 17). It's easy to plant false memories, study finds. *Pittsburgh Post Gazette*, p. A6.

Woodside, D. B., Bulik, C. M., Halmi, K. A., Fichter, M. M., Kaplan, A., Berrettini, W. H., Strober, M., Treasure, J., Lilenfeld, L., Klump, K., Kaye, W. H. (2002). Personality, perfectionism, and attitudes toward eating in parents of individuals with eating disorders. *The International Journal of Eating Disorders*, April 2002, 31(3), 290–300.

World Health Organization (2001). *Mental health: the bare facts*. Retrieved May 7, 2004, from http://www.who.int/mental-health/en/

Young, J. Z. (1978). *Programs of the brain*. Oxford, England: Oxford University Press.

Young, R. M. (1970). *Mind, brain and adaptation in the nineteenth century*. Oxford, England: Clarendon Press.

Zanarini, M. C., Frankenburg, F. R., Hennen, J., & Silk, K. R. (2003). The longitudinal course of borderline psychopathology: 6-year prospective follow-up of the phenomenology of borderline personality disorder. *American Journal of Psychiatry, 160*, 274–275.

Zeki, S. M. (1992). The visual image in mind and brain. *Scientific American, 267*(3), 69–76.

Zeki, S. M. (1993). *Vision of the brain*. London: Blackwell.

Zeki, S. M. (2001). Artistic creativity and the brain. *Science, 293*(5527), 51.

Zhou, M. (2001). Better mouse memory comes at a price. *The Scientist, 15*(7), April 2, 21.

Zilboorg, G., & Henry, G. W. (1941). *A history of medical psychology*. New York: Norton.

Zilbovicius, M. (2000). Temporal lobe dysfunction in childhood autism: A PET study. *American Journal of Psychiatry, 157*(12), 1988–1993.

Zimbardo, P. G. (1972). Pathology of imprisonment. *Transaction/Society*, 4–8.

Zimbardo, P. G., & Leippe, M. (1991). *The psychology of attitude change and social influence*. New York: McGraw-Hill.

Zlotnick, C. (2001). Gender differences in patients with posttraumatic stress disorder in a general psychiatric practice. *American Journal of Psychiatry, 158*(11), 1923–1925.

Zrenner, E. (2002). Will retinal implants restore vision? *Science, 295*, 1022–1025.

Zuckerman, M. (1991). *Psychobiology of personality*. Cambridge, England: Cambridge University Press.

Zuckerman, M. (1995). Good and bad humors: Biochemical bases of personality and its disorders. *Psychological Science, 6*, 325–332.

GLOSSARY

16PF: a test of personality traits devised by Raymond Cattell that theoretically measures all 16 factors that make up personality.

abnormal psychology (psychopathology): the branch of psychology that studies mental illnesses, their causes and treatments.

absolute threshold: for a particular sense, the smallest amount of energy it takes for an average person to notice it.

accommodation: changing the thickness of the lens of the eye in order to focus on things near or far.

acetylcholine: one of the most common neurotransmitters in the brain.

action potential: the firing of a neuron. An electrical charge travels from one end to the other.

active phase: the term used for the stage of schizophrenia when a person exhibits severe positive symptoms such as hallucinations and delusions.

actor-observer effect: the fact that people are more likely to see the influence of the situation when finding causes for their own behavior than for the behavior of others.

affect: emotions, moods, or temperaments, including fear, love, depression, nervousness, anger, and happiness; the subjectively experienced feeling of emotion.

afferent (sensory) nerves: the set of nerves that carry signals from the body's parts to the spinal cord and brain, providing the sense of touch and feeling.

agoraphobia: very broad fear in which a person is nervous about going out in public.

all-or-none law: refers to the fact that when a neuron fires the signal goes all the way and at full strength.

alpha waves: the brain waves that occur when a person is awake and relaxed. They are short and regular.

alternate personalities (alters): the different identities experienced by a person with dissociative identity disorder.

altruistic (prosocial) behavior: the act of helping people in trouble.

Alzheimer's disease: the most common form of dementia, which results from an abnormal buildup of amyloid protein in the brain.

American Psychological Association (APA): the largest professional association of psychologists in the world. It is divided into dozens of divisions and focuses on counseling and therapy rather than on purely scientific pursuits, as does the APS.

American Psychological Society (APS): a professional association formed to meet the needs of scientific psychologists. This group publishes information and hosts meetings aimed at the scientific exploration of behavior and the mind, rather than focusing on psychological applications or therapy as does the APA.

American question: a term used by Piaget to refer to the question commonly asked by Americans: How can we push children through the four stages as fast as possible?

Ames room: a distorted room shaped like a trapezoid (one side is much taller than the other) in which objects in one corner appear much larger than objects in the other corner.

amygdala: Greek for "almond," a brain area located at the end of the hippocampus that is a center for emotions, such as fear and anger.

anal: the second psychosexual stage centering around toilet training, beginning around the age of two and extending up to preschool.

anal-expulsive: a personality trait including being undisciplined, messy, disorderly, late, impulsive, and overly generous. A concept used in psychoanalytic theory.

anal-retentive: a personality trait including neatness, orderliness, punctuality, cleanliness, and stinginess. A concept used in psychoanalytic theory.

analysis of resistance: a technique used in psychoanalysis in which the therapist analyzes things that a patient resists talking about in the belief that those things are held in the unconscious mind and are therefore causing the person's disorder.

analysis of transference: a technique used in psychoanalysis that assumes that a patient will transfer some feelings he has for significant people in his life to the therapist. This transference is then analyzed.

analysts: See *psychoanalysts*.

anima: an archetype in Carl Jung's theory of personality—the feminine side of men.

animal magnetism: the idea that animals have magnetic energy; proposed by Anton Mesmer, who claimed that mental disorders were produced by disruptions or interference in a person's magnetic field.

animus: an archetype in Carl Jung's theory of personality—the masculine side of women.

anorexia nervosa: an eating disorder in which a person does not eat enough. This person refuses to maintain a normal body weight, has an intense fear of becoming fat, and has a disturbance in the concept of her or his body shape.

anterograde amnesia: an inability to form new memories caused by damage to the hippocampus and surrounding regions of the medial temporal lobe.

antianxiety medication (minor tranquilizers): medicines that slow down the nervous system.

antidepressant drugs: medicines that increase the activity of certain brain neurotransmitters, such as serotonin and norepinephrine; used in the treatment of depression and other disorders.

antimanic drugs: medicines, such as lithium, that alleviate the wide mood swings typical in the bipolar disorders.

antipsychotic drugs: See *neuroleptic drugs*.

anxiety disorder: a groups of psychological disorders in which people suffer from nervousness, fear, worry, or tension.

aphasia: problems in the use or understanding of language due to damage to specific brain areas.

aqueous humor: the fluid that lies in the front of the eye between the cornea and the lens.

archetypes: the elements, or content, of the collective unconscious, including the persona, the anima, and the shadow.

attachment: a term coined by John Bowlby to refer to the emotional relationship between an infant and a caregiver, such as the mother.

attention deficit/hyperactivity disorder (ADHD): a disorder seen more often in children that causes difficulty in paying attention and sitting still.

attitudes: archetypes proposed by Jung including extraversion and introversion.

attribution: a person's idea or beliefs about the causes of a behavior.

atypical antipsychotics: new neuroleptic drugs that have physiological properties different from those of traditional antipsychotics.

autism: a serious disorder that causes debilitating symptoms including bizarre behaviors, lack of language development, lack of social development, impaired nonverbal behavior (such as eye-to-eye gaze), impaired peer relationships, and lack of social reciprocity.

autonomic nervous system (ANS): the nerves that work mostly automatically in the control of body organs and basic life functions.

aversive therapy: any psychotherapy that uses unpleasant circumstances to treat a disorder.

axon: the relatively long branch that extends out of the soma of a neuron and carries a message.

axonal transmission: the electrical process by which a signal travels from one end of a cell to the other.

backward conditioning: the type of classical conditioning in which the US is presented before the CS.

Barnum effect: people's tendency to accept a personality description if it is general and ambiguous. Named after P. T. Barnum, the circus owner who said, "There's a sucker born every minute."

basilar membrane: the membrane inside the cochlea of the inner ear that contains tiny hair cells that transduce sound waves into neural energy producing hearing.

behavior: anything that an animal does—an action, either overt (directly observable) or within the animal's body, such as heartbeat; the main topic of scientific study in psychology.

behaviorism: the school of psychology founded by John B. Watson and promoted by B. F. Skinner that argues that psychology should give up its aspirations of being a science of the mind and should focus instead on being an objective science of observable behavior.

beta waves: the brain waves that occur when a person is awake and very alert; short, irregular, but very active brain waves.

Bethlehem Hospital: one of the first hospitals; an asylum in London that imprisoned mentally ill people. It was so chaotic that the word *bedlam* was derived from its name.

Big Five: five personality traits that appear to show stability over long periods of time.

binocular cues: depth perception cues that require having two eyes.

binocular disparity: the fact that each eye sees a slightly different image of an object than the other eye.

binocular rivalry: when each eye is presented with a different stimulus, the brain will flip back and forth between the two perceptions.

bioethics: a field of study that contemplates ethical issues regarding biological and psychological research.

bipolar cells: the cells in front of the rods and cones in the retina of the eye.

bipolar disorder: a type of mood disorder in which a person experiences mania as well as depression.

blind spot: the field of vision (or no vision!) in which light strikes the optic disk.

bloodletting: a previously common treatment for a variety of problems, practiced even in the twentieth century, in which blood was removed from a person.

body dysmorphic disorder (BDD): a type of somatoform disorder in which people believe that they are extremely ugly and repugnant to others.

bound anxiety: anxiety that is connected to some object or situation; anxiety that only occurs in certain conditions.

brain stem: the brain area just at the top of the spinal cord where the brain and spinal cord meet. The brain stem includes a number of regions responsible for basic body functions.

brain waves: the electrical patterns created by groups of brain cells. Brain waves can be measured by the EEG.

Broca's (expressive) aphasia: problems in the use of grammar or pronunciation of language due to damage to Broca's area.

Broca's area: a region in the left frontal lobe that controls grammar and pronunciation of language.

bulimia nervosa: an eating disorder in which a person binges and purges.

bystander apathy: the fact that people who witness an emergency often do not help.

bystander effect: the fact that people in trouble are far more likely to be helped if they are seen by only one person rather than by a group.

cardinal trait: one trait that describes a person very accurately and completely, that nearly totally represents the person's personality.

case study: the study of an individual case. One individual is observed and described, sometimes in great detail.

castration anxiety: a concept used in psychoanalytic theory to refer to the unconscious fear that preschool boys have of knives, scissors, being bitten by dogs, or similar things that represent a loss of manhood.

cataracts: patchy white spots in the lens of the eye that often develop in old age.

catatonia: a symptom of schizophrenia that involves body movements. Sometimes a sufferer will stand perfectly still for hours and then suddenly will run wild.

cell assemblies: theoretical neural networks proposed in 1949 by Donald Hebb.

central fissure (fissure of Rolando): a major brain fissure that runs mostly vertically dividing the frontal and parietal lobes.

central nervous system (CNS): the brain and the spinal cord.

central traits: five or six or seven traits that give a fairly complete description of a person's personality.

cerebellum: the part of the brain attached to the back of the brain stem. Its main job is to control coordinated body movements.

cerebral cortex: the outer, surface layer of the cerebrum.

cerebrum: the top section of a brain that is very large in humans.

chromosomes: the long strands of DNA that are the units of inheritance received from mother and father.

chronological age (CA): a term used in intelligence testing to refer to the age of a child.

chunks: the meaningful bits of items in short-term memory, such as UCLA. Using chunking, many more than seven items can fit into short-term memory.

circadian rhythm: literally, "circles around the day"; this is a term for the body's biological rhythm.

civil commitment: See *involuntary commitment*.

clanging: a symptom of schizophrenia in which a person talks in rhymes.

classical conditioning: the type of learning studied by Pavlov that occurs when things are associated together and a reflexive reaction is learned to a new stimulus.

client-centered: a major part of humanistic therapy; the therapy focuses on the client.

clinical psychology: the branch of psychology in which licensed psychologists provide therapy and counseling to those suffering from behavioral or emotional concerns, similar to psychiatry.

closure: a simple Gestalt principle in which partial information about a sensed stimulus is filled in by the brain to form an image of a complete figure; the stimulus is closed.

cochlea: the organ inside the ear that contains the cells that respond to sound waves, thereby producing hearing.

Cogito, ergo sum: Latin for "I think, therefore I am." The statement made by René Descartes expressing the fundamental beginning of his rational understanding of reality.

cognition: mental acts, whether conscious or unconscious, including memory, sensation, perception, thinking, reasoning, intelligence, problem solving, and similar processes performed by the brain.

cognitive-behavior (CB) therapy: a common type of psychotherapy developed by Aaron Beck in which patients are taught to change their thinking and their behaviors.

cognitive dissonance theory: a consistency theory proposed by social psychologist Leon Festinger.

cognitive map: a mental idea of a maze or other space, supposedly learned by laboratory animals with experience running a maze.

cognitive neuroscience: a multidisciplinary field that includes philosophy, psychology, neuroscience, and computer science. Researchers attempt to uncover the exact details of the brain events that produce various cognitions, behaviors, and emotions.

cognitive psychology: the branch of psychology that studies cognitive processes such as memory, perception, and thinking. Perhaps the fastest growing branch of psychology.

cognitive restructuring: a therapeutic technique aimed at changing faulty or dysfunctional ways of thinking into more realistic, rational ones.

collective (transpersonal) unconscious: Jung's notion that all humans share certain elements in their unconscious minds.

community psychology: a new approach that is not so much a set of practices as it is an attitude or a way of thinking. The focus is on the prevention and containment of mental disorders, rather than on their treatment.

comorbidity: the condition when psychological disorders occur together.

comparative psychology: the branch of psychology that scientifically studies animal behavior.

compulsions: behaviors (not thoughts) that people feel they must do lest something horrible happen.

concrete operational period: the third of Piaget's stages of cognitive development in which school-aged children begin to understand basic mental operations whose contents are concrete or easily imagined.

conditioned response: a learned reflexive reaction to a new stimulus via classical conditioning.

conditioned stimulus: a stimulus that an animal learns through classical conditioning to give a reflexive reaction to.

conditioning: the same thing as learning.

cone: a type of photoreceptor that responds to wavelengths of light, producing the sensation of color. There are three kinds of cones in the normal human eye.

confabulation: the cognitive process in which people make up good sounding reasons to explain their behavior, particularly noticed with split-brain patients.

congruence: a state of accord when our experiences in the world match our sense of self; a concept used in humanistic psychology.

conscience: a part of the superego that gives people feelings guilt when they do something morally wrong; a concept used in psychoanalytic theory.

conscientiousness: a personality trait that includes things such as hard-working versus lazy, punctual versus late, orderly versus disorderly, neat versus messy, and responsible versus careless.

conservation: a term used in Piaget's theory that refers to the mental ability to understand that the amount of liquid or substance does not change if it only changes in appearance.

consistency theories: social psychology theories that suggest that humans have a driving force to be consistent in their beliefs, attitudes, and behaviors.

consolidation: the physiological process by which memories are stored in the brain.

construct: See *hypothetical construct.*

contact comfort: the close physical hugging that Harry Harlow discovered was important for normal development in infant monkeys.

containment: the approaches used in community psychology aimed at keeping mental problems from spreading.

continuous reinforcement: the schedule of reinforcement in which a behavior is reinforced every single time it occurs.

contralateral: the opposite connection between the brain's hemispheres and the body; the left hemisphere is connected to the right side of the body, and vice versa.

control group: in a controlled experiment, the group of participants who are not given the independent variable, but instead receive a placebo; the comparison group.

controlled experiment: the scientific method of research that is carefully designed to find out which variables have an influence on a specific variable.

convergence: a depth perception cue in which the eyes swivel inward a good deal more when focusing on something near than they do when focusing on something far (see stereoscopic vision).

conversion disorder: a type of somatoform disorder in which people believe they have physical impairments, but there is no organic cause; see hysteria.

cornea: the front of the eye, the window on the world.

corpus callosotomy: See *split-brain surgery.*

corpus callosum: literally, the "hard body," a brain region that connects the left and right hemispheres.

correlation coefficient: a number between 0 and 1.00, computed by a formula, that indicates the amount of relationship between two variables. Represented by the letter *r*.

correlational study: the scientific method of research that attempts to discover to what extent variables are related to each other.

counterconditioning: a classical conditioning therapy in which a reaction is conditioned to a stimulus that is opposite from the existing one. If a person has an unpleasant reaction to something, then counterconditioning attempts to condition a pleasant reaction to that thing.

CREB gene: a gene that influences the LTP process, typically by influencing the NMDA receptor.

crisis: a term used by Anton Mesmer to refer to the violent convulsions his patients sometimes experienced as he supposedly realigned their magnetic fields.

criterion scoring: See *empirical scoring.*

critical period: the peak time for the expression of a particular characteristic; or the time when a characteristic can be most influenced by environmental conditions.

cross-sectional study: a research method that measures two groups of people of different ages and then compares them on certain behaviors or characteristics.

crystallized intelligence: a person's knowledge of general facts and the ability to use them, as opposed to fluid intelligence.

cued recall: a type of memory retrieval that requires finding something in memory given a cue to narrow the search.

culture-bound: disorders that arise as part of the folklore, the superstitions, or simply the common beliefs of a particular culture of people.

culture-fair: a term used for IQ tests that were constructed to be completely free of any cultural norms.

cyclothymia: a bipolar disorder in which mood swings are mild.

dark adaptation: the process of adjusting to dark after bright light has depleted the chemical rhodopsin in the rods of the eye.

decay: the process by which memories fade away over time.

declarative (explicit) memory: a kind of "conscious" or "aware" memory; what most people call memory.

defense mechanisms: the ways in which the unconscious mind protects us from unpleasant thoughts. An idea from psychoanalytic theory.

deinstitutionalization: the decrease in the number of people in mental hospitals that began in the 1950s and continues today.

delay conditioning: the procedure in classical conditioning when the CS remains on when the US is presented.

delta waves: the brain waves that occur when a person is in deep sleep; brain waves that are very slow and regular. On an EEG chart, they have the shape of the Greek letter delta (a D).

delusion: false beliefs that are held despite clear evidence to the contrary. Often, experienced by people with psychotic disorders, such as schizophrenia.

dementia: injury or disease of the brain that permanently decreases a person's cognitive abilities, such as memory.

dendrites: the branches of a neuron that extend out of the soma to receive signals.

denial: a defense mechanism in which the unconscious mind denies things that produce anxiety.

dependent variable: the variable that is the result, effect, or influenced variable in a scientific experiment. The variable that is measured at the end.

depersonalization disorder: a type of dissociative disorder in which a person feels detachment or estrangement from himself. Some sufferers report feeling like a robot or automaton or as if living in a dream.

depolarization: the process that occurs as positively charged sodium ions enter a neuron and the inside of the cell becomes more positively charged.

developmental psychology: the branch of psychology that scientifically studies how people develop and mature.

Diagnostic and Statistical Manual of Mental Disorders (DSM): a book published by the American Psychiatric Association that lists the criteria of mental illnesses.

diathesis-stress theory: the idea that a disorder is caused by a combination of a genetic potential (a diathesis) and something in the person's experience (stress).

dichromat: a person or animal that has only two kinds of cones in the retina of the eye. Such a human is colorblind.

difference threshold: the amount of change in the intensity of a stimulus that is required for the average person to notice that the level has changed.

diffusion of responsibility: in a large group, each person feels only a small amount of responsibility to help someone who is in trouble.

discrimination learning: the type of learning in which a behavior is conditioned to occur under one set of circumstances but not under another.

discriminative stimulus (S^D): a stimulus that acts as a cue or trigger for the occurrence of an operant behavior.

disorganized type: a subtype of schizophrenia in which the patient shows very disorganized speech and behavior that may be very juvenile and accompanied by silliness and excessive laughter.

displacement: a defense mechanism in which a person's unconscious wishes are displaced to a dream or to another person.

displacement: the process of dislodging items from short-term memory as new information is added.

dissociative amnesia: a form of repression, a blocking of memory retrieval, that occurs when a person has experienced a psychological shock.

dissociative disorder: a group of disorders in which people experience a disassociation, a split or break, in their conscious awareness or identity.

dissociative identity disorder (DID): a psychological disorder in which people alternate between different identities.

dizygotic (DZ) twins: commonly known as fraternal twins, the product of two zygotes that developed in the womb at the same time (two-egg twins).

DNA: deoxyribonucleic acid, often called the molecule of life. What genes and chromosomes are made of.

dopamine: one of the most common neurotransmitters in the brain.

dopamine hypothesis: the idea that schizophrenia is caused by excessive dopamine activity.

double blind: an experimental condition in which neither the participants nor those in contact with the participants are aware which group the participants are in.

double depression: the diagnosis used when a person meets the criteria for both major depression and dysthymia.

double helix: the shape of a chromosome—two spirals wound around each other—like a twisted ladder.

Down syndrome (trisomy 21): the condition in which a child inherits an extra chromosome #21, resulting in a total of 47 chromosomes instead of 46. Causes mental retardation and certain physical features.

dropout effect: a bias of longitudinal studies because the participants who drop out are likely to have certain traits different from those who continue in the study.

dualism: the view ascribed to René Descartes that divides everything in the universe into two categories: physical and nonphysical. Dualism proposes that the mind is a nonphysical entity.

dysthymia: a depressive disorder in which a person has at least two symptoms that persist for two years or more.

echoic memory: the type of sensory memory in which auditory information is stored for a brief moment.

echolalia: parrotlike speech common in autism and some cases of schizophrenia.

ectomorphs: in Sheldon's theory, people who were thin.

efferent (motor) nerves: the set of nerves that carry signals away from the brain and spinal cord to the body's parts, providing movement of the skeletal muscles.

ego: Greek and Latin for "I" or "me," the personality structure that evaluates what is real. A concept used in psychoanalytic theory.

ego ideal: a part of the superego that gives people feelings of pride when they do something morally right; a concept used in psychoanalytic theory.

egocentric: the inability of preschoolers to see the world from more than their own perspective or point of view. The inability to hold multiple things in mind at the same time.

eidetic imagery: the rare ability, sometimes called photographic memory, in which a person can recall visual information in extreme detail.

Electra complex: a term sometimes used for the Oedipus complex in preschool girls.

electroconvulsive therapy (ECT): commonly called *shock treatment*. A treatment for mood disorders that uses electrical current to cause a brain seizure.

emotional expression (EE): the degree to which families use lots of criticism and threats with their family members who have schizophrenia; a circumstance that causes symptoms to be more visible and severe.

emotional intelligence: the ability to deal socially with self and others using emotional skills; promoted by Daniel Goleman.

empathy: a therapeutic technique used in humanistic therapies in which the therapists attempt to put themselves into the mind of the client.

empirical (criterion) scoring: a scoring system on a test that compares test takers to some known outside standard rather than using opinion.

empirical question: a scientific question that can theoretically be answered through observation and measurement.

empiricism: the approach to science that is based on observation and measurement, as opposed to rationalism, which is based on logical reasoning.

encoding: the first step in memory in which items get into the brain; dependent on paying attention.

endocrine system: a system of glands located throughout the body that secrete chemicals (hormones) into the bloodstream, often influencing moods and behaviors.

endomorphs: in Sheldon's theory, people who had a lot of fat on their bodies.

engram: the physiological change in the brain that represents a memory; a neural network.

enzymes: housekeeping chemicals in the body, such as MAO. One of their functions is to recycle neurotransmitter chemicals that have been released.

epidemiology: the study of the frequency and distribution of a disorder within a population.

epilepsy: a disorder in which a person has repetitive seizures.

episodic memory: the storehouse of episodes in one's life that are connected to time and place.

erectile dysfunction: a man's inability or difficulty in achieving an erection.

eros: in Freudian psychoanalytic theory, the life wish.

ethologist: a scientist who studies animal behavior.

etiology: the various causes and influences of a disorder.

evolutionary psychology: a subdivision of psychology that focuses on how behavior and mental processes developed by principles of heredity and evolution.

exhibitionism: the type of sexual disorder (paraphilia) in which a person exhibits his genitals to strangers.

existential philosophy: a branch of philosophy that deals with issues of existence such as free will and the meaning of life. Had great influence on humanistic psychology.

existential therapy: a variation of humanistic therapy that attempts to help people who are struggling with issues involving philosophical ideas about existence, such as free will and making choices.

experimental group: in a controlled experiment, the group of participants who are given the independent variable.

experimenter effect: the effect on a variable by the actions of the experimenter because of his or her beliefs about the variables. An experimenter might inadvertently treat participants differently because of his or her beliefs, and that may affect the outcome of the experiment.

explicit memory: another term for declarative memory.

exposure therapy: a type of extinction therapy used to treat fears and other conditioned responses by exposing the patient to the source of the fear.

expressive aphasia: See *Broca's aphasia*.

extinction: the unlearning of a response.

extinction bursting: an increase in the rate of a learned operant behavior at the beginning of extinction when the reinforcer is first removed.

extinction therapy: a type of therapy in which behaviors are decreased by removing their reinforcement.

extraversion: the personality characteristic of being very outgoing, friendly, and gregarious.

factitious disorder (Munchausen syndrome): a psychological disorder in which a person purposely makes himself sick or pretends to be sick solely for the purpose of receiving medical attention.

factitious disorder (Munchausen) by proxy: the psychological disorder in which a person purposely makes someone else sick, typically his or her child, solely for the purpose of getting medical attention.

factor analysis: a statistical procedure that provides correlation coefficients for all possible pairs of traits that were measured; used to find personality factors.

false memories: memories that a person believes are correct but were implanted and are false.

fear hierarchy: a list of things that produce fear, in order of their strength. Used in systematic desensitization.

feature detectors: cells of the visual system that are specialized to respond to certain features of the environment.

fetish: the type of sexual disorder in which a person uses an object or a part of the body to achieve sexual satisfaction.

figure-ground: a simple Gestalt principle by which brains organize the world of sensations into a figure and a background.

fissure: a wrinkle or crease in the brain's cerebrum.

fissure of Rolando: See *central fissure.*

fissure of Sylvius: See *lateral fissure.*

fixation: when a person exhibits personality traits characteristic of a certain psychosexual stage, according to psychoanalytic theory.

fixed interval (FI): a partial schedule of reinforcement in which the occurrence of a behavior is reinforced only after a fixed amount of time has passed.

fixed ratio (FR) schedule: a partial schedule of reinforcement in which every nth instance of a behavior is reinforced.

flight of ideas: a symptom of mania in which a person's mind cannot hold attention to one idea for very long.

flashbulb memory: A memory of an event that was surprising and consequential, such as an assassination or major disaster. Such a memory sticks in the mind very vividly and for a long time, almost like a photograph.

flooding: an extinction therapy in which the patient is asked to imagine upsetting stimuli in a very intense manner for a long period of time.

fluid intelligence: a person's ability to think quickly and agilely, to figure out original solutions, and to shift gears nimbly, as opposed to crystallized intelligence.

formal operational period: the fourth and final stage of Piaget's theory of cognitive development in which adolescents begin to think abstractly.

formal thought disorder: a core symptom of schizophrenia that involves disorganized thinking, such as loosening of associations.

fovea: the area of best vision in bright light; the area in the middle of the retina where cones are most densely packed together.

free-floating anxiety: general anxiety; anxiety that is not bound to anything.

free recall: a type of memory retrieval that requires finding something in memory without any help—it must be freely recalled from memory.

Freudian slip: a mistake that is influenced by the unconscious mind; a mistake that is not a real mistake but has a meaning.

fugue: a type of dissociative disorder in which people travel away from home and lose some memory for their identity; the term literally means "flight."

functionalism: an early school of psychology led by William James who argued that psychology should attempt to discover how the conscious mind functions. How do we remember, think, learn, and reason?

fundamental attribution error: the mistake people make in attributing behaviors to personality variables more than they deserve and giving less credit to situational variables.

ganglion cells: the cells in the very front of the retina whose axons form the optic nerve.

gender identity disorder: the type of sexual disorder in which an individual's biological sexual characteristics do not match his or her mental idea of his or her gender.

gene: a particular sequence of base pairs on a chromosome; a unit of heredity that represents a recipe for the body.

general paresis: a disorder caused when the syphilis germ infects the brain; also known as neurosyphilis.

generalization: the spread of a conditioned response to other, similar, stimuli.

generalized anxiety disorder: the diagnosis that is used when a person complains of experiencing anxiety at all times and under all conditions.

genital: the final psychosexual stage that arises during adolescence when teenagers begin to show sexual interests; a concept used in psychoanalytic theory.

genius: a term with no official definition that is often used to refer to people with very high IQ scores.

Gestalt psychology: an early school of psychology that proposed that a whole is greater than the sum of its parts. Gestalt psychologists studied perception and identified many principles by which people perceive their environment.

Gestalt therapy: a humanistic psychotherapy that was pioneered by Fritz Perls.

gifted: a term with no official definition that is often used to refer to people with very high IQ scores.

glaucoma: an increased pressure in the eyeball due to the lack of drainage of the aqueous humor.

glial cell: Greek for "glue," a type of brain cell that mostly surrounds and nourishes neurons.

glove anesthesia: a type of conversion disorder in which a person complains that his hand is numb, but that he still has feeling in his arm.

gyrus: the bumps that are formed on the brain's cerebral cortex by the wrinkling of the cerebrum.

hallucination: a false perception; experienced by people with psychotic disorders, such as schizophrenia.

hebephrenia: the previous term for "disorganized schizophrenia," that literally refers to a "childlike mind."

hemispheres: the left and right sides of the cerebral cortex.

hierarchy of needs (pyramid of needs): a conceptualized system, proposed by Abraham Maslow, that orders human needs from most basic to most supreme. Physiological needs are at the bottom, and self-actualization is at the top.

higher-order conditioning: classical conditioning using an already learned CS in place of the US.

hippocampus: Greek for "seahorse"; the part of the brain that bends around the inside of the temporal lobe. An important region for the formation and storage of conscious memories.

hormones: the chemicals released by the glands of the body's endocrine system.

humanism (humanistic psychology): the school of psychology initiated by Abraham Maslow that argues that psychology should include an approach centered on the normal conscious mind and self-actualization.

humors: the body fluids, such as bile, blood, and phlegm. Old theories linked them to personality.

Huntington's disease: a form of dementia caused by a dominant gene on chromosome 4 that strikes late in life and eventually results in death due to destruction of major brain areas.

hypochondriasis: a type of somatoform disorder in which people are excessively and irrationally worried about their health.

hypomania: mild manic episodes.

hypothalamus: an important brain area located just below the thalamus that serves as a regulator or control center for a number of motivations, such as hunger and thirst.

hypothesis: a statement about variables that someone intends to measure to find out if the statement is true. Every scientific study begins with a hypothesis.

hypothetical construct: a variable (such as love, creativity, and frustration) that is not directly measurable and therefore must be defined in a scientific experiment.

hysteria: a form of mental disorder in which people experience physical impairments (blindness, deafness, paralysis, numbness, pain, etc.) without any apparent organic illness or trauma. The term is ancient Greek for "wandering womb" and has been replaced by the term *conversion disorder*.

iconic memory: the type of sensory memory in which visual information is stored for a brief moment.

id: Latin for the term "it," this structure of mind includes our basic instincts, inborn dispositions, and animalistic urges. A concept used in psychoanalytic theory.

identification with the aggressor: the term used in psychoanalytic theory to refer to the process by which a preschool child resolves the Oedipus complex. The child begins to internalize the values, morals, and behaviors of the same-sex parent.

implicit memory: another term for procedural memory; sometimes used to mean memories that are unconscious.

imprinting: a term coined by Konrad Lorenz that refers to the inherited process by which baby ducklings or goslings will follow their mothers.

incidental learning: See *latent learning*.

incongruence: the state of discord between the inner self and the world of experience; a concept used in humanistic psychology.

independent variable: the causative (influencing) variable in a scientific experiment; the variable manipulated or controlled by the experimenter.

inferiority complex: a personality characteristic in which adults feel inferior; a major part of the theory of Alfred Adler.

information processing: the view of cognition that the brain is an organ that analyzes or processes information, much like a computer.

insanity: a legal term, not a psychiatric one. A court judgment that a person will not be held responsible for a crime he committed. The criteria vary from one jurisdiction to another but typically rely on evidence that the person had a psychological disorder.

insight therapies: approaches to psychotherapy in which the goal is to help patients gain insight into the causes and dynamics of their disorders.

insomnia: a sleep disorder in which a person has difficulty sleeping that persists for at least one month.

instincts: defined in sociology as the complex, inborn behavior patterns of animals. In evolutionary psychology, the inherited tendencies of a species.

instrumental conditioning: the term used for the type of learning investigated by Thorndike in which an animal's behavior was viewed as an "instrument" that led to success.

intelligence quotient (IQ score): the score on an intelligence test that has an average of 100 and standard deviation of about 15 points. In the past, it was derived by dividing a child's mental age by chronological age and multiplying by 100.

intermittent explosive disorder: a disorder in which a person cannot control aggressive impulses and aggressive acts that result in serious assaults or destruction of property.

intermittent reinforcement: another term for partial reinforcement.

internal attribute: See *personal attribute*.

intrapsychic conflict: the conflict between the id and the superego. A concept used in psychoanalytic theory.

introspection: a technique for investigating the mind that asks people to look inside themselves and report on their mental experiences.

introversion: the personality characteristic of being very quiet and shy and preferring to be alone.

involuntary commitment (civil commitment): a person can be taken into custody for mental health care against his or her will. Today, such commitment depends on judging a person to be dangerous to himself or herself or to others.

iris: the colored part of the eye located behind the cornea, shaped like a donut or inner tube.

just-noticeable difference (JND): for a particular intensity of stimulus, the amount it must change for people to notice that it changed.

kinase: a protein involved in the physiological changes that occur in the brain during learning.

kinesthetic: the sense of body position and body movement.

Klinefelter's syndrome: a condition in which a person has two X chromosomes and a Y chromosome.

knockout mice: genetically altered mice missing a certain gene; used to determine the functions of genes.

Korsakoff's syndrome: a type of memory loss, mostly anterograde amnesia, that occurs in people who use alcohol so heavily that it impairs their intake of vitamin B$_1$ (thiamine).

Krause end bulbs: receptors in the skin that are stimulated by things that are cold.

latency: the fourth psychosexual stage in which school-aged children's sexual urges are dormant or resting. A concept used in psychoanalytic theory.

latent content: the hidden representations or meanings of dream elements.

latent (incidental) learning: the kind of learning when extraneous things are learned as a side effect of learning something else.

lateral fissure (fissure of Sylvius): a large fissure that extends horizontally from the middle front of the cerebral cortex toward the back.

lateral geniculate nucleus: the region of the thalamus that specializes in relaying visual information from the eyes to the brain.

lateralized: to the side; used to refer to brain functions that are more localized in one hemisphere than the other, such as language.

law of effect: the behavioral law suggested by Thorndike that says that a behavior followed by something pleasant will become more common, and a behavior followed by something unpleasant will become less common.

L-dopa: a medicine used to treat Parkinson's disease because it is a precursor of dopamine and helps the brain to make more of that neurotransmitter.

learned helplessness: apathetic behavior shown by animals that have been in an unpleasant situation with no possible escape; a model for how depression might be caused.

learning: a relatively permanent change in behavior that occurs because of some experience or practice. The same thing as conditioning.

least restrictive environment: the principle that mental health providers should not restrict patients any more than is necessary.

lens: the part of the eye just behind the iris that focuses the incoming light onto the back of the eye.

light therapy: See *phototherapy*.

limbic system: a series of interconnected structures that lie between the brain stem and the cortex. The limbic system processes emotional feelings and reactions.

linear perspective: a depth perception cue in which parallel lines seem to converge in the distance.

lithium: a naturally occurring element that has good success in the treatment of bipolar disorder.

lobes: the four anatomical landmarks or boundaries that divide each hemispheric cortex.

lobotomy: (prefrontal lobotomy) a formerly common treatment for extreme mental disorders in which the patient's prefrontal lobe was surgically destroyed.

localization of function: the idea that certain mental states and behaviors are controlled by a specific location in the brain.

locus coeruleus: the part of the brain that triggers the physiological reactions to danger.

logotherapy: literally, "therapy for the spirit"; a type of existential therapy that concentrates on helping people to find meaning in their lives.

longitudinal fissure: the wrinkle that divides the cerebrum front to back.

longitudinal study: a research method that measures one group of people at different ages in order to determine the effect of aging on certain behaviors or characteristics.

long-term depression (LTD): a physiological event in the brain that weakens the connections between brain cells.

long-term memory: the memory storage system that includes information that has been stored relatively permanently.

long-term potentiation (LTP): a physiological event in the brain that strengthens the connections between brain cells.

loosening of associations: a symptom of schizophrenia in which a person makes odd and loose connections between ideas or words.

lunacy (lunatic): terms derived from the notion that behavior can be influenced by the phases of the moon.

lycanthropy: the idea that people can turn themselves into animals.

magic eye pictures: drawings that take advantage of the brain's stereoscopic vision—the eyes turn inward to focus on an object, and the brain uses that information to compute depth. Repeated images are seen by each eye, and the brain fuses them into a three-dimensional image.

mainstreaming: the idea that mentally retarded and children with psychological disorders be placed in normal classrooms as much as possible.

major depression: a serious mood disorder in which a person suffers from a number of symptoms including low mood or disinterest in things.

major tranquilizers: See *neuroleptic drugs.*

malingering: faking an illness.

Malleus Malifecarum **("Hammer of the Witch"):** a book first published in 1486 that told people how to recognize witches and how to destroy them.

manic episodes: extremely high moods that occur in bipolar disorder and are associated with impulsive, irresponsible behavior.

manifest content: the things that are present and the events that happen in a dream.

MAO: an enzyme that recycles several neurotransmitter chemicals.

MAO inhibitor (MAOI): a category of antidepressant drugs that inhibit the enzyme MAO, resulting in increased neurotransmitter activity.

maturation: the course of natural and normal development of the individuals within a species, such as growth, that occurs regularly and orderly as a result of heredity.

McGurk effect: the phenomenon that occurs when a person sees a film of someone speaking and hears a syllable on the sound track that is different from the syllable seen spoken by the person's lips. The observer reports hearing a syllable that is a combination of the two (sight and sound).

mean: a statistic derived by adding a set of scores and dividing by how many scores there were; commonly referred to as the average.

median: a statistical average for a group of scores that is the score exactly in the middle.

medical school syndrome: the tendency for people to imagine that they have the disorders that they are studying.

meiosis: the process by which 46 chromosomes are divided into two sets of 23 for inclusion into an egg or sperm cell.

melancholy: sad, despondent, or depressed; often used when the source of the depression is an inner biological state rather than an experience.

melatonin: a hormone that helps to regulate the sleep-wake cycle.

mental age (MA): a term used in intelligence testing to refer to the score a child gets that equates that child's results to those of children of a certain age.

mental retardation: the term used for people whose IQ scores are significantly below average. The current definition requires scores more than two standard deviations below average. About 3% of people fall within this criterion.

mesmerism: an early form of hypnosis derived from the name of Franz Anton Mesmer, who believed that mental disorders were caused by disruption in a person's magnetic field.

mesomorphs: in Sheldon's theory, people who were muscular.

method of loci: a mnemonic device in which places are used as triggers for memories.

mildly retarded: the highest level of mental retardation; IQ scores between 55 and 70.

Minnesota Multiphasic Personality Test (MMPI): a personality test that is criterion scored; used mainly to diagnose psychopathology. The most frequently used personality test in the world.

minor tranquilizer: antianxiety medicine.

mirror cells: certain brain cells that apparently are used by the brain when a person is imitating observed behaviors.

mitosis: the process by which cells copy and divide. One cell becomes two, two cells become four, four become eight, and so on.

M'Naghten rule: a legal test of insanity named after Daniel M'Naghten, who in 1843 in England shot and killed the Prime Minister's secretary in an attempt to kill the Prime Minister because "the voice of God" ordered him to. The criterion is whether a person knew the difference between right and wrong.

mnemonics (mnemonic devices): memory aids or tricks that move information into long-term memory by connecting it to things that are already there.

mode: a statistical average for a group of scores that is the most often occurring score.

modeling: an operant conditioning technique in which a therapist uses imitation and reinforcement to teach a patient certain appropriate behaviors.

moderately retarded: a category of mental retardation; IQ scores between 40 and 55.

monism: the modern scientific view that mental phenomena (the mind) emanate solely from the physical brain, and are therefore physical products that do follow physical laws.

monochromat: a person or animal that has only one kind of cone in the retina of the eye. Such a human is colorblind and sees the world in black and white and shades of gray.

monocular cues: depth perception cues that require having only one eye, such as texture, linear perspective, and size constancy.

monozygotic (MZ) twins: commonly called identical twins, the result of one fertilized egg that split in two in the womb and developed into two individuals (one-egg twins).

moral treatment (therapy): the view that people with psychological disorders are not crazed animals but suffering individuals who would benefit from being treated with dignity.

motion parallax: a depth perception cue in which things that are close seem to move in a wider arc than things that are far away when one moves their head.

motor cortex (strip): the gyrus at the top of the cortex, at the back of the frontal lobe just in front of the central fissure, extending from the top down vertically, that controls muscle movement.

multiple sclerosis: a serious disease that destroys the myelin that protects and insulates nerves.

multisensory (multimodal) neurons: brain cells that receive information from more than one sensory system.

Munchausen syndrome: See *factitious disorder.*

myelin (myelin sheath): the white, fatty substance that surrounds portions of the axon of a neuron.

Myers-Briggs Type Indicator: a personality test that divides people into 16 categories based on their answers to items.

narcolepsy: a neurological sleep disorder in which a person suffers from "sleep attacks."

natural selection: the fundamental process of evolution in which characteristics that lead to survival are passed from one generation to the next, while characteristics that are a disadvantage for survival will drop out.

naturalistic observation: the study of humans and animals by gathering information via observation in the natural setting.

nature-nurture question: the question that asks what things are inherited (nature) and what things are learned (nurture); or the extent to which a certain characteristic is inherited or learned.

Necker cube: a two-dimensional drawing that is perceived as a cube, but the perception shifts between two perspectives.

negative correlation: a relationship between two variables in which scores that are high on one variable tend to go with low scores on the other variable and low scores on one variable tend to go with high scores on the other variable.

negative punishment: the type of learning in which a behavior is followed by the removal of a positive reinforcer and the behavior then decreases in frequency.

negative reinforcement: the type of learning in which a behavior is followed by the removal of a negative reinforcer and the behavior then increases in frequency; escape learning.

negative reinforcer: a reinforcing stimulus that strengthens behavior when it is subtracted following an instance of the behavior.

negative symptoms: the symptoms of schizophrenia, such as social withdrawal, that are absent and that we want to increase, as opposed to positive symptoms.

neo-Freudians: early followers of Freud who splintered off and formed their own theories.

neologism: any word made up by a person with schizophrenia.

neural network: a system of brain cells that act together in a fashion to produce problem solving. Neural networks are a common model for thinking about computer software as well as a model for understanding how the brain creates cognitive states.

neurogenesis: the brain's creation of new cells; a process that occurs in the hippocampus area even in adults.

neuroleptic (antipsychotic) drugs: medicine used to treat schizophrenia and other psychoses that blocks dopamine receptors in the brain.

neuron: the major type of cell in the nervous system that sends and receives signals. Often called a brain cell.

neuropsychology: the branch of psychology that studies the biology of actions, emotions, and mental experiences.

neuroticism: a personality trait that is an indication of the degree to which a person is calm or nervous.

neurotransmitters: the chemical messengers that send signals from one neuron to another.

NMDA receptor: a chemical receptor in the hippocampus involved in the physiology of learning and memory.

nondirective: a major part of humanistic therapy—the therapist does not direct the client.

non-securely attached: the term used in attachment theory to refer to infants who have not formed a close emotional relationship with their caregivers.

norms: the standards on a psychological test to which people are compared.

NREM (non-rapid eye movement) sleep: the stage of sleep when a person's eyes are not moving about (as opposed to REM). When awakened from NREM sleep, the person does not usually report dreaming.

nuclei: clusters of brain cells.

nucleus: Latin for "center," an area in the center of a cell.

observational learning: the learning of behaviors via seeing or listening; similar to imitation.

obsession: an idea or thought that intrudes uncontrollably into a person's mind. The thought is something horrible that causes a person great anxiety.

obsessive-compulsive disorder (OCD): an anxiety disorder in which a person experiences obsessions and compulsions.

Oedipus complex: a concept used in psychoanalytic theory to refer to a preschool child's affection for the opposite-sex parent and rivalry with the same-sex parent. This unconscious process is named after the Greek story of Oedipus, the man who was raised by foster parents and grew up to unwittingly kill his biological father and marry his biological mother.

olfactory bulb: a brain area that receives and processes information from the smell receptors in the nose.

operant behavior: a type of behavior such as walking, talking, and moving that is a way of operating on the world. Behavior that is influenced by its consequences.

operant conditioning: the type of learning studied by Skinner that occurs when a behavior is learned through reinforcement.

operant level: the natural rate at which a behavior occurs.

operational definition: a practical definition of a hypothetical construct that makes it measurable for scientific study.

opponent process: the visual process in which cells work in opposition to each other.

optic chiasm: the point in the brain where the two optic nerves meet and where cells from the left travel to the left hemisphere, while cells from the right travel to the right hemisphere.

optic disk: the place in the retina where the optic nerve exits the back of the eye.

optic nerve: the cable of ganglion cell axons that extends out of the back of each eye and carries electrical signals from the eye to the brain.

oral: the first psychosexual stage in Freud's theory when babies are interested in activities involving the mouth.

orgasmic dysfunction: a woman's inability to achieve orgasm.

ovum: the egg produced by a woman, normally containing 23 chromosomes.

p value: a number (derived by formula) that tells the probability that the results of a scientific experiment would have been produced if there was no relationship between those variables within the population.

panic disorder (PD): a type of anxiety disorder in which a person has attacks of extreme anxiety that seem to come out of nowhere.

paradigm: a diagram, drawing, or model that shows the essential features of something. Used to analyze behavior in cases of classical and operant conditioning.

paradoxical intention: a therapeutic technique in which a person is asked to try to *worsen* his or her symptoms.

paraphilia: the type of sexual problem in which a person has an unusual way of achieving sexual gratification.

parasympathetic division: a division of the autonomic nervous system consisting of nerves that slow one down, relaxes one, and help conserve energy by digesting food and reducing heartbeat and blood pressure.

Parkinson's disease: a common form of dementia in which damage to a particular brain area reduces the production of dopamine and thus causes muscle tremors (shaking) and eventual death.

partial (intermittent) reinforcement: the schedule of reinforcement in which a behavior is reinforced once in a while but not every time it occurs.

partial reinforcement effect: behaviors that are reinforced only once in a while are difficult to extinguish.

pegword method: a mnemonic device in which certain words are used as association "pegs" for new information to be remembered.

percentile: a statistic for a particular score that tells the percentage of scores that are lower.

peripheral nervous system (PNS): the nerves that bring messages from the body to the spinal cord together with the nerves that send messages out from the spinal cord to the body.

person-centered: See *client-centered*.

persona: an archetype (from Carl Jung's theory of personality) that represents the fake side of our personality that we show to others.

personal (internal) attribute: a person's belief that someone's behavior is caused primarily by factors within the person's personality.

personal unconscious: Freud's notion that each person has his or her own particular elements within their unconscious mind, as opposed to Jung's notion of the collective unconscious.

phallic: the third psychosexual stage, which occurs approximately during the preschool years. The term *phallic* means any representation of the penis.

phantom limb: the feeling that persists in a limb that has been amputated. This demonstrates that the sense of feeling is not in limbs, it is in the brain.

phenomenology: the personal, subjective view that a person has of the world.

phi phenomenon: if similar images appear within a split second of each other (as in a film at the cinema, or pictures on cards fanned quickly in front of your eyes), the brain perceives not separate images, but one image that is in motion.

phobia: a psychological disorder in which a person experiences irrational fears.

photoreceptors: the receptors in the back of the eye that respond to light; rods and cones.

phototherapy: a treatment for SAD in which patients sit in front of a bright light source for a few hours each day during the winter months.

phrenology: the old-fashioned idea that by feeling the bumps on a person's head it can be determined what psychological functions the person is good at.

pineal gland: a gland that is part of the endocrine system, located about in the middle of the brain, that secretes melatonin. Helps to regulate the biological rhythms. In the dualist view of René Descartes, the pineal gland was where the mind and soul are located.

pituitary gland: a gland in the brain that is sometimes called the "master gland" because it releases hormones that influence other glands in the body.

placebo: a fake independent variable given to the control group in a controlled experiment.

placebo effect: the effect on a variable by a person's belief that something will cause the effect.

plaques: brain cell clumps seen in Alzheimer's disease and caused by the buildup of amyloid protein.

plasticity: the brain's ability to change.

pleasure center: a region in the hypothalamus that when electrically stimulated produces a feeling of pleasure.

pleasure principle: the operating principle of the id—it aims toward pleasurable things and away from painful things.

polarized: an electrical difference. While the cell is at rest, the outside of the neuron has a positive charge and the inside of the neuron is negatively charged.

population: in a scientific experiment, the group that we are interested in drawing conclusions about.

positive correlation: a relationship between two variables in which scores that are high on one variable tend to go with high scores on the other variable and low scores on one variable tend to go with low scores on the other variable.

positive punishment: the type of learning in which a behavior is followed by the addition of a negative reinforcer.

positive reinforcement: the type of learning in which a behavior is followed by the addition of a positive reinforcer.

positive reinforcer: a reinforcing stimulus that strengthens behavior when it is added following an instance of the behavior.

positive symptoms: the symptoms of schizophrenia, such as hallucinations and delusions, that are present and that we want to reduce, as opposed to negative symptoms.

postreinforcement pause: the pause in responding that occurs just after reinforcement when an animal is on a fixed ratio schedule of reinforcement.

postsynaptic: the neuron that is receiving a chemical signal from another neuron.

posttraumatic stress disorder (PTSD): an anxiety disorder in which people experience traumatic events and continue to experience significant problems many months and even years later.

Prader-Willi syndrome: a rare genetic disorder that causes a person's hypothalamus to malfunction. The sufferer has an insatiable appetite, always feeling hungry. Other problems include shortness, low muscle tone, and mental retardation.

precursor chemicals: substances used by the body to manufacture neurotransmitters.

premature ejaculation: when a man ejaculates too soon for a woman's pleasure. The most common of the sexual dysfunctions.

preoperational period: the second stage in Piaget's theory of cognitive development in which preschoolers think egocentrically but are incapable of solving mental operations that require holding more than one thing in mind at a time.

prepotent: the priority that needs lower on the hierarchy of needs have over needs that are higher.

presbyopia: a condition literally meaning "old eyes" that occurs around the age of 45 when the lens of the eye will not accommodate to focus on objects close to the eyes.

presynaptic: the neuron that is sending a chemical signal to another neuron.

primacy effect: the fact that things at the beginning of a list are the first ones to get into the brain and therefore have an advantage in being recalled.

primary mental abilities: theoretically, the fundamental types of intelligence as derived by factor analysis.

primary reinforcers: reinforcing stimuli that influence behaviors because of natural biology, such as food, water, and pain, as opposed to secondary reinforcers.

priming: a physiological event that happens at a synapse when a signal passes in which the cells change in such a way as to make it a little easier for a signal to pass again.

proactive interference: a disruption of long-term memory when something learned in the past "moves forward" to interfere with the learning of new material.

procedural (implicit) memory: a kind of body memory in which one remembers body movements, such as typing, or reactions to stimuli.

prodromal: a term that refers to the early signs of an illness.

profoundly retarded: the lowest level of mental retardation; IQ scores lower than 25.

prognosis: the expected course and outcome of a disorder.

projection: a defense mechanism in which the unconscious mind projects unacceptable feelings onto other people.

projective test: a personality test in which the test taker can give any possible answer, as opposed to a structured test. The belief is that the answers given will be a projection of the person's personality.

proprioceptive: sensations coming from inside the body, such as kinesthesis.

prosocial behavior: See *altruistic behavior.*

prosopagnosia: the disorder in which a person cannot recognize familiar faces caused by damage to a specific brain region.

proximity: a simple Gestalt principle by which things that are arranged close to one another are perceived as belonging together.

psyche: the ancient Greek word for the mind/soul, from which the term *psychology* was derived.

psychiatrist: a medical doctor who specializes in helping people with emotional and behavioral problems.

psychoanalysis: the psychotherapy that Freud developed that attempts to uncover a patient's unconscious mind.

psychoanalysts (analysts): psychiatrists who use Freudian methods of therapy, focusing on helping patients uncover things in their unconscious minds.

psychoanalytic theory: the school of psychology founded by Sigmund Freud that teaches that behavior is usually caused by unconscious mental processes.

psychological autopsy: an investigation of the cause of a person's suicide.

psychometrics: the field of psychology that studies and creates tests for assessing people's characteristics.

psychophysical laws: mathematical laws that describe the relation between physical energy and our sensation of it.

psychophysics: the branch of psychology that studies how physical energy is related to the mind's experience of it.

psychosexual stages: that occur during childhood and adolescence that shape personality according to psychoanalytic theory.

psychosis: a mental disorder in which people are out of touch with reality, as evidenced by their experience of hallucinations and delusions.

psychosomatic (psychophysiologic): the term for real physical symptoms that are caused or worsened by stress.

psychosurgery: the general term for brain operations that are performed in order to help people who suffer with psychological disorders.

psychotherapy: any therapeutic approach to treating psychological disorders.

psychoticism: a personality trait that borders on the extreme characteristics of the severely mentally ill. This trait denotes such behaviors as recklessness, disregard for conventions, and inappropriate emotional expression.

punishment: the type of learning in which a behavior is followed by something unpleasant.

pupil: the black hole in the middle of the iris of the eye.

pyramid of needs: See *hierarchy of needs.*

pyramid of sciences: a hierarchical organization of scientific disciplines that is based on their domains with physics at the bottom and anthropology at the top.

radical behaviorism: the view ascribed to B. F. Skinner that conceptualized scientific psychology as only the study of behavior, giving no attention to the mind.

random selection: the process of selecting a sample for a scientific experiment in which every member of the population has an equal chance of being selected.

rapid cyclers: people who have more than three cycles of mania and depression in a year.

ratio strain: extinction that occurs when reinforcers do not come often enough.

rationalization: a defense mechanism in which the unconscious mind makes up a good-sounding reason to explain something that is too unpleasant to face.

reaction formation: a defense mechanism in which a person's mental and emotional energy is so threatening that the person adopts the reverse, the opposite, of what he or she really wants.

reality principle: the operating principle of the ego — it attempts to help the id get what it wants by judging the difference between real and imaginary.

recency effect: the fact that things at the end of the list have nothing after them to interfere with them and therefore have an advantage in being recalled.

receptive aphasia: See *Wernicke's aphasia.*

recognition: a type of memory retrieval that requires recognizing information stored in memory.

reflection: a therapeutic technique used in humanistic therapies in which the therapists repeat back to the clients what they have said.

regression: a defense mechanism in which a person reverts to developmentally earlier forms of behavior and thinking.

reinforcing stimulus (reinforcer): a stimulus that follows an operant behavior and has an influence on its frequency.

reliability: a statistical measure of a test that indicates the degree to which a test is consistent, trustworthy, or dependable, rather than influenced by extraneous, changeable factors.

REM (rapid eye movement) sleep: a stage of sleep when a person's eyes are moving about rapidly (as opposed to NREM). Often thought of as "dream" sleep, since people who are awakened during REM report dreaming about 85% of the time.

REM latency: the amount of time that passes after falling asleep before a person enters REM sleep.

replication: the duplication of scientific experiments with different participants in different places to confirm the findings.

repression: a major defense mechanism proposed by Freud in which unpleasant ideas and thoughts are pushed out of awareness and into the unconscious mind.

residual type: a subtype of schizophrenia for patients whose symptoms have improved but are not completely gone.

resistance: a term used in psychoanalytic therapy to refer to patients resisting the therapist's suggestions that probe the anxiety-producing contents of the unconscious mind.

respondent behavior: a reflexive reaction to a stimulus.

resting potential: the electrical charge on the inside of a neuron at rest. It measures precisely −70 millivolts.

reticular activating system (RAS): a system of nerve cells that extends from the spinal cord up into the brain that can be compared to the channel selector and volume control on a TV set. The RAS determines what we pay attention to and how intense our attention is.

retina: the inside back layer of the eye where the photoreceptors are located.

retrieval: The final step in the memory process is to get information out of storage when you want it.

retroactive interference: a disruption of long-term memory when something learned recently "moves backward" to interfere with the retrieval of previously learned material.

retrograde amnesia: memory loss for things that happened in the immediate past caused by a blow to the head.

reuptake: the process by which a neuron sucks some of a released neurotransmitter chemical back inside the sending cell.

reuptake inhibitors: a category of antidepressant drugs that decrease the reuptake process, thereby increasing the activity of neurotransmitters.

reversible figures: figures that can be perceived in more than one way.

rhodopsin: a chemical used by the rods that is very sensitive to light.

rod: a type of photoreceptor in the back of the eye that is very sensitive to light.

Rorschach Inkblot Test: a commonly used projective test in which a person gives responses to inkblot patterns.

Rubin vase: a drawing of a vase in which the background can be perceived as profiles of two faces.

Ruffini cylinders: sensory receptors in the skin that become active when something warm touches them.

ruminate: to mentally go over and over certain thoughts.

sample: in a scientific experiment, the group that is selected to be studied. The sample is selected from the population.

savings score: the difference in time between learning something once and twice.

schemas: mental representations of objects and events.

schizophrenia: the most common of the psychotic disorders. Contrary to the popular view, this is not multiple personality. Schizophrenia is a severe brain disorder in which a person loses touch with reality and lives in a mental world full of confusion and falsity.

seasonal affective disorder (SAD): a mood disorder in which a person is especially sensitive to fluctuations in the amount of light and therefore experiences low moods during the winter in high latitudes.

secondary reinforcers: reinforcing stimuli that have strengthening power because they were learned through classical conditioning, such as money, praise, and attention.

secondary traits: personality characteristics that are not very important or complete in describing a person.

securely attached: the term used in attachment theory to refer to infants who have formed a close emotional relationship with their caregivers.

selective serotonin reuptake inhibitors (SSRIs): a category of antidepressant drugs, including Prozac, that decrease the reuptake process, thereby increasing the activity of serotonin.

self-actualization: the highest human motivation, according to humanistic psychology. The process of self-fulfillment, of finding our true inner self, of becoming true to our inner identity.

self-concept: our subjective feelings and ideas about ourselves; the basis of the personality theory of Carl Rogers.

self-serving bias: when attributing causes to our own behaviors, we are likely to use situational attributes more when we experience failure and are more likely to use personal attributes when explaining our success.

semantic memory: memory of general facts; information about the general world, facts that are not dependent on personal experience.

semicircular canals: three curved tubes in the inner ear that help the vestibular sense detect balance.

semipermeable: the surface membrane of a neuron is so called because some things can enter it and some cannot.

sensitive period: a term used for human development in place of critical period, because humans are the most flexible of all animal species and the time of expression of inherited characteristics is less narrow.

sensory adaptation: the process by which sensory receptors, such as warm and cold, adapt to the environment and send a weaker signal to the brain. The person feels less warm or cold after the adaptation.

sensory memory: the very brief memory that is stored in our sensory systems when we sense something and that fades within a split second.

sensory-motor period: the first stage in Piaget's theory of cognitive development, in which an infant depends on sensation and movement and is unable to use mental representations.

separation anxiety: the fear of being separated from their mothers that infants show in the first year of life. A by-product of emotional attachment to their caregivers.

sequential study: a research design that combines cross-sectional and longitudinal designs.

serial position effect: the fact that when learning things in a particular order it is much easier to recall things from the beginning or end of the list than from the middle.

serotonin: one of the most common neurotransmitters in the brain; implicated in mood disorders.

serotonin/norepinephrine reuptake inhibitors (SNRI): a category of antidepressant drugs that decrease the reuptake process, thereby increasing the activity of serotonin and norepinephrine.

severely retarded: a category of mental retardation; IQ scores between 25 and 40.

sex chromosome: genetic sex is determined by these two chromosomes known as X and Y.

sexual dysfunction: the type of sexual problem that has been extensively studied by Masters and Johnson; problems that couples have with sexual performance.

shadow: an archetype—the dark, cruel side of us that contains animal urges and feelings of inferiority.

shaping: a procedure used to speed up operant conditioning in which behaviors that come close to the target behavior are reinforced in successive approximations; learning by small, successive increments.

shock treatment: see electroconvulsive therapy.

short-term memory: the memory storage system that holds things in mind, and that is limited to about seven chunks for about 30 seconds.

similarity: a simple Gestalt principle by which things that are similar to one another are perceived as a group.

single blind: an experimental condition in which the participants do not know which group they are in but the experimenters in contact with the participants do know which group the participants are in.

situational (external) attribute: a person's belief that someone's behavior is caused primarily by factors within the situation.

situationism: the psychological theory proposed by Walter Mischel that says that behavior is greatly influenced by the variables in a situation, as opposed to being influenced by personality traits.

Skinner box: an experimental device for studying operant conditioning in laboratory animals invented by B. F. Skinner.

sleep apnea: a sleep disorder in which a person cannot sleep and breathe at the same time.

smart mice: genetically engineered mice whose NMDA receptors stay open a bit longer than normal, thereby strengthening synaptic connections between cells.

social phobia: fear of being around people, such as a fear of signing your name in public.

social skills training: a type of behavior therapy in which patients are taught effective skills for relating to other people, controlling anger, being more assertive, and acting appropriately in social situations.

sodium gates (channels): the openings on the neuron that allow sodium ions to enter the cell when it is stimulated.

sodium pump: the process a neuron uses to regularly move positively charged sodium ions out of the cell.

soma: the body of a cell.

somatic nervous system (SNS): the nerves that serve the senses and that go to the skeletal muscles.

somatoform disorder: a group of psychological disorders in which a person's psychological problems are converted into simulated body problems.

somatosensory cortex (strip): the gyrus just behind the central fissure in the parietal lobe, extending from the top down vertically, that receives body sensory information and gives the feeling of touch.

somatotypes: various body types, such as fat or skinny, that William Sheldon believed were linked to personality.

source traits: a term used by Raymond Cattell to refer to personality traits that are the underlying causes of personality (as opposed to source traits).

specific phobia: fear of a particular thing, such as snakes, heights, water, flying, or any object.

spinal cord: the series of nerves traveling up and down the back that carry signals to and from the brain and the body.

split-brain surgery (corpus callosotomy): an operation that severs the nerves that carry signals between the left and right hemispheres, the corpus callosum.

spontaneous recovery: an increase in response strength following a rest period during extinction of a classically conditioned response.

squeeze technique: a classical conditioning procedure used in the treatment of premature ejaculation.

St. John's wort: an herb, an extract from a flowering plant, that is currently being studied as an antidepressant treatment.

standard deviation: a statistic referring to the amount of spread in a group of scores.

Stanford-Binet test: a commonly used IQ test that was devised by Lewis Terman in 1916.

statistically significant: the results of scientific experiments that are highly probably true. Most scientists require a *p*-value of 0.05 or smaller. This means we can be quite sure that the results did not happen by chance, that in fact there really is a relationship between those variables within the population.

stereogram: See *magic eye picture*.

stereoscopic vision: the brain computes the depth of objects by the fact that the eyes turn inward (converge) a certain amount.

stimuli: things in the environment that can be sensed by an animal and that are responded to.

stimulus control: changing the rate of a behavior by controlling the discriminative stimuli that precede it or trigger it.

strange situation: an experimental procedure developed by Mary Ainsworth for studying the emotional attachment between children and their mothers.

stranger anxiety: the fear of strangers that infants show in the first year of life. A by-product of emotional attachment to their caregivers.

stream of consciousness: William James's analogy that the conscious mind is like a stream that flows from one thing to another.

striving for superiority: the fundamental human drive and determiner of personality according to Alfred Adler.

structuralism: the early school of psychology led be Edward Titchener that taught that psychology should attempt to find the structures of the mind.

structured test: a personality test that has a structure, such as multiple-choice or true-false, as opposed to a projective test. A test taker must choose from the answers provided.

subcortical: the areas of the brain that lie below the cerebral cortex.

sublimation: a defense mechanism in which undesirable emotions and thoughts are redirected or rechanneled into a socially acceptable activity.

substance P: a neurotransmitter that was so named because it was found to be involved with pain reception but has since been identified as a chemical transmitter for a number of other processes. It is currently being evaluated for its effects on depression.

sulcus: a wrinkle or crease in the brain's cerebrum.

superego: literally means "above the ego." The personality structure that includes the moral ideas that a person learns within their family and society. A concept used in psychoanalytic theory.

surface traits: a term used by Raymond Cattell to refer to personality traits that we observe and measure in a people, as opposed to source traits.

surrealism: the artistic and literary movement in which writers and artists used their works in an attempt to reveal the contents of their unconscious minds. An artistic incorporation of Freud's ideas about the unconscious mind.

sympathetic division: a division of the autonomic nervous system made up of the nerves that use energy in situations of danger.

synapse: the process of chemical transmission between neurons.

synaptic gap (cleft): the space between two communicating neurons.

synaptic transmission: the chemical process by which a signal is sent from one neuron to another.

syndrome: a group or cluster of symptoms (complaints) that are associated with a disorder.

systematic desensitization: a therapy used to extinguish conditioned responses that pairs relaxation with a gradual presentation of the fearful stimuli.

tabula rasa: Latin for "blank slate"; used to refer to the idea that newborns do not have fixed characteristics, but rather that they are shaped by experience.

tangles: twisted, deformed brain cells seen in Alzheimer's disease.

tardive dyskinesia: a side effect of extended use of antipsychotic drugs which causes uncontrollable muscle twitches, writhings, and other body movements.

teratogen: a substance that interferes with prenatal development, such as alcohol, certain drugs, and toxic materials. A teratogen passes the placental barrier and disrupts the hereditary recipe for normal development, resulting in defects in the body.

terminal buttons: the enlarged regions at the end of a neuron's axons that hold the vesicles of neurotransmitters.

terminals: the branches at the end of the axon of a neuron that send a chemical signal to a muscle, an organ, or to another neuron.

texture gradient: a depth perception cue in which objects appear near or far based on their texture.

thalamus: a brain area that serves as a relay center for the senses.

thanatos: in Freudian psychoanalytic theory, the death wish.

Thematic Apperception Test (TAT): a commonly used projective test in which test takers write stories about ambiguous drawings of people in various situations.

token economy: a learning technique used with large groups in which each person is given a token as a reinforcer for behavior. The tokens can be traded in for desirable things.

trace conditioning: a type of classical conditioning in which there is a space of time after the CS was presented when the CS is no longer present and the US is presented.

trait: an enduring or lasting personality characteristic.

transcranial magnetic stimulation (TMS): a procedure in which an electromagnetic coil is placed on a person's head and magnetic pulses are applied to the brain.

transduction: the conversion of one form of energy to another, as when sensory receptors change physical energy into neural energy.

transpersonal unconscious: See *collective unconscious*.

transsexualism: an adult gender identity disorder in which there is a mismatch between the biological sexual characteristics and the psychological gender identity.

transvestism: a type of sexual fetish in which a man wears women's clothing to get sexual satisfaction.

trephining (trepanation): punching or drilling a hole in the skull of a person; a procedure done in the Middle Ages intended to release evil spirits.

trichromatic: the condition in which the eye's retina contains three kinds of cones, as in humans.

tricyclic antidepressant (TCA): a medication used to treat depression that is a reuptake inhibitor.

trisomy 21: See *Down syndrome*.

Turner's syndrome: a condition in which a woman has only one X chromosome.

unconditioned response: a natural reflexive reaction to a specific stimulus.

unconditioned stimulus: a stimulus that causes a natural reflexive reaction.

unconscious mind: thoughts, ideas, and wishes that are in a person's brain, but are not accessible by the conscious mind. Ideas in our brains that we are not aware of. The cornerstone idea in Freud's psychoanalytic theory.

undifferentiated type: a subtype of schizophrenia in which the patient's symptoms do not fit into any of the other subtypes.

unipolar depression: a mood disorder in which a person suffers depression but not mania.

unipolar ECT: ECT treatment in which the electrodes are applied to only one brain hemisphere, typically the right side.

vaginismus: the sexual dysfunction when a woman's vaginal muscles tighten before sexual intercourse making it painful.

validity: a statistical measure of a test that indicates the degree to which the test is actually measuring the thing that it claims to be measuring.

variable: the thing that is studied in science. Variables are things that can vary, that is, that can have varying values.

variable interval (VI): a partial schedule of reinforcement in which the occurrence of a behavior is reinforced only after a fixed amount of time has passed, but the time interval keeps changing.

variable ratio (VR) schedule: a partial schedule of reinforcement in which every *n*th instance of a behavior is reinforced, but the *n* is an average and the number of instances varies.

ventricles: the hollow cavities of the brain through which spinal fluid moves.

vesicles: the bags of neurotransmitter chemicals inside the terminal buttons of a neuron.

vestibular organ: the organ in the inner ear that detects balance.

visual cliff: a clear glass tabletop with a checkerboard below it arranged so that it appears that there is a drop off—a cliff—in one place; used to study depth perception.

vitreous humor: the fluid in the eye that lies between the lens and the back of the eye.

voyeurism: the type of sexual disorder (paraphilia) in which a person secretly watches other people engaged in sexual activities.

Weber fraction: the constant fraction that indicates the ratio between the JND and the intensity of a stimulus.

Wernicke's (receptive) aphasia: problems in understanding the meaning of language due to damage to Wernicke's area.

what pathway: the cellular pathway in the brain that flows into the temporal lobe and processes information about what an object is.

where pathway: the cellular pathway in the brain that flows into the parietal lobe and processes information about where an object is.

working memory: holding things in mind; thinking about something; short-term memory.

X chromosome: one of the two sex chromosomes. Women have two, men have one.

Y chromosome: one of the two sex chromosomes. Women have none, men have one.

Yerkes-Dodson law: states that performance decreases when arousal level is too low or too high; performance is best when arousal is medium.

z-scores: a scoring system in which scores are expressed as standard deviation units; for example, a *z*-score of +1.00 would be one standard deviation above average.

zygote: a fertilized egg; the union of sperm and ovum.

Answer Key Chapter 1

Fill in the blank

1. general psychology
2. behavior, mental processes
3. scientific
4. clinical
5. comparative
6. industrial/organizational
7. psychiatrist
8. psychoanalysts
9. affect
10. biology
11. philosophy
12. Socrates, Plato, Aristotle
13. psyche
14. study, mind
15. Hippocrates
16. hysteria
17. wandering womb
18. unconscious
19. defense mechanisms
20. René Descartes
21. I think, therefore I am
22. dualism
23. empirical
24. EEG; brain waves
25. REM
26. REM, 85%, NREM, 15%
27. REM
28. brain, monism
29. physiology, Wilhelm Wundt
30. Leipzig, Germany, 1879
31. philosophy, physiology
32. structuralism
33. introspection
34. greater (more)
35. functionalism
36. stream
37. psychoanalytic; psychoanalysis
38. surrealist
39. dreams
40. Watson
41. behaviorism
42. Skinner, Skinner boxes
43. humanistic; positive
44. Maslow
45. self-actualization
46. biological
47. cognition
48. Piaget
49. object
50. schema
51. operations, preoperational
52. conservation
53. abstract
54. formal operational
55. Kohlberg
56. cognitive, information
57. evolutionary
58. instincts
59. Darwin
60. natural
61. attachment
62. imprinting
63. critical period
64. contact comfort
65. strange

Matching

1. h	3. g	5. d	7. e	9. a
2. k	4. r	6. j	8. b	10. l

11. c	13. o	15. n	17. m
12. q	14. p	16. f	18. i

Multiple choice

1. d	4. c	7. c	10. d	13. c
2. a	5. b	8. c	11. d	14. a
3. c	6. c	9. a	12. b	15. b

16. c	19. c	22. b	25. c	28. d
17. a	20. a	23. a	26. a	29. a
18. a	21. d	24. b	27. d	30. b

Answer Key Chapter 2

Fill in the blank

1. empirical
2. case studies
3. Sacks
4. Goodall
5. comparative psychologists
6. Kinsey
7. sexual
8. variables
9. describe, explain, predict, control
10. perfect correlation
11. population
12. randomly
13. hypothesis
14. hypothetical constructs
15. operational
16. r
17. 0 (zero)
18. positive, low
19. negative
20. straight line
21. p value
22. 0.05
23. statistically significant
24. causation
25. "A causes (influences) B"
26. independent
27. dependent
28. experimental
29. placebo
30. experimenter
31. double blind
32. meta-analysis
33. replication
34. antiscience
35. not treated
36. animal rights
37. bioethics

Matching

1. p	3. d	5. o	7. e	9. c
2. h	4. b	6. k	8. m	10. n

11. a	13. i	15. l
12. f	14. j	16. g

Multiple choice

1. d	4. d	7. b	10. c	13. a
2. d	5. c	8. d	11. a	14. d
3. b	6. b	9. a	12. a	15. c

16. c	19. c	22. c	25. c	28. b
17. d	20. c	23. c	26. a	29. a
18. a	21. b	24. b	27. a	30. c

Answer Key Chapter 3

Fill in the blank

1. cerebrum
2. sulci, gyri
3. spinal cord
4. corpus callosum
5. split-brain surgery
6. lateralized
7. optic chiasm
8. left
9. confabulation
10. cortex
11. central, Rolando, lateral, Sylvius

12. lobes
13. left
14. localization, function
15. occipital
16. temporal
17. paralysis
18. somatosensory
19. Broca's
20. Wernicke's
21. aphasia
22. plasticity
23. phantom limb
24. EEG
25. CAT
26. PET, fMRI
27. thalamus
28. olfactory
29. hypothalamus
30. endocrine
31. master
32. hippocampus, conscious memories
33. amygdala
34. brainstem
35. reticular
36. cerebellum
37. central
38. autonomic
39. sympathetic, parasympathetic
40. neuron
41. glial
42. dendrites
43. terminal
44. −70 mv
45. positively, depolarization
46. action
47. all-or-none
48. myelin
49. nodes, Ranvier
50. neurotransmitters
51. excitatory, inhibitory
52. enzymes
53. presynaptic, reuptake
54. Parkinson's, l-dopa
55. neuroleptics
56. ovum, chromosomes
57. zygote
58. DZ, MZ
59. X, X, X, Y
60. DNA
61. gene
62. Huntington's
63. 21, Down
64. Klinefelter's
65. teratogens
66. nature-nurture

Matching

1. h	4. r	7. m	10. a	13. l	16. o	19. p
2. u	5. g	8. c	11. k	14. b	17. f	20. e
3. q	6. t	9. j	12. s	15. d	18. i	21. n

Multiple choice

1. c	5. a	9. b	13. a	17. c	21. c	25. c	29. d	33. a	37. a
2. d	6. a	10. d	14. b	18. a	22. b	26. c	30. b	34. d	38. a
3. b	7. d	11. c	15. d	19. c	23. a	27. d	31. d	35. c	39. c
4. c	8. b	12. a	16. b	20. c	24. b	28. c	32. c	36. b	40. d

Answer Key Chapter 4

Fill in the blank

1. transduction
2. sensation
3. perception
4. cochlea, basilar
5. gustation
6. smell, thalamus
7. hot
8. pain
9. proprioceptive
10. kinesthetic
11. vestibular
12. psychophysics, Fechner
13. absolute
14. signal detection
15. difference, just noticeable, JND
16. $JND/I = k$
17. cornea
18. iris, pupil
19. accommodation
20. presbyopia
21. cataracts
22. aqueous humor
23. vitreous humor
24. retina
25. photoreceptors, rods, cones
26. fovea
27. rhodopsin
28. 3, trichromatic
29. monochromat
30. feature detectors
31. opponent
32. bipolar
33. ganglion, optic
34. optic, blind spot
35. lateral geniculate nucleus
36. Gestalt
37. proximity
38. reversible
39. linear perspective
40. visual cliff
41. Ames
42. binocular disparity, convergence
43. binocular rivalry
44. altered
45. blindsight
46. paradoxical, awake
47. NREM
48. hypnosis, suggestible
49. depressant, stimulant, dopamine
50. mimicking

Matching

| 1. r | 3. i | 5. h | 7. k | 9. m | 11. j | 13. f | 15. e | 17. p | 19. c |
| 2. g | 4. s | 6. d | 8. t | 10. a | 12. b | 14. n | 16. q | 18. o | 20. l |

Multiple choice

1. b	5. a	9. a	13. d	17. a	21. b	25. b	29. b	33. c
2. a	6. a	10. b	14. c	18. b	22. c	26. c	30. c	34. a
3. b	7. b	11. a	15. b	19. a	23. a	27. c	31. d	35. a
4. d	8. a	12. d	16. c	20. c	24. d	28. a	32. d	

Answer Key Chapter 5

Fill in the blank

1. conditioning
2. changes, experience
3. operant
4. respondent
5. classical, operant
6. unconditioned
7. Ivan Pavlov
8. bell
9. 1/2 second
10. backward
11. trace
12. taste

13. *tabula rasa*
14. extinction
15. systematic desensitization, relaxation
16. generalization
17. discrimination
18. behaviorism, Little Albert

19. counterconditioning
20. Thorndike
21. puzzle boxes, cats
22. Effect, pleasant, more common, unpleasant, less common
23. Skinner, Skinner box
24. reinforcers

25. operant level
26. primary, secondary
27. bursting
28. negative reinforcement
29. negative punishment
30. shaping
31. continuous
32. ratio, interval

33. token
34. observational learning
35. latent, incidental
36. long-term potentiation

Matching

| 1. c | 3. p | 5. g | 7. e | 9. l | 11. m | 13. k | 15. f | 17. d |
| 2. i | 4. q | 6. b | 8. a | 10. h | 12. n | 14. o | 16. j | |

Multiple choice

1. b	5. d	9. b	13. d	17. b	21. b	25. c	29. a	33. d	37. c
2. a	6. b	10. c	14. d	18. b	22. b	26. c	30. a	34. d	38. d
3. c	7. c	11. c	15. d	19. d	23. b	27. a	31. a	35. d	39. b
4. c	8. c	12. c	16. c	20. b	24. b	28. d	32. a	36. d	40. c

Answer Key Chapter 6

Fill in the blank

1. learning
2. engram
3. neural networks
4. hippocampus, anterograde, H. M.
5. retrograde
6. declarative
7. procedural
8. semantic
9. episodic
10. cerebellum

11. limbic, amygdala
12. encoding
13. external, internal
14. consolidation
15. retrieval
16. free recall
17. recognition
18. middle, serial position
19. decay
20. eidetic imagery

21. the magic number 7 plus or minus 2
22. displacement
23. chunks
24. rehearsal, mnemonics
25. mnemonic
26. pegword
27. loci
28. Ebbinghaus
29. repression
30. false

31. Loftus, implanted
32. flashbulb, details
33. interference
34. Hebb, cell assemblies
35. NMDA
36. long-term depression
37. hippocampus
38. smart, genetic

Matching

| 1. j | 3. k | 5. e | 7. l | 9. g | 11. o | 13. c | 15. i | 17. r |
| 2. d | 4. f | 6. b | 8. p | 10. a | 12. q | 14. m | 16. n | 18. h |

Multiple choice

1. d	5. d	9. c	13. a	17. d	21. b	25. b	29. a	33. b	37. d
2. a	6. a	10. b	14. c	18. d	22. a	26. a	30. d	34. c	38. d
3. b	7. a	11. d	15. c	19. a	23. c	27. c	31. d	35. b	39. d
4. c	8. c	12. b	16. c	20. a	24. d	28. d	32. b	36. b	40. d

Answer Key Chapter 7

Fill in the blank

1. types, traits, behaviors
2. humors
3. physique (body shape), somatotypes
4. Barnum effect
5. stereotyping
6. trait
7. 16PF
8. neuroticism, extraversion-introversion, psychoticism

9. longitudinal
10. Big Five
11. situation, situationism
12. electric shock
13. conformity
14. bystander effect
15. diffusion of responsibility
16. cognitive dissonance, Festinger
17. attribution
18. personal

19. Binet
20. MA/CA × 100
21. standard deviation
22. Stanford-Binet
23. Wechsler
24. Verbal, Performance
25. mentally retarded
26. mild, moderate, severe, profound
27. Down syndrome
28. crystallized, fluid

29. structured, projective
30. Minnesota Multiphasic Personality Inventory
31. validity
32. reliability
33. validity
34. Rorschach Inkblot
35. TAT

Matching

| 1. f | 3. o | 5. p | 7. n | 9. g | 11. h | 13. d | 15. j |
| 2. b | 4. m | 6. l | 8. k | 10. a | 12. i | 14. c | 16. e |

Multiple choice

1. b	5. b	9. a	13. c
2. d	6. d	10. c	14. a
3. b	7. d	11. b	15. a
4. b	8. d	12. d	16. d

17. b	21. c	25. b	29. b	33. a	37. a
18. c	22. d	26. a	30. d	34. b	38. c
19. c	23. c	27. a	31. b	35. a	39. c
20. d	24. a	28. c	32. c	36. d	40. a

Answer Key Chapter 8

Fill in the blank

1. Sigmund Freud, psychoanalytic
2. unconscious
3. repression
4. manifest, latent
5. Freudian slip
6. resistance
7. defense mechanisms
8. rationalization
9. sublimation
10. reaction formation
11. regression
12. pleasure
13. reality
14. superego
15. intrapsychic conflict
16. fixation
17. oral
18. anal-retentive
19. Oedipus complex
20. collective
21. archetypes
22. persona
23. Erikson
24. 8, Man
25. Karen Horney
26. Adler
27. behaviorism
28. Skinner
29. genetics, personal history, current situation
30. Social Learning
31. observational
32. Bandura
33. Abraham Maslow, humanism
34. existential
35. phenomenology
36. self-actualization
37. pyramid
38. self-concept
39. nondirective
40. nature, nurture
41. +0.90
42. Twins Reared Apart
43. extraversion, neuroticism
44. climate, weather
45. affect, physiology, expression, cognition
46. fight, flight
47. James-Lange
48. the brain
49. Schachter-Singer
50. people around us
51. intrinsic, extrinsic
52. homeostasis
53. Yerkes-Dodson, medium

Matching

1. h	3. q	5 g	7. d	9. a	11. c	13. n	15. t	17. r	19. o
2. f	4. m	6. p	8. b	10. j	12. i	14. s	16. l	18. e	20. k

Multiple choice

1. b	5. a	9. a	13. a
2. b	6. c	10. c	14. c
3. c	7 b	11. c	15. c
4. b	8. c	12. c	16. a

17. c	21. c	25. c	29. d	33. c	37. d
18. d	22. b	26. c	30. a	34. d	38. a
19. d	23. d	27. a	31. a	35. a	
20. a	24. a	28. c	32. b	36. b	

Answer Key Chapter 9

Fill in the blank

1. illnesses
2. 80%
3. shame
4. homosexuality, alcoholism
5. Diagnostic, Statistical Manual
6. syndromes
7. Alzheimer's
8. Parkinson's
9. psychotic
10. bipolar
11. factitious, Munchausen
12. sexual dysfunctions
13. paraphilias
14. gender identity
15. bulimia nervosa, purges
16. comorbidity
17. insomnia
18. circadian rhythm
19. melatonin
20. narcolepsy
21. apnea
22. personality
23. antisocial
24. borderline
25. split personality
26. hallucination
27. delusions
28. loosening, associations
29. catatonia
30. positive, negative
31. disorganized
32. paranoid
33. undifferentiated
34. 1%
35. prodromal
36. active
37. emotional expression
38. diathesis
39. ventricles
40. dopamine
41. antipsychotic, neuroleptic
42. women
43. hypomania
44. cyclothymia
45. double
46. seasonal affective
47. attempt
48. higher
49. psychological autopsy
50. light (photo)
51. antidepressants
52. electroconvulsive, ECT, shock
53. cognitive-behavioral
54. bound, free-floating
55. generalized
56. panic
57. agoraphobia
58. obsession, compulsion
59. posttraumatic
60. psychosomatic
61. stress
62. stressor
63. general adaptation syndrome, Hans Selye
64. alarm, resistance, exhaustion
65. conversion
66. body dysmorphic
67. dissociative
68. fugue
69. identity
70. depersonalization
71. etiology
72. Huntington's
73. learned helplessness
74. culture-bound

Matching

1. j	3. n	5. a	7. g	9. l	11. h	13. b	15. s	17. t	19. f
2. d	4. i	6. e	8. r	10. p	12. c	14. q	16. k	18. o	20. m

Multiple choice

1. d	6. b	11. b	16. a	21. a	26. d	31. b	36. a	41. a
2. c	7. d	12. a	17. a	22. d	27. b	32. b	37. a	42. d
3. b	8. d	13. c	18. d	23. a	28. d	33. d	38. b	43. d
4. a	9. a	14. a	19. b	24. d	29. c	34. c	39. d	44. c
5. d	10. a	15. b	20. a	25. d	30. d	35. a	40. a	45. d

Answer Key Chapter 10

Fill in the blank

1. trephining
2. removing evil spirits
3. *Malleus Maleficarum*
4. lunatic
5. bedlam
6. Pinel, moral
7. Mesmer, animal magnetism, hypnosis
8. Charcot
9. antipsychotics, neuroleptics, dopamine
10. atypical
11. serotonin
12. reuptake
13. lithium
14. tranquilizers, antianxiety
15. L-dopa
16. electroconvulsive
17. magnetic
18. psychosurgery
19. unconscious, psychoanalysis
20. dream
21. self-concept
22. unconditional positive
23. reflection
24. Gestalt
25. directive
26. client
27. existential
28. logotherapy
29. Behavioral
30. Systematic desensitization
31. flooding
32. counterconditioning
33. reinforcement
34. token
35. rational-emotive, thinking
36. cognitive behavior
37. narrative
38. outcome
39. Dodo Bird verdict
40. deinstitutionalization
41. Alliance
42. insanity
43. community

Matching

1. e	3. s	5. l	7. p	9. t	11. d	13. o	15. n	17. f	19. g
2. r	4. b	6. a	8. q	10. k	12. c	14. i	16. j	18. m	20. h

Multiple choice

1. c	5. b	9. d	13. d	17. a	21. a	25. d	29. d	33. a	37. a
2. b	6. d	10. d	14. a	18. a	22. c	26. b	30. a	34. b	38. b
3. c	7. c	11. d	15. c	19. b	23. d	27. d	31. d	35. a	39. d
4. a	8. a	12. c	16. a	20. b	24. d	28. c	32. c	36. a	40. b

NAME INDEX

SUBJECT INDEX

PHOTO CREDITS